# Acquiring Modernity

# Studies in Critical Social Sciences Book Series

Haymarket Books is proud to be working with Brill Academic Publishers (www.brill.nl) to republish the *Studies in Critical Social Sciences* book series in paperback editions. This peer-reviewed book series offers insights into our current reality by exploring the content and consequences of power relationships under capitalism, and by considering the spaces of opposition and resistance to these changes that have been defining our new age. Our full catalog of *SCSS* volumes can be viewed at https://www.haymarketbooks.org/series_collections/4-studies-in-critical-social-sciences.

*Series Editor*
**David Fasenfest** (SOAS University of London)

*Editorial Board*
**Eduardo Bonilla-Silva** (Duke University)
**Chris Chase-Dunn** (University of California–Riverside)
**William Carroll** (University of Victoria)
**Raewyn Connell** (University of Sydney)
**Kimberlé W. Crenshaw** (University of California–LA and Columbia University)
**Heidi Gottfried** (Wayne State University)
**Karin Gottschall** (University of Bremen)
**Alfredo Saad Filho** (King's College London)
**Chizuko Ueno** (University of Tokyo)
**Sylvia Walby** (Lancaster University)
**Raju Das** (York University)

# ACQUIRING MODERNITY

An Investigation into the Rise, Structure, and Future of the Modern World

PAUL B. PAOLUCCI

Haymarket Books
Chicago, IL

First published in 2019 by Brill Academic Publishers, The Netherlands.
© 2019 Koninklijke Brill NV, Leiden, The Netherlands

Published in paperback in 2020 by
Haymarket Books
P.O. Box 180165
Chicago, IL 60618
773-583-7884
www.haymarketbooks.org

ISBN: 978-1-64259-191-0

Distributed to the trade in the US through Consortium Book Sales and Distribution (www.cbsd.com) and internationally through Ingram Publisher Services International (www.ingramcontent.com).

This book was published with the generous support of Lannan Foundation and Wallace Action Fund.

Special discounts are available for bulk purchases by organizations and institutions. Please call 773-583-7884 or email info@haymarketbooks.org for more information.

Cover design by Jamie Kerry and Ragina Johnson.

Printed in United States.

10 9 8 7 6 5 4 3 2 1

Library of Congress Cataloging-in-Publication Data is available.

# Contents

    Preface     IX
    Acknowledgements     XI
    List of Illustrations     XIII

1    No Rest Until Modernity is Acquired     1

2    Speculation Ends, Science Begins     9

3    Divesting Philosophy's Ultimate Word     17

4    The Concept of Society     28

5    History and Human Development     34

6    A History of Struggles     42

7    Mystical Consciousness     47

8    Illusions to this Day     53

9    An Inverted World     58

10    Educating the Educator     66

11    Windy Idealists and Frothy Youth     71

12    Middle Class Snobbism     74

13    Pauperism and Artificial Impoverishment     79

14    Social Scum     94

15    Of Souls, Sighs, and Opium     98

16    The Cult of Nature     112

17    World Literature     117

| | | |
|---|---|---|
| 18 | Modern Society's All-dominating Power | 120 |
| 19 | An Impulse Never Before Known | 126 |
| 20 | Head of the Movement | 134 |
| 21 | Absurd Epidemics | 138 |
| 22 | Swindling Joint-stock Companies | 145 |
| 23 | Machines | 153 |
| 24 | Rule of the Towns | 159 |
| 25 | Feverish Anxiety and Astonishment | 162 |
| 26 | Solids Melting into Air | 165 |
| 27 | Civilization and Barbarism | 179 |
| 28 | Celebrating Orgies, Blood, and Fire | 186 |
| 29 | Bureaucracy and the Bureaucrats | 194 |
| 30 | The Economic Existence of the State | 200 |
| 31 | Democracy for their Truth | 203 |
| 32 | Parliamentary Disease and the Holy Ghost | 214 |
| 33 | The Executive Committee | 217 |
| 34 | Modern Mythology and its Goddesses | 225 |
| 35 | Rolling Back the Wheel | 230 |
| 36 | The Goal of Popular Desire | 234 |
| 37 | National Egoism | 237 |

| | | |
|---|---|---|
| 38 | Every Sect is Religious | 239 |
| 39 | Disgusting Despotism | 247 |
| 40 | The Sycophantic Babblers | 256 |
| 41 | Applying Chemistry to Industry and Agriculture | 269 |
| 42 | The Measure of Social Progress | 290 |
| 43 | Defiling Republics | 300 |
| 44 | A Fetish Dark and Mysterious | 316 |
| 45 | The World Market | 330 |
| 46 | The Political Chessboard | 346 |
| 47 | Throwing Dust in People's Eyes | 364 |
| 48 | Gravedigging Megalomaniacs | 368 |
| 49 | The Sorcerer | 376 |
| 50 | Prevailing Tendencies | 380 |
| 51 | Common Ruin | 392 |
| 52 | Chains, Riddles, Worlds | 402 |
| 53 | Socialist Sentimentalizing | 410 |
| 54 | Whether We Want it or Not | 414 |
| 55 | Afterword | 423 |
| 56 | Postmodernism? | 451 |
| | References | 465 |
| | Index | 534 |

# Preface

A comment to the reader about the following subject matter. This book is about the basic origins, structure, and development of the modern world, though it does not presume its account is exhaustive. Many important historical details are, by necessity, either touched on all too briefly, embedded in broader discussions, or omitted altogether. My purpose is to provide a general snapshot of modernity, though one not steeped in arcane academic jargon or minutiae but rather a portrait painted in a language familiar to an everyday reader. Any such reader will be the final judge of my success on that score.

A word or two on my selection bias. While I often attempt to provide historical and cross-cultural examples to demonstrate main points in the following pages, there is heavy, though certainly not sole, reliance on the American experience. This is for several reasons, some of which were unavoidable. First, being from the United States—and having a non-insignificant portion of my studies focused on it—meant that demonstrations of ideas often came most readily from my personal knowledge of this society, both experiential and academic. Second, America—with its contemporary political, economic, military, and cultural dominance—has been the focal point of modernity's recent historical development—say the last 80–100 years or so, after previous European ascendance. Analytically, then, it makes sense to appeal to what happens in America as indicative of modernity's overall thrusts, just as a similar book on modernity written 100 years earlier would rely on the nature and influence of European development, with England most likely playing the leading role. Of course, this also means that the extent to which modernity has features less expressed in the American experience is the extent to which my narrative here is incomplete.

Extending from the points above, a book like this could organize itself around alternative perspectives. In one instance, a book on modernity could easily mobilize the themes of these chapters from the vantage point of those areas of the world—e.g., Africa, the Caribbean, or South America—that have experienced modernity's historical rise and present conditions as societies in its colonial sphere. In another vantage point, modernity could be investigated from the perspective of a country sitting historically astride different geopolitical locations of modern development, between East and West, between the struggles of the older and the newer, such as Iran, Turkey, or Egypt. Or, again using the themes of these chapters, a book such as this could be written from the vantage point of an ascendant global power—such as China—should it increasingly assume cultural, political, economic, and/or military leadership in the future. This period of decline of one systemic leader—this time the United States which followed England's previous dominance and decline—and the rise of another is perhaps one we are living through today. That said, it is not always necessary to reinvent the wheel, as, if successful, the themes of this book will still be applicable to the next period of modern development and the dominant social force driving it forward. That judgment on the book's "success" is for both history and readers, too, to decide.

A few final notes on the themes of this book. It begins with several general observations about the modern world and then turns to consider aspects of scientific versus philosophical inquiry as ways to analyze past and present human experience. It builds on these foundations slowly as it returns to examining modernity in more detail, with each chapter focusing on its various but interconnected dimensions until a broader picture comes into view. The themes that inspire and are used to organize the book's narrative—i.e., its chapter titles—are not my own, so I make no claim on their originality. Though they are hardly opaque or impenetrable, my sources for these themes are revealed by book's end, as is my reasoning behind both choosing them and their method of presentation. And, again, it will be up to the reader to render judgment on the wisdom and efficacy of their choosing and my method of presentation. But that said, I do hope that the reader will agree that the picture of modernity from the book as a whole, its selection of themes, and the informational details contained throughout is at once both familiar and illuminating.

# Acknowledgements

Books such as this, like all others, neither write themselves nor are they made possible solely through the efforts of the person whose name graces the cover. They only can come into being because of a wide support network the official author enjoys, nay, relies on. Though these names will not appear on any bibliographic entry, one must give credit where and when it is due, and it is only right and proper that I do so here.

I first want to thank Dr. Jen Koslow, plant biologist, after-dinner conversationalist, and romantic partner extraordinaire. Her input and patience were invaluable in many stages involved in writing this book and I could not have done it without her. Love, hugs, and kisses to you Jen Jen!

I would also like to extend my thanks to Dr. David Fasenfest, Series Editor for Brill International Publishers and Editor for *Critical Sociology*. David has supported my work in various forms over the years and his advice, direction, and encouragement have been invaluable. I owe him a great debt that literally cannot be repaid.

Several individuals and organizations also granted me permission to use their images or illustrations. Thanks here goes to the following: Art Resource, the Economic Policy Institute, Emma Johansson (Department of Physical Geography and Ecosystem Science, Lund University, Sweden), Euratlas, the FRED Blog of Economic Research, the editors at *Perspectives on Politics*, and Saji George (of Tom's Doubts).

I would also like to thank my colleagues at Eastern Kentucky University, several of whom I am sure I bored with my discussions about my project over the years and others who were kind enough to give me a University Fellows Award that provided crucial financial support so that I might see this book through to its end.

Last, and certainly not least, I owe my friends and family a tremendous debt for their encouragement. As I matured in my studies over the years, they would often ask to read my publications. But as these were often written with a professional audience in mind, my friends and family patiently wed through the academic jargon and the minutiae about much of which they were unfamiliar. They often asked whether and when I would write something an everyday audience could read and understand. These friends, usual suspects, and unindicted co-conspirators include (alphabetically): Brandon Cartner. Bill and Tiffani Cavatassi. Elizabeth Case. Matthew "Zip" Irvin. James Nobbe. Craig and Laura Sheehan. Jamie Skaggs. Dionne Smith. Bryan and Robin Swearinger. Tricia

Watts. Deborah and John Weber. Chad and Kristen Whalen. Shannon Williams. Apologies to anyone left off of this list. The oversight is wholly unintentional.

Someone who had a similar request was my mother, Mary Paolucci. Though no longer with us, she always encouraged me in my work and sometimes even served as copyeditor and critic. Moreover, she believed in a life of the mind, in education, in science, and in a social consciousness. Her calm demeanor combined with her intellectual and political passion probably influenced me more than anyone and perhaps more than she ever knew. You are missed more than any of us can now say.

Finally, I must acknowledge my father, Bernie Paolucci, who has always supported my life-long efforts to study sociology and often comes to me for my opinion about current events and human behavior. My father's steady familial guidance, along with the example of my mother, always made our home one where opinion and debate were as welcome as friends, food, and drink. Thanks dad!

# Illustrations

## Figures

13.1 US unemployment rate, 1910–1960. Source: Lawrencekhoo. Public Domain: Wikimedia commons - https://commons.wikimedia.org/w/index.php?curid=7875410   82

13.2 Top charts of 2016. Source: Economic Policy Institute (December 22, 2016). See: http://www.epi.org/publication/the-top-charts-of-2016-13-charts-that-show-the-difference-between-the-economy-we-have-now-and-the-economy-we-could-have/   84

13.3 Top Charts of 2016. Source: Economic Policy Institute (December 22, 2016). See: http://www.epi.org/publication/the-top-charts-of-2016-13-charts-that-show-the-difference-between-the-economy-we-have-now-and-the-economy-we-could-have/   85

13.4 Top Charts of 2016. Source: Economic Policy Institute (December 22, 2016). See: http://www.epi.org/publication/the-top-charts-of-2016-13-charts-that-show-the-difference-between-the-economy-we-have-now-and-the-economy-we-could-have/   86

23.1 Compensation of Employees: Wages and Salary Accruals/Gross Domestic Product, 1950–2015. Source: US Bureau of Economic Statistics, FRED BLOG, Economic Research—Federal Reserve Bank, St. Louis. June 9, 2016. See: https://fredblog.stlouisfed.org/2016/06/2393/?utm_source=series_page&utm_medium=related_content&utm_term=related_resources&utm_campaign=fredblog   156

26.1 Asymptotes. Source: Kmhkmh. Creative Commons BY 4.0. Wikimedia Commons - https://commons.wikimedia.org/w/index.php?curid=63918126   165

26.2 World Literacy Rate, 1970 to 2015. See: Public Domain: Wikimedia Commons - https://commons.wikimedia.org/w/index.php?curid=544969   170

26.3 Microprocessor Transistor Counts 1997–2011 & Moore's Law. Source: Benzirpi. Creative Commons BY-SA 3.0. Wikimedia Commons - https://commons.wikimedia.org/w/index.php?curid=29600339   177

31.1 Average Citizens' Preferences. Source: Gilens and Page (2014: 573). Used with Permission of Cambridge University Press   210

31.2 Economic Elites' Preferences. Source: Gilens and Page (2014: 573). Used with Permission of Cambridge University Press   210

48.1 World Population and Growth Rate Curve   373

49.1 Kondratieff Wave. Source: Internaszonalderivative work. Copyrighted Free Use. Wikimedia Commons - https://commons.wikimedia.org/w/index.php?curid=7814202   377

50.1 Global Distribution of Wealth. Source: Marius xplore. Creative Commons BY-SA 3.0. Wikimedia Commons - https://commons.wikimedia.org/w/index.php?curid=1461356     385

50.2 Lorenz Curve of Annual GDP Distribution in the World, 2013. Source: Tbap. Data Source: World Bank. Creative Commons BY-SA 4.0. Wikimedia Commons - https://commons.wikimedia.org/w/index.php?curid=37064699     385

## Images

9.1 Illustration of the Camera Obscura Principle. Source: Public Domain (PD-1923): Wikimedia Commons -https://commons.wikimedia.org/w/index.php?curid=52154597     58

11.1 British Students at Eton, 1932. Source: Aktuelle-Bilder-Centrale, Georg Pahl. Bundesarchiv, Bild 102-13350. Creative Commons BY-SA 3.0; Creative Commons BY-SA 3.0 de. Wikimedia Commons - https://commons.wikimedia.org/w/index.php?curid=5480996     72

11.2 Vietnam War Protesters at March on Washington, 1967. Source: Lyndon B. Johnson Library. Public Domain: Wikimedia Commons - https://commons.wikimedia.org/w/index.php?curid=19267316     73

11.3 Students at Tiananmen Square, 1989. Source: by Jiří Tondl. Creative Commons BY-SA 4.0. Wikimedia Commons - https://commons.wikimedia.org/w/index.php?curid=68125236     73

11.4 A Protester on Tahrir Square Holds Up a Poster Comparing Morsi to Former Fascist Leaders Mussolini and Hitler, November 30, 2012. Source: Public Domain (USA): Voice of America - http://gdb.voanews.com/9120A890-5B07-44B3-89D2-0F62758F0EB4_mw1228_mh548_s.jpg Wikimedia Commons - https://commons.wikimedia.org/w/index.php?curid=31357188     73

12.1 World's Highest Standard of Living, *Life* Magazine, 1937. Source: Margaret Bourke-White / Masters / Getty Images     77

15.1 The Egyptian God Harsaphes. Source: Public Domain (PD – 1923): Wikimedia Commons - https://commons.wikimedia.org/w/index.php?curid=121759     103

15.2 The Creation of Adam, by Michelangelo. Source: Public Domain (PD-1923): Wikimedia Commons - https://commons.wikimedia.org/w/index.php?curid=8118862     103

15.3 Tom's Doubts #14, September 3, 2011. Source: Saji George; Used with Author's Permission. See: https://twitter.com/s_a_j_i/status/110040087445782528     105

ILLUSTRATIONS                                                                                         XV

16.1   Medium and Séance. Source: William Marriott—On the Edge of the Unknown.
       Pearson's Magazine. March-October 1910. Public Domain (PD-1923):
       Wikimedia Commons - https://commons.wikimedia.org/w/index.
       php?curid=55652019     113
16.2   Couple with a Young Female Spirit. Source: National Media Museum.
       Public Domain (PD-1923): Flickr - https://www.flickr.com/photos/
       nationalmediamuseum/2780177093/ Wikimedia Commons - https://
       commons.wikimedia.org/w/index.php?curid=12215098     113
16.3   Houdini Displays Tricks of Fraudulent Mediums, 1925. Source: Public Domain.
       Library of Congress- http://memory.loc.gov/rbc/varshoud/3b13893u.tif
       Wikimedia Commons - https://commons.wikimedia.org/w/index.
       php?curid=12503991     114
16.4   A Group of Druids Summoning their Spirit Animal at Stonehenge in
       Wiltshire, England, 2018. Source: Wikipedia. Creative Commons – 1.0.
       Wikimedia Commons - https://commons.wikimedia.org/w/index.
       php?curid=69158791     115
16.5   Wiccan Event at Avenbury, 2005. Source: Creative Commons BY-SA 2.0.
       Wikimedia Commons - https://commons.wikimedia.org/w/index.
       php?curid=135486     115
16.6   New Age Shop and Healing Centre, Market Place St. Albans, Hertfordshire,
       UK, 2009, by Graham Hale. Source: Creative Commons BY-SA 2.0.
       Wikimedia Commons - https://commons.wikimedia.org/w/index.
       php?curid=11014753     115
19.1   English Ships and the Spanish Armada, 1588. Source: Public Domain (PD-
       1923): Wikimedia Commons - https://commons.wikimedia.org/w/index.
       php?curid=284027     128
19.2   Canadian Stamp Depicting the British Empire, circa 1898. Source: Bibliothèque
       et archives Canada. Public Domain: Wikimedia Commons - https://commons.
       wikimedia.org/w/index.php?curid=5057700     129
19.3   Victim of Congo Atrocities, Congo, ca. 1890–1910. Source: Public Domain (PD-
       1923): University of Southern California Libraries -http://digitallibrary.usc.edu/
       cdm/ref/collection/p15799coll123/id/78038 Wikimedia Commons - https://
       commons.wikimedia.org/w/index.php?curid=30895485     129
24.1   London, 1600s. Source: Columbia University - http://www.columbia.edu/itc/
       mealac/pritchett/00generallinks/munster/britain/aa_britain.html Public
       Domain (PD-1923): Wikimedia Commons - https://commons.wikimedia.org/w/
       index.php?curid=55205406     160
24.2   Shakespeare's England, 1910. Source: Internet Archive Book Images. Flickr
       The Commons - https://www.flickr.com/photos/126377022@N07/14594699267

Wikimedia Commons - https://commons.wikimedia.org/w/index. php?curid=43536727     160

24.3 Palace of Westminster from the Dome on Methodist Central Hall. Source: Colin. Creative Commons BY-SA-4.0. Wikimedia Commons - https://commons.wikimedia.org/w/index.php?curid=35768815     160

24.4 Super Moon Over City of London from Tate Modern, 2018. Source: Colin. Creative Commons BY-SA 4.0. Wikimedia Commons - https://commons.wikimedia.org/w/index.php?curid=66185487     160

25.1 Christmas Illumination Champs-Elysées, Paris, 2011. Source: ACT Lighting Design 20011 - http://www.actlightingdesign.com/ Creative Commons BY 3.0. Wikimedia Commons -https://commons.wikimedia.org/w/index.php?curid=18613005     163

25.2 Times Square, New York City, USA. Source: Flickr - https://www.flickr.com/photos/22240293@N05/3845692998/ Creative Commons BY 2.0. Wikimedia Commons - https://commons.wikimedia.org/w/index.php?curid=10048145     163

25.3 Night in Shinjuku - Tokyo, Japan. Source: Martin Falbisoner. Creative Commons BY-SA 3.0. Wikimedia Commons - https://commons.wikimedia.org/w/index.php?curid=31796038     163

26.1 Two Women on Beach, 1900s. Source: Flickr - https://www.flickr.com/photos/53035820@N02/sets/72157625672172059/with/5345544894/ Public Domain (PD-1923): Wikimedia Commons - https://commons.wikimedia.org/w/index.php?curid=18876231     168

26.2 Women Walking at the Beach, 2013. Source: Flickr: Dr. No Redux. Creative Commons BY-SA 2.0. Wikimedia Commons - https://commons.wikimedia.org/w/index.php?curid=31992739     168

26.3 Women at the Beach, 2007, Ukraine. Source: Flickr. Creative Commons BY-SA 2.0. Wikimedia Commons - https://commons.wikimedia.org/w/index.php?curid=5246896     168

26.4 Men's Fashion, 1700s. Source: Nordiska Museets Fotoateljé. This file was donated by Nordiska museet to Wikimedia Commons as part of the Europeana Fashion collaboration. Public Domain (PD-1923): Wikimedia Commons - https://commons.wikimedia.org/w/index.php?curid=25100254     169

26.5 Humphrey Bogart, 1942, Trailer Screenshot. Source: *Casablanca.* Public Domain: Wikimedia Commons - https://commons.wikimedia.org/w/index.php?curid=67227366     169

26.6 Lundi Gras in New Orleans. Before the Start of the Red Bean Parade, Royal Street, Lower Faubourg Marigny, 2015. Source: Infrogmation of New Orleans. Creative Commons BY-SA 2.5. Wikimedia Commons - https://commons.wikimedia.org/w/index.php?curid=38578564     169

ILLUSTRATIONS                                                                                                    XVII

26.7   Early US Census Machines, 1960. Source: US Census Bureau. See: https://www
       .census.gov\/multimedia/www/photos/census_history/early_census_
       machines_2.php. Public Domain: Wikimedia Commons - https://commons.
       wikimedia.org/w/index.php?curid=33471424     176
26.8   Firing Room 2, Launch Control Center, Apollo 12, November 14, 1969. Source:
       Kennedy Space Center Photo Archive. Public Domain: Wikimedia Commons -
       https://commons.wikimedia.org/w/index.php?curid=7330252     176
26.9   Young Woman with Cellphone—Outside Sheikh Lotfollah Mosque—
       Isfahan–Iran, 2012. Source: Flickr - https://www.flickr.com/photos/adam
       _jones/7433220770/ Uploaded by mrjohncummings. Creative Commons
       BY-SA 2.0. Wikimedia Commons - https://commons.wikimedia.org/w/index.
       php?curid=30320500     176
27.1   Native American Looks Out Over Transcontinental Railroad, Western
       Territories (USA), 1867. Source: Library of Congress. Public Domain
       (PD-1923)     181
27.2   Barbarie and Civilisation—Drawing from 1900. Source: https://imgur.com/
       QRMtuWq     182
27.3   1984 Winter Olympics Opening Ceremony at Koševo Stadium, Sarajevo. Source:
       BiHVolim. Creative Commons BY-SA 4.0. Wikimedia Commons - https://
       commons.wikimedia.org/w/index.php?curid=43623035     184
27.4   Government Building Burns After Being Hit by Tank Fire, Sarajevo, 1992. Source:
       Wikipedia. Creative Commons BY-SA 2.5. Wikimedia Commons - https://
       commons.wikimedia.org/w/index.php?curid=357728     184
28.1   Triangle Shirtwaist Fire, Front Page, *New York Tribune*, March 26, 1911. Source:
       Library of Congress. Public Domain     186
28.2   Bodies of Workers Who Jumped from Windows to Escape the Triangle Shirt-
       waist Fire, 1911. Source: Public Domain: Wikimedia Commons - https://
       commons.wikimedia.org/w/index.php?curid=50405402     186
28.3   Taino (Arawak) Genocide via Columbus's Conquest in Cuba. Source:
       Las Casas's, *Brevisima relación de la destrucción de las Indias*. Public Doman
       (PD-1923)     188
28.4   Punishment Meted Out by Columbus for Failing to Meet Gold Quotas. Source:
       Las Casas's, *Brevisima relación de la destrucción de las Indias*. Public Doman
       (PD-1923)     188
28.5   Natives of Arrakan Sell Slaves to the Dutch East India Company at Pipely/
       Baliapal (in Orissa), January 1663. Source: Columbia University | De Oost-
       Indische Voyage van Wouter Schouten - http://www.columbia.edu/itc/mealac/
       pritchett/00routesdata/1700_1799/trade/dutch/view1708.jpg. Public Domain
       (PD-1923): Wikimedia Commons - https://commons.wikimedia.org/w/index.
       php?curid=63232379     188

28.6 Child Coal Miners, West Virginia, 1908. Source: National Child Labor Committee. Library of Congress Prints and Photographs Division - http://hdl.loc.gov/loc.pnp/nclc.01052. Public Domain: Wikimedia Commons - https://commons.wikimedia.org/w/index.php?curid=1075220     189
29.1 Chart of Sales Department, 1905. Source: Systematizing (1905). Public Domain (PD-1923): Wikimedia Commons - https://commons.wikimedia.org/w/index.php?curid=38581494     195
29.2 Outline of Organizational Chart, 1914. Source: Graphic Methods for Presenting Facts. The Engineering Magazine Company. Public Domain (PD-1923): Wikimedia Commons - https://commons.wikimedia.org/w/index.php?curid=37942798     195
29.3 NASA Organizational Chart, November 1, 1961, by NASA. Source: Mariner-Venus 1962 Final Project Report. Public Domain. NASA - https://history.nasa.gov/SP-59.pdf. Wikimedia Commons - https://commons.wikimedia.org/w/index.php?curid=26290609     196
29.4 US Government, 2011, Office of the Federal Register National Archives and Records Administration. Source: The United States Government Manual 2011. Public Domain: Wikimedia Commons - https://commons.wikimedia.org/w/index.php?curid=42227191     197
31.1 A Chart Illustrating Gerrymandering in its Most Basic Form. Source: Steve Nass. Creative Commons BY-SA 4.0. Wikimedia Commons - https://commons.wikimedia.org/w/index.php?curid=38869847     208
31.2 1990s Supreme Court Redistricting Decisions. Source: Minnesota Legislative Services; Office of Senate Counsel & Research for the Minnesota Senate - https://www.senate.mn/departments/scr/REDIST/red907.htm     209
34.1 Slogans in Revolutionary France—"Liberty, Equality, Fraternity, or Death." Source: Hector Fleischmann, La guillotine en 1793, Paris: Librairie des Publications Modernes, 1908. Public Domain (PD-1923): Wikimedia Commons - https://commons.wikimedia.org/w/index.php?curid=4021551     225
34.2 Slogans in Revolutionary France—"Unity and Indivisibility of the Republic. Liberty, Equality, Fraternity or Death." Source: Bibliothéque Nationale de France | Gallica - http://gallica.bnf.fr/ark:/12148/btv1b69503876.r=Unit%C3%A9+indivisibilit%C3%A9+de+la+R%C3%A9publique.langFR. Public Domain (PD-1923): Wikimedia Commons - https://commons.wikimedia.org/w/index.php?curid=30577458     225
35.1 The Iranian Revolution Meets Reaction, 1978. Source: Public Domain: Wikimedia Commons - https://commons.wikimedia.org/w/index.php?curid=6254904     231
35.2 Women in Afghanistan, 1927. Source: Afghanistan On My Mind – Blog. Public Domain: Wikimedia Commons - https://commons.wikimedia.org/w/index.php?curid=18694989     231

ILLUSTRATIONS                                                                  XIX

35.3   Women in Afghanistan after Taliban Takeover. Source: Public Domain: Wikimedia Commons - https://commons.wikimedia.org/w/index.php?curid=18599    231

35.4   Alt-right Members Preparing to Enter Emancipation Park Holding Nazi, Confederate, and Gadsden "Don't Tread on Me" Flags, Charlottesville, Virginia, 2017. Source: Charlottesville "Unite the Right" Rally. Creative Commons BY 2.0. Wikimedia Commons - https://commons.wikimedia.org/w/index.php?curid=61769434    233

39.1   Mutilated Children from the Belgium Congo, before 1905. Source: *King Leopold's Soliloquy: A Defense of His Congo Rule*, by Mark Twain, Boston: The P.R. Warren Co., 1905, Second Edition. Public Domain (PD-1923): Wikimedia Commons - https://commons.wikimedia.org/w/index.php?curid=1221821    247

40.1   Joel Osteen, Multimillionaire Preacher of the Prosperity Gospel, at Lakewood Church, July 17, 2017. Source: Robert M. Worsham. Creative Commons BY-SA 4.0. Wikimedia Commons - https://commons.wikimedia.org/w/index.php?curid=50224944    265

41.1   Black Country – Borinage (Belgium). Source: Photo by Szilas—the Meunier Museum, Brussels. Public Domain (PD-1923): Wikimedia Commons - https://commons.wikimedia.org/w/index.php?curid=9792677    270

41.2   Nant Y Glo, Monmouthshire, Wales – 1830. Source: National Library of Wales (also see NLW Catalogue). Public Domain (PD-1923): Wikimedia Commons - https://commons.wikimedia.org/w/index.php?curid=42001750    270

41.3   Nelson's Column during the Great Smog of 1952, London. Source: Geograph. Creative Commons BY-SA 2.0, Wikimedia Commons - https://commons.wikimedia.org/w/index.php?curid=4094275    271

41.4   Two Photos Taken in the Same Location in Beijing, August 2005. Source: Bobak. Creative Commons BY-SA 2.5. Wikimedia Commons - https://commons.wikimedia.org/w/index.php?curid=2190112    272

41.5   Smog Near New Delhi, India, November 2016. Source: Saurabh Kumar. Creative Commons BY-SA 4.0. Wikimedia Commons - https://commons.wikimedia.org/w/index.php?curid=52945685    272

41.6   New Delhi, India, November 2017. Source: Sumitmpsd. Creative Commons BY-SA 4.0. Wikimedia Commons - https://commons.wikimedia.org/w/index.php?curid=63957099    272

41.7   Alberta Tar Sands, 2008. Source: Flickr: Tar Sands, Alberta. Creative Commons BY 2.0. Wikimedia Commons - https://commons.wikimedia.org/w/index.php?curid=33395825    273

41.8   Methane Leaking Through the Cracks, 2009–2010. Source: NASA Earth Observatory - https://earthobservatory.nasa.gov/IOTD/view.php?id=77868 Public Domain: Wikimedia Commons - https://commons.wikimedia.org/w/index.php?curid=20106634    276

41.9 Image Microplastics. Source: Flickr - https://www.flickr.com/photos/noaamarinedebris/7656713582/ Creative Commons Attribution 2.0 Generic License / Public Domain: Wikimedia Commons - https://commons.wikimedia.org/w/index.php?curid=65695792    279

41.10 The Great Pacific Garbage Patch. Source: NOAA. Creative Commons Attribution 2.0 Generic License.    280

43.1 Capture of Slaves in Africa by African Slavers. Source: Wellcome Collections Gallery (2018-04-03), Blog Post - https://wellcomecollection.org/works/vyfyapx2?query=V0050563&wellcomeImagesUrl=/indexplus/image/V0050563.html Creative Commons BY 4.0 International. Wikimedia Commons - https://commons.wikimedia.org/w/index.php?curid=36674214    301

43.2 Slave Ship Poster. Source: Library of Congress. Public Domain (PD-1923): Wikimedia Commons - https://commons.wikimedia.org/w/index.php?curid=2203871    302

43.3 Sugarcane Cutters in Jamaica (after 1838 Abolition of Slavery), circa 1880. Source: Royal Museums Greenwich - http://collections.rmg.co.uk/collections/objects/261996. Public Domain (PD-1923): Wikimedia Commons - https://commons.wikimedia.org/w/index.php?curid=62377660    303

43.4 Official Medallion of the British Anti-Slavery Society, 1795. Source: British Abolition Movement, Public Domain (PD-1923): Wikimedia Commons - https://commons.wikimedia.org/w/index.php?curid=121448    304

43.5 Rescued Slaves Aboard the HMS Daphne, 1868. Source: Flickr – The Commons, No Known Copyright Restrictions. Wikimedia Commons - https://commons.wikimedia.org/w/index.php?curid=51242802    304

43.6 Convict Leasing, Children, 1903. Source: Library of Congress, Prints & Photographs Division, Detroit Publishing Company Collection. Public Domain (PD-1923): Wikimedia Commons - https://commons.wikimedia.org/w/index.php?curid=65943203    307

43.7 Sharecropper Sam Williams with Family Members and Laborers in Cotton Field, 1908. Source: Library of Congress. Library of Congress Catalog: https://www.loc.gov/pictures/item/98506914/. Image download: https://cdn.loc.gov/master/pnp/cph/3c20000/3c20000/3c20700/3c20752u.tif. Original url: https://www.loc.gov/pictures/item/98506914/. Public Domain (PD-1923): Wikimedia Commons - https://commons.wikimedia.org/w/index.php?curid=68226492    308

43.8 Lynching and Burning of Will Brown, Nebraska, 1919. Source: University of Washington. Public Domain (PD-1923): Wikimedia Commons - https://commons.wikimedia.org/w/index.php?curid=2205643    308

43.9 Logo from the Second International Congress on Eugenics, 1921. Source: Scanned from—Harry H. Laughlin, The Second International Exhibition of Eugenics, held September 22 to October 22, 1921, in connection with the

ILLUSTRATIONS

Second International Congress of Eugenics in the American Museum of Natural History, New York (Baltimore: William & Wilkins Co., 1923). Public Domain (PD-1923): Wikimedia Commons - https://commons.wikimedia.org/w/index.php?curid=135048     310

43.10   Map Indicating Sterilization Legislation in US States, 1921. Source: Scanned from—Harry H. Laughlin, The Second International Exhibition of Eugenics, held September 22 to October 22, 1921, in connection with the Second International Congress of Eugenics in the American Museum of Natural History, New York (Baltimore: William & Wilkins Co., 1923). Public Domain (PD-1923): Wikimedia Commons - https://commons.wikimedia.org/w/index.php?curid=135044     310

43.11   German Eugenics Propaganda, 1935. Source: Aktuelle-Bilder-Centrale, Georg Pahl (Bild 102), Bundesarchiv, Bild 102-16748. Creative Commons BY-SA 3.0; Creative Commons BY-SA 3.0 de. Wikimedia Commons - https://commons.wikimedia.org/w/index.php?curid=5415569     310

43.12   Tom Torlino, Native American Before and After Forced Assimilation. Source: Beinecke Rare Book & Manuscript Library, Yale University. Public Domain (PD-1923): Wikimedia Commons - https://commons.wikimedia.org/w/index.php?curid=10867044     311

43.13   Rally at State Capitol, Protesting the Integration of Central High School, Little Rock, Arkansas, 1959. Source: Library of Congress, *U.S. News & World Report* Magazine Photograph Collection. Public Domain: Wikimedia Commons - https://commons.wikimedia.org/w/index.php?curid=887311     311

43.14   US Marshals with Young Ruby Bridges on School Steps, William Frantz Elementary School, New Orleans, 1960. Source: US Marshals Service. Public Domain: Wikimedia Commons - https://commons.wikimedia.org/w/index.php?curid=27473461     312

43.15   "Japanese Only" Sign at Yunohana Onsen, Otaru City, Hokkaido, Japan, 1999. Source: Debito.org - http://www.debito.org/onsenyunohanasign.jpg. Creative Commons BY-SA 3.0. Wikimedia Commons - https://commons.wikimedia.org/w/index.php?curid=12734726     313

49.1   The Sorcerer Calls Up Spells He Cannot Fully Control—*The Witches of Warboyse*. Source: Wellcome Collection Gallery. Wellcome Blog Posts: https://wellcome.ac.uk/press-release/thousands-years-visual-culture-made-free-through-wellcome-images. Creative Commons BY 4.0. Wikimedia Commons - https://commons.wikimedia.org/w/index.php?curid=36012782     377

50.1   Horse Drawn Plow, Ring of Kerry, 1963. Source: Flickr - https://www.flickr.com/photos/47290943@N03/35623519404. Public Domain (No Known Restrictions): Wikimedia Commons - https://commons.wikimedia.org/w/index.php?curid=65162599     383

50.2 Wheat Harvest with a Claas Lexion before Sunset Near Branderslev, Lolland, Denmark, 2008. Source: Flickr - https://www.flickr.com/photos/criminalintent/2720980560/. Creative Commons BY-SA 2.0. Wikimedia Commons - https://commons.wikimedia.org/w/index.php?curid=6209017  383

52.1 Slavers Bringing Captives on Board a Slave Ship on Africa's West Coast. Source: Public Domain (PD-1923): Wikimedia Commons - https://commons.wikimedia.org/w/index.php?curid=51783662  402

## Maps

19.1 Europa Ortelius, 1572. Source: Euriskodata CD-ROM. Public Domain (PD-1923): Wikimedia Commons - https://commons.wikimedia.org/w/index.php?curid=3176655  126

19.2 Europe, 1864. Source: Public Domain (PD-1923). Original from: David Rumsey Historical Map Collection - https://www.davidrumsey.com/luna/servlet/detail/RUMSEY~8~1~206519~3002702 Wikimedia Commons - https://commons.wikimedia.org/w/index.php?curid=12863171  127

19.3 Map of Colonial Africa, 1897. Source: Public Domain (PD-1923): Wikimedia Commons - https://commons.wikimedia.org/w/index.php?curid=29328147  129

19.4 World Empires and Colonies in 1914, Just Before the First World War. Source: Andrewo921 (2010). Creative Commons BY 3.0. Wikimedia Commons - https://commons.wikimedia.org/w/index.php?curid=11022316  131

20.1 Map of English as the Official or De Facto Language. Source: Public Domain: Wikimedia Commons - https://commons.wikimedia.org/w/index.php?curid=637466  135

26.1 Europe 1300. Source: Euratlas, The History and Geography of Europe and the World. See: http://www.euratlas.net/history/europe/index.html Used with Permission.  172

26.2 Europe 1400. Source: Euratlas, The History and Geography of Europe and the World. See: http://www.euratlas.net/history/europe/index.html Used with Permission.  172

26.3 Europe 1500. Source: Euratlas, The History and Geography of Europe and the World. See: http://www.euratlas.net/history/europe/index.html Used with Permission.  173

26.4 Europe 1600. Source: Euratlas, The History and Geography of Europe and the World. See: http://www.euratlas.net/history/europe/index.html Used with Permission.  173

ILLUSTRATIONS XXIII

26.5  Europe 1700. Source: Euratlas, The History and Geography of Europe and the World. See: http://www.euratlas.net/history/europe/index.html Used with Permission. 174
26.6  Europe 1800. Source: Euratlas, The History and Geography of Europe and the World. See: http://www.euratlas.net/history/europe/index.html Used with Permission. 174
26.7  Europe 1900. Source: Euratlas, The History and Geography of Europe and the World. See: http://www.euratlas.net/history/europe/index.html Used with Permission. 175
26.8  Europe 2000. Source: Euratlas, The History and Geography of Europe and the World. See: http://www.euratlas.net/history/europe/index.html Used with Permission. 175
33.1  Free Trade Agreements with Three or More Participants, 2009. Source: Primarily based on the WTO list, with exceptions for African Free Trade Zone, Association of South East Asian Nations +3 (ASEAN Free Trade Area) and ASEAN Australia New Zealand Free Trade Area. Public Domain: Wikimedia Commons - https://commons.wikimedia.org/w/index.php?curid=5616150  223
41.1  Aquatic Dead Zones, 2010. Source: NASA Earth Observatory - https://earthobservatory.nasa.gov/images/44677. Public Domain: Wikimedia Commons - https://commons.wikimedia.org/w/index.php?curid=10946843  278
41.2  Map of the North Pacific Subtropical Convergence Zone (STCZ) within the North Pacific Gyre. Source: NOAA Marine Debris Program - http://marinedebris.noaa.gov/info/patch.html. Public Domain: Wikimedia Commons - https://commons.wikimedia.org/w/index.php?curid=6808542  280
41.3  2011–2014 Hydraulic Fracturing Water Use (sq. meters/well), 2015. Source: USGS - http://www.usgs.gov/newsroom/images/2015_06_30/water_use_for_fracking.jpg. Public Domain: Wikimedia Commons - https://commons.wikimedia.org/w/index.php?curid=41337487  282
43.1  Slave Trade of Africa, 1899. Source: From The New York Public Library - https://digitalcollections.nypl.org/items/510d47df-fd20-a3d9-e040-e00a18064a99. Public Domain / No Known Restrictions  302
43.2  US Coast Guard Survey's Map of the Slaveholding States. Source: United States Coast Guard. Public Domain: Wikimedia Commons - https://commons.wikimedia.org/w/index.php?curid=12273096  305
45.1  Transasian Silk Trading Routes, 500BC – 500CE. Source: Creative Commons BY-SA 3.0. Wikimedia Commons - https://commons.wikimedia.org/w/index.php?curid=721591  330
45.2  The Modern World Market. Source: Untitled Map by Emma Johansson, published in: J.W. Seaquist, Emma Li Johansson, and Kimberly A. Nicholas. 2014. "Architecture of the Global Land Acquisition System: Applying the Tools of Network

Science to Identify Key Vulnerabilities." *Environmental Research Letters* 9 (11): 1–13. Used with Permission.   333
46.1 Eurasia. Source: Central Intelligence Agency, World Factbook. Public Domain: Wikimedia Commons – https://commons.wikimedia.org/w/index.php?curid=35753   351
46.2 The Strait of Hormuz. Source: w:en:Kleptosquirrel (talk | contribs). Creative Commons BY-SA 3.0. Wikimedia Commons - https://commons.wikimedia.org/w/index.php?curid=17987147   362
52.1 Supply Chain for a Laptop Computer, 2011. Source: Sourcemap | Massachusetts Institute of Technology—Free Use. Source map - https://open.sourcemap.com/maps/57d0d127dd378od6272b3f8c   403

CHAPTER 1

# No Rest Until Modernity is Acquired

There is something unique about our world. It is a world whose basic structure came into being during the sixteenth century and its history is still maturing, unfolding, and morphing before us. Some have termed our period "modernity," a term the meaning of which this book elaborates. As a unique social system, modernity has properties that we need to grasp and understand if we are to make sense of our contemporary experience.

People have not always felt a need such as this. Historically speaking, most societies have not been built in such a way as to release many people from the daily struggle for survival—and to have enjoyed certain forms of inquiry—so that reflecting on the nature of their society was (or is) a real accessible possibility. Early in modernity—its exact date of birth subject to debate—those with social, personal, and historical memory of the recent past had a vantage point from which to realize a new world, one that would bear only a passing resemblance to what had preceded it, was being born. With modernity already accomplished, our society seems as given to us, as if it is what a natural and normal human reality is and should be. But, no doubt, modernity had a birth, a period of maturation, and, as such, it will eventually pass away. And, in doing so, it will prepare a future for us. Perhaps today we sit as did the barely-aware peasant of yesteryear—sensing an event on the horizon and scarcely able to make out what lies just beyond view but approaches closer every day. And we sense this, even if only vaguely and intermittently.

You no doubt have heard and used the term "modern" before. We often speak of "modern art" or "modern architecture." But the use of "modernity" here is not meant as a generic "recent" or "new."[1] Any person at any time could, conceivably, refer to life in their own world as being "modern" as in the strict definition of "current." That said, there is only one social world we call *modernity* and what people experience of and in modernity is unique to and in history. Modernity is our society and we are the moderns. What does this mean? Who and/or what is included or excluded?

Social systems—for example, hunting-gathering, early agricultural societies, or forms of feudalism—produce different experiences for those who live in them. Hunter-gatherers experience a level of goods that waxes and wanes

---

[1] For an example that makes exactly this problematic connection, see Haque's (2018) discussion on "Why Didn't America Become Part of the Modern World?"

across migrations, seasons, and/or the ecology and climate in which a people lives, which are often things outside of their control. Their gods—more like spirits and forces, really—animate animal and material life and they keep time through movements of herds, stars, weather, and other cyclical events. Their "history books" tend to be lore, fables, memory, and myths, orally told and retold and passed down over generations like an extended version of the child's game "telephone." Societies that first developed agriculture produced more food and goods, and, with these, people. These systems also initiated the first forms of slavery and built the earliest city-states and professional-like armies (societies such as Rome, Chinese dynasties, the Mayan Empire, and so on). Their gods were different too, more people-like, with names, personalities, and histories, instead of forces animating nature. Later, feudal peasants in Europe suffered bouts of great want, enjoyed no social mobility, feared, loathed, and loved their kings and their queens and had to deal with a singular, jealous, and angry god. Individuals born into any or all of these societies had no hand in choosing their parents, their methods of production and reproduction, their forms of labor and political authority, or the nature of their gods. You and I would have thought and behaved in the same was as such people had we been born at any of these times and/or in any of these places.

Likewise, we have been born into the modern world and it has shaped us. But the issue is more than just or simply that human experience is based on the type of system into which one is born. That is a sociological truism. Perhaps the first sociological novelty about modernity as a socialization force is that we are more aware than those before us that we live in a *type* of system, particular and distinguishable from other systems. It is doubtful that the earliest human foragers or the serfs of Middle Age Europe spent much time pondering what it is like to live as hunter-gatherers, much less even knowing their society was/is a *type of society as such* nor that other types existed (not always true, of course). But we moderns know what type of society we live in, we are occasionally aware we are new and different, and we sometimes wonder what it *means* to live in our world. We discuss it constantly, even if we do not exactly realize this is what we are doing.

Modernity is not wholly without traits it shares with other systems. As nature is not ready-made for us, we must produce a world in which to live. Likewise, we organize ourselves into family units for raising children and passing down knowledge, morals, and skills (even if those families are organized in different ways at different times and in different places). All societies contain sets of rules for interpersonal interaction, many of which are based upon various statuses, such as the class, kin/clan, ethnic, or gender category of those doing the interacting. We have sets of rules on who can have sex with whom, who may marry whom, and the forms of socially recognized rituals that "count" as a birth rite or a marriage ceremony. We learn about what is acceptable food from our families and our wider culture. We have formal and informal norms of attire and style when presenting ourselves in social settings. We have forms of governance, whereby relationships between individuals, groups, and even whole cultures, are regulated. And both cooperation and conflict are pervasive between all of these levels of human interaction. At a general level, these things are all true of our society just as in any and all others, even if the specific details may vary.

But modernity also has some important differences from other systems, things which we find nowhere else. In modernity, barter generally gives way to a money economy which comes to dominate more and more of social and public life. And it is no exaggeration to argue that without production and monetary exchange linking up global sectors, modernity would never have emerged in the first place. Further, while other historical societies had external trading links uniting corners of the world, modernity is *based on* such trading links.

Modernity embraced the scientific revolution, won from hard battles during the medieval period (also known somewhat erroneously as "The Dark Ages"). Moreover, modernity was in part forged *by that* scientific revolution. Science—as a key to improvements in living conditions, knowledge, education, transportation, medicine, and so on—is a central feature of modernity. Indeed, today, more and more of the natural world is understood, from the DNA that provides the blueprint that makes us up to the expanse of the cosmos. Modernity has brought us mass agriculture unlike we have seen before, knowledge about electricity, germ models of disease, electron microscopes, vaccines, antibiotics, microchips, bioengineering, and so on. It is hard to imagine what part of a modern person's life has not been thoroughly influenced by science, its practices, and its products.

The modern world is chaotic, though its forms of power have no center in one consistent person, state, or army. Modernity has seen many contenders to the throne of state and its military apparatus. Nation-states have been belligerents in wars almost without end for modernity's lifespan and in the process some have risen and many have declined. The world economy grows and contracts only to grow once again, bringing states into clashes, and both make mass migrations the norm in modernity's historical scope, with abundance and famine dancing around one another in different parts of the globe as the tune the world economy plays changes from one tempo to another.

Modernity has witnessed a decline of superstition and church authority and we no longer burn witches nor do we venture on religious crusades or inquisitions. Today, while many people are still religious, rejection and criticism of religious authorities and traditions are no longer capital offenses in most places (though death for apostasy still remains in some sectors of the world). The Catholic Church is still the world's largest, but no political body or civilian population really answers to them anymore as they would to a gendarme or judge. The Church cannot officially pass legal judgments nor legally do *direct* physical harm to citizens, as such practices have been passed over to state authorities or remain as residual effects of religious teaching. Other sectors of the world still struggle under the yolk of theocracy and we moderns feel sympathy for such victims and wish it were otherwise.

Though modernity has not seen the passing of religion, it has seen the proliferation of multiple religions. One hallmark of the social freedom endorsed by modern thought is that a society is best run where individuals are free to choose their own religion or have none at all. Further, modern states tend not to support one religion over others and, as such, in modern societies multiple religions flourish (and even decline), as do individuals who proclaim no creed whatsoever. In some places, the United States especially, churches enjoy attendance and, as physical structures dotting the landscape, a level of social respect, even from many non-believers. In other places, Europe, Japan, and China especially, few people practice any religion at all, though their churches, cathedrals, and temples remain standing as reminders of a past not very far behind them.

The idea of "modernity" has historical roots. Europe was experiencing dramatic spasms as the feudal order was cracking at the seams, the encompassing authority of the Catholic Church was increasingly challenged, masses began to demand participation in public affairs, and a new class of merchants and traders were vying for power against an increasingly obsolete and parasitic aristocracy. Industry and invention flowered across the Continent. But so did abundance, filth, crime, modes of transportation unseen before, and a level of crushing poverty visited upon laborers who no longer had access to land (which became the norm for more and more people). This is the period and place that birthed modernity.

Let's take a look at some of the other changes wrought on the world since the birth of our modern system.

It is easy to forget, but the nation-state is a relatively new phenomenon. This geographically bounded and defined territory ruled by a (usually) armed sovereign government containing a people who identify themselves in terms of nationality is new on the historical scene. Added to this, the American and the French Revolutions brought to the world the idea that the authority of the state rested on the consent of the governed. It was and still is a revolutionary proposition, one not yet ubiquitous across the entire world but, nevertheless, today exists as an enduring socially motivating force that continues to unfold before us.

In modern society, more and more people continually transform from rural to urban living. The city is a major center of commerce, transportation, tourism, culinary arts, literature, and so on. Though rural life still often contains these things, today more and more people live in urban centers, which become locales of culture and cultures, people and peoples, innovation and stagnation. Such processes of urbanization—metropolitanism, really—began with the rise of modernity and continue today.

The modern world is awash in constantly changing and developing technology. Indeed, technological change is built into the very notion of modernity. Communication has changed from hand-carried letters to telephones to cell phones and cyber-technology where one can exchange ideas with people around the globe in a practical instant. Transportation has changed from foot and animals to coal powered trains to automobiles, airplanes, and high speed rail. Today we hear about the prospect of driverless cars. With electron microscopes, we can see atoms that were once unimagined and then later simply a theoretical conjecture. With modern telescopes, we are now mapping the universe and discovering planets in solar systems that are, for the average person, inconceivably far from our own. In 1975, no other planets were known to astronomers; a simple internet search reveals the known existence of 5291 confirmed planets (plus other Kepler candidates) as of July of 2018.[2] And we have also heard about possible Earth-like planets found in the habitable "Goldilocks zone" (i.e., conditions that are "just right" for life) around far away suns. Further, change in our society is often rapid, where what occurs very quickly over our lifetime may have taken several generations in earlier societies, if it happened at all. Think of the fact that one person could have lived long enough to witness the belief that lighter-than-air travel was physically impossible to seeing the invention of airships and planes and later still a moon landing. We could make a similar observation about the change from mail to Morse code to phones to transatlantic cables to satellites and the Internet.

Modernity is rife with material abundance, at least in the wealthier sectors of the world. Americans have more food than they can eat, throwing about 40% of it away from field to grocer to restaurant and home (Gunders 2012). And still obesity is an epidemic of social concern, which is historically unheard of. The average square feet per person allotted to us in housing is extensively larger than seen in earlier systems. In the West, most families have cars, televisions,

---

[2] See: http://exoplanets.org/. Also see: http://adsabs.harvard.edu/abs/2014PASP..126..827H - This research has made use of the Exoplanet Orbit Database and the Exoplanet Data Explorer at exoplanets.org.

indoor heat, multiple sets of clothes, more appliances than they use during the average day, and so on. Further, not only do we have these things, but our stores are chock full of replacements should we need or want them. And the world economy is reliant on constantly reinvigorating this state of demand.

In modernity, science as applied to human life has given us anthropology, sociology, economics, geography, history, and other quests for understanding our past as well as our present and future. We learn different languages—if not outright, we certainly learn *about* them and come to a wider awareness of peoples in many parts of the globe. We write history in a way that encompasses a vast array of social forms across time and space, where all societies of the past become "history" in comparison to what arises today. In fact, this knowledge is often one thing that we juxtapose to our knowledge of our modern selves, often seeing pre-modern societies as primitive or backward (though this is starting to be more of a relic with each passing year) and our own culture as superior. However, we also wonder whether some accomplishments are hard to depict as "progress" in comparison with the past; only has modernity produced the technological capability to destroy the planet, e.g., nuclear weapons.

We know more of us live longer than did many people of the past.[3] Most people in the modern world live well beyond 30 or 40, some places even having a median age of death twice these figures, e.g. Japan. Further, we often know *why* we get ill. We have confirmed that certain pathogens cause certain diseases (e.g., small pox, malaria, influenza) and we know how lifestyle results in other illnesses (e.g., heart disease, lung cancer, type II diabetes). We no longer use amulets to ward off vapors (though we do still have lots of hocus-pocus when it comes to various forms of healing, e.g., homeopathic medicine). We see fewer of our children die in our own lifetimes, expecting them to bury us instead of us them. We like to think of this as progress and, indeed, it is hard to argue that it is not.

The modern world made it possible to challenge institutionalized male authority like never before. This has been one of the more recent developments, where women's struggles for social equality both came later in modernity and were met with resistance from many men and some women, and the dominant

---

3   In modern society, median age has progressively increased over the past few centuries. This is not to repeat the myth that in pre-modern societies people died around 40 years of age. This myth, whether applied to hunter-gatherers or even feudal societies, stems from the fact that high rates of infant mortality brought down the median age overall. However, if one calculated a median age based on those who lived past, say, age 5, then the likelihood of aging into the 50s, 60s, or even 70s was not rare or extraordinary. Today, more people have a chance to do this because of our lower infant and maternal mortality, more consistent potable water and calorie supply, and medical advances.

social institutions of the times. But it has been those very institutions—governmental, economic, educational—that have been crucial to the advances women have enjoyed. Today, the idea of gender "equality" is on the social agenda and is less and less waved off as naïve or impossible in much, if not most, of the modern world.

Around the time of modernity's rise, many people spent most of their life within about 20 or fewer miles from where they were born. Today, many people travel that far each day to go to their jobs. Not only has our knowledge of the world community grown but more people than before can go to where other people in other cultures live, whether on business trips, while on vacation, being reunited with family members whose sons and daughters migrated long ago, or even moving and relocating there. And such travels no longer take months or years but now weeks or even a few days or hours or less. Modernity has indeed made the planet seem smaller in our lived experience.

Conversely, the universe has greatly expanded during modernity, both figuratively and literally. As mentioned before, astronomers are finding more and more evidence of planets outside our solar system but they also have discovered that the universe is expanding more rapidly all the time. But this comes with a societal-wide psychological cost. Prior to modernity, planet Earth was all there was. More specifically, it did not make sense, for the vast majority of people, to wonder if other "planets" with civilizations existed near other "suns." For most people, Earth was reality and the shiny things in the night sky were part of Earth's existence, its backdrop or canvas. More specifically, they did not even know we lived on a "planet" as we understand it today, even if they knew their own world was round. Stars were not understood as suns millions or even billions of miles (or "light years") away and other planets in our solar system were just seen as peculiar stars, i.e., they did not know these were planets revolving around the Sun just as Earth does. The idea that we exist in a massive galaxy with a massive number of stars and that the number of galaxies was/is also massive was not part of popular consciousness. One result of learning all of these things was an obvious question, Are we the only ones here? As Earth's relative place in the great expansiveness of the universe has become increasingly known, the lack of confirmed lifeforms from other planets makes us a lonely people on a planet drifting in a vacuum we have only begun to investigate. This idea was not even thinkable for most people before modernity.[4]

---

4  A qualification is necessary here. Clearly, people did posit that others might exist on other planets in our solar system. The point here, however, is that it was not until modernity and its technological development that we understood that stars are other suns billions (and billions) of miles away and that we exist in a galaxy among millions and billions of other galaxies.

Our sense of self is increasingly inward in modernity. We have developed forms of knowledge that increasingly require that duties to tribe, clan, master, lord, king, and leader increasingly lose their place of priority and are supplanted by a focus on the self. We look out for "number one." And in many ways, we must. Before anything else, we must secure the money needed to keep a roof over our heads, clothes on our backs, and food in our stomachs. For many people in the world, to the extent that these are just within reach, this becomes their primary daily activity. But for many others, these concerns are secured to such a reasonable extent that they move on to cultivate style, tastes, and pleasures. They worry about their blood pressure and cholesterol level. They go to counsellors for psychological evaluation and constantly reflect on their mindset, happiness, and desires. They measure themselves against others in terms of their selection of wine, the new clothes they own, the special features of their cars, and so on. And modern people are increasingly depressed and dysfunctional. They love and hate themselves at the same time, presume a type of normalcy that leads to fear and over-diagnoses of conditions such as ADHD and autism, and take pharmacological "remedies" at the highest rate ever seen (see Weale 2014; Cha 2016; J. Wright 2017, and references therein). Modern society is a society of the (literal) self-centered self.

This litany of observations about the modern world is not exhaustive. In order to really "grasp" modernity, we must add to, elaborate on, and go beyond these observations, as something lies behind them and unites them. Given what modernity has in store for us—real results, potentials, and possibilities—it is wise counsel that we do not rest until we acquire what that something is.

CHAPTER 2

# Speculation Ends, Science Begins

More than one culture proposed that a god's locomotion directs the Sun across the sky. During The Black Plague, the story goes, Pope Clement used fire to purify the air around him to keep away suspected vapors. It is thought that George Washington's death was hastened by the bloodletting he received when ill. Today, one hears that some people in South Korea believe an electric fan can kill someone in his or her sleep ("fan death"), while in Germany one finds the less dramatic belief that being cooled by such air can cause a cold or flu.[1] All of this was and is guesswork about the mechanisms entailed in observable events. All of it was and is wildly off the mark.

What counts as trustworthy knowledge? It is not if something sounds or seems correct or makes us feel good. The Sun certainly does not orbit the Earth, even though it looks that way. A mother's kisses do not heal our wounds, even if they may soothe our pain. Many elixirs and potions may have no direct therapeutic healing properties outside our own minds. The Placebo Effect is real.

For much of human history, our knowledge was bound with religious thought and thinkers. Shamans, monks, priests, lamas, and imams were the arbiters of how people should understand the world and the forces they confront in it. Pharaohs, kings, and potentates joined in this quasi-monopoly on official knowledge, telling their subjects who they should fear and whom to obey, what to eat when and how, with whom to have sex and which acts were forbidden, when and where to fight and how to die with honor. This is only partly true, however. People developed other forms of everyday knowledge—such as when to plant, how to kill livestock, where to find clean water, how to make folk medicines, cheeses, and breads, and so on—that did much more for human survival than did the dictates of authorities.

---

[1] The claim about South Korea is a "general knowledge" fact. Though the belief is in decline there, the belief itself has been documented. The claim about Germany comes from both personal experience and from something I read in *Der Spiegel*. In terms of personal experience, someone I knew from Germany told me that sleeping with a fan on can cause a cold or flu, no matter my protestations otherwise. In terms of what I read in *Der Spiegel*, the magazine asked readers, during the summer of the 2006 World Cup, to contribute to a "Germany Survival Bible Travel Guide." An ex-pat who had lived in Germany wrote of their experience in a car where fellow passengers would roll down their windows at stop lights to let in fresh air, only to wind them back up as the car was moving. They later learned this practice was because of the belief that exposure to cooling air leaves one susceptible to getting ill.

The Romans, Greeks, and Persians (among others) also developed a class of individuals that did not fit in either camp above. Some of these were historians, others were philosophers, and, collectively, they made up the earliest intellectuals and scientists. They thought deeply about the world and the space that contains it (actually, for many it was the other way around—our world contained the universe, nay, it was "the universe"). They sometimes came up with ingenious ideas, inventions, and insights. And, they passed this tradition of investigation and invention down through time to new generations. Their progress was slow, though often impressive. They learned much about the world and helped build great civilizations and their products—Weapons. Aqueducts. Medicines. Surgery. Astronomy. Mathematics. Agriculture. And so on.

What these thinkers and their students seemed to lack, however, were today's complement of tools used in systematic, empirical, and experimental inquiry. This may be easy to overstate, given we cannot know how much ancient knowledge we have lost.[2] Still, even given the advances these ancestors made, their inquiries often remained in the orbit of speculation, a tradition of thought that even marked many Enlightenment thinkers.

What is "speculation"? In common everyday language, it is guesswork. But "guesswork" might be too harsh a label. Maybe we can refer to speculation as theorizing about a reality without *sufficiently* systematic empirical foundations and without the consistent use of sound analytical devices. To speculate is to make assertions about reality that we cannot ultimately and positively verify with a high degree of confidence.

Speculative work is not necessarily directed toward things without value, of course. Such work might try to piece together why we get sick or what stuff makes up stars. For instance, scientists at one point thought miniature human beings were contained in sperm and grew into birth-ready babies. This is not an outrageous guess, even though our modern knowledge makes it seem so. Though speculative work might inquire about real things in the world, it was not until modern scientific inquiry (plus a dash of advanced technology) emerged that many things about which we remained mystified, ignorant, or ill-informed became better understood.

The concept of "speculative philosophy" used to carry with it more respect than this depiction allows, as some of the world's most respected intellectuals

---

[2] The destruction of Alexandria's library is often cited as an event where great stocks of ancient knowledge were lost. While that is possible, historians debate the accuracy of the claim, suggesting its books had long been copied and/or moved elsewhere. That said, perhaps the story is repeated so much to indicate the obvious fact that we have lost knowledge from the ancient world and, by definition, cannot know what that knowledge was and how much of it was in fact lost.

may be categorized this way. Advances, that is, *were* made. People such as Immanuel Kant, for example, provided modern thought with invaluable tools with which to work. But Kant was not a specialist in data collection but rather an expert in musing philosophical (even if we grant his genius for it). Much, if not most, of his work (and that of others like him) remained in the realm of pure thought (even when giving examples of core concepts) and remained there in such a way that developing a clearer picture of the world would remain within its limits. And this is less a criticism of Kant but more of a recognition that modes of thought, even as advances on what came before, often have their built-in limits that, in turn, inherently limit what can or cannot be discovered when working within that framework. Newton's theories might help us build a bridge, but it took Einstein's theories to lead to the discovery of how to split atoms.

We can philosophize and theorize and guess all we like but it is only upon the careful inspection of the empirical evidence of the real world and its painstaking and systematic analysis that we can build a base of knowledge in which we can have confidence. Science—with its experimental model—is the best method to get at this goal that humans have yet produced.

What is science? Science is not the results of investigation. Nor is it the material things used in investigation or the technology we can see as its occasional product. Though science can use and help produce such things, these are not what science is *per se*.

Science is a systematic method of inquiry that aspires to discover the laws and/or causal mechanisms that account for a variety of subject matter. To do this work, scientists rely on data collection, methods of reasoning—including both induction and deduction—and a community of open debate. Scientific practice's openness to debate is based on the willingness, even the necessity, of scientists admitting that certain conclusions might be or are erroneous. As such, science builds into its method of investigation a way both to acknowledge and to self-correct its errors. Thus, science is not dogmatic and eschews appeals to authority or tradition to establish the validity of its knowledge.

It is possible, or even likely, that the reader has no problem recognizing the descriptions of the scientific enterprise depicted above. It is just as likely the reader sees these principles as uncontroversial. This has not always been the case. It required centuries of struggle with religious and political authorities for scientific knowledge and scientists to win respect, relative autonomy, and public acceptance (things that nevertheless seem to wax and wane). Both Copernicus and Galileo risked their safety and comfort in studying the heavens and making known their conclusions. At the Roman Inquisition, where Galileo was investigated for heresy, the Pope refused to look into the telescope, as it was seen by many as a tool of Satan. Copernicus and Galileo were not alone. Many investigators aspiring to study the world—some bent more scientifically than others—had to hide their endeavors and some were killed for them.[3] Later, even if death was not a punishment, a scientist could be run out of their profession for breaking with orthodoxy. For example, in 1846, Ignaz Semmelweiz suggested that doctors wash their hands before delivering babies as a way to reduce puerperal fever and maternal death. He was ridiculed and ostracized by his peers for the suggestion (as there was no germ theory of disease yet; even he was unsure of why the practice reduced maternal deaths). And today there are religious leaders still waging a war on science.[4]

How life emerges from nature has vexed thinkers and scientists for countless generations. Beginning with Aristotle, one leading theory was "spontaneous generation"—that the organic material from one lifeform spontaneously generated into other lifeforms. Over centuries various proto-experiments were done to inspect the theory's veracity. More than one investigator used things like animal broth, meat, or dead fish exposed to air, placed in containers that were sealed (or some combination thereof) and observed whether or not the broth turned cloudy or if maggots or flies emerged.[5] Different arguments were made for and against the accepted theory, criticisms of methods and conclusions were drawn, and the methods of investigation grew more sophisticated. It was not until 1859 when Louis Pasteur formulated a definitive experiment and shared his findings which were then tested by others that spontaneous generation was relegated to history's dustbin.

In experiments, systematic data collection occurs with conditions and variables specified in a consistent and controlled manner. It begins with some observation about a regular phenomenon in experiential reality (How do flies form on meat? What makes people get the flu? and so on). The scientist makes an initial observation without those conditions (e.g., fresh meat without flies, people without flu symptoms, etc.). Variables with conjectured causal properties of interest are introduced as elements of the initial conditions are carefully changed (meat in a jar, meat in cloth, meat exposed to air; quarantined person, person exposed to cold air, person exposed to another person with the

---

3  For example, though not a "scientist" strictly speaking, see the story of Giordano Bruno for a case of what happened to someone questioning church authority on the cosmos, its size, our place in it, etc.
4  It should be noted here that both the Vatican of Catholicism and Buddhism's Dali Lama have increasingly admitted to science's value, importance, and validity.
5  This short summary of many years of investigation, some forms sounder than others, as well as debates and personalities will necessarily gloss over many interesting details in order to capture the basic gist of the principle.

flu, etc.). Outcomes are again measured and compared to samples not exposed to the variables of interests (i.e., the control group). In a pure and adequately done experiment, the addition (or subtraction, as the case may be) of a (real causal) variable should account for observed differences between the control group and those exposed to the stimulus.

As such, several principles accompany this basic model: (1) control all variables that might influence the outcome, (2) repeat the experiment to confirm findings, (3) replication of the experiment by others following the exact methods of the original experiment, and (4) peer-review from specialists in the field to check methods of data collection, forms of analysis, and conclusions drawn. Finally, not only does the experimental model allow for uncovering thus far hidden causal forces but, when done properly, it should remove observer bias and allow for a form of an objective testing of claims that opinion, conjecture, speculation, authority, or assertion could never achieve. It was a long struggle to get there but this method of knowing was a significant achievement in human history, one that we often take for granted today.

The experimental model, however, is not the be-all and end-all of scientific inquiry. Theories, concepts, and sampling methods are subject to criticisms for internal inconsistencies and biases. Data collection may eschew the use of experimental tests but rather search for correlations between objects of interest (associations where one variable changes along with changes in one or more other variables; here a form of control variables is used to eliminate spurious correlations and to uncover partial correlations). Data collection may even be more rudimentary, where, rather than statistical correlations, uncovering broad empirical patterns that need to be explained across a subject matter is of interest. Also, there are issues in what is called "the philosophy of science," where forms of and errors in reasoning are hashed out through discussion, demonstration, and debate and where, it is hoped, eventual agreement on such principles is reached.

Ultimately, science wants to know why things are the way they are and what happened to bring them to be this way. What forces account for the world we observe? And how do these forces interrelate? After long periods of inquiry, scientists can put such forces together in what may be termed a "model." As a heuristic device, a model depicts the causal mechanisms of a phenomenon in a manageable arrangement of its most important parts and how they interconnect with and/or influence one another. We have models of the universe, the atom, and the human body. We also have models of disease, climate, and plate tectonics, and so on.

The social sciences produce models, too. Social research establishes the core relationships of phenomena through a controlled comparison of different social forms. In this work, the scientist examines regular social practices, investigating their various dimensions and concrete manifestations. They collect data on these practices and look for other social relationships and practices they share associations with, decipher which associations are inherent to the issue at hand (excluding those statistical correlations that are simply artifacts of the math), and attempt to piece together a model that accounts for such practices, their variations, and their deviations from predicted outcomes. Like the natural sciences' approach to nature, the social sciences have as their goal nothing less than a complete understanding of human social action and organization as possible.

Science is not in the business of revealed Truth, such as may be a soothsayer or prophet. Scientific truths rest on the internal validity of its assertions and their empirical verification. This is one reason why systematic data collection, use of logical reasoning, and a community of inquiry and debate are essential for its practice. And in scientific practice, claims are subject to systematic verification rather than appeal to authority, such as may happen with a shaman, priest, pope, king, or president.[6] For proper verification to be possible, scientific statements have to be constructed in a way where it is possible to show that they are incorrect, or what philosopher of science Karl Popper called the principle of *falsification*. The contrast between the idea of "intelligent design"—which some religious activists want added to US school curriculums—and the theory of evolution demonstrates this issue.

Evolutionary theory asserts two general principles. First, those members of a species that possess traits that are advantageous to their survival in a given environment are more likely to reproduce and pass those traits down to their offspring. Second, either in the process of reproduction where genetic variations occur (mutations) or because of external changes in the environment (climate, new predators introduced, etc.), and sometimes both, some traits that provide

---

6  However, this does not mean that individual scientists do not have an air of authority as we commonly use the term. When a scientist has a long period of productive and influential work, their opinion often brings with it a level of gravitas and deference from others. Newton. Galileo. Einstein. There is a fine line between saying "it is true because so-and-so said it" versus "so-and-so has vast experience with this subject matter and their opinion holds great weight." By extension, one way that scientific authority works is that when an individual of renown speaks about a subject matter on which they have invested a great deal of research and study it is more likely they have better knowledge about that subject than the layman or dilettante. But they too *can be shown to be wrong*. Indeed, an honest scientist wants to be proven wrong so as not to cling to erroneous beliefs about the nature of the world. Priests, should they be proven wrong about the nature of the world, would theoretically be out of a job. This explains religion's long history of avoiding and even forbidding inquiry into it and the world it purports to minister.

advantages become important when perhaps they were not before (or the reverse, some traits that were previously advantageous no longer are). Over time, as offspring with advantageous traits tend to survive more often than those without them, the dominant numbers of a species will possess these traits too. As members of a species both with and without a trait reproduce, the resulting process is one of "natural selection." Given these conditions and a *long* period of generational reproduction, species best fit for survival tend to do so and can also "drift" into new species (or, "speciation")—thus, the longer phrase, "evolution by natural selection."

After it became legally impossible to keep biblical creationism in school curricula, religious activists came up with the idea of "intelligent design" as a way to inject theological models into the classroom. Intelligent design holds that certain characteristics in some species are so complex and specialized that (1) they could not have developed from prior, less developed organs—or "irreducible complexity"—and, therefore, (2) only the existence of a creator can account for them. So, for instance, intelligent design proponents might argue that the human eye is so complex that its existence cannot be explained through evolution by natural selection. This is an assertion, of course, but it is less an appeal to biblical authority than it is a form of argumentation. That is, instead of saying that god made the species we observe because it says so in Genesis, the theory of intelligent design uses an empirical observation upon which to base its assertion.

There is a crucial difference between this model and the theory of evolution, however. The principles of evolution are constructed in a way where they can be tested and falsified, while those of intelligent design cannot. While one could empirically verify whether or not certain traits conferred survival advantages that are passed to offspring and whether or not those offspring over long periods branched off via speciation, there is simply no way to establish that a deity *did not* create the living world we observe. And even if and when any particular trait is pointed to as so irreducibly complex that science is yet to explain it, we have seen that over time such traits are eventually scientifically understood. Moreover, even if one demonstrates that something like the human eye clearly had relatives in the primate family, the intelligent design proponent can always claim "yes, god guided that evolution." Finally, while the leading principle of intelligent design *could hypothetically be true* this would not change the fact that its principles *cannot be experimentally tested or falsified*. Intelligent design, then, is not a scientific discourse but rather one that rests on assertion and faith, i.e., it is a form of speculation.

Where would the modern world be if humans remained reliant on unfalsifiable assertions and authority for the establishment of truth-claims rather than the principles of logic, reason, data collection, verification, and falsification? While this is hard to say exactly, the modern world most certainly would lack almost every advance we employ in everyday life today: readily available clean water, fuels, computers, cars, cellphones, medicines, radio, television, mass production, flight, use of electricity, medicines, vaccinations, and so on. The development of all of these things would have been impossible through a knowledge system reliant on appeals to tradition or authority or guesswork. The modern world is one that moved past speculation so that real science could begin.

CHAPTER 3

# Divesting Philosophy's Ultimate Word

For most of its history, philosophy has been a search for "Truth." This search has had two central and interdependent tracks. First is the search for a finalized set of categorical knowledge that has been so perfected that it is subsequently unchanging. Second is the search for Truth whose proof is obtained from an abstract schematic existing in a pure conceptual realm outside and independent of us and, therefore, uninfluenced by human exigencies. These two visions overlap in their concerns to a considerable degree and characterize a great deal to which philosophy has put its efforts.

Many questions in philosophy orbit around the issue of, what is the nature of reality? We can treat this question—where philosophy's "reality" can stand in for theology's "god"—as an empirical one rather than as an abstract speculative one. Moreover, the issue is not *can* we but *should* we? We first come to know reality by experiencing and observing the world. And if this is so, then the nature of reality is a question about which we must turn to history and our real observations of everyday life to answer. As this approach is not one where answers exist in a supposed pure abstract realm outside of us, such an assumption challenges the very foundation of philosophy.

What is wrong with the search for Truth as it may exist in the abstract? First, it is problematic to assume this abstract realm exists as something real outside of us when, understood as such, there is no way to *observe* and *verify* this supposition. The best we can do is develop "true" axioms, premises, and laws and see how well reality matches them, even if only proximately. Though better than an appeal to authority, this approach remains at the level of the speculative. The realm of the abstract, of categorical knowledge, is the product of our imagining how the world we observe works. If this is the case, then an estimation of any claimed Truth must rely on what we can observe in the material world for that estimation's basis. This tack is the opposite of that found in speculative philosophy.

Second, the presumption that Truth is real as an abstract existence must also presume both this Truth and the realm it inhabits are unchanging realities. This principle, however, clashes with the first. Since we know the material reality upon which knowledge has been and is based is one that is always changing (given a broad enough temporal lens), then we cannot presume an unchanging realm of Truth in the abstract, especially so when it comes to human social questions.

This is only true to a point, however. The world contains things whose properties retain some consistency while their other features change, a point of decisive consequence and one to which we will return to later.

How do we develop knowledge steeped in the assumption that reality is a changing thing? In such an inquiry, we must develop a set of logical categories that help us grasp dynamic change in both our methods of analysis and the subsequent language we use to depict the results of that analysis. These concerns—forms of analysis, logical categories, language, and our presentation of results—relate to what "dialectics" is meant to address.

The central thinker in popularizing dialectical thought in philosophy (after Aristotle's contribution) is the German thinker, Georg Hegel (1770–1831). Hegel was what is called "an idealist" as well as a "speculative philosopher." In his period, an "idealist" was someone who believed that a world of abstract principles existing outside of our material existence establishes what we observe in that material world. In this outlook, humans and our history are moved by the invisible world of abstract laws and dictums just outside our complete reach. But Hegel's philosophical assumptions do not mean he failed to help us escape philosophy's dilemmas, an ironic part of his genius and a subject to which we will return to below. For now, it will suffice to say that an alternative exists to traditional notions of static truth in philosophy and it was Hegel who did much to open doors to this alternative.

Hegel's philosophy was notoriously difficult and flawed. His writing could be obtuse and his meaning not always clear or obvious. Understanding him is not particularly easy. And where his system ultimately ended up was flat nonsensical. These difficulties resulted in an early reading of Hegel that was erroneous, though it has remained one interpretation of dialectical concepts ever since. It will be useful to clear this path before continuing.

An early reviewer of Hegel forwarded the idea that his dialectical logic could be reduced to the triad of "thesis-antithesis-synthesis." In this formulation, something exists as a "thesis," which produces or calls up its "antithesis"—its opposite. These two things stand in tension with and against one another. This tension-filled relationship produces changes in each and produces a "synthesis," or a new form that contains elements of both. It will not help going further into this idea except to say that Hegel rejected it as an inaccurate oversimplification of his ideas. Worse, several later thinkers that aligned themselves with a dialectical outlook were also interpreted in this triadic and formulaic framework. And, erroneous as it may be, many others *did* accept this interpretation as an accurate reflection of dialectical reason and adopted it.

In any case, why might one consider Hegel the ultimate word in philosophy? That is a bold statement. It seems hardly demonstrable, even counterintuitive.

It is not as if philosophy departments world over shut their doors after he wrote.

Prior to dialectical thought, philosophy struggled to uncover—or at least tried to develop a method to do so—Truth as a permanent, stable, and reliable set of knowledge. Dialectical thought assumes that, with reality composed of things undergoing flux and change, the best way to make sense of the world is discovering how such things relate to one another and give each other meaning through their interrelationships, interrelationships that ultimately refer back to the material world that sustains human existence and its history. Knowledge must be grounded, therefore, in empirical observations and framed in a material, historical, and *relational* way. In this perspective, knowledge no longer requires positing an idealist abstract realm outside of us for establishing meaning.

Several of Hegel's categories of dialectical logic, stripped of their idealism and non-empirical bases, help us capture the dynamics of change in thought, analysis, and writing. Let us take a look at a few of these categories and concepts.

Perhaps the appropriate place to start is with the concept of identity/difference. Aristotle's analytical philosophy tells us a thing is what it is and it is not another thing. This is often summed up with the phrase: A is equal to A and it does not equal non-A. This construct tells us to be careful and precise when we match a word with something real in the world. As such, it asks for consistency in linguistically establishing an identity and using it analytically. This is good advice and has served philosophers and scientists well for centuries. But this is only a place to begin our thinking about the relationship between words and the objects they identify, not end it.

Establishing identities is important because this allows us to make general statements about the properties of things and this aids in comparing one thing with another. Things that share essential qualities with one another might have similar origins or may be caused by similar forces and cause similar effects, a principle dependent on investigation instead of assertion, nevertheless. Further, as science is interested in the properties of things and their causal relationships, its method of knowing requires comparing one thing to another in order to isolate their identities and thus their qualities, and all of these combined allow for making successful generalizations, such as scientific theories, laws, and models.

However, if we are to understand both the limits of general statements and the insight and utility of comparing one thing with another, then we also need to know how things are *different* from one another. That is, some things share some properties with others and sometimes the properties they share are the most important and telling; other times it is their differences that matter the most. When we confuse one for another—that is, mistake difference for identity (or vice-versa)—then our analyses and evaluations are likely to make important errors, rendering comprehension and communication less effective than possible.

For example, when former US President Jimmy Carter claimed (years out of office) that the attitudes and actions of some members of the Southern Baptist Convention were similar to those of the Taliban, he was excoriated from many quarters. The Taliban were murderers of innocent men, women, and children. They forced women to wear the burqa. They banned music, television, kite flying, and other forms of entertainment and recreation. The Southern Baptist Convention never had done any of those things, not even close. Had the former President taken leave of his senses? Such criticisms were legitimate only by way of confusing these differences for the identities Carter was trying to stress. Both the Taliban and the Southern Baptist Convention practice literal interpretation of their holy scriptures, advocate that women should subjugate themselves to the will of men, demand conformity to authority, and enforce a strict set of social rules and practices (e.g., no drinking of alcohol or sex before marriage). From this point of view, the comparison had legitimacy, though his critics lacked the tools to root out such identities and differences and tell them apart.

The above example uses two cases to compare and contrast them in terms of shared/not-shared identities and differences. It is also possible for a single object to have multiple identities and differences within it, such that we often find ourselves debating which claims are true, as if accepting one version negates the other. For example, many people throw the word "freedom" around quite a bit, especially Americans and their debates over the conditions of their country and the policies of their government. Freedom's opposite is tyranny and oppression. However, sometimes one person's freedom is another's tyranny. Had the British defeated the American colonists, it is possible the slaves in British colonial holdings would have been freed, given that they had offered liberation to colonial slaves who fled to join their side in the war.

Relaxing the global rules of trade gives large corporations the ability to move more easily from areas of high wages (usually the modern West) to those of low wages (usually places like Central America, Africa, South East Asia). When this happens, large business owners and their investors certainly experience more "freedom" in the world market. What real history teaches us, however, is that business leaders and their host governments in such a world have had little reticence cozying up to dictators in poorer sections of the world, a combination of power that often oppresses local populations. And if not dictators, we still often find states in poorer sections of the world handing over land and resources (e.g., water, minerals, etc.) to foreign investors because of "free trade" policies while local people often experience deprivation and violence when they protest (e.g., see Frontline 2002 and sources therein). Further, the abundance global markets produce necessitates conditions where businesses can sell their goods, and this requires a certain amount of social and cultural freedom to move, mingle, shop, grow affluent, and participate in civic life. And, *at the same time*, government policies in consumer societies seem to gravitate toward wealthy elite interests via funding of elections, land ownership, ownership of media, support for think tanks, and whatnot. When does such freedom for one group stop and the subjugation for others begin? While we often know it when we see it, the line of demarcation is not a clear, precise, or Manichean one.

The concept of identity/difference tells us we do not have to make either/or choices in such matters. The freedom for large social forces to function the way they do often entails the loss of freedom elsewhere. All too often, however, our intellectuals, our media, and our social discourse become wrapped up in ideological baggage that does little to help us think clearly. From the traditional right, the idea that free markets can produce something other than freedom, and that in fact the history of market society has contained tyranny and oppression, are claims hardly worth considering and are seen and treated as absurd on their face. Conversely, should one accept many traditional leftist arguments, one could come away thinking that it is *only* some coalition of lies, falsehoods, ideology, propaganda, etc. that explain why working classes have often rallied to the defense of free markets.[1] If we are stuck with "freedom"

---

1 For example, see *Hillbilly Elegy* and the critical responses to it. In this work, J.D. Vance (2016) discusses his struggles being born into a poor Appalachian family in Kentucky, his middle class upbringing further north in Middletown, Ohio, and how he witnessed both lack of opportunities as well as behaviors and values amongst the poor (e.g., drugs, alcoholism, failure to maintain steady jobs, early pregnancies, and so on) that are dysfunctional for seizing the opportunities that did exist. He credits his grandparents for instilling in him values of education and hard work and sees himself as one who overcame significant obstacles and odds to make something of himself (e.g., finishing high school, going into the military, paying his way through to a university diploma, and eventually earning an Ivy League law degree and finding work at a prestigious firm). His narrative does seem to imply that if he could do it, so can others but that they are held back by their own limiting beliefs and actions. His critics view his analysis as overly simplistic, relying on stereotype, and lacking in the sort of structural analysis necessary to understand poverty's persistence (for indicative examples, see Jones 2016; Yates Sexton 2017). There is no reason, however, to see factual elements in both points of view without reducing them to either-or arguments. That said, his analysis was seized upon by right-wing politicians as evidence justifying gutting policies meant to assist those in poverty.

and "tyranny" as our mutually exclusive categories sans any notion of identity/difference, it is no wonder we have repeated the same debates for the last five centuries.

In terms of identity, it is important to be clear about what qualities must be present for a particular concept to be applied to an object so that we may improve our precision in language and thought. The concept of "essence" addresses this concern. As dialectical thinking assumes a world in the process of change, the "essence" of something does not necessarily refer to a permanent identity. At the same time, we would be misdirected if we assumed that language is not meant to connect our ideas to the world's real features. If we use the words "food," "liquid," "transportation," "nausea," or "sleep," it is not difficult for most people most of the time in our language community to understand to what we are referring. Some characteristics must be present for something to be "food," "liquid," "transportation," or "sleep." In terms of social relationships, we use the terms "the family," "governance," or "economics" to refer to certain social practices that have characteristics that must be in place for these concepts to be useful and relatively accurate. "Essence," then, refers to the basic, core properties of a thing, a relation, or a process that allows words we use to refer to them to carry the meaning attached to those words.

That said, it is not always easy or unproblematic to settle on what sort of "essence" constitutes a thing. What makes something a "sport"? No doubt, when you read that term you imagined something to which the concept refers. We would probably find close to universal agreement that soccer, basketball, baseball, tennis, cricket, and track and field are sports. But what about cheerleading, hunting, or chess? It is likely the level of agreement here will vary by person, country, and/or time period. All of these activities require skill, as does any sport. But if athleticism is required for an activity to be a sport, then hunting or chess might not qualify. This is not true of cheerleading, though. However, if being a competition is required, then most cheerleaders do not compete (or historically have not, until recently when competitions have been put together and awards given out). Hunting is a competition of a sort and certainly chess is and few would deny that any and all sports are in essence competitive activities. But what about rock climbing? The issue is more complicated still. Better athletes are likely to win a "three-legged race," but few people would consider that a sport more than a "recreational activity" or a "contest." So what is the essence of sport? We use the word freely but coming up with an "essential" identity all will agree upon is not so easy.[2]

---

2   The American monthly, *Sports Illustrated*, once had a regular feature called "A Sport or Not a Sport?" (or something like that) where they asked professional athletes to weigh in on the

Social sciences use the concept of "essence" in several ways but its practitioners are not always aware that this is what they are doing. First, at a structural level, the concept of essence is in-use in the following questions: "What makes a social system *a system per se*?" "What makes a society a hunting-gathering one rather than a simple agricultural or a pastoralist one?" "What has to exist in a governing system in order for the words 'authoritarian' or 'democratic' to be accurately applied?"

In a second use of essence, this time in quantitative sociology, a step in methodological practice is the use of "operational definitions" to establish who or what gets included or left out of a measurement. For instance, if we want to know the average age of students at a particular college, we could include only those "enrolled full-time and attending classes during the fall semester" in the sample we use for measurement. That definition becomes the "essence" of what will be considered a "college student," at least for that particular research agenda.

In sociology and other social sciences, there has been much debate and controversy over the issue of "essentialism," especially as this relates to issues of race/ethnicity, sex/gender, and sex/sexuality. It will be important to address this matter and to distinguish this debate from the dialectical usage of "essence" before continuing. In the social sciences, critics of "essentialism" object to the idea that there are natural and unchanging identities affixed to categories such as "male," "female," "white," "black," "heterosexual," "homosexual," and so on. Further, such critics argue, the supposed unalterable meanings that accompany these categories are/have been established by more powerful groups in society that can create and enforce categorical norms and the social mechanisms of control that accompany them. "Anti-essentialism" is the school of thought with which such critics align.

A dialectical use of "essence" is not the same as this debate on questions of race and/or sex and/or gender. Because of their sensitivity to historical social change, dialecticians do not require racial/ethnic, sex/gender/sexuality categorical knowledge to be inflexible. Further, as they tend to be materialists, dialecticians assume that meanings not only change but are profoundly influenced by relations of power in a society and that this can significantly shape

---

question as it applied to a particular activity, like archery, chess, hunting, and whatnot. The subtext, of course, was that it would be uncontroversial for most people that some activities, such as soccer or basketball, are considered sports. But other activities are more ambiguous as to their identity as a "sport." And, of course, lively debates were had when both athletes and readers weighed in and defended their respective positions. This was a real life example of a debate where identity/difference was the central issue, whether or not it was recognized there as a dialectical category.

what societal members accept and believe as normal and acceptable, even if it is socially constructed with only some, little, or no scientific basis at all. Dialecticians are, therefore, essentialists in one way and anti-essentialists in another.

Because dialectical thinking and language are concerned with the logic and processes of change, the concept of "transformation" is a key conceptual issue. Transformations exist all around us, from forces of nature to ways we organize our social relationships. Plants transform sunlight, air, water, and soil into leaves, flowers, wood, and other forms of energy use and storage, such that animals can eat them to live or other plants absorb their nutrients when they die and decay, with both animals and new plants becoming transformed in the process. Energy from plants and animals are consumed as food that transforms us from infants to adults. Humans also extract wood, ores, water, rubber, and minerals from the earth to build houses, cities, roads, and forms of transportation, transforming social relationships as well as themselves.

The issue of transformation is not simply a term or analytical category for dialectical thought; it is a central subject dialecticians study. How did traditional hunting and gathering societies transform into agricultural systems and how did this transform other social relationships, such as familial relations or religious practices? In our modern world, how do policies of states transform the social conditions for the population, in both the wealthiest and the poorest sectors of the world? It would be hard to be a social scientist and not be concerned with such issues.

One of the most important ideas about transformation is the concept of "quantitative to qualitative change." Quantity refers to the magnitude of something, e.g., the amount of money in one's wallet or the degrees of heat in atmospheric conditions. Quantities can go up or down and, when they do, a qualitative change in the properties of an object can occur. Some of the time, when the transformation of quantitative to qualitative change happens is not always set in stone, though cases of this are plentiful. When liquid water (at sea level) reaches $32\frac{1}{2}$ F it turns to "ice" and at $212\frac{1}{2}$ F it boils and jets off as steam. Ice is a solid and steam is a vapor and, as such, both have different properties while still composed of water (identity/difference). But when does the growth of money's magnitude become "potential capital" ready for investment? A number of variables, all in flux, make this determination, e.g., the value of the money compared to other forms of money and commodities, the prices of raw materials, the number of competing outlets available for the money to function as capital investment, the cost of labor and technology, the rate of inflation, and so on.

When one thing or relationship transforms into another, one or another or both (or more) of the participants in the change—because of how they interact—result in the "negation" of (one or more) of the others. Here we find several of our dialectical concepts interconnecting. The quantitative decrease in the temperature of water results in its qualitative transformation into ice, which negates its previous state as a liquid (and its properties). Money's accumulation transforms it from a simple amount of wealth where one might buy a car or a house to where, given enough of an increase, one can buy factories, land, and/or entire corporations, a difference that differentiates middle and/or upper-middle class people from the upper echelons of modern society. When such large stocks of money accumulate into a few hands, the economy can become dominated by a few but powerful economic actors, which can negate the principles of the competitive market and gravitate toward monopoly.

Other terms help us capture the various stages and features involved in transformations. Think of the concept and reality of "value" in our society. We can say that value has many "expressions," "manifestations," or "moments" in free market systems. When human labor produces goods that we can exchange, the value that such objects "express" (now in a new form) can be "manifested" (made real) in various ways, such as barter, price, money, profits, or credit. Each of these latter terms express different "moments" in the circulation of social value, though none are value *as such*. Each term captures some feature of value relations, from their "embryonic" stage (labor and barter) to their more "crystallized" forms (price, money, profit, credit). In this example, barter represents a form of trade based more on qualitative features that transform over time into more quantitative measures such as price and money. The terms above help us capture in word, thought, and analysis such multifaceted relationships.

Though there are many other dialectical concepts one could discuss, I will finish with the issue of "contradiction." For some dialecticians, this is the most important category. I will not quarrel with them here while agreeing that the question and reality of contradiction is vitally important. The first thing to note is that a "contradiction" is not simply a paradox (e.g., a square sphere) or a logical puzzle such as one might encounter in a word game or some other logical conundrum (e.g., Schrodinger's Cat). Rather, our concern here is with *how contradictions exist in the real world*. A contradiction exists when two (or more) elements built into a relationship undermine one another and do so in such a way that neither can reach its full potential without negating the other. The important feature here is that such contradictory elements are required in these incompatible relationships in that these elements are "essential" to the relationship in question while the contradictory nature of that relationship transforms each of them.

For example, an *essential* relationship built into the very principle of private enterprise is property ownership and the performance of labor. However, owners and laborers have several contradictory interests. Owners are in business to earn profits; workers work for wages. Should workers have the ability to extract a higher wage level through, for example, striking and withholding their labor, this would cut into the amount of profits available for the business owner to accrue to himself or herself. The business owner can try to recover those profits by raising prices—i.e., inflation—but unless there are similar price rises for their competitors' goods, they risk losing market share, while if prices rise too high across the market as a whole, this will negate previous wage increases. At the same time, if business owners accrue so much in profit that the amount of wealth available for wages declines, then access to the means of life for workers shrinks. And, if this decline goes on unchecked, then the spending power of workers contracts to such an extent that businesses lose potential purchasers, which in turn threatens their profits and the survival of an increasing number of them. Neither side can achieve a full development of their interests without the negation of the other. In the interim, they struggle over these interests and this struggle transforms things like state and corporate policy, types of technology used in production, standards of living, worker organization, employer market strategies, and so on.

Let us return to the issue of the "ultimate word" in philosophy. Hegel shared with traditional philosophy the idea that Truth exists abstractly outside of human practical activity and our job is to uncover this, preferably using a justifiable method to do so. Traditional philosophy went so far as to posit that the principles of Truth were independent of human intervention. Hegel went further, positing the real world was *the product* of an ideal realm beyond us that exerts its influence on that real world, or, even further, that the real world is but a manifestation of the abstract world's principles and truths. This argument was beyond where traditional philosophy had taken its claims before, as Hegel inserted a self-moving metaphysical existence to the ideal realm, with humans existing as only intermediaries of invisible, non-material forces laying beyond us.

Using his dialectical categories but reversing the ideal-material relationship advances our ability to analyze, understand, and depict our world. In studying this material world on its own terms without speculation and building concepts upon observation of material existence, we can use dialectical concepts in our thinking and our writing to help us overcome our tendency to think in terms of stasis and permanence and rather focus on flux and change. Further, mobilizing dialectical logic (thinking in terms of change) and terms (manifestation, transformation, contradiction, and so on) while investigating how relationships in the real world interact and evolve over time means that we no longer have to search for "Truth" in a singular locale but rather truths with many loci grounded in our observations. When we ground the question "How does reality work?" in systematic empirical analysis where it belongs and animate that analysis with dialectical logic and reason, we divest ourselves of philosophy's idealism and metaphysics and are better prepared to move forward scientifically.[3]

As our inquiry moves forward, we will increasingly see why we need a mode of thought that allows us to think about and analyze the world in terms of its essential relationships and its internal processes. Like any society, modernity is one composed of historical and structural relationship that we must grasp if we are to truly understand it. Unlike other systems, modernity's structural relationships are as such that change is an inherent part of its normal functioning and its real history. We need to acquire a quality of mind equal to the match and speculative theory will only get us so far. What we need, therefore, is a form of inquiry that allows us to harness tools that incorporate the logic and the language of change, development, dynamism in our analysis and our thinking. Dialectical reason is geared to do just that.

---

3   It is important to point out here that "dialectic" itself is not a material property causing these changes, something unmeasurable except by the residues it leaves behind. This would put us back on the grounds of speculation again, not positive knowledge. "Dialectic" (sometimes "dialectics") refers to a set of terms and logical categories that assist us in grasping material and social changes in thought, words, and writing. That is, "dialectic" is not a *thing*. It is a term that denotes a conceptual framework for thinking, analyzing, and writing about the forces of change we observe. It is neither a world view, as in a philosophy of life or politics or spirituality, nor a causal force in the world making things happen.

CHAPTER 4

# The Concept of Society

For much of history, the way humans have thought about and explained their behavior has been through positing forces beyond their ability to fully understand, such as spiritual forces, god or gods, a model of universal human nature, or genes, or some other mechanism to which we only had partial access. Religious thinkers told us about devils, sin, grace, redemption, and eschatology, i.e., some final conflict and resolution through god's intervention on Earth. Even many Enlightenment thinkers forwarded arguments about our innate tendencies to do things like truck, barter, and trade (Adam Smith), though life was often nasty, brutish, and short (Thomas Hobbes).

Religious traditions and proto-social thought shared the idea that Truth existed in an abstract world of hypothetical laws, only some of which are actually true and our job is to discover them. In such a world, the real world we could see, taste, and touch might indicate what these hypotheticals are, but it is the hypothetical principles themselves that account for real reality and our material world is just their reflection, though often a poor or incomplete one. This is the path of inquiry often followed by the speculative philosophers like Immanuel Kant (Chapter 2) and Georg Hegel (Chapter 3).

Of course, human culture always intercedes between the positing of hypothetical Truth and observance of the real world. Different cultures at different times have held different goals and/or values to be of high regard and worthy of pursuit. The pattern *over time* is for the knowledge of what is valuable in life to solidify and remain for a period of time only to be changed or transformed with a culture's transformation. But, *at any one time*, the pattern is for the members of a culture to hold such institutionalized goals as personally dear to them, as if they represent transcendent and timeless values. Thus, there is a tension between the personal experience of "Truth" and basic historic-sociological processes. Neither one holds absolute sway for very long; both enjoy challenge and constant flux, whether welcomed or not. Or, another way to put it is that humans, by and large, live with a modest level of certainty of what is true and good, though these standards have been neither consistent nor universal across time and space. Nevertheless, our society's values become *our* beliefs, its norms *our* rules, and its practices *our* behaviors. After we fill our gods and Truths with our culture's norms, our culture then presents itself as a reflection of the *real* reality that exists in the abstract world. This is true not just for us in our society, but this seems to be a general sociological truism...at least thus far in history.

This approach to knowledge—what the previous chapter termed "speculation"—only gets us so far indeed. An alternative way to go about investigating human reality is starting with what we can observe, see, touch, taste, smell, or otherwise measure in some way. That is, rather than start in the clouds of abstraction, we should start our investigations in the real world, with society and its parts, practices, norms, structures, and so on. Beginning here, we can move beyond guesswork and hypotheses that can only find support through confirmation bias (i.e., finding what we hope, expect, and/or want to find) and start with careful and systematic inquiry into the nature of real things, real relationships, and real history. And it is upon such investigations that we can better understand the whys and wherefores of human behavior and limit how our own cultural assumptions influence us and the knowledge we produce.

It is no stretch of the sociological imagination to see humans as a *homo symbolicus*, i.e., a symbol creating animal. Symbols are products of the human mind and, as such, we do not derive their meaning from outside of our social relations. Take, for example, the Christian cross. This religious iconography was not picked from thin air but rather came directly from the story of the crucifixion of Jesus. Symbols, always meaningful to some degree (as they are, by definition, carriers of meaning), are not always religious. Everyday life functions with a symbolic code, of which language is a key form. Language allows us to create and exchange a seemingly infinite range of ideas, beliefs, messages, philosophies, signals, moods, directions, and so on. But without being born into and raised within a social system that is rich with symbolic content, we would never learn this skill of communication for which we seem to have an innate capacity to excel at once exposed.

Humans are social beings at their core. We learn the languages and norms to which we are exposed. We are dependent on each other for our daily bread. Without society we fail to develop and die before we even have a chance. This is why we must study humans in their *social* context, where society is an object of study in its own right.

Food is one of the best arenas of human activity to demonstrate the power of socio-cultural forces, their symbolic character, and how these relationships shape us in turn. There may be some food in your culture you do not like. I, for instance, do not like beets or sweet potatoes or sea urchin. These are personal tastes and as such they do not concern us here. Our concern here is that what one culture defines as "food" another culture might define in a completely different manner. Many Americans eat meat from cows (beef), something that would seem to someone from India just like how eating the family pet would appear to someone from the United States (not exactly, but the point should stand). Speaking of the family pet, there are places in China and South Korea where dogs are considered food (less prevalent with newer generations and their killing of dogs for meat was made illegal by a South Korean court in June 2018). In Peru, you might be served guinea pig and, in the Philippines, half-formed duck embryos still in the shell (balut). The Maasai in Kenya sometimes stick their cattle in the neck with a sharp stick and drink the blood that spurts out.

As you read this list of examples, did you feel a slight twinge of nausea? If you did, it probably felt as if it came from somewhere interior to your being, as a biologically built-in reaction just the same as it is to feel pain when touching hot metal. But just as not feeling emotions of reverence for another country's flag is socially determined, feeling revulsion at the prospect of eating roasted cat is equally socially conditioned. Beyond evolutionarily programmed things like being repelled by rancid meat and excrement, many things we find distasteful are simply social products without any biological basis. Society shapes us at our most visceral level.

But even closer to home, in modern society we eat things all the time we might not have eaten had we an alternative point of view. Look on the back side of pre-packaged food available at your local grocery store. How many of those ingredients do you recognize as "food"? And do you think someone from an earlier culture would recognize them as such either? We are constantly reminded that you do not want to see hotdogs or sausages being made and for good reason. We moderns are accustomed to our food as a final product. If the average modern person saw a deer hit by a car, it is doubtful too many would feel comfortable going up and actually touching the bloody carcass. However, kill a cow in a slaughter house, cut it up into pieces, call them "steaks," package them, ship them in cool containers to grocery stores, cook the flesh over a grill, and many, many modern people will put it *in their mouth* without thinking twice. Finally, should they have encountered the dead deer early in the day and refused to even touch it, it is highly unlikely that when they sit down later for their steak dinner they will even notice the inconsistency in their attitudes and behaviors. Such is the power of society's ability to condition us.

But the relation between food and our social conditioning runs even deeper. Food is an especially good example of an "embedded" knowledge. What is edible versus poisonous has long been worked out in most cultures and if they do not work this out they risk not being around as a culture for very long. So worked out have been methods of cooking and storage that, while taught anew per generation, they rarely need to be "rediscovered." This knowledge is embedded in culture and practice, but its origins are often lost to our immediate understanding. Simple things are collected in memories. Just as tying our shoes, sewing on a button, and standards of hygiene (e.g. a child does not really understand why brushing one's teeth now is a good idea for their life fifty years later) are living embodiments of mental and physical labor of previous generations, so do recipes for dishes contain an untold number of traditions, personal styles, and previous know-how developed long ago through everyday trial and error.

Cultures associate food with their rituals and holidays, even if they no longer remember the origin of the association. The Christian Bible makes no mention of eggs as representative of the resurrection they claim for their Christ-figure. How many British children know from where their culture's obsession with tea comes? How many Americans can imagine a Thanksgiving feast without a turkey on the dinner table, even though that particular dish played a minor (or maybe even no) role in the holiday's earliest observance of lore? How did hotdogs become associated with a baseball game? Sport historians might know the answer, but the average person likely does not.

It would be impossible to list here the entire manner in which society inscribes its rules and rituals upon us, often in ways about which we remain unaware. The religion people practice has an unmistakable correlation with the geographical location of their birth. The same is true with language, political systems, family structures, and so on. Many gender roles are prescribed by societal history, relations of power, and the teaching of norms that are culturally expected, and so on. We become, in innumerable ways, what our society makes of us. Even the sound people make when they sneeze differs depending on whether they are American, French, Japanese, Filipino, or deaf, i.e., it is culturally conditioned (see Tracey 2013).

Of course, the relationship is not one-to-one, but it would be foolish to deny the power society has over those who participate in it over their lifetimes. Human behavior is not a smorgasbord of infinite choices where individuals *just happen* to freely choose behaving and believing the same way over and over again each day. If we reject that explanation as an impossible coincidence, then we must accept that some manner of conditioning is always at work. The fact that "cultures" exist at all over time and that we can conceptualize "culture" itself tells us much about the power that society has to shape individuals prior to any agency they might or do have.

These observations bring us to the idea that it is possible to study the social world and the outcomes it produces in a scientific way, without recourse to speculation. We can observe, measure, see, study, and analyze societies and the regular patterns of behavior they produce. These are real. These do not exist outside of us as a specter or an invisible world of Truth that is non-material at root. And such patterns of behavior serve as indicators of the reality and logic of a social structure, as systems write their prescriptions and proscriptions upon us and we live them out. We can see how this is so and learn how it works via methodical investigation.

Positive knowledge of the relationship of the human species to nature and to its own social constructs require a working model of both, given that it is an objective social world that provides for our survival—individual and collective—in nature. That is, just as we can develop models of atoms, of chemical bonds, or automobiles, we can model social worlds in a similar way. We can examine the structures of societies in general—what they all share—and we can construct models of unique societal configurations. And from these models, we can construct various laws, discover central tendencies, and understand why regular practices develop the way they do. We can construct a science of society that explains much more about human behavior than can philosophical speculations about human nature or the dictates of religious lore.

A science of society focuses on the real social relationships external to the inner lives of individuals, whether these be social norms and rules of interaction, familial, economic, and/or political ties between groups, and wider social structures that define systems *as types of systems*. These external forces—i.e., social facts, social structures, and social relationships—often shape us and our behavior in ways we rarely consider or realize, though they are just as real as are trees, bacteria, and gravity.

Social structures have orders of causal magnitude. That is, some social structures determine more outcomes than do others. But which structures are the most determinative? How many are involved? To what extent? Are these relationships necessary to a structure (part of what it is) or are they historically contingent ("accidents")? *How* do some social phenomena determine the range of possibility for other(s)? In which historical periods does this or that social structure, social relationship, or social fact predominate? Towards answering such questions, one analyzes how the connections of specific parts of systems determine the range of limits and conditions of possibility for other phenomena. Just as in the natural sciences, the social sciences build models that provide for the discovery of such causal relationships. These parts and their relationships are often in conflict with the operation(s) of other parts, closing or opening the range of their limits and possibilities in turn. And, consequently, the entirety of all societies' dynamics and changing features as a whole are what we call "history."

This latter claim is not intuitive by any means. Typically, we think of "history" as the actions of individuals—sometimes collectively but often singularly—usually in positions of influence, authority, and/or power. Other times, "history" is written in terms of the actions of states and/or political decision-makers. But none of what gets catalogued as "history" happens outside of the social relations interior to social systems. Do a people stop their nomadism and learn to engage in agriculture? Then they better also learn to wield weapons to protect their newfound territory (which another group may have a claim on). Leaders of kingdoms must make decisions based on the tactics other leaders use and this is often in pursuit of needed land, resources, materials, etc. Systems have requirements necessary to keep them running and actors in positions of leadership must adjust their strategies accordingly. Further, from top to bottom, social systems shape people, constrain them, give them the space to act and realize themselves, and provide the options available to them. And this is not even to mention long-term cyclical patterns systems experience because of their own internal logic, which are imperceptible in day-to-day life. To make a very long story short, "history" is a product of the way social systems have a logic, how that logic unfolds, and the way actors perform within that unfolding logic. Given this, it is the logic of systems, of societies, that we must grasp before anything else if we are really to understand the human condition.

What can we learn from this discussion? First and foremost is that human beings are constantly surrounded by social forces that shape them and have always been this way. This is not to deny the reality of either how the psychology of mind works nor the existence of human agency. Rather, it is to hold that social forces have their own reality and force of influence. Further, and more boldly, if we really want to understand humans, the world they build and live in, and how they act in that world, we must grasp the concept of society and the forces it contains. It was not until the mid-nineteenth century that this idea took root. This is where sociology originated and it is a field of scientific inquiry broader than most others, one whose work not only is not yet finished but in fact in many ways has just begun.

CHAPTER 5

# History and Human Development

One could prioritize a variety of things when interpreting history. What has the history of religion been? Here, one could examine changes in beliefs about spiritual forces across different societies, from animism to polytheism to monotheism. If one studied societies through their size and the complexity of their armaments, they could arrange human history from stone weapons to those forged from metal to the invention of gun powder and so on. If a telling of the human story followed its forms of technology from simple to the more complex, this reading might emphasize tools that required human force, animal power, and then the replacement of those with various machines and fuels. Of course, using other criteria—e.g., art, philosophy, music, food—would each reveal something interesting about historical life on our planet.

What if we examined history as the history of human development? Such a view would prioritize the relationships between humans as a species, the natural world, the social worlds they build to survive in that natural world, and the effect all of these have on the individuals that different systems produce. A lens that captures our earliest societies and our latest and everything in between will bring into focus how we have transformed the world and how it has transformed us: from the distance between chipping away at a rock in order to make an arrowhead or a spear versus the creation of atomic weapons; the distance between gathering nuts and berries for immediate and local consumption and mass factory farming, where meat and vegetables are produced by the ton and shipped across thousands of miles to global markets; and the distance from complete ignorance of the microscopic world and its influence on our health to germ theories of disease, vaccinations, and antibiotics. But are these separate and disconnected realities or does something tie them together? To better make sense of that question, an analytical framework would need to examine general forms of social organization, the various methods of production different societies have practiced (and the social relations these spawn), and the way such systems shape individuals who comprise them and the potential destinies they lay out before them.

When we look across history, using the modern world as a baseline from which to look backward at our collective past, it is clear that societies have grown more complex and individual capabilities have changed in turn (not always for the better). This growth has not been uniform, linear, or inevitable, but it is, nevertheless, possible to discern a general trend over time.

Let us start with and isolate the human individual as a social animal.

Viewing the world as a thing in transformation suggests that there are limits to using a generalized "human nature" as an explanatory model for understanding humans at the abstract individual level. Such a concept implies a static existence—as in, "such-and-such behavior is just a reflection of human nature and therefore there is not much we can do about it." In a model such as this, the concept of "human nature" is an inherent part of being human in that it applies to everyone by matter of being a member of the species and is part of their core being whether conceptualized in spiritual or biological terms. This model assumes this interior nature of humans is unchanging and common across history and is a determinative part of our individual selves, i.e., it explains much of our perceptions and concrete behaviors. Such proposed characteristics, however, are confounded by several known sociological realities.

What we experience as a self is neither static or wholly in-born but rather is dependent upon learning the language, views, and ideas and behaviors of others, others that stand in both significantly meaningful and close relationships to us, as well as more general, distant and often temporary relationships (Mead 1934). As we develop, these others are mirrors of a sort for us, reflecting back to us how others receive us and in this way we learn our social identities through this external relationship to those with whom we interact (Cooley 1902; for recent research dealing with a similar idea, see: Neal, Durbin, Gornik, and Lo 2017). This reality poses two problems for the model of human nature recounted above. First, because of the dependence on outside sources for parts of our sense of self, human behavior in general cannot be reduced solely to an interior core individuality. Second, the relations outside of us in which we move and our interactions with others are things that constantly change over time, which means that so too do humans change over time.

And we are formed by more than just our interactions with others or our genes. The development of human productive powers across history has changed our forms of governance, religion, social practice, norms, values, and even language and skills. That is, humans are born into and are formed by *types* of societies that produce and reproduce their means of life differently. Some rely on hunting and gathering, some on agriculture, and still others use complex forms of industrial technology (with today cyber-technology growing all around us). Hunter-gatherers were/are basically illiterate (because many do not need written language) nor do they regulate their movements by precise schedules or clocks; by the same token, modern people are less likely to develop hunting skills while they experience the passage of time marked by a Christian calendar and with weeks and workdays shaped by commercial life. Such social conditions and experiences translate into different inner lives, world views, understandings of nature, and so on, and this makes viewing human nature as a static, universal, and determinative thing problematic.

There are other reasons to remain cautious and circumspect in using human nature as an explanatory model. First, in its conventional usage, the concept of human nature assumes something that requires explaining—e.g., "Why did she/he do that?" "Well, it is just human nature." Here, human nature as an explanation only pushes back behavioral questions into an abstract generality that does not identify what *it is about this human nature* that accounts for the observed action and why human nature might be such as it is and not some other way. Pushed further, if an explanation rooted in human nature encounters examples of behavior out of accord with the proposition, this undermines the position's basis. And even if we can pinpoint human characteristics rooted in our "nature," these are always filtered through socialization and culture. For example, some forms of mental illness are culturally specific and found only in one or just a few societies (e.g., "culture bound syndromes"), while others, such as schizophrenia, are experienced differently in different cultures.[1]

Second, as it is pitched at the universal level, if human nature accounts for as much human action as its conventional usage implies, we should see more cultural similarity than we do. A strong form of this critique is that if a static and universal human nature exists, then all cultures would be identical. Or, rather, we would only see one culture historically around the world—all cultures would be the same given the same genetic make-up of humans as a species. A weaker and mirror-image (i.e., opposite in the way a mirror reverses our sense of right hand versus left) but no-less-relevant form of this critique is that if there is a universal human nature then we would not see the wide range of behaviors as we do. Even a cursory reflection tells us that people are profoundly conditioned by their external circumstances, from language to morals to tastes and so on. We would have almost no preferences for things in these terms if we were not socialized into a certain but limited set of choices that includes some possibilities and excludes others.

Are humans simply empty shells, born *tabula rasa*? Well, no. If it is only culture and learning that inscribes all of our personalities and capabilities into us, we would take many more years to develop language and interpersonal skills than we do. The brain is prepared to rapidly learn language and read cultural tropes and norms, i.e., we are pre-wired to learn (an argument made famous by the linguist, Noam Chomsky). We know we learn things and we also know

---

1  According to Stanford anthropologist, Tanya Luhrmann, people with schizophrenia that do hear voices (i.e., not all do) tend to hear benign and playful ones in India and Africa and harsh and threatening ones in the United States (see C. Parker 2014 and references therein).

we learn to learn how to do things. But if we had to learn to learn how to learn first, it is hard to imagine how we would progress or even start.

The *tabula rasa* theory of individual development is also incompatible with our knowledge of evolution. As should bear little repeating, individual members of a species pass their genes on to their progeny. Individual members of a species possess traits that either help or hinder their survival and those individuals that have the greatest advantages here are more likely to successfully pass on their genes; thus, their offspring tend to share those same characteristics. As such, it makes no sense to assume that after over at least two-hundred thousand years of human existence (in its present form) that it all occurred through passing down blank slate infants from one generation to the next. For this to be true, somewhere in the past that we share with other primates, a species (i.e., us) emerged that passed down physical traits but suddenly ceased in passing down cognitive faculties, personality dispositions, and so on. This makes little sense. There would have to be a first blank slate or at least an observable *decrease* in inherited faculties from our primate ancestors, not the increase so obviously observed. More damning still for blank slate theory considering what we know about evolution is the fact that the slow withdrawal of biological imprinting on the mind from primates to humans would have been disadvantageous and prevented humans from moving ahead, as we clearly saw them do.

We can view human nature in a way that is comparable to the relationships among an alphabet, a language, and a grammar. Human biological make-up is similar to an alphabet: it creates the basic tools within which all subsequent relations must work, but it does not determine their content, i.e., an alphabet is like our DNA options. Combined, letters make isolated words, but words in themselves do not pre-determine the sentences we will say or write. A language's grammar, much like a set of social norms, creates the rules of discourse we must operate within, where that grammar is similar to our biology's basic tools. Over long periods of time, the words, their meanings, even the grammar can change somewhat, while the alphabet stays intact (or changes even more slowly). But, by using words, sentences, and meanings in interaction with others over time, the words, concepts, ideas, individuals, and rules (and so on) are thus changed too. Words and meanings change most rapidly, rules of grammar less so, and letters even less. Letters, and in part grammar, are the genes passed down and these set up possibilities, limits, and capacities. Cultures are the words, and these are the carriers of meaning to which we are exposed, that we adopt, have available for criticism and debate, etc.

Our biological conditions—DNA, genes, our brains and bodies—make up a blueprint upon which our culture can inscribe directions. A computer has a blueprint for its use, a structure that provides it potential utility, but that structure does not allow it to do just anything its user wants. We may fill it up with nothing, our shopping list, or simply use it for email. Or we can use its vast potential to calculate immense numbers, run statistics, tap into data bases, communicate with others around the world, and so on. The human being is similar. Our genes have no will but can organize how our bodies and minds are structured. Given identical genetic background, individuals may be left uneducated, filled with superstition, and/or their physical capacities left underdeveloped—e.g., "feral" children who have been locked away from interaction by abusive parents and that remain physically and mentally stunted even if rescued from the situation. Or individuals may be highly educated, infused with a high degree of analytical sophistication, and/or trained in a variety of physical skills and capabilities.[2]

So, we can think of history as a history of human development. As our socially productive capacities have changed, so have we changed our individual abilities and capabilities. What has been behind this change and what sort of changes has this brought to society and to ourselves? To answer these questions, we must first address what is at the basis of society. To survive and thrive, humans must construct a world in which to live. Nature does not provide ready-made houses, clothes, and tools that we need. We must transform nature into these things. At the core of this transformation is human labor—the outward physical expression of our inner creative capacity—and, in this transformation of nature, labor builds *society*.

Labor is something more than simply producing goods for market trade or personal consumption, though it does include these things. Human labor is *creative* activity, whether this be planting, building, harvesting, sewing, or burying. And it is more than that. The arts are a form of labor, where painting, sculpting, composing, or performing are outward expressions of our creative capacities. Even forms of leisure are *part* of the labor process as a whole, though we normally separate these two things in thinking about them. When people play sports, not only are they engaging in physical activity (which often requires mental creativity) but they are also playing with equipment, and on fields and courts, i.e., with apparatuses that require producing. And leisure itself helps us *reproduce* and *prepare* ourselves for future laboring endeavors by allowing us to rest, to supply our bodies with nutrition and energy, and to escape mentally for a while.

---

2  For example, Lázló Polgár, a Hungarian chess teacher and educational psychologist, believed geniuses are made not born. He raised his three daughters to become chess prodigies and two of whom became the first and second highest rated women players in the world.

So, labor in this expansive sense is the basis upon which society exists. And different types of societies distribute people's labor—including skills, tasks, and roles—differently, or what social scientists call the "division of labor." This social-structural trait is an integral feature of all social systems, some of which are more "complex" than others. And thus, we can connect several ideas in envisioning history as one of human development—how different types of systems have different divisions of labor and how these shape individuals.

Let us view labor in the broad view of history and human development. The earliest societies were hunters and foragers. Much of their productive labor went into securing calories, whether by killing game or finding plants to eat. Most of these peoples were (and are) nomadic and thus part of their labor includes traveling for food and/or new encampments. Such peoples build tools for hunting, sew skins for clothing, sharpen bones and rocks for weapons (and other tasks), and often leave visual articulations of their lives on stones and cave walls (among other things). Though such societies probably experience more leisure time than we moderns suppose (see Just 1980) and probably more than modern people do today (see Kaplan 2000), their technology was/is rudimentary, as were/are too the limits of their knowledge (though, clearly, some of their knowledge greatly surpasses the average person's today; for instance, how to hunt or find food or predict future weather from current visual observations).

At some point in many parts of the world and at different times (but beginning approximately 10,000–15,000 or so years ago), humans discovered how to grow food (horticulture) and attend to and/or pen up animals (pastoralism). Use of digging sticks, slash and burn techniques, the saving of seeds, simple metallurgy, and more sophisticated weapons developed here, as did more permanent forms of housing, techniques of securing water and food, and thus so did grow more calories available to more people over their lifetimes. One result here was such systems produced and supported more people. And with more people such societies could devote more time to creating things like pottery, art, and even mythmaking. Also, with improved tools and more people, the expanse of the territory they needed for settling would tend to grow (though not always the case; in some early sedentary societies, if a village grew in numbers beyond its capacity, they would often split off some members to form new villages elsewhere and thus the culture would grow, expand, and even morph and change over a wide territory). These societies also developed new forms of weapons and military arts, as settling down on land also meant an increased need and opportunity to defend it.

Some simple horticulturalist societies eventually transformed into large-scale agriculturalists and grew quite large. In such societies, more people either could specialize in a smaller set of skills, while others were relieved of physical labor and focused their work on mental labor (e.g., early philosophy and the proto-sciences). And, while doing so, they increased their mastery of metallic and maritime arts, learned better ways to transport fresh water, expanded their visual arts, invented more detailed religious theologies and traditions, and so on. These societies also developed methods of writing, built large temples, created a permanent armed force, and often enslaved defeated rivals.

It would arguably be pedestrian here to continue this type of analysis as it would move through mass agriculture and industrial society. The reader probably can see around that corner on his or her own. But let us look at the scope of human historical development via additional categories that direct us to how it has grown over time.

Humans have developed knowledge increasingly over their history. Things like mathematics, physics, and astronomy have advanced by leaps and bounds (with some setbacks, of course). Though the Greeks and Romans had their own mathematical knowledge (e.g., Pythagoras) and calculus came to us several centuries ago (Newton and Leibniz, though independently of each other), today's mathematical knowledge has developed far beyond these periods. Physicists have used the knowledge of mathematics and geometry to figure out things such as the speed of sound and light and that the universe is expanding more rapidly all the time. We have learned the whys and wherefores of the seasons, what stars are, that trillions upon trillions of stars (about 10 to the 22nd to 24th power) and (roughly) one or two hundred billion galaxies exist, as well as the existence of the atomic and subatomic world and the mysteries they contain. Our sense of the world, the heavens, and our place in them has irrevocably changed.

Human skills, social infrastructure, and technology have advanced over time, though in mixed and uneven ways. Though few people today know how to grow and make all the food they need or produce their own clothing, at a global level illiteracy numbers have been dramatically reduced since 1800 and more people today can read than at any time in human history.[3] Use of things like cars, appliances, industrial technology, and computers would have probably confused people into thinking they were magical devices less than 200 years ago. We have mastered flight and reached the moon. We send up satellites that allow global communication. We have learned how to cure diseases and ease pain in ways that the ancients and even our great-grandparents could only dream about.

---

3   See Max Roser and Esteban Ortiz-Ospina, "Literacy" (Our World in Data) and sources therein at (URL retrieved August 31, 2018): https://ourworldindata.org/literacy.

These results in human development are not evenly distributed nor are their effects all in a direction that speaks of progress. Much of the world is still illiterate, struggles for daily bread, lacks fresh water, and dies of curable diseases (e.g., malaria is the one of the largest killers of children and adults in Africa). Our cars and televisions reduce our exercise and our mental acuity, and we become overweight, lazy, and less informed than entertained. Industry pumps out commodities and pollution at equal rates. Our reliance on fossil fuels for cars and fertilizers is destroying our air and our use of plastics is soiling our nest and ruining our bodies.

These are not issues to take lightly and covering them here briefly does the magnitude of the problems they cause us a disservice. But these issues are not the point of this chapter and we will return to them later. The point to stress here is that a large enough temporal lens cannot help but bring into view how human history has been a history of change in society, technology, knowledge, and human individuality, and not one of stagnation or suspended animation. Human history, that is, is a history of their own development.

CHAPTER 6

# A History of Struggles

The last chapter discussed history from the vantage point of human social, technological, productive, and individual development. But this is not the only lens we could use.

What is history? Is history just a series of nations and their conquests and rivalries, great names and personalities, actions taken and results, accidents and flukes? This view is familiar, but it is a history without coherence other than a timeline. And if we inspect such a timeline with a theme in mind, our inner-historian may write the history of religion, of states, of warfare, of art, and so on for us. This is a common way to view the world and it is not without merit.

Another way to think of history attempts to grasp the range of human behavior from the earliest wandering bands to the most recent technological metropolis. A lens carved at this broad level brings with it three interesting observations and one important possible conclusion. First, this view sees social change as the norm, even if most of that change has been relatively recent historically speaking (for about 95% or more of their existence humans have lived in hunter-gatherer societies). Second, the existence of distinct social classes has marked the *minority* of linear social history but a majority of the *types* of social systems observed over time. Third, periods of the least rapid change extensively overlap with the periods without a developed class structure (in general, nomadic hunter-gatherers are relatively egalitarian systems); the period, relatively shorter by comparison, where social change is more common and rapid overlaps extensively with the history of social class systems. For this observation alone, therefore, a study of class history is suggested.

Let us first make a distinction between a "category" and a "class." A category of people is made up of those who share some characteristic in common as individuals, such as redheads, the left-handed, circus clowns, or parking attendants (we could think of many other categories, no doubt). But what constitutes a *class*? First off, a class is irreducible to its members as a unit of analysis; it is its own unit. The examples above are only a product of our categorizing them mentally on some characteristic that interests us, and they are thus categories and not classes. Even if the criteria are meaningful and real (as opposed to arbitrary and unmeasurable, i.e., those with unkempt hair, those yawning in the last hour), we would still have a category on our hands and not a class because, importantly, none of the examples above can *act as a structural unit of analysis* outside of the individuals that compose it. A class, on the other hand, is something *built into* a social structure.

Second, therefore and by extension, the concept of "class" is meant to capture an *essential* set of structured relationships inherent to a system's very logic. We can imagine a society without clowns or clam diggers. But feudalism and market systems have landed gentry and businesspersons, respectively, built into their signature practices. Regardless of their individual traits as persons in a feudal system, when an individual in a well-placed family dies off, there are rules of inheritance and obligation that keep the wealth in certain hands. At the bottom of society, there are serfs who are required to provide labor and other resources—e.g., farmers, masons, carpenters, ironsmiths—that keep the system functioning a certain way, which here means producing the material goods upon which the system depends. These people are often "tied" to the land and cannot freely move or withdraw their labor under threat of punishment. Thus, individuals in each case are compelled to do certain things given their structural position in the class system and, as such, class relations can be analyzed as a unit of analysis because they exist and operate in ways that are analytically meaningful.

What justifies examining some societies as "class" systems? For one, a real pattern exists that the criterion "class" captures and we can make real observations of its existence in history. Second, such a criterion reveals relevant and insightful knowledge. Looking at human history going back, say 200,000 years, we see that most of this time humans were nomadic hunter-gatherers. Afterward we saw the rise of early village life, small cities, and even city-states, etc., shaped by the rise of simple agriculture (i.e., horticulture) and pastoralism and later mass agriculture and trade, and so on. In hunting-gathering systems, we observe a sort of early communal life where food, tools, etc. are collectively owned and new goods and surpluses are seen as the property of the group as a whole. With the rise of sedentary agricultural societies, we witness the rise of individual, family, clan, and subgroup ownership in land, resources, the origins of slavery, and the ensconcing of (often hereditary) leaders in positions of political authority and military power. One of the most salient differences between hunting-gathering periods versus societies afterward is the emergence of mechanisms for the "appropriation of wealth." Though not all early simple agricultural societies were class systems (some maintained common property), this transfer of produced wealth from one group to another is an important feature of human history that delineates systems and epochs, so it makes sense that we address it.

The appropriation of wealth is a method of transferring wealth from those who do the labor that produces it to those who own and control the resources the system of production is based upon. If the structure of a society does this systematically, then it is a "class system." We have seen multiple types of classes and class systems—slaves, plebeians, slave masters, and landowners in ancient societies, serfs, bondsmen, monarchs, and aristocratic lords in feudalism, and wage-laborers, corporate owners, and investing classes in modern society. Slaves produce the material wealth that accrues to slave owners, serfs produce the wealth upon which a landed gentry sits, and wage-workers produce the goods upon which businesses depend to make their profits. And outside of hunter-gatherers, most other social systems in history have been based on a class structure such as those above. This is true whether we are speaking of Rome, Carthage, Chinese and/or Japanese dynasties, the large agricultural societies of Mesoamerica, European feudalism, or the modern world system.

Sociologists use the notion of class to categorically organize different social systems because *a system whereby one much larger group produces the vast majority of wealth while a much smaller group controls and enjoys that wealth is a salient and essential trait.* This numerical imbalance plus an opposite but equal material imbalance in the other direction tells us that class societies have not only inequality built into them but that inequality itself produces a certain antagonism between the classes. This antagonism rests on the terms of labor, the conditions under which labor is undertaken, what is done with the product of that labor, how wealth is thus distributed (i.e., quantity of wealth appropriated, how, and at what rate), and what is done with it afterward. One class, the ownership class, sets these terms more often than not, as well as all that stems from these terms. Or, said more precisely, the former class does not so much as create these terms but rather sets the details of their practice, e.g., how much labor is to be done and when (the working-day) and at what level and method of remittance (in kind products such as food or things such as wages). And this class reaps the rewards while the laboring classes struggle to get what they can to improve their lot.

Business owners, for instance, often try to keep wages low, hire overseers and managers, employ strikebreakers, and whatnot. Owners work to shape state policies in their favor, e.g., using state police to keep strikers from disrupting production, supporting anti-union policies, lobbying for tax breaks, demanding free trade policies when advantageous, urge using state policies for breaking into new markets, and so on (e.g., see Kozik 2016; Elliot 2018b). In their turn, workers can sabotage equipment, slow down work, disobey orders, abandon the production apparatus, organize themselves for collective bargaining, and withhold their labor or even revolt. In addition, worker movements have pressured the state to improve working conditions, such as workplace safety regulations, higher minimum wages, eliminating child labor, mandatory days off (e.g., the weekend), and/or other benefits like health care or pensions.

Still, the deck can be stacked, as owners of industry come from the same class as the owners of the mass media, which often sets the social agenda for what gets publicly discussed. The wealthy can more easily fund politicians and the educational apparatus and influence the clergy. The ownership class also engages in struggle to improve their own lot against other competitors within their class, sometimes in terms of trade wars or even shooting wars. As a result, the ownership class has significant advantages when it comes to social and political influence and even military power.

The relationships and resulting practices such as those above have a direct influence on the quality and even length of life of workers. For instance, Amazon is the world's largest retailer (outranking Walmart in 2018) and its CEO, Jeff Bezos, is one of the world's wealthiest individuals (est. $140+ billion in 2018). However, while the company enjoys subsidies and tax breaks from the state, it pays its warehouse employees wages that are so low that many are eligible for food stamps, which, in short, is a state subsidy of its labor costs (see Brown 2018). Not only is pay low but workers are often forced to skip bathroom breaks and are not permitted to sit down for rest or talk to one another. In 2018, conditions such as these led to walkouts and calls for boycotts of Amazon throughout Europe to mark "Prime Day" and a "CEO vs. Workers" town hall meeting organized by Senator Bernie Sanders in the United States (see Johnson 2018b).

In another example, at the urging of the business community and its allied politicians, many US states have instituted "right to work" laws. These laws allow employers to hire non-union workers in industries that are commonly unionized. The result is weaker unions overall and an associated harm to the working class's ability to defend itself over the terms and conditions of labor. One study of the 1992–2016 period, for instance, found that a 1% decline in unionization related to right to work laws resulted in a 5% increase in occupational fatalities, with a total of a 14.2% increase overall associated with such laws for that timeframe (Zoorob 2018).

What does it mean to say that the history has been a history of struggles between the classes? To better answer this question, we must first juxtapose the long history of slow change in non-class systems with the rapid changes that come with class history. Here we see that most of *temporal* history exhibits slow change as, generally, one type of system has usually remained in place during any one individual's lifetime. On the other hand, most of *socio-cultural* history is a history of multiple types of systems and more types and spaces of social change. The imbalance in wealth and power across these many systems is thus associated with a much higher pace of social change as well as conflict. A world of various class systems is a world of myriads of struggles, not only between owning and working classes but also between factions within the owning and/or the working classes, familial and national rivalries, and a whole variety of clashes, regional wars, and so on. And this history is not simply or only a modern one but extends back to the earliest class systems.

The struggle between classes is not an inevitable forward projection of progress from one step or system to another. History is not universally predictable nor is it moved in some predetermined direction. While the lens I have carved at certain points in this chapter and previous ones has been so broad that progress and change are easy to see over long periods of time and space, none of this was predetermined. Hunter-gatherers sometimes ran into population shortages and many died out. Others collapsed because of ecological destruction, sometimes of their own making. Other societies have disappeared because of invasion by outsiders, some of whom were not always known.[1] Rome collapsed and now its residue is a tourist draw and a lesson in the history books. World War II and a few times during the Cold War, the destruction of modern society was at risk. Progress can always be turned back and often times one group's progress is another group's defeat.

The class dynamics of the past provide us invaluable insight into the nature of the present, to the extent that *any and all* class systems will share some forms of activity (identity/difference). As such, while history is not a linear projection, examining it through its class relations does reveal important features that are necessary for understanding how it has unfolded and continues to do so. And to better understand our present, we must, therefore, start from a place that prioritizes part of its fundamental structure—that is, its class relationships—and then investigate its past to discover how the present came to be. In sum, classes, their structural role, and the struggles this relationship produces are essential sociological variables we must acquire insight into if we are to grasp modernity adequately.

---

1 For example, the "Sea Peoples" were a group that invaded many Mediterranean civilizations, wiping many out, with Egypt being apparently the only one to withstand the onslaught at the time (approximately from 1276 to 1178 BC). Their identity to this day remains unknown.

CHAPTER 7

# Mystical Consciousness

To "mystify" something is to distort its reality in thought. And cultures instill in their members pre-worked out ways of understanding the world and many of these ways have often been ideas that mystify them as to their real conditions of life. Hence, such mystified knowledge produces mystical consciousness—or how we mentally comprehend and respond to our observations of and experiences in the world. We learn these ways as children, adopt them as our own, and act them out as we age. The crucial question is whether we can learn to recognize mystifications and understand how they work when we encounter them.

Some people believe that "evil" causes war and the suffering it brings. In this notion, the lethal endpoint to which at least two groups have come is produced by a malevolent force either outside of human will and agency or found within certain individuals driven by ill-intent. But just as social systems author individual lives and beliefs, systems also author war and how it is waged. Anthropologists find evidence that violence even among normally peaceful hunter-gatherers usually resulted from situational needs for protecting or gaining resources and was not a typical feature of their system building, i.e., they could engage in mass violence if needed but their societies were not built upon warfare in general (for discussion of a mass grave among hunter-gatherers and the issues it provoked, see Handwerk 2016).

The introduction of agricultural systems introduced methods of waging what we would term "warfare" in the sense of systemic conquest of others, seizing territory, and so on. And those practices continued to develop further as societies grew more complex to such an extent that some societies worked external conquest into their planning. So, whether we write warfare off as a capacity for humans to inflict violence or as a clash of systemic needs acted about by people from such systems, in either case, war and violence are not the result of a non-human force evoked by terms like "evil" or simply the result of specifically violent individuals who wish to do harm to others.

It is easy to write-off war as the product of the dispositions of those organizing it. After all, it takes little imagination to conjure up individuals we have either met or learned about who seem violent, belligerent, obtuse, and/or power-hungry. No doubt, such people exist and it is easy to imagine war as the outcome of when such individuals gain control of political decision-making and military power. But this idea constructs war as simply the individual's capacity for violence writ large to society as whole and this is only a surface appearance, i.e., what sociologists call "individualistic reductionism." As Hannah Arendt ([1963] 2006) pointed out, even the suffering the Nazi regime caused resulted from forces more "banal" than we suppose—i.e., everyday people following orders in pursuit of their jobs within a larger institutional framework. If people do their jobs and follow orders within a setting with conflicting interests and competition over resources, war can result from the clash between the needs, goals, and interests of different relationships structured into social systems. And if that is true, and if we persist in thinking about war as a product of our individual capacities for violence writ large, then we fundamentally mislead ourselves as to the essential causes of war.

We can approach many social practices and issues and questions this way. For instance, think of all the possible ways humans have answered the question, What is valuable in life? Getting married and having children. Acquiring things. Acquiring land. Acquiring money. Making the gods happy. Making parents happy. Being free to think and do as one wants. Dying a warrior's death. Serving the king. Serving the state. Serving knowledge. Serving others. Serving tea. The historical record reveals instances where these roles and norms were presented, taught, and treated as if they were a "natural" or "god given" ideal for one group or another. When we juxtapose such everyday norms and "what everyone knows" with their changes over socio-cultural history, it is easy to see how human beliefs often rest on mystified ideas and certainty.

Being makers of a symbolic world of meaning sets humans apart from the animal kingdom. And this has both served humanity well and inspired some of our worst behaviors. With skills in symbolic manipulation we can create language, record history, make long-term plans, preserve methods of production and reproduction in thought, word, and writing. Language allows for complex forms of communication and we can produce an imaginary world of ideas, visions, metaphors, aphorisms, and so on. And through the symbolic world we invent things out of thin air, believe they are real (at least for a while), and act on that basis. While we moderns cannot imagine killing our children to appease gods, influence our fortunes, or change the weather, such ideas were not only previously thinkable but were once put into practice (for two recent finds, see BBC News 2018; Pavid 2018).[1] And just as no one in modern societies believes in royal blood anymore, one wonders what beliefs today will seem

---

1 More recently, a religious guru in India (Gurmeet Ram Rahim Singh) convinced 400 men to cut off their testicles to get closer to God (Sura 2018). And in Malawi (and other places in Africa), people born with Albinism are believed to have magical powers and thus are seen as witches and often killed (Essa and Furcoi 2017).

similarly nonsensical and fantastic hundreds or even thousands of years from now.

Humans are skilled at inventing concepts for interpreting the world but often forget they invented them and come to believe such things are real. We say someone has "luck" when they win the lottery and then act similarly with our own money, despite the staggering odds, hoping that this force will be visited upon us. But luck does not exist *as a force or thing*, even if good fortune does occur. A parallel idea is that of a balance sheet of deeds, where "karma" doles out some reward or punishment for one's actions depending on the weight of the ledger. Such an idea is similarly found in the "just world hypothesis," where people believe that those who do wrong in the world will eventually get what is coming to them. And then there is "fate," the idea that some outcome was preordained and meant to be, whether by gods or karma or just by fate itself. Each of these ideas shows how humans create mental constructs to help them understand, interpret, and explain the world around them but then such ideas take on lives of their own, as if they exist as external things moving human beings and their destinies around on the chessboard of life.

Rituals, by definition, are repetitive, are specifically contextualized, and convey special institutionalized meanings meant to recognize significant markers of time or the gravitas of an event. As such, they are taken very seriously. In the modern world, we see ourselves as American, Italian, or Argentinian and have inscribed national identity into public rituals. In the United States, for instance, we have symbolic public rituals such as the National Anthem before athletic competitions from high school up to the professional ranks. For some, the connection between flags, anthems, and national identity take on a tone that verges on religious devotion. At their most religiously important, rituals are enacted during life's great passages: birth, transition into adulthood, marriage, and death. In situations of such importance, the participants in a belief system will tend to relate to the ritual with reverence and assume that the ritual's transformative powers are set in motion only if certain performative expectations are met.

For example, the wedding ceremony transforms two individuals into a "couple," but only if certain stipulated rituals are correctly performed. These rituals vary per society and per belief structure and have included things like providing cattle to a bride's father, the mixing of blood, the use of specific dress codes and verbal passages, the eating of certain foods, exchanging of vows and ornaments, among a host of other possibilities. In each custom, the ceremony has ritual performances scheduled into it and their enactment sets off the meaning of the whole. As rituals, these performances represent a connection with past ancestors and with the realm of the "sacred." They put a "holy" sanction on the event and "bless" the couple and their union. It is strange but true, then, that the power of one society's sacred rituals is null and void when and if the act's symbolic meaning is not shared with an audience from a different society.[2] This tells us much about the real origins of the rituals' supposed power, i.e., the minds of a community of believers and their everyday interrelations.[3]

Shamans sometimes use chants to curse enemies and cure allies. The Babylonians and the Assyrians believed repetition of a word gave it power, sometimes to help in curing diseases and ailments. The Greeks and Romans had magic dolls and potions for love and spells to win chariot races. Modern people often think themselves exempt from such magical thinking. But consider how people today think of "curse" or "cuss" words. These words are meant to express strong emotions. But there is more to them than that. We censor television

---

2 Even in complex societies, human groups have little problem keeping their meaning structures intact and thus rituals survive, even if only for a while. But meaning structures can be transformed as well. Think of the typical American marriage ceremony. There remains a tradition of it being "bad luck" if the groom sees the bride before the ceremony on the day of the wedding. Most people who participate in this practice have no idea it is a holdover from an era of arranged marriage—long gone in the West—where the groom did not see the bride at all until the actual wedding ceremony when he lifted her veil (thus it would be bad luck to try to get an early look at a bride and be cursed with a not-so-attractive wife). When a bride and a groom of different religious faiths marry, the more orthodox their families, the more likely conflict will arise over which rituals must be performed in order for a "real" marriage ceremony to have occurred. In secular societies, these conflicts are often worked out, especially with the rise of state-sponsored ceremonies at courthouses, the acceptance of Las Vegas "chapels" for weddings, etc. But even in secular culture, the stricter a believer the more likely they will not accept that two people have been transformed into a "couple" in the eyes of (their) "god." It is *their* rituals, not someone else's, that make a union holy.

3 Even *within* a society, humans may not share meaning structures perfectly with one another, often in the same cultural tradition. Catholicism can mean something very different to two, three, or more family members. As a system grows more complex, or the more conflicting and contradictory its various social relations, the more likely there will be disagreements over important ideas. Moreover, even in small religious communities, as the number of adherents grows the likelihood of disagreement over interpretation of scripture and ritual increases. And, the odds of this grow further the more fundamentalist in orientation its believers. Think of it this way: Have you ever tried to get six people to agree on what to have on or leave off a pizza? This is probably not too hard with two people but as you gain a third person, and a fourth, and so on, the likelihood of a collective agreement on something as innocuous as pizza toppings goes down. Now, apply that same logic to a group of people who believe in the literal inerrancy of a religious text (especially if it has its own internal contradictions) and that eternal torment of their souls are at stake. Such disagreements can tear a religious community apart, figuratively and literally. Again, the problem is that believers inside a belief system legitimately take their symbolic universe, their moral codes, and their ritual behavior as sacred realities, while to outsiders it is relatively meaningless at best and misleading or even pernicious at worst.

programs so that our children are not likely to hear certain sounds (i.e., words) at certain times. We censure comedians, professors, and politicians if they are too loose with their tongues. It is as if there is a corrupting power in the arbitrary sounds and letters we use to communicate. We are told to say "darn" instead of "damn," "frick" instead of "fuck," and "shoot" instead of "shit" around children and in polite company. It is as if our intended meaning does not matter; all that matters is the formal content of our communication. We, too, believe that magical spells can contaminate us because of the sounds we emanate.

Though we are a tool-making animal, because of our symbolic skills and capacities, we are great mystifiers, too. When individuals live at a time when these practices are in force, their sacred character appears obvious and compelling. Retrospectively, they no longer do. For instance, traditional Indian/Hindu beliefs depict cows as a "sacred animal" and the Ganges River to be a holy site. The changes modernity brings to the country and culture can erode such beliefs as well as the structure of the caste system, especially in more modernized and urban settings (see Ahuja 2016), though such changes happen unevenly and slowly (see Desai and Dubey 2012). What one era takes as a given, natural reality, another era shrugs off as ancient superstition.

Let us look at an example of a mystification taken from news headlines. On August 31, 2018, the *Los Angeles Times* published a story, "The Economy May Be Booming, but Nearly Half of Americans Can't Make Ends Meet." Its author, David Lazarus (2018), opens the article with, "By virtually any yardstick, the US economy is doing great. Unemployment is near a two-decade low. The stock market is strong. Corporate profits are at record highs. Yet a report out this week finds that almost half of Americans are having trouble paying for basic needs such as food and housing." Later chapters of this book will show why all of these claims save the latter mislead us in multiple ways, but there are two things relevant for current purposes here.

First, note how the idea of "the economy" is constructed as such that it is "booming" when the stock market is up, corporate profits are high, and unemployment is low, even while failing to serve the needs of half the population. One problem here is that the first two indicators can improve significantly but may only be relevant for a small proportion of the population, not "the economy" or the population as a whole.

Second, both history and conventional economic theory suggest that low unemployment should lead to wage gains in the labor market, which should also then improve the ability of the population to pay for basic needs. During the period in which this article was written, there was much consternation from economists and other observers over why wage growth did not accompany low unemployment amidst high corporate profits. The answer resides in three places: (1) low levels of unionization; (2) declines in labor force participation (which is not counted in official unemployment statistics); and (3) underemployment. While the former two issues are addressed in later chapters, here it is important to stress that the third issue is normally absent from conventional models of the unemployment-wage relationship, even though it plays a significant role in suppressing potential wage gains (see Bell and Blanchflower 2018).[4] When "the economy" is constructed on measures mainly relevant to a small proportion of the population, when unemployment is mismeasured, and when underemployment is not taken into account in conventional thinking at all, observers can easily be mystified by the conditions they witness but are unable to explain.

The list of human mystifications might be so long that it is impossible to tally all that have occurred before us and those still existing today. Many gods, once worshiped, are long dead and forgotten. Almost no one sees cats as having special powers anymore. Criminology has long dropped theories of atavism. Some men wear earrings today, whereas not long ago this was still primarily seen as women's prerogative. We are taught that we should respect those in authority, whether priest or president, whether we know them or not, or whether they have earned that respect or not. We treat babies as "miracles" (even after billions of births), see homosexuals as some exotic species, and invoke a belief in "soulmates" in our romantic lives. We humans, whether ancient or modern, have always lived in a world of mystifications of our own making. What parts of our world today will seem frivolous or arbitrary in one or two hundred years hence?

---

4 Bell and Blanchflower's abstract reads: Large numbers of part-time workers around the world, both those who choose to be part-time and those who are there involuntarily and would prefer a full-time job report they want more hours. Full-timers who say they want to change their hours mostly say they want to reduce them. When recession hit in most countries the number of hours of those who said they wanted more hours, rose sharply and there was a fall in the number of hours that full-timers wanted their hours reduced by. Even though the unemployment rate has returned to its pre-recession levels in many advanced countries, underemployment in most has not. We produce estimates for a new, and better, underemployment rate for twenty-five European countries. In most underemployment remains elevated. We provide evidence for the UK and the US as well as some international evidence that underemployment rather than unemployment lowers pay in the years after the Great Recession. We also find evidence for the US that falls in the home ownership rate have helped to keep wage pressure in check. Underemployment replaces unemployment as the main influence on wages in the years since the Great Recession.

CHAPTER 8

# Illusions to this Day

This chapter continues the investigation of mystifications. Here, I first look at illusions seemingly built into the very nature of society—or at least so far. Toward the end, I examine how such illusions are manifest in modern society, a discussion which sets up the following chapter as well.

Not every society reinvents all of its own wheels with each generation. Some wheels are continually passed down over many generations and even across cultures. Such things can appear to be natural or normal or universal, things we must simply accommodate. This does not mean we cannot overcome them.

We see the shaman trying to conjure up a spirit and conclude they have fooled themselves with gods of their own making. If someone told you that Thor does not exist, it would probably not bother you at all. If someone told a Hindu that the Abrahamic gods were nonexistent, his or her reaction might be the same. But tell a Hindu the Vedic gods are fictions or tell a Jew, Christian, or Muslim that the Abrahamic god is equally fiction and one would expect a less-than-friendly reaction.[1] Our gods are true, their gods false.

There are no spirits above the Earth, nor are they in it either. Nature does not *care* about us or *about anything for that matter*, for it cannot. It does not nurture us. It does not notice us, as a mother would a child. Nature does react to activity upon it, but it has no consciousness, motive, or reasoning ability. We may find it beautiful, awe inspiring, or even at times fearsome but nature has no such emotions or senses to feel our presence, though cultures world over have attributed such human characteristics to it.

As humans created a world of time and space so did they create a moral universe. Moral codes tell us what to do and not to do, when to do this or that, and, in general, how to act or not to act. We insist our children and neighbors follow certain rules—whether they be not to lie, cheat, steal, or kill, what to eat when and where, who to have sex with, when and where or who not to have it with, and so on. Such moral codes are socially constituted and collectively enforced, though some people may also have their own personal moral codes. In any case, when we dictate to one another that we not harm our neighbors

---

1 In 2015, Wheaton College suspended a professor for saying the Christians and Muslims worship the same god. This is true. Both worship the Abrahamic god, though they have different beliefs about this god's activities in the world, his message for humans, and what it takes to reach the afterlife (see Pashman and Eltagouri 2015).

or allow each other to remain safe in our possessions and be truthful with our words, we tend to believe these rules come from a sacred realm outside of us, discovered through the revealed intentions of this or that god. And once handed down over generations, we learn not to inspect such rules or their origins too closely for we may be surprised at what we might find.[2]

We do not need to posit a theological source to understand that moral codes function as a method of social control, whether tacitly or explicitly, or why this is so. Many moral rules develop through practice, as it would be difficult for any society to sustain itself if its members do not have security in their communications, persons, and property. As such, casting strictures against lying, cheating, stealing, killing, and rape in an armor of sacred morality gives such rules more heft and meaning and, therefore, increases odds people will

---

2  Within the Abrahamic traditions, it is widely believed that core moral codes came down through Moses, to whom god gave "The Ten Commandments." However, there are more than one set of "commandments" and those explicitly titled as the "ten commandments" are not what a believer might suppose. Should a Christian open the King James bible to the chapter and verse that lists the "ten commandments" (Exodus 34:10–28), they would find the following:
1. Thou shalt worship no other god: for the LORD, whose name is Jealous, is a jealous God.
2. Thou shalt make thee no molten gods.
3. The feast of unleavened bread shalt thou keep.
4. Six days thou shalt work, but on the seventh day thou shalt rest.
5. And thou shalt observe the feast of weeks, of the first fruits of wheat harvest, and the feast of ingathering at the year's end.
6. Thrice in the year shall all your men children appear before the LORD God, the God of Israel.
7. Thou shalt not offer the blood of my sacrifice with leaven.
8. Neither shall the sacrifice of the feast of the Passover be left unto the morning.
9. The first of the first fruits of thy land thou shalt bring unto the house of the lord thy God.
10. Thou shalt not seethe a kid [young goat] in his mother's milk.
This list is not the one Christian children are taught nor does it contain those rules the faithful are expected to obey. Rather, those commandments are found as "my commandments" (Exodus 20: 20–17):
1. Thou shalt have no other gods before me.
2. Thou shalt not make unto thee any graven image.
3. Thou shalt not take the name of the LORD they God in vain.
4. Remember the Sabbath, and keep it holy.
5. Honor they father and thy mother: that they days may be long upon the land which the LORD they God giveth thee.
6. Thou shalt not kill.
7. Thou shalt not commit adultery.
8. Thou shalt not steal.
9. Thou shalt not bear false witness against thy neighbor.
10. Thou shalt not covet thy neighbor's house...or any thing that is thy neighbor's.

obey them.[3] Most, if not all, societies have developed moral codes against such practices. But rather than treat these rules as grounded in the sociological requisites of running a society, people treat them as if they came from a sacred source. Rules about things such as dress, diet, rituals, and so on are largely wholly invented, though we often treat them, too, as if they come from the same extra-social sources, i.e., rules such as "don't eat this animal" (arbitrarily-based) are treated as if coming from the same otherworldly realm as "don't lie" (socially-based).[4] Thus, in both cases, to declare that religious moral armor and the world it protects and controls have origins outside of human history and agency is to distort the sociological roots of such rules in our thinking, mystifying these rules and our own consciousness about them in the process.

Not only do we invent some moralities out of whole cloth, but then we also condemn other cultures for their own lack of commitment to them, or we find their behaviors distasteful or immoral. For example, modern Westerners have culturally specific and rather new notions of hygiene and look down on those who do not follow suit.[5] Devout Muslims tend to find both the more revealing fashions that Western women wear and how free speech rights allow for access to sexually explicit materials to be deeply immoral. Each group is equally convinced of their convictions and that those very convictions themselves are a product of nature, transcendent morality, or god. These are comforting illusions in that we do not have to explain the source of our morality because we often do not know. We thus mystify ourselves as we reproduce the past and pass it down to our children over and over until we no longer remember the source of our social rules.

With some exceptions, most humans are born with either a penis or a vagina. The former we call "male" and the latter we call "female" (at least in the English language, with other languages having their own appellations). Culture, then, assigns certain behavioral traits considered appropriate for the male or

---

3   Earlier social rules against rape combine the latter two into a crime against four victims: a woman's father (who needs her a virgin in order to keep her available for an arranged marriage), her husband (or future, potential husband), her family and its community reputation, and, lastly, her.

4   The qualification here is that some rules, such as dietary ones, were less arbitrary in their cultural origins but rather based on certain material and/or cultural conditions for that time and place. However, over time and generations, such rules get detached from their origins and are treated as is universal codes and religious dictums.

5   Of course, they tend to forget that their standards of hygiene were made possible by the invention and spread of indoor plumbing as well as manipulated by advertisers over decades to make people fear social reprobation. As a result, a whole historically new set of standards became "real."

the female—or "masculinity" and "femininity." Most cultures assume their versions of masculinity and femininity are the natural and normal versions as well as how other societies *should* perform gender. This sort of ethnocentrism is quite common, where cultures that fail to conform to our norms and roles are anywhere from criticized to condemned for it. However, most cultures developed gender norms long before modern knowledge of hormones, chromosomes, and genes and this knowledge tells us that both sex and gender are not as clear cut as cultures have historically constructed them. And even with such knowledge, most cultures still today treat masculine and feminine social roles as rooted biologically just as vaginas and penises are rooted in the body. Though *some* gender activity may indeed be part of our biology (e.g., building muscles requires testosterone and men naturally have more of it than women), we still tend to treat *all of it as if it is*, another illusion.

We also treat things other than genitalia as if they have marked significance in an individual's and/or a group's stature, meaning, behavior, and whatnot. Human collective groups often appear somewhat different in shape, color, size, and so on. Given cultural isolation (relatively speaking) and ethnic solidarity, some peoples have developed identifiable differences in appearance from others. People indigenous to today's Peru look a bit different than those from Iceland. Most people could successfully divide a group between Hungarians and Senegalese with a high degree of success. Less successful, however, has been the widespread attempt to claim correlations between behavior (and other traits) with these outward physical appearances. Whether it be sexual behavior, athletic ability, moral standing, intellectual capacity, work ethic, and so on, none of these are associated with the same biological components that account for the way hair, eyes, noses, and/or skin appear. This idea that different physical appearances identify any group via anything other than superficial outward characteristics is an illusion that has continued over time.[6]

Modern people often hear the assertion that humans are naturally competitive creatures. We are told that hierarchies of status, power, and control are inevitable products of the human condition that we must simply accommodate and to think otherwise is naïve. But competition does not come naturally—it

---

6 It may be the case that certain traits, characteristics, behaviors, aptitudes, and whatnot correlate with one supposed "racial" group more so than others. However, such correlations are not so much "biologically" determined but rather are accounted for by marriage patterns. Groups tend toward in-group solidarity and within that dynamic, a trait (hair, eye, or skin color, diseases, height) or behavior (accent, food preferences, commitment to certain social skills, etc.) is typically based on socialization and/or genes being common among mating pairs and their offspring. This does not require a hypothesis of the existence of races and/or traits reduced to being racial in character.

is built into certain social relations. Parents in all societies do not compete with their children for food. Hunter-gatherers only compete externally while internally they are cooperative. Modern individuals share tax burdens to facilitate avenues of transportation and public education for the common good, while at the same time compete for jobs and status just as products compete for their money. As putative employees, we compete for jobs and later promotions. Competition and cooperation are *capacities* that are systemically encouraged, not ironclad destinies to navigate. As such, modern competition is so normal for us that we mistake it for human nature, forgetting that societies have not always been organized this way.

What are illusions to this day? Simply put, people across societies tend to mistake the cultural scripts and norms of their *own society* as a reflection of some wider *human nature*. This is quite predictable and simply not a mistake indicative only of pre-modern thinking. Humans everywhere habitually overgeneralize from their own specific and systemic behavioral norms to what it means to be human in general and this is one of the most long-lasting ways of thinking in our existence. Once we recognize this tendency, we can acquire the tools to progress past it.

CHAPTER 9

# An Inverted World

Another form of mystified consciousness stems from how our world teaches us to get things backwards in our thinking. Several examples demonstrate the idea.

Scientists have debated whether human behavior is best explained by genes or social forces, i.e., the famous "nature versus nurture debate." For sociologists, understanding humans requires first understanding the social structures that contain them and all that this implies. Every human ever born was born into a social system that already had rules, norms, relationships, statuses, and so on. They also had forms of production and distribution established, forms of communication worked out, familial forms institutionalized, gendered roles enforced, and so on. Some of these systems were hunter-gatherer or pastoralist, animist, polytheistic, or monotheistic. Some had few if any neighbors. Some were peaceful and others warlike. But rarely, if ever, can we pinpoint any individual "author" of these realities. Moreover, humans never have had a myriad of choices of institutional options set in front of them—e.g., language, religion, production system, familial organization, etc.—and then the ability to simply pick from and then implement them. Instead, the systems humans are born into choose those options for them. That is, thus far in history societies have created humans more than humans have created societies and to suggest otherwise is to get the causal order backwards.

If you would ask the average modern person what caused the transatlantic slave trade, it is likely they would respond with something akin to, "The racist attitudes of European and American slavers." That explanation, however,

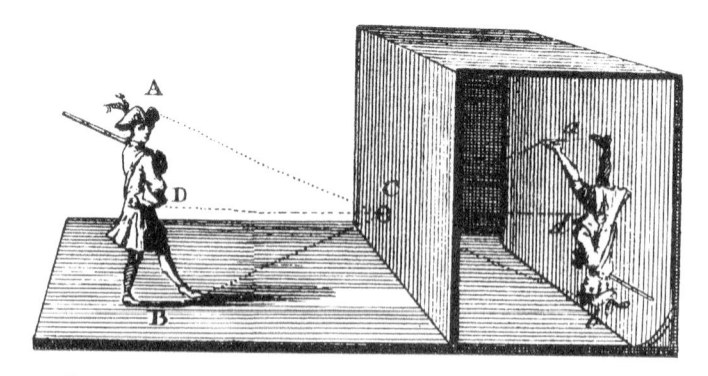

IMAGE 9.1   Illustration of the Camera Obscura Principle

overlooks several facts. First, slaving practices in early modernity made no racial distinction on who was forced into servitude. In fact, "race" as we understand it today was not an operative belief system nor a social ordering mechanism in the 1500s and 1600s; that would develop later.[1] The enslaved, at least in early modernity, could be from Africa, the Americas, Ireland, and even southern or eastern Europe (among other places). The closest distinction law and custom made in early modern slavery—i.e., during colonialism—was between Christian and "heathen" (or "savage"), not black or white. Second, in early modernity, the supposed race or ethnicity of an individual did not determine whether or not they could own slaves. There were slave owners that were European, Arabian, African, and Native American in origin. In short, early modern slavery was a *labor system* first and foremost, not a racial system. The color line that grew to demarcate free (white) and non-free (black) developed later in modern slavery and was an effect of it, not its cause.

Adam Smith's *Wealth of Nations* is perhaps the quintessential apology and justification for the modern economic system. Commentators on the right tend to view it as a sort of bible for a free market economy (though they often overlook most of Smith's critical evaluation of some practices his book discusses, e.g., capitalism rewards greed and avarice; the rich tend not to care about anyone but themselves and even conspire against the public). The basic assumptions of Smith's analyses go something like the following: God created human beings and thus with them he created human nature. Competition for resources and the drive to accumulate wealth are, therefore, collectively expressed products of that human nature. It further follows from these premises that the free market system is intended by god's design and, thus, to interfere with it is to go against human nature, god's will, and only courts folly. This, then, is the early moral argument for "laissez faire" economic policy—and it also explains the connection between modern religious and economic conservativism (also see Hill 2001).

---

1 As opposed to a general xenophobia, what I mean by racism as a modern phenomenon is that racism is the belief (and actions based on it) that humans beings (1) can be subdivided into subtypes, (2) based on some physical characteristic (often skin color but also hair type, nose shape, and/or other biological markers), whereby (3) these biologically-based subtypes are supposed to have differential rates/possession of certain dispositions such as intelligence, moral capacity, initiative, physical prowess, sexual appetite, etc. based on that very biology, and (4) these supposed subtypes and their associated appearances are worked into culture and law in terms of status, privilege, power, authority, etc. Understood this way, "racism" is new in modernity. That said, it is true that in the early modern European mind dark skin was seen as something anywhere from exotic to dirty to savage, certainly not "civilized" or normal or even necessarily human.

Should one reply to this thesis that the vast majority of human history has not been lived in a free market system and then ask how could a market economy be the result of god's will (and, thus, human nature) if it took so long to come into being, what sort of Smithian response would they likely get? The free market apologist would likely argue that human beings have long lived estranged from their natural selves, overcome by technological ignorance (tribes) or religious superstition (non-Christian systems) or illegitimate powers over them (feudalism). Once humans overcame these unnatural forces and became more self-actualized they could live in accordance with their true nature. With the defeat of Muslims in Spain and the later overthrow of the feudal order, human nature and its free market companion stepped forward and achieved victory over the alienation that thus far in history distorted our true human selves.

This is the inverse of another view of this same history. This point of view holds, like Smith, that human labor is the source of social wealth. Further, though, it is humans' ability to think abstractly and forge things into reality through transforming the world that is at the root of "human nature." We transform the world into a place to live and then that world transforms us. Rather than static, human nature is therefore a dynamic mix of biology, structural influence, and historical development. To be free, then, means to control the means, terms, and products of your own labor. But the existing social structures thus far in history have controlled us and our labor, rather than us controlling them—e.g., ancient civilizations and their massive kingdoms (like Carthage, Rome, Egypt, Mesopotamia, and so on), all forms of slavery, and Asiatic and European feudal systems. In these prior systems, this control over the means, terms, and objects of labor was in the open, as in everyone knew how it worked and to withdraw one's labor was usually illegal and resulted in physical punishment, even death. In modernity, rather than overcoming this alienation of humans through their own control of their labor, our labor is more alienated than ever in that its control by external forces is not openly admitted and remains hidden to many people, while we tell ourselves we are free as we have ever been.

In modernity, we are not owned by others. We are not forced at the point of a sword or the end of a gun to go to work. We freely sign contracts, get up in the morning, and go to our jobs. We are legally free to leave them when we choose. We are not tied to the land and cannot be kidnapped and forced into servitude on any one person's estate (at least lawfully). We are free agents in that sense. It seems nonsensical to claim our labor is controlled and manipulated by someone else. But if we do not work for wages, we starve and/or go homeless. This threat, not law or a sword or a gun, forces us to sell our labor to others for money, a fact we do not and cannot control. And this social fact is an obdurate and built-in reality of our social system. As a result, we suffer from alienation of and from our labor, its product, each other, and the species as a whole. We have not overcome alienation but rather experience its most sophisticated form yet.

Once on the job, we are disciplined by the clock, watchman, the overseer, the manager, the computer, the spreadsheet. We must produce more wealth via our labor than what our bosses pay us in wages if we are to remain employable. At least this is what the average worker must do for the average business. We are ledger sheet numbers for management and bureaucrats under the entry, "labor costs." Our personal interests and talents really do not matter much to employers. Our system cares for our individual well-being even less than feudalism did for that of the peasant; at least a peasant had rights to land and resources and had more time off work than the modern (American) citizen (see Schor 1992). At work, we have the right to sell our labor and reap the agreed upon remittance in our paycheck and not much else. Even if we are not as physically broken down as the peasant or slave (though some of us are), the fact that the market system hides its exploitation of labor and describes itself as the height of human development just goes to show how mystified we are about our alienated existence in modernity. It is all backwards.

We often look upon business owners as those who produce wealth in our society. The scions of Wall Street today or the robber barons of yesterday are said to be the "wealth creators" of modernity. But we know that's not true. Andrew Carnegie and Cornelius Vanderbilt did not pump the oil, extract the ores, or staff the banks that produced the wealth their families enjoyed. Steve Jobs did not personally build the computer-based gadgets that brought him his billions in riches. Jeff Bezos is not making any physical things nor is he staffing his warehouses personally and filling orders. Even Adam Smith knew that workers, everyday people, produce social value that is at the root of wealth. When the owners of a business fail in their endeavors, their workers go unemployed. Should those workers turn to welfare for survival, then free market devotees call them social parasites. Again, this is all backwards. Corporate tax breaks, subsidies, and bailouts cost taxpayers more money than all the social welfare benefits for individual citizens combined.

Ask modern people from where "the family" originated and most, it seems a sure bet, will say "love" and/or "commitment" or some such. Marriage, the belief goes, is based on our love for each other and that such a union should produce children, which we then raise. Though today we may marry for "love," for most of history most marriages were arranged by parents, which is still the case for a significant part of the world. While the motives were often political, economic, strategic, and cultural, what was not at play, at least in terms of the *origination of the institution*, was an initiation of the union because the couple "loved" one another. Typically, parents arranged marriages in order to produce children as heirs, to make sure their daughters gained social respect via leaving home and producing descendants, to secure economic and social alliances between families and clans. Though a couple *could* come to love one another, this was not why the institution was established; nor was whether or not love ever developed consequently relevant for the social "success" of the coupling. Duty, honor, children, and so on were at its base.

Modernity produced "romantic love" as the basis for marriage. People in modernity still raise children, just as in the past. Today, however, we tend not to pass down honorary titles, trade resources in terms of daughters and dowries, or cattle and land, require political alliances between families or clans, and so on. We still marry because it is custom and we want stability for ourselves and our children. But if the traditional means for marriage disappear while its bases (domestic stability/security; as a socialization mechanism for children) remain, then the motive-source for marriage shifts to individual choice and this means emotional intimacy. Assuming that "romantic love" is the origin of the family and not the changes brought about in modernity reverses the temporal order of things.

What comes to mind when you think of "crime"? Likely things like robbery, larceny, murder, rape, arson, auto theft, and assault. These are crimes against persons and property and most often are "person to person" crimes. But what about white-collar crimes committed via business dealings, ledger sheets, and so on? Which one—white-collar or blue-collar—costs the public more in terms of lost lives, property, and money? Which one takes up more of our mental space and budgets for public policing and imprisoning? White-collar crime—bribery, embezzlement, price fixing, graft, unsafe products, dumping of dangerous chemicals, and so on—costs the public *vastly* more in terms of loss of life, loss of money, and loss of property. Unsurprisingly, our police spend much more time in poor neighborhoods instead of rich boardrooms. And our prisons bear out this inverted priority and resource allocation.

In the 1980s, it seemed as if crack cocaine was everywhere in America. In the mass media, crack was often aligned with images of reckless and angry black male inner-city youths, usually armed with weapons and willing to use them. And the 1990s (and 2000s) seemed to return to the 1950s and 1970s, when heroin was around more than its "usual" presence. It was as if these drug epidemics were fueled by the demand of users as well as small time dealers, both of which were considered plagues on society and justifications for draconian policing measures and imprisoning large segments of the population. But where were all these drugs coming from? Poor African-American kids weren't growing, harvesting, processing, and transporting cocaine from equatorial countries and bringing it to their neighborhoods. The junk killing rock stars anew in the 1990s–2000s was not grown and processed by them or their crew. In each of these cases, government actors—as well as massive foreign criminal cartels in places like Bolivia and Colombia—were behind these drug epidemics through agencies involved in covert activities, especially those related to foreign warfare and subversion.[2]

What do leaders of covert operations do when a war is not officially declared yet they need local allies to help fight it and money to help pay for it? The reader will be forgiven if "drug dealing" did not immediately occur to them. Nevertheless, when the US government took over from the French in Vietnam, it aligned with the same local power-centers the French had used for safe-houses, black-market weapons, allies in the dark arts of espionage, and so on. In Vietnam, these were the Hmong people and the United States allied with them against the Viet Cong. The cost was helping protect poppy growing fields and assisting in heroin export. In the 1980s, under Ronald Reagan, a similar dynamic played out in the undeclared wars in Central America and the United States' strategic alignment with the Contras (in Nicaragua especially). This time cocaine made its way into the United States. In the 1990s, it was opium again but now from Afghanistan after the United States aligned with the Mujahedeen against the Soviet occupation there. In the 2000s, after the September 11th, 2001 terrorist attacks in New York City and Washington, D.C., this process continued with the fight against the Taliban and the United States' alignment with the Northern Alliance. Thus, the United States has a heroin problem again in 2010–2019 (and likely beyond), a problem not *originating with* users or small-time dealers (see McCoy [1972] 2003; Cockburn 1998; Webb 1998).

Modern society's abundance of products does not overflow on the shelves because consumers collectively wanted things and companies simply responded and accidentally made too many. Rather, business leaders have learned that the market cyclically produces situations where the consuming public does not have enough money from wages to buy enough goods that have been produced and this means that a satisfactory rate of profit becomes harder to achieve (this systemic process is explained in later chapters). Consequently, today's business community spends billions of dollars on advertising that is not simply "informational" in the sense of making consumers aware of this or that company making this or that product but instead is meant to manufacture demand that was not "naturally" there. And if advertising did not stimulate

---

2  Juan Pablo Escobar Henao, son of Medellín cartel kingpin, Pablo Escobar, in Colombia, recently wrote a book where he claims his father worked with the CIA in cocaine smuggling (up to 15 tons a day into the United States) (see Bernish 2017 and reference therein).

consumption in this way, the business community would not continue to spend the money on it they do decade after decade as such an expense would only contribute to their losses.

What product do television companies produce and sell? "Programming" is not a ridiculous answer, as it seems so obvious. But that is incorrect.

Does the quality of a program determine if it stays on the air? Clearly not. Great television shows get canceled all the time and lousy ones remain way past their sell-by date. What determines if a program stays on air or not is the size of the desired audience. Programs with larger audiences command a higher price extracted from advertisers that buy air time. If television executives kept high quality but lower-rated programs on the air while canceling low quality highly-rated programs, if they did not lose their jobs outright, they would certainly feel pressure to change their policies from both their higher-ups and from those shareholders who invested money in their business (their ultimate bosses). So, television broadcasters feel a structural pressure to perform their jobs in a certain way, which is to maximize market share and, therefore, profits.

What results is something different than how television broadcasting began. Today, the industry is in the business of selling a product, no doubt. But what, then, is that product if it is not programs? Who is paying the costs of production? Clearly, the advertisers are. Advertisers pay money to networks to air their commercials. And the larger the audience for those commercials, the more advertisers must pay. So, in short, television networks sell audiences to advertisers. The audience is the product, not the programming. The programs are only there to get you to watch the commercials. To see it any other way is to get it backwards.

The examples above are instances where we experience and think of things in an inverted way. We see society as the product of individuals rather than the other way around. We see business persons as the creators of wealth instead of workers. We embrace modern marriage as a product of pair-bonding for love rather than its progenitor. We believe street level drug users and distributors are the source of the scourge and not larger forces. Advertising's goal is to stimulate demand rather than respond to it. We get it all backwards. As a result, we have a hard time getting our bearings in a world that we not only *experience* backward but one that gives us *inverted knowledge* to understand it.[3] It is no

---

3  In 2015, a Kentucky (USA) County Clerk by the name of Kim Davis refused to sign marriage licenses because her religious beliefs led her to conclude that same-sex marriage was against god's will. However, in order not to discriminate against gay couples specifically, she decided to decline marriage licenses for all couples, same or opposite sex. Courts intervened and ordered her to comply with the law. She was jailed after refusing to do so. Some people came to her defense, holding demonstrations and claiming her religious freedom was being violated.

wonder we feel confused, lost, and helpless in modernity much of the time, as this backwardness is built into the very nature of our society.

---

Critics wondered if her supporters would also support a Buddhist man refusing to sell fire arms, a Muslim worker refusing to sell bacon or alcohol, or a Rastafarian refusing to arrest someone for marijuana possession. All fair questions. But for the purposes of this chapter, these critical observations do not demonstrate how Kim Davis's supporters got it backwards. Her religious freedom was not being attacked. Her church was not shut down. Her pastor was not being forced into marrying same-sex couples. She was not arrested for teaching her flavor of Christianity to Sunday school children. The issue was that she wanted her religious beliefs to supersede state and federal law. Rather than the case demonstrating an attack on religious freedom, her and her religious supporters were attacking freedom, democracy, separation of church and state, and due process. Here, her supporters and her critics both got it backwards and the real issue was misunderstood completely.

CHAPTER 10

# Educating the Educator

A newborn child does not possess the knowledge it needs to survive. Babies are truly dependent and helpless for quite a long period of time, especially in comparison to our mammalian relatives. Beyond things like breast feeding and crying for attention, newborns have to learn things from experience and/or from external sources, whether formally or informally. Some societies leave the process of learning to doing things with others, i.e., through practice and instruction. A boy learns to hunt via hunting with his elders. A girl learns to tend fields through working alongside her mother, aunts, and other young women (of course, in some societies, these designations could be reversed). And other forms of learning are done via lore, storytelling, mythos, and whatnot. We are told by others what things mean, the lessons of life, and the story of our people. So, no matter the society, all of them have a method to make sure their knowledge gets passed along anew to each generation as the previous one ages. It *must* be done and so crucial is it that every society that survives any appreciable length of time has, by definition, discovered its necessity. Educating children is truly a cultural universal.

As systems become larger and more complex, some interesting things happen. First, growth in the division of labor brings with it more skills, roles, positions, and so on. From hunting-gathering to agriculture and from there to larger city-states and, much, much, later, industrial societies, there are more things to do and to know.[1] But as systems grow more complex it becomes impossible for any one person to know all of that culture's products and master all of its skills. So, with growth in the division of labor there comes a growth in *specialization*. One person digs clams, another makes clothes, another watches the stars, another practices warfare, and still another butchers the meat. And some people specialize in the art and science of education, where "the educator" becomes a role society formally recognized, filled, and institutionalized.

We can say that the function of an educational system is to teach the standardized cultural knowledge of a society. In modernity, we must learn to read, write, and do arithmetic, things people in a hunting-gathering society would lack for they had no need for such skills. We also teach skills in cooking, car

---

[1] Despite the phraseology, society does not grow on its own and develop step-by-step from one system to another as if a predetermined set of stages.

repair, how to debate, world history, the history of art, human psychology, social science, and so on.

It is common, however, for the way we think about and teach such subjects above to become a passive reflection of the systemic rules within which they exist, for them to be influenced by common mystifications and illusions, and/or for them to become passé. Social systems often shape their institutional practices and official knowledge forms toward the requisites and needs and goals of the system as a whole. And one thing that is common to all systems is to simply forget that they are *specific types of historical systems* and thus they present the knowledge and the education they foster in neutral or uncritical terms. Of course, we must educate you how to do math because how else are you going to be able to balance a checkbook, understand how taxes work, and/or figure out how to save for rent and retirement? But these are rules of a *free market society* specifically and other systems do not need to teach these things.

Education can become weighted down by its own past, by the knowledge and victories of the dead. We often do well to acknowledge the mastery of thought and inquiry the people who came before us won. We hold their ideals high and respect their insights. But should we do this for too long and too uncritically, the world might pass us by and with that such knowledge becomes old, stale, and stagnant, worse than unproductive but rather inhibiting. As society evolves, changes, and develops, so too does knowledge, ideals, technology, and so on. A book or some other form of knowledge from a prior decade (or century) or two may seem like a quaint but antiquated trifle when viewed contemporarily. Education must keep pace with the society that contains, nourishes, and encourages it, less it stagnates and brings that stagnation to those exposed to it.

But this is not the end of the obstacles facing education and the educator. On the one hand, it is a sort of default mode for education to be shaped by the institutional framework that supports it. British education not only teaches British history but probably has Britain playing the role of good guy, leader, innovator, fighting the noble fight, having leaders with the best of intentions, etc. An educator here or there might be allowed to speak up critically about Britain's past, but, by and large, the general pattern is that education, British or Brazilian, will tend to support that society's, culture's, or country's institutional moorings. But that is often not enough and often not left to chance. Education can be intentionally shaped by those with some leverage, influence, and/or power. And this shaping is often in the direction of specific goals.

Students in Turkey are unlikely to hear a word of the Turkish government's role in the genocide of the Armenians living in the Ottoman Empire circa WWI. Similarly, Japanese school children will have to go elsewhere other than school to learn about the Rape of Nanking or Unit 731's use of prisoners of war in experimentation during WWII. In 2015, the Texas Board of Education attempted to rewrite the past with its standards for school history books. The post-slavery era curriculum, it decided, would omit Jim Crow laws, other segregationist initiatives, and even terroristic activities, including that of the Ku Klux Klan. These are all intentional omissions of crimes because their inclusion would paint the wrong picture.

But it is not only crimes of omission and it is not only specific acts that shape the contours of education. Inclusion of officially pleasing generalities also play a significant role in educating a child into the worldview considered right, true, honest, honorable, and worth upholding. That same Texas Board above also endorsed standards of educating students that included teaching the wonders of free enterprise and the beneficent role of the United States in world affairs, a role where the usual standards imposed on other states simply do not apply, i.e., "American Exceptionalism." In this sort of education, unlike reading, writing, and arithmetic, a certain set of interests are being served.

The professional educator that teaches things that serve certain interests might do so with a wide range of intentionality, ranging from cluelessness to being fully aware of what they are doing. That said, very often knowledge masked as neutral and/or non-political is anything but. Let us take a simple example that might not seem relevant for the topic at hand: the weather. The weather reporter comes on television and tells us about a "beautiful" and "amazing" day in store, where it will be "warm and sunny, high of 75 degrees and low of 50." She continues, "Get out and enjoy this early February break in winter." Her voice is comforting and enthusiastic. And it is hard to see anything political here ... except the facts that it should almost never be 75F in February in much of the Northern Hemisphere, we have a warming planet on our hands, we continue to see increasing average yearly global temperatures, and so on.[2] Warm winter days should sound an alarm, not be a cause to pronounce the good news. Even during heatwaves US broadcasters routinely omit "climate change" in their reporting—e.g., there was one mention of climate change in 127 segments between three major networks over a two-week period during a heatwave from late June to early July in 2018 (see Macdonald 2018). But not only do we have weather reporting like the above, but we also have state officials trying to keep *scientists* from studying and reporting on such things.[3]

---

2  For tracking the "global land-ocean temperature index" and other climate data, see NASA's "Fact" page at (URL retrieved August 31, 2018): https://climate.nasa.gov/vital-signs/global temperature/.

3  In 2015, Florida Governor, Rick Scott, tried to prohibit state employees in the Department of Transportation, Department of Health, and the South Florida Water Management District from using the terms "climate change," "global warming," and "sustainable" in their papers.

Conversely, we have also seen scientists censor themselves in order to make their conclusions more palatable to state officials.[4] In the examples above, we see both unintentional and intentional shaping of the discourse to which the public is exposed.

Knowledge is rarely neutral, though that is not impossible. One does not need a political agenda to calculate the rate at which objects fall in a vacuum, the speed at which galaxies are moving away from one another, or what the most popular name for girls was in Spain in 2013.[5] Plenty of knowledge has no agenda attached to it that favors one political or economic faction over another, or subtly endorses the requisites of one system over others. But these do exist, we must recognize and understand them when we see them, and educators must learn the difference or they risk becoming propagandists. That said, not all knowledge developed within and/or by systems of institutional hierarchies and power are only malformed ideas and nothing else. Human progress would have scarcely occurred if that were the case. It may be that many things we enjoy today came about in the search for technologies that might help win a war, e.g., radar.

The point is that we must be able to parse out what sort of knowledge is essential to know while having no propagandistic agenda for the powers that be smuggled into it. We must know how to do math, how to write, how to dig ditches, and how to get planes aloft and keep them there. We also must learn how to see through knowledge that presents its as neutral but supports one agenda or another, usually a hidden one. Such knowledge is fundamentally dishonest as it does not present itself as a faction or as an endorser. Finally,

---

In 2016, Wisconsin, under Governor Scott Walker, removed mention of human contributions to climate change from their state website. In 2017, after taking helm at the White House, the Trump administration eliminated mention of climate change from its website. In 2018, the same administration canceled NASA's Carbon Monitoring System, which would contribute to measuring greenhouse gasses as a way to verify national emission cuts as agreed upon at the Paris climate accords.

4  In 2018, Robin McKie (2018a) of *The Guardian* reported that climate scientists preparing a draft of summary findings (*Special Report on Global Warming of 1.5C*) for a major international climate meeting in South Korea (October 2018) altered it and omitted key conclusions in order to make it more palatable to countries such as the United States, Australia, and Saudi Arabia. Notable omissions included: any mention of the idea that temperature rises above 1.5C could lead to increased migrations and conflicts; any discussion of disruptions in the Gulf Stream from cold water from the Arctic caused by increased ice melts; warning about the danger of how a 1.5-2C temperature rise could trigger irreversible loss of the Greenland ice sheet and result in a 1–2 meters rise in sea level over the next century; how poverty has increased with recent global warming trends; and, the potential for significant population displacement in the tropics with increased sea level rises.

5  It was Lucía (see Jones 2015).

we must also produce knowledge that allows us to exercise the critical capacities of our minds. And this type of knowledge *is positively political* in that it is knowledge that allows us to think, process, analyze, and conclude for ourselves about the veracity of ideas, practices, and beliefs we are exposed to—in everyday life, in the media, and in our education itself.

In an era of mass media, being lazy in our thinking makes us more susceptible to "fake news," lies, and manipulation, regardless of political ideology (see Pennycook and Rand 2018). And that sort of dishonesty is more likely to be successful when an audience cannot distinguish factual claims from opinions, a skill many Americans struggle with (see Mitchell et al. 2018). The recognition of these problems is rising in several European countries, with efforts to counter fake news and disinformation through campaigns to raise public awareness of the problem, cultivating an understanding of how to distinguish fake news from valid sources, educating the public to resist propaganda, and coordination between government agencies, the media, and civil society (see Willard 2018). While the problem of propaganda is not new, several methods of moving the public mind are and learning to recognize them and understanding how they work are keys to not falling susceptible to them.

That person in the division of labor who becomes the educator must be taught how the mind works, how learning happens, and what people must know to survive in the system in which they live. The educator must be educated on the skills involved in critical analysis, skepticism, and independent thinking. The educator must be educated on those powers that be who want to interfere with their work, to have a worldview projected that serves special interests, and to keep the public unaware of the inconvenient facts that undermine their positions of privilege. And just because one is in a position to be an educator, there is no guarantee that he or she will not fall prey to the mystifications, illusions, and inverted knowledge common in history in general and in their own society specifically. For all these reasons, the educator too must be educated.

CHAPTER 11

# Windy Idealists and Frothy Youth

In an oft repeated story, it is said that Plato told of Socrates' complaint about the youth of his time:

> The children now love luxury; they have bad manners, contempt for authority; they show disrespect for elders and love chatter in place of exercise. Children are now tyrants, not the servants of their households. They no longer rise when elders enter the room. They contradict their parents, chatter before company, gobble up dainties at the table, cross their legs, and tyrannize their teachers.[1]

Whether or not Socrates ever said such a thing is of no matter here. What does matter is that the quote has been widely repeated not only because it sounds like something an elder teacher would say about his or her students but also because, with just a little bit of word change, this quote could pass for something an adult said in 1960, 1970, 1980...right up to the present.

As a modern vocation, many in the middle classes are dependent on educators and their institutions—especially college—to replicate their class standing. But at modernity's onset, a university education was reserved mainly for children of privilege. Over time, the industrial apparatus grew and thus needed more skills and educated workers and education was extended to more people. This became one of the foundations for middle class growth. Part of this process involved the state, which allotted land and money for building public universities and set aside funds to subsidize the costs of running them. The project turned into one of the most successful state programs in modern history and it paid off as well. Populations grew not only in literacy, education, and skills, but they also participated in research and development both of scientific knowledge and commercial goods. And today it is no wonder that some working class families aspire to find ways to get their children into the hallowed institution.

---

1  The website, Quote Investigator, claims to have tracked down the original quote to Kenneth John Freeman's 1907 dissertation for Cambridge. See (URL retrieved August 31, 2018): http://quoteinvestigator.com/2010/05/01/misbehaving-children-in-ancient-times/.

IMAGE 11.1
British Students at Eton, 1932,
Unknown Author

The commonality across these class distinctions is that a university education is a place where young people predominate. And their behavior there is something that adults have often remarked upon with some amusement, charity, and dismay. Many college students have just left home for the first time and are exposed to new levels of social freedom, ideas, behaviors, and beliefs. They usually have little experience in the real world but act as if they have it all figured out and will "do" life better than their parents. Their level of assuredness often does not match their knowledge or accomplishments and they can come off as almost petulant in their naivety. They are easily excitable.

Be all of that as it may, university students are often at the forefront of social change and upheaval. They participated in the European revolutions of 1848, where workers' rights and other social reforms were forged on the Continent. There were worldwide revolts in 1968, where students opposed the Vietnam War (Image 11.2) and condemned the arrangements between the establishment Left in the Soviet Bloc (as well as the West) with the authorities in the centers of power (Paris, New York, London, Washington). Movements in the United States, France, Mexico, and Japan forced into public consciousness the idea that old ways were no longer going to work and put women's rights, environmental concerns, racism, and sexuality on the political agenda. In China, students also put democracy on the agenda in their demonstrations at Tiananmen Square in 1989, only to find themselves in the scope of soldiers' guns and in the path of tanks (Image 11.3). More recently, students were central in the opposition to the old guard of authoritarian rulers from Egypt to Libya and elsewhere in what became known as "The Arab Spring" (Image 11.4).

WINDY IDEALISTS AND FROTHY YOUTH 73

IMAGE 11.2
Vietnam War Protesters at March on Washington, 1967, by Frank Wolfe

IMAGE 11.3
Students at Tiananmen Square, 1989, by Jiří Tondl

IMAGE 11.4
A Protester on Tahrir Square Holds Up a Poster Comparing Morsi to Former Fascist Leaders Mussolini and Hitler, November 30, 2012, by Y. Weeks/VOA

Modern youth have continually challenged their elders and forged into being their own ideas, actions, and practices, only for their children to do the same. Youth may be filled with foment and folly but also demand that old ways be periodically wiped away. As university education has become a central feature of modernity, so has its windy idealists and frothy youth.

CHAPTER 12

# Middle Class Snobbism

One idea that prevails in modernity is that people should rise and fall within the system according to their talents, hard work, marketable skills, intelligence and so on. This model of social mobility and inequality is known as "meritocracy," or how individuals are sorted out based on their merits. As such, the middle classes like to think they are the authors of their situations and destinies. But talents and efforts mean little to nothing if the socio-structural context is not one that allows them to payoff, to find a place in the system where they will be rewarded. If a social system contracts, by definition, there are fewer positions available for everyone who might want one and thus even some hard-working people with talents will be left out. And the reverse is true as well. As a system expands, more people are needed to do the work, staff the offices, and so on, and thus there are more positions available for more people and even those with less qualifications or talents can find a place to sell their labor for decent wages. In short, part of the modern class structure relates to the division of labor, periods of systemic growth and/or contraction, and what we might call an "opportunity structure." And these realities tell us a lot about the middle class.

Let us use the US experience as an example. Education is the gateway to middle class life for many. For others, that gateway might be learning a highly sought-after skill that pays well, such as woodworking, plumbing, or electrical work. For still others, the entry into the middle class might be ownership of some small to moderate business concern. These professions are an important feature of modernity's signature. The feudal system that birthed modernity destined the majority of people to a "nasty, brutish, and short" (Hobbes) life among the peasantry, so it should be no wonder that the relative comfort of being in the middle class became something for modernity to tout, even if the great middle classes were not formed at modernity's birth, as most people for the next few centuries would remain rural and/or endure hard labor. And though they made an appearance prior to it, it was not until after World War II that the Western world saw the middle classes proliferate, a historic achievement in many respects.

After World War II, the United States emerged intact industrially. They were situated to supply other nations on their needs for food, appliances, cars, textiles, and machine goods. The United States co-sponsored the Bretton Woods Conference, where an agreement was made to create the International Monetary Fund (IMF) and the World Bank. Together they would provide currency stability by using the US dollar for international trade while also providing devastated European countries loans to rebuild (thus flooding the United States with additional money). Accompanying these policies was The Marshall Plan, whereby the United States provided additional loans to European allies (plus other countries that were belligerents in the war). Funds would often be spent purchasing US goods, which bolstered its own economy. In addition, the GI Bill provided low-cost loans to returning soldiers (and sometimes their family members) to get an education, vocational training to enter the workforce, and/or loans for housing, which, collectively, placed these individuals in a strategically advantageous position for advancing.

In short, the US economic structure expanded after WWII because of global and national economic conditions built on non-market mechanisms, i.e., government programs and tutelage. Consequently, the US state bureaucracy and educational system also expanded with this economic growth. With housing demand increasing and an interstate highway system being put in place, there was an immense blooming of the opportunity structure in the United States. Should individuals from that period mention the hard work they put in to attain a middle class status, such efforts (as real as many of them were) must be understood within the macro-economic and historic context outlined above. *The middle classes did not just sort of happen*, whether in the United States, Europe, or Japan, or elsewhere even today. This dynamic above is a form of "structural mobility," where a whole section of society is elevated upward into a new social position.

The middle classes are buffered on the one side by poorly paid working classes and the poverty-stricken, groups that function to keep the middle class working diligently in their offices and their children studying for a future they hope to retain, producing a constant anxiety from their "fear of falling" (see Ehrenreich 1989). This fear is enough to encourage middle class youth in places like the United States—which counts on market forces more than government involvement to financially support its university system—to take on great amounts of debt to pay for the costs of college, a debt load that in the 2010s (over $1 trillion and rising) appeared ready to explode into a default crisis as increasing numbers of graduates were unable to earn enough through wages and salaries to repay their student loans. And such debts cause delays in marriage (about 12% or so say they have put off marriage because of student loan debt) and delayed marriage is the most significant factor in deciding not to buy a home (e.g., US millennials are down 3.4 million fewer homeowners compared to rates of previous generations) while today dual incomes and homeownership are keys to maintaining a middle class life (see Nance-Nash 2012; Ellis 2013; Weisbaum 2016; Scott-Clayton 2018; Hyun Choi, Zhu, and Goodman 2018, and references therein). But the risk of taking on such debt can be worth it to many, given that, as of 2015, a college degree translated into 56% higher earnings than high school graduates (see Rugaber 2017 and references therein).

On the other side, the middle classes are buffered by the upper-middle classes and the very rich. The upper-middle classes are composed of well-paid professionals such as doctors, lawyers, dentists, mid-level executives, people with advanced degrees, and so on. They are mostly white and increasingly are geographically, culturally, and financially separated from the bulk of the middle class, accumulating wealth, pensions, property, and know-how to isolate themselves from the many slings and arrows those below them must dodge. Their kids go to the best schools, have tutors, and do not lack for health care. This upper portion of the middle class has been able to consolidate its advantages to the point of even hoarding them away from others (for discussion see M. Stewart 2018).[1]

The upper-middle classes envy the material goods that wealth can obtain and are not beyond putting on their own displays of affluence, or what Thorstein Veblen called "conspicuous consumption" in reference to the *nouveau riche* at the turn of the twentieth century. But those in the middle of the middle class temper such envy with cautious misgiving, suspecting that the very wealthy either inherited their money or did not earn it honestly through hard work. The middle classes also have little taste for the regular sex and drug scandals of the very wealthy but usually see them as the result of people understandably succumbing to the temptations that wealth brings (while similar behavior from the working class is reacted to with an attitude ranging from pity to reprobation). In any case, a sense of moral superiority reigns among many in the middle classes. For the bulk of them—still strongly shaped by Catholic and Protestant notions of modesty and thrift—having some nice gadgets and being able to retire and play with their grandchildren is good enough.

The middle classes tend to see themselves as the epitome of respectable living. Work hard at school, at home, at the job. Devote time for worship and teach your children respect for authority. The poor did it to themselves and are at best to be pitied and too much wealth threatens to degrade one's soul. They believe that they are truly better and their station in life is to be aspired to. Dirty work must be done but it is for the dirty, not for them.

---

1  From the point of view of the poor, the working class, or even those right in the middle, the upper-middle class appears relatively wealthy, though from the point of view of the banking community, "the rich" start at around $25 million, which, in monetary terms, is far beyond the upper-middle class (for discussion, see Woolley 2018).

IMAGE 12.1  World's Highest Standard of Living, *Life* Magazine, 1937
SOURCE: MARGARET BOURKE-WHITE / MASTERS / GETTY IMAGES

But the middle classes have other tasks that cast suspicion on such self-images. Educated office workers find that their life experiences have been reduced to reports, stifling work culture, and answering to bosses they dislike.[2] Many in the middle class devote a majority of their adult lives to producing goods in which they have no personal connection or emotional stake. The highly skilled worker who fixes our car or our wiring or our plumbing has little respect for the manager or the banker or the boss. This is not work, they think, convinced that those who get their hands dirty are superior. And the small business owners fancy themselves innovators and hard workers who have built up their businesses by their own toil. They labor and work for themselves and they pride themselves on their loftier aspirations and struggles. In all these cases, the middle classes compare themselves to each other and they chase each other's tastes and styles. One cannot be caught *not* being up-to-date on the news, new fashions, new music, or new gadgets, rarely considering how such

---

2  One in four Japanese employees admit to wanting to kill their boss (see Grannum 2018 and reference therein).

things—like the global electronics industry—are dependent on a massive supply of workers in far off lands, many trafficked persons forced to work against their will and living in overcrowded migrant work camps without clean water or plumbing (e.g., see Ramchandani 2018). And should people find themselves attuned with the times, they can never rest for the times change and so must they—i.e., newer cars, newer club memberships, newer schools, shoes, and friends for their children.

At the end of the day, the middle classes have nowhere to go but down or across. Should a child fail in his or her lessons, succumb to drugs, or just become a lay about, downward mobility awaits. Statistically speaking, more often than not, children of the middle class reproduce their class standing, acquiring the schooling, training, discipline, sacrifice and knowledge to do so. Though this is not simply handed to them on a platter, they tend to underestimate both how privileged they are and how hard those below them must work.[3] Simply being born into a middle class family will often put one in the "right" geography where opportunities are more easily seized. And the poor often work more hours—both on the job and off—than their relative level of wealth might suggest. Still, the middle classes feel as if they are the authors of their destinies and those without their life chances only have themselves to blame, a view reflecting a certain level of unwarranted snobbism.

---

[3] Less than 1% of Americans between 1996 and 2007 moved from the bottom 20% of income brackets to the top 20%, while roughly 10% moved out of the bottom 20% by working 1000 extra hours. Respondents guessed about 16% would rise from the bottom to the top brackets and 35% would make it out of the bottom bracket should they work 1000 extra hours (see Pomeroy 2015 and references therein).

CHAPTER 13

# Pauperism and Artificial Impoverishment

The existence of classes suffering from poverty is not unique to modernity, as history reveals no lack of plebeians, serfs, and peasants. And not only were peasants and serfs lacking in luxury and sometimes in want of sustenance, but should the king or queen desire a lavish banquet to impress foreign dignitaries or to celebrate a child's betrothal, the serfs might find their cupboards barer than usual and the winter longer and more trying than it might otherwise have been. But prior to modernity, normally, it was the level of avarice and greed on one side, the amount of work and technological development on another, and the fortunes of ecological richness and the weather still on a third, that usually determined the degree of bounty or want a feudal peasant "enjoyed." In modernity, poverty is built into the system in a very different but systemic way.

Here, when we speak of wealth and poverty, we are interested in more than simply "inequality." After all, if we hypothetically observe that the top household income was $1,000,000,000 and the bottom was $100,000, we could speak of inequality while still imagining a scenario where the second household could live decently well (if we assume a low level of price inflation). In modernity, wealth concentrates in fewer hands over time while being pulled from the total amount of money available in the system. So, rather than inequality per se, the issue is how *the accumulation and concentration of wealth relate to the impoverishment of others* in the system's normal operations across the class structure and across generations.

By 2015, the richest 400 Americans owned more wealth than the bottom 61% of the population (Collins and Hoxie 2015). According to the US Census Bureau, the United States had 320.9 million people in 2015, making those 400 richest individuals only .00000125% of the population. Globally, according to Oxfam International (2016) and by 2015, wealth was even more concentrated, with the "wealth of the poorest half of the world's population [having] fallen by a trillion dollars since 2010, a drop of 38%. This has occurred despite the global population increasing by around 400 million people during that period. Meanwhile, the wealth of the richest 62 has increased by more than half a trillion dollars to $1.76tr." In that report, Oxfam found that these 62 people had the same amount of wealth as half the world's population, a level of concentration that was also increasing (in 2010 it was 388, in 2011 it was 177, in 2012 it was 159, in 2013 it was 92, and in 2014 it was 80). If we estimate the 2016 world population at about 7.4 billion, that means that .00000000838% of the world's population had as much wealth as the bottom 50% of it that year.

Such wealth concentration is likely to persist across time. Economic historian, Gregory Clark (author of *The Son Also Rises: Surnames and the History of Social Mobility*), found that only after 10 to 15 generations does a family's wealth (or poverty) dissipate (see his interview in Robb 2014). By investing their inherited stocks of wealth into industry and finance, class advantages passed on to children are parlayed into new accumulated wealth and this allows a select few to maintain its position atop the class structure. Further, we see wealth increasingly concentrate as the number of those at the top decrease overtime while the amount of wealth they control only grows. And this is not an infinite pie; wealth concentration relates to how a pie is divided, where wealth accumulated in one class means less of it available for others.

What about the other classes? A 2015 study by the International Monetary Fund investigated the drivers of inequality in both advanced market economies and those still developing. Its authors expressed concerns stemming from previous studies that found increased income inequality reduces economic growth, which, they suggest, means that wealth does not trickle down and its concentration limits the growth of the size of the pie to be divided. Before presenting its findings, the report makes observations about recent trends. Between 1998 and 2008, the largest global income gains were for median incomes (50th percentile) and the top 1% (with the former an indicator of middle class growth in emerging economies and the latter demonstrating concentration of wealth in advanced ones). Across all economies, executive salaries have been "strikingly high." In advanced economies, the middle 20% has shrunk, marked by declining or stagnant wage growth, often while productivity has risen amid a decline in middle-skilled occupations. Poverty is on the decline in emerging economies (unsurprising given poverty's greater levels there), though it is rising in advanced ones (more below). Some effects of inequality include cutting off peoples' paths to wealth, education, and health services.

Among the drivers of these trends, their study found that technological growth increased a "skill premium" for better paying jobs and also induced job loss through automation (which had a larger effect in advanced economies). Also contributing to inequality is (what they call) "financial deepening," or the ability to accumulate assets (e.g., savings, retirement, investments in education) that allow households to withstand wider economic shocks (this had a greater influence in developing economies). Relatedly, there was an overall growth in both financial globalization and the "skill premium" in modern economies, which favored those with access to education and accumulated assets, especially those in the top 10% income brackets of advanced economies.

Finally, both a decline in organized labor (i.e., unions) and a decline in governmental redistributive policies (e.g., welfare spending, food subsidies, and so on) increased levels of inequality (Dabla-Norris et al. 2015).

Note that while the above study addresses what might *change levels* of inequality, it does not really discuss how inequality is a structural product. How does the system produce the impoverished? And, if it is built into the system, how does the system benefit from that production?

It first will be useful to discuss poverty at the individual level, that is, the extent to which someone is the author of his or her own conditions. Imagine a person who declines to get educated and/or declines to learn a trade and/or succumbs to impulsive self-destructive behavior, thus becoming inarticulate, dull in mind, and incapable in deed. Should he or she be born outside of the ranks of the wealthy, all things being equal, it is more than likely that they—instead of someone more intelligent, diligent, and with sought after skills—will become downwardly mobile until they suffer poverty, even destitution. Whether he or she drinks or gambles or idles their way into poverty, it is not hard to see how their destiny is the product of a long line of personal choices and behaviors. The common modern person's explanation of poverty in general is usually along these lines, i.e., as the result of many people—millions even—making similar choices and mistakes, doing it to themselves, and getting what they deserve.

Look at Figure 13.1. Notice that US unemployment begins to grow in 1929 and by 1933 over 20% of the workforce was out of work. If we use the model in the previous paragraph to explain such a trend, we must conclude that within a few years more and more people in the United States grew either too lazy, too stupid, too drunk, too idle, too unskilled (etc.) to want a job, to attract one, and/or to keep one should they get it. That makes little sense, though. Rather, in 1929 the stock market crashed and the United States (and much of the world market) entered into The Great Depression. And if you look at the graph, it was not a sudden return to the work ethic but rather a combination of the New Deal (which helped so that things did not get worse) and the war-time economy of WWII that brought the unemployment rate back to a more even keel. Thus, just as we saw with the middle class in the previous chapter, it is necessary to understand such structural and historical relationships if we are to understand poverty in modern society.

In modernity's early development, the state tended not to regulate economic activity very much, leaving each business concern to its own devices. There were no workplace safety laws or environmental regulations, no unions, no minimum wages, no pensions, and so on. And welfare states did not exist to catch those who fell through the cracks. In such a system, workers found

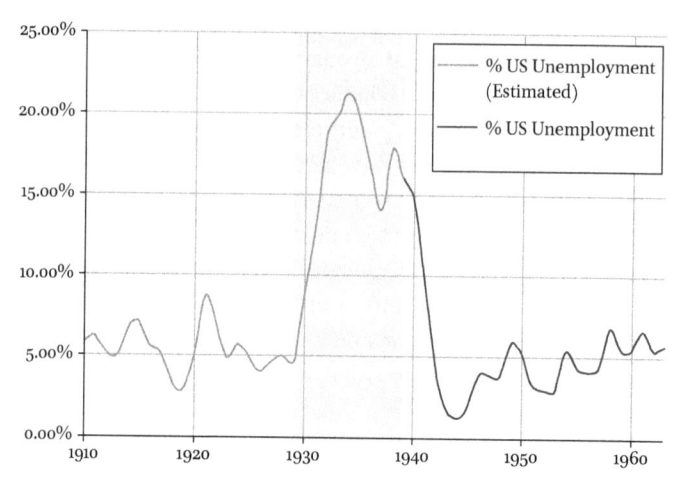

FIGURE 13.1 US Unemployment Rate, 1910–1960, by Lawrencekhoo
Caption from Source: US Unemployment rate from 1910–1960, with the years of the Great Depression (1929–1939) highlighted. Data for 1910–1930 from Christina Romer (1986), "Spurious Volatility in Historical Unemployment Data," *The Journal of Political Economy* 94(1): 1–37. Data for 1930–1940 from Robert M. Coen (1973), "Labor Force and Unemployment in the 1920's and 1930's: A Re-Examination Based on Postwar Experience," *The Review of Economics and Statistics* 55(1): 46–55. Data for 1940–1960 from the US Bureau of Labor Statistics, Employment Status of the Civilian Noninstitutional Population, 1940 to Date (URL retrieved March 6, 2009): ftp://ftp.bls.gov/pub/special.requests/lf/aat1.txt.

employment as they could, and employers paid as little as they could get away with. A person might work full-time (60–100 hours a week even) and still be dirt poor, as such coal miners or migrant farmers or those working in the cotton mills. This is because the ideal situation for a business owner would be where an employee produces a great deal of output and the employer pays that worker very little. So, before states stepped in with regulations on wages, allowing unions, collective bargaining, and such things, the working class could be kept as poor as the conscience of their bosses allowed.

But this is only taking into account those who had jobs. There exists in modern society a structural and permanent underclass, a section of the population unemployed at any one time (the individuals may vary, but the existence of the unemployed in general remains). The existence of this class provides a somewhat positive function to the system. First, full employment tends to drive wages up—when employers needs workers they have to offer wages and benefits at a level greater than what workers can find elsewhere in order to attract them and/or keep them. Simultaneously, when there are always people out of work the odds of finding someone to take a job at whatever wage is offered is higher. And in both cases, wages paid will be apportioned out of the profits from the previous investment cycle. Simply put, the more an employer must set out in wages, the less money is available for profits, something that both employers and those who invest in their companies know too well (e.g., Weissmann 2018). As a result, in an unregulated market economy, there will tend to be suppressive pressures on wages as a matter of course, unless there are other factors that will push them upward—i.e., governmental policy, strong unions, less unemployment, productivity growth in light of the latter two, and so on.

What happens when workers are placed in a position to both (1) work harder and more productively while (2) being unable to extract additional compensation out of the wage-bill for that work? As we see in Figures 13.2–13.4, their wages and standards of living tend to lag and decline. Additional compensation for harder work is not something that naturally happens or that employers freely offer. Rather, it is something that has to be extracted through worker negotiations and demands and, should those fail, withholding their labor, i.e., collective bargaining with the threat of strikes. And this is something, among other things, that union organization makes possible—improving working conditions, raising standards of living, and reducing overall income inequality. Consequently, union decline also means declines in those same things (see Valenti 2018; Dynarksi 2018, and references therein).

In addition to a polarizing trend between the top 1% (and top .1% and top .01%) and everyone else, today we are witnessing a divide among those in the middle classes, where the top portion of that class accumulates advantages while a new form of impoverishment—where wages, salaries, debt, and living standards once visited upon those with lower levels of education—is being thrust upon new generations of (often) educated young people. For instance, Peter Temin (2017) sees the United States increasingly divided along a dual-track economy. The first is the FTE sector (finance, technology, electronics), which is populated by the college-educated, good jobs, and social networks that boost odds of success. The second is the low-wage sector, filled with about 80% of the population, straddled with poor education, job and health insecurity, crumbling infrastructure, debt, and so on. As poor education and poor neighborhoods weigh down those in lower income brackets, the top 20% finds ways to benefit from what Richard Reeves terms "opportunity hoarding," i.e., making it harder for the economically less-privileged to rise upward. Kids from the middle class are better prepared for scholastic success, their parents vote

**The minimum wage would be much higher if it had kept up with a growing economy**

The inflation-adjusted minimum wage, and hypothetical minimum wage values if it had grown with average wages and productivity since 1968

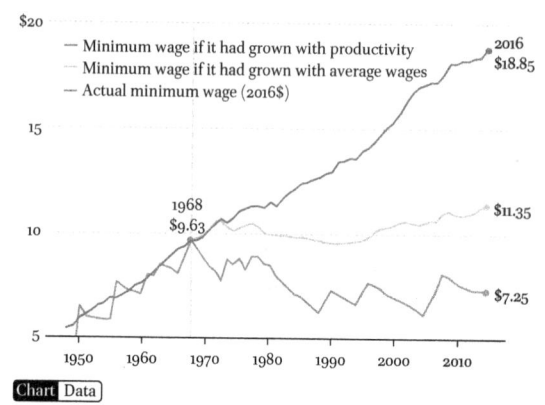

- Minimum wage if it had grown with productivity
- Minimum wage if it had grown with average wages
- Actual minimum wage (2016$)

2016 $18.85
1968 $9.63
$11.35
$7.25

Note: Growth in average wages measures average wages of production/nonsupervisory workers in the private sector.

Source: Adapted from David Cooper, *The federal minimum wages has been eroded by decades of inaction*, Economic Policy Institute Snapshot, July 25, 2016.

FIGURE 13.2   Top Charts of 2016. Used with Permission of The Economic Policy Institute

for tax breaks for themselves, families benefit from class-based zoning laws (which doubles back on access to better education in safer neighborhoods), and their children have more opportunities for professionalization through internships, among other benefits (for discussion of Reeves' theses, see Helmore 2017).

In the professional labor markets, according to US Census Bureau's numbers, while employed US women have seen a steady rise in median earnings, employed US men earned less in 2014 ($50,383) than in 1973 ($53,294). When asked about these figures, Harvard University labor economist, Larry Katz, attributed the stagnation in men's wages to, among other things, the fact that labor's share of national income has been declining since 2000 and a gap between middle- and low-wage jobs that has been steadily widening since about 1980 (see Wessel 2015).[1] Costs of health care, education, and housing have

---

1  Katz references the Economic Policy Institute's Josh Bivens' and Larry Mischel's work that shows that this decline coincides with policy initiatives aimed at lowering the bargaining power of low- and moderately-waged workers.

## Boosting productivity is necessary but not sufficient for wage growth

Disconnect between productivity and a typical worker's compensation, 1948–2015

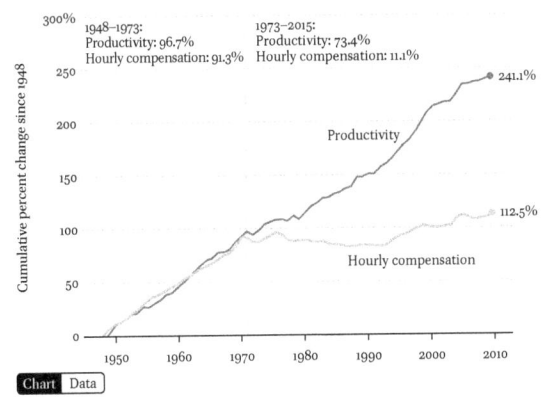

1948–1973:
Productivity: 96.7%
Hourly compensation: 91.3%

1973–2015:
Productivity: 73.4%
Hourly compensation: 11.1%

Productivity: 241.1%
Hourly compensation: 112.5%

Note: Data are for average hourly compensation of production/nonsupervisory workers in the private sector and net productivity of the total economy. "Net productivity" is the growth of output of goods and services minus depreciation per hour worked.

Source: Adapted from Figure K in Josh Bivens and Hunter Blair, *Financing recovery and fairness by going where the money is*, Economic Policy Institute Report, November 15, 2016.

FIGURE 13.3   Top Charts of 2016. Used with Permission of The Economic Policy Institute

continued to climb while wages for young people in manufacturing, professional and business occupations, retail and wholesale, and leisure and hospitality have fallen (more than 10% since 2007). Outsourcing and computerization have helped drive these trends (Thompson 2014).

Such an economic situation is reflected in real life living conditions and decisions. We are witnessing more Americans (32%) ages 18–34 living with their parents recently (as of 2017) than in the last 130 years, something that men (35%) experience more than women (29%), crosses racial lines, and is more concentrated among all groups without college degrees (Fry 2016). And how are working class and middle class students supposed to keep up or even get by when the cost of college has gotten 12x more expensive than for the previous generation (Rose Quandt 2014)? Reflecting such costs and a polarized labor market, as of 2016, over 40% of student borrowers were no longer making payments on their loans (Mitchell 2016), which grew to $1.5 trillion in 2018, up $500 billion since 2010–2011 (Wigglesworth 2018). However, those strapped with such debt are no longer able to appeal to bankruptcy court because of changes in federal law, chaining many individuals to these debts for life (see Chen 2018).

**Drop in union membership has taken $14 to $52 out of nonunion workers' weekly wages**

Additional weekly wages that nonunion private-sector workers would earn, had the sharke of workers in a union (union density) remained the same as in 1979, 1979–2013 (2013 dollars)

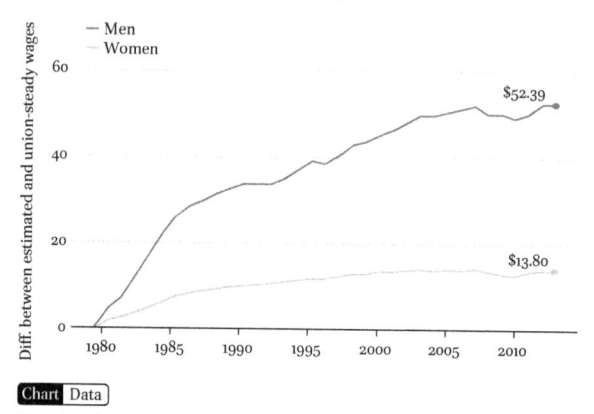

Note: Sample restricted to nonunion full-time workers in the private sector ages 16 to 64.

Source: Adapted from Figure C in Jake Rosenfeld, Patric Denice, and Jennifer Laird, *Union decline lowers wages of nonunion workers*, Economic Policy Institute Report, August 13, 2016

FIGURE 13.4    Top Charts of 2016. Used with Permission of The Economic Policy Institute

Facing such dilemmas, establishing new families and households becomes extra difficult. To wit: young people in the United States today are having even fewer children than before, citing as their reasons the desire for more leisure time and personal freedom, not having a partner yet, and costs of childcare (see Cain Miller 2018 and references therein).

Matching these trends, then, is the decline in upward mobility and an increase in poverty in the middle class, with education being no panacea. Young people from wealthier households who drop out of high school are just as likely to remain in their income quintile by age 40 as are college graduates from poor households likely to find themselves at age 40 in the same income quintile of their youth (see O'Brien 2014 and references therein). Being born into a poor household in a poor neighborhood will tend to limit the odds of oneself or one's children being upwardly mobile (a fact that is more pressing for non-whites in the United States) (see Bouie 2014 and references therein). For instance, 42% of American men raised in the bottom fifth of incomes stay there, compared to 25% of men in Denmark and 30% of men in Britain, while only 8% of American men at the bottom rose to the top fifth, with figures of 12% for the British and 14% for the Danes; and 62% of men and women born in the top fifth stay in the top two-fifths, while 65% born in the bottom fifth stay in the bottom two-fifths (see DeParle 2012 and references therein).

These figures are reflected in quality of life measures. Increasingly, people living in what was once the middle class are stuck in a cycle of unequal family resources, disadvantaged neighborhoods, insecure labor markets, and declining conditions of K-12 education (see Duncan and Murnane 2011). Thus, as well-paying, low-skilled jobs in manufacturing have disappeared in developed countries like the United States, we are seeing rising rates of poverty in the suburbs (about 17 million in suburban poverty as of 2016–2017, growing 43% between 1990–2012, as compared to 17% in urban areas), accompanied rising costs of health care, drug addiction, and suicide rates (McGreal 2016; Kopf 2017; Centers for Disease Control 2018; Fox 2018; Hellman 2018). In terms of suicide, not only do the rich live longer than their poor counterparts (rich Americans live 15 years longer on average; see Cuthbertson 2017 and references therein), but suicide rates correlate with poverty and inequality outside the United States, such as in Japan (Inagaki 2010) and South Korea (Lee et al. 2017). And as income inequality rises, so does the rate of hate crimes, reflecting rising strife among working people (Majumber 2017). Further, inequality tends to perpetuate itself, as higher levels of income disparity result in lower levels of social mobility, as those in lower income households have curtailed access to educational opportunities, are more likely to be burdened by debt and long work-days, become single parents as teenage girls, and find themselves involved with violence (see Pickett and Wilkinson 2017 and references therein).

Concurrently growing with the decline of the middle class and retracting opportunities for upward mobility has been the rise in extreme poverty in the United States. The number of US households living on less than $2-a-day went from 636,000 in 1996 to around 1.46 million by early 2011, or a growth of 130%, with about 2.8 million children living in extreme poverty in the same period (Shaefer and Edin 2012). One in 30 US children were homeless in 2013, an 8% rise from 2012, with growth found in 31 states (Yuhas 2014). A Federal Reserve Survey found that four in 10 Americans would be unable to cover a $400 emergency expense in 2017 (see Guardian Staff and Agencies 2018 and reference therein). In 2018, a United Way report found that nearly 51% of Americans, or about 160 million people, could not afford a "bare-bones" household budget for housing, child care, food, transportation, and health care (see Corbett 2018a and references within). Given all these facts, it should not be surprising that optimism about their economic future is higher in developing countries than it is in wealthier ones (Pew Research Center 2014a).

One sociological idea is that systems will tend toward eliminating those realities that are dysfunctional for it. Not only is poverty a problem for those who suffer it, but a market system is also dependent on consumer spending, which poverty works directly against. Even if that is so, it is also the case that poverty is persistent in the modern system because it is both built into the very structure of our economy and it provides a positive function for the system as a whole. When the distribution of a pie concentrates among fewer hands, this leaves less for everyone else to divide among themselves and this will mean more people will be left behind and/or less and less wealth is available for all those who remain. The prospect of poverty keeps people working hard at jobs they do not like but jobs they need for fear of falling into destitution. And structural unemployment suppresses the level of wages employers have to pay, as there will always remain people willing to work for what is offered. For these reasons, the existence of poverty in market systems is not exceptional but a rule.

Outside of structural features, artificial impoverishment can be simply a matter of pulling levers of the state or having no regulatory levers at all (the libertarian dream), as state actions and/or corporate policies can increase or decrease the level of poverty and its severity. States can raise minimum wages or keep them behind inflation. The business class can increase their wage-bill or invest overseas in search of cheaper workforces. And in the global economy of the 2000s, wages often do not even rise with lower unemployment. For instance, David Dayen (2018), writing for the *New Republic*, notes that wages have not increased in real terms during the 2017–2018 recovery period, even with low unemployment, and points to several structural features: lower levels of unionization and the subsequent rise of independent contract work, non-compete clauses that prevent workers in an industry from moving to higher paying jobs, creeping monopolization that allows companies to corner markets without sharing profits, workers in abandoned geographical regions cannot bid up wages, and a greater level of people ages 25–54 who have dropped out of the work force entirely, which depresses wage gains for those entering it. These dynamics suggest something beyond how certain individuals may author their own conditions. They tell us to inspect the very structure of our social system.

By the 1970s and 1980s, the world economy had basically recovered from the devastation of World War II. Europe and Japan were both back on their feet and competing with the United States in global markets. The World Bank and the International Monetary Fund had done their jobs, it seemed. However, rather than closing up shop, these institutions refurbished themselves and set out to transform the "Third World." Rolling out a variety of "development programs," lending organizations offered loans to less wealthy societies as a way to assist in their "modernization." Development loans were ostensibly geared toward building infrastructure, purchasing industrial equipment, installing modern transportation and communication systems, and so on. Such projects would then make recipient countries attractive investment opportunities for businesses interested in setting up there. However, such loans would have conditions attached to them (often called, "conditionality"). A list of typical conditions included wage freezes, devaluing currency, removal of price supports (i.e., let inflation rise without state intervention via price controls), reduction of social spending (e.g., on health, education, etc.), reduction in environmental laws, privatization of public utilities such as water, lowering regulations on foreign investment, and moving to an export-based economy centered on agricultural products.

The result of such loaning practices was entirely predictable. In some places, given the largesse of some of these loans, regional elites often first skimmed vast riches off the top. People became poorer as their wages stagnated and prices rose. Their access to public services declined and with it the social safety net. Resources they once had access to, such as fresh water, were put in private hands. Multinational corporations moved in, taking land and releasing pollution into water, soil, and air and traditional peoples were often pushed off their lands and forced to find work where they could. National resources such as land for agriculture and other products (ores, oil, natural gas, etc.) were put on international markets to fetch money to pay back the development loans that states had agreed to; many states, nevertheless, found themselves in a "debt trap" and unable to pay back what was owed. Hunger and poverty rose almost immediately and to such an extent an international outcry against these practices arose. All that said, such areas did lead to attractive investment opportunities and this led to increased offshoring of jobs and services, from wealthier countries to poorer ones. Such a series of developments were a significant causal force for the emergence of our period of "globalization" and further weakened the ability of "First World" workers—professionals and blue-collar—to find work while forcing that same labor force to compete with global labor markets, which in turn put additional downward pressure on their wages at home.

Poverty, then, is not only built into a market system but it can be artificially imposed both through active measures and acts of omission or neglect. In the economic sector, what corporations do with either profits or tax windfalls can be a matter of choice, but only to a point. One issue, as Michael Hiltzik (2018) puts it, is "the long-term trend of funneling gains from labor productivity not to the workforce, but to shareholders. As with any addiction, this process produces short-term euphoria, reflected in share prices, but long-term pathology, reflected in income inequality, poverty, and social unrest." And the same can be said about what corporations do with their tax breaks. As we will see in a later chapter, much of the freedom of choice corporations have had in such matters has been usurped by their shareholders who demand short-term gains on their investments as the priority over wage increases or any long-term social planning from corporate boardrooms. So, while business leaders could direct profits and gains toward higher wages and increased productive capacity, they often do not do so for fear of capital flight away from their companies to others promising more short-term profits for their stockholders.

In the political sector, states can do several things that influence poverty levels. States can make it easier for investment capital to transfer overseas, as just discussed above. Internally, if states fail to increase mandated minimum wages and/or adjust levels of state pensions to keep pace with inflation and other cost of living increases, then the number of those in poverty, or threatened with it, will rise. For instance, minimum wage in the United States originally was set so that a full-time worker could support a family of four and keep them out of poverty.[2] As such, the minimum wage was regularly raised to keep pace with the costs of certain necessities, especially food. During the Reagan administration, such regular cost of living increases in the minimum wage were ended and have been only sporadic ever since. Indicatively, a study from the National Low Income Housing Coalition, released in 2018, concluded that in no single US state could a worker paid minimum wage afford a 2-bedroom rental and, in order to do so, they would have to work 122 hours a week (i.e., three full-time jobs) all year long (see Andone and Campisi 2018 and reference therein).[3] Such conditions often prompt calls for increasing government mandated minimum wages, with objections mainly coming from the business community and economic conservatives, many of whom claim that such increases will cost the economy jobs. A study of six metropolitan areas (Chicago, Washington, D.C., Oakland, San Francisco, San Jose, and Seattle) published in 2018, however, found that minimum wage increases to over $10 per hour (federal minimum

---

[2] When initiated, and demonstrating the operative assumptions of the time period, the original policy assumption about minimum wage was that it was for a male worker supporting a wife and two children.

[3] It is similar with benefits for the elderly, as one study found that retiree benefits for US Social Security buy 34% less in 2018 than they did in 2000, an imposition of poverty also based on policy decisions (O'Brien 2018).

being $7.25) produced no significant employment reductions (Allegretto et al. 2018).[4]

It should be no wonder, then, that a United Nations human rights officer—citing the faults of "successive administrations," personal observations made on a two-week trip to Alabama, California, Georgia, Puerto Rico, West Virginia, and Washington, D.C., and the recent $1.5 trillion income tax cut directed mainly at the very wealthy—described poverty in the United States as a "political choice" and a problem that "With political will ... could be readily eliminated" (Associated Press 2018b). Such conclusions provoked a backlash from US officials, e.g., US Ambassador to the United Nations, Niki Haley, in a letter to Sen. Bernie Sanders, wrote, "It is patently ridiculous for the United Nations to examine poverty in America" and that the study "wasted the UN's time and resources" (see Shelbourne 2018).

But evidence supported the UN view on the political aspect of poverty, or at least how to decrease it. For instance, in the post-crash / post-recession recovery period—between 2008 and 2018—about $30 trillion in the United States was distributed to the top 10% of households (who were rewarded with tax cuts), while the average net worth for the poorest half decreased from $11,000 to $8,000 (see Buchheit 2018 and references therein). By contrast, Norway, a country with nationalized offshore oil reserves and a healthy corporate sector, has made it social policy to distribute the fruits of such resources among its population, e.g., profits from oil are invested into a sovereign wealth fund and dividends there are used for social development. In addition, its strong working-class politics and union participation in policy-making have resulted in higher minimum wages, higher taxes, and wage compression, i.e., lower distance between top and bottom income earners because of union negotiations. And rather than stifling economic development, Norway scores at the top among 110 countries in the Legatum Prosperity Index; its youth demographic has enjoyed an increase in its per capita income by 13% in comparison to Gen Xers at a time when income share is in decline across Europe (down 9% in Germany and as much as 30% in parts of southern Europe) and the United States (down 5%) (see Savage 2018 and references therein). This is just one demonstration of how just as poverty can be exacerbated by state policy, so can it be alleviated by it.

Poverty, personal health, and national politics all connect with one another. Beginning with the Reagan administration the US government made it easier for corporations to fire workers that attempt to organize, strike, and collectively

---

4   A PDF of the Center on Wage and Employment Dynamic's study can be found here: http://irle.berkeley.edu/files/2018/09/The-New-Wave-of-Local-Minimum-Wage-Policies.pdf.

bargain, for businesses to conglomerate into mega-corporations, and for states to pursue and enact "right to work" laws, all of which decimated unions and thus the ability of labor to negotiate higher wages, pensions, and benefits—while CEO pay skyrocketed. Further, as corporate conglomerates increasingly dominate labor markets, this creates less real competition for workers and this means that lower rates of unemployment do not translate into a situation where a higher demand for workers with a lower supply available compels employers to raise wages (see Ghilarducci 2018; Reich 2018; N. Smith 2018a, and references therein). And what wage gains do occur are often negated by inflation, as happened from June 2017–2018 when 2.9% inflation wiped out those wage increases that did exist and US workers had to work more hours just to come up with 0.1% growth in weekly earnings (Long 2018; Mitchell 2018).

While companies—despite evidence showing that the relationships are the inverse of what they suppose—expect that layoffs and longer work-hours increase worker productivity, both overworked employees and those in poverty suffer higher levels of stress and stress related illnesses such as depression and heart disease while suicide rates double for those laid off from their jobs, making the workplace the fifth leading cause of death (Pfeffer 2018).[5] And as the poor die at younger ages than the affluent, the affluent dominate the age groups where people are more politically active and thus have a greater influence on which politicians are elected and thus the policy decisions that result (Rodriguez 2018). Such politicians, for instance, have allowed for the existence of predatory lending agencies that mass-mail loan checks to low-income Americans, hide exorbitant interest rates, and sue those who cannot repay their loans; one outfit—Mariner Finance—is even run by former Obama administration Treasury Secretary, Timothy Geithner (Johnson 2018a). The rich, then, even often prey on the poor and vulnerable for their own benefit, another way that impoverishment can be induced.

We see above how, first, poverty is part of modernity's economic system, as it is built into its normal functioning. We also see, second, that additional poverty can be imposed on people by decisions that are made and thus is a choice. But this choice is one we often conceptualize in backwards terms. That is, *to the extent* that poverty is a choice, it is a choice made by bankers, employers, policy-makers, and other elites more than it is a choice made by the population at large. These former groups possess great stocks of wealth and/or

---

5   And in an example of how we perceive things backward, modern poverty keeps those with jobs overworked to such an extent that they put in *more* hours per day, week, and year than did workers had in feudal times, not less, giving modern workers less leisure time than medieval serfs (Schor 1992).

can institute practices that direct wealth in one direction but not another. While some people are poor because of decisions they make, there is an entire condition of modern pauperism that is both structurally systemic as well as a product that has been artificially manufactured.[6]

---

[6] Also see extract from the 2013/2012 book, *The Price of Inequality: How Today's Divided Society Endangers Our Future*, by the economist Joseph Stiglitz. Reprinted: "Nobel Laureate Economist Says American Inequality Didn't Just Happen. It Was Created: How to Keep Power at the Top of Society." Evonomics.com. March 18, 2016 (URL retrieved July 21, 2017): http://evonomics.com/nobel-prize-economist-says-american-inequality-didnt-just-happen-it-was-created/.

CHAPTER 14

# Social Scum

To meet their needs, the poor and the working class often have to make their money stretch or find other ways to secure the goods and resources their paychecks cannot obtain. This situation often leaves them vulnerable to predators who use other-than-legitimate pursuits to secure the money that runs our economy and dominates our lives. These are the ways of graft, thievery, violence, and the con employed by people exploiting the edges of our social system.

In Victorian London or New York City of the same period, worries about the safety of one's person or property during daily activities were perfectly reasonable. One might be robbed by street thugs, have his or her pocket picked by professional thieves, or fall prey to scam artists or snake oil salesmen. Or imagine living in Seattle in the 1800s. You go into a bar, are served poisoned alcohol, pass out, and then are dropped into a chute that lands you in a holding pen in the basement, only to wake up as impressed labor on a boat to Shanghai. This is more than just mythos or fancy storytelling. It actually happened.

Modernity has had several waves of drug problems, the main ones being those associated with opiates and cocaine. After the British forced open China in the Opium Wars, the drug made its way further and further into Western society. Opium dens flourished in several urban centers for a time and later poppy extracts could be found in common over the counter medicines. Eventually, though, laws were passed that made opiates harder and harder to obtain and soon they became street drugs, as a black market for heroin and cocaine developed.

We have seen drug problems related to narcotic pills and synthetic drugs emerge every few years, much of this due to the work of large pharmaceutical companies pushing their wares through the medical establishment's willing participants. In a particularly egregious example, one town of 392 people in West Virginia had 9 million doses of oxycodone dumped into one of its pharmacies in a two-year period (Pierce 2016). Worse, one investigation concluded that in six years that same state was flooded with 780 million hydrocodone and oxycodone pills, during a period in which four counties there outpaced the nation in overdose deaths, while the state as a whole totaled 1,728 deaths (Eyre 2016). Addiction, disease, death, destroyed futures, families, and communities are left in the wake of these drugs. By 2017, overdoses were the leading cause of death for Americans under 50 (Katz 2017), made possible by individual, professional, and corporate drug dealers.

In many of the world's major cities there are outdoor markets and bazaars. Here, one can find Rolex watches, Jimmy Choo shoes, or a Gucci handbag at astoundingly low prices. Counterfeit goods, each and every one.

People who struggle to find productive work sometimes find themselves appealing to state welfare services for subsidies for rent, utilities, and/or food. These benefits come at the taxpayers' expense. There is a faction of people, however, that do not use such services only in times of need but rather use them as a regular source of income, effectively becoming dependent on the state and public largesse. And sometimes welfare dependency becomes an inter-generational reality; here we do not refer to those stuck in impoverished communities that cannot get out and wish they had access to productive work but to those actively staying on welfare rolls, finding ways to extract more from state coffers, and teaching their children this trade. Though hard to establish how often or common this is, such a collection of people lives off the work and effort of others—many of those workers among their own working-class neighbors—and what they contribute back to their society, if anything, is difficult to tell. Liberal sensibilities often do not like to face up to such realities but there is no doubt that a portion of people on welfare reflect this reality. It is a testimony to the helplessness and graft our society facilitates.

Poor and working-class neighborhoods encounter a particularly tricky problem: grocery and hardware stores, restaurants, and banks often flee with urban decline or simply refuse to set up shop there in the first place. What is a working person to do if there are no banks near where they live? Such individuals often find they have little choice but to appeal to legal loansharking businesses. Here, those in need can either cash, say, a $100 check for only $85 in return, or, should they run out of money before their next paycheck, they can get a "payday loan" at the same rate. If caught in the cycle, they might go further and further into debt, seeing less and less of a return in cash on subsequent paychecks. Many such businesses out there to "help" the weak and vulnerable actually prey on them. Similarly, others who do not have access to a cash flow (or not enough of one) might find themselves selling off household items, from televisions to weapons to jewelry to family heirlooms. Some of these people might suffer from low wages, some from crippling addiction (drugs, alcohol, gambling), and some from both. Such desperate people can find willing buyers at local pawnshops. By their very nature pawnshops rely on people selling items they would rather not give up and often buy from those who have stolen items from others. In either case, such shops function as sops for those trying to stop from falling further down the ladder, all the while assisting in that fall.

Sometimes the weather turns against us. Floods, tornadoes, earthquakes drought, tsunamis, and so on plague societies from time to time. In their wake often come scam artists who prey on the vulnerable. They suddenly appear in ravaged cities and communities and offer to repair homes, to remove fallen trees, to provide fresh water, food, and medicine, only to disappear once the target's money is collected. And in our modern cybernetic world, other scam artists discovered a new method of defrauding the naïve and vulnerable. More than one scheme has emerged where thousands of emails are sent out via a bot that dumps its payload into unsuspecting victims' accounts. Asking for their bank account number so newly found "inheritance money" can be sent to them, those falling for the trick soon find their own savings and/or checking accounts emptied. This is not the only cyber-scam, but it is indicative of the practice.

We hear that prostitution is the world's oldest profession. True or not, it is a fact that the exchange of sexual services for money predates our period. Rome had legal brothels with signs hanging outside advertising the services available inside. And while it is also true that prostitution has been legal in some modern states, one thing we find in our period is the practical ownership, control, and even trade in women coerced into performing sexual acts with paying customers. Sometimes the circumstances of women drive them into the trade, while others are simply forced into it by family, acquaintances, manipulators, and those who threaten them with violence should they refuse. In either case, pimps and traffickers make their living preying on the weak and destitute.

And this trade is growing today rather than dying off. From the 1980s on, many politicians and nation-states embarked on a series of policy changes subsequently dubbed "neo-liberalism." The goal of such policy changes was to "deregulate" the economic system and encourage more "free trade." Governments reduced or eliminated laws on workplace safety, wages, environmental protections and allowed for freer movement of goods and financial investments in and out of countries. The laws of supply and demand would rule which goods and which companies would predominate. Instead of government oversight, production practices and the quality of goods would determine which industries thrived or failed. Human traffickers and modern slavers stepped into this vacuum of reduced oversight of global trading links. Poor people from the world's poorest countries have been conned or forced into coerced labor, sometimes in cocoa fields, coffee plantations, diamond mines, shrimp boats, and brothels, a topic to which we will later return.

In the chaos of modern development, we find that a portion of the population turns against their neighbors and, rather than working for the common good, threaten them with violence and death, often following through with such threats. Groups such as the Taliban in Afghanistan or The Islamic State in the Middle East strive for a society ordered and run by religious authority, hoping to stave off the modern world and create their ideal utopia.[1] They demand obedience to their dictates, which are most often directed toward their fellow citizens and religious cousins. Women are forced into strict conformity to gender roles under Sharia law and some are killed for stepping outside of them. Some of them are sold as wives and raped. Children are killed for seeking education, or even flying kites. Homosexuals come under constant threat of execution, none-too-seldom suffering it. In Mexico, drug gangs seize territory, fight over turf, execute rivals, informants, and politicians, often posting videos of their crimes online and even littering civic centers with the bodies of their victims. Across Europe and the United States, neo-Nazis are drawn predominantly from working class ranks and instead of aligning themselves with their laboring compatriots across their class they embrace racial supremacy and far-right politics. Rather than ordinary theft or graft, in these cases the working class becomes the target of violence and is caught up in the political intrigue of factions seeking advantage rather than solidarity.

In modernity, a section of people feed off others, often people that share a relative class position as their own. While the business person might be dependent on the legal labor of others, this bottom-feeding class leaches off of the extra-market niceties and dysfunctions of life among the working and middle classes, using non-market tactics of fraud, coercion, threat, and violence. This class of social scum only identifies with the working and middle classes as predator does to their prey. They are, nevertheless, an endemic feature of our modern system.

---

1 Terrorist groups do not operate in a vacuum. Many would be unable to operate and spread without assistance, knowingly and/or unknowingly, from international banking and offshore financial institutions (see Algar 2014; Kennedy 2016; Croucher 2017).

CHAPTER 15

# Of Souls, Sighs, and Opium

It would be easy to go to any library or bookstore and find a book entitled, *The History of Art*. In fact, there are probably dozens, if not hundreds, of books similarly titled. In such a book, an opening chapter may give a broad survey of types of art across a variety of world cultures. If that chapter does not exist, one would likely find very near the beginning of such a book a series of depictions of the earliest "ancient art" known to us, such as cave paintings. The book would then likely move on to types of pottery, statuettes, and so on found during archeological digs. These figurines, necklaces, and everyday material would be described in terms of craftsmanship, style, and the possible symbolic meanings embedded in the objects. As the book moved forward, it would likely provide examples of old Mesopotamian, Egyptian, and Chinese art, including hieroglyphics, vases, plates, and idols. Eventually, the book would move through religious art in early Islamic cultures, in medieval Europe, and then the impressionist, futurist, and modernist movements of the last few centuries. All of this would seem logical and maybe even impress us with its comprehensiveness. And, from this vantage point, art would appear as if it is a true human universal.

Perhaps using "art" as the coverall term for all these forms of human creative expression might mislead us in ways about which we are unaware. Today, "art" as a concept means something specific to us given its historical development as a form of expression, i.e., concepts like "art" and others have their own historical origins and their meaning changes over time. When modern people say "art," what we often mean is something done by "an artist." This person and his or her activities intentionally work toward the end of producing something we, they, and/or our culture consider to be "art." Putative artists are often trained—directly or indirectly—and work in a style, learn specific techniques, and are often familiar with past masters and traditions. In modern times, many aspiring artists may go to art school and/or major in art in college. Fewer may even be trained directly by a modern "master," something more common in feudal and medieval Europe and other civilizations of the past.

We must ask a question here. Given these observations, does it make sense to refer to our hypothetical cave-painting ancestors as "artists" and their products as "art"? Of course, *identities* are there for all to see (see discussion on "identity/difference" in Chapter 3). There are the materials used to transfer one medium to another. There are colors and techniques. And there are abstract images imbued with symbolic expression and thus with meaning. But were the people doing this trying to create "art" as we understand it today and was this their "profession"? Were there styles and schools that people aligned with like in our period or were there patrons of artists as in times past? Were there "good" cave painters and "bad" ones who had a hard time making a living? Were there critics, traditions, and standards? As a linguistic term and a category that orders our experience, "art," like "sport," applies in some ways across time but less so in others.

The relevant point here is that a category that makes sense in organizing our experiences and refers to our cultural practices may increasingly lose its relevance/applicability the further back in time we go when applying it. If we go back only 100 or 200 or even 500 years, it is very likely we can apply the concept of "art" to practices in those periods and lose very little of its meaning. But if we go back further, much further, does not the concept of "art" increasingly lose *some* of the meaning with which *we* imbue it today? While what such people in pre-historic societies did can be "artistic," would our cave-painter have the same linguistic tools and conceptual framework to employ when we discuss art? Imagine posing these requests and questions to our putative cave artist:

- Tell me about your art.
- Why do you paint?
- What is life as an artist like?
- Did you always want to be an artist?
- What is your favorite style?
- What do you believe the role of art is in the human experience?

Our cave painter likely would be unsure about what exactly we were asking. Just because some identities or similarities exist between these earliest forms and our own, the differences that emerge over time may increasingly change in a way that they become the foundation for a term in use later in time (a quantitative to qualitative change). In other words, the new features that develop in such practices are what made a concept possible in the first place—in this instance, "art."

Perhaps we can refer to what came before as "proto-art forms." To understand what this means, an appeal to the example of money is instructive. In broad terms, as a thing, money is a universal medium of exchange. But as a concept, the material conditions needed to develop "money" as a framework of our thinking did not exist until it became more fully matured. While early societies might use clam shells or stones in their exchange relations, these "proto" forms of money do not have all the characteristics later more fully developed money forms would acquire—e.g., one could not take clam shells to a culture that uses stones and find the former converts into the latter.

When metals like gold and silver became used to represent value, the human medium of exchange matured further. And with this development soon came use of metals by states, such as Rome or Greece, where depictions of leaders (i.e. political power) were stamped on coins and standards of exchange became more codified, and money matured yet again with added characteristics of more universal values more fungible across time and place. That is, once certain metals were considered valuable across different cultures, then they could function as a medium of exchange even in raw form, as gold and silver could be melted down and reminted by one kingdom victorious over another. Money, then, shifted from its proto-form to more crystallized forms and this made the concept of "money" more materially possible. Today, money still functions as a universal medium of exchange, can be transformed from one currency to another (now without needing to melt down coins), and is backed by political-economic power detached from the value of metal and political personages on coinage. So, while we can use the concept clearly for today's bills and coins and not lose much meaning when applied to many earlier forms of currency, if we go back further to shells and rocks many of the traits that made the concept of "money" possible do not exist in those proto-forms. This is the sense in which we mislead ourselves when we assume that a concept that is fully applicable to our present world applies equally to all practices in the past with which it shares some traits. That is, those past practices were embryonic stages of what would more fully crystalize later while adopting new traits in the process.

Let us apply this same type of analysis to religion. Historians, sociologists, and anthropologists have cataloged thousands of social practices organized around beliefs in matters and beings of a spiritual and/or supernatural sort. Such practices have doctrines, dogmas, rituals, high priests, and sacred texts. But, if we call what the shaman and the animist do "religion," does this do justice to both that term and to their activities? Some researchers find that the term "magic" or "magic rites" is a better description for these proto-religious practices, something with which today's monotheistic believer would probably agree. In any case, what we observe today as "religion" is a more fully formed institution that has increasingly separated from other institutions and developed an independent existence (a process still incomplete and uneven across the world, however). In the earliest social groups, spiritual beliefs and practices were not a distinct reality from daily life—from planting, hunting, birthing, illness, and so on. Spirits animated everything. In later city-states, religion became an official doctrine of ruling authorities, even if local beliefs were often tolerated. Under Asian and European feudalisms, state power and religion drew even closer together. But in modernity, as states have increasingly secularized, religion has become its own institution, even though individuals, families, and communities have their beliefs and practices of favor. In this institutional separation, "religion" is thus more fully formed materially and thus so is our concept for it.

These are not just academic questions. If a human activity develops more fully in a later period in a way that allows for a conceptualization of it to be made, it is illogical to apply that concept to every period before this full development with equal weight or with its full meaning intact. Such practices may share some identities, but often their differences are just as or even more important. Though the transitions are difficult to precisely identify, should we equate all partial identities under a concept like "religion," we make the activity seem as if it is a timeless practice, when in fact what we understand today has been the product of historical development. Further, once we call the earliest shamanistic practices a "religion," this makes our contemporary religious practices simply the most recent examples of a sociological universal human practice. Every priest, pastor, preacher, and/or religious apologist would agree—though they would likely disagree if we reversed the lens and referred to their practices as "magic rites."[1]

Not only is popular knowledge subject to the problem of reading the historicity of concepts backward with full application but so are social theories. For instance, one principle in some forms of sociological theory is the idea that if some practice is found in all societies, it is likely because it is a requisite for society as whole and thus a practice that we must embrace. For example, many approaches to "the family" assume that it is a universal institution (it is) because all societies must produce and socialize children (they do). But not all of today's institutions represent timeless forms, though sometimes they do and we must, therefore, discern what practices are or are not universal and not mistake *our* forms for universal forms if they are not. And if this is done, that is, if we interpret our current institutional framework as the product of a universal human condition and thus a social requisite, then we give it a mystified appearance in our imaginations and in our putative scientific sociological models. For religion, we often come to see it as a permanent and necessary feature of social life, even though it was something we invented and something we lived without at one point in time.

---

[1] It is possible that some readers are unfamiliar with the term "apologist" as it is used here. Though it is common to read this term as derogatory in nature, in religious studies it is used to describe a defender of a religious faith, especially Christianity, and thus the term is more categorically descriptive than it is critical.

But the permanent appearance of religion is more than simply a conceptual trick we play on ourselves. It works its way into our core social relationships, especially those involving power—over society as a whole and over us as individuals. History shows us how religion has, at times, participated in the most egregious violations of human well-being and how it has often deformed the thinking of those exposed to it. Religion has produced human sacrifice, mass murders, killing of children for imaginary crimes (e.g., witchcraft, albinism), and capital punishment for things such as having sex with the "wrong" person even if they are consenting adults. Religion has condemned rape victims to additional gang rape, marrying the perpetrator, or even stoning. Religion has been at the center of burning supposed witches and heretics at the stake, child marriage (and rape), lynching, impaling, and throat slitting. The apologist will respond, of course, that religion has produced many good things in the world, such as feeding the hungry, treating the sick, housing the homeless, bringing water to the thirsty, and so on. Many religious organizations have done and continue to do these things, no doubt. But none of these things require religion to do and, more importantly, given their doctrines, they are compelled to do these things—i.e., they are in their scriptural directives. And so are many of the violent acts previously mentioned.

The earliest nomadic hunter-gatherers, overwhelmed by the forces of nature, depicted a natural world animated with powers and spirits that controlled the origins of life, changes in the weather, the onset of disease, the outcome of the crops, and so on. Over time, with the development of agricultural-pastoral societies, many of these spirits and forces took on human traits, such as vengeance, nurturing, planning, mischief, and so on, and became gods with personalities, names, and specialties, e.g., Mars, Eros, and Poseidon. Sometimes these gods mixed humans and animals, with similarly associated skills and powers. Later, monotheism brought us the idea of a single god, containing all of humanity's characteristics, such as wrath, love, jealousy, compassion, and so on. And today, god for many is no longer an Abrahamic god per se (i.e., Yahweh) but instead is a general idea of a singular god though now without name, history, or specificity while still in charge of the forces of nature and the universe. Across this history, we see that human ideas about gods became inverted and the gods were seen as the authors of nature, ideas, and human life rather than humans being the author of the gods.

But if religion served a sociological function in the past, modern social development clashes with its foundations. Knowledge based on faith and authority, over evidence and critical thinking, is averse to the scientific process, one core advance modern knowledge has brought us. And this antagonism has been expressed in multiple ways. While it is true advances in knowledge have come from cultures steeped in religion, both Islamic and Christian zealots

IMAGE 15.1 The Egyptian God Harsaphes

IMAGE 15.2 The Creation of Adam, by Michelangelo

have, nevertheless, attacked and even killed those who pursue knowledge outside of religious dictates. One must consider that the explanation for this is that they fear what will be found. However, religion approaches science today for a peace agreement, pleading that science and religion are "compatible," as if religion's past (and even present) history of opposition to scientific inquiry tells us nothing about the form of knowledge it represents. Genesis, after all, tells us that Adam and Eve were kicked out of the Garden of Eden for eating from the Tree of Knowledge of Good and Evil. And given the authority science has taken on in the last two centuries, it is no wonder that only recently have religious leaders tolerated the evaluation of their texts based on external sources, such as historical data and cross-cultural comparisons.

Philosophers of science rightly deride circular thinking as an invalid form of knowledge, i.e., fundamentally in error and an obstacle to clarity in thought.

Circular thinking is called a "tautology" and, as such, tautological thinking is a telling example of one of the divides separating science and religion, where tautology is hostile for the former and the essence of the latter. Believers hold The Torah, The Bible and The Koran to be true because they (and their advocates) say they are true. Why should people not engage in same-sex relations? Why this food forbidden? Because the Bible presents itself as a true book with rules sent by god. But religious books say they are true only because religious discourse cannot expect to attract and keep adherents if they claim to contain only partial truths or simply suggestions. To believe that religious claims are true *because* such claims appear in a text self-asserting its own providential veracity is in effect to say: This is true because it says it is true. Such a tautology does not past scientific muster.

Our modes of thought on religion are apt to fall prey to other problems in reasoning, one of them being "teleological" argumentation. In teleological thinking, an end result was/is the initial reason for a causal force in the first place. This might make sense in something labor-like, such as cooking. That is, the end point of cooking—a consumable meal—is entailed in the action initiated earlier. But when we use this model for our social relationships and institutions, problems begin almost immediately. Was the purpose of the agricultural revolution to push women back to a more subservient role to men? Clearly not. Was the goal of the Pilgrims coming to the "New World" to create "The United States"? Clearly not. Was the car invented so that Western societies might later create interstate highway systems, build suburbs, and develop new forms of dependence on resource rich regions of the world? Clearly not.

In the religious mind, by contrast, one's religious tradition as they know it is an intended result of their prophet/savior/messiah, no matter all of the changes a religious theology and practice have gone through from its initial inception up to current times. Christians generally, for instance, project the idea that the goal of the ministry of Jesus was to produce the Catholic Church, the Eastern Orthodox Church, the Southern Baptist Convention, multiple fundamentalist doctrines, and so on, even if they do not agree on key aspects of that same ministry. But any such assertion confronts confounding historical facts. Jesus was a Jewish rabbi who preached to other Jews that the coming of their Lord's kingdom would be in their lifetime. And at the time, Judaism was for Jews, not a universalist theology as we understand religions like Christianity (and Islam) today. After Jesus failed to return as promised, his ministry was then reinterpreted as him being the incarnation of a universal god and the savior of all of humanity. By extension, there is no sense in the Bible that the goal of Jesus's ministry was to establish a 2000-year-old tradition that broke away

IMAGE 15.3 Tom's Doubts #14, September 3, 2011

from its roots and spread worldwide. It is only teleological thinking that allows such a conclusion, something upon which religious faith depends.

This is not unique to Christianity, though. It is likewise with all institutionalized religious traditions, where each believes to be in contact with the original intent of the religion's origin and with present-day rituals entailed in a causal way in the founding of the tradition. And should this fail to be the case, then a return to purity is called for (e.g., Islam). But the truth that modern religious practitioners proffer is still subject to broader sociological processes that change the content of their religion, making any such truth *always partial at best*. Though "God's Truth" ideally is unchanging by definition, we also know that religious doctrines have constantly changed over time. A randomly selected Christian today versus one in the first century are unlikely to recognize each other's beliefs and certainly not each other's rituals. Nevertheless, religious reasoning, regardless of time period, posits that the outcome for their historical period was the outcome intended in the initial cause, which is a teleological model that underpins the foundation of faith and devotion. That said, there are reasons as to why religion has persisted in many parts of the world.

The world we live in is relatively indifferent to us. The natural world does not have emotions for me or you as individuals. It unleashes earthquakes and tsunamis on hapless victims. Volcanoes destroy entire cities at a time. When climates shift, mass starvation is set in motion. Bacteria and/or viruses that are invisible to our naked eyes are carried on the wind, on fleas, on mosquitos, on cattle, on others and wreak havoc on large swaths of people, year in and year out. We can plead and try to negotiate with nature all we want, but to no avail. We must outpace it. We must learn where not to build our cities, or how to build them to withstand certain natural forces, though we still often lose. We must learn how to get water to our crops when the rains fail to come. We must endeavor to discover cures for the diseases we suffer and/or try to prevent them in the first place. With the natural world stubbornly indifferent toward us, we must attribute meaning to that world.

Living as we do in a soulless world—that is, a natural world without feeling or emotion, which is often matched by our social world—religion is but one (though not the only) way to give it meaning and a sense of humanity. Religion tells us our place in the cosmos, why nature works the way it does, and how we should relate to it and those around us.

We not only invent such meaning, but we also construct social systems in which to live. As a general rule, we did not invent our social systems with forethought so much as we developed them over time through responding to situations and needs confronting us. By trial and error, many people in many places learned how to successfully hunt and gather, harvest seeds, corral animals and irrigate water, erect sturdy housing, and so on. One thing that developed during and after the emergence of mass agricultural societies was the development of very powerful groups, such as political rulers and their militaries. So, though we have existed for most of our actual history in *relatively* peaceful nomadic groups, much of our *recorded history* has been in societies with dominant groups ruling by fiat and force. And when the ruled were relatively compliant with the ruling relations under which they lived, they still often feared outside invaders, which could be as brutal and violent as any despot ruling over them. As such, one can see religion as the sigh of such oppressed human creatures, a response to an unjust world, and a belief that things will be better either in the future or in a netherworld beyond our mundane confines. Religion's story is one where heretics and oppressors will be vanquished, the meek shall inherit the Earth, and where there will be some justice in some place at some time.

Human societies have not always taken care of their members with equal benefit and comfort. Some go hungry, some go lame, and some go homeless. Some people have debilitating diseases for which there is no cure. Some people lose spouses and/or children, for reasons outside of anyone's control. People go broke and lose all their possessions. We live in a world where the downtrodden have forever been with us. Religion provides them a haven, a place to go for succor, food, shelter, and comfort.

In Europe in the 1800s, opium was primarily a legal pain killer and widely used. But, as was widely known, opiate-based drugs simply ease symptoms of injury or disease and then only temporarily; they do not cure the cause of the pain. And worse, medical opium derivatives make their users addicted to them well beyond the time that they are useful. It is in this sense that religion is like opium. It is addictive and it cures pain, but it leaves the underlying causes of that pain intact.

Just as social systems do not always explain their origins to us accurately, social systems also depict their own institutional forms as necessary ones. And a social system treats its religious beliefs and practices no differently than its other institutions, i.e., it trains us to see them as eternal institutions we cannot live without. At the same time, dominant ideas across societies try to get us to not notice how the power relations within them have transformed religion over time and shaped it toward its current form, which in fact contradicts the idea that a religion is timeless. And one step further, as social systems change over time, older religious doctrines that could undermine new systemic power relations must be eliminated and forgotten, as if they never existed in the first place.

Modernity shapes all manner of social institutions, and religious beliefs and practices have not escaped its forces. Though many people today are unfamiliar with the term "usury," scholars, the educated, and religious leaders usually are. One reason is because the practice of usury is forbidden in the Torah, Bible, and Koran. What is usury? It is the charging of interest on money loaned. And though sectors of the Muslim world not-yet-fully-modernized still forbid it, most modern people in the Americas, Europe, Canada, Australia, and Japan live in societies built upon it. Their car loans, mortgages, and credit cards all charge interest. Banks could not exist without it. And without banks, there really is no modern market economy. But in modernity we have little experience with popes, priests, or preachers warning against the sin of usury that shapes so many aspects of the modern world. This is but one way in which religion has changed with the onset of capitalism.

Early in the social sciences, a predominant theory held that the modern world would increasingly secularize, and that religion would succumb to such forces and eventually fade away. If we examine just those societies that forged modernity and took the lead in its development, the accuracy of this theory-prediction is decidedly mixed.

In 2018, the Pew Research Center examined 15 countries in Western Europe. Among their key findings were: (1) though the number of those non-affiliated religiously are rising and half or more people in multiple countries claim to be neither religious or spiritual, most people still identify as Christian if given a list of options (e.g., 71% in Germany and 64% in France); (2) in every country except Italy, the number of non-practicing (attending church no more than a few times a year) Christians outnumber those who attend church weekly or monthly (e.g., in England 55% identify as non-practicing Christians versus 18% practicing); (3) practicing Christians are more likely to believe in god "as described in the Bible," while non-practicing ones who do not believe the same still believe in a higher power or spiritual force in the universe; (4) Christian identity is associated with higher levels of nationalism and negative attitudes toward Muslims and immigrants, while majorities, including Christians, also favor legal same-sex marriage and abortion; and (5) while the share of non-affiliated adults in several countries is similar to that in the United States, US "nones" are often more religious than self-identified Christians in Europe (Sahgal 2018). It should not be surprising, then, that in the United States, Pew found: (1) 90% believe in a higher power (99% among Christians), with 56% believing in a Biblical god (80% among Christians), 33% believe in another type of higher force, and one in 10 claim belief in neither; (2) 48% expressed belief in a god active in what happens to them most or all of the time (nearly eight in 10 claim protection from god and two-thirds say they have received rewards from god); (3) those with a high school education or less were more likely to believe in god or a higher power (94%) while college graduates were less likely (84%); and (4) adults under age 50 were less likely to believe in a Biblical god and more likely to profess no belief in any higher power or spiritual force (see Fahmy 2018).

So even in the most "advanced" modern societies, belief in god remains relatively high, though active religious practice measures at a lower rate. These measures do indicate ongoing secularization, but this is both uneven (e.g., much higher in the United States as compared to Europe) and at a slower rate than theorists once expected.

Still, measurements of demographic cohorts portend that such trends will continue in the future. For instance, the European Social Survey for 2014–2016 examined the religiosity of young adults (16–29) across the Continent. The top five countries with the most youth identifying as having no religion were the Czech Republic (91%), Estonia (80%), Sweden (75%), the Netherlands (72%), and the United Kingdom (70%), with the lowest five (i.e., more religious) were Ireland (39%), Slovenia (38%), Austria (37%), Lithuania (25%), and Poland (17%) (see McCarthy 2018 and references therein). And though the numbers are not mutually consistent, and measures are fraught with methodological hurdles, the general pattern in the United States strongly suggests that the percent of people self-identifying as Christian is on the decline while non-affiliated, no religion, and atheists are on the increase and possibly larger than what previous measures assumed (see Cox 2017 and Shermer 2018, and references therein). For instance, the percent of Americans claiming "none" for religious affiliation rose from 6% between the 1970s and 1991 to 14% by the end of the 1990s to 20% by 2012 and hit 25% in 2016. The top reasons given for disaffiliation with their childhood religion were lack of belief in a religion's teachings (60%), lack of family religiosity growing up (32%), negative teachings about and/or treatment of gays and lesbians (29%), clergy sexual-abuse scandals (19%), a traumatic event in their life (18%), and their congregation becoming too focused on politics (16%) (Cooper et al. 2016). And on top of these trends, atheists are also increasing worldwide (Bullard 2016).

When modernity pushes in one direction, it often experiences pushbacks in the other. Three seemingly disconnected examples here will suffice. In the first, with a past history of military dictatorship and externally imposed modernization, Brazil underwent rapid economic transformation and growth, only to see recession, mass unemployment, and violent crime return in the 2000s, leading to the collapse of its Workers' Party. Such conditions in the past in multiple countries have resulted in the rise of populists, often of a conservative, reactionary variety colored with religious fervor and Brazil is no exception. Buoyed by the Assemblies of God and other evangelical support, Jair Messias Bolsonaro, an ultraconservative and former military officer, has enjoyed increasing support. He professes nostalgia for its military past and openly expresses skepticism of human rights, supports homophobia, and makes misogynistic comments about political opponents (see Polimédio 2018). And, second, attendees at a 2018 Vatican conference (attended by over 250 priests, theologians, psychologists, and criminologists) were told that the number of exorcisms was booming because of declines in Christian faith and because of how the Internet allowed easy access to black magic, the occult, and Satanism and that demand was high enough that priests had to resort to delivering prayers of liberation by mobile phone—about which Cardinal Ernest Simoni intoned, "thanks to Jesus" (Squires 2018). Third, failure to endorse the correct religious dogma still can be life-threatening in some places. For instance, in 2015, Saudi Arabia declared that atheists were to be considered terrorists and killed. What all three cases share is that when people are placed in conditions of fear, desperation, and where a vacuum of meaning and hope exists, people become susceptible to returning to religion's promises. Despite all of modernity's secular trends, should it continue to produce such social and material conditions, it is very likely it will continue to prove that the secularization thesis was only partially on point.

Religion controls the mind with the mind's own creation. Christianity and Islam tell believers and non-believers alike that after death eternal punishment awaits those unconvinced of their doctrines. It is a formula for obedience. Further, their sectarian divides promise the same punishment to each other. It would be of little public matter if such doctrines remained in the halls of religious organizations, but they do not. Such doctrines work their way into secular institutions such as education and government and sometimes with grave implications. For instance, in 2018, US President Donald Trump nominated Mike Pompeo to the position of Secretary of State. Pompeo has held Bible studies in the White House, adheres to an evangelical brand of Christianity that envisions a Muslim versus Christian apocalyptic holy war leading up to "the rapture," and is on record as saying that faith in Jesus "is the only solution for our world" (see Burton 2018). Pompeo is in a position to escalate global tensions in a way that brings about this envisioned end-game scenario. And, in this belief system, it is justifiable for him and fellow believers to perpetrate such a result upon people who either do not believe in this version of Christian doctrine or do not practice any religion at all, as these groups are among those heretics and non-believers destined for judgment and deserving of punishment.

Proto-religion was the product of the human species emerging from an evolutionary past where ignorance was no mere choice, living in a world they could fully control or understand. Religion survived and grew as the product of human beings that did not, and most often still cannot, control the means and terms in which they interact with the external world, both naturally and socially. Once magical thinking was established as a way to provide meaning to nature and society, societal evolution continued and powerful groups atop of ancient societies adopted religion as they consolidated their position, influence, and control. And with humans in need of meaning, they were and still are preconditioned to receive, embrace, and internalize such ideas. This is perhaps why Seneca the Younger—Roman statesman, philosopher, satirist—is said to have believed that "Religion is regarded by the common people as true, by the wise as false, and by the rulers as useful." And many centuries later, Napoleon was quoted similarly as saying, "Religion is excellent stuff for keeping common people quiet. Religion is what keeps the poor from murdering the rich." Whether or not either actually said this is less relevant than no one would be surprised if they had, so congruent is the sentiment with how experienced thinkers and leaders understand the rise and tenure of political rulers and the people under them. Religion can be wielded by the powerful to enhance their power while offering the powerless a type of knowledge that allows them to more mentally withstand the effects of that power and oppression. It is both the product of a species alienated against itself and the false solution to that very same alienation.

This chapter began with an analogy about how "art" as a concept was made possible by historical development and argued that reading that concept backwards to all time and place can be misleading. We must be careful to not treat "religion" the same way. "Art" is something we named much later than the earlier practices that expressed human visual creativity and symbolic representation. And it is these latter traits of expression, creativity, and symbolic capacity that the cave painter, Michelangelo, and today's art student share. It is similar with religion. Religion, like art, had proto forms in early human history and from then into modernity religion has become more codified and institutionalized as a social practice. However, this does not mean that "religion" is a social universal required by any and all social systems for their functioning and survival. It is not a supposed human need for spirits, gods, or doctrines that is universal but rather it is *the need for meaning*, especially meaning shared within community. And as long as humans live in a world they cannot fully understand and are subject to social forces outside their control, they are likely to continue to create religious forms of knowledge they posit to exist outside of them. But as more of nature is understood and should humans create a world that does not leave them subject to social forces they cannot manage, then the presence of religion as we know it should fade, leaving us to create a meaningful world the content of which is yet to be determined.

CHAPTER 16

# The Cult of Nature

Sometimes, spiritual imaginings attract a following, bloom for a period, and then wilt like a thirsty flower in the summer heat, only to reemerge again in a new form. Part of this recurring pattern is explained by how human beings—in their need of and search for meaning—tend to anthropomorphize the world around them, seeing in inanimate things reflections of themselves, attributing personalities and other qualities to animals and an indifferent physical world, believing such things have powers beyond the physical realm they do not have. In addition, throughout modernity people have at times felt the religion of their upbringing was somehow failing them and turned to other claims about supernatural sources to provide meaning in their lives. This pattern testifies to a real human need. We are a species that does so poorly without meaning that we constantly drive to create new forms after old ones fail or simply fade away.

Pagan religious rites thrived in the Roman Empire. Some of these practices and beliefs were more sophisticated than others, but the use of idols, temples, oracles, and sacrifices was common, so much so that Jewish scripture had Moses denouncing the worship of the Golden Calf. But such practices were not isolated to the Empire's center, as similar forms of mythos, supplication, and worship could be found in (what later became) the British Isles, Scandinavia, among the Germanic tribes, in large swaths of Africa, and the continents of North and South America. With the ascendance of Christianity in the Empire, many old pagan traditions were absorbed and some abolished. When the Empire's fall left Christianity intact as the leading power center during Europe's middle period, the suppression of non-Christian traditions accelerated. With the rise of modernity, its nation-states, and their colonial projects, large numbers of pre-modern religious traditions were swept away. But this did not put an end to the creation of a spiritual mythos.

In the 1800s, England (and some other parts of Europe and the United States) experienced a fad of spirit mediums convincing others they could talk to the dead. The spiritualist would meet with people—very often in a home where the deceased once had lived—and conduct a séance that they purported would contact the spirit of those once living (Image 16.1). The tricks they used were so akin to those of magicians that Harry Houdini (among others) went out of his way to debunk them, rather successfully (see Image 16.3). This was also a time period where photography was somewhat new, and charlatans took

THE CULT OF NATURE                                                                 113

IMAGE 16.1
Medium and Séance

IMAGE 16.2
Couple with a Young Female Spirit, by Unknown Author

the opportunity to convince the bereaved that their dead relatives appeared in their photographs that would be considered cringe-worthy today (Image 16.2).

Astrology is the notion that the position of stars and planets in the sky at the time when we are born influences both our personalities and the course of our lives. Astrologers also claim the ability to soothsay and are often appealed to for advice from people across the spectrum.[1] Scientists criticize these principles and have tested them in several ways. First, astrological divinations are usually written in such a way that they could apply to anyone at any time. "You have a lot of curiosity." "Listen to the advice of a loved one or family member today." And so on. But when stated at such a broad generality, any claimed accuracy of a description or prediction is rendered meaningless. Second, in terms of testing, scientists have randomly mixed up characteristics claimed to be associated with star signs (i.e., Leo, Aquarius, Taurus, and so on) and have found that the descriptions for a star sign are just as likely to resonant with the seeker

---

1  During Ronald Reagan's presidency, his wife, Nancy, consulted an astrologer when making his travel and meeting plans.

IMAGE 16.3
Houdini Displays Tricks of Fraudulent Mediums, 1925, by Anonymous Photographer

as would randomization or chance. Further, when purported astrologers are given such descriptions to look at, they have no agreement on what characterization fits which individual person (see Carlson 1985; Matthews 2003). This is thus less a pseudo-science than a parlor trick.

In the 1970s and 1980s (and beyond), we began to hear about a "New Age" movement. Many Westerners were questioning and sometimes rejecting the old guard religions modernity inherited. For many, older faiths did not seem to have answers for the modern world and failed to resonate with their psyches. While some people turned to a new sort of "religious fundamentalism," others turned toward a mix of Eastern spiritualism, Native peoples' beliefs, and an assortment of spiritual doctrines—e.g., tarot cards, the I Ching, crystal healing. Yoga and acupuncture also attracted audiences and practitioners and people went to sweat lodges and tried to cleanse their bodies of toxins and other bad things. More recently, we have witnessed the resurrection of old practices such as Wicca and witchcraft, with their claims about being in touch with nature, the Goddess, and the casting of spells and use of potions (see Doyle 2015; Ferguson 2017). And homeopathic medicine has attracted followers as well—the idea here being that trace amounts of some substance provides healing power in a solution and the less of the "active ingredient" there is the more effective the potion. More recently, we have heard parents claim that a new special spiritual breed of children is among us, the "indigo children" who possess extraordinary insight, intelligence, and empathy. Rather than parlor tricks, what these claims and beliefs amount to are "speculative" knowledge but this time more akin to magical beliefs and religious devotion than philosophical inquiry.

# THE CULT OF NATURE

IMAGE 16.4
A Group of Druids Summoning their Spirit Animal at Stonehenge in Wiltshire, England, 2018, by sandyraidy

IMAGE 16.5
Wiccan Event at Avenbury, 2005, by ShahMai Network (http://www.shahmai.org/)

IMAGE 16.6
New Age Shop and Healing Centre, Market Place St. Albans, Hertfordshire, UK, 2009, by Graham Hale

Modernity has not been simply the march of reason and rationalism. It has seen its oscillating share of religious cults rising and falling and others rising again anew. Some, like Mormonism and Scientology, have made a push for mainstream acceptance and have found a level of success. Others have imploded, either from an orgy of violence or just from running out of steam. We have witnessed religious charlatans such as the People's Temple or The

Children of God or seemingly insane UFO cultists such as Heaven's Gate and The Raelians. The search for meaning and the aspiration for belonging are not creations of modernity and therefore not unique to it; these are long-term human behaviors. That said, modernity has prided itself on overcoming ancient superstitions, though perhaps this accomplishment has been more in content than in form (and even then, incompletely). Modernity still has a cult of nature haunting it, with the above but a small sample of how the human need for meaning and community leads them to vulnerable gullibility and the particular way that modernity harnesses and expresses it. What is new to modernity is that today's peddlers in spiritual claims have a wide range of material across time and space from which to draw. As the modern world unites ideas across global cultures and brings together a mix of hocus pocus and the nonsensical, things in which our real human need for meaning in a meaningless world can still find a home.

CHAPTER 17

# World Literature

While it was said that the sun never set on the British Empire, the same was probably true about the Spanish before them. Where the Spanish and British empires went, so did their languages and culture. For instance, Cervantes' *Don Quixote* is by far the highest selling novel of all time, while Shakespeare's collected works likely surpasses it in terms of readership, longevity, and influence. Later writers like Charles Dickens, Agatha Christie, and yarns about Sherlock Holmes and John Watson were and still are read the world over. Less than a century after its independence from Britain, American writers such as Edgar Allen Poe garnered audiences and became internationally known. And Britain's and America's expansion also brought with them a wider appreciation of Western "classics," such as Homer's *Odyssey*. Later, Americans Mark Twain and Ernest Hemingway also put their stamp on world literature, each becoming modern classics. And today, J.K. Rowling's Harry Potter novels and those by Stephen King capture wide swaths of the reading public. The home countries driving modern development have been and still are progenitors of those who drive much of its words, ideas, and culture.

Modern technology changed forms of human communication and soon words and pictures soared invisibly through the air. The "motion picture" industry thrived out of Hollywood, enthralling audiences in the United States, then Europe, and then the world. Once they became more affordable, home radios delivered information once read only in newspapers and magazines and broadcast songs that previously were usually only heard live. Soon, multiple societies heard similar news reports and danced to similar tunes. With television, moving pictures were brought into the home and it quickly became a new device around which people gathered and culture continued to spread with it. Britain's and America's idols became modernity's idols. Elvis. Marilyn. The Beatles.

Modernity's world culture combines disparate national and regional cultures. Nazi Germany consumed Disney productions; American children today eat sushi. India's Bollywood produces the most films per year; America's Hollywood enjoys the lion's share of audiences worldwide. Christianity, Islam, and Buddhism are world religions whose literature is sold in almost every society. While living in the United States, one can listen to the BBC (British Broadcasting Company) news in the early morning and then turn to National Public Radio (NPR) or Telemundo for the morning news broadcast across America or online. One can dine on kimchi while a colleague from South Korea eats a Big Mac, as both of you read *The Economist* or learn from a variety of internet news outlets about the victims of the shooters at *Charlie Hebdo*'s offices. Youth in the Middle East listen to rock-and-roll, drink beer, and go drifting with their hotrods (though they often must hide these activities from authorities). There are subcultures of heavy metal fans in Botswana and Mozambique. The whole world is on Facebook and can scour news and enjoy cat pictures on Reddit.

Our world culture facilitated by education, mass media, and migration is a product of the world economy and has brought advantages and disadvantages with it. Exposure to world culture can reduce our xenophobia and expand our horizons, sweeping away old prejudices and provincialisms of those both living in the center of modern society and those at its periphery. Social media platforms like Facebook allow us to keep up with family and friends, share news of life's ups and downs, and engage with communities of our own making. But such communication platforms also lock out other information and isolate us from real social interaction. We often remain stuck at our computers instead of socializing publicly or, when we do venture out, we find our attention still focused online via an all-too-convenient access made possible by our phones.

It should be no wonder, then, that we are learning how modern forms of communication and our technology-dependent interconnections with others have potential for serious harm. Using Facebook can lead to disorders comparable to addictions and to feelings of envy and depression, while quitting it can make us happier (Tandoc, Ferrucci, and Duffy 2015; Happiness Research Institute 2015; Tromholt 2016; Brailovskaia and Margraf 2017; Burnett 2018). Facebook, too, is a business, worth billions of dollars and its users are its product. As we communicate there we share not only family pictures, news articles, and reports of our daily lives with loved ones, but we also answer questions and quizzes that are created as a way to collect information on us so that Facebook knows what advertising to expose us to as we have provided them, usually unknowingly, a profile of our beliefs and habits. Further, the applications linked in Facebook for such data collection can be penetrated and/or leak out to external sources, where, in one instance, up to 120 million users had sensitive information exposed (see Murdock 2018). This was not the only time Facebook left its users vulnerable to others outside the platform, nor will it be the last in high likelihood.

And just as communication and culture shifted from books to radio to television and movies, the internet age finds new ways to adapt to and mold these former modes by which ideas and norms are diffused. Television networks that once dominated entertainment with over-the-air broadcasts, as well as movie studios of old, must today compete with Netflix, HBO Now, Amazon, and other organizations that deliver programming through cable wires and satellites.

YouTube provides a mechanism by which everyday people can find viewing audiences for their individualized productions and tastes. Twitter provides a borderless platform for opinions in addition to and other than elite commentary and allows users to immediately express their views on the day's events and happenings around the world.

The changes such technologies and mediums have brought us are decidedly mixed. On the one hand, such developments represent a sort of democratization of information, entertainment, and culture. On the other, they also provide for a degrading of civil society by making it easier to insert vitriol into public discourse without threat of personal consequence and by facilitating a way to further manipulate public consciousness with unsupported assertions, outrageous accusations, and conspiracy theories. For instance, when, in 2018, news programs broadcast audio and video evidence of undocumented immigrant children crying and begging for their parents because of the Trump administration's policy of separating and detaining them in metal cages, someone on Twitter claimed that such children had been "coached" by liberals, similar to claims made by other conspiracy theorists that some survivors of mass shootings and their relatives were actually "crisis actors." The President's son, Donald Trump Jr., "liked" this tweet as a way of supporting the claim (see Sinclair 2018). Further, as President, Donald Trump has made it a habit of Tweeting all manner of insults, unfounded accusations, and other diatribes via Twitter at all hours of the day, a comportment that has only degraded the office that he holds. Moreover, people in such positions set standards others follow, in effect normalizing such behavior. While this does not portend well for public discourse going forward, it is also true that the very same platform allows citizens and public intellectuals to call out the president on his nonsensical declarations with retorts that can also reach audiences far and wide.

The world market that cultivates world culture reveals much about modernity's possibilities and problems. Humans today are interconnected across geography like never before, know more about each other than they ever have, and share more ideas and things than could have been imagined before this time. But modern culture also is often vacuous, impatient, and capricious. Today, the whole world has read of Anne Frank's travails and knows things go better with Coke. The type of culture modernity spreads is increasingly planned, manufactured, and homogenous and molds previous world cultural diversity as if it were like any other commodity, where literature, music, movies, and television all resemble one another just in the same way as cans of beans on the shelf. A question that such an observation brings up is, Why? What sort of mechanism is in place that shapes the world the way we find it today? To answer this, we must investigate the very basis of the structure of the modern world, a topic we turn to in the following chapters.

CHAPTER 18

# Modern Society's All-dominating Power

Even if science and rationality are cornerstones of modernity, it is nevertheless a society that worships at an altar that profoundly influences our behavior, just in the same way so-called "primitives" were believed to throw virgins into a volcano to appease a god of their own creation. Modernity's all-dominating power, though, is real. This all-dominating power is not a habit of mind or something produced because many separate individuals *just happen* to do a similar thing repeatedly. Rather, this all-dominating power is modern society's central organizing mechanism, something so pervasive that it is less as a regular pattern of behavior and more something interior to the very structure of the modern world. It accounts for modernity's origins and rise. This something is what we call "capital" and the drive for its ceaseless accumulation. As we live in a society based on this dynamic, it is perhaps imperative to take pause and investigate what this means and implies.

What is capital? In simplistic terms, capital is the process of investing money into buying up elements of the production system—in part or in whole—to produce commodities to sell at a profit, profits used for both personal gain and for reinvesting back into continued producing, selling, and additional profiting. This cycle thus contains the profit-motive plus competition plus the cost of production plus the ability to attract enough buyers, all of which require this circuit of capital to maintain itself as well as to *constantly grow*. And what is meant by constantly grow is that there is no logical end to the cycle of investment, production, sales, profits, reinvestment, as this process is set up to continue *ad infinitum*, i.e., without logical end.

This set up is more than a simple model for the humble street corner business but, in fact, has had world-historical implications. Several very large, rich, and powerful groups began engaging in this type of economic activity about 500 years ago and were successful enough that it transformed the feudal economy and brought down its political system. As feudalism crumbled, this new method of production and distribution based on capital and its accumulation took its place. Today, most of the modern world (save outside communist states such as North Korea and Cuba, as well as the last remnants of hunter-gatherers and tribal groups that still exist) is organized around capitalist forms of producing and distributing food, goods, services, and information. Capital transformed a previous world, made a new one, and has become so pervasive that it connects with almost all aspects of our lives, even our leisure time.

Imagine you are reading this book in a dwelling in which you live. If you rent, you live in a structure owned by an individual landlord, a company that owns housing, or a bank. You must purchase the right to (temporarily) live there. Those you give your money to in "rent" make a living, often quite a handsome one, off that money. And when you pay this rent, that money is gone from you forever, as it is not an "investment" in something which you have a right to claim a future return on. But maybe you own a house. If you are like the vast majority of homeowners, you probably did not buy it outright with cash. You probably borrowed money from a bank or a mortgage company. Each month you send in a portion of your wages or salary to them in order to retain your right to live in this house. You might check "homeowner" on a survey question, but should you miss your payments for too long, even your very last one, the real owner will take possession of this house. And that owner is a capitalist, either a person who owns the bank or, more likely, a family or shareholders who claim ownership of it or a similar lending institution.

If you are like most people, you get money to purchase living space from the wages earned from a job. You sell your labor to an employer, either a specific person or a company and, like how someone else owns your dwelling, these people own the business in which you work. Most people do not own their own businesses and must work for those who do (or they sometimes work for the state or some other bureaucratic organization). They do this because they do not have the means to produce their own goods and services with productive tools and/or land they might need. So, they must sell their labor and skills to others and receive a wage for that work. Much of peoples' days and weeks in capitalist societies are taken up securing these wages.

Inside our dwellings, how do we stay alive? First, we must make sure we have running water and access to electricity and/or natural gas. We buy these utilities from organizations that sell them to us, whether they be government run or privately owned. Once these are secured, we can fill up our homes with appliances that help keep us alive and/or increase our level of comfort. We buy stoves, refrigerators, ovens, heating and cooling units, and so on. We also buy food, drink, and toiletries to maintain our vigor and health. And like our homes and even our labor, all of these things are "commodities," things we buy with money we typically make from our jobs. This transformation into commodities bought on the market of almost all things we need to survive is a historic event, as none of these have ever been commodities like this before. With the exception of very few, these are things we no longer produce in the domestic sphere. We have to buy these commodities from the businesses who legally own them, even though the owners of these businesses usually did not personally make them—their workers did.

Many of us have children. We must access goods and services in order to keep ourselves and our children alive. We also must secure a mode of transportation to and from the places of employment where we earn money to access these goods and services. As our children grow, we hope they can be positioned to make their life as good as possible. Part of our income is taken from us in the form of taxes to educate our children to a basic social standard, usually indicated by a high school diploma. If we are fortunate, we can apportion part of our wages to purchase the tuition necessary for our children's college education. If we cannot, that is, if we do not have access to socialized college education (such as in European countries like Germany, Spain, Norway, Denmark, and Sweden), often our children will take out loans on their future wages to pay this cost. If *they* are fortunate, they can get this cost paid for with a scholarship, though most people do not have such luck. In any case, the reason why large sums of money are spent on securing a college education is so that people can be successful in selling their labor (mental and/or physical) to a business owner (or one of the other organizational structures in capitalist society) in order to secure the wages they need to secure the commodities they need and, very often, simply want.

Not everyone sails smoothly through life's passages. Our eyes require correction, bones break, illnesses strike us, tonsils must be removed, and teeth need straightening. In many parts of the world, such problems are collectively addressed, usually through something called "national health care" (and they often are not solved at all for the unfortunate ones). In the United States, health care must be purchased, and fortunate workers have some form of insurance through an employer that assists with the inevitable bills that come from accessing for-profit health care. Others, less fortunate, make enough money to buy this insurance on their own. Still others, even less fortunate, have no access to any health insurance whatsoever.[1] In either case, in the United States at least, health care is treated as a commodity and is bought and sold like any other.

When we age, we reach a point where we "retire." If we are fortunate, we have had an employer that apportioned part of our wages or salaries into a "pension." Many modern governments also have social security policies for the

---

1 The advent of "Obamacare" in the United States reduced the number of people without access to health insurance and/or health care. But not only did it not eliminate the problem of cost and universal access but there was also no guarantee that the law and policy would survive changes in administrations or objections from Congress. Additionally, not everyone is fortunate enough to live in Cuba or Europe (where there is socialized health care) or the United States (where there is at least a modern system for those who can afford it). It would be foolish and one-sided to act as if the standards of access to health care are similar worldwide.

aged (something similarly extracted from the compensation for our labor), which can cover costs of living and medical expenses. In any case, after a lifetime of work one is not relieved of the need to access the means of life through the purchase of commodities via money. In a capitalist society, this need follows us cradle to grave—from being born to being buried (which also costs money).

Other aspects of modern daily life are organized in the service of capital as well. Assuming an eight-hour workday and a five-day work week, the average worker spends about a third of their waking hours in pursuit of an income that will allow them to keep a roof over their head and food on their table, to access utilities, and to secure transportation. And, a significant portion of the hours that are left are spent keeping a house together, buying and preparing food, and washing clothes. After we feed our bodies to sustain our laboring ability and entertain ourselves with television to relieve the stress from the workday, we go to sleep for the remaining hours of the day so that we might be rested enough for the next day on the job. There we meet fellow employees dealing with conditions, problems, and exigencies similar to our own. The roads we use to get from home to work link us to gas stations, food outlets, places to buy furniture, appliances, medical care, etc. These roads also connect to interstate highway systems created for transporting goods over long distances. Our countries are lined with railroads and dotted with ports to facilitate trade, often of the international sort.

When we relax, we have a veritable smorgasbord of entertainment to distract us from our daily travails. On our televisions, in magazines, newspapers, and on the Internet, we are bombarded with advertisements that tell us what is on sale, what we can and/or should buy, and how we should organize our leisure time. When we escape to other forms of entertainment, we find ads on race cars, jerseys, billboards, buildings, train car walls, and even on the clothes we wear. We go to movies produced by huge corporate entities striving for the next blockbuster or indie house flicks produced by filmmakers hoping to make a living in the market. Most of our books are produced by huge profit-making entities striving for the next bestseller. Theme parks, music venues, opera houses, and public festivals must all make profits if they are to continue doing what they do.

We rarely ask who is making and selling all of this stuff and why? To what end are we working besides endless consumption (on the worker side) and endless accumulation (on the capitalist side)? We sometimes have a vague sense that larger powers are at work and that they do not have our best interests at heart, but we rarely venture very far down this path of inquiry. Modern society's all-dominating power dominates us individually, personally, and psychologically. We rarely realize it and when we do it is typically not for very long, as it is a powerless feeling that is uncomfortable to entertain. More likely, we are so surrounded and inundated with the stipulations of life in market society that it appears to us as if this existence is normal, unexceptional, nothing to be thought about for too long if at all.

Is it possible to understand modern life without grasping the nature and functioning of capital? To the extent that it is, such an examination would be anywhere from incomplete to distorting to hollow. Capitalism is our world today and we must understand it if we are to come to an adequate and satisfactory understanding of ourselves, both individually and collectively. While some elements of modernity may pre-date the capitalist system, once it took root, capitalism became internally related to all pre-existing social institutions within our society, e.g., familial relations, education, health, religion, governance, entertainment, leisure. Thus, in order to better grasp how capitalism shapes our lives, we must piece together the prevailing tendencies of capitalism *as a system* in conjunction with the institutional configurations of the societies in which it is developing.

Life in capitalist society and its division of labor experiences a tension between two poles. On the one hand, there is the tendency toward the standardization of the individual in much the same way as the standardization of commodities. Similar cans of corn, similar jobs, similar fashions, similar political ideologies, and so on produce a similarity between individuals. On the other hand, individuals in capitalist society are shaped by many different roles and practices within these same institutions, institutions that are in tension, incompatible and/or in struggle with one another. Thus, amidst the homogenization of individuals and their styles and personae, there coexists tendencies toward heterogeneity, diversity, and freedom, creativity, spontaneity, and complexity. It is a system that expands while it contracts, standardizes while facilitating individuality, provides freedom within constraint, and produces vast wealth while it impoverishes.

We should not, therefore, limit our understanding of social relations in capitalist society to the individual level. Capitalist society, like other systems, rests on relationships between classes—i.e., those who own the means of producing goods and services and those who work for them. This is more than simply a recognition of different social categories or groups structured into the economic system. Rather, the relationship between the classes—as we have seen—is an antagonistic relationship in many ways. Capitalists earn profits by paying workers less in wages than those same workers produce in terms of goods through their labor; if capitalists did not do this, there would be no profits. Capitalists can take measures to increase the rate of their wealth extraction from the labor of workers, such as speeding up machinery, lowering wages, extending the working-day, and so on. In addition to these methods, other measures include reducing pensions, restricting access to health care, moving jobs overseas when it becomes profitable, preventing workers from organizing, funding political candidates for favorable policies, and so on. This antagonism produces a sense of opposition and struggle between these groups, though it is usually the capitalists that are more consciously aware of this struggle and act on this awareness.

Geography and levels of education are internally related to class dynamics, too. Ownership of the productive apparatus is correlated with accumulating wealth, which is correlated with the location of housing, both of which are correlated with high levels of educational attainment and attendance at elite institutions by the children of wealth. Capitalist class relations are thus internally related to social polarization, both of which are accompanied by economic and geographical segregation, and variable levels of parental social capital, e.g., literacy, access to social networks, multiple routes to skills and connections, and so on. Because of public policy, therefore, another reality of capitalism is simply differential access to educational institutions and social mobility for children born to parents of different classes. Within such a relationship, a surprising finding would be if geographical location and educational attainment *were not* correlated. However, if the educational system is conceived as geared toward "all children," then policies intended for "all" will actually augment the benefits already provided to the privileged children of wealth.

The discussion above has only touched on some of the ways capital is modern society's all-dominating power. Taken together, the cycle of production, sale, and consumption of things that results in profits and reinvestment comprise the central organizing principle of the modern world and distinguishes it from other historical systems. Capital, its needs (profit-making and accumulation) and imperatives (growth), dominate us like water dominates fish. It is at the root of our environmental problems. It creeps its way into our bedrooms and sex lives. It provides us food that makes us fat and sick. It teaches us to see each other as obstacles to overcome in the labor market. It keeps us so busy that time for study and personal growth become increasingly precious and is none-too-seldom seen as frivolous. Spiritual teaching is increasingly shaped by the celebration of wealth and largesse. It steers our politics and politicians in their drive to war. Capital, capitalism, and capitalists are not simply adjuncts to "modern society" but are in fact its prime movers and shakers. We do not live in a "society" but in a *capitalist* society. Understanding this is crucial and necessary if we are to understand ourselves, our experiences, each other, and the realms of possibility that modernity lays before us.

CHAPTER 19

# An Impulse Never Before Known

When the last chapter looked at capital as the all-dominating power of modern society, it focused on how capital shapes daily life. This chapter addresses how the drive for capital accumulation fundamentally reshaped the world, producing the one in which we live in the process.

Compare the two maps 19.1 and 19.2. One thing to note is that the nation-state system that we know in modernity was not yet consolidated in the first, nor was it finished in the second (nor is it today!). In the first map, Europe was in the medieval period that was beginning to collapse with modernity's rise. As various burghers and merchants began to attain wealth in different regions, they also gained political influence. Over time, agreements were reached (e.g., The Peace of Westphalia, 1648) that recognized geographical consolidation of sovereign territory and, consequently, bureaucratic administrative apparatuses were further constructed, professional armies raised, and national identities congealed.

MAP 19.1    Europa Ortelius, 1572, by Abraham Ortelius

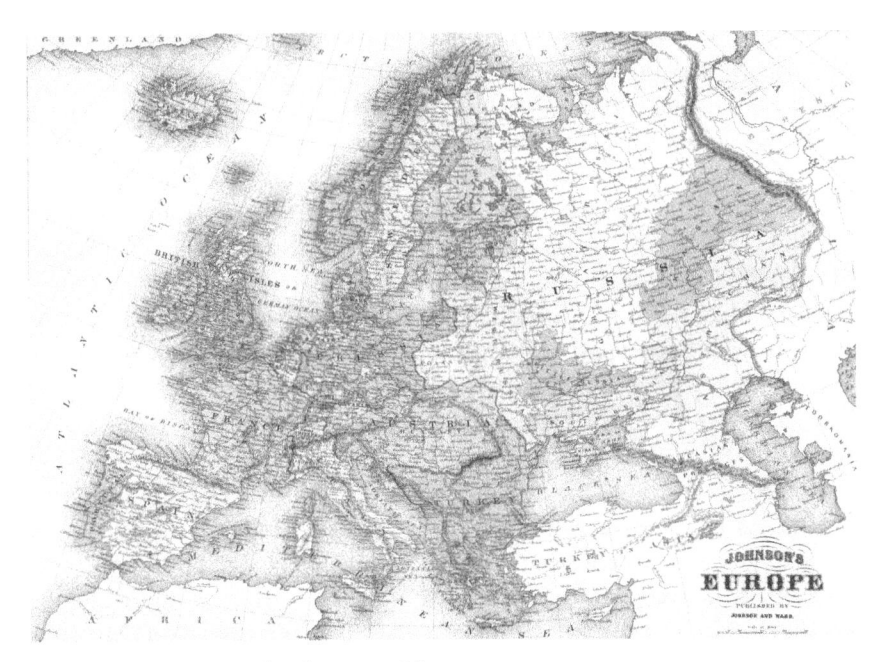

MAP 19.2   Europe, 1864, by Alvin Jewett Johnson

Today, we are more familiar the modern names for such regions—Portugal, Spain, Holland, England, France, Belgium, Germany, Italy, etc.—than the prior regional ones—Iberia, Saxony, Gaul, Brittany, Bohemia, the Ottoman Empire, Castille, Prussia, Flanders, etc.—which have meant less and less to us over time. Each modern country's rise involved trading interests, sources of external conflict with other powers, and internal ruling and working classes locked in struggles both within their own ranks and between each other. Primarily, they—countries, ruling classes, trading companies, and other business concerns—were interested in accessible land, cheap labor, and raw materials, whether home or abroad. This every-direction-competition produced an impulse never before known, i.e., the era of colonialism.

The Colonial Era (1400s–1800s).[1] Portugal and Spain were the first modern empire builders, though what they began would continue with vigor by other Continental powers. The Portuguese ended up in North Africa and parts of its

---

[1] All areas mentioned here will use the modern-day name for the territory, though it should be understood that many of these places did not go by these names before and/or at the time of colonization. Also, given the massive scale of colonization of the world by European powers, the following in no way should be considered exhaustive.

coast, Spain, the Azores, Africa (Angola, Benin, Cape Verde, Senegal, Mombasa, Morocco, Nigeria, Mozambique, Tangier, Zanzibar), the Caribbean (Barbados), Brazil, India (Goa), China (Macau), Papua New Guinea, Hormuz (Persian Gulf), Japan (Nagasaki), and East Timor.

Spain created an empire larger than that of the Portuguese, with colonial outposts and interests in Italy (for a time), parts of the American west coast, the Philippines (also Guam, the Mariana Islands, Caroline Islands, and Palau), Florida, the Caribbean (Cuba, Puerto Rico, Haiti, Bahamas, Trinidad, Dominican Republic), Central and South America (Mexico, Nicaragua, El Salvador, Guatemala, Belize, Panama, Costa Rica, Colombia, Ecuador, Peru, Bolivia, Argentina, Chile, Paraguay, Uruguay, Venezuela), and parts of Asia (e.g., Brunei, Taiwan) and Africa (e.g., parts of Guinea, Morocco, Algeria, coastal islands such as the Canary Islands).

Holland ended up in Africa (west coast regions, Ghana, Senegal, Mauritania), South Africa, Sri Lanka, Malacca, Ceylon, the Philippines (defeated by Spain), Indonesia, the Caribbean (Aruba, Curaçao, Saint Maarten, Saint Croix), Bangladesh, Burma, North America (New York and Hudson River region), South America (Guyana, Brazil—defeated by the Portuguese), Suriname, New Guinea, and Taiwan.

England established colonies (or tried to) in much of the world, including Ireland, the United States, Canada, the Caribbean (Bermuda, Bahamas, Barbados, Jamaica, Grenada, Saint Lucia), South America (Guiana, Falkland Islands), Africa (Sudan, Lesotho, Botswana, Kenya, Somalia, Ghana, Egypt, Nigeria, Rhodesia, Malawi, South Africa, Namibia, Zimbabwe, Tanzania, Uganda), Mosquito Coast, India, Myanmar, the Middle East (Iraq, Kuwait, Qatar, Saudi Arabia),

IMAGE 19.1
English Ships and the Spanish Armada, 1588, by Unknown Author (before 1700)

IMAGE 19.2
Canadian Stamp Depicting the British Empire, circa 1898, by American Bank Note Company, Ottawa. Engraved by Charles Skinner. Designed by Warren L. Green

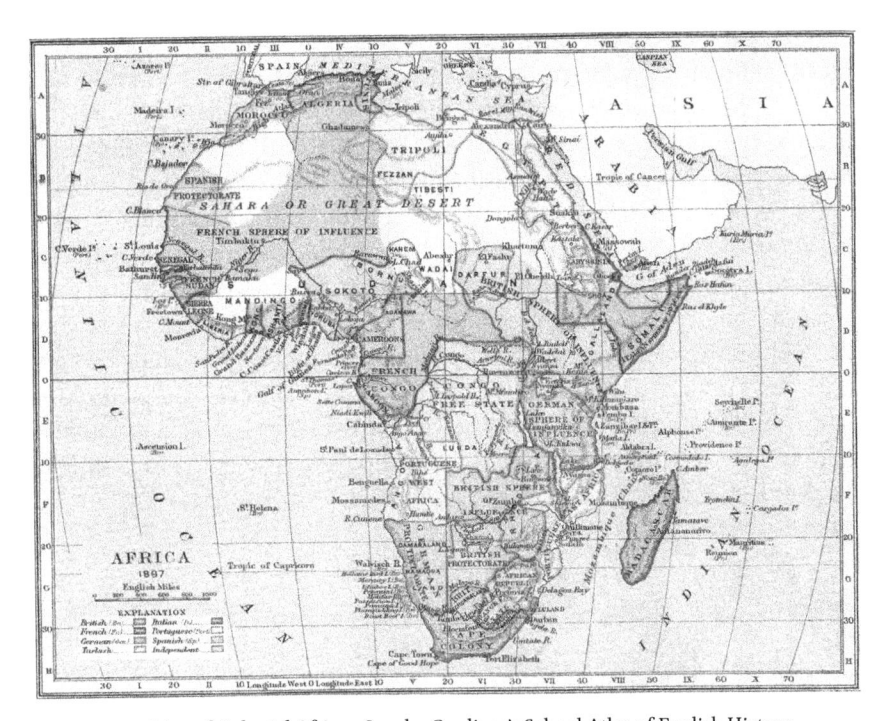

MAP 19.3    Map of Colonial Africa, 1897, by Gardiner's School Atlas of English History

Australia (also the Solomon Islands, Brunei, Fiji, Cook Islands, Malaysia, Borneo, Papua New Guinea, Tonga), and Hong Kong. One examination concluded only 22 countries in the world were not invaded by Britain (see Copping 2012 and McCarthy 2015, and references therein).[2]

---

2   The list for the British is extensive but such a figure can be misleading. First, not all countries in the study made the list for British activity during its colonization efforts. Second,

France ended up in Newfoundland, Africa (Algeria, Gambia, Benin, Cameroon, Congo, Chad, Guinea, Upper Volta, Mali, Togo, Ivory Coast, Mauritania, Central African Republic, Niger, Rwanda, and Tunisia), the Indian Ocean (Madagascar, Seychelles), North America (Quebec), South America (French Guiana), the Caribbean (Antigua, Dominica, Grenada, Haiti, Montserrat, Saint Croix, Tobago), and the Middle East (Yemen).

Belgium conquered the Congo and sent colonizers to parts of the Asian Pacific (Caroline Islands, Samoa, Marshall Islands, Marianas Islands, Palau). Germany colonized areas of Africa (Burundi, Rwanda, Tanzania, Namibia, Cameroon, Nigeria, Togo and Ghana). Italy ended up in Africa as well (East Africa, Eritrea, Libya, and Somaliland).

Not only is this list of areas that European powers colonized incomplete, the list of European points of origins is also incomplete. Countries like Norway, Sweden, Denmark, and Russia (and even Scotland) have been left off, mainly because their attempts were fewer and less successful. This does not mean, however, that they did not feel the impulse to join in the spoils of conquest.

Colonization was a long-term, arduous, and immense undertaking. In reading about the various countries involved, one finds a plethora of expeditions, treaties, wars, taking of boodle, enslavement, massacres, alliances, counter-alliances, border wars, and so on. This is the period of modernity's origins. In this history, we first find European powers conflicting over land, territory, rights, and resources within its borders (e.g., Spain had control of parts of the Netherlands for a while and had its own internal struggles). And as Europe's powers expanded outward overseas, many indigenous peoples lost their land

IMAGE 19.3
Victim of Congo Atrocities, Congo, circa. 1890–1910, by Unknown Source

some countries were listed because Britain engaged in some sort of transitory battle there, though no colonization took place. Third, other countries made the list because of privateer activities there sponsored by the British government but, again, without a colonial regime established.

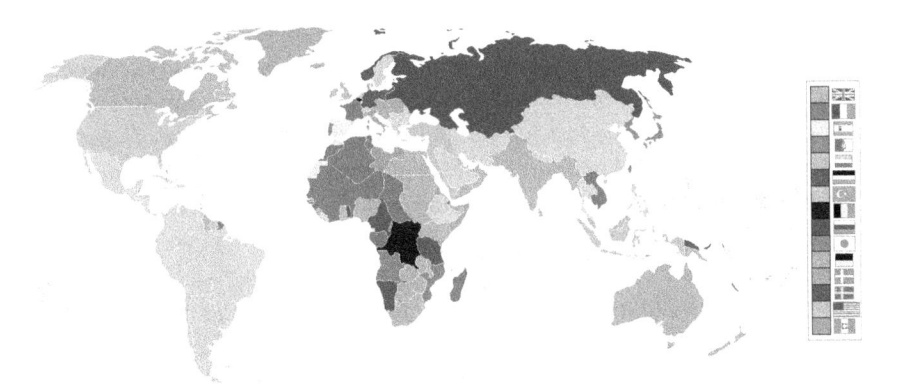

MAP 19.4   World Empires and Colonies in 1914, Just Before the First World War, by Andrewo921

and lives. Weapons and diseases brought by invading armies eliminated both cultures and populations. How many is next to impossible to count. Religions, languages, and traditional clothes were banned in many places. Christianity was imported while resources and materials were exported. In the process, while several powers rose and fell, many colonizers still remain among the most powerful and influential nation-states today—e.g., England, France, Germany. The impoverished areas often became places of colonial and civil war, which were the "birth pangs" of our modern world economy.

Now we can return to a question broached earlier in this book but from a new angle: If the market system simply was and is a product of our propensity to truck, barter, and trade and thus the result of human nature, why did it take so much violence and conquest to forge it into place? After all, a corollary to the human nature argument is that human nature produces behavior on its own accord without the need for external interference. If capitalism is a product of human nature, why did it not emerge earlier in history? If capitalism is but a reflection of human nature, one would think such a system would be relatively easy to install, or even would require little to no force to establish in the first place. But without this period of violent subjugation, the modern world would never have come into being and, as such, by the twenty-first century we would probably be debating very different theoretical models to explain a very different world in which we would be living (while likely still finding "human nature" arguments for *that* world).

Why would we consider this era of colonization something "new" and unique to modernity? Did not the Mongols have an empire? Was there not an Ottoman Empire in existence around the same time of European colonialism? Were not these empires (and others) out for land and wealth as well? While this is all true, there was a key difference. Prior to modernity, former empire builders were typically interested in expanding the geographically connected land they already controlled. True, they were expanding their domains and often driven by greed, the lust for conquest, and the vanquishing of enemies. And even in the feudal period, a king might covet the gold, soldiers, land, etc. of his neighbors and/or finance a Crusade or two. But generally, the pressure to expand outward was not particularly systemic in these prior systems. And, to the extent it was, it remained a localized outward pressure.

But empire building in modernity contained no impulse for *simply and only* expanding the boundaries of one's geographical territory. Rather, many colonial holdings were disconnected over space, as the shipping and warmaking technology available at the time provided modern empire builders the *whole world as their target*. And while their motivation may have been greed, of course, the systemic thrusts to colonialism rested on external competition between ruling classes in competing nation-states and the race to accumulate wealth related to both internal and external competition among those same classes. Countries and capitalists went seemingly everywhere in search of land, labor, and raw materials for individual wealth, for profits for their business enterprises, and for the enrichment of the homeland. These combined features make modern empire building a new historical phenomenon.

The colonial period is still with us in innumerable ways. It birthed the most powerful nation-states we have today. The most geographically widely-spoken languages in the world (English and Spanish) were spread via colonization. International law sprung from the conflicts colonial powers came into and failed to settle or settled because of the cost-loss from too much aggression. Some former colonial domains today experience violent conflict, as internal factions that remain in their homelands after decolonization struggle for power, authority, sovereignty, and whatnot. Other former colonial areas today are tourist destinations, flooded by the affluent from countries that were former empire builders. Should one visit these former colonial areas, they might encounter majestic halls, palaces, cathedrals, museums, mansions, and other architectural wonders and achievements that reflect the styles from their former colonizing countries. It is easy for those in the modern West to forget that these accomplishments—in both places—were products of the looting of the world's pre-modern lands and the rivalry among Europe's rising powers. And, further, many of the world's peoples who suffer second class status as racial or ethnic minorities in their countries of birth had ancestors forcibly brought there to serve a colonial power—e.g., Indians and Pakistanis in England. Or, they have migrated from conquered lands to those of the colonizer. The sense of anger and humiliation felt in places like China and the Middle East stem from these centuries' old defeats. The late colonial period (1800s) produced the European invasion of Africa, which brought the Continent's leading colonizers into conflict with one another and contributed to the outbreak of World War I, whose failed settlement (The Treaty of Versailles) was a foundation for the outbreak of World War II, which set the groundwork for the middle-late twentieth century, American ascendance, the Cold War, and all that has come after.

It is for all of these reasons above that in order to grasp modernity we must grasp the world-making results of the colonial period, the impulse never known before that set it off, and how these set the foundation for the world we know and live in today. The history of colonialism is not one of simply the past but rather it is the author whose words and deeds account for the story of the present.

CHAPTER 20

# Head of the Movement

There are several additional ways the legacy of European colonialism still shapes the world we live in today.

While a capitalist economic system theoretically could have developed at other times and in other places, this was in Europe during the sixteenth century where the right pieces fell into place. Though this was not an inevitable event, Europe of that period had preconditions—an increasingly unbounded ruling class involved in trade—and presuppositions—a money economy—that facilitated capital's emergence and growth. And once a system based on capital accumulation crystallized, its structural features asserted themselves, toppled feudalism, and created a world based on those people, places, and things that were at the head of its initial movement.

Most obviously at the head of the movement was getting in the capitalist game, which meant, as we have seen, the colonial project—i.e., those in Europe slower to move in the capitalist direction risked falling behind and risked being outdone on several fronts or even being conquered and/or absorbed by their counterparts. It is no coincidence that Germany was an aggressor in World War I, given its late and modest entry (comparatively speaking) into the colonial theater. Starting a war on the Continent was an attempt to have its enemies—especially England and France—spend their fortunes and might on a war, giving Germany a chance to catch up or at least diminish the level of dominance of the former two. Though this did not work, it does tell us much about what happened later. Anyway, those parts of the world nowhere close to the head of the movement became areas most subject to being colonized.

With the spread of capitalist development came the spread of European culture—language, education, sexual norms and familial organization, religion, sports, and so on. In modern colonial development, language not only became a lingua franca used to facilitate trading activity, but it became enforced culturally, ensconced in the legal framework of colonial governments, taught in colonial schools (as did Spanish previously with Spain's colonial efforts), and eventually became the language of international relations. Victorian notions of modesty, compulsory heterosexuality, and the nuclear family also followed the British Empire across its sphere of influence. Christianity spread globally mainly because of colonial conquest and the missionaries that came with it, where conversion often was required for maintaining one's life. In addition to football (i.e., soccer), the most popular sports in the world even

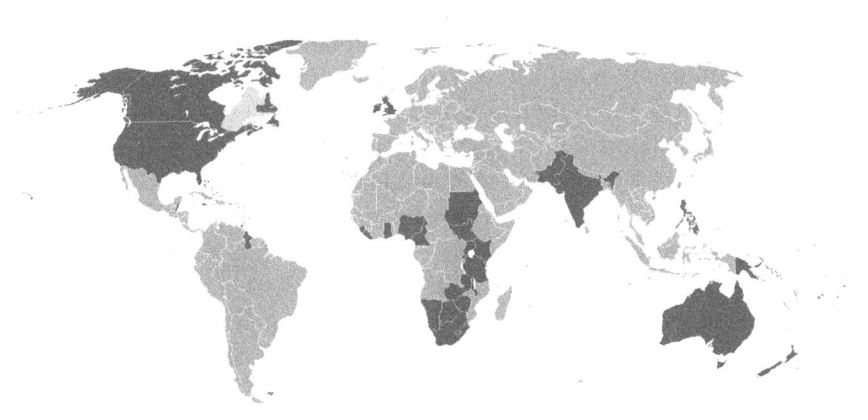

MAP 20.1  Map of English as the Official or De Facto Language, by Vardion

today are cricket, tennis, track and field, and rugby. All of them British in origin and all of them following the British colonial footprint.

After World War II, when England was essentially bankrupt and began to decolonize, the Americans assumed leadership in rebuilding the world economy. This left the English language intact as the world's language of first resort. And with the United States next at the head of the movement, American culture played the role that English culture once did. Hollywood movies and television programming began to dominate worldwide. Musical styles from Britain and the United States were the template for others. McDonald's today is a global food franchise. The longer these and other forms of cultural hegemony last, the more the people of the world come to resemble Westerners in general and Americans specifically. It would be different had another country come out of the war in the US position. Thus, such dominance is not a trait of US culture *per se* but rather a trait that is passed along with the country and culture that finds itself at the head of the movement of the world economy.

One of the most pernicious examples of mystified beliefs about modernity goes something along the lines of "white people created colonial conquest, racism, and genocide," as if these things were a product of a unique drive particular to a people because of their race per se. Though capitalist market practices are not inherently racist on their own *structural* logic, its historical development *did* build racism into that very history and structure. But how did this happen? Capitalism as a system is built on expansion, in two important ways here. First, any particular firm will tend to reinvest a portion of its profits into further production. On its own, nothing appears to be racially built into this logic. On the other hand, competition between firms and between nations is also a structural (and historical) element of this system. And this means that the system tends to expand outward as competing firms and nations search for cheaper raw materials, cheaper labor, and new markets. Given its center of origination in one culture, it tends to expand outward to encompass other cultures and, in doing so, it finds people elsewhere whose labor they can use. This means that the nation of origin in capitalist development becomes the ethnic majority of favor and those groups brought under foreign exploitation become the "races" and "ethnicities" of subordination (see Wallerstein 2000). Afterward, racial ideas and categories work their way into science, education, law, popular culture, and everyday life as "racial projects" that create, recreate, and reinforce such constructed and imposed hierarchies (Omi and Winant [1986] 2015).

It would be a misnomer to assume that at the head of the European colonial movement was a unified and shared identity in terms of kin and ethnicity. At the time of early colonial conquests, the differences of significance between conqueror and conquered were understood more in terms of "civilization" versus "savages" or "Christians" versus "heathens." At that point, "European" did not yet equal "white," which is what people of European extraction have become today. That said, similar to what was and is common to many cultures then and now, the various colonizing societies *did* view themselves as superior to all others, others who were degraded peoples, sub-human or even akin to animals. If we think of why capitalism initially spread, we realize it was not developed or spread because it was a program rooted in race but rather economic interest and drive, often dressed up in religious and nationalistic garb.

As capitalism spread through the colonial program, European gender roles and norms also followed. European men were the heads of households, owners of most property, ran the military, and staffed the bureaucratic apparatus of state. Women's roles were mainly confined to the domestic sphere, tasked with producing and raising children, and in charge of maintaining the household. These institutional roles are not specifically endemic to capitalism as a structure but rather come from socio-cultural norms established in societies prior to modernity. Nevertheless, the political-economic structure of capitalist society incorporated patriarchal norms into its own, which is why traditional gender norms and roles both have persisted during modernity while changing along with it.

Capitalism at its most systemic level, then, does not need the variables of "white supremacy" or "patriarchy" to function. Even without known forms of European racism or sexism, it would have subjected people where it first developed to the same impulse to expand outward to find cheap labor and resources. Had capitalism developed in China first, *its* religious traditions, *its* gender norms, and the supremacy of its dominant ethnic group would have followed its path of expansion, as would xenophobia toward its colonized ethnic groups.

It just so happens that capitalism first developed in Europe. As the system historically matured and expanded, its religious principles, its gender system, and its form of ethnic dominance became affixed in forms of law (e.g., sexual norms, miscegenation laws, voting rights, etc.), science (e.g., heteronormativity, racial sciences), and culture (e.g., religious hegemony, ethnic and racial prejudice and discrimination, stereotypes, and so on). In this sense, racism is built into the *historical*-structural logic of capitalist development as a predictable set of formal relationships (i.e., colonizer versus colonized) but its content (i.e., white versus non-white) was contingent on the point of origin of the system. Similarly, given the commonality of male authority and dominance in European colonial culture, capitalism also carried such gendered institutional forms and norms along with it. There was or is nothing uniquely Christian, white, and/or male and/or even European about capitalism *as a system*; these historically-rooted traits simply were at the head of the movement of capitalism's original development.

CHAPTER 21

# Absurd Epidemics

In 1636 in Holland, the story goes, a mania erupted, where, in a very short period of time, everyone suddenly wanted to buy tulip bulbs. Demand drove the price for some bulbs up to approximately ten times the annual income of the average worker, though by February 1637, the bubble burst and prices returned to "normal," signaling the craze was over. While this event was absurd by any measure, it was the product of a form of collective hysteria, a sociological phenomenon no doubt but one that only concerns us here as a point of departure on what the relation of supply to demand can force upon us.[1]

In a market, there is a supply of goods and a level of demand for those goods. Supply, stated simply, is the amount of some product available for sale (plus perhaps an amount of similar already manufactured goods in warehouses waiting to take their place on the shelves). Demand is slightly more complicated. We can say there is the totality of *possible real demand* for a product, which would be all of those individuals who would like to have or need a product. However, not all of them might have the spending power needed to actualize such demand through purchases. And then there's "aggregate demand" (John Maynard Keynes), which is the total amount of *potential* spending power available in a population. Here, however, there is no guarantee people *will* spend that money instead of saving it. Finally, there is "effective demand," which is the amount of money ready to be used or already in-use for purchases.

When there is a certain amount of supply of a product ready for purchase, its price (assuming competition in the market) is determined, in part, by the amount of people ready, willing, and able to purchase it. If there is more supply of a product than demand for it, prices will tend to fall (a problem for sellers but less so for buyers, at least initially). This is because sellers will have to lower prices to attract buyers away from other sellers, i.e., it's a "buyer's market." If there is more demand for a product than the supply of it, prices will tend upwards (which is good for sellers and not so great for buyers). This is a "seller's

---

1  Though this story has been told and retold for generations, recent analysis suggests that "tulip mania" never in fact happened to the extent originally claimed. Though prices did rise for the new commodity in Dutch markets, demand was relatively circumspect to a few traders and not society-wide, nor did the market's collapse bring down the wider economy in Holland (for discussion, see Boissoneault 2017 and references therein).

market" because sellers can demand higher prices for their goods if buyers really want or really need them and have money available to buy them.

But what happens if supply outstrips demand to such an extent—a change of quantity to that of quality—that it drives the sale price down to where it is no longer worth it for sellers to bring their products to market? For instance, imagine that it costs me $10 to grow a bushel of corn and another $5 to bring it to market. To make it profitable enough for me to stay in business, I must charge $20 per bushel and use the excess $5 to cover my personal expenses such as mortgage payments, food, clothing, savings, and so on. If enough *other* corn producers bring enough product to market so that there is more corn overall than can be bought, there is now an "overproduction" of it. This overproduction will likely drive down the price as sellers reduce what they are asking for their corn in order to fetch enough buyers to prop up their overall profits. If this dynamic continues to the point where buyers will only purchase corn that cost $14 or less per bushel, I am forced to sell at a loss. Should prices drop to $9 or below, I would lose less if I simply did not bring my corn to market at all, though my entire business and personal life are now at risk. If a few other producers also stopped bringing their corn to market (or go out of business), then this would reduce supply to an extent that prices could creep back up and profits again could still be made by those who stayed in the market. Moreover, those who can *produce* corn for less than $14 a bushel can withstand such a decline in market demand, while those for whom it costs more risk having a balance of payments problem on their hands.

What would happen if those who did not bring their product to market decided to put ads in newspapers: "Free corn! Come to my farm, take away all you can!" That would save them the cost of getting product to market, but it would also exacerbate the problem of excess of market supply as a whole, i.e., it would pull effective demand from elsewhere and sop up some aggregate and total demand potentially. This would both pull purchasers from other producers and that excessive supply would keep the price of the remaining corn for sale low or even lower it. In this sense, then, excess supply is additionally dysfunctional for sellers as well as a market system dependent on prices and profits as a whole.

But something must be done with excessive supply, given that these are physical things and they do not simply vanish from warehouses. Though producers *could* store that corn and wait for current supply to decline and thus drive prices back up to a profitable margin, that is no long-term solution if a commodity has a sell-by date, whether corn or cars. And producers that store excess commodities leave themselves susceptible to unforeseen future market shocks, so this strategy is risky at best. They also might have to withhold future production until current supply dwindles but this means idle production facilities and stagnation, creating potential losses in the next cycle. Production of too many goods, then, can lead to economic stagnation and decline. If this sounds like a contradiction, it is, and this contradiction is a central problem in modern economics.

Not only does the market system have a tendency to overproduce goods, it can also overproduce profits. Overproduced profits are those that cannot find a new home for reinvestment, in which case, rather than commodities being overproduced, *capital has been overaccumulated*. And as both overproduction and overaccumulation can have disastrous ripple effects throughout the system, let us take a look at their interrelation, starting with the latter.

Overaccumulation of capital results from excessive investment. In a prior expansionary cycle, businesses invest in raw materials, labor, production equipment, storage facilities, and what not. As they do this, so do their competitors, each looking to maximize potential market share. And when the market contracts, as it inevitably does, they are overextended in these areas and products cannot be brought profitably to market. Think about global competition between US, German, Japanese, and South Korean automakers. Collectively, they may produce 60 million cars a year but sell only 50 million. In such a case, the auto sector experiences bottlenecks, where cars remain in warehouses without buyers and additional capital cannot be moved to new production investments for lack of expected effective demand, producing likely future losses where past profits have already been sunk into facilities and products that are not moving and thus such past profits are eaten up. This is an inevitable part of the system and from this extends other forms of overproduction and their results, e.g., recent industry moves toward "just-in-time" manufacturing and supply chains.

First, there is overproduction of industrial plant. When the market is in a growth pattern of production and consumption, businesses do not want to lose out on profit opportunities and will tend to hire new workers, have facilities working at capacity, and even build new ones. Once market demand pulls back, a business now has too many machines and too much raw material and thus too many workers. In response, they reduce their capacity and output, with machines, and even whole factories going silent. Entire towns may go under economically as a result. Another solution is to set out investment in new, more efficient production techniques, often ones that save labor costs, e.g., more output in the same amount of time and/or technology that requires fewer workers. The modern world previously saw the complete overhaul of manufacturing with the introduction of assembly lines, which, while more technologically complex, required fewer workers and thus saved businesses money in the short-medium run. Today, we see a replay of this with the incipient robotic revolution, a shift that threatens to consume millions of jobs and professions worldwide (a topic to which we will return in Chapter 23).

Second, often accompanying the above is the overproduction of commodities—too many goods made and not enough buyers to purchase them. This problem, too, is endemic to the logic of the system and, as such, it periodically springs its effects upon it. In the Great Depression, for example, livestock and other agricultural products were destroyed to relieve market gluts and price crashes. In 1933, the US Agricultural Adjustment Act (AAA) worked to reduce the supply of livestock and cotton on US farms as a matter of policy. Around one million pigs were purchased and killed by the government and, in the American South, farmers were paid to plow under over 10 million acres of cotton. This destruction of perfectly good resources saved many farmers, either through direct subsidies for their products and/or propping up market prices by reducing supply, which would in turn support the purchasing power of farmers from their sales (eventually, the Federal Surplus Relief Corporation was created to distribute goods such as beans, apples, and meat to relief organizations). The AAA also worked to control the supply of tobacco, peanuts, corn, wheat, milk, and rice. Similar subsidies for farmers to not produce at maximum capacity are still in place today.

In the 1980s, a series of national and global economic developments intersected to produce a similar result, i.e., overextended US farmers. After World War II, advances in machinery and new techniques using designer seeds, fertilizers, and pesticides resulted in greater productivity and output in US agriculture. Stockpiles grew and were then drawn down to reduce oversupply. In the 1970s, demand for US agricultural products again exploded, especially after the United States in 1972 signed a multiyear deal with the Soviet Union for wheat and grain feeds. Within two years, prices for wheat doubled and tripled for corn and farmers responded with increased production. Good times were ahead. However, in 1979, the Federal Reserve tightened its monetary policy to address inflation and the prime lending rate went from 6.8% to 21.5% by 1981. As farmers often rely on borrowing money for seeds, equipment, pesticides, etc., interest rates at that level were a burden many could not bear. Also, in 1979, the Soviet Union invaded Afghanistan and after, in 1980, US President Jimmy Carter ordered grain shipments to them stopped. With collapsing demand and growing supply, prices crashed, and US farms started going under. A farm crisis rippled across the rural economy, taking with it families, rural communities, and banks.

American farming took another hit in the late 1990s. In 1996, the Republican Congress and the Clinton administration enacted the Freedom to Farm Act, which phased out government supports and subsidies remaining from the

Roosevelt/New Deal era, just as record harvests were driving down prices. Financial shocks and crises hit Asia, Russia, and Latin America, which collectively reduced their demand for agricultural imports. World stocks of corn and soybeans multiplied and US stores of wheat from harvests from 1996–1998 piled up in grain elevators. Wheat prices subsequently dropped, as did those for soy, corn, and pork. Emergency legislation was needed to stem the bleeding with new subsidies (which were supposed to have been eliminated). Nevertheless, during the decade, the number of farmers either going bankrupt and/or leaving the business went up.

One social-epidemiological result of these gluts was the search for new ways to use overproduced agricultural goods. Excessive corn production was transformed into new forms of sugar, e.g., high-fructose corn syrup. Because of the misplaced and hyped-up fear of natural animal fats urged on the public in prior decades, new forms of industrial food production turned to replacing animal fat with sugar (and not just high-fructose corn syrup).[2] Excessive amounts of soy were transformed into other forms of added fat (and thus flavor to replace eliminated animal fats) for food products. Collectively, they added caloric value into foods that would normally have lower levels, e.g., sugar in pasta sauce, breads, soups, and so on—from field to shelf to waist.

Third, overproduction of industrial plant and commodities means there are more people who want or need work than the business community requires. And this can be true across the economy, not just in the production of durable goods. The introduction of computers has increasingly reduced the number of personnel needed for office work, while the Internet as a source of information has had a dramatic negative impact on newspaper and magazine industries. Throughout the 1980s and 1990s, new strategies of "downsizing" and "lean manufacturing" took root, each being euphemisms for reducing workforces and having those workers that remain take on additional responsibilities. In the manufacturing sector, many companies introduced "just in time" delivery methods, which tightened up supply chains through filling orders and delivering goods from factory to retailer more rapidly, bypassing traditional methods of stocking warehouse shelves. Computers made this possible, while also allowing for reducing workforces, the odds of bottlenecks, and, by extension, reducing the amount of capital tied up in unsold goods.

---

2  For a discussion of the personalities and scientific politics that denied sugar's role in the obesity epidemic and persistent high death rates from heart disease and pushed fear of high-fat, low-carbohydrate diets, see Leslie (2016). Even today, governmental guidelines and popular knowledge still see dietary fat and cholesterol as culprits for rising obesity rates despite growing scientific evidence that shows no link between them and instead that sugar and refined carbohydrates are very likely the causes.

There are a few "solutions" to overproduction in a market economy. One is some form of "devaluation" or "depreciation," whether by chance or by design. Companies can lower their total wage-bill by keeping wages stagnant, reducing working hours by reducing output (thus reducing their excessive capacity and the resulting supply of commodities), or shutting down plants and/or firing workers. Other times companies can reduce their wage-bill by moving facilities to low-wage areas, either within their host nations or abroad to other countries. Businesses can invest money in real estate and buildings as speculative ventures (a gamble at best) which can be a motor for new urbanization initiatives. They can also look for and/or invest in faster forms of transportation and communication which can reduce the time and the costs of doing business. At a more macro level, devaluation might come in the form of mass bankruptcies, crashes, depressions, or even war (which can eat up economic deadwood in the system). Another solution is finding new investment markets in which to sell stockpiles of commodities, such as foreign lands, which often calls for either breaking those markets open forcibly or negotiating trade deals with other governments.

The twins of overaccumulation and overproduction mean that additional capital is unlikely to be spent in the short-run on new investments in the productive sector. However, the logic of capitalism requires the perpetual expansion of capital. Like commodities sitting unsold on shelves, capital requires flow, movement, expansion, and this means reinvestment and additional profits (*ad infinitum*). So, when reinvestment in production in one sector seems unprofitable, money will move to new areas that promise better odds of (higher) returns and this can create market bubbles. Sometimes bubbles occur in sectors investors believe have a pent-up demand or otherwise expect profitable growth, i.e., like the tech bubble in the 1990s. Other times capital flows to the financial sector when commodity markets are not seen as profitable. So in the 2000s, the "FIRE" economy—Finance, Insurance, Real Estate—was not only the fastest growing sector but also overtook manufacturing as a percentage of the US GDP—with the FIRE portion of the economy going from 10.5% to 21.5% from 1947 to 2009 and manufacturing dropping from 25.6% to 11.2% in the same period (see Bureau of Economic Analysis | Global Macro Monitor 2011). That period also saw the rise of housing derivatives, growth of credit card debt and auto loans, and auto manufacturers stockpiling their cars. This shift also ultimately led to the housing bubble and the financial crisis of 2007–2008. And, as we will see in Chapter 44, the effects of this crisis were felt in declines in household wealth that persisted a decade later.

In the modern market economy, the expansion of capital requires priority attention. Production and distribution of what people *need* is ancillary, a byproduct of what businesses owners think they can *actually sell*. Further, once sales have been made and profits accrued, those profits are reinvested (i.e., the circuit of capital) and reinvestment must target those areas in the market that are expected to have high enough effective demand to produce a satisfactory rate of return on that investment. If, because of their level of spending power, people cannot buy enough commodities that transform into desired profit rates, then capital reinvestment must find other outlets, whether those be office buildings, more efficient machinery, new industries or financial markets, and so on. Sometimes the investing classes create whole new instruments in which to sink accumulated capital, such as derivatives or the privatization of public resources. Though excess goods that cannot be sold can be withheld for a time period, that is a limited solution. Total product must be reduced, so that supply reaches a closer equilibrium with effective demand and if that means withholding needed goods from the market, then so be it, as that is what best serves the process of capital accumulation.

And this is ultimately absurd. When food was overproduced in every other system in history, it was often a cause for celebration, of feasts, of making new alliances through trade, of additional ways to feed animals and even grow a herd, and so on. What it was not was a "crisis" that threatened to spread throughout the economic system. And the idea that food (including animals) and other goods would need to be destroyed while people go hungry and homeless would be an unthinkable proposition, literally. Destruction of consumable goods would not have occurred to those living in prior systems because there would be no need for it, no advantage for it to be done, no structural crisis that would require constant addressing. But in capitalism these *are* things that need attending given the structural logic of its market. Such are the absurd epidemics inherent to the modern system.

CHAPTER 22

# Swindling Joint-stock Companies

The Appalachian region of the United States is blessed with natural beauty and resources, which have often been its people's curse. Residents there were once offered a "Broad Form Deed," an agreement where a property owner relinquished his or her mineral rights to the coal (or other stipulated mineral resources) that might be found under their land. The contract's terms were often for well-longer than the lifetime of the property owner and such terms transferred to those who inherited or bought the land. The deed also relieved any new holder of it from responsibility for damages resulting from any extraction methods used. For a poor and none-too-seldom illiterate citizen, being paid, say, $100 in 1910 for transferring rights to coal they would never dig (or which might never be found) seemed like a good deal. As a result, many people were taken advantage of by these contracts. By 1981, for instance, over 40% of the land and 72% of the mineral rights were absentee owned, with 47% out-of-state owners and 53% out-of-country (Appalachian Land Ownership Task Force 1981). Though these contracts were legally binding, they swindled the people and the region out of their prosperity and legacy for generations, right up to the present day.

Corporations—called "joint-stock companies" in times gone by—are often collectively owned by a multitude of individuals (and even other companies). Stock is a small "share" of a company one can buy and thus making one part owner of that business. The more stock one buys, the more of a share of ownership they have. And if several companies combine and/or are bought up by a larger one, they become a "conglomerate," often a very powerful economic entity with investments and production practices in a variety of fields and often crossing multiple global borders.[1] Today, there are thousands of corporations in the world and hundreds of conglomerates. And together they account for the largest share of criminal swindling in the world.

Very often, even before a person even gets to the marketplace, they have been inundated with advertising containing imagery and information about products businesses want them to buy. In order to entice consumers to buy their goods, advertisers often offer misleading and even flat out false images and information about their products. Words like "organic," "cholesterol free," and "natural" have almost no meaning for a variety of foods. Advertisers can

---

[1] The largest 25 corporations wield more economic resources than many of the largest states in the world (Khanna 2016).

omit or speed through important information—like the side effects of over-the-counter drugs—or hide these and worrisome fees in the fine print. Fillers, such as saltwater injected into meats, can pad the weights of foodstuffs. Highlighting the one perceived healthy ingredient in a product filled with other suspect ones misleads as to its overall quality. Companies pushing diet pills and schemes often hire athletes that have gained weight because of an injury for a "before" picture and pay them to use their product once they heal up and get back to working out and then take their "after" picture. In this way, they can legally state that this is what this person looked like before and after using the product. Meaningless terms like "important part of a healthy breakfast" are used to sell cereals whose white flour and sugar content matches that of cookies. Pictures of serving sizes can give the impression they are larger than what is actually used on the nutritional label. A company might claim their food has "21 essential vitamins and minerals" though several of them are actually only in miniscule quantities. Examples are legion.

While advertising might mislead, some products are simply dangerous, even deadly. Tobacco companies, for instance, publicly denied their product's threats to health for years, intentionally made them more addictive, paid for spokespersons to manipulate the findings of research on tobacco's dangers, though internal documents revealed they perfectly well knew the connection between tobacco use and illness and death (Bates and Rowell 2004; Brandt 2012; Karagueuzian et al. 2012; Kodjak 2017). Pharmaceutical companies, such as Bayer, continued to sell blood-related products infected with HIV—often shifting sales of older, more dangerous stock to Latin America and Asia—even after coming to understand HIV's connection to AIDS (Bogdanich and Koli 2003; Goldenberg 2003).

A famous case of dangerous products involves the Ford Pinto. It was claimed that its gas tank was at risk for exploding when the car was rear ended, even at relatively minor speeds. Even though Ford held that it had placed the fuel tank aligned with industry standards of the time, critics argued that the Pinto had smaller real "crush space," less structural reinforcement, and a rear bumper that was poor at absorbing impacts. By 1973, Ford received reports of their car catching fire after low-speed rear accidents, but their recall team decided that the data was not actionable. A scandal erupted when it was discovered that Ford had calculated and compared the cost of fixing millions of cars ($11 per car for 2.5 million cars/trucks for a total of $137 million) to the societal costs of injury or death (estimated at 180 deaths, 180 serious injuries totaling $49.5 million; referred to as the "Pinto Memo"). With the social cost estimated lower than the cost of recalling and fixing these cars, even if it was relatively inexpensive per vehicle, Ford decided not to recall the car. In response to pressure from the National Highway Traffic Safety Administration (NHTSA), Ford held that the Pinto was no more prone to fire hazards than other cars, that NHTSA used worst case tests on it (weightier equipment than standard, weighing down the front of a test vehicle so that it would slide under the Pinto's rear bumper), that accident reports often did not indicate whether death was caused by impact or by a subsequent fire, and that the number of deaths attributed to fires was the same as those that could be attributed to the car's transmission. Nevertheless, under pressure from NHTSA, Ford issued a recall in 1978, the largest in automotive history at the time (see Wojdyla 2011; Dowie 1977). And even if Ford was correct that a faulty case was being made against the Pinto alone (other cars in its class showed similar risks and these were by no means the most dangerous ones), the fact that they did cost-benefit analysis shows that balancing profits over people's lives is a variable calculated in the way businesses operate. And though the logic of market competition for profits makes this inevitable, such an equation would be anywhere from illegal to unthinkable should it be used in our interpersonal interactions.

Price fixing occurs when two or more companies in the same market collude and agree to set a price for a commodity outside of market forces. In 1993, the US Justice Department investigated Archer Daniels Midland executives for manipulating prices of lysine. ADM employee Mark Whitacre informed the FBI that he and other executives had been involved, on ADM's behalf, with rival companies from Japan and South Korea in fixing the price for the food additive in global markets. In 1997, ADM was fined $100 million (the biggest fine for breaking anti-trust laws in US history at the time), three top ADM officials were sentenced to federal prison in 1999, and its 2005 annual report stated that ADM settled a class action anti-trust lawsuit for $400 million. Purdue professor and agricultural economist, John M. Connor, called on as expert witness in the civil suit, testified that the US public alone was overcharged between $155–166 million and, according to secretly recorded tapes of the meetings, a top ADM executive referred to their customers as enemies and competitors as friends (see Wissman 1998:1). This case of collusion and price fixing is by no means a singular one.

One attempt at summarizing the extent of this type of corporate swindling can be found in, "Statistics on Modern Private International Cartels, 1990–2005" (Connor and Helmers 2007). This report relied on data collected by anti-trust authorities since January 1990 on private, international hard-core cartels.[2] The researchers found that cartel sales totaled about $1.2 trillion, with

---

2 Cartels referring to "an association of legally independent firms that aims to raise their joint profits through explicit agreements" and "hard core" defined as those that "fashion

about $300 billion (in 2005 money) in overcharges. About 47% of the cartels resided in Europe, 16% in the United States, 12% in other continents, and the remaining 25% being global or international in scope (i.e., operating across two or more continents). Cartels in manufacturing measured the highest (79% of sales, with most in chemicals, nonmetallic minerals, paper, and electronics), followed by services (21%), and then raw materials. Though penalties at that point were the highest in history, they concluded that widespread levels of recidivism imply that such penalties are inadequate deterrents.

A bribe offers an individual or organization money or some other compensation in exchange for some desired behavior the bribe's recipient otherwise might not do. In the commercial world, such rewards might be kickbacks or good deals, lucrative contracts, money for a political campaign, stock options, a job, or a promotion. For instance, though the American Medical Association has ethical guidelines for accepting gifts from industry, it is widely understood that pharmaceutical companies regularly curry favor with doctors to use their drugs, whether by kickback, direct payment, funding tropical vacations, etc. In 2012, a survey by Ernest & Young (a multinational professional services firm) of 400 Chief Financial Officers found that 15% of them admitted they were willing to pay bribes as the cost of doing business (Nitsche 2012). A World Bank study ("Governance Matters, 2007: Worldwide Governance Indicators 1996–2006") estimated that bribery involves about $1 trillion in transactions worldwide.[3]

Such political corruption can lead to other forms of economic distortion. Political leaders, often in underdeveloped countries, sometimes skim billions off the top from charitable donations, foreign aid, subsidies for food, and development loans. Corruption from bureaucrats and politicians can raise the cost of doing business—and thus the cost of consumer goods and services—when businesses must take into account the need to pay off officials for contracts and inspections. Business leaders can bribe government officials to overlook environmental regulations, increasing risks to the public from polluted water, air, soil, and consumer products. Additionally, corrupt officials directing business to capital projects where bribes and kickbacks are common raises the costs for governments and therefore for taxpayers.

---

agreements to control market prices or restrict industrial supply (or both)" (Connor and Helmers 2007: 3).

[3] A copy of the World Bank's report can be found here (URL retrieved September 1, 2018): http://siteresources.worldbank.org/INTWBIGOVANTCOR/Resources/Englishpressrelease.pdf.

Insider trading occurs when people with knowledge of non-public information use that information to buy or sell stocks or securities. This is illegal because it is considered a distortion of fair market practices. For instance, if an insider knows a stock is about to fail, they can sell before that happens and not suffer a loss. Conversely, if they know a stock price is about to rise (for legal or non-legal reasons), they might buy large shares at the lower price, see their value inflate, and make significant gains they would not have otherwise.

It is also possible to manipulate the stock market by creating misrepresentative or deceitful appearances of the price or market for commodities, currencies, or securities. The following are just a few examples. In a "pump and dump," stock promoters put out false information to millions of unsuspecting potential investors that tout a stock's value to drive up its price, only to sell their own shares once that value has gone up, causing the value to crash. "Churning" is done by placing both buy and sell orders at the same time, an increase in activity that is supposed to draw attention and attract new investors and thus increase a stock's price. Similarly, a "wash trade" is where the same security is repeatedly bought and sold, also creating the appearance of activity, drawing attention, and driving up the price.

Another form of fraud is the misrepresentation of financial statements. Funds may be misdirected, revenues overstated, and expenses understated. The value of assets may be falsely inflated, or liabilities hidden. A particularly pernicious form of this is the reverse: presenting an under-valued picture of a business's assets and health. For instance, if an executive successfully makes a company appear to be worth less on paper than its real market value, the value of that company's stock might decline. Should that company get bought out at this lower price, the buyer gets a bargain and might reward that executive with a "golden handshake" worth millions or even billions of dollars. Bankruptcy fraud is another example. Here, individuals or corporations can file for bankruptcy to deal with debt while protecting their assets from creditors. In the process, they might conceal assets, destroy documents, make false statements, and/or misrepresent their financials in other ways.

The former US energy corporation, Enron, is perhaps the leading candidate for a host of swindling activity. In 1999, they developed a scheme where they counted anticipated future profits as part of their current assets, allowing them to record what might be future losses as gains. This assisted them in manipulating their stock price and thus encouraged continued investor contributions and confidence.

In 2000–2001, Senator Phil Gramm (recipient of the second largest amount of Enron campaign contributions and whose wife was an Enron board member) worked to deregulate California's rules for trading in energy commodities.

Afterward, the state had 38 rolling blackouts declared because of manipulation from traders and marketers. The resulting decrease in supply allowed Enron traders to exact a premium price for energy. In another example, which would later contribute to the company's demise, they created Special Purpose Entities where they could keep their financial liabilities off of or mask them from their financial statements, making the company seem profitable when it was in fact losing money. This, in turn, helped raise their stock value, after which executives used insider information to trade billions worth of stock to enrich themselves, hide losses in offshore accounts, and continue to encourage investors to keep buying stock even as the price went down. As the company stock shrunk to junk status, Enron went bankrupt, executives were charged with insider trading, conspiracy, and fraud. It was the largest Chapter 11 bankruptcy in US history. The scandal also brought down Enron's accounting firm and one of the world's largest, Arthur Andersen (found guilty of obstruction of justice for destroying audit documents they had for Enron).

Research has found that banking culture, which places "financial gain above all else," is particularly prone to promoting dishonesty among its employees (see Cohn, Fair, and Maréchal 2014). In 2016, Deutsche Bank agreed to settle a suit brought by bullion investors after it was accused of having fixed silver and gold futures since 2007. After the financial crisis of 2007–2008, Lehman Brothers, a US investment bank over a century old, went under (having $639 billion in assets and $619 billion in debts). This played a significant part in the subsequent stock market crash that rippled through global markets. They were accused of short-selling their customers, betting against their own investment advice, and having their executives walk away handsomely rewarded. Despite the suspicions about possible misdeeds, none of the upper management was prosecuted. However, another investment bank, Goldman Sachs, decided to settle a lawsuit for $5.1 billion after agreeing on a list of "facts" that delineated its part in the crisis, facts which included assuring investors that the securities it sold were sound all the while knowing that the home mortgages that backed them were likely to fail. Other banks that also agreed to settlements included J.P. Morgan Chase ($13 billion), Bank of America ($16.6 billion), Citigroup ($7 billion), Morgan Stanley ($3.2 billion), and Wells Fargo ($2 billion) (see Shen 2016; Scipioni 2018). Additional examples of banking fraud include money laundering for drug cartels and/or dictators (Wachovia, HSBC, Bank of Credit and Commerce International), fixing currency markets (the Forex scandal), submitting fraudulent interest rates for short-term loans (the LIBOR scandal), and shaving money from pension accounts (Bank of New York Mellon).

This is not an exhaustive list of methods used to swindle consumers, the public, and even other corporations. Conflicts of interest are common, such as pharmaceutical companies subsidizing journals and/or reviewers while providing grants to researchers to study their planned medications so that favored outcomes are more likely to be published and unfavorable findings withheld. Companies collude in rigging bids, where a competitor agrees to over-bid on a project, allowing their rival to win a contract, only for a *quid pro quo* in return on other bids on other projects so that those that over-bid the first time will win the next time around. "Pay-to-play" involves providing financial gifts to decision-makers in business or politics, with the implied assumption that such gifts will provide access to new contracts or lawmakers at some later point.[4]

There is also an extensive use of tax havens and shelters by individuals and companies to avoid paying their share of taxes to the government. Bermuda, Panama, Seychelles, the British Virgin Islands, and the Cayman Islands all host operations that allow individuals and corporations to place their assets there in order to avoid taxes (often legally and sometimes illegally through hiding such assets) in their home countries (sometimes these "businesses" are no more than a mailing address). For instance, in 2016, the "Panama Papers" scandal erupted when over eleven million files were leaked from the world's fourth-largest offshore firm, Mossack Fonseca, revealing accounts that world leaders, celebrities, sports stars, and other global elites used ostensibly for hiding their wealth from their home governments (see Harding 2016).[5] In terms of outright tax evasion, in December of 2011, Public Campaign called out General Electric for the $84.35 million it spent on lobbying, while not paying any taxes from 2008 to 2010 and receiving $48.7 billion in tax rebates, making $10.4 billion in profits while laying off over 4,000 workers. Hundreds of billions of unpaid tax dollars from such techniques remain unavailable to governments for keeping infrastructure and services sustained.

Not only are governments and the public funds entrusted to them swindled out of money due, so are workers and customers. One study found that in just three cities (New York, Chicago, and Los Angeles), minimum wage workers annually lost $2,634 (out of $17,616) through employer practices such as shaving off one half-hour per day from time sheets. The yearly total of lost wages from

---

4 In 2017–2018, Donald Trump and his administration were accused of such activities (see Heath et al. 2017; Victor 2017; Fritze 2018; Korte 2018).

5 As of 2005, overseas tax evasion by individuals was costing the American public about $40-$70 billion in lost tax revenue (Guttentag and Avi-Yonah 2005). It was estimated in 2017, that Fortune 500 companies held a record $2.6 trillion in offshore accounts, costing US taxpayers over $700 billion in lost revenues (ITEP 2017). Another estimate found that, in 2012, the United States lost between $77-$111 billion in tax revenue because of profit shifting and this was expected to reach about $94-$135 billion for 2016 (see Merle 2016 and references therein).

these three cities was $3 billion and, if generalizable to the United States as a whole, the total stolen from workers is an estimated $50 billion per year (which the authors compare to $340,850,358 lost from reported robberies) (Meixel and Eisenberry 2014). In 2017, JP Morgan Chase, the largest bank in the United States, agreed to $53 million in fines for charging African-Americans and Latinos higher rates than whites for home mortgages (Mattera 2017b); the Consumer Financial Protection Bureau hit Citigroup with $28.8 million in fines failing to disclose actions borrowers could take to avoid foreclosure (Mattera 2017a); Bank of America received a $45 million penalty for the way they treated one couple attempting to save their home (Stech 2017); and a class action lawsuit against Wells Fargo resulted in $142 million in fines for creating fake accounts on 3.5 million customers who had not applied for them (Coleman 2017; also see Prins 2017 and references therein).

That corporate managers and leaders are tempted to swindle others and cheat the system should not surprise us for a number of reasons. First, both the amount of money available and the ways to manipulate transactions are enormous. The temptation must be similar. Second, a business's profitability is what matters most to investors and for a CEO, COO, or CFO to keep his or her job, their business must be as profitable as possible (especially in comparison to others) so as to not encourage those with investment-ready money to look elsewhere. Third, corporate crime is less policed than street crime, as is well-known by criminologists. And if caught, one is less likely to be tried and convicted of wrongdoing. White-collar crime is thus advantageous, insulated from prosecution, and lucrative. And if convicted, the likelihood of a heavy fine or even jail time is less than the average criminal.[6] Given such observations, that many of our largest companies engage in swindling behavior should perhaps be expected and not be seen as exceptional.

---

6   Even with historically loose enforcement, a 2018 study found that the civic penalties handed out by 11 of the 12 federal agencies declined during the Trump administration's first year in office. Compliance penalties handed out by the Environmental Protection Agency dropped around 94%, those from the Department of Justice against corporate rule breakers were down 90%, and those from the Federal Communications Commission and the Securities and Exchange Commission had declined 85% and 68% respectively (see Lartey 2018).

CHAPTER 23

# Machines

Unlike fish born as fry in a stream, we must learn to transform nature's materials for our own ends, making clothes, hammers, levers, pulleys, pottery, etc. Our everyday lives are so steeped in things made by manipulating and transforming nature that we tend to take this for granted, forgetting that tools and technology are testimonies to the human stamp on the world. It has been said that tool-making is what separates humans from other species. Today, we know this is not true, as several species from crows to primates have been observed making tools. Still, we are certainly the *most advanced* at this practice among the animal world. And over history our tools have grown increasingly complex, varied, and interconnected.

The search for ever-more useful tools is not unique to people in any one system, as the human imagination appears evolutionarily selected to transform nature's products in the mind in order to forge new objects into reality. Those individuals and/or those societies that could take advantage of this skill and/or exchange its knowledge with others found an edge in the game of social survival. Stagnation and lack of imagination were costs paid for with possible social decline. That said, not all systems witness the same type and rate of growth of technological development. For some, just a few tools are enough to negotiate survival in nature. Though not thoroughly stagnate, hunter-gatherers remain at a rudimentary level once tools for needed tasks are created; agricultural societies develop tools of more complexity but their development there has limits, too. By contrast, technological development is built into the very fabric of the capitalist system. But why?

First, the modern division of labor has more types of work, skills, professions, and specialization than any system before it. Each specialty—such as transportation, education, electronics, sewer systems, and so on—develops techniques and technologies to improve its operations and to respond to new conditions, new problems, and/or new technologies developed elsewhere. And such development has feedback loops, where technology in one or more arenas can be adapted by others, creating the potential for exponential growth.

Second, the modern marketplace can handsomely reward inventors at times. Given the right mix of start-up capital, patent law, and consumer demand, riches can be made. Bill Gates and Microsoft are but a recent example. Though he invented very little, if any, of the technology for which his company is known, Gates did court investors, buy patents from inventors, and paid attention to market changes that could help stimulate demand should computers be made affordable and useful to everyday people. He succeeded on all counts and is now one of the richest persons in the world.

Third, in a competitive market, those that produce more efficiently and/or develop new desirable products are more likely to outdo their rivals. In this competition, firms that reinvest profits into "research and development" find that this can help improve older products and develop new ones, both of which aid them in the struggle against economic peers. Car companies today have engineering departments to craft new designs, models, and other improvements. They also invest money in computers and robotics for updating their production lines, which in turn require fewer workers to staff them. Overtime, output efficiency–and potential quantity–rises and those that first adopt such methods outpace competitors and win market share (compelling competitors to catch up to new industry standards).

Fourth, while market competition can be understood as a form of "intraclass" struggle amongst the owning-selling class, there is also a struggle between the owning and working classes and machines can be a weapon in it. And why? Workers and business owners have built-in antagonistic interests. The more conscious a business owner is of the need to control the movements, thoughts, and deeds of workers, the more likely it is that he or she spends part of their profits on machines that aid in labor control and productive efficiency. Below are just a few examples of how this might be done.

In the division of labor inside a factory, the task at hand—whether building a bicycle or a car—is broken down into simpler steps, with each accomplished by some specialized action, e.g., attaching wheels on a bike, inserting seats in a car. Over time, machines have tended to replace human labor in this process, though machines still often must be tended—there are buttons to push, gears to adjust, moving parts to lubricate or repair, and so on. When the human becomes an appendage to the machine, they become another moving part and their movements are dictated by the quality and pace of the machine's movements. A machine can be set to be, relatively speaking, slower or faster. The slower the pace of work, the more time there is for a worker's mind to wander, to converse with fellow employees, to slack off on the job, etc. Such a worker may begin asking troublesome questions, like whether or not there's more to life than tending a machine for someone else's enrichment. They might discuss their mutual problems with fellow employees—the unhappiness they have with their working conditions, how to extract more from the employer's wage-bill, and other thoughts unwanted by employers. Speeding up machinery means less time to think, less time to be idle, less time to mingle with one's peers. In this way, a machine's pace can be used as a disciplining mechanism.

Industrial work has been, very often, physically intensive and destructive. Mining the coal to fuel the industrial apparatus left hundreds of thousands of dead worldwide, either in the mines themselves or at home dying from black lung and other diseases. Those not killed sometimes found their bodies crippled. Like the mines, large industrial factories often relied on child labor and that of women and desperate fathers and many in all of these groups found themselves sacrificing limbs to machinery's might. In factories producing textiles, workers suffered from brown-lung, a condition similar to black lung. Mines for aluminum, steel, uranium, diamonds, and so on all visited health problems on their workers and still do. Today, we witness a resurgence of sweatshops, where long hours, lack of ventilation, and hazardous working conditions keep workers in a state of constant pain and dilapidation. This is true for clothing and electronics industries, conditions often kept away from the eyes of consumers who enjoy the fruits of such labors. In all of these industries, there has been a constant introduction of new machine technology that requires fewer workers but long hours on the job, leaving little opportunity for things other than work, sleep, and more work.

Office workers are not immune from the effects of machines and advanced technology, either. Though their labor is not as physically demanding, office workers are often tied to their desks and stuck behind their computer keyboards. These modern machines can keep track of your keystrokes, how often you enter information and data, where online you visit, and with whom you communicate. Workers no longer need to have a manager over their shoulders in order to be watched and surveilled. These same technologies follow us when we leave the office as workers and venture into the marketplace as consumers. Data on how we spend our money, on what, where, and when are compiled into databanks and we are then inundated on our computers and in our home mailboxes with ads to entice even more money out of our pockets.

Having machines replace workers has been a continuous trend in modern society. Fewer workers mean fewer human beings to interfere with the production process. Machines do not unionize, make fewer mistakes, do not get sick, and never ask for a maternity leave, childcare, health insurance, worker's compensation, or a pension. Machines can make almost everything for us, including new machines to take additional work away. This, of course, creates a contradiction at the heart of industrial society: the more workers that are replaced with machines, the less the total amount of money that is set out to workers as wages (see Figure 23.1); the less wages in circulation in the system, the less

FIGURE 23.1   Compensation of Employees: Wages and Salary Accruals/Gross Domestic Product, 1950–2015. Data: US Bureau of Economic Statistics. Used with Permission of Federal Reserve Economic Data (FRED) at https://fred.stlouisfed.org/

effective demand there will be for consumer goods; the less demand for consumer goods means that less spending is available to sellers to accrue as profit from the productive sector; and, the less profit available, the less cash flow the business class involved in production has available to stay afloat. This is a fundamental contradiction the capitalist system has no way of solving. And this is one of the keys for understanding its periods of contraction and recession.

In the 2010s and afterward, we heard about the advancement of robotics and computer technology in the productive sector as well as in office work and the outlook for jobs was often grim. It is not difficult to find articles where it is predicted that half of the jobs in the United States and/or Britain will be automated by 2025. While only time will tell if such claims are exaggerated, it is no exaggeration to say that the replacement of human labor with machinery is a core feature of the modern world economy. For instance, in January 2016, the World Economic Forum published, "The Future of Jobs: Employment, Skills and Workforce Strategy for the Fourth Industrial Revolution."[1] They explain that this new industrial revolution is the result of "previously disjointed fields

---

1   A copy of the World Economic Forum's report can be found here (URL retrieved September 2, 2018): http://www3.weforum.org/docs/WEF_Future_of_Jobs.pdf.

such as artificial intelligence and machine learning, robotics, nanotechnology, 3D printing and genetics and biotechnology...building on and amplifying one another." The Forum expected transformations in homes, factories, farms, electrical grids and whole cities that will shape "broader socio-economic, geopolitical and demographic developments" in the next five years and beyond, shaping employment in both manual labor and white-collar professions (with a possible total loss of 7.1 million jobs, two-thirds being routine office jobs) (p. 1). This process of replacing human labor with that of machines has marked the entire history of capitalist development and there is no reason to assume it has a logical end.

Machines, while providing for increases in productivity, also deskill us. While we no longer need a whole day to wash and dry our clothes, hardly anyone knows how to make them either. Though we no longer need to chop wood in order to stoke our stoves, few moderns can kill, skin, and clean their own meat or make their own bread. And, when we leave our jobs in the production system as employees, we confront other machines all around us. In the guise as cell phones, we become dependent on computers in our pockets for not only communication but for news, weather, traffic reports, directions, and constant entertainment. Phones, televisions, and home computers now seem required for navigating modern life, while we become ever more distracted, dumbed-down, and anti-social. And once these break down or a new model is made available, old ones are discarded as obsolete and sent to landfills.

This ascension of computer technology is touching our lives across the board, from work to home, from civil society to government, from one nation to another. And it is doing this in ways we control less and less and often in a manner we increasingly cannot understand. Computers today interconnect our phones, laptops, home appliances, shopping habits, video games, health care, voting booths, and workstations. Information about our behavior and our personal data are stored in "the cloud," made up of phone lines, fiber optics, satellites, and ocean floor cables. Hackers can steal our passwords through breaking into smart appliances such as refrigerators, thermostats, or home security networks. Outsiders have breached the power grid in the United States on more than one occasion. Military grade cyber-weapons such as the Suxtnet virus have been developed by persons unknown, with at least one use on a nuclear facility in Iran that destroyed its centrifuges. Programs can monitor our gaming and sleep habits. The spread of false news stories and outlandish conspiracy theories go unchecked online. And we have created computing networks so advanced that the engineers who work with them are incapable of understanding how they work, while such computers have learned to keep their secrets from their users (see Bridle 2018).

We live in a world today where machines appear to be outpacing our ability to manage them, a striking difference than simply changes in employment markets and the growth of output seen during the Industrial Revolution. Computers, for instance, have been changing the way stocks are bought and sold and this can have a dramatic impact on the market. High-frequency trading (sometimes called micro-trading) is an emergent form of stock exchange, where computer algorithms look for micro-margins on stocks, often in fractions of cents. These computers can make thousands, even millions, of trades in minutes to seconds. Businesses are in a sort of arms race to make their equipment micro-seconds faster than others in beating the margin and improving their share, even moving their physical locations closer to Wall Street from places like Chicago to improve such speed. These algorithms, however, operate without human input most of the time and can get out of control. On May 6, 2010, the US stock market experienced a trillion-dollar loss in 36 minutes (the Dow Jones Industrial Average dropped 998.5 points). Though concerns about the Greek debt crisis hung over the day, the market recovered quickly. A trader was blamed for manipulating the market through micro-trades (and a series of illegal trading practices, exploitation of loopholes, and off-shoring tax evasion of the type discussed in Chapter 22; also see Vaughan 2017) but an official and widely accepted explanation of the "flash crash" remains to be found. We are, then, building a world where our machines are increasingly things we cannot control or understand, a world of unknown and portentous possibilities.

We have grown not only dependent on machines but also, by extension, on those who own those machines. We must sell our labor to the business class, whose profits keep the apparatus of machinery moving. We become parts in that apparatus, separated from each other just as one cog is separated from another, mutually interdependent but at the same time kept at arm's length because of how the system is configured. The modern world increasingly resembles one large machine—moving parts, breakdowns, faceless, impersonal, and narrowly tasked—that ultimately functions as variables in capital's constant and ceaseless need for accumulation.

CHAPTER 24

# Rule of the Towns

In feudal Europe, landed gentry were the dominant political force, their lands the major source of their wealth, and what we know today as the "metropolis" did not really exist. There were places like London or Lisbon or Madrid that were "cities" to the extent that a city could and did exist then, but economic life at the time was based on agriculture and animal husbandry, with some seafaring trade in goods, food, and luxuries. In the 1500–1600s, however, economic power began to increasingly shift to banking houses, trading companies, shipbuilders, and landowners who used it to produce commodities for export. These business concerns were organized around capital accumulation and this would be made easier the closer in time/space they existed to each other, as their day-to-day operations were often with each other and others like them in other cities.

Eventually, the gentry's land became something they could sell to investors for agricultural development and trade, both regionally and globally. With the "Enclosure Laws," peasants, once tied to the land and unable to leave it without permission, were cut off from their traditional source of livelihood. The cities already in existence increasingly became centers of foreign trade as goods flowed into their harbors and storage facilities and soon they experienced an influx of migrants looking for food, work, and relief from their collapsing rural economy. Urban populations exploded while cities possessed an infrastructure unprepared for the influx of people. Modern sewage systems as we know them did not really exist, nor did modern plumbing of any real sort. Homes were overcrowded and the desperate roamed the streets in search of handouts and scraps, bits of sustenance where they could find them.

Modernity birthed urbanization, in short, which was no accident. Industrialists need banking services and factories need workers, markets, and infrastructure for export. As cities like London, Amsterdam, Venice, and Florence (among others) became financial centers, business owners found loans there for additional investment and this in turn spurred more economic development, free trade, and capital accumulation and, with them, additional urban growth and its associated population explosion. Combined, these dynamics made many cities logical places to locate production facilities. Water was harnessed for mills, shipping, and other forms of transport and also became the major avenue for waste runoff, including sewage and industrial pollution. Smog choked out the air in many places as a vast army of workers staffed the machines that kept the wheels of modernity rolling. And as cities generally did not and could not produce their own food, farmlands used to produce commodities like vegetables, animals, and wood were increasingly directed toward servicing urban life. Nation-states, with their vast bureaucracies, coalesced and changed regional and cultural relationships, developing national seats, forging laws on trade (e.g., the repeal of the Corn Laws that led to the Irish Potato Famine, etc.), adopting a dominant language for law and business, and creating standing armies that needed feeding. The rule of the towns thus made rural life subservient to urban life and rural people had to organize their lives around it.

Urban centers are loci of modern culture and modern social life. During modernity's period of rapid growth, World Fairs were held in New York, Chicago, London, Paris, St. Louis. In urban centers, one can find markets for food, clothes, and the hardware needed to navigate modern society. Migrants and immigrants constantly arrive, mix, and produce new forms of culture. Small

IMAGE 24.1 London, 1600s, by Sebastian Münster

IMAGE 24.2 Shakespeare's England, 1910, by William Winter (1836–1917)

IMAGE 24.3 Palace of Westminster from the Dome on Methodist Central Hall, by Colin

IMAGE 24.4 Super Moon Over City of London from Tate Modern, 2018, by Colin

businesses sprout like weeds and the city center becomes a locale of things, deals, transportation, intrigue, and "progress." One can find libraries, museums, and expositions displaying the new world and its technology being formed right around us. Increasingly, cities burst at the seams with more people while rural life falls further and further behind, cut off from social life, new conveniences, and up-to-date education.

To the modern city dweller, rural life can look stagnant, dull, and increasingly backward. It was this way at modernity's birth and it is still this way today. And though the city has often been the locale of the forces that have driven modernity, cities are not independent and self-sufficient. They depend on rural life for their very existence and this means that rural life is a crucial element in the survival of the city. And with the same forces that drove urbanization in the past are still with us today, more and more of the world's population have become city dwellers with an accompanying decline in those working on farmland and living in areas of low density. Like rural life, the quality of such urban areas also varies greatly, as does the level of income and standard of living city dwellers enjoy, from exclusive high rises to block apartment housing to slums and favelas. Given the structure of the modern system and how it is compelled to develop, this rule of the towns, all they have to offer, and their sense of adventure and menace are not things that will end any time soon.

CHAPTER 25

# Feverish Anxiety and Astonishment

Some things commonplace to the people experiencing them might be remarkable to others. Though many of us moderns are typically accustomed to its environs, not everyone is familiar with urban life. A transplanted person from a rural farming community may find the big city such a jarring experience that they come across as naïve, as someone unfamiliar and perplexed towards the experience. In fact, this experience of the new and the urban by traditional/rural people makes the stereotypical epithet "hayseed" or "bumpkin" possible. Though such characterizations may not always be true, they do point to the observation that the people of modernity live in and come from environments that have been shaped differently.

To stand on a street corner in a major metropolitan area can be quite an experience. One must contend with the pace of the traffic and the pedestrians, which combined create a sense of non-stop movement and activity. The noise of trains, cars, cabs, and conversations can overwhelm one's attention. Everywhere one looks they find shop windows filled with candies, cakes, meat, cheese, jewelry, shoes, and commodities of every sort and from every corner of the world. Buildings are plastered from top to bottom with advertisements, some very creative and overwhelming. As day turns into dusk turns into night, the city lights up like a Roman candle and a shift in energy changes from the daily workers traversing the streets to and from home to a raucous and rowdy night life, with its promises of excitement and even danger. The city provides a cover of anonymity that small-town rural living never can, so varieties of lifestyles, ideas, and norms blossom beyond which many imaginations can dream up. But even for someone from a garden variety major city, what is it like to be in Times Square or Piccadilly Circus for the first time? These places represented "the metropolis" multiplied. Everything said in the previous paragraph is larger, faster, bigger, more intense.

This slice of modernity is new in the human experience, so anxiety and astonishment should come as no surprise. But for some, urban life is not a new experience but rather is daily life. While a portion of this latter group adapt to such environs, others struggle with them as living in cities increasingly places pressure on mental health to the extent that individuals not only have to deal with overloaded senses, overcrowding, pollution, crime, traffic, and whatnot, but also many urban dwellers become increasingly disconnected

FEVERISH ANXIETY AND ASTONISHMENT 163

IMAGE 25.1
Christmas Illumination
Champs-Elysées, Paris, 2011,
by Didier Boy de la Tour

IMAGE 25.2
Times Square, New York
City, USA, by Francisco Diez

IMAGE 25.3
Night in Shinjuku—Tokyo,
Japan, by Martin Falbisoner

from family, lack integration into social groups that provide them meaning and a way to release daily stress (i.e., social isolation), and experience poverty and/or discrimination (e.g., residential segregation). In this sense, mental illness—especially depression and anxiety—cannot be reduced to only biological factors, as its risk is doubled by living in cities (see Srivastava 2009; Benedictus 2014; Fitzgerald, Rose, and Singh 2016; Kwon 2016; Gruebner et al. 2017; Levine 2017).

Modern urban life has rhythms and novelties all its own, that which one cannot experience elsewhere. Its experience can make us excited and shocked, impressed and repulsed. And as just seen above, it can ruin our mental health. Nevertheless, the city is a central feature of modernity, maybe its most recognizable symbol. It is physically imposing and seems to have a life of its own. It survives as people move into and out of it, as generations pass and make way for new ones. And it never seems to cease to produce a sense of astonishment and feverish anxiety.

CHAPTER 26

# Solids Melting into Air

It is easy to notice the changes human society has gone through if one uses a long period of time and the right subject matter with which to think about it. Changes in human communication—from storytelling and lore to cave paintings to messages carried by runners and on horseback to national posts, telegrams, the telephone, satellites, and cyber-technology and the Internet arc across time/space and include many different types of societies. More often than not, most people have lived in societies that changed very little, if at all, from their birth to their death. In modernity, change often occurs in such a way that it is perceptible within our own lifetimes. More than that, this fact shapes our experience in and of the world and of ourselves.

An asymptote is a graphed curve that increasingly approaches an axis but never quite manages to get there, even though the further it goes the closer it gets to that axis (Figure 26.1). If we graphed social change on an asymptote, most of human history would reflect that portion of the curve where change is slow, gradual, and hardly perceptible. Today we live at a time when that arc shoots rapidly upward, where change, rather than the exception, seems the rule. And the pace of modern change does not stay at a steady rate but rather accelerates over time, getting faster and faster. In such a condition, what we experience as solid one moment melts into air the next. Let's take a look at a few examples.

What makes something "far" from or "near" to us is not as an objective measure as one might suppose. Our sense of distance can be shaped differently in different cultural contexts. So, say, a nomadic desert dweller like the Bedouins have a sense of what counts as a "long distance to travel in a day" that is much different than someone in the modern world. But this sort of cross-cultural

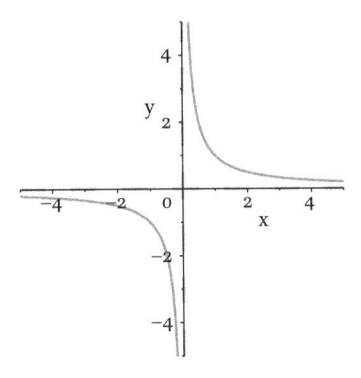

FIGURE 26.1 Asymptotes, by Kmhkmh

comparison, no matter how informative, is only a preliminary point here. Think of how modern people have experienced distance only within the last 100 years. At one time, a horse-drawn vehicle (or just the horse itself) was the dominant form of transportation and reliable roads easily traversed were not always available. A trip from one's home to "the city" might take days or weeks and required many preparations, such as caring for horses and securing food supplies and lodging (if one could get it). With the advent of trains, trollies, and cars, horses suddenly went from expeditious transportation to arduous and slow. And as the vehicles got faster, the distance we could go got longer and our sense of distance changed, as did how we prepared for our travels.[1] Similarly, from boats that had sails to coal/oil powered ships to airplanes, our experience of international travel has changed, and our sense of the world's size has thus shrunk psychically, if not physically. What is "far flung" for us today would be very different than what our grandparents considered the same way.[2]

Societies very often treat moral codes very seriously. At one time, the "virginity" of a young woman was closely guarded, whether by her, her parents, social pressures, or some combination thereof. Her future prospects as an adult depended, rightfully or wrongfully, on her ability to attract and keep a mate (and impress his parents). If she would attract a man and marry him, his future mobility conferred benefits on her both materially and socially. Thus, her virginity represented several things—e.g., her ability to delay gratification, to abide by certain cultural expectations and traditions, her treatment of her future husband's provisioning with prior restraint evidenced her ability to honor her future commitment (i.e., chastity before marriage would be assumed to be an indication of sexual fidelity during it and thus increasing the odds that

---

[1] This was an even greater concern for African-Americans traveling in the southern United States no more than a generation or two ago. As more of them gained higher incomes, they purchased cars and, like many others, traveled on vacation or to visit relatives. However, parts of the United States remained entrenched in virulent racism and many people acted on it. As such, *The Negro Motorist Green Book* (published by Victor Hugo Green from 1936–1966) advised African-Americans on what towns to avoid, where food and lodging could be obtained, where to get cars repaired, and what cities were "sundown towns" where it was best to be out of town at a certain time.

[2] Many older people in modernity perhaps remember when much of their food was seasonal and/or regional. As a boy growing up in the Cincinnati, Ohio / Northern Kentucky area in the early 1970s, I still vaguely recall when citrus baskets were sometimes given out at Christmas as a moderately expensive and seasonal gift, as oranges and grapefruit were grown in Florida and rarely available and/or cheap that far north, especially in winter months. Today, they are not only inexpensive but available year round at grocery stores because of new methods of production and transportation. Further, in the middle of winter today all over the United States one can get mangoes harvested from groves half way around the world.

any offspring were indeed co-created by her husband), and her willingness and future ability to pair-bond with one person through sexual intercourse. The point here is not whether these were either fair or reasonable norms held and followed by everyone but rather that such norms did exist and had an institutionalized logic behind them.

Eventually, with the advent of the birth control pill, the Women's Movement, and other social trends, women entered college and the workforce *en masse*, put off marriage and children, and challenged social norms that limited their sexual expression. As more people supported such changes and challenges, the rules about premarital sex, the number of sexual partners, and children out of wedlock all changed too. Today, with puberty happening sooner—around 13–15 years of age (for reasons not yet fully understood)—and age of first marriage rising—around 28–29—the social proscription to "save it" for marriage seems even *more* unrealistic. If we compare this to what grandmothers of these women were taught, the difference seems universes and cultures apart, though this change has occurred in less than 50 years.

It is increasingly unlikely that any modern person who gets married will experience any of the following: (1) their parents arranged with other parents that their children would be married to each other, (2) their wedding day will be the first time they meet their spouse, (3) their future spouse is/was a virgin on their wedding day, and (4) that the marriage will be their first and last. While arranged marriage is relatively unheard of today in Western culture, it does exist among immigrants there and in developing countries it is still common, though in decline as love marriages become more popular. Premarital sex—both acceptance of it and its practice—is also on the increase worldwide (see Chamie 2018 and references therein). And divorce in modern society has long lost its stigma and is not uncommon (between 40–50% in some countries). Marriage and the family as an institution have undergone other changes as well. We see governments stepping in for ceremonies that churches once monopolized. Single, educated, career women are increasingly having children without husbands. Same-sex marriage is increasingly accepted and legal in more of the world. All of these trends will only continue in the future. Marriage and the family and how we think about them have undergone a sea change in less than 100 years.

Think about modern notions of feminine modesty. There was a time that a woman on a public beach could be arrested for exposure of ankles, legs, or arms. This slowly changed to where only so much of a woman's leg could be seen then to eventually more dramatic changes with the bikini and the later "French cut" suit. Today, there are "thong" bathing suits that cover very little of the body and would have been scandalous and illegal less than a century

168  CHAPTER 26

IMAGE 26.1
Two Women on Beach, 1900s, by Adolf de Meyer

IMAGE 26.2  Women Walking at the Beach, 2013, by micadew

IMAGE 26.3
Women at the Beach, 2007, Ukraine, by Oleksandr Bezpalko

SOLIDS MELTING INTO AIR 169

IMAGE 26.4
Men's Fashion, 1700s

IMAGE 26.5
Humphrey Bogart, 1942, Trailer Screenshot

IMAGE 26.6
Lundi Gras in New Orleans.
Before the Start of the Red Bean
Parade, Royal Street, Lower
Faubourg Marigny, 2015

ago. Moreover, both men and women regularly post photos of themselves unclothed online for strangers to view. And, for all intents and purposes, the Internet is a public space.

The words "wigs, face powder, panty hose, and high heels" bring to mind women's fashion accessories. But they should not if we are talking about European men around the 1700s. Today, we look at those men's fashions and find them peculiar. A similar attitude arises when we look at a wedding album from 20, 30, 40 years ago and wonder how people could have worn their hair that way or could have thought their clothes looked good. True, a few styles are more resilient over time than are others—e.g., the classic tuxedo or dinner jacket—though most have only a moment in the sun and fade into obscurity—e.g., the modern hipster.

It is possible that the ground upon which you stand or sit right now, if you go back far enough in time, once did not have housing on it but instead was used for agricultural purposes. If not this, then at minimum the area in which you live certainly was more rural in the past than it is now. With modern urbanization and suburbanization have come technological growth and with all of these mass education and an increasingly literate population have grown, so much so that you are more likely now to encounter people who can read and write than you are those who cannot. The reversal of this norm is a historic achievement and has mainly come within about the last 100 years (Figure 26.2).

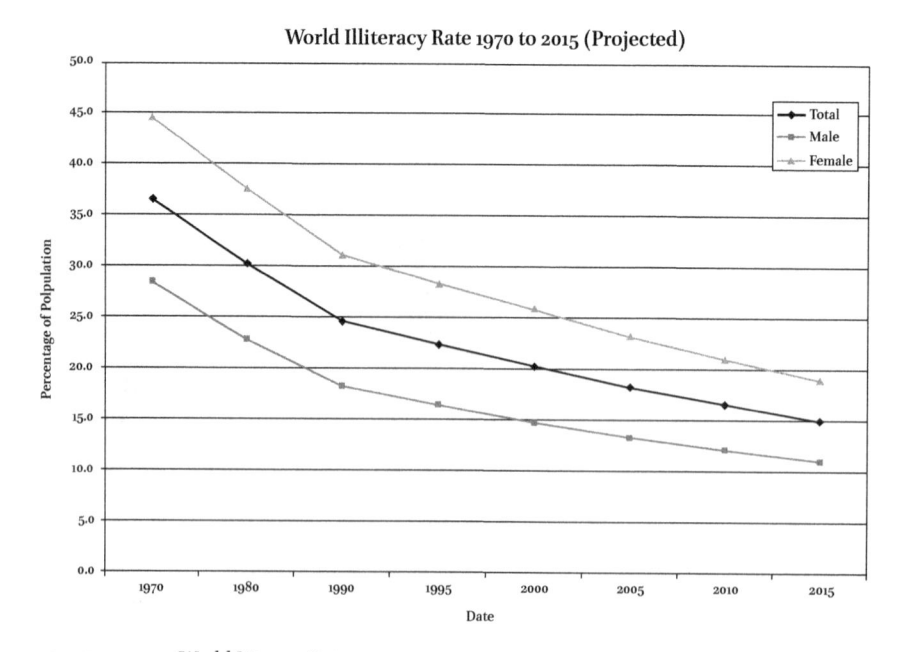

FIGURE 26.2   World Literacy Rate, 1970 to 2015

After World War II, the pace of change in modernity was worrisome for religious institutions. Post-war populations in many countries considered participation in church life less and less appealing. Some went to other churches/other religions and some went religiously AWOL altogether. In an attempt at stemming the tide, the Catholic Church held the Second Vatican Council (or Vatican II for short) and instituted several changes: Mass could be said in the local language instead of Latin; priestly garb's ornamentation was reduced; Eucharistic prayers were revised; priests could face the congregation rather than east (where god supposedly was); and changes in liturgical music. This path was not without controversy, especially among the older generation. However, the changes stuck and for a child growing up Catholic today these changes feel like the way Catholic faith and practice have always been.

State boundaries have shifted regularly over time. Take a look at the various configurations of Europe depicted on maps at 100-year increments (Maps 26.1–26.8). One notices the maturation of feudal Europe, the rise and fall of states, and the shifting of their borders with capitalist development and regional wars. As interesting as these maps of Europe's transformations are, they are also revealing for what they leave out. Can you identify what that is? The maps between 1900 and 2000 make it look like the entire Soviet Bloc and the Cold War never existed. The former USSR occupied one of the world's largest land masses and, perhaps outside the rise and defeat of the Axis powers, its competition against the liberal democracies of the capitalist sphere was *the* defining feature of twentieth century geo-political history. Its defenders, allies, and enemies saw the Soviet Union as a great communist bear, one not easily defeated, and whose influence would project forward indefinitely into the future. The idea that by the 1990s-2000, it too would melt into air would be a hard proposition for an adult or even a child of the 1950s, 1960s, 1970s, or 1980s to believe.

As stated by "Moore's Law," in our age the number of transistors in a dense integrated circuit doubles about every two years (see Figure 26.3). Computers were once few, roughly the size of a small room, and with low to modest computational ability. Over time, computers shrank and got more powerful and soon it seemed as if every business was using them. By the 1990s, electronic stores regularly published full-page newspaper ads with sales bargains for hand-held stereos, digital clock-radios, calculators, computers, mobile cellular phones, portable music players, video recorders, answering machines, and voice recorders.[3] Each of these gadgets were not only separate items but

---

3 A well-known example of this has made the rounds on the Internet at multiple sites. You can find a copy of this 1991 Radio Shack ad at this link: https://imgur.com/gallery/koXqycM.

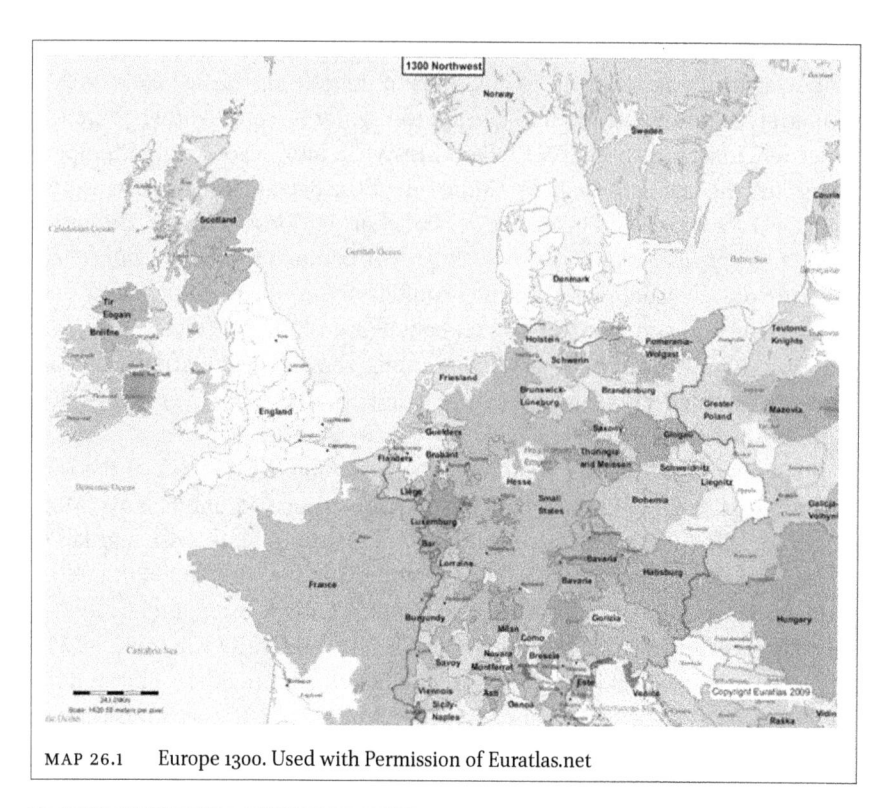

MAP 26.1   Europe 1300. Used with Permission of Euratlas.net

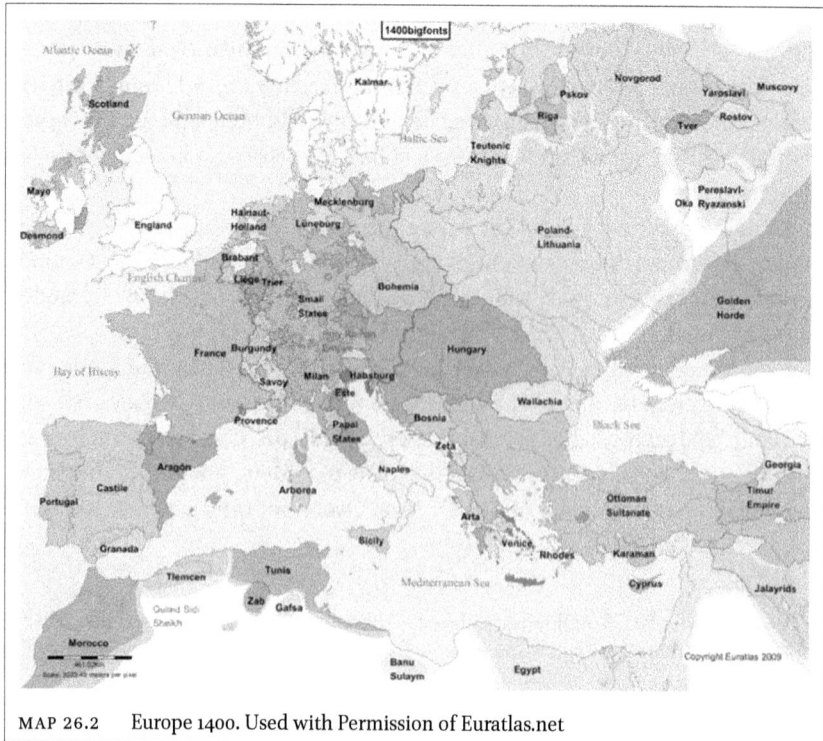

MAP 26.2   Europe 1400. Used with Permission of Euratlas.net

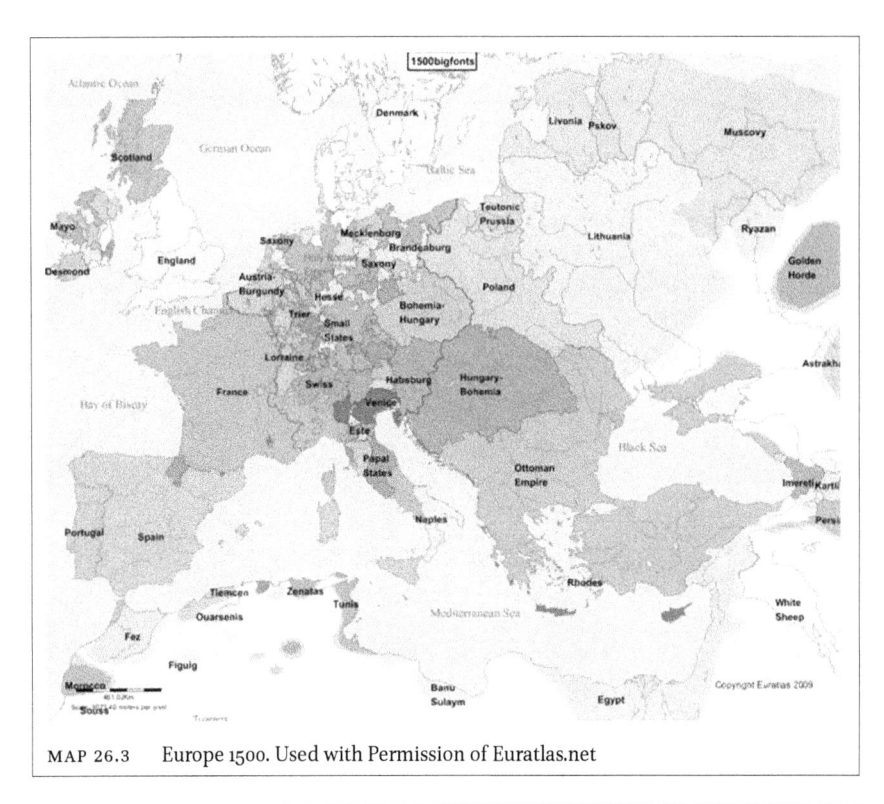

SOLIDS MELTING INTO AIR 173

MAP 26.3    Europe 1500. Used with Permission of Euratlas.net

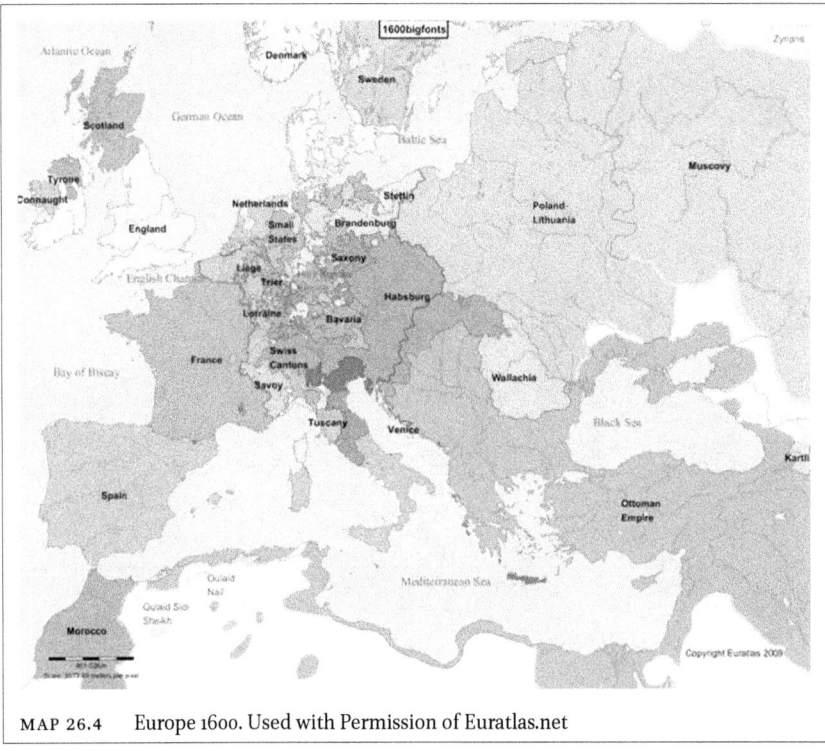

MAP 26.4    Europe 1600. Used with Permission of Euratlas.net

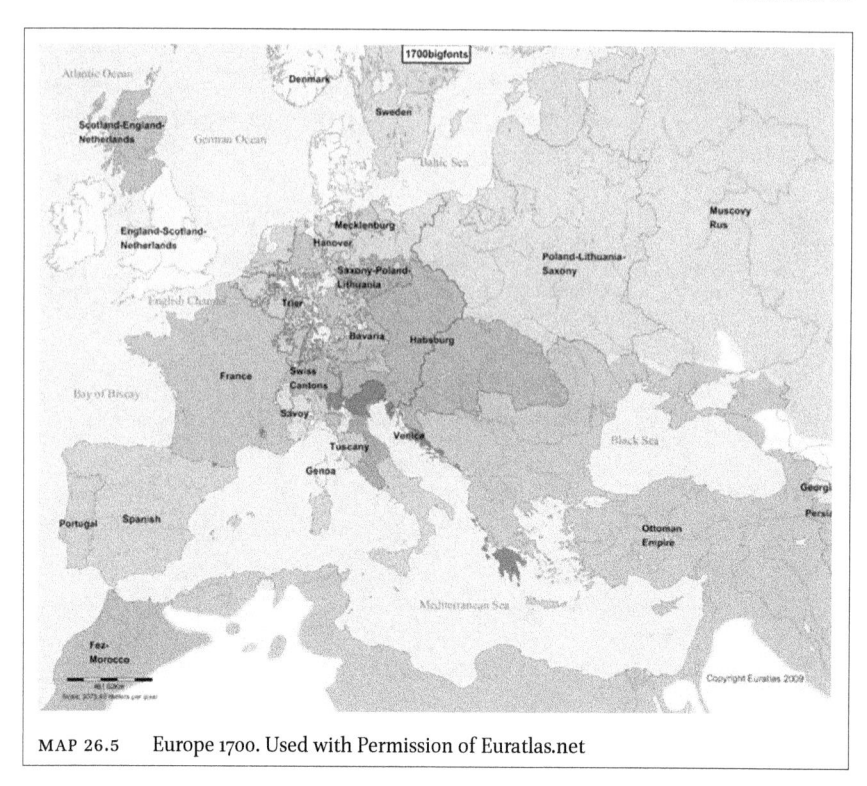

MAP 26.5   Europe 1700. Used with Permission of Euratlas.net

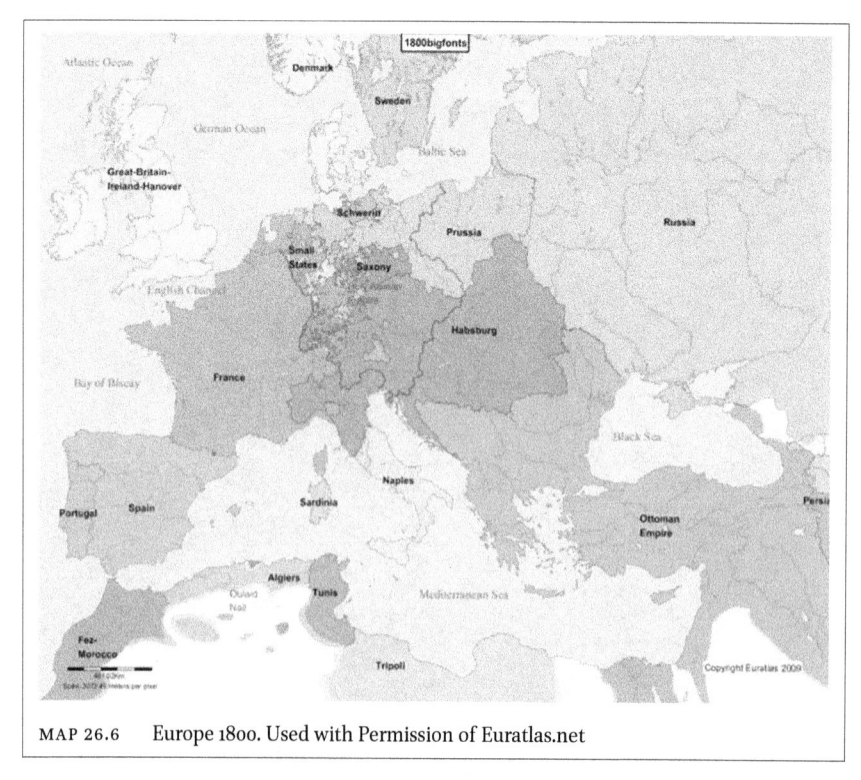

MAP 26.6   Europe 1800. Used with Permission of Euratlas.net

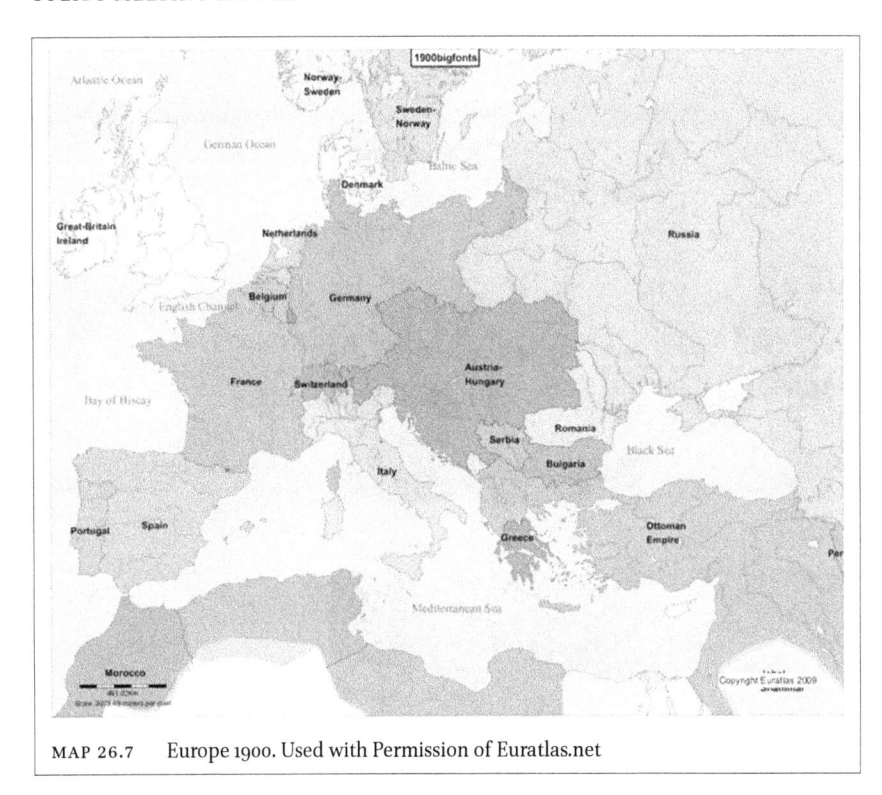

# SOLIDS MELTING INTO AIR

MAP 26.7  Europe 1900. Used with Permission of Euratlas.net

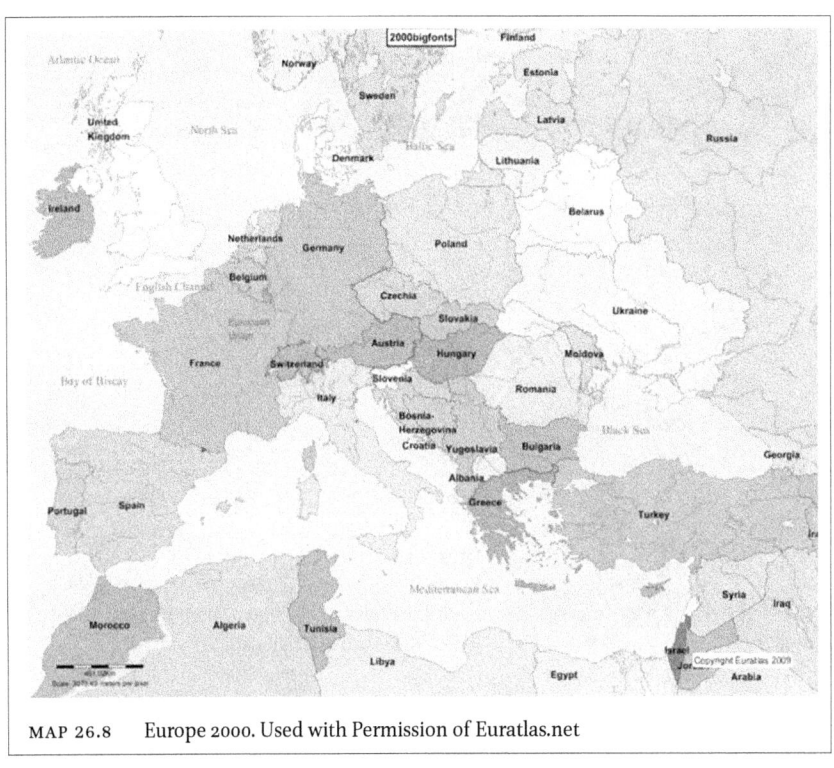

MAP 26.8  Europe 2000. Used with Permission of Euratlas.net

IMAGE 26.7
Early US Census Machines, 1960

IMAGE 26.8
Firing Room 2, Launch Control Center, Apollo 12, November 14, 1969

IMAGE 26.9
Young Woman with Cellphone—Outside Sheikh Lotfollah Mosque—Isfahan—Iran, 2012, by Adam Jones (Kelowna, BC, Canada)

SOLIDS MELTING INTO AIR                                                177

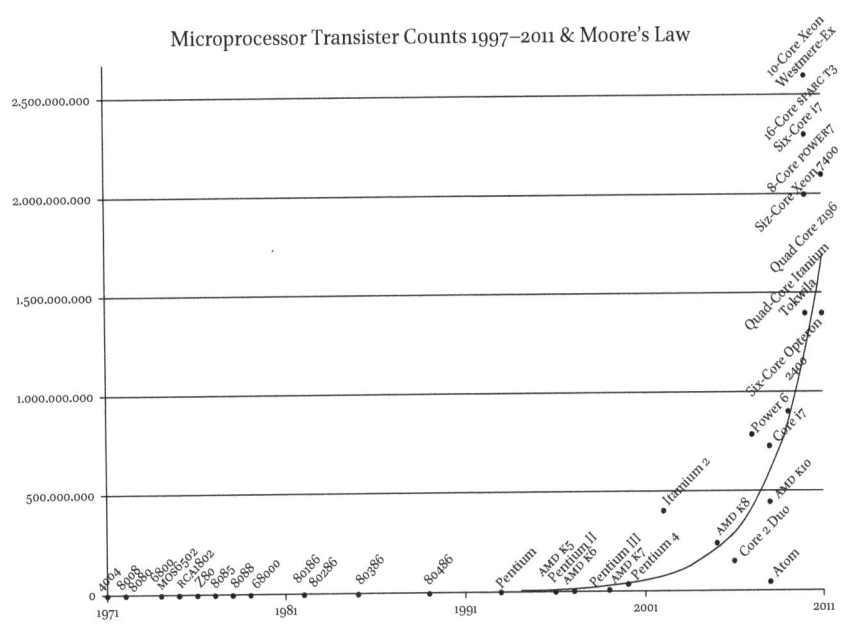

FIGURE 26.3   Microprocessor Transistor Counts 1997–2011 and Moore's Law
PLOT OF CPU TRANSISTOR COUNTS AGAINST DATES OF INTRODUC-
TION. NOTE THE LINEAL VERTICAL SCALE; THE LINE CORRESPONDS TO
EXPONENTIAL GROWTH WITH TRANSISTOR COUNT DOUBLING EVERY TWO
YEARS (BY BENZIRPI).

the cost of all of them in 2018 dollars would be between $5,000-$6,000. By 2018, however, one could buy them for about $800 in a new cell phone or for around $100 in a used one. Speaking of cell phones, NASA's computing power not only during the first Apollo missions but also with their Voyager 1 and 2 expeditions was significantly less than that of modern cell phones.[4] And today, not only adults but almost every teenager, and even pre-teens in some places, has a cell phone, not only in wealthy societies but in much of the world. As an adjunct, not only has the size, speed, and utility of our computer technologies rapidly increased in the late twentieth and early twenty-first centuries, but the amount of *knowledge* produced in this era has increased even faster. We are producing knowledge in ten years that used to take hundreds of years. And it is speeding up in a trajectory of an asymptote.

---

4   According to NASA, Voyager 1 and Voyager 2 have 69.63 kilobytes of memory each. An iPhone 5, with 16 gigabytes of memory, has about 240,000x the memory of a Voyager spacecraft. You can find this information at NASA's link here (URL retrieved September 3, 2018): https://www.nasa.gov/mission_pages/voyager/multimedia/vgrmemory.html#.W19tUtVKjIU.

What will it be like to experience the world in 10, 20, 30 years? How fast will styles and morals change? What rules that seem sacrosanct today will be forgotten tomorrow? Will the pace of change continue its upward climb until it is so fast that people are unable to find *any* footing? Given our long evolutionary history in more stable systems, what will the future pace of change do to our psyches, social relations, and political, spiritual, and religious beliefs? These are questions whose answers we cannot foretell. But one certainty in modernity is that change is the norm and what that change will look like is uncertain. In such an accelerating world, will we become more susceptible to those who play on our fears, who promise us stability and certainty? What sort of brave new world lies ahead?

CHAPTER 27

# Civilization and Barbarism

In early modernity, it was often characterized as "civilization," with pre-modern societies being seen as "primitive," "savage" or even "barbaric." Civilized society was technologically complex, regulated by the rule of law, and honored a singular true god. Civilized people are modest, dress in clean clothes, eat farmed food, are literate, studious and hardworking. They live in housing with bedrooms, indoor plumbing, a bathroom and kitchen. Barbarism was the life of the savage living in the outback or hinterlands, barely clothed, ignorant, lascivious and licentious, eating meat raw, unleashing violence on neighbors, believing in magic and/or gods that do not exist except in their superstitious minds. The comparison gave modern people a sense of moral superiority about themselves and their society, one which they felt lucky to be born into. Though people think this way less so today somewhat, the juxtaposition of these two ideas is not without its insights.

How accurately, first off, is this characterization of pre-modern people? The depiction of the "savage" evokes a being somewhat out of control, beastly, hardly human, and one that needs either the taming influence of civilization or, barring that, elimination as a threat to it. Even early anthropologists had a difficult time pulling away from such a view, as Bronislaw Malinowski titled his classic, *The Sex Life of Savages of North-Western Melanesia*. Eventually that discipline reined in its terminology for and understanding of "primitive" people and explained to us that we find hunter-gatherer and tribal societies to be the most common forms of human organization historically speaking. Should they find themselves blessed with abundance of resources and/or relative isolation from other groups, many of these peoples live lives one might call peaceful or at least somewhat harmonious. Though we should not over-romanticize the idea of the "noble savage"—especially because life did pose its problems, their understanding of the world was often wildly inaccurate, and they could in fact be violent when necessary—any depiction of such people as some sort of atavistic monsters tells us more about those viewing pre-modern people than it does about those pre-modern people themselves.

A cousin of the pre-modern as "savage" is the "barbarian," as in "barbarians at the gates" laying siege to the city. Such groups were not known for simple hunting-gathering or placid village life but for pillage and plunder. Several groups, including the Vandals and the Visigoths, sacked Rome on more than one occasion. Coming out of the steppes of Asia, Genghis Kahn and his Mongol "horde" are still infamous today, associated with wanton violence, cruelty, and conquest (though we make better sense of their practices if we consider this was a society based on cattle herding for food, clothes, and wealth generally). A seaside village in (what is today) England or Ireland might wake to the shock of longboats pulling shore full of armed Norse Vikings bent on killing the inhabitants, looting their food and goods, and maybe even kidnapping women. The "barbarian," then, is not meant to depict the proto-human, atavistic savage but instead to capture the personage of the unethical, avaricious marauder who shows lack of empathy for and humanity to his targets and earns his wealth through violent (thus illegitimate) means.

By extension, as a literary flourish and potential reality, "barbarism" is the threat posed by the breakdown of civilization, or so say modernity's spokespersons. Modernity is that period when humanity harnessed technology and science to conquer nature. Modernity is that period where industrial productivity, mass agriculture, and free trade find humanity conquering privation and want. Modernity is that period where enlightened inquiry and mass literacy conquer ignorance, stupidity, and superstition. Modernity is that period where the extension of the franchise and the rule of law conquer outdated notions of royalty and despotism. Civilization, as a result, must be defended lest we court our own destruction by allowing barbarism to rise once again. Civilization tames the beast.

For the citizen of civilization, these are comforting notions as they are not totally illusory or wholly invented. Civilization does have many of the traits depicted above and it has had its successes and victories for which its members should be proud and guard jealously. Just think of how easy modern people can get clean water or speak their mind without government or religious repression. These things above are significant achievements that most modern people today take for granted—until compromised, that is. The problem with the "civilization versus barbarism" image, however, is that, first, the depiction comes into play when the game is already half over. How did "civilized" society come to be? What methods did it take to get it established? Second, is there anything about our current modern system that this depiction overlooks? In answering these questions, one finds that "civilization," with all its benefits, often offers a rather self-congratulatory depiction of itself that neglects many inconvenient facts.

Look at Image 27.1. It is both iconic and telling. What do you see? This picture was taken in 1868 in the western United States (or what would eventually become states in the then Western Territories). The person standing there is native to the land and is looking at the now completed Transcontinental Railroad. This, settlers, technology, government expansion, and the US Calvary

IMAGE 27.1 Native American Looks Out Over Transcontinental Railroad, Western Territories (USA), 1867, by Alfred Hart

basically sealed the fate of this person's people and culture. The people living there and their culture were destroyed in a process that saw the forces of modernity grow and prosper. It has been called a "genocide" and this strong term has its merits. Native peoples were killed outright, and their land was stolen, in the United States as well as in Canada, New Zealand, and Australia, just to name a few. This is not to say that many indigenous tribes did not have war-like relations with each other; they did. The point is that when we look at the list of characteristics outlined above, it was the use of the techniques of "barbarism" by "civilization" that allowed the latter to grow and thrive in the first place.

This is not an isolated case. The transatlantic slave trade was the back upon which significant portions of early modern development was carried. Spanish, Portuguese, Dutch, British, French, and American colonies all participated in slavery and sent the boodle they pillaged in their colonies back home for personal and national enrichment. It is impossible to name how many native peoples world over died in the process, but we do know that "civilization" was built by either enslaving, killing, or assimilating multiple native peoples. This project has by now been relatively accomplished in much of the world and to

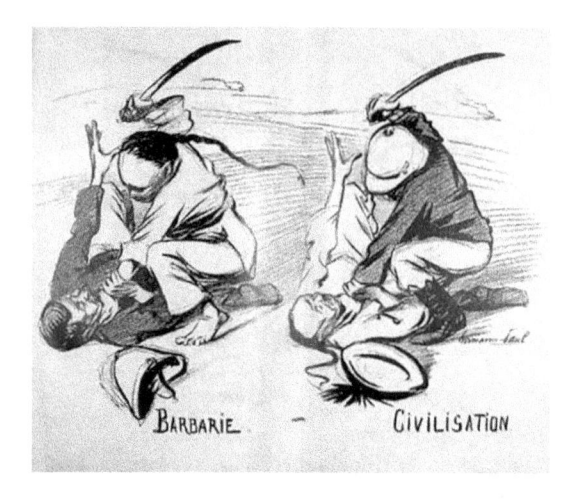

IMAGE 27.2
Barbarie and Civilisation—
Drawing from 1900

simply point out the advances and benefits of modernity without acknowledging this part of the story is to tell a story so incomplete that it verges on a fable.

What about the behavior we find *in* "civilized" society toward people that are disadvantaged? Canada and Australia rival the United States in their removal of indigenous people from their lands, the theft of their children, and negation of their cultural traditions. The Nazis adopted eugenics from the United States and set out to sterilize those deemed too mentally feeble or physically unfit to reproduce and took this beginning and weaponized it towards Poles and Czechs, Jews and homosexuals, and others. The Reich's reign was *planned on* land theft and mass killing. In just the last 80 years, we have witnessed lynching of African-Americans and the internment of Japanese Americans in concentration camps in the United States, use of concentration camps by the British in Kenya, mass killing and the theft of land in Central America by US sponsored terrorist groups, a policy for the benefit of multinational capital. China gunned down its own citizens in 1989 for the crime of simply asking for more say in government representation via protesting at Tiananmen Square.

Also, in the 1980s-1990s, the United States continued its historical meddling in the Middle East, the Persian Gulf, and the Pacific Rim. It supported both sides of the Iran-Iraq war (1980–1988), providing the latter poison gas to use in its fight. It supported murderous dictators in Indonesia and Saudi Arabia, among other places. After the United States pushed Saddam Hussein's forces out of Kuwait (1990–1991), US representatives worked with the United Nations to place sanctions on the regime and, by extension, the country. Limitations were put on exports of oil for food, as well as imports. The country, not unexpectedly, ran low on food, medicine, and clean water. In response to claims that around 500,000 children were estimated to have died because of such sanctions and other fallout from the war (a *British Medical Journal* study later claimed such numbers were based on dodgy data collection and analysis), US Ambassador to the UN, Madeleine Albright (later Secretary of State under President Bill Clinton) said, "we think the price is worth it" (*60 Minutes*, May 12, 1996), a claim she later argued (in *Madam Secretary: A Memoir*) was "something she did not mean."

Not only has civilization behaved in barbaric ways against its opponents (modern or otherwise), but when the structure of civilization breaks down it can devolve into a barbarism of the most extreme kind. Prior to World War II, Japan invaded China as part of the Second Sino-Japanese War. Japan's ransacking of Nanking was not limited to military targets but included the killing and rape of civilians caught in the crossfire, even those the Japanese encountered on the road from Shanghai to Nanking. During World War II, the Japanese ran Unit 731, which engaged in chemical and biological weapons research on men, women, and children, often on Chinese as well as Russian, Korean, Mongolian and Allied POWs. Deaths were estimated to be over 200,000 (Kristof 1995; Harris 2002; Keiichi 2005). During its closing and after the war, many German women chose suicide as an option as Soviet forces occupied their cities and towns due to the fear, and reality, of the mass rapes that were expected and did occur (Teo 1996; Beevor 2002; Ash 2015). Later in the century, Yugoslavia, caught in the disbanding of the Soviet Union and the Eastern Bloc, broke up in 1990 and divided along ethnic lines. In the process, war broke out between the Republic of Bosnia and Herzegovina and Bosnian Serb and Croat forces (supplied by Serbia and Croatia). The former capital and 1984 Olympic host, Sarajevo, was torn to pieces and atrocities on both sides commenced, including ethnic cleansing and mass killings (over 100,000 killed). Civilization turned into barbarism once again, with World War II style violence and massacres just across from the Italian Peninsula and near the heart of a Europe that wanted to believe such days were in its past.

Barbarism also awaits us "internally," as it were. Today, many of the clothes and gadgets enjoyed by "civilized" peoples are made in sweatshops, both near and far. People living in the developed world whose ancestors were brought there through slavery still suffer a disproportionate amount of poverty, imprisonment, and early death. Across our social classes in the modern world, the rates of obesity continue to rise, reflecting a hoarding of the world's calorie supply. We wantonly discard our wastes as if producing trash was a birthright. Our forms of entertainment increasingly devolve from reading well produced literature to watching reality television, listening to racist radio jocks spouting political invective, and spending billions of dollars on the circus we call "sports." While we once accused the "savage" of having uncontrolled sexual

IMAGE 27.3 1984 Winter Olympics Opening Ceremony at Koševo Stadium, Sarajevo, by BiHVolim

IMAGE 27.4
Government Building Burns After Being Hit by Tank Fire, Sarajevo, 1992, by Mikhail Evstafiev

drives, today we find that, instead of an "information superhighway," the Internet has turned into a pornography delivery device, as porn is one of the largest users of bandwidth and the wealthier countries are among its largest consumers.

Humans behaving in barbaric ways is not specific to a time or place. It results when social relations and institutional forces either breakdown or are as such where the powers that be can act with impunity, allowing for people to unleash violent behavior upon others without fear of retribution or consequence. It can be suppressed or encouraged by social-systemic developments, whether in forging them or in their dissolution. After years of Hugo Chavez's putatively socialist rule and the attacks upon it from the United States (among others), Venezuela today still has an obstinate and obdurate ruling class, suffers from free market experiments, and experiences hyperinflation, scarcity, and social breakdown. As such, a UN human rights commission described the rule of law there as "virtually absent" and concluded that its security forces participated in extra-judicial killings, torture, and arbitrary detention (United Nations 2018). Testimony collected by UN human rights experts in the Congo describe atrocities committed by rebels and government troops there that include mass rape, forced rape of relatives, cannibalism, and dismemberment (Miles 2018). There are reports that the Chinese have forced more than a million Uyghurs into concentration camps, having previously taken over their land, cultivated a Chinese population there, banned their language and religion, and demolished their mosques (Tohti 2018).

The forging of modernity via the colonial project required extensive violence, as capitalism as a system pits the strong against the weak, the rich against the poor, the favored races against the degraded ones. It makes community ties hard to establish and undermines the ones that exist. It rewards the avaricious. Left unchecked by other forces, capitalism has unleashed barbarism upon us in the past, all the while telling us that "they" are the barbarous tribes and "we" are the keepers of civilization. And even feudalism contained a barbarism in need of taming, as royal caprice and avarice was replaced with law, courts, and trials. But however soothing this story may be, our civilization was, nevertheless, built upon doing to the barbarous tribes what we feared they would do to us, all the while our own civilization and behavior increasingly resembles what we have been told to fear. Should those elements of civilization that keep a modicum of social order fail us, barbarism anew stands in the waiting.

CHAPTER 28

# Celebrating Orgies, Blood, and Fire

On March 25, 1911, the Triangle Shirtwaist Factory caught on fire. It was located on the eighth, ninth, and tenth floors of a building just east of Washington Square in New York City. The owners often locked the doors to the stairwells and exits to prevent unauthorized breaks and thefts. Unable to escape the smoke and flames, 146 garment workers (123 women and 23 men), many recent immigrants, died from smoke inhalation, fire, or from jumping to their deaths. It was the city's largest in industrial disaster at that point (see Images 28.1 and 28.2).

If capitalist development was something that simply and naturally springs forth from the practice of producing, selling, and buying—and thus the product of our biology—then to critique it or suggest it is anything but natural is to talk about a fantasy world that denies reality. But capitalist development required extensive violence to forge into place and the function of conventional

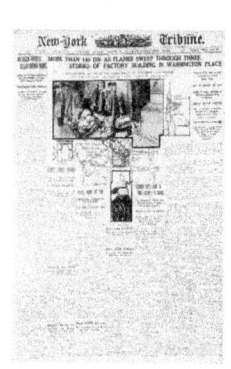

IMAGE 28.1
Triangle Shirtwaist Fire, Front Page, *New York Tribune*, March 26, 1911

IMAGE 28.2
Bodies of Workers Who Jumped from Windows to Escape the Triangle Shirtwaist Fire, 1911, by Brown Brothers

thought—whether institutionalized in the media or the academy or the state—is to mediate between the actual practice of historical capitalism and the prospect that its machinations be uncovered, seen through, criticized, and/or rejected. All of this said, the violence needed to put capitalism in place and to keep it there stands at contrasting odds with the celebratory views and words of its spokespersons.[1]

Looking for a new route to Asia (the Turks had cut off more convenient eastern routes), Columbus found financial backers, took a risk, and, in 1492, sailed west. After a few months he hit ground in what we today call "the Bahamas" (and in miscalculating the Earth's size and thinking he was in India, he gave the name "Indians" to the people living there). After this initial and then later ventures, his record there was one of extensive killing, maiming, rape, theft, and slavery. That is not hyperbole. People native to the land were forced to gather gold and had limbs amputated should they not fulfill their quota. His men sexually assaulted women, sometimes killing them afterward. Unable to get him as much gold as he wanted, many people found themselves shackled, placed on ships, and transported back to Europe as slaves. Within a few decades, the inhabitants on some islands—originally numbering in the tens of thousands—had been reduced to basically zero. This was the initial salvo of Spanish, Portuguese, Dutch, French, English, and later American colonization of the region.

Established just after 1600, the Dutch East India Company, perhaps the first multinational corporation, specialized in trade and colonization in Asia, sending over one million Europeans in over four-thousand ships. As an organization, it was close to being its own state-power, with the ability to print coins, sell stocks, imprison people, execute prisoners, and make treaties and even war. Lasting almost 200 years, the company specialized in the spice trade and took land from India, Africa, Sumatra, Cambodia, and Indonesia (among other places). In the process, an uncountable number of people were displaced and/or killed outright. Nevertheless, the company was a crucial component in elevating the Netherlands into one of the dominant economic powers of the time.

In the middle 1600s, the Dutch brought sugar from Brazil to the West Indies. Over the next two centuries, sugar plantations would supplant cotton and tobacco concerns in Barbados and eventually spread throughout the Caribbean (including Martinique, Grenada, Saint Croix, Saint Domingue [Haiti], Cuba, and other islands). Given the low level of technology available at the time, the

---

1 Much of the information in the following section comes from the work of Zinn (1980), Wolff (2007), and Chomsky (2015).

IMAGE 28.3
Taino (Arawak) Genocide via Columbus's Conquest in Cuba, by Theodor de Bry

IMAGE 28.4
Punishment Meted Out by Columbus for Failing to Meet Gold Quotas, by Theodor de Bry

IMAGE 28.5
Natives of Arrakan Sell Slaves to the Dutch East India Company at Pipely/Baliapal (in Orissa), January 1663, by Wouter Schouten

vast majority of this endeavor was built on the backs of slaves from Africa, who increased in number as the size of sugar plantations grew. Overwork, disease, and malnutrition resulted in the death rate of slaves being higher than their birth rates. Because of this, plantation owners depended on a constant supply of new slaves being imported to sustain their business model.

During the Industrial Revolution, many regions on both sides of the Atlantic Ocean were transformed from dependence on agrarian work to a dependence on machine work. Labor in such factories was often hot, dirty, exhausting, dangerous, and none-too-seldom fatal. In London and New England, textiles and flour were two of the main goods produced. Often relying on child labor and that of young women, the working conditions in these new industrial facilities were so severe that some referred to them as "Satanic Mills." A new era was emerging in modernity, one based on industrial technology where human beings were often consumed by machines along with the natural resources fed into them.

The eastern Appalachian Mountain range in the United States extends from New England to Georgia. It was originally home to numerous groups of original peoples. It also became home to westward travelers and some malcontents fleeing the eastern cities of early colonial America. It is filled with old-growth forests, natural beauty, foothills and vistas, waterways, and widely sought-after ores, especially coal. "King coal" attracted investors from the outside and it would fuel the American Industrial Revolution, just as coal from Wales fed the British industrial machine. Initially supplying their mines with immigrants and the poorly educated, operators found their workers would put up resistance to dangerous conditions, child labor, and the company scrip forced upon them. So needed was the labor that agencies such as the Pinkertons as well as the federal government unleashed bullets and bombs to squelch unionizing, which would later become a right of workers everywhere in the country. Today, the region remains resource rich and money poor, welfare and drug dependent. Religion thrives.

The American corporation, The United Fruit Company (officially formed in 1899), came to control plantations and transportation facilities in Central America (Costa Rica, Honduras, Guatemala), Colombia, Ecuador, and the West Indies. Accompanying this control were deals with military authorities, bribery, worker exploitation and oppression, espionage, suppression of people's organizations and revolt, and so on. They backed dictatorial military juntas

IMAGE 28.6
Child Coal Miners, West Virginia, 1908, by Lewis Wickes Hine

which participated in killings, disappearances, and suppression of democratic initiatives (also see Schlesinger and Kinzer 2005). This was not the only US company or foreign enterprise to invest in the region, meddle in its politics, and cozy up to repressive regimes, as this was a general pattern for the US approach to the countries of the area.

After negotiations with Germany in the early-mid 1880s, the British established control of Kenya and by the early 1900s, the region was being inundated with white settlers. Its people—especially the Kikuyu—reacted predictably with various forms of resistance. One movement, the Mau Mau Uprising, and the British reaction to it, set off a spiraling sequence of violence, which included land seizures, massacres, and concentration camps. As the settlements increased, so did the need for cheap, local labor in order to produce the cash crops the British desired. By the 1950s, the Mau Mau rebellion on the Kenyan side upped the ante on violence and resistance and atrocities on both sides commenced. Tens of thousands of Kenyans were killed, maimed, captured, detained, and/or brought to trial. The British even bombed forests where people hid. Failing to stamp out the resistance, the British officially withdrew in 1963 (also see BBC News 2011).

Similar stories could be told about the British in Rhodesia, the French in Algeria, and the Belgians in the Congo.

In the mid/late 1960s, the US Central Intelligence Agency began undermining the Sukarno regime in Indonesia because it had not opened up the archipelago fast enough to Western investment. Their activity ultimately helped overthrow Sukarno's regime, with up to one million people losing their lives, something the CIA admitted, and Western media celebrated. Within a few years, the newly installed Suharto regime decided to take East Timor, a nearby island nation and former Portuguese colony. Though Indonesia had previously admitted it had no claim to it, the problem was that (1) East Timor had plenty of resources (timber, minerals, oil, natural gas) and (2) Indonesia feared a free Timor would inspire other people within Indonesia's vast collection of islands to also seek independence. With knowledge and help of Western powers, Indonesia invaded, killed mass numbers of people, annexed the island, and declared itself the sovereign ruler. Between 1974 and the 1990s, over one-third of the Timorese were killed, women were sterilized, villages starved, and indigenous religions and languages were banned, among other crimes. The United States, England, France, and other Western leaders provided arms and political cover (also see Jardine 1996). In John Pilger's documentary, *Death of a Nation*, one can observe footage of powerbrokers and Western energy representatives celebrating their good fortune with champagne as they fly over the Timor Gap while finalizing an exploration, export, and trade deal.

Starting in the 1950s, Royal Dutch Shell started drilling for oil in Nigeria. In the 1990s members of the Ogoni Tribe protested the company's activities, especially their environmental record. Documents from the 1990s (released in 2009) showed that Shell made regular payments to the Nigerian military in order to prevent and/or put down the Ogoni protests (Vidal 2011). The Nigerian military was later accused of summary executions, torture, and arbitrary arrest and detentions. Reflecting just a modicum of its involvement, Shell paid out $15.5 million to settle a case involving the killing of protest leader, Ken Saro-Wiwa (eight other leaders of the tribe were also hanged) (Pilkington 2009).

In 1970, the people of Chile elected Salvador Allende, a physician, to their highest office. He would be killed in a coup within a few years. His crime? He was a socialist who determined that the land and natural resources of Chile should be used for the benefit of its citizens and not that of foreign multinational corporations. The military junta that took over the country was led by Augusto Pinochet. Thousands of people were rounded up—often in local soccer stadiums—arrested and disappeared. Estimates range from over 25,000 arrested, about 3,000 killed, and others tortured and/or exiled. Henry Kissinger, US Secretary of State at the time, perhaps summed up the leading attitude among Washington powerbrokers when he said, "I don't see why we need to stand by and watch a country go communist due to the irresponsibility of its people. The issues are much too important for the Chilean voters to be left to decide for themselves" (cited in Fagen 1975).

Nicaragua, too, once made the similar mistake of electing a socialist, Daniel Ortega, to its highest office (in 1979). He was buoyed by wide national support for his rebel cohorts, the Sandinistas. He initiated multiple reforms, features of which included repatriating national land and resources and demanding that foreign multinational corporations leave the country. In response, local elites and the Reagan administration sponsored the creation of a mercenary army, the Contras, to overthrow his government. One of their key tools was terrorizing villages and towns. Documented in the process was nothing less than rape, murder, and the disappearing of women, children, nuns, union leaders, teachers, and local activists. To top it all off, when the US Congress cut off funds for the Contras between 1982–1984 (The Boland Amendment), the CIA participated in shipping arms to Iran and in drug running with Contra rebels to pay for their operations, with cocaine ending up back in the United States (Cockburn 1998; Webb 1998). Similar events transpired in El Salvador, Honduras, and Guatemala in the same period.

After decades of military rule, Bolivia came under civilian government in 1982. However, they soon experienced hyperinflation and appealed to the

World Bank for assistance, which they would do several times in the next two decades. World Bank loans required Bolivia to privatize airlines, energy systems, railways, and communications. In the late 1990s, Aguas del Tunari, along with a joint-venture with Bechtel, proceeded on a project to build a dam and privatize the city of Cochabamba's water supply. It was claimed that the dam would provide not only greater water access but electricity as well. However, given that several previous years saw little to no rate hikes, and given that community norms allowed peasants and farmers access to traditional resources, it would be difficult to complete the project with the already established revenue stream. Upon receiving the contract, Aguas del Tunari agreed to pay the debt of the previous water system, complete the dam, and expand the system, but this would require an increase in water price rates, which went up to $20 a month, more than what many people spent on food with their $100 per month incomes. Protests quickly started in the city in January of 2000 and included irrigation workers, sweatshop employees, street vendors, as well as street children and others. Over the next several months, the people of the city would experience tear gas, rubber bullets, mass arrests, injuries, and death. Though protestors were ultimately victorious, the water system was not updated and much of the remaining infrastructure remained in the hands of private contractors (also see Sadiq n.d.).

After the 2001, September 11th terrorist attacks in Washington D.C. and New York City—officially attributed to several Saudi nationals and their allies—the Bush administration directed the military the United States to attack Afghanistan and later Iraq. While the former had supposedly provided safe-haven to Osama bin Laden (suspected mastermind behind the Sept. 11th attacks) under Taliban leadership, the latter (Iraq) had no ties whatsoever to the terrorists and/or the violence wrought on US soil. After the war against Iraq, Paul Bremmer, head of the Coalition Provisional Authority, signed several directives that privatized much of its economy and took bids from international oil and gas conglomerates for control of the oil fields. After disbanding the Iraqi army and failing to provide for the population, Sunnis and Shiites soon turned on each other, unleashing unspeakable violence. The oil, however, continued to flow to international markets. Over one million were estimated dead in the wake of these events (e.g., the British medical journal, *Lancet*, estimated almost 655,000 deaths by 2006 in the Iraq War alone). The terrorist movement, ISIS, grew out of the wake of this boondoggle.

Market "mechanisms" and the global commodity trade are not things that just sort of happen when people are "free" to truck, barter, and trade. Capitalism's leading stewards have unleashed orgies of blood and fire in pursuit of their economic interests and have done so in a way that goes beyond the drive for profits and capital accumulation and becomes indistinguishable from simple greed. This chapter has highlighted only a few instances of this. As a case in point, on September 3, 1991, the Imperial Foods chicken processing plant in Hamlet, North Carolina, caught fire. Because of locked doors to prevent thefts, 25 people died from smoke and flames and another 55 were injured in North Carolina's worst industrial disaster. It was as if the Triangle Shirtwaist Factory fire was replayed, just at a different time and place but a tragedy for similar reasons nonetheless.

CHAPTER 29

# Bureaucracy and the Bureaucrats

In a way very similar to the asymptotic curve of technological growth we observed earlier (Chapter 26), the human population skyrocketed around the time of and after the Industrial Revolution. How is one to efficiently organize these masses into productive activities? How can a business build and staff the machines that produce textiles or transportation on a large scale? How are societies to organize health care, postal delivery, and the educational system? How are states to shape its agencies and its military? And how are these things to be done in an orderly and predictable manner so that the goals of these institutions are met?

In modernity, as sociologist Max Weber long ago noted (see his essay "Bureaucracy"), bureaucratic organization promised an answer to such questions. Create a hierarchy of offices. Allot more physical labor, lower status, and lower pay at the bottom and more mental and symbolic labor, higher status and pay at the top. Place some layers in between. Create offices in each layer with jurisdictional authority and supervision over responsibilities. Allow for performance examinations and career advancement to encourage hard work and increase the odds that talented workers find their way into positions that can best use them. So ubiquitous are these ways of arranging organizations that bureaucracies seem to be a natural, normal, and an unexceptional state of things. Or, at least they seem this way to our modern eyes and minds. But they are not. They are not so much as "unnatural" (as in false or artificial) as they are a non-natural human invention for particular times, places, and goals.

Bureaucracies seem like a necessary nuisance needed to organize and to serve social needs and stability. That they do. They also make sure authority rests in offices, policies, regulations, and laws, rather than in the idiosyncratic whims of a specific person or hereditary family. But more than that, they are a social power unto themselves too. Those on the higher rungs have—because of the resources these organizations wield and the authority they concentrate—a greater impact and higher level of social influence over everyday people by the fact that their decision-making affects not only those in the bureaucracy but all those whom it serves (and even more people than that). Because bureaucratic authority resides in its offices and not individual personalities, the power and influence of the organization outlasts its members. Bureaucracies are not, therefore, so easily dismantled and, in fact, tend to grow larger over time.

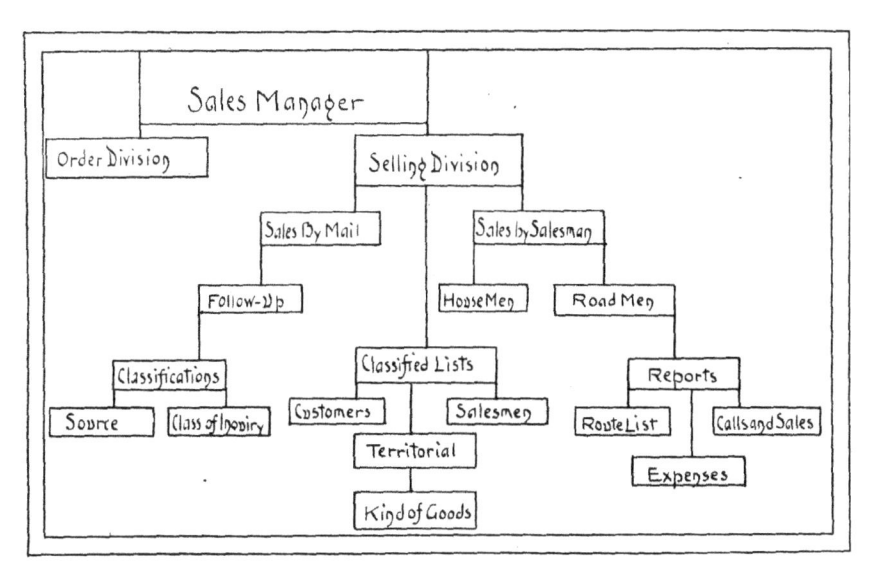

IMAGE 29.1  Chart of Sales Department, 1905, by James B. Griffith (ed.)

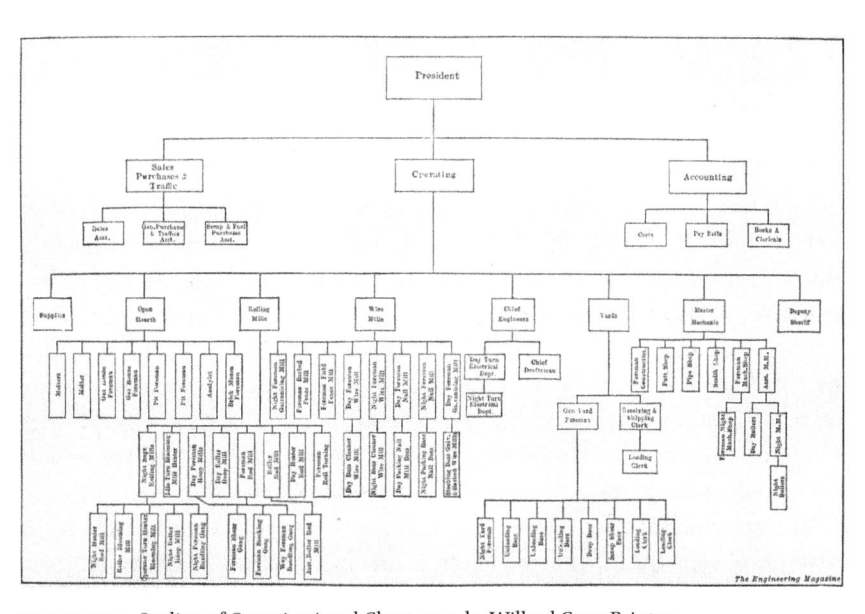

IMAGE 29.2  Outline of Organizational Chart, 1914, by Willard Cope Brinton

Bureaucratic managers do not hire just anyone. Candidates for work must prove themselves worthy of employment—and later promotions—through acquiring qualifications. Such qualifications are established via examinations—in high school, college, and/or the trades—demonstration of skill and/or

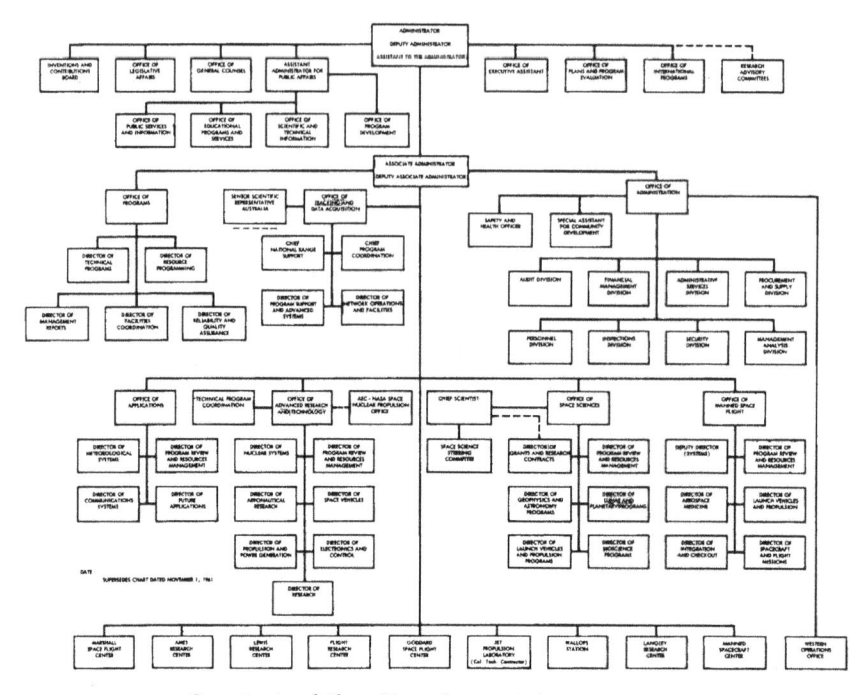

IMAGE 29.3 NASA Organizational Chart, November 1, 1961, by NASA

accomplishment, and by periodic evaluations from superiors. Aspirant office holders must show they know the instruction manual, how to pull organizational levers, and remain compliant to its rules. In return, the bureaucracy—whether the state, a business, or some other type of enterprise—promises regular work and a regular paycheck. Moreover, the organization holds out the carrot of moving up in the hierarchy ahead of the stick of unemployment or social stagnation. One may go from day-to-day petty office holder to one with more status and pay and, on such a journey, become a member of the middle class—educated, literate, respectable, hardworking, and disciplined.

The bureaucrats, then, serve the bureaucracies and, by extension, become servants of what the bureaucracies serve. And in modernity, this is mainly capital, its markets, and its accumulation. Often, though, the bureaucrats do not see it that way. For them, the bureaucracy is an extension of "society" and its needs. Modern society is a mass society and the masses must be attended to and that means administration. The only way to do that is by treating humans as faceless subjects dealt with in terms of numbers, procedure, policy, and red tape.

As the bureaucratic order serves the needs of capital and the class upon which it rests, this order increasingly becomes the order of the state. The state, then, becomes part of a state-capital nexus—i.e., "the bureaucracy." This is a shorthand for not only elected officials but also day-in-day-out workers who staff state agencies, the unelected mass of office-holders, decision-makers, and rule-enforcers. For example, states contain ministries of defense, departments of labor, of foreign affairs, of environmental protection, and/or of public information, education, and societal overseeing in general.

These organizations can be wielded in multiple directions by multiple forces. In an ostensibly democratic society, bureaucracies, like large cargo ships, can be slowly but deliberately steered by changes in law, changes in political administration as a result of elections—which can influence changes in law and/or changes in administrative heads—and even decisions made by the judiciary on the legality of policies and whatnot. In theory, the idea is that each section of the state bureaucracy is "checked" and "balanced" by others so that influence, control, and power do not become concentrated in one organization or person. At the other end of the spectrum, dictatorial and/or authoritarian states are as such where bureaucrats can be ordered by an individual potentate or the party in power's leadership. Checks and balances here may come from internal factions within a party or the state as a whole, but the general set up is that bureaucrats must obey the orders they are given by those in power, who

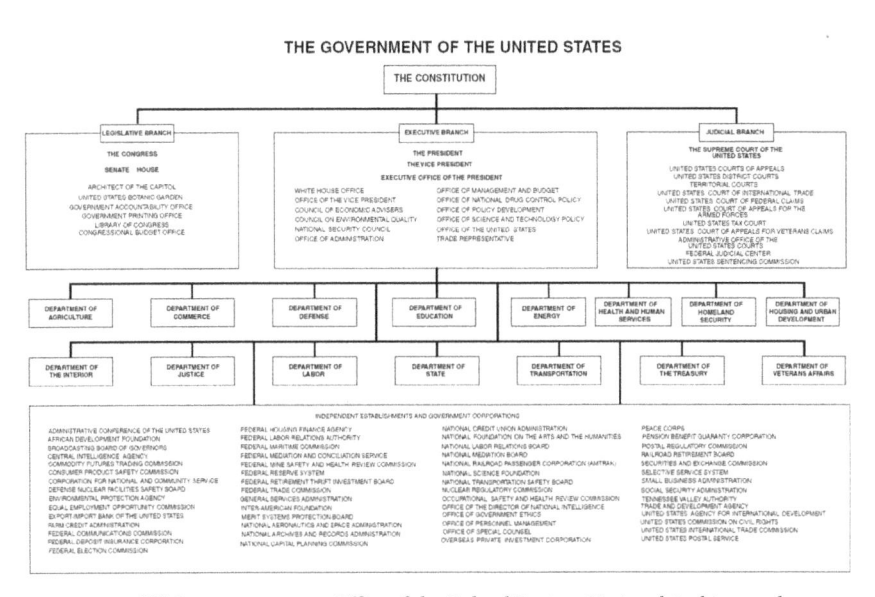

IMAGE 29.4  US Government, 2011, Office of the Federal Register National Archives and Records Administration

generally are the top bosses of the system. And here there is little if any consideration of public will, desire, or participation in the decision-making process.

We should not think of these as dichotomous options that have no linkages between them. Modern state-apparatuses are not an "either or" proposition, as many of them have moved from one end of this sliding scale to another, and sometimes back again. Adolf Hitler's rise to power began in an ostensibly democratic Germany. Once elected to office, Hitler worked his way up the bureaucracy, made allies, and eventually convinced the state to grant him emergency authoritarian powers (the specific details are not important here). Afterwards with the developments of World War II and his aggression against external neighbors and internal people (i.e., the Jewish population, the Roma, Czechs, Poles, and so on), Hitler's regime was able to not only become dictatorial but also brought many everyday citizens to participate in his militaristic and genocidal plans. One way this was accomplished was to simply have organizational leaders pass down rules, regulations, and orders to their underlings and have bureaucrats—governmental, corporate, and military—follow such orders. In fact, after the war, the "I was only following orders" defense was common for many Nazis put on trial. Today, Germany has returned to its place as one of the world's leading democracies.

Dictatorial powers are not the only threat to democratic societies that come from bureaucratic hierarchies. In the modern state, the military leadership sits atop of its own bureaucratic order. The military needs weapons and orders to fight wars. Weapons come from munitions industries. Combined, weapons manufacturers, the business class as a whole, their political representatives, and military leaders drive the foreign policy of nations, often to the path of war. This is a development about which Dwight D. Eisenhower alerted the public. As former Supreme Allied Commander for the European theater in WWII and later Republican President of the United States, he had an insider's view of post-war developments. In his farewell address to the American public, he warned against the "unwarranted influence, sought or unsought, of the military-industrial complex," concluding that the "potential for the disastrous rise of misplaced power exists, and will persist."[1] He was concerned, in short, that this military-industrial complex would usurp the public's input on directing the ship of state and undermine modern democratic principles and institutions. His prognostications have proven just as insightful as they have been unheeded.

---

[1] For discussion and analysis of the relevance of Eisenhower's warning today, see the Eugene Jarecki 2005 documentary, *Why We Fight*.

With many bureaucrats being unelected and retaining their offices regardless of a changing of the guard of elected officials, the bureaucracy and the bureaucrats become persistent parts of the state apparatus, a self-sustaining framework of modernity. This society does not perpetuate itself simply by its collection of individuals making the same autonomous choices every day. Rather, its order is sustained by the operations of its structure, which continues after individuals are born, raised in it, serve it, and pass on to their graves. As such, bureaucracy has a sort of life of its own and is the skeleton upon which the organs of modernity's body hang.

CHAPTER 30

# The Economic Existence of the State

If you have ever ventured outside of a modern home and gone to work, to school, or went shopping, you have likely encountered many, if not all, of the following things. Outside your place of residence there is likely a road for vehicles and sidewalks for pedestrians. There are street lights that illuminate these roads and sidewalks at night for our collective safety, just as there are painted lines between the lanes and the walkways that cross them. Every so often along these roadways are fire hydrants for easy access and use. Under these and out of sight (and mind) we find sewers to take away our waste products, from feces to water from showers and washing, even run off from storms and our gardens. When it snows, plows are staffed and sent out to the roadways to clear the way, to improve safety, and to allow our travels and commerce to continue.

If you have ever been near the ocean, you might have seen massive ships—the capillary cells of world trade—arrive in a port, bringing cargo from lands far and near. Also, near oceans you can find public beaches, often lined by boardwalks with lovers, locals, and tourists wandering along them. Connecting one border to another you can find railroads and the stations positioned for their stops, unloading people and things as they go. And in the skies are airplanes similarly requiring airports for safe landing and unloading.

Should you explore one of the many metropolitan areas in the modern world, you will no doubt come across city parks, public libraries, museums, pools filled with neighborhood children, and monuments to influential persons of the past. Extend your explorations to rural areas and you find similar city and county parks and fairgrounds abutting public lands and forests established by national governments, open to all citizens and visitors from far and wide. These depictions should not sound unfamiliar to anyone who has spent any time in a modern country.

Very often people in modern societies must call on services of which they are in need. Homes are robbed, people assaulted or killed, or even, more pleasurably, parades held. In each instance, police are called upon to investigate and find culprits or to provide order. Fire departments douse the regular infernos that erupt, from houses to businesses to forests. A national guard is called upon to monitor the borders and help out in the case of a national emergency. A professional military is at the ready when called upon to protect the nation or its allies. When soldiers return home with their battle scars—physical and/or mental—we provide hospitals for their care. Should they be less fortunate, those who fell during their service may find a final resting place in a national cemetery.

We often think of taxes as a burden and they can be, especially when money is tight. Consequently, state taxes and how they are spent are often used to stir up public antipathy and anger toward government. Our propaganda machine directs our attention to the tax money taken out of our paychecks and this can make us feel taken advantage of, weighed down, and otherwise under-served. And while that may be true, the directing of our ire toward taxes redirects it away from something else. And that something else is the level of wealth we produce via our labor which is not returned to us in wages but is siphoned off as profits. This portion of wealth is usually a good deal larger than our tax burden. Taxes, however, provide some social benefit we can see and share in, while the personal profits of others mainly subsidize the largesse in their style of living. In this way, irate rhetoric toward taxes and government focuses our attention towards the very organization meant to serve us and away from the class that benefits most from our laboring efforts.

We also often think of "the state" as simply the buildings, policies, and people of government. And while this is part of what "the state" is, the state is also something more and has expressions other than what the common idea might bring to mind. The state provides us a series of necessary things, services, and people central to the existence of modern society. Our taxes pay for teachers in grade school and the playgrounds upon children run and pull each other's hair. Taxes pay for highways on which we drive our cars for our vacations and jobs, as well as being arteries for a massive fleet of trucks at the heart of commerce. The state is in existence in our sea ports, airports, and train stations. Our parks, libraries, and museums all rest on our collective contribution in taxes paid to the state, whether local, regional, or federal.

It is hard to imagine modern society without the economic existence of the state. Not only is it expressed in these things above, but our market system *depends* on the state. Individual businesses have no incentive to build their own private roads, ports, and schools and modern society would be unmanageable if each of them did build such things but only for their own use. How many railroads, highways, and ports would inundate our shared public space if private businesses had to construct their own infrastructure to get goods and costumers to and from their establishments? What would our electrical grid look like if each business and household had to pay for and put up wiring for their own personal use? Not only would this be unwieldy, but it would also be immensely expensive. Some third organization is needed to build these things for the common good, as the business community's individual members would lose profits should they provide the capital outlay to do it. And given the vital services such infrastructure plays in the operations of the market, states are part of the structure of modern society without which capitalism could not function.

CHAPTER 31

# Democracy for their Truth

Historical social systems have had multiple forms of governance: collective decision-making, a council of elders, a chieftain, a warlord, potentates, dictators, kings, queens, authoritarians, and democratically selected representatives. Today, the majority of modern societies are governed by bureaucratic entities made up of elected officials that make laws that are enforced, ultimately, by the threat and use of legal violence—i.e., police and military—if they are not followed (Max Weber). While they may share these characteristics, democratic societies vary on how they choose representatives and function politically. In a parliamentary system with proportional representation, people vote for a party that receives a number of seats relative to the proportion of votes cast for them, i.e., if a party gets 20% of the vote, they get 20% of the available seats. In a "winner take all" system, citizens vote for a candidate and the one that gets a majority of votes wins the seat. In both cases, modern liberal democratic theory holds that it is through electing such officials that modern states enact the will of society in general and represent and serve the individual people that make it up. This is why democracy is a baseline by which to evaluate whether states truly do and act as they claim. The extent to which a state (1) is *not* composed of a cross-section of the people it purports to represent and/or (2) does *not* serve the interests of those same people is the extent to which a state participates in a false pretense.

In modern democracies, adult citizens have the right to vote for candidates for office. In order to win a seat, an aspirant must make his or her candidacy as well as their political views and policy positions known to enough people who do then eventually vote. At the end of a campaign and the subsequent election, winners and losers are announced and the system is declared a success in its peaceful transfer of power, even if the losers and their voters are unhappy about the outcome and the eventual policy decisions made. But here we must ask how a candidate's exposure comes about? Most commonly, it is from the combined influence of two different factors: money and the candidate selection process.

If a randomly selected person contemplated traveling the country to run for office, they would need to secure lodging, food and travel expenses, hire a staff, make speeches, do interviews, and so on. Few people could do this without external sources of funds. In fact, such an individual would first need enough money to hire a staff whose job it is to raise *more* funds to secure *more* opportunity to get the desired message out—buying airtime on television and radio, hiring staff in multiple cities, renting out halls for speeches, paying for air travel, and so on. Poorly funded candidates are thus hamstrung in reaching the widest audience possible, putting candidates with more funds at a distinct advantage, at least in societies with privately funded campaigns (e.g., the United States).

And it is no easy task to secure the needed funds. There must be *enough* individuals donating *enough* money. If a candidate finds sufficient individuals and/or organizations with *large* amounts of expendable money who wish to donate it, then that candidate is in a better position to secure the requisite funds through soliciting fewer people. What this means is that access to money—and very often the people and/or organizations behind it—shapes who gets to run. This, therefore, means that the political arena cannot be reduced to a simple marketplace where an infinite range of ideas and political aspirants reign and the public chooses among them as if they are being provided a buffet of across-the-board choices.

First and most obviously, wealthy sectors can and often do pony up the money their favored candidate needs and do so expecting their candidate to support policies toward which the funder is inclined. Focusing on the United States (rather than countries that have publicly financed campaigns), the creation of "Super PACs" (or political action committees) allows for wealthy individuals and corporations to contribute unlimited amounts of money to a candidate without directly funding them. How this works is that, over here is the candidate's actual campaign organization (with legal limits as to how much money can be given to them) and over there are the Super PACs for a candidate (and funders can give them as much as they want). These Super PACs can buy exposure (television, radio) and/or create propaganda (letters, websites) for the candidate without directly being *from* the candidate's organization. This allows for several things: the campaign proper can save money; funding sources are limited only by the number of entities willing to give money and how much they do actually give; and plausible deniability for a candidate when a Super PAC does something questionable, accuses a competitor of malfeasance, slanders an opponent, and so on. This sort of "purchasing" of the government was legalized by the US Supreme Court in its "Citizens United" ruling under the auspices that money given to political candidates was a form of free speech. The result has been a narrowing of those individuals and organizations who pay for the electoral process (Gold and Narayanswamy 2016).[1]

---

1    For example, between 1989 and 2010, the top donating industries of political candidates and/or policy initiatives were: (1) Finance, insurance, and real estate ($2.4 billion), miscellaneous

In order to increase odds of election, then, a candidate must secure enough money to ensure enough exposure, a process that benefits those candidates who can attract wealthy funders and/or other significant pools of money. And this means that upper classes and the corporate sector have a disproportionate influence on candidate selection.

Another way candidates that elites prefer are selected and narrowed for voters is through the vetting process via a party's political apparatus. Former US President, Barack Obama, wrote in his book, *The Audacity of Hope*:

> Increasingly I found myself spending time with people of means—law firm partners and investment bankers, hedge fund managers and venture capitalists. As a rule, they were smart, interesting people, knowledgeable about public policy, liberal in their politics, expecting nothing more than a hearing of their opinions in exchange for their checks. But they reflected, almost uniformly, the perspectives of their class: the top 1 percent or so of the income scale that can afford to write a $2,000 check to a political candidate. They believed in the free market and an educational meritocracy; they found it hard to imagine that there might be any social ill that could not be cured by a high SAT score. They had no patience with protectionism, found unions troublesome, and were not particularly sympathetic to those whose lives were upended by the movements of global capital. Most were adamantly prochoice and antigun and were vaguely suspicious of deep religious sentiment.

---

businesses that included manufacturing, casinos, and breweries ($1.4 billion), lawyers and lobbyists ($1.3 billion), health ($902 million), communications, electronics, and entertainment ($808 million), labor unions ($699 million), energy and natural resources ($511 million), agribusiness, including supermarkets and tobacco ($486 million), construction ($478 million), transportation ($416 million), and defense ($153 million). And in the 2008 elections, of the $2.64 billion donated, business donors accounted for 74%, ideological groups 8%, labor 3%, with "other" coming in at 15%. Among the $1.96 billion from business donations, 83% was from individuals, while 17% was from PACS (Gilson 2010). And in 2011, gifts of $1 million or more accounted for half of Super PAC's money (Merkelson 2012). In Merkelson's analysis of the presidential campaign of 2012, 17 donors gave $1 million or more (total, $28 million, with a $1.7 million average), 73 donated $100,000 or more (total, $21 million, with a $289,000 average), 81 gave $50,000+ (total, $8 million, and a $96,000 average), and 543 offered up $200+ (total, $6 million, with a $10,000 average). The top recipients were Restore Our Future ($30 million), American Crossroads ($18 million), Make Us Great Again ($5 million), Priorities USA Action ($4 million), Our Destiny ($3 million), Winning Our Future ($2 million), FreedomWorks for America ($2 million), Endorse Liberty ($1 million), and Red White and Blue Fund ($0.8 million). All of these Super PACs worked on behalf of conservative candidates and/or causes, except for Priorities USA Action, which is/was the largest Super PAC behind the establishment-liberal Democratic Party.

And although my own worldview and theirs corresponded in many ways—I had gone to the same schools, after all, had read the same books, and worried about my kids in many of the same ways—I found myself avoiding certain topics during conversations with them, papering over possible differences, anticipating their expectations. On core issues I was candid; I had no problem telling well-heeled supporters that the tax cuts they'd received from George Bush should be reversed. Whenever I could, I would try to share with them some of the perspectives I was hearing from other portions of the electorate: the legitimate role of faith in politics, say, or the deep cultural meaning of guns in rural parts of the state.

Still, I know that as a consequence of my fund-raising I became more like the wealthy donors I met, in the very particular sense that I spent more and more of my time above the fray, outside the world of immediate hunger, disappointment, fear, irrationality, and frequent hardship of the other 99 percent of the population—that is, the people that I'd entered public life to serve. And in one fashion or another, I suspect this is true for every senator: The longer you are a senator, the narrower the scope of your interactions. You may fight it, with town hall meetings and listening tours and stops by the old neighborhood. But your schedule dictates that you move in a different orbit from most of the people you represent.

And perhaps as the next race approaches, a voice within tells you that you don't want to have to go through all the misery of raising all that money in small increments all over again. You realize that you no longer have the cachet you did as the upstart, the fresh face; you haven't changed Washington, and you've made a lot of people unhappy with difficult votes. The path of least resistance—of fund-raisers organized by the special interests, the corporate PACs, and the top lobbying shops—starts to look awfully tempting, and if the opinions of these insiders don't quite jibe with those you once held, you learn to rationalize the changes as a matter of realism, of compromise, of learning the ropes. The problems of ordinary people, the voices of the Rust Belt town or the dwindling heartland, become a distant echo rather than a palpable reality, abstractions to be managed rather than battles to be fought.

President Obama's reflection above is a long way of saying, *people who pay for the party pay for its candidates and work to make sure those whom they deem unfit for office have a tougher hill to climb, where approved contenders, already vetted, receive the needed financial support. And over time, successfully re-elected candidates succumb to this system because of either fatigue, compromised morals, or both*.[2] And, if we are to believe the former President, it only follows that the longer elected individuals are in office, the more likely it is that money will control their activities and thus the legislative agenda as a whole.

This process does not always determine the winners of elections, but it does increase the odds that candidates *who do* reach a wide and visible public stage will be those conducive toward working for the interests of the funders of the major parties. And if a candidate achieves a modicum of popular support but demonstrates they are unlikely to be compliant with the party apparatus, that party can deny them funds, organizational tools like offices and volunteers, and whatnot. For example, the in 2015–2016 presidential race, both Republican and Democratic party leaders in the United States failed to support the candidacies of Donald Trump and Bernie Sanders, respectively, and worked to undermine them in the primary elections. Dominant parties can also determine the rules on who gets included on the ballot and/or invited to influential debates, e.g., see the presidential candidacies of Ross Perot (1992), Ralph Nadar (2000), and Rand Paul (2016). In short, those in power, funded by the elite, control the political discourse, the rules of access, and the likelihood and direction of additional power.

The process above funnels approved of and well-funded candidates into positions of political influence. Once such positions are achieved, the political class pulls the levers of state with two main goals in mind: (1) maintaining power and (2) steering state policy towards desired ends. Very often, however, achieving the second goal supports the first, as successfully instituted policies desired by funders encourages them to provide additional funds for the next round of elections. Let us take a look at a few ways both funders and politicians maneuver the state to achieve the goals above.

One common technique funders—individual and/or corporate—use for influencing politicians that win office is to finance both opposing candidates during a contest. This could and does occur to curry favor with whichever candidate wins, of course, but importantly the election winner is now aware that such funders are willing to support his or her political rivals. This places constraints on the winner to the extent they are concerned about funders possibly revoking their support and sending cash only to political foes, especially if the elective representative sponsors and/or supports legislation that goes against the funders' interest. And the reverse is true as well, i.e., politicians often expect to be rewarded with campaign donations based on the way they vote (e.g., see Talking Points Memo 2014).

---

2  For an insightful listing of quotes of US politicians' admittances about their pursuit of money and how it corrupts them and the political process, see Schwarz (2015).

Once in office, political officials can work to make sure they and/or members of their party remain in power. Gerrymandering—where the lines of political districts are drawn in advantageous ways by and for the favored party—is one way of doing this. Gerrymandering allows for disparate areas which may otherwise be divided among a plurality of districts to be brought into a district-based voting bloc. It is a way to reorganize voters along geographical-ideological lines, which can turn a minority voting base into a majority one. Below are two images that demonstrate how this works, first in conceptual form (Image 31.1) and second with maps from real-life examples (Image 31.2).

In the United States, gerrymandering is used to provide a party more seats than it would have under more "naturally" drawn districts. And this works at both the level of state houses and, nationally, in the US House of Representatives and the Senate. With additional numbers in those seats, parties that enjoy higher representation have the advantage in steering the legislative process, as gerrymandering reduces the representation of potential oppositional majorities, thus moving the state further in an anti-democratic direction. Such machinations of geo-political balance are still active today, as seen in political leaders' private communications where they explicitly discuss methods of marginalizing opponents and consolidating power (e.g., see Wines 2018).

Spread the dynamics outlined above across many candidates and over multiple successive election cycles and the funding classes have a powerful tool to control and maneuver the ship of state.

Elite strategies translate into policy-making on two interconnected fronts: the staffing of agencies and the legislative process. Should a well-funded and supported candidate win a position high enough in the state bureaucracy, they

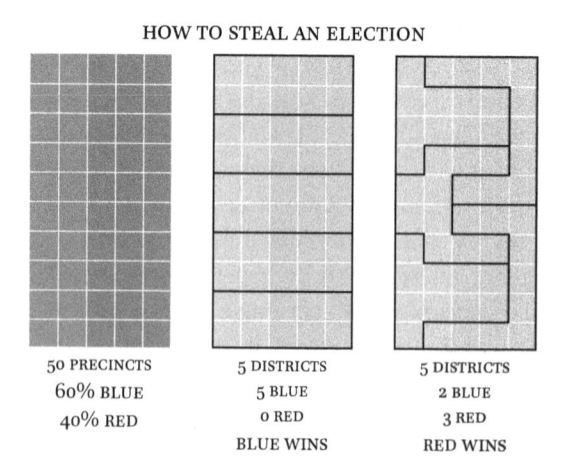

HOW TO STEAL AN ELECTION

| 50 PRECINCTS | 5 DISTRICTS | 5 DISTRICTS |
|---|---|---|
| 60% BLUE | 5 BLUE | 2 BLUE |
| 40% RED | 0 RED | 3 RED |
|  | BLUE WINS | RED WINS |

IMAGE 31.1   A Chart Illustrating Gerrymandering in its Most Basic Form, by Steve Nass

**Illinois**
*Congressional District 4*

**Georgia**
*Congressional District 11*

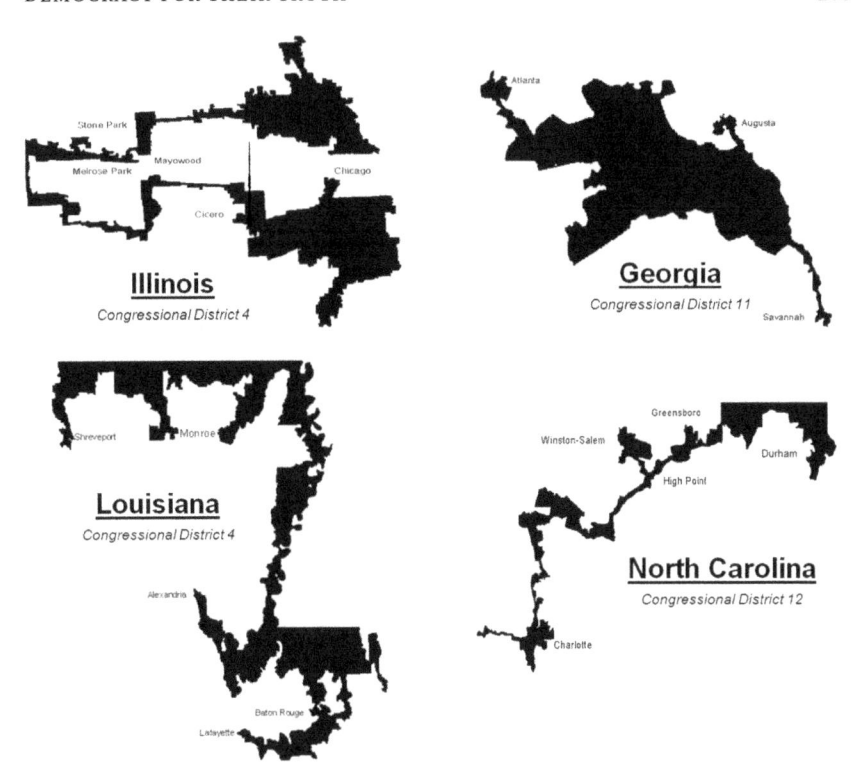

**Louisiana**
*Congressional District 4*

**North Carolina**
*Congressional District 12*

IMAGE 31.2     1990s Supreme Court Redistricting Decisions, by Peter S. Watson

can place economic leaders—i.e., prior funders and/or allies—in positions of political authority, whether as ambassadors, members of a cabinet, or heads of influential governmental agencies related to economic, environmental, or military issues. For example, in 2017, Donald Trump, as President-elect of the United States, named billionaire Republican contributor, Betsy DeVos, to the position of Secretary of Education (she had no experience in higher education, nor had she attended college). He also placed several former Goldman Sachs employees on his staff and at the head of federal agencies. But Trump was/is not unique in these regards, as similar practices have been common across multiple US administrations.

In terms of actual priorities that governments pursue, one influential study looked at 1,779 policy issues between 1981 and 2002 and concluded that "economic elites and organized groups representing business interests have substantial independent impacts on US government policy, while average citizens and mass-based interest groups have little or no independent influence" (Gilens and Page 2014: 546). Two graphs from the Gilens and Page study showed that public preferences had almost *no effect at all* on what policies were pursued and/or enacted (Figure 31.1), while the preferences of economic elites (support/opposition) were much more likely to move the legislative needle in favor of those very preferences (Figure 31.2). This is simply another way of saying that what the public desires has no effect on what policies are enacted, while what elites want does.

Given the observations above, it is no abuse of language to conclude that the US political system is better defined as an "oligarchy," or rule by the few. It is certainly not a democracy or even a republic as those terms have traditionally been understood. Former US President, Jimmy Carter agreed: "So now we've

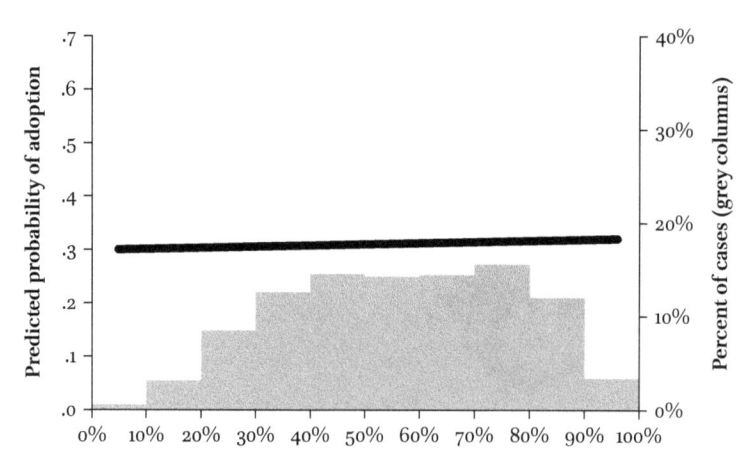

FIGURE 31.1   Average Citizens' Preferences. Gilens and Page (2014), Used with Permission of Cambridge University Press

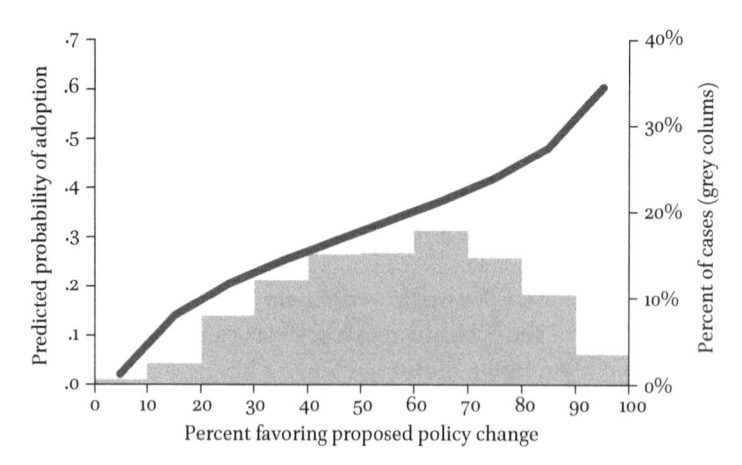

FIGURE 31.2   Economic Elites' Preferences. Gilens and Page (2014), Used with Permission of Cambridge University Press

just seen a complete subversion of our political system as a payoff to major contributors, who want and expect and sometimes get favors for themselves after the election's over" (McLendon 2016). But observations such as Carter's are not new. In 2009, *Monthly Review* (Volume 61, Issue 1, May) republished an article by Albert Einstein they had run decades earlier. In it, he argued:

> Private capital tends to become concentrated in few hands, partly because of competition among the capitalists, and partly because technological development and the increasing division of labor encourage the formation of larger units of production at the expense of smaller ones. The result of these developments is an oligarchy of private capital the enormous power of which cannot be effectively checked even by a democratically organized political society. This is true since the members of legislative bodies are selected by political parties, largely financed or otherwise influenced by private capitalists who, for all practical purposes, separate the electorate from the legislature. The consequence is that the representatives of the people do not in fact sufficiently protect the interests of the underprivileged sections of the population. Moreover, under existing conditions, private capitalists inevitably control, directly or indirectly, the main sources of information (press, radio, education). It is thus extremely difficult, and indeed in most cases quite impossible, for the individual citizen to come to objective conclusions and to make intelligent use of his political rights.

Einstein's diagnosis fits with our times as much as his, as this dynamic has only become more acute as modernity has matured.

In what ways do states act *against* the preferences of the people? Just looking at the United States, majorities of Americans have long wanted a better health care system, including support for a nationalized model (see Blendon and Benson 2001), and few want spending cuts for government programs overall nor cuts for heath care programs for low income families and individuals, such as Medicaid (see Gramlich 2017 and references therein). After Donald Trump's election and contrary to legislation passed later, one poll showed that only about a quarter of Americans favored lowering taxes on corporations and the wealthy, while majorities were in favor of raising them (Pew Research Center 2017a). Surveys show that the public wants less spending on defense (see Cary 2017 and references therein) and more of the public (59%) believes stronger environmental laws and protections are worth the cost than those (34%) that believe such laws and protections threaten jobs and/or hurt the economy (Pew Research Center 2016). Slim majorities want federal job guarantees (52%), community job creation (54%), government produced generic life-saving drugs (51%), and the creation of a public utility for those without Internet access (56%) (see Data for Progress 2018; Nwanevu 2018). As of this writing, US policy and legislation are the opposite of the views of the public majority on all of these issues.

And it would not be a stretch to argue that the public does not want more of their children to die in wars in far flung lands. The public wants and needs an adequately funded education system. Public health requires tighter regulations to ensure clean water, air, and food. The public has long supported national health care in the United States, but this has been kept out of reach. Workers want better pay, more job protection, and safer working conditions and consumer goods. Clean parks, safe neighborhoods, and well-kept streets improve everyone's quality of life. Modern societies need safe and up-to-date rail, interstate, and air transport. While all of these things create a more vibrant civil society, none of them assist *immediately* in the accumulation of capital and some might even impede it.[3] And it, therefore, requires an act of political will to accomplish these things and this requires that the public have the ability to use their own power to turn the wheels of state. However, not only have the tactics recounted here politically disarmed them, but states also require taxes to accomplish such goals, and taxes cut into the total amount of wages citizens have available for spending as well as into the salaries and profits of the elite, all of which reduces profitability and the accumulation of capital. Further, not only is there little stomach for using the tax system this way amongst elites but, *politically,* such activities would strengthen the position of the working and middle classes. From the perspective of capital, the working classes should work hard on the job and be otherwise compliant and docile rather than activist and demanding. From the perspective of the working class, the state is a place they can focus their efforts for legislative and policy redress. That said, most often there are enough strategically placed individuals and organizations with money and connections in the higher political-economic classes to sway the actions of the state toward the side of moneyed interests and away from the needs and interests of the public.

---

3 A qualification and clarification is necessary here. Many of the elements listed here can in fact assist capital accumulation, but mainly for the business class as a whole and mainly in the long-run. However, as political actors, the representatives of capital plan economically and engage politically at the level of the firm and household and most often for the short-term, with perhaps medium-term considerations added on. As such, the business class most often, but not always, acts for more immediate factional advantage than it acts in concert as a whole for overall and long-term societal planning.

Modern society provides an appearance of democracy in that people have the right to vote and they are not routinely hauled off to jail for voicing unpopular opinions (though sometimes they are). But if by "democracy" we mean that our elective representatives enact laws and policies the public at large desires, then this is an inaccurate depiction of how modern states function. In fact, modern states appear, for all intents and purposes, to operate in the interests of the wealthy and the elite. And this relationship is so striking that even stalwart organs of traditional conservative thinking cannot help but take notice, though they often come to different conclusions. For instance, Britain's *The Economist* (2018a) noted that increasing inequality additionally augments the political power of the wealthy, effectively undermining the public's desires for decreasing inequality and increasing social spending; and in Europe increasing inequality results less in a legislative agenda to address it and more of one focused on "social order" issues such as crime and immigration. In the United States, *The National Review*'s Joe Albanese (2017), on the other hand, argued that trying to limit corporate political spending was a "dangerous assault on constitutionally protected corporate speech," a favorable view of the role of money in politics that inverts the relationship classical liberal-democratic theory asserts should exist between the public will and the state. To the extent this disavowal of public will and desire is the political rule of modernity rather than the exception, the truth of the modern state negates its own democratic pretenses and possibilities.

CHAPTER 32

# Parliamentary Disease and the Holy Ghost

Two pillars of modern political philosophy are (1) that public voting provides democratic substance to governing executives, legislative bodies, and their decisions, providing each with the appearance that (2) "the state" represents "the people" and their will and thus the public get the governments they want and deserve. This interconnected process is at the basis of the modern state's "legitimacy," i.e., that its position of social dominance is agreed to and accepted by those whom it stands over (Max Weber). There are several reasons to question whether the purported connection between these two principles accurately reflects the reality of the relationship.

First, legal governing is limited to and by what a constitution does or does not allow and/or address. If a constitution's primary function is managing the interests of a particular class, the everyday activities and policies of a state's bodies will, as a result, be directed toward just that. In such an instance, it does not matter *who* does the voting. By way of analogy, if I am a basketball player and I am asked to vote on the offside rule in soccer, that I get to vote, whether or not my vote counts, and/or whether or not that rule is changed will have no bearing on my sport or how I play it. While the hypothetical given here is in more absolute terms, the political principle here is that *the extent to which* a legal apparatus focuses on one faction of a society over another is the extent to which the potential impact of voting rights and privileges will nevertheless be limited to the subject matter of that legal apparatus.

Second, putting the first stipulation now aside and assuming a constitution that favors no one class, then the next issue is who runs for office and/or is elected. If those running for office, or the parties for which they run, represent ideological commitments that support one class or faction over another, then, once elected, legislation and policy will tend to favor the class and/or faction that enjoys such ideological support now transformed into electoral representation.

Third, when a governing system is as such that elites have more influence than the public over the candidate selection process, then even *if* a constitution's authors did not write it with elite interests in mind, it will nevertheless be more likely that the governors who are selected will represent the interests of those who do most of the funding.

Fourth, it is only after these factors come into play that we can examine who gets a voting voice in electing candidates for office. The United States, as modernity's first representative democratic republic, granted voting rights only to white male landowners, restricting political participation and decision-making to the country's property owners. It was only after long struggles with their working class men (who claimed the franchise was necessary if they were going to be subject to military impressment) and later with their freed slaves that voting rights were initially extended. And it was only because of later struggles again—with half of the population, this time women—that the franchise was further extended (those 18 years of age would have to wait a bit longer). These groups have, at times, been able to steer legislation toward their interests and goals, but only with mixed and often temporary success. All of that said, if this broadening of the franchise occurred within the context of the first stipulation above, then *what extends from that stipulation will still hold*, i.e., who votes matters less than whose interests are constitutionally embedded.

Fifth, the members of a deliberative body ostensibly determine what issues they will legislatively address. Today we find lobbyists and corporate lawyers writing the legislation upon which elected representatives vote. So again, even if all other things were equal—a non-elite tilted constitution and elected officials chosen by voters cutting across all sectors of society—we would still find that *what* elected representatives voted on were bills introduced by wealthy sponsors.

Sixth, *unelected* bureaucrats also make rules and decisions influencing vast swaths of the population, rules and decisions on which they have no input. For example, the population at large has no say in the regulations that supranational institutions—such as the World Trade Organization (WTO)—create and enforce. Very often the rules established by such global organizations relate to whom—immigrants and laborers—and what—products, investments, profits, jobs—are allowed in or out of a country and under what conditions and what standards. Recent historical trends have liberalized the ability for investment capital to flow from high-wage to low-wage areas, reduced environmental laws and their enforcement, allowed for cheaper products to infiltrate a country where they can outcompete local industry, and relaxed taxation on profits made overseas. These developments subject everyday people to social conditions over which they have little influence, even with free and fair elections. When faced with such conditions, it is not usually the corporate sector that the public blames for their situation but rather they tend to direct their ire at the state and its functionaries, where the veil of legitimacy makes it appear that the people, or some faction of them more accurately, brought such conditions upon the society at large. In this dynamic, publics turn on each other and on "the government" as the source of their problems.

Democracy promises people participation in decision-making about general public affairs, especially those that shape their everyday lives. But if the councils of government are imbued with charters that reflect the needs and interests of the few over the many, then formal participation is only procedural, not substantive. In such a condition, formal public electoral participation stalks the halls of state as if it were a ghost seldom heard or seen and usually ignored until the next voting cycle. And when we peel back the curtain, we more clearly see that the results of formal modern democracy are more closely related to a shell game than its actual promise. The belief that voting for establishment candidates reflects a real democratic choice and process, that modern governments operate in the interests of those so ruled, and that laws and policies enjoy the stamp of legitimacy is a form of mystical consciousness and a sort of parliamentary disease. Symptoms of this disease include the belief that the people get the governments they want and therefore deserve and that if an elected deliberative body makes a decision, then that decision is legitimate, just, and binding, as it reflects the common will. And when demonstrated otherwise, we are told the cure for this disease resides in the election of a new slate of candidates churned out by the same machinery as the last slate of candidates. Nothing changes, and the patient becomes more and more ill when the disease and the cure come from the same poisoned well.

CHAPTER 33

# The Executive Committee

A university has a president, a board of regents, and a provost. A business enterprise, especially as they get larger, has levels of management, a board of directors, and a chief executive officer. In each case, these upper echelons decide on staff and worker relations, investment ventures, policy, vision, and long-term projects. Modern capitalist systems, too, have an executive committee—writ large commonly known as "the state"—that passes and enforces laws, enacts policies, and makes treaties with other countries. It also builds and maintains infrastructure for commerce, keeps civil order, backs contracts, adjudicates conflicts, and wages war. These functions manage the common affairs of modern society's dominant social class—the business class.

In modern society, the class that owns productive resources—land, factories, companies, stocks, and whatnot—has many factions, some in competition with one another, some indifferent to one another, and still others with allying interests. But they nevertheless share a common interest in the social conditions that provide for profitability and capital accumulation and that these conditions not be hindered. As a consequence, they apportion some of their cash-assets for political donations in pursuit of securing these interests (either this or a candidate with private wealth can use his or her own money to run for office and gain governmental access to pursue their own and/or their class's interest without the need to pursue outside money). Among the goals for such political activity are keeping advantageous markets open, that state policy be attuned to profitability (e.g., low taxes on profits and low interest rates on federal loans), that an infrastructure be in place to aid the continuation of commerce, the existence of a stable money supply, unhindered access to energy resources, and so on. It would be naïve to expect the business class *not* to use its money in pursuit of such goals.

Tasked as they are with several crucial economic functions, state bodies monitor social conditions, listen to important constituents, and shift and shape their tactics as stewards of the conditions of profitability, turning knobs, adjusting machinery, opening valves or shutting them off. And this puts states in the center of struggles within and between the classes. Sometimes this struggle is between the owning classes in the home country versus classes abroad. Sometimes this struggle between factions of the owning classes is within the state's territory. But most often the struggle is between the owning class and the working class.

States engage in stewardship of the general conditions of profitability, for example, when they maintain avenues of commerce, such as roads and ports. They manage relations *between* classes when they relax or tighten a money supply to deal with inflation or unemployment or foreign trade. States will side with an internal faction of its owning class when it increases import tariffs to protect local industry until that industry is competitive in the world market and then drop such policies in the name of "free trade." Similarly, states can favor class factions by giving tax breaks to encourage (or discourage) certain types of industry—e.g., subsidies for agricultural or fossil fuel companies.

In terms of the struggle between owners and workers, states operate as a mediator when they establish rules of the workplace, such as whether or not there will be a minimum wage and at what level, workplace safety regulations, environmental protection (or lack thereof), and/or rules of unionization. Each side—owners versus workers—tries to influence this mediation, though capital's representatives often prevail. Too much worker freedom to pursue their interests leads to increasing the odds they will threaten to withhold their labor in seeking a more favorable wage-bill, protest by impeding the flow of goods to markets, and so on. Historically, states have often responded to such practices by limiting worker rights and even using police to break up worker demonstrations. More recently, we have seen a growth in "right to work" laws that prevent union workers from negotiating labor contracts with employers that prohibit them from hiring non-union workers, i.e., a way to weaken worker organization, solidarity, and strength.

One of the reasons to weaken organized labor is because of its past and potential future successes. If you are reading this on a Saturday or a Sunday, perhaps it is while you have the "weekend" off from school or work. Perhaps you are tired from working "overtime" and will receive additional pay for it. And in addition, hopefully your job has a measure of "safety regulations" ensuring your well-being is not jeopardized unnecessarily and should you get hurt at work there is "worker compensation" for your loss of health, just as overtime pay compensates you for your loss of personal time. Should you be a modern Western person, it is very likely that you also did not work for wages as a child but rather went to school, played in the park, and had an active childhood. "Labor laws" made sure no one could hire children as they would other employees until they reached a certain age. There was a time when none of this—wage regulations, weekends, overtime pay, laws on child labor, and worker compensation—existed. It was only a struggle waged by workers from below that forced states to carve out such provisions to which the business class had to acquiesce.

Given that pressures can move the state in ways favorable to capital or to labor, the business class and its political allies have learned ways to disguise the biases that betray the state's claimed democratic grounding. While states announce their mission statements in a language that makes their goal seem to be common welfare of "the nation" and "the people," the majority of the state's functions and activities involve caretaking the conditions needed to accumulate capital. This is usually done by equating the needs of the business community with the common interests. For example, the business class establishes and funds think tanks and other policy-forming organizations—such as the Brookings Institute or the Heritage Foundation—that specialize in writing policy papers and publishing thought pieces that advise party leaders and governing representatives on their preferred laws, practices, and policies, often phrased in terms of the "national interest." International conferences—such as the G7 (the seven largest industrial economies), The World Economic Forum, and Bilderberg Meetings—invite state, corporate, and intellectual leaders and meet at the global level for discussions and making policy-decisions for the world economy, where the goal of capital accumulation is phrased in terms of "jobs" and "prosperity," i.e., a language use that makes the interest of the business class correspond with those of the working class.

As policy-making and policy-enforcing institutions, state practices always relate to other states, especially in terms of the intimately related issues of trade, foreign policy, and war. For instance, under influence of British and American oil interests, the US and the British secret services (CIA and MI5) helped overthrow the democratically elected government of Mohammad Mossadegh in Iran (1953). The United States also helped overthrow popular governments in Guatemala (1954) and Chile (1973), either in supporting local military strongmen or through direct military support. These were not minor incidents, nor were they new. Within the United States, Major General Smedley Butler was asked by several industrialists to lead a coup ("The Business Plot") against President Franklin Roosevelt, whose New Deal and other redistribution policies they considered suspiciously leftist. Not only did Butler testify in front of Congress as to the seditious solicitation (though no one was ever prosecuted), he later explained how across his career he "spent most of [his] time being a high-class muscle man for Big Business, for Wall Street and for the bankers. In short, [he] was a racketeer for capitalism."[1]

---

1   In his work, *War is a Racket*, Butler—a two-time Congressional Medal of Honor recipient—explains that much of his service in the US military was in support of corporate interests, ranging from military action in China, Central and South America. Prior to this, the United States goaded Mexico into a war and took half its territory in the 1800s. And historians today generally agree that World War I was spawned by the competition amongst European powers to colonize Africa, a war whose settlement laid the groundwork for World War II. This competitive struggle for resources—either direct possession of them or making sure they remain open for capital investment and export to the world market—was also behind

Market economies have "business cycles," or periods of boom-and-bust. As a depressive period sets in, states find limited options on reversing a sagging economy and a populace can grow impatient, restless, and even, at times, violent. Anti-business sentiment sometimes rises. In the 1930s, the Great Depression struck the United States and rippled worldwide. Businesses failed, people were thrown out of work, and hunger and desperation rose. After it worsened and traditional strategies failed (i.e., mainly relying on the market to rebound on its own), working people responded with anger, organizing, and even radicalism. Membership in socialist parties surged, as did civil unrest. One response states eventually adopted was to provide welfare provisions, which had a two-pronged class-based strategy with the one interconnected goal of saving the market system from itself.

In a depressive market phase, the economy contracts because businesses suffer from lack of sufficient profitability and thus hemorrhage money, go out of business, and lose their employees (who lose their wages), a cycle which can then spread further throughout the economy. "Keynesian" approaches (named after their chief architect and advocate, Lord Maynard Keynes, a British economist) to the problem attempt to stimulate the economy by addressing the needs of both workers and business owners.

On the worker side of the ledger, states enact welfare state policies such as works programs for the unemployed, unemployment insurance, social security measures for the retired, minimum wage regulations, retraining programs to help workers adjust to new economic conditions, and so on. Economically, the goals here are to create both a safety net to prevent people from falling through the cracks and to stimulate consumer demand by providing spending power the market needs for recovery, i.e., sales = profits. Politically, the welfare state also functions as a release valve for social pressures stemming from economic malaise, as the safety net makes it less likely people will revolt when it eases the burdens of unemployment and privation. But even here, too, these efforts ultimately keep the system afloat by tempering pressures on states and from deflecting anger away from the business class.

On the capitalist side of the ledger, the welfare state provides a stimulus to consumption, a needed remedy as commodities must be bought and sold to keep the wheels of the economy turning. Other capitalist-centered initiatives involve state subsidies for industries, loans for businesses, regulating interest

---

US wars recently in Iraq. Other times it may not be resources themselves but rather global powers making sure less powerful countries do not get so confident in their independence that they decide they might want to withdraw their membership in global trade or at least control their own resources in ways they see fit (e.g., Vietnam, Falkland Islands, East Timor, Nicaragua, to name a few).

rates on such loans, adjusting the money supply, regulations on imports and exports, and so on. For instance, interest rates can be kept low to encourage more borrowing by those wishing to invest in economic ventures. Interest rates can also be adjusted to deal with unemployment and inflation, two conditions also of concern to capital accumulators.

And while such policies ultimately are geared toward propping up the system until it can get its legs back underneath it, welfare state/Keynesian approaches are often unpopular with the business community, at least to the extent those approaches are directed at supporting the working class. Such objections usually are rooted in both economic and political reasons. Economically, these programs often involve states raising taxes—e.g., a social security tax on wages, taxes on corporate profits, luxury taxes, and/or inheritance taxes. The former one cuts into workers' immediate spending power; the latter three cut into current profits. As such, none of these benefits the real need for current profit-making and capital accumulation. Politically speaking, a working class that has a safety net is more politically empowered and less likely to accept wages below the level that welfare state provisions provide, which then requires the business community to compete with state guarantees against worker destitution in order to attract the needed labor, which again can harm profit rates as wages will be higher in societies with strong welfare states than in those without them.

All of that said, collectively, this series of policies did bring a level of economic stability to the market (or at least tempered its swings) after the Great Depression struck. These policies also reduced economic inequality in modern societies via their redistribution mechanisms (though the influence of World War II's wartime economy on employment and wage levels cannot be overstated either). But the welfare state as it was historically constituted would not and did not last.

By the end of World War II, the United States emerged as the world's largest economic, military, and political power. It used its position to rebuild the world economy, especially war-ravaged Europe and Japan. By the 1960s–1970s, countries like Germany and Japan had largely recovered and rose as competitors to the United States. In addition, new countries were increasingly entering the fray of international competition and, as a result, profit rates enjoyed by US investors began to wane. States were called on to do something. As a result, from the 1970s to 2000s and beyond, modern states adopted a series of policies meant to dismantle Keynesian approaches and to liberalize their economies, i.e. "neo-liberalism."[2] By the late 1970s and 1980s, the business class, politically

---

2  This should not be confused with traditional "liberal" economic approaches (which slant more toward the welfare policies just recounted above), as neo-liberalism is more aligned

spearheaded by conservatives Margaret Thatcher (UK) and Ronald Reagan (US), directed policy-makers to reduce state involvement economic matters via several distinguishing approaches: (1) free trade laws, including lower taxes on both foreign investment and repatriation of profits made outside the home country; (2) lower capital gains (profits on investments) taxes; (3) less regulations on air, water, and land pollution, as well as reducing them on workplace safety, consumer goods, and so on; (4) privatization of public institutions such as water supplies, publicly owned land, utilities, schools, and prisons; and (5) cutbacks in Keynesian policies such as welfare provisions, redistribution of wealth through taxes and state services, and other safety-net programs (e.g., housing and heating subsidies, lunch programs, support for reducing hunger in families, and so on).

In the 1990s-2000, this agenda was perhaps best exemplified by the North American Free Trade Agreement between the United States, Canada, and Mexico (NAFTA). Here, laws related to workplace safety, the environment, and wages were weakened while obstacles to capital investment and movement were liberalized. The public was told that such policies would benefit everyone but the results were job losses from higher-wage areas to lower-wage areas (e.g., from the United States to Mexico) while the lower-wage areas saw an influx of multinational capital that devastated rural economies, e.g., family-farming communities in Mexico could not compete with subsidized mass agribusiness industries whose economy of scale put downward pressure on commodity prices (see Carlsen 2013; Darlington and Gillespie 2017). This not only explains the increase in migration of workers from lower-wage to higher-wage areas throughout the continent, but it also contributed to the resurgent drug flow from and drug wars in the region during this era (see McKibben 2015). Similar policies, such as the Trans-Pacific Partnership, were later developed and proposed between the Pacific Rim and the United States. Globally speaking, these are only two of several regional free trade agreements seen in the era of neo-liberalism (see Map 33.1).

One way to identify both the real function of the state and the practices of neo-liberalism is to examine what states do in times of economic downturns and crises. While Keynes's proscriptions were a way to save capital while saving its workers, today the latter half of that equation is increasingly being eliminated from policy initiatives. For example, after the financial crisis of 2007–2008 rippled across world markets, many countries embarked on bailouts of banks and

---

with economic policies that argue for *less* government regulation of business and reducing welfare state provisions.

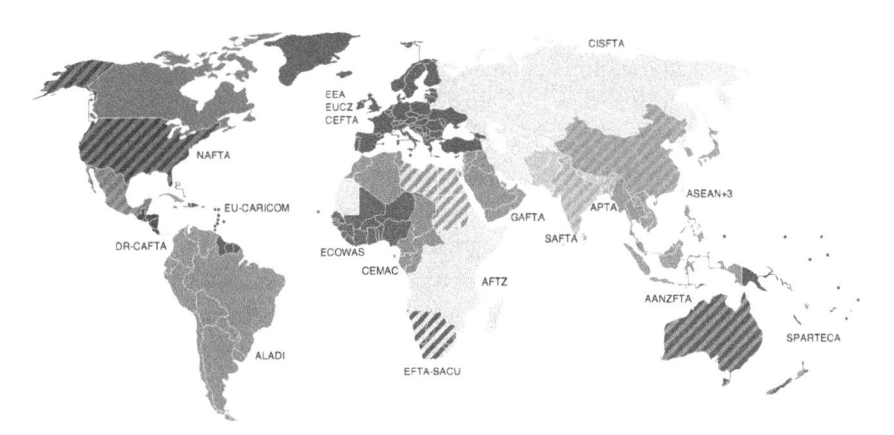

MAP 33.1   Free Trade Agreements with Three or More Participants, 2009, by Emilfaro

austerity measures, pension cuts, and higher taxes for citizens. Riots erupted in places such as Greece against such measures. And since that time, taxes on corporations have plummeted globally speaking, as corporations shift their profits to offshore tax havens and states—fearful that taxes on profits will harm their ability to attract business investment—shift tax burdens to citizens through taxing goods and other forms of consumption (see Stein 2018). In short, in order for states to fulfill many services for the public like health care and social welfare programs *on top of* normal infrastructure management and national defense, they must rely increasingly only on taxes taken from workers' wages and consumer purchases (basically the same people). In the process, the corporate class is increasingly relieved of any responsibility for contributing funds to keep either physical infrastructure in working order or the laboring classes afloat, two things upon which profits depend. Suggesting that there are parallels here to feudal labor relations would not be outlandish.

In the modern world, the police state has grown as a method of population control during an era of increasing economic uncertainty and growing inequality. In being shifted away from state-administrated organizations, many prisons are now privately-owned business enterprises. The product of privatized prisons is prisoners and, to be a viable investment, growth in the number of prisoners is crucial. Beginning in the 1980s in the United States and Britain under Reagan and Thatcher and gaining momentum in Australia (mid-1990s) and New Zealand (2000s), today we find Britain and Wales leading in the percentage of inmates in private prisons (18.46%), followed by Australia (18.28%), Scotland (15.3%), New Zealand (10%), and then the United States (8.41%) (see Kuek Ser 2016). For such prisons to be profitable, there is also a need to incentivize states to create more criminals and/or more laws.

Perhaps it is no coincidence that such developments have come during growth in the militarization of policing. Over time, for example, the US military has increasingly invested in high tech weaponry while lowering the number of individuals in its ranks. Add in the ratcheting down of periodic wars, both personnel and war-making equipment have been channeled toward civilian police forces, militarizing the latter. In fact, domestic police forces have grown in their level of high tech, military-grade weapons, antipersonnel devices and vehicles, and use of violence against citizens (American Civil Liberties Union 2014). Recent evidence suggests, however, that such practices not only do not reduce crime but in fact erode public opinion toward law enforcement (Mummolo 2018). Neo-liberalism's manifestations such as these are not usually those that one will find in an economics textbook but they are, nevertheless, real parts of its overall practice of population management.

The state in modern society, as an executive committee, is charged with monitoring the market and its conditions of profitability. This role includes managing the public as a whole and the struggles between classes that result from each pursuing its interests. Early modern states were tasked with returning fugitive slaves to their legal owners and treated many attempts at unionization as subversion and even treason, unleashing violence on working people in the process. In policing channels of commerce such as roads and ports, states have declared it illegal to impede such commerce with laws directly targeting union striking activity. A free market system and the struggle embedded in it, that is, cannot be left to chance. An organization is needed to attend to its needs and the state was created in order to fill that role. Though it can be moved via external pressure from below, its ultimate function is as a steward of the conditions of profitability and capital accumulation. This is not the reality with which the state announces itself nor upon which its public legitimacy rests. However, when we listen closely to its insiders or observe its behavior in times of crises, this reality of the state as the executive committee of the ruling class is made all the more apparent.[3]

---

3   In August of 2018, members of the Texas petroleum industry supported a $12 billion taxpayer funded state project to build a 60-mile "spine" composed of concrete walls, earthen barriers, floating gates, and steel levees for the purposes of protecting Texas Gulf Coast oil facilities and other infrastructure against the effects brought on by climate change (see Pierce 2018).

CHAPTER 34

# Modern Mythology and its Goddesses

A new set of political ideals that emerged in modernity was summed up in a slogan from the French Revolution, i.e., "Liberty, Equality, Fraternity!" It is hard to argue with such principles. Who can object to the ideas that people should have liberty in thought and deed, be equal under the law, and embrace solidarity amongst each other? But looking at the modern social context and systemic implications of these principles reveals levels of complexity easily missed. Let's take them in turn.

Liberty, at its root, refers to liberation. But does this mean liberty "from" something or liberty "to do" something? In its historical origins, liberty usually meant freedom from some overarching power, such as colonial America's liberty from British rule or the French peasantry's liberty from the monarchy. Those opposed to this idea were mainly the ruling powers being liberated from, so self-validating was the concept among much of the population at the time (though, it should be noted, not with everyone, as those who remained loyal to monarchial norms and principles were not rare). In terms of liberty and doing,

IMAGE 34.1 Slogans in Revolutionary France—"Liberty, Equality, Fraternity, or Death"

IMAGE 34.2 Slogans in Revolutionary France—"Unity and Indivisibility of the Republic. Liberty, Equality, Fraternity or Death"

liberty *to do* what? In its historical roots, this sort of liberty usually meant freedom of conscience, whether political or religious, i.e., freedom to think, feel, believe, worship as one sees fit. These are laudable ideals that modern people should defend regardless of political orientation, and they often do. But additional notions of liberty none-too-seldom have been smuggled in with these traditional ideals in a way that mystifies them and the principle of liberty generally. Here we speak of the liberty of the marketplace, i.e., the freedom to buy land, machinery, raw material, and the labor power of workers so that they will build things for owners to sell at a profit; the freedom of these owners to find markets to sell their goods, whether down the street, across the border, or across the world.

Unlike the liberties from external domination and/or of conscience above, the liberty of the market is not universal in principle, but when these three forms of liberty are constructed and treated as if of the same order, then peculiar linguistic-ideological tricks happen. First, market liberty is a liberty of a type that only 1% of the population or less has been in a position to enjoy. In a capitalist system, however, "private" property is usually treated legally as of the same quality as "personal" property. The owner of a shipbuilding empire owns all the things involved in that business just in the same way you or I own our shoes, clothes, or cars. Thus, as an *ideological* construct, the liberty to buy land, factories, or the stocks that represent them (i.e., private property) is treated as the *same type of liberty* to buy your neighbor's car (i.e., personal possessions). But a transaction for an exchange of personal possessions between two individuals—say, trading or buying cars or clothes between neighbors—is qualitatively different than the freedom to buy up productive resources (land, machinery, natural resources, etc.) on a massive scale. The former only directly involves two individuals while the latter can shape the destiny of entire communities, for good or ill. Second, if a group of people in a large enough voting bloc supports a state policy to restrict businesses in some way (e.g., minimum wages, environmental laws, and so on), opponents can argue that such policies are "restricting liberty" and construct this conceptually as if it is identical to a state regulating interpersonal behavior. This *sleight-of-hand* is possible when the possessions of individuals are linguistically and legally of the same status as the private property of business owners. In this way, public and political discourse can convince many people that preventing the state from interfering with the interests of business is of the same order as protecting their personal freedom. And this is one way to rally large numbers of working people around the interests of the corporate few.

It has been this type of liberty in the marketplace that has been most often pursued by states, those organizations said to represent "the people." Aspirant governors *run on* promises of liberty of movement, conscience, and keeping the republic safe but *govern on* making sure the rules of the market are as liberal as possible. And usually this means keeping wages low, gaining access to natural resources, keeping the rules on pollution and product safety lax, opening borders for export of investment, and so on. And in such class relations, the individual person is "free" but in mainly terms of a freedom to sell his or her labor for wages or go homeless and starve. Thus, the idea of "liberty" here can be wielded as a weapon in the class struggle, where only the "enemies of freedom" oppose it.

"Liberty," and thus "freedom," are tenuous realities in modernity. It is easy to mistake our social freedoms—of movement, of association, of assembly—with "liberty" in general. Capitalist society requires a modicum of freedom in its core sectors, so people can move to and from work, to and from centers of commerce, and to and from areas of entertainment and leisure. But increasingly, "liberty" for the average citizen is freedom to work, freedom to spend, and freedom to be entertained quietly at home. Freedom of conscience, freedom of speech, freedom of body and mind, and freedom of assembly are secondary, even tertiary, concerns and are none-too-seldom curtailed. And none of these things are required for capital accumulation to proceed—but they can undermine it if left unchecked by power from above.

Equality is another hallmark of modern political philosophy. No longer do we honor hereditary titles and we work hard to delegitimize social inequalities rooted in social status, such as race, gender, and sexuality. Modern legal theory assumes that all individuals, even heads of state, are equal under the law. To the extent that people and groups remain unequal is and has been a wedge constantly used to attack those very inequalities as illegitimate. Liberal political theory has its roots in such notions and has been on the ascendant for over the last three centuries of modernity.

But what sort of equality is it, to borrow from Anatole France, that makes it illegal for the rich and poor alike to beg on the street, to sleep in the park, or to camp under the bridge? Both the poor and the rich have equal rights to legal representation in the court of law but unequal ability to find quality representation. Both poor and the rich have the same legal right to move the levers of state, but only the rich have the resources to regularly shape legal procedures and/or access those very levers. Both the rich and the poor alike have a right to free public high school education, but the rich can afford private schools and tutors and tuition at elite institutions—even the middle classes more and more cannot afford college costs. Both the rich and the poor alike have the right to free speech and the right to criticize the government, but only the rich can own media industries and guide the agenda of public discourse. Both the rich and the poor have an equal right to bear arms, but only the rich own armaments industries and lobby for the use of those arms. And, by extension, the poor and the rich alike have the right to vote, but only the rich have the means to invest heavily in candidates to do their bidding and/or to steer the state towards war for economic gains, while those without such resources usually provide the bulk of the fighting personnel.

Formal legal equality is quite a different thing than the ability to use those freedoms and rights. And class relations are square in the center of this difference.

Fraternity was another slogan of the French Revolution. Echoing the US slogan of "United We Stand, Divided We Fall," the idea of fraternity is that, "We are all in this together." And is there a more accurate and vital truism? But what does this mean in societies divided by class, class interests, and a political sphere that pits these against one another? Fraternity under the banner of the nation rallies the working and marginalized masses to the side of those who own that society's productive resources and control its political machine. Modern fraternity is often similarly framed by state borders. Modern people are nationalist in identity and their fraternity extends across borders not to those of the same station (i.e., class solidarity) but rather to everyone in another state that has been attacked by their enemy. Fraternity of flag and alliance, not of social class. And ruling classes hardly embrace the idea of fraternity at all and, when they do, it is as a way to rally working classes to carry the arms for the wars that periodic breakdowns in the political system call up.

Liberty, equality, and fraternity, as goddesses of our modern political mythos, are undermined by a one-sidedness that obscures the class nature of the modern world. Liberty, in capitalist society, means freedom to work or starve, obey orders or be fired, vote for establishment candidates or don't but be disenfranchised either way. Modern society has narrowed down its conception of "liberty" away from not being subject to an oppressive power to the liberty of the market. In this construct, the liberty to buy up productive resources, the liberty to sell goods on the market, and the liberty to accumulate wealth unimpeded by the constraints of states or other classes are treated as of the same order of the liberation of a people from an external power. Or, another way to say the same thing, "liberty" though originally used to mobilize a people to fight against their domination by an external power has been transformed into market freedom for a new ruling class. And the liberty that is increasingly left for everyday people is to sell their labor and to consume commodities, while their ability to organize themselves and to have something to say about the quality of their jobs, water, air, land, and communities are redefined as constraints on the market and thus activities that undermine freedom and liberty. And here we are reminded of how things in the modern world appear backward to us.

Without a class consciousness, ideas about equality also develop in peculiar ways in modern society. Liberals often pursue a form of "equality" with two sets of interconnected goals. First, social statuses such as race, gender, and sexuality should no longer carry socially relevant messages or stigmas that result in biases, harms, prejudices against individuals in those groups, and so on. This goal carries over to a second, where those same groups no longer face discrimination in their efforts to climb through the meritocracy. This is the equality of opportunity, with the barriers of racism, sexism, homophobia, and nativism torn down. Though perfectly acceptable goals, should such liberal social reforms be successful, the result would be that groups formerly marginalized on the basis of their racial, sex/gender/sexuality, and nationality statuses would be equally represented in the ownership class, in management strata, in the houses of government, military leadership, and thus no longer overrepresented in the ranks of the poor. There is nothing objectionable about this, but it should be clear that such a program is only geared toward equal opportunity to own, get rich, and climb the bureaucracy but is not a program directed toward addressing the concerns of working classes themselves. Liberal reform, that is, would do nothing to alter the basic nature of the class structure (outside its race-gender-sexual composition) and the nature of capital accumulation itself.

Fraternity, in these contexts, is shallower than its aspirations project. As it does not place capital and the class structure upon which it rests within its targets, liberalism is blunted from having any real impact toward *fundamental* social change. Liberalism, in short, is at base reformist. And as a reformist project, liberal political action *can* transform modern life in a progressive direction but, as its political program supports solidarity *outside of a class context*, liberal progress means little more than eliminating status inequalities as a mechanism for sorting who gets to work for the needs of capital, its state, and the bureaucratic apparatuses associated with both.

In short, we could imagine a situation where all three ideas—liberty, equality, fraternity—are upheld without a single challenge to the class relations that rule in modernity. In this sense, liberalism's modern mythology and goddesses are less objectionable than they are limited and incomplete. And without imbuing them with a notion of social class and its structural roots, the aspirations which these ideals imply will remain similarly out of reach.

CHAPTER 35

# Rolling Back the Wheel

If "Liberty, Equality, and Fraternity!" was the early call of modern liberal political philosophy, rolling back the wheel is the modern conservative's vision. Conservatives warn us that modernity has headed in the wrong direction and continues to do so—i.e., too much liberty, too much equality, too much fraternity. For instance, conservatives were in favor of maintaining slavery and later segregation and, today, some still claim eliminating slavery was a mistake, with the implicit suggestion that it would be best if we returned to it (see White 2016). US conservatives today want to repeal environmental protection laws, prevent national health care, and repeal the Voting Rights Act (which extended protections to historically oppressed racial and ethnic groups). They also have opposed women's reproductive rights (abortion, birth control) and Affirmative Action. One poll (from YouGov, with a sample of 1,500, April 2018) found that 59% of Republicans did not want to see a woman as US President in their lifetime (see Marchin 2018 for discussion and reference). Similarly, US conservatives generally reject equality for homosexuals and the transgendered. In the 2000s, the fascist right made social and electoral gains in areas where wars were fought to defeat it, such as in England, Germany, and France.

Islamic conservatives, too, desire to turn back of the wheel of modernity's efforts for democracy and equality. In the Iran of the 1970s—under the rule of the despotic and US sponsored Shah, as it was—women had a public face and social independence and Iranian society was undergoing modernization. However, the Shah's brutal rule provoked revolutionary reaction from students, workers, activists, and religious quarters who demanded democratic and economic reforms (see Image 35.1). After the Shah's successful deposing, religious forces turned on their former allies and instituted additional reaction under Islamist auspices. And it was similarly the case in Afghanistan, where, after the 1988–89 Soviet withdrawal, the Taliban forced women back under the veil, thwarted democracy, and reinstituted clerical rule (see Images 35.2 and 35.3). Across the Muslim world, Islamic conservatives desire for a return to a Caliphate, with vast areas of land from Central Asia and across the Middle East to North Africa and Spain under the rule of an Islamic leader and Sharia law.

While there have been many attempts to put the genie back in the bottle, what if the bottle to put the genie back into is only a figment of a mystified historical tale? When prayer was still allowed in American schools, segregation and lynching still existed in more than one place and women's "place"

IMAGE 35.1
The Iranian Revolution Meets Reaction, 1978, by Unknown Photographer

IMAGE 35.2
Women in Afghanistan, 1927, by Unknown Photographer

IMAGE 35.3
Women in Afghanistan after Taliban Takeover

was still in the home, Appalachia was even poorer than it is today, and people prayed desperately that their sons be brought home safely from World War I and World War II. A lack of intellectual curiosity and humility stands behind such reactionary religious worldviews (Krumei-Mancuso 2018; also see Mujezinovic 2018). As such, many Jewish, Christian, Islamic, and Hindu fundamentalists reject much of modern science, e.g., that evolution is a mechanism of change in the natural world. Some American conservatives view colleges as having a more negative impact on their society (58%) than do religious institutions (14%) (Pew Research Center 2017b). Conservative religious leaders of multiple faiths tell us that earthquakes and tsunamis are the result of angering god for one infraction or another, usually the existence and/or toleration of homosexuals, none-too-seldom believing that they are unnatural, perhaps an abomination, and warrant the death penalty. And such conservatives work to limit the social freedoms of homosexuals as much as they can, even trying to stop them from the charitable and loving practice of adopting and giving orphans a home (e.g., see Toce 2018). Such religious reactionaries often want to roll back scientific progress, save, however, its use in creating arms with which they hope to fight their final battles. And that's the issue. Such believers are not content with consigning their regressive and prejudiced beliefs to their places of worship, their homes, and their private lives. They want nothing other than a reshaping of society and the beliefs and behaviors of others in a way that fits a narrow, restrictive, and repressive vision.

During the 2016 US Presidential election, one of Donald Trump's major campaign themes was, "Make America Great Again." This slogan explicitly intoned the idea of rolling back the wheel to a supposed bygone era by directly lifting it from the 1980 campaign of Ronald Reagan, whose slogan was "Let's Make American Great Again." Trump promised to return coal and manufacturing jobs and to crackdown on undocumented immigrants whom he accused of being criminals. But this was just coded racial language for making America white again. After his election to the presidency, there were increasing reports of violence by whites against Hispanic/Muslim/immigrant persons or verbal assaults where people from these groups were told that they were no longer welcome and that the country was being taken back (see Southern Poverty Law Center | Hatewatch Staff 2016; Mindock 2017; Petulla, Kupperman, and Schneider 2017; also see Crandall, Miller, and White 2018). Much of Trump's actual legislative and policy agenda was rolling back President Obama's achievements mainly, it seemed, because it was Obama's administration that had passed them.[1]

Some conservatives are embarrassed by their past, such as support for racism, segregation, sexism, vilification of gay people, and disastrous environmental policies. But others are less so. A portion of Trump's supporters appear to want to roll back the wheel so far that "reactionary" does not really seem to

---

1 As of 2018, this rollback included 17 executive actions, 96 cabinet level decisions, 14 congressional review acts, and three new pieces of legislation (see Eilperin and Cameron [2017] 2018).

IMAGE 35.4
Alt-right Members Preparing to Enter Emancipation Park Holding Nazi, Confederate, and Gadsden "Don't Tread on Me" Flags, Charlottesville, Virginia, 2017, by Anthony Crider

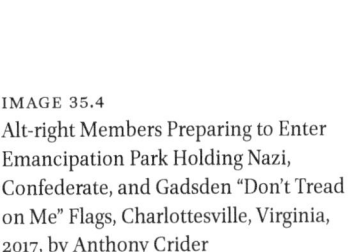

apply. Shortly after the Trump's election, for example, white nationalists gave the Nazi salute in celebration of his victory (see Lombroso and Appelbaum 2016). Elsewhere, there was a "Unite the Right" rally in Charlottesville, Virginia, which harkened back to a darker American era of open racism as some of his supporters there openly carried Nazi flags (Image 35.4). The idea of walling off the United States from undocumented immigrants and Trump claiming current border control efforts allow rapists and drug dealers to enter unimpeded was a selling point of his campaign, not a misstep. The banning of immigrants from several Muslim majority countries was a campaign plank and buoyed his support among key constituents. His Supreme Court picks appear to favor restricting abortion rights and repealing *Roe. v. Wade*. Trump also promised to bring back coal at a time when global demand lagged and the future looked to be one of solar, wind, and other renewables. The future will show how successful Trump—like Islamic clerics and radicals before him—will have been in rolling back the wheel, a testimony to the fact that the progress of modernity is neither written stone nor can it be taken for granted.

CHAPTER 36

# The Goal of Popular Desire

Imagine you are tasked with selecting the dog catcher for your city. Should it matter what church that person goes to? Or even if he or she attends church? Should it matter what sex—male or female—they have intercourse with? Should it matter if they are married, single, divorced, or a swinger? Should it matter if they have served in the military? No, none of this would probably matter. What would matter would be things like basic honesty, lack of a (serious) criminal record, and job effectiveness—showing up for work on time, staying on the job for the allotted hours, and, of course, the likelihood of their success in catching dogs—but not much more.

In a modern, secular form of government, what are national elections for a country's leader all about? One would imagine the foremost priority would be the policies a candidate hopes to enact. Other important traits would be basic honesty and integrity and a desire to work for the common good. Still other traits might be knowledge of how a system of governance works and effectiveness at navigating it. And it is true that candidates in modernity will often tout these traits in their pursuit of votes. But these are not the traits that often win the day and/or sway a voting public. What does win the day in the electoral process?

When someone decides to run for national office, it goes without saying that person must love their mother and babies and appear clean, hardworking, and diligent. Military service can help but is not specifically necessary. Traits such as national pride and patriotism, holding relatively the same sorts of values as enough voters, and personality, looks, and charisma (stage presence, language use, oratory skills) also go without saying. It can be either some combination of these traits or others, but what is key is that a candidate elicits the needed emotional response from an audience. That emotion might be fear, anxiety, calmness, resolve, or aggression. What matters is that the candidate's appearance and demeanor match up with that set of emotions most likely to gather crowds and produce supporters' adoration. A candidate on the national stage should love the same sports as "the people," follow the same god as "the people," and hate all the same groups as "the people"—or at least enough of "the people" who eventually cast votes. They should partake in the nation's rituals and eat its popular dishes. Thus, an individual on a national stage should personify the country's image of itself in its most idealized form for that time. This is because the goal of popular desire is for the head of state to personify both the ideal characteristics of the nation and the aspirations of "the people." Notice, however, none of these traits have much if anything to do with honesty or the policy initiatives a candidate will likely pursue.

This does not always have to be the case. Certainly, people do vote based on an element of their desired policies. However, before that decision is made, they must like or at least identify with a candidate. Hitler was laughed at as a clown when he first sought elected office. But after his arrest because of his coup attempt in the Beer Hall Putsch (November 1923), once released from jail he ran for office again and, in doing so, he appealed to the German people's sense of post-WWI humiliation, national pride, and economic desperation. This gained their attention. He stood as a proud German (he was Austrian), a fighter of the good fight, and a person who would restore the country's honor. It was similar for the British, as Churchill stood for British resolve, supporter of the Empire, and never, ever, giving up. Exit polls told of the swing voter in the United States where, after a close election, the undecideds pushed the winner's column in favor of George W. Bush. This was because he seemed, according to the pundits, more like a guy they would rather have a beer with compared to Al Gore. In later elections, the "beer" vote was often a topic of prognosticators, so telling about electorate behavior was this idea.

National leaders become repositories of personal aspirations, of characteristics individuals would like to imagine in themselves and their ideal form of "their country." This contains the kernel of a cult of personality, of course. Kennedy, Reagan, Clinton, Obama, and now Trump all fit these depictions. Kennedy reflected a young, energetic optimistic America maturing as a world leader after the trauma of World War II and a liberal stalwart against a feared Soviet threat. Reagan provided the soothing faith of a grandfatherly figure for a country suffering still from Watergate, the economic doldrums of the 1970s, and the hit to the national ego from the Iranian Hostage Crisis. He was also another reliable Cold Warrior. After his first term in office, George Bush (I) could not compete with Bill Clinton's charisma, especially among citizens ready to move past the older politics of the Cold War. Barack Obama allowed a public to feel renewed optimism in a confident, smart, and executive figure after the bumbling disaster of the Bush II Era (especially the Iraq War fiasco), while easing their guilt over a racist past. And Trump presented himself as the accomplished outsider from the business community who was going to address the economic malaise brought to white, rural America, reinvigorate their pride in their culture and nation, and stand against the hated liberal political elite and the feared supposed influx of foreign threats. Thus, not only did this appeal rest, in part, on economic grounds, but, as research discovered, there was a real fear on the part of white, Christian, male voters of losing their status (Cox, Lienesch, and Jones 2017; Mutz 2018).

All of these depictions of US leaders above are fanciful, of course. But if you compare these images to those whom each defeated, you will find their opponents simply did not appeal to the same sentiments. And those like Bush I and Carter were defeated after their first term because of an inability to match and adjust their appeal to popular desire of the time. Each of these victors of the executive branch resonated with popular desire enough to harvest the needed votes in winning the contest for dog-catcher-in-chief.

What does this tell us about the structure of political rule in modernity? While there could be many answers to this question, one likely answer is that the further up the ladder a position—from dog catcher to council member to mayor to state representative to governor to senator to president—the more necessary it is for those aspiring to become elected representatives to appeal to the emotional sentiment of the masses. Whether this is a weakness of the human condition or a predictable side effect of mass bureaucratic governance under the nation-state, or some combination of both, is less important here than is the observation that this is the political dynamic modernity has passed on to us. And this leads us to the question of whether we are able to change this situation (as it leaves us susceptible to demagogues and despots) or if this is something which we must always endure and manage, in this world or in its successor.

CHAPTER 37

# National Egoism

Prior to modernity, people had deep personal connections to their clan, region, religion, or even kingdom. Today, we identify ourselves with a nation-state, as being of a "nationality," as "British," "French," "Japanese," "Chilean," "Canadian," and "American." This is new in our historical experience, as a nation-state might contain people of multiple ethnic backgrounds, different language communities, various religious beliefs and political ideologies, different families and clans, and so on. The uneven way this has or has not taken root in places such as Papua New Guinea or portions of Africa, where family, tribe, and clan still predominate in many areas, reveals the extent to which this is a reality of and in those societies pulled more thoroughly through modernity's sieve. As such, it is easier to rally people around a flag, the state, and a central leader in those areas where nationalism has taken root, whereas those parts of the world with less of a national identity are often more susceptible to internal factions and rivalries (often over control of the national seat itself).

With this national identity comes a certain amount of national egoism. Part of this is based on humanity's natural predilection towards xenophobia (or fear of the stranger or outsider). Xenophobia has both what we might call a "soft" and a "hard" form. First, there is a sort of predicable "soft" xenophobia that results from outsiders coming into a new environment. People often encounter outsiders with suspicion, i.e., "Who are you and what are you doing here?" Even hunter-gatherers act with suspicious caution when they encounter unknown outsiders on land they consider their own territory and often demand an accounting of their presence. This is a sort of "natural" gatekeeping mechanism societies engage in to monitor potential threats. And because of this strangeness with which outsiders present us, whether in traditional cultures or modern ones, we find their food, clothes, sexual norms, and even gods peculiar, weird, strange.

This sort of soft xenophobia can be juxtaposed to its more "hard" relative, that of outright feelings and beliefs of superiority and even hatred, which usually come with a moral condemnation of others as individuals and groups. Your food is not only weird but you are judged negatively for eating it. Your gods are false and ours will punish you. Your sex is immoral and angers us (and our gods). These notions are not unique to modern societies either.

But in modernity, our national egoism merges with both soft and hard xenophobia. Our country is superior by almost every measure: where our food, sex, clothes, politics, religion, morality, economics, language, policy, and so on are the best, even if we have not traveled to other parts of the world.[1] But this false sense of superiority is not satisfied with its own stature. It is driven to stroke its ego by admonishing other people from other nations for being crass, as due for little respect, and as suspect of harboring the worst characteristics humans have to offer. They are cheap. They cheat. They are dirty. They are lazy. They are licentious. They are criminal and a threat to *our* [sic] women. They are godless. But not just those of *that* clan or *that* pastoral region or of *that* family, but *all of those* different races, families, ethnicities, and religions inhabiting the boundaries of a different nation-state than ours.

But that is not the end. National egoism can grow into rabid nationalism and blind patriotism. Our country is not only superior but our history must be depicted in the most pristine and ideal terms. Past heroes should be whitewashed of any racism they might have exhibited or crimes they might have committed. National disgraces such as enslavement of others or unspeakable acts of brutality should be understood, if mentioned at all, as unfortunate exceptions, misguided but well-intended ventures, or simply mistakes of the ignorant. And not only are we superior but we *deserve* to dominate others. Our interests and priorities and "way of life" should prevail and those who say otherwise are our natural enemies. Should our leaders decide that we must punish some other society, they must have done something to deserve it. Do our leaders require the mobilization of the military to go to some far-flung land and kill its inhabitants? No questions asked. In a sense, nationalism is a tribalism writ large but this time with state boundaries and identities as the mechanism of cohesiveness. Modernity took this older habit of humanity and shaped it in a new form and to new ends.

---

1 American author, Mark Twain, was quoted as saying that, "Travel is fatal to prejudice, bigotry, and narrow-mindedness, and many of our people need it sorely on these accounts. Broad, wholesome, charitable views of men and things cannot be acquired by vegetating in one little corner of the Earth all one's lifetime."

CHAPTER 38

# Every Sect is Religious

While past kings, princes, tsars, and potentates all had to deal with internal struggles and court intrigue, it is not until we have formal parliamentary procedures with elected officials and an enfranchised public that we have "politics" as we know it today. Politics is about the struggle over what publicly binding decisions will be made by whom and how in social, economic, political, and military worlds. Most modern societies have a few major political parties representing "the mainstream" in this struggle, with other sectarian groups at the margins. Such sectarian political movements can often resemble a religious cult, whether or not such a sect represents a leftist or a rightist political philosophy. What are some of their identifying characteristics?

*The Existence of a Charismatic Leader or Idea.* Political movements often coalesce around an individual with striking personal traits and/or a set of ideas that are dramatic, extreme, sometimes utopian in nature.

*Worshipful of Leaders.* Leaders of such movements often receive a level deference from their constituents that borders on the worshipful and pathological in that such leaders are often seen as beyond questioning and their actions as the correct course, not because it was/is the right thing to do but because it was something *they* have done.

*Moral Certitude.* Like religious cults, sectarian political movements often believe their cause is one of moral certitude. This belief not only augments the non-questioning of leaders, but it also allows for a Machiavellian attitude that if the ends represent an absolute moral good, then any means of furthering those ends is justified.

*Dogmatic and Doctrinaire.* Because of such moral certitude, sectarian movements often develop beliefs and/or tenets that are never to be questioned and always obeyed. Over time, these dogmas and doctrines tend to expand to cover more areas of not only social policy and life but of individual behavior and belief as well.

*Fearful of Criticism and Debate.* Because of their oppositional juxtaposition to mainstream political (or religious) power and policy, sectarian social movements tend to be fragile. Their initial low numbers often means that they are. But if and when their numbers grow, there also grows a likelihood of multiple opinions on ideology, practice, strategy, and so on. And this means an ever-growing tendency toward codifying beliefs, values, and principles into doctrine and even dogma. With their tendency toward ever more dogma and doctrine, there arises a fear of criticism—internal or external—which instills a threat of potential existential crisis. Criticism, therefore, cannot be allowed, as it is dangerous, just as is simple debate. This disposition, of course, runs counter to the idea of the cause being one of moral certitude.

*Paranoia.* The result of all of the above is paranoia. Enemies are everywhere, maybe even inside the movement itself. Few, if any, can be trusted and those who can tend to dwindle over time (for reasons that we will see shortly).

*Appeal to Emotion over Objectivity.* To avoid paranoia over enemies and to avoid the sort of debate and self-criticism that would help refine ideas, sectarian movements appeal to emotions over objective facts. What feels good or right or furthers political goals becomes what is acceptable as "true." What feels bad or incorrect or does not further political goals is anywhere from neutral to "false" to "subversive" or even "evil." And anything that subverts such goals should be attacked with vitriol at minimum, with violence if necessary.

*Censorious.* Because debate and dissent might challenge doctrine and threaten the movement as a whole, dissent and/or differing opinions must be censored. Even lack of complete unanimity can be seen as seditious. The narrative must be controlled, and this means controlling speech and narrowing the parameters of allowable word and deed and thus, it is believed, thought.

*Linguistic Control.* It is for these reasons that language must be controlled. People must have the right thoughts and be prevented from having the wrong ones, which can occur if they are exposed to the wrong words, ideas, and even people. Thus, sectarian groups begin to police language and punish those who fail to toe the party line.

*Vilification of Opponents.* Opinions of outsiders, especially those once in the in-group but who have since left, must be squelched. If this cannot be done, then their personality, their morals, and/or their integrity must be brought into question. If their unflattering opinions are known, they and/or their views must be defeated through shouting them down or otherwise derided, mocked, and ridiculed as not worth considering. The actual content, logic, or factual basis of an opponent's view must not be taken into account, as this will open up the group to subversion.

*Strict Gatekeeping and Loyalty Oaths.* As it is important to only let the right people into the group, ever-stricter gatekeeping mechanisms may be necessary. And since with growth in a group's size grows the likelihood of different opinions, a method is needed to make sure those who are in The Party have the right thoughts and The Party's (and its leader's) interests at heart. Thus, there develops a need for loyalty oaths as a mechanism for keeping the ranks pure, obedient, and loyal.

*A Tendency Toward "Gaslighting."* Group members of suspect loyalties require disciplining, often through punishment, re-education, ostracism, or other mechanisms of control. One method sect leaders and their followers use is "gaslighting," where someone is made to question his or her perceptions and sanity when others around them deny something has happened when it in fact has; or the opposite, i.e., affirming the reality of something that does not exist. For instance, perhaps a leader has claimed to have taken some action or made a claim that later appears unflattering or even criminal in nature. The leader and/or his or her followers can deny that any such thing ever happened. And such denials, when held by authorities and/or their collective followers, can make witnesses start to question their own perceptions and even sanity. And people in such conditions are more pliable to suggestion and following orders.

*Quick to Punish and/or Exile Dissenters or Those Who Stray.* It is important that dissenters—those who fail to use the right words and/or work toward the right ends—be exiled as quickly as possible. This will help keep the ranks pure and the exiled serve an example to those that remain of what fate awaits those who make trouble.

*Eating and Purging their Own.* Because of all of the above, the spectrum of allowable thoughts, words, and deeds increasingly narrows over time and this means it becomes easier for individuals to stray, violate codes, cross the line. Eventually, it is impossible to maintain purity. People who believe they are saying the right thing and see themselves as allies will slip up eventually and use the wrong word or take the wrong action, often not even realizing the offense or intending one. Whether they be leaders, members, allies, or whatnot, sectarian forces eventually turn on their own.

After the October Revolution of 1917 and Lenin's subsequent death, Josef Stalin worked to consolidate his power and with this he consolidated the apparatchiks and rules that would govern the Soviet Communist Party. The party line was strictly enforced, and dissenters were subject to show trials and either "re-educated," sent to psychiatric institutions, shipped off to Siberian work camps, jailed, or executed. Citizens were encouraged to turn in suspicious neighbors. Political freedom ground to a halt and an iron curtain descended on the continent, in Winston Churchill's famous words. Similar things would happen with the Maoists in China, where intellectuals were purged, often jailed or even killed, and classic art and even chickens were declared to be "bourgeois" and expunged from society. Pol Pot would enact similar practices with similar results in Cambodia in the 1970s. Leaders there were seen as demigods, not to be questioned, and party loyalists and even family members were urged to out dissenters or anyone whose views strayed from orthodoxy. Millions died, many from executions.

In the United States, protagonists during "The Red Scare" declared the country and government had been infiltrated by communists. Its leading instigator, Senator Joseph McCarthy, convened his Committee on Un-American Activities and targeted private citizens, public employees, scientists, and even Hollywood celebrities, musicians, and authors. People were encouraged to turn each other in and report suspicious goings-on, something similar to what communist authorities did in the USSR and Eastern Europe at the time. Those suspected were hauled in front of congressional hearings, interrogated for their views, behaviors, and loyalty and many were impugned, blacklisted, and their reputations and careers destroyed. McCarthy, however, had no evidence for his accusations.

More recently, we find economic theories and philosophies treated with a sort of reverence saved for religious doctrine. Sometimes the thinking of economists becomes "siloed," where they are isolated from ideas that challenge orthodoxy and wedded to mathematical models that make them seem "almost priestlike" to outsiders (see Tett 2015). This results in the creation of ideological blinders, where ideas within them are treated uncritically and those outside of them are heretical. Similarly, libertarians and supporters of unrestricted free market doctrines defend these policies without evidentiary support, where rhetoric about "the wisdom of markets" and how economic liberty is the basis of freedom is all that is required and data on accumulated and concentrated wealth and political power does nothing to bring pause to such beliefs; nor does the fact that when capitalism concentrates wealth in fewer and fewer hands—as it inherently does—it undermines competitive markets. It is the screeds of the Ayn Rands, the Friedrich Hayeks, and the Milton Freidmans that matter. And when radical free market approaches crash the economies where they are applied, the response is that these principles *were not applied enough* and thus the solution is *even more of the same.* The lessons are never learned because the theory's proof is self-contained (for discussion, see Rapley 2017).

Though a market-fundamentalist outlook would seem to have little if anything to do with religious fundamentalism, one cannot help noting that both religious and economic conservatives tend to gravitate toward the same political policies and parties. How might we account for this? Social systems often produce an outlook, a set of beliefs and philosophies, articulated by a "priesthood," a concept we do not have to confine to just religious instruction. A priesthood articulates a distilled and crystallized institutional logic and defends it as if it is a sacred product. Nuance, historical variation, and evidence are not important, while fidelity to approved doctrine is. As both religion and economics are structural relations in a society, there arises a category of people who pronounce the fundamental tenets of that structure as sacrosanct and an audience exists ready to accept such pronouncements as self-evident. And in a way, they are: a sacred idea is an expression of a society's core social relations put into spiritual terms (which results in its mystification).

Whether or not a political philosophy is inside or outside the mainstream, right-wing or left-wing, does not immunize it from such tendencies. And sectarian drift does not require party organization either, as more than one of the tendencies above can be found in some espousing feminist and social justice ideals. For example, professors who stray from feminist orthodoxy have been silenced and their careers exiled (e.g., Camille Paglia). Battles rage between more inclusive feminists and those that have been called "Terfs," or "trans-exclusive radical feminists."[1] A shaping and policing of language has also emerged among the social justice oriented, with an itemization of "microaggressions."[2] One internet activist/educator (YouTube "celebrity," Laci

---

1 The former believe those assigned "male" at birth but who have transitioned to living as women (some having gone through hormone treatment and surgery) are in fact "women," while the latter believe that one must be born with a vagina to be included in that category.

2 The term "microaggression" was coined by Harvard Professor, Chester M. Pierce, in 1970. The original idea was to recognize and even catalogue situations where African-Americans were recipients of things like insults, dismissals, leers, sneers, slights, rudeness, and so on, from those with whom they interacted, especially whites, in everyday life. Today, this idea has changed in several ways. The concept has been applied to the treatment of other ethnic groups, the LGBTQ community, and those who have hearing or other physical impairments. This should raise no objection and, in fact, is a logical and reasonable way to extend the concept. But other things have also changed in the contemporary usage of "microaggression" that transforms the concept beyond its original intent into something new. In Pierce's formulation, the aggressor is putatively acting with some level of prejudice, racism, hostility, and/or otherwise malign intent. In addition, the focus in his original model is on the attitude and intent of the one delivering the message. Today, microaggressions are often understood to be "unconscious bias" that makes someone else feel uncomfortable, marginalized, lesser-than, and so on. This is a crucial change. The point here is not that such things do not happen nor that they do not cause harm to their recipients, especially as they build up over time. This can clearly be the case. Rather, the concept of microaggression has been flipped on its head, where—in addition to previously identified actions undertaken with malevolence—the antagonist can be completely unaware of what they are doing, may have no malign intent, and the recipient's subjective opinion—not the objective action—defines what gets counted as an offense. In this reformulation of microaggressions, there is lack of clarity, consistency, precision, and, thus, coherence as to what words and deeds to which it applies or should apply. As such, the bar for including something as a microaggression can be moved without regard to an agreed upon standard or demonstrable measure. In a prior period, a racial epithet was a clear word or phrase that carried unmistakable meaning and was understood by all as derogatory, hostile, and inflammatory. Here all that was needed was to discredit use of such words and phrases, which in some ways has been successful. Under the current model of microaggressions, the type and level of offense can be redefined in perpetuity and, therefore, there might be no conceivable limit to their quality or quantity nor a way of measuring the success

Green), having already angered the reactionary right for her liberal views, was called transphobic by social justice activists for using "male" to refer to those born with penises and "female" to refer to those born with vaginas. Later, when Green engaged in dialogue with conservative critics of her and of other social justice activists, she was accused of betraying the cause, providing aid and comfort to the enemy, and even had her well-being threatened.[3]

This tightening of rules and opinions on both the left and the right occurs because of a dynamic that develops without regard to political orientation. Whether political or religious, this dynamic is real, and its progenitors rarely recognize the implications of their actions, as ambition and high-minded moral certitude guide them while they protect their flanks and keep their ranks pure with methods of gatekeeping, censoring, expelling, and physical threat.

Sect-like behavior is not restricted to oppositional radicals on the margins of the mainstream. A large political party can drift into extremism over time and, as they do, they adopt many of the behaviors above. The US Republican Party of the twenty-first century is an apt example. As he tested the waters as a candidate prior to announcing his run, Donald Trump courted conservative evangelicals via appearances on the Christian Broadcasting Network. There, his style, wealth, and attitude meshed well, despite his apparent lack of religiosity, with the sect-like tendencies of televangelism and the prosperity gospel (see Graham 2018). During his campaign, his supporters seemed unmoved by several of his actions and words that would have sunk candidates in prior elections. He refused to release his taxes, an expected practice going back several presidents. The Democratic candidate, Hillary Clinton, was questioned for not releasing transcripts of her speeches to Wall Street executives, while Trump,

---

in their elimination. What we see here is a case where an agreeable goal of social equality and justice provides cover for a method of changing minds through policing language via a model of targeting offences that can be defined in almost anyway the activist wishes. This model, then, when stripped of its social justice goals, is one conducive to sectarian politics whether from the right or left.

3 If the reader is unfamiliar with the reasoning behind why someone would object to associating penises with men and vaginas with women, it is because in the activist community (i.e., activism related to sex, gender, and transsexual issues), there is the belief that not everyone's genitalia (their physical selves) is appropriately matched with the sex-category assigned to them at birth. And thus one can have the outward physical traits of one sex but have the inner-life of and/or mental identification with another sex. This, of course, is also confirmed by scientists who study issues of transsexuality and transgenderism. The activist community, as a result, takes umbrage with our traditional language use that attaches sex-categories with genitalia, claiming that it erases the trans community. For insight on Green's situation, her views on it, and what happened over time, see "Words You Can't Say," *This American Life* (WBEZ Chicago | PRX – The Public Radio Exchange, February 2, 2018), at this link (URL retrieved September 6, 2018): https://www.thisamericanlife.org/637/words-you-cant-say.

with his non-disclosed tax records, made a living working with Wall Street and real estate. He was shown on film, shot several years before the election cycle, talking about grabbing women's genitals without their consent, an act that most reasonable people would consider sexual assault. Several women, in fact, had accused him of acts that were reflected in what his words had depicted. He repeatedly made statements shown to be untrue.[4] He mocked military veterans and people with disabilities. He cultivated fear of immigrants and those of different religions. He said that he "alone" could solve America's problems. His supporters appeared to hang on his every word regardless if there was any truth to them or even if they did not make any sense. A cult of personality was in the making for everyone to see and was broadcast worldwide.

Parallels between the rise of Trumpism and cultish behavior do not end there. Both Trump's base and the television network that buoys his support appear to uncritically embrace his words and deeds, not because of their substance but because it was Trump himself who said or did something (see Holmes 2018). For instance, as President, he cultivated relationships with Russia, though conservatives had previously excoriated President Obama for similar moves. The Republican Party (as well as its base) had long criticized North Korea's Kim Jong-un as a dictator and an enemy of freedom and of the United States (not without reason), a position Trump initially held during his early presidency. This changed, however, after he engaged in overtures toward Kim for a détente over escalating nuclear threats. In June of 2018, FOX News, in an apparent reversal of its own previous position and an apparent endorsement of Trump's new friendliness toward Kim, criticized Republican Senator Marco Rubio for denying that Kim was "talented." After his base and other supporters were accused of engaging in cult-like behavior because of such positions, FOX News asked Donald Trump Jr. his opinion on that charge, to which he replied, "If it's a cult, it's because they like what my father is doing."

The problem here runs deep. After Trump won the election, he began appointing advisers and making nominations to his cabinet and a shift from "religious sect" as metaphor to reality began. Several of his advisors and appointees were/are "Dominionists." And as religious tests tend to be an anathema in American politics, this issue was little covered by a media that should have done so. Dominionism, generally sect-like but loosely organized, is an

---

[4] Politifact, a Pulitzer Prize winning website, found that a majority of his claims (near 60%) were of dubious accuracy or simply false—e.g., 33% of the statements Trump made in his campaign could be listed as "false," 19% as "mostly false," and 17% as "pants on fire"; see: "Donald Trump's File." Politifact (URL retrieved August 6, 2017): http://www.politifact.com/personalities/donald-trump/.

American religious movement that believes their form of Christianity should have dominion over the "seven mountains," i.e., the family, religion, media, arts and entertainment, government, and business. More than one person who had Trump's ear was aligned with the movement directly or indirectly (e.g., Vice President Mike Pence, Attorney General Jeff Sessions, Education Secretary Betsy DeVos). A close Trump adviser, Steve Bannon, was/is associated with a radical Catholic sect, "The Church Militant." These two groups are not interested in traditional liberal democratic values such as separation of church and state, freedom of conscience, secularism, and so on. Rather, they want to control social and political institutions, whether the public at large wants this or not. And they believe god has given them the charge to pursue and accomplish this task. The growth of the extreme right-wing of the Republican Party and this extreme religious doctrine have (what Max Weber called) an "elective affinity" for each other. Now that they have found electoral success, they are not unlikely to go through the phases outlined here.

CHAPTER 39

# Disgusting Despotism

World history is littered with leaders who ruled with avarice, violence, and disdain for those over which they reigned, both people their armies had conquered and people of their own domain. While feudal lords of all stripes ruled with caprice, their degree of cruelty often varied with the personality at hand and what other nobles would tolerate. Modernity, with its dissolving of feudal norms and regimes, claimed its states would constrain such behaviors through the rule of law and with checks and balances on the powerful. But modernity has not always reigned in the violence of despotism with such balancing forces. Rather, individuals and parties none-too-seldom have been able to harness the state's power toward tyrannical ends. Though the list is too long to exhaustively recount, some overview is a valuable lesson on this feature of the modern world.

King Leopold of Belgium ruled over a short-lived colonial regime in what is today the Democratic Republic of Congo. At the 1884–1885 Berlin Conference, European powers acknowledged his claim over the "Congo Free State," a region he used for personal enrichment. With his own mercenary force, he presided over the forced labor of millions (including children) in the harvesting of ivory and, after international demand increased, rubber. To ensure the securing of such resources, he had the hands cut off of those who did not do the work and/or failed to meet quotas (so many hands were cut off that they functioned as a sort of currency). Anywhere from 1–15 million people died under his rule, with the most systematic estimate being 10 million (Hochschild 1998).

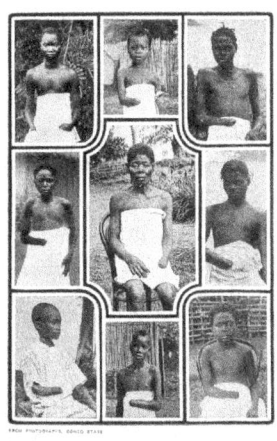

IMAGE 39.1
Mutilated Children from the Belgium Congo, before 1905, by Alice Harris, Daniel Danielson, Others

In the twentieth century, modern states updated their ideologies and their bureaucratic-military machinery for new despotic ends. In Germany after World War I, Adolf Hitler, with help of his staff, military leaders, and state bureaucrats, built one of the most violent and despotic regimes the world had seen before or since. Though initially elected to office, he orchestrated a takeover of a state apparatus that organized the invasion of foreign lands, concentration camps, secret police, propaganda, and systematic genocide. Approximately 6 million people of Jewish heritage were systematically killed during the Holocaust, and about 4 million Roma, homosexuals, communists, Catholics, and those seen as physically and/or mentally impaired also fell victim to the Nazi killing machine. During roughly the same period, in communist Russia, Josef Stalin presided over forced collectivization, kangaroo courts for dissidents, state run media, impressment, extermination of opponents, ethnic cleansing, and a general police state. Tens of millions died under his rule from famine, purges, and labor camps (more than died under Hitler's regime).

In Chile in 1973, General Augusto Pinochet took over after a military coup displaced and killed the democratically elected, Salvador Allende. Workers, unionists, teachers, and other protestors and supporters of Allende were rounded up and "disappeared." The free press, public education, and free association were repressed. Similarly, from 1965 to 1986, Philippine dictator, Ferdinand Marcos, brutally silenced opposition, shut down critical media, used martial law, and generally ran the nation as potentate, growing rich in the process.

Since the end of the US war on the Korean Peninsula, North Korea has been ruled by the Kim family—most recently (as of 2018) headed by Kim Jong-un—with an iron fist. Though the regime keeps tight control of education, media, and the freedom of tourists, refugees and investigative journalists have witnessed concentration camps, starvation, torture, collective familial punishment for actions of individuals, slavery, and systematic rape. Not restricting such violence toward the population, the Kim family has also executed political and military leaders suspected of insufficient loyalty and obedience. North Korea is considered by many as the most repressive regime in the world.

These are but just a minority in the despotism experienced in modernity (e.g., François "Papa Doc" Duvalier of Haiti, the Shah of Iran, Idi Amin in Uganda, and Saudi Arabia generally come readily to mind).

Part of what makes despots what they are is the violence they inflict on people, some their own and some in far flung areas of the world. Sometimes this violence is from neglect in taking care of societal needs. Sometimes this neglect is maliciously planned, such as forced famines, e.g., the Hungarian Holodomor. Sometimes this violence is inflicted with brute force, such as Pinochet's regime and their method of disappearing those who might cause trouble for his fascist government.

Other times despotism transforms from the constitutional rule of law toward rule by fiat. Part of the social contract of the modern state rests on due process and enacting the will of the people through legal means. Despots do best when they seize power in states that are armed but weak with such legal restrictions. Other despots aspire to power in stronger states where there are more checks to their efforts to rule than exist in weaker states—such as stronger constitutional protections and limits on executive power.[1] As a result, despotic behavior can still find fertile ground in states of any sort. How do we know a despot when we see one?

Despots use the government and/or military to further their own economic interests, either through policy, bribes, extortion, or looting the public treasury, sometimes all of the above.

Despots embark on ventures whose plans and goals are not made immediately explicit to the public (and sometimes not at all) and are often disguised as policies for the public welfare and the good of the nation.

Despots restrict the information about which the public is made aware. When the press is free, a state executive can try to control the free flow of information by putting out disinformation, spin, and alternative facts. They can discipline recalcitrant media members with lack of access should they probe too much with pesky questions at press conferences and/or print inconvenient or unflattering stories. In states without constitutional press protections, despots often shutdown uncooperative media and/or jail journalists and even sometimes have them killed.

Despots cultivate a cult of personality around themselves, where they are adored by the public and enabled by their staff. They surround themselves with sycophants who do not question the leader, do what they are told, repeat fabrications to the public, and/or go along with questionable and dangerous plans.

Despots threaten to purge and/or jail real or potential dissidents from their staff and the organs of state, often acting act on such threats.

---

1 A "weak" state may be internally strong in the sense of having a monopoly of power and being highly repressive. What is meant here by a "weak" state is that it is a state that, in comparison to others in the international community, is relatively small, has a legal apparatus that is not well-developed, has ruling dynamics that gravitate more toward personalities and coalitions than procedure, is relatively isolated in terms of its international relations and allies, and has minor to modest ability to project outward military force. A "strong" state is on the polar end of such things, while other states land along this continuum.

Despots use the language of nationalism and patriotism to inculcate loyalty and cast suspicion on critics. Blind obedience to dictates from and acts of fealty to the leader are treated as identical to a commitment to state, country, and culture.

Despots know that when a populace perceives a threat—external or internal, real or imagined—they often bind more tightly to rulers for protection and use this to their advantage. Despots will often therefore manufacture crises so that the public rallies to their side.

Despots view the public as either a loyal herd to be used or as an enemy to be corralled. When the public, or a faction of it, is no longer useful, they become a threat, with suspect loyalties and even perhaps traitorous in their designs. This allows for their jailing, exiling, or even murder.

Despots are paranoid and see conspiracies against them everywhere, which, if true, they often bring upon themselves. As such, there is often the need for show trials and/or detentions as ways of expunging rivals and sending a signal to those who remain.

Despots enforce rules on their people they do not intend to follow themselves. They often live lavishly while expecting sacrifice and austerity from their people. They may take drink or engage in sexual acts that are forbidden by local religions and/or the beliefs and morals of their followers.

Despots fear not being adored by their people, so they stage public demonstrations of their authority and power, such as military parades, extravagant birthday celebrations, and other displays that bear witness to victories over rivals or tout national holidays. Such events encourage citizens to submerge their identities into a collective whole, making it easier for them to forsake their individuality for the glory of a common national cause.

Despots often enjoy the company of other despots, especially if their interests coincide or at least do not conflict. They state their mutual admiration and flatter each other during official state visits. They join in on each other's birthday celebrations and consider the enemies of their friends their enemies as well.

Despots fear losing the power and authority that the aura of the state casts upon them. They often augment that halo with ceremony, dressy uniforms, public displays of wit, wisdom, strength, and will.

Despots suffer from weak egos and are quick to anger. They demand supplicating praise from underlings, handle bad news poorly, and often act like children when they cannot get their way.

Despots have problems with self-control. They fire staff willy-nilly, over-indulge in pleasures of the flesh, act on impulse, and sometimes inflict pain on others as a method of comfort or retribution.

Despots often resort to torture as a means of disciplining others, punishing infractions, and/or extracting information. Rule of law being a nuisance or even non-existent, despots rely on extra-judicial methods of control and often do not worry, or sometimes in fact hope, that knowledge about such punishments becomes publicly known.

Despots divide and conquer their own people and make examples out of a few to instill fear in others. Those parts of the populace insufficiently loyal may have food embargoed or be visited by police or military forces as a show of who is in charge and what happens to those whose loyalty is not without question. Suspect populations are sometimes required to register on state lists or may be rounded up and sequestered in camps or reservations or even "cleansed" from the society altogether.

Modernity may have birthed the democratic republic but it adopted the despot (see Davies 2014; Goni 2016; Norton 2016). Today we still find authoritarian regimes in both weak and strong states as well as those in between, where despotic behavior is not confined only to personalities but also comes from juntas, bureaucratic organizations, and even elected deliberative bodies. Multiple states, as we will sample below, have demonstrated various forms of the behaviors listed above.

In military-ruled and predominately Buddhist Myanmar, for example, Rohingya Muslim refugees report government security forces killing children in front of their parents, participating in gang rapes, torture, and burning villages to the ground, while the world powers do nothing effective to stop it save a UN designation of the repression as a form of "genocide," their investigators' conclusion that Myanmar's military leaders be sent to the International Criminal Court, and an effort to find hosts for refugees (Guterres 2018; Withnall 2018). Physicians for Human Rights affirmed that forensic examinations and medical records are consistent with the Rohingya's reports of being raped, hacked, or wounded by explosives, which doctors called "crimes against humanity" (see Baldwin 2018). In September 2018, Myanmar tried and jailed two Reuters journalists reporting on a recent atrocity for breaking a colonial-era law, even though two police officers testified they were ordered to frame them (Chalmers 2018). Further, any attention such events did receive from the world community provided cover for Myanmar's infliction of similar atrocities on its Christian Kachin population in the north (Breaking News 2018).

In dealing with a militant Islamic movement within its borders, Pakistan's military used indiscriminate force, collective punishment, bulldozing homes of families of suspected militants, punishments for entire villages, and detention in internment camps without charges for months and years on end, resulting in a backlash of protests there (Gannon 2018).

In 2018, Turkish government forces used tear gas to break up a Gay Pride march, enforcing a ban in place there (Agence France-Presse 2018b), while in Egypt members of the gay community are subject to discrimination, arrest, and jail time should they make their identities publicly known (H. Stewart 2018).

In Nicaragua, Daniel Ortega and his government have grown increasingly authoritarian, with the placing of his wife in the office of Vice President, the banning of opposition parties, the stacking of electoral councils, consolidation of the military, crack downs on non-state media, and security forces firing on protesting citizens, which killed at least 127 (perhaps up to 400) and injured 1,000 (*The Economist* 2018c; Wierson and Arguello Lacayo 2018).

In 2017, Philippine President, Rodrigo Duterte, encouraged vigilante violence against drug dealers or those just accused of the offense. Victims of such extra-judicial killings were said to be between 7,000 (according to police estimates) and 20,000 (according to research cited by an opposition senator there) and provoked protests in the capital, Manilla. His political opponents were suspected as being targets of these killings, which subsequently drew attention from the International Criminal Court (see Amnesty International 2018; Deutsche Welle 2018; Hincks 2018; Regencia 2018).

Stronger states allow for despotic behavior if they contain few if any internal checks or balances and/or if they can withstand pressure from the international community. For instance, China confined millions of Uyghur Muslims in its western region of Xinjiang in concentration and re-education camps, jailed their activists, and shut down their mosques, while much of the world's Islamic leadership remained silent (see Coca 2018; Nebehay 2018; Niewenhuis 2018; Rauhala 2018; Thum 2018, and references therein). And, less violently but still indicative of the fragile despotic mindset, there was widespread suspicion that Chinese censors deleted images and other material related to Winnie the Pooh from internet access there because of Chinese President Xi Jinping's sensitivity to suggestions he resembles the fictional character.

In Russia, Vladimir Putin jailed gay activists, dissidents, uncooperative oligarchs, and journalists. He or his government were believed to be behind the killings of Sergei Magnitsky (oppositional anti-corruption lawyer), Alexander Litvinenko (former KGB), and the use of chemical weapons on Russian nationals living abroad in England. In 2018, three journalists investigating connections between the Kremlin and Russia's "troll army" (often behind "fake news" distributed worldwide) were killed in the Central African Republic (Ayres 2018). Russia backed the Syrian government in its "civil war" there, with civilians deliberately targeted (including hospitals) in their joint bombing operations (Mackintosh 2018).

Donald Trump, as US President, exhibited similar behavior and practices as some of those seen above during his time in office. His lies and false claims regularly numbered 100 or more per week (Dale 2018). He called the media "the enemy of the people" and upon learning of negative stories in the press, threatened to revoke media credentials (Embury-Dennis 2018b). When bodyguards for Turkish President, Recep Tayyip Erdogan (who censors his own press, jails dissents, and relies on military backing), beat up US citizens protesting his state visit in Washington, D.C., Trump did not voice outrage or objection. He shrugged as if unconcerned when reminded that North Korea's Kim Jong-un, with whom he had just had a meeting, was a "killer" who was "clearly executing people" (P. Weber 2018). He later told a television interviewer that he wished Americans would obey him just as North Koreans obey Kim (Reed 2018). In a 2017 nationally televised interview during Super Bowl Sunday, he reiterated his respect for Russia's Putin, even as he acknowledged Putin's reputation as a "killer" (Pengelly 2017). In 2018, he met with Putin in Helsinki, in a meeting that was widely interpreted as Trump demonstrating alliance with and subservience to the authoritarian Russian leader. Despite widespread coverage of the significant rise in murders associated with the drug war in the Philippines, reports suggested Trump's administration was working on setting up a meeting with the authoritarian Duterte in the United States (Philstar.com 2018). And in September 2018, after the *New York Times* published an op-ed said to have come from an administration insider that claimed many of his staff feared he was mentally unstable, Trump publicly said that he wanted that person turned over to government authorities.

In addition to his words and behaviors, Trump favored several policies that smacked of despotic tendencies. He backed a policy of detaining undocumented immigrants and putting their children in cages, where these children claimed they were forcibly drugged, handcuffed, and abused (Chan 2018). Military personnel opined that such a policy "smacks of totalitarianism" and was an "enormous moral offense" that "beggars the mind" (see Laporta and Ackerman 2018).[2] In discussing his policy, Trump said such immigrants "infest" the country, language that was compared to that of the Nazis (see Sapolsky 2018). After there were additional parallels drawn between the policy and practice and the Nazi regime's treatment of Jews during World War II, acting Director of Immigration and Customs Enforcement, Thomas Homan, rejected the comparison and defended ICE agents as "simply enforcing laws" (see Rupar 2018), apparently without a sense of either irony or history, given that the defense many Nazis used at the Nuremberg Trials was that they were "just

---

2 In another affront to the military, Trump reportedly clashed with his national security officials and in one indicative case he complained to National Security Adviser H. R. McMaster that the military was not doing all that it could to make money off of Libya's oil reserves, a suggestion military leaders found distasteful (see Maza 2018).

following orders." And even the last living judge from those very same Nuremberg Trials, Ben Ferencz, said these detention policies were a "crime against humanity" (Germanos 2018). After international and national outrage ensued, Trump later ordered the detention policies to end, an order he later said he regretted (Blitzer 2018).

As of 2018, certain trends did not portend well for the spread of democratic society in the immediate future. One study concluded that dictatorship was on the rise in the twenty-first century, as an increasing number of rulers were consolidating power and wealth at the expense of their own people. The number of people living under such regimes had risen from 2.3 billion in 2003 to 3.3 billion in 2017; the number of countries scoring highest for free and fair elections dropped from one in six in 2006 to one in fourteen by 2017; and the number of countries considered to have unrestricted freedom of the press and opinion went from 17 of 129 countries to 10 in the same period of time.[3] Former US Secretary of State, Madeleine Albright, expressed similar concerns in her 2018 book, *Fascism: A Warning*. There she noted the global resurgence of authoritarianism, that Italian fascist Mussolini once (like Trump) had promised to *drenare la palude* (i.e., "drain the swamp"), and that Hitler claimed part of his success lay in how he "reduced [complicated political problems] to the simplest terms. The masses realised this and followed me" (see Rawnsley 2018). In respect to the United States, it is difficult to miss the parallels here to Trump's opinions, words, and behaviors.

We cannot write off the recurring emergence of despots as simply and only the unfortunate result of the wrong people with corrupt personalities and morals reaching office. It is true that ruthless and amoral people attain state power and that this outcome is bad fortune. But if this were the only way to account for despots, then the solution would be to have mechanisms in place to thwart their ambitions and prevent their ascendance. Those mechanisms, however, become easier obstacles to overcome should a voting public support someone with despotic tendencies.[4] And that said, one explicit goal of the modern state's model of liberal democracy was preventing any aspiring despot from exercising such authority, so there must be something else going on here. Yes,

---

[3] See the Bertelsmann Stiftung "Transformation Index BTI 2018" at this link (URL retrieved September 7, 2018): https://www.bertelsmann-stiftung.de/fileadmin/files/BSt/Publikationen/imported/leseprobe/LP_978-3-86793-848-8_1.pdf.

[4] One study found that it was not "financial stress" but that, when holding constant factors such as education, age, and income, the primary variables that distinguished Trump voters were characteristics associated with "authoritarianism", such as targeting women and minorities and favoring dominant and intolerant leaders who are uninhibited about their biases (Smith and Hanley 2018).

non-despotic personalities and/or proper checks and balances can prevent a drift of states toward more fascistic ends. Those potentialities, however, *must be already embedded in the structure in the first place*. Rather than manufacturing authoritarianism out of thin air, the individual despot simply maneuvers the right levers to inflate this inherent potential in the state and unleash its power. Thus, the state itself, the power and riches the system offers, and the ways that these can be wielded guarantee that modernity has not seen the last of despots.

CHAPTER 40

# The Sycophantic Babblers

An anthropologist goes back in time and lives with the Aztecs, collects data, records the culture's practices, and estimates several possible trajectories in which their society is likely to develop. The level at which so many individuals—both child-bearing women and laborers—are killed through ritual human sacrifice leads the anthropologist to conclude that total births will decline to the point where they will be too low to sustain the labor hours needed for both agriculture and warfare. As a result, a shortage of people needed to maintain the society looms and, if the current path is continued, the society is likely to collapse. After the anthropologist shows them the data, what sort of reaction would the Aztec elders likely have to such a warning? They would probably reject it outright—as this is how they have always done things, the way the gods intended—and the priesthood and tribal leaders would wave the warning (and the data) off as fearmongering, ignorance, and intellectual elitism and shoo away the troublesome messenger.

Our society is subject to a similar dynamic. In our world, too, there exists a group whose function is to defend the institutional structure and its practices and to reject out of hand perspectives that cast a critical eye upon such things. This class of individuals exists for several reasons. For one, powerful groups do not leave to chance what ideas dominate public discourse; rather, they direct resources toward cultivating intellectuals and institutions for that task. Second, even without the influence of the powerful, our institutional framework rewards those whose worldview corresponds with elites' interests with upward mobility and social esteem. And such intellectuals and the institutions they serve—whether in the media, academia, public relations, or the pulpit—facilitate a conditioning process that begins in childhood and continues throughout our education and our learning of professional trades, both directly and indirectly. In addition, we take cues from our elders and the wider society in which we move. If we start to forget the needed lessons, professionals—in the universities, on news programs, from think tanks, via talk radio, and so on—repeat them for us, presenting their knowledge as disinterested inquiry or as the result of hard won experience forged in the "real world." If these dynamics are successful, then ideas that conform to the interests of the wealthy and powerful will tend to dominate, enjoy receptive audiences, and be regularly repeated and defended, while oppositional and contrary voices will tend to be muted and/or rejected. In democratic capitalist societies, such an institutional set up works much in the same way propaganda does in authoritarian states (for analysis and discussion of this topic, see Chomsky and Herman [1988] 2002).

The mass media and its sycophantic babblers are the most pervasive of these forms of public discourse. One principle of liberal democratic society is that the public must be informed on the issues of the day and this is better accomplished when they have access to a wide range of news, information, and opinion. Indeed, one of the criticisms directed toward communist regimes during the Cold War was that their media was not only state controlled but also that this limited the range of perspectives and news sources to which the public was exposed to just one, maybe two. Today, in modern capitalist societies, we are witnessing a similar dynamic. In the early 1980s, for instance, there were about 50 companies that controlled 90% of US media output, while by 2012, it was less than 10, closer to five (Bagdikian [1983] 1997; Lutz 2012). This narrowing of sources was facilitated, in part, by The Telecommunications Act of 1996, which aimed to deregulate the media market and inject more competition into it but in fact led to more mergers and consolidations.

Along with the narrowing of sources has also come a narrowing of perspectives to which the public is exposed. In the United States in 1987, the Federal Communications Commission under the Reagan administration repealed "the Fairness Doctrine" (in place since 1949), which directed broadcasters with a public license to report on issues of public importance and do so in a way that was honest, equitable, and balanced in offering contrasting views. This repeal has often been identified as a major influence in the growth of US conservative talk radio, which dominates the political radio market (Barker and Knight 2000; Clogston 2016).

Corporate mass media are not simply or only national broadcasters but also own many local stations and can shape what perspectives and types of information are available there. The Sinclair Broadcasting Group, for instance, is the largest broadcasting company in the United States by number of stations owned and total viewers. One of its former reporters, Suri Crowe, was instructed by management to make her coverage of climate change more "balanced" and to include oppositional voices against the scientific consensus; she was even given a script to read on air (which she did) that included the opinion of Donald Trump before he was the official Republican nominee for President (see Perlberg 2018).[1] Sinclair also made headlines nationwide when

---

1   This is a common practice—where individuals representing two sides of an issue are brought on a news program to discuss it, which provides an appearance of "balance." However, in the case of something like climate change, where the vast majority of climate scientists (1) agree that it is happening and (2) have concluded that it is the result of human activity, then having

it was revealed that it forced reporters at its local stations to read a script aimed to sow distrust in the mainstream media by depicting it as suspiciously biased, presumably liberal, and a danger to the country (see Burke 2018). They later engaged in a similar tactic requiring local stations to broadcast segments casting doubt on the media's coverage of the Trump administration's policies of detaining undocumented immigrants and their children (see A. Chang 2018), as well as "must-run" segments in support of Trump's Supreme Court nominee, Brett Kavanaugh (see Vogel 2018).

With market and organizational dynamics such as these above, it does not require state-controlled media to centralize and control information.

To the extent that major and important news is covered without such interference, news reporting is often augmented by feel-good human interest stories, celebrity gossip, or the latest natural disaster and/or local house fire. The roots of foreign policy, the funding of governing candidates, covert operations, meetings and proceedings of the powerful, and other crucial information necessary for understanding the world are routinely left out. This can be done via vetting of job candidates to make sure they are not "subversive," either by use of government plants, as was done at the BBC in Britain (Reynolds 2018), or by hiring managers and editors that share the worldview of media owners, the latter of whom are typically drawn from the upper class. Whether for reasons of obedience, ignorance, and/or simply adopting an uncritical worldview, the result is the control of and a narrowing of the flow of information all the same.

Sometimes newscasters are cowed into conformity and/or lack of relevant reporting via political fiat or by their own timidity. In 2012, North Carolina's legislature passed a law (HB 819) that banned state and local agencies from basing their coastal policies on scientific models indicating an accelerating rise in sea level in favor of historical linear predictions. Canada, under Stephen Harper, in another instance, forbid its media weather forecasters from mentioning global warming, one of the central threats to humanity today. Wisconsin, under Governor Scott Walker, removed mention of human contributions to climate change from their state website. In Florida, under Governor Rick Scott, state funded scientists were told not to use the terms "climate change," "global warming," and "sustainable" in their papers. In 2018, with heatwaves, wildfires, extreme rain, droughts, floods, crop failures, and deaths mounting in

---

a climate scientist discuss the issue aside a climate change denier is a "false balance," where it makes it appear as if there is more debate and disagreement among specialists than there really is. In September 2018, the BBC publicly admitted to the practice in the past—in addition to failing to challenge climate change deniers—and, as a result, they "get climate change coverage wrong" because of it (see Carrington 2018b).

the United States, Europe, and Japan, a large majority of media stories made no mention of climate change (e.g., see Grit Post Editorial Board and references therein), or demonstrated a disciplined lack of sufficiently explaining the wider institutional problem, its main actors (e.g., the fossil fuel industry, the climate change denial industry, major political parties), and the consequences of inaction (e.g., see Seymour 2018; Meyer 2018a).

Other times service to power is directly intentional. Rupert Murdoch built a media empire in Australia and England upon tabloid journals and right-wing talking points. Afterwards, Murdoch and his lieutenant, Roger Ailes, created FOX News in the United States as a platform for mobilizing right-wing audiences. Reportedly, Ailes believed that the resignation of US President, Richard Nixon, came about because US media did not have a conservative counter-narrative to what he considered an irredeemably liberally slanted media. Since at least that administration, he worked on plans to develop a media mouthpiece in support of conservative / GOP causes (see Cook 2011). As a businessman, Murdoch was proven prescient, in that in his decision to develop a media outlet to cater to conservative audiences that felt the mainstream media did not speak to or for them has been wildly successful both economically and politically (e.g., it boasts the largest US television audience for news programming).[2]

Intent to deliver such a product, former employees report that Murdoch and Ailes (since deceased) regularly interfered with and directed the content of news broadcasts. As such, the amount of jingoism, fearmongering, distortion, and fabrication on the network is obvious to any non-partisan observer. A case in point: when taken to court, FOX lawyers argued that intentionally reporting untruths to the public was not against the law; they won their case.[3] Today, the

---

2  Data from 2018 found the audience for FOX News as 94% White, 3% Hispanic, 2% Asian, 1% Black (see Price 2018 and reference therein). According to the Pew Research Center (Mitchell, et al. 2014), US conservatives "are tightly clustered around a single news source, far more than any other group in the survey, with 47% citing FOX News as their main source for news about government and politics" and they "[e]xpress greater distrust than trust of 24 of the 36 news sources measured in the survey. At the same time, fully 88% of consistent conservatives trust FOX News."

3  A note of general clarification. This story was often interpreted as a case where FOX News lawyers argued for the right to deliberately lie. Rather, the real story was more nuanced and in a way only a lawyer could appreciate. FOX appealed a case they previously lost after former reporters sued them because they were fired for refusing to change their story to include a rebuttal from a Monsanto spokesperson the reporters knew to be untrue. FOX lawyers argued they had a right to broadcast the story as management saw fit, even if this meant including what their own reporters knew to be a false account from one of the parties involved. Five other major news corporations filed an Amici Curiae (i.e., friend of the court) brief on FOX's

standards to which they hold themselves are murky enough that Ailes admitted that they are mainly in competition with entertainment channels rather than serious news channels. Finally, though it might have been said in jest, in a telling remark that revealed the actual role he saw the network serving, as US President, Donald Trump said that he thought that North Korean state television was a propaganda arm comparable to FOX News, though the Korean dictatorship was better at it (Hartmann 2018).

On mainstream television news, when anchors are not reporting on what government spokespersons have said, then the newest fashions, kittens saved from sewers, courageous children flying planes, and the most recent outrage (usually reported as a way to stir up fear, passions, and ratings) tend to reign. News programming is often either bookended by, or placed near, talk shows. Talk radio is an endless stream of cacophonous rhetoric, often of a right-wing variety. In conjunction with these offerings are sports-talk programs, commanding one of the largest segments of the radio audience and, ultimately, a distraction when juxtaposed to the real issues facing society today. In between segments, advertisers also distract us, this time with imagery of the good life, the newest convenience or alcoholic beverage, and the never-ending demand to consume ever more. The people at the head of these endeavors are handsomely paid and should they experience pangs of conscience, others stand at the ready to replace them. It should not be a surprise, then, that the more exposure one has to mainstream mass media the less they actually know about the issues of the day.[4]

Politicians do not fail to reflect on how to use language to shape our thoughts and perceptions with finely crafted double-speak. Honest, candid, informative, and politically useful discourse is not favorable to many political leaders, their ends, and/or their sponsors and they use our language and words as weapons against us. They have spent much time, energy, and money figuring ways to do so. For instance, US House of Representatives member, Bill Foster, the only scientist in Congress at the time, said that, "It has taken me a while to adjust to politics where, for many who practice it, the question is not 'Is it true?' but 'What can I convince the voting public is true?' That psychology has bled into

---

behalf to, in their words, "ensure that a news story about a scientific controversy regarding a commercial product was presented with fairness and balance, and to ensure that it had a sound defense to any potential defamation claim" (see Project Censored 2010).

4 On Monday November 21, 2011, Fairleigh Dickinson University sent out a press release of a poll of 612 New Jersey adults done in October of that year ("Some News Leaves People Knowing Less"). While they found those watching the Sunday morning news programs and talk shows had the most accurate knowledge of current events, outlets such as FOX News "lead people to be less informed than those who say they don't watch any news at all." For original Farleigh Dickinson study, see link here (URL retrieved August 12, 2018): http://publicmind.fdu.edu/2011/knowless/final.pdf.

politics more than it should" (see Fine Maron 2018). But the trend Foster was observing was not new. To wit: In 1996, US politician Newt Gingrich issued a memo for his GOPAC political action committee entitled, "Language: A Mechanism of Control," where he encouraged Republicans to use certain words to describe political opponents versus allies.[5]

### The Gingrich Memo

As you know, one of the key points in the GOPAC tapes is that "language matters." In the video "We are a Majority," Language is listed as a key mechanism of control used by a majority party, along with Agenda, Rules, Attitude and Learning. As the tapes have been used in training sessions across the country and mailed to candidates we have heard a plaintive plea: "I wish I could speak like Newt."

That takes years of practice. But, we believe that you could have a significant impact on your campaign and the way you communicate if we help a little. That is why we have created this list of words and phrases.

This list is prepared so that you might have a directory of words to use in writing literature and mail, in preparing speeches, and in producing electronic media. The words and phrases are powerful. Read them. Memorize as many as possible. And remember that like any tool, these words will not help if they are not used.

While the list could be the size of the latest "College Edition" dictionary, we have attempted to keep it small enough to be readily useful yet large enough to be broadly functional. The list is divided into two sections: Optimistic Positive Governing words and phrases to help describe your vision for the future of your community (your message) and Contrasting words to help you clearly define the policies and record of your opponent and the Democratic party.

Please let us know if you have any other suggestions or additions. We would also like to know how you use the list. Call us at GOPAC or write with your suggestions and comments. We may include them in the next tape mailing so that others can benefit from your knowledge and experience.

---

[5] You can find The Gingrich Memo at the Information Clearinghouse: (URL retrieved August 6, 2017): http://www.informationclearinghouse.info/article4443.htm.

## Optimistic Positive Governing Words

Use the list below to help define your campaign and your vision of public service. These words can help give extra power to your message. In addition, these words help develop the positive side of the contrast you should create with your opponent, giving your community something to vote *for!*

- active(ly)
- activist
- building
- candid(ly)
- care(ing)
- challenge
- change
- children
- choice/choose
- citizen
- commitment
- common sense
- compete
- confident
- conflict
- control
- courage
- crusade
- debate
- dream
- duty
- eliminate good-time in prison
- empower(ment)
- fair
- family
- freedom
- hard work
- help
- humane
- incentive
- initiative
- lead

- learn
- legacy
- liberty
- light
- listen
- mobilize
- moral
- movement
- opportunity
- passionate
- peace
- pioneer
- precious
- premise
- preserve
- principle(d)
- pristine
- pro- (issue): flag, children, environment, reform
- prosperity
- protect
- proud/pride
- provide
- reform
- rights
- share
- strength
- success
- tough
- truth
- unique
- vision
- we/us/our

## Contrasting Words

Often, we search hard for words to define our opponents. Sometimes we are hesitant to use contrast. Remember that creating a difference helps you. These are powerful words that can create a clear and easily understood contrast. Apply these to the opponent, their record, proposals and their party.

- abuse of power
- anti- (issue): flag, family, child, jobs
- betray
- bizarre
- bosses
- bureaucracy
- cheat
- coercion
- "compassion" is not enough
- collapse(ing)
- consequences
- corrupt
- corruption
- criminal rights
- crisis
- cynicism
- decay
- deeper
- destroy
- destructive
- devour
- disgrace
- endanger
- excuses
- failure (fail)
- greed
- hypocrisy
- ideological
- impose
- incompetent
- insecure
- insensitive
- intolerant
- liberal
- lie
- limit(s)
- machine
- mandate(s)
- obsolete
- pathetic
- patronage
- permissive attitude
- pessimistic
- punish (poor ...)
- radical
- red tape
- self-serving
- selfish
- sensationalists
- shallow
- shame
- sick
- spend(ing)
- stagnation
- status quo
- steal
- taxes
- they/them
- threaten
- traitors
- unionized
- urgent (cy)
- waste
- welfare

This manipulation of language in order to steer one's audience toward preferred thoughts and behaviors is nothing new. The public relations industry was shaped and perhaps even founded by Edward Bernays, nephew of Sigmund Freud.[6] He believed that the public should not be trusted in public affairs and propaganda was required to maintain order and discipline. Toward these ends, he studied techniques from psychology and the social sciences and started a new professional discipline that would have lasting influence.[7] Today, those who shape the public mind often come from elite educational institutions with degrees in "advertising," "business," "communications," and "public relations" and they sell their skills to corporations and political parties. These specialists use language and imagery to steer audiences in needed directions and have them embrace the wanted fashions, political views, and products through appealing to emotions and impulses such as fear, desire, and the need to fit in.

The university presents itself as a bastion of inquiry that is disinterested—meaning they do not take sides or have a hidden agenda—and enlightened—meaning that they apply the highest standards of intellectual and scientific thought. For some working there, this is no doubt true. However, compare intellectuals who challenge the official institutional ideological framework of our system to those who embrace, endorse, and defend it. Who makes a better living? Who rises through the ranks in think tanks and other elite institutions? Who shows up more to be interviewed on the talk shows, the newspapers, and the arbiters of public discussion? These questions practically answer themselves. And these are not issues limited to liberal democracies. In China—politically communist in name, economically capitalist in practice—the university system, in a fundamental abdication of principles of scientific practice, has been enlisted through online courses, funding, and new research institutes to promote the ideas of its President, Xi Jinping, to its citizens and to the world (e.g., see Shepherd 2018).

Overlapping with the university system are public intellectuals and experts. While it would be counterfactual to claim that all such individuals lumped

---

6  For insight, see *The Century of the Self*, a four-part series from BBC TWO that explores the origins and techniques of the public relations industry to manipulate the public mind, techniques which were subsequently harnessed by politicians, opinion-makers, and the advertising industry.

7  For instance, in one of Bernays' early successes, he placed women in public view smoking Lucky Strike cigarettes during an Easter parade in New York City, exposure that was credited for the surge in women's smoking during the period. So effective was his work and the professions it spawned that *Life* magazine (September, 1990) listed him as one of the most influential 100 Americans of the twentieth century. He was also behind the campaign that convinced Americans that bacon and eggs was a mainstay of a normal, healthy breakfast.

here are simply sycophantic babblers, none-too-few of them are. If the President is bent on war, there will be no shortage of people ready to explain why this course of action is necessary and is in fact an emergency of national consequence. Should a massive and significant trade deal catch some public notice, plenty of "experts" exist to explain why this is in the public interest, even though this agreement has been written by and for those working for corporate interests. Need someone to deny global warming, to put the right spin on the Israeli-Palestinian conflict, or to convince the populace that on-going surveillance is inevitable in modern society? There are specialists on speed dial who will climb over one another to provide such services.

The public must not only be misinformed on the important issues of the day, but they also must be distracted from them. The priesthood and public moralists (again, overlapping categories) tell us why global warming is a hoax, that homosexuality is abnormal, and why safe, legal abortion is a crime against god's will. At the same time, other moralists either remain silent on real biblical sins at the foundation of modern society—e.g., usury—or they rework the message of Jesus's ministry into one where he wants you to get rich—e.g., Joel Osteen's "prosperity gospel" (Image 40.1).

Whether in music, television, movies, or sports, celebrities in modern society receive an extensive amount of attention. And this serves a function beyond simply an entertaining distraction. The celebrities enjoy media platforms that allow them a participation in public discourse that often does not match their expertise. What makes a singer, actor, or athlete someone to listen to on matters of foreign policy (e.g., George Clooney or Sean Penn), dietary advice (e.g., Gwyneth Paltrow), or the efficacy of vaccines (e.g., Jenny McCarthy and Jim Carrey)? That such people are listened to and can have more influence than scientists tells us much about the type of society in which we live and the social discourse and standards of knowledge it perpetuates.

The sycophantic babblers serve several functions in our society.

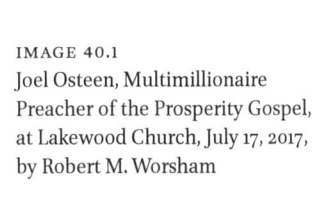

IMAGE 40.1
Joel Osteen, Multimillionaire Preacher of the Prosperity Gospel, at Lakewood Church, July 17, 2017, by Robert M. Worsham

First, they tell us that market society is the height and limit of human achievement and an inevitable product of human nature. Second, they keep alive the fiction that modern society, and especially its governing bodies, reflect democratic practice. Third, they deflect attention away from the lie that modern society is a meritocracy and keep us convinced the rich and the poor alike get what they deserve. Fourth, they obfuscate the roots of government policy, why we go to war, and why new villains must be regularly conjured up to unite the populace around the leader. Fifth, the babblers deflect attention from the reality that modern society is a class society run by and for its owners and that the ruling class gives not one whit about the population, unless it as potential voters, taxpayers, consumers, soldiers, or until they become unruly (this is why corporations spend billions subsidizing the babblers—keeping the behemoth hidden is expensive). Sixth, they must make sure that the public never considers possible alternative ways organizing their world, much less that they start to work toward those ends. Seventh, like our hypothetical Aztec priesthood, the sycophantic babblers convince us criticism of our civilization based on real information is not worthy of discussion at best or crazy talk at worst. And they are handsomely rewarded for all of these services.

After 2016 US Presidential election, there were reports about the "fake news" that inundated the media during the campaign. Some Trump supporters were concerned about a story, spread online and through Facebook, dubbed, "pizzagate," a supposed conspiracy involving pedophilia, a pizzeria, code words in secret emails, and the Hillary Clinton campaign. It was widely suspected that this story came from Russian hackers bent on swaying American voters. Though this fake news was ridiculous, there were other similar stories related to sordid sexual predation that *were* apparently true but relatively untouched by the press. Before running for President, Donald Trump had associations with billionaire Jeffery Epstein, who was known to visit Trump's resort, Mar-a-Lago. Evidence also indicates Trump's name (as well as Bill Clinton's) appeared on flight logs to Epstein's private island, where sex parties were known to take place. While Epstein was convicted of illegal sex acts with minors at his island parties, it is not known if Trump was involved in such crimes. That said, we *do* know Trump had called him a "terrific guy" and admitted his own knowledge of Epstein's interest in "younger" women (see Gerstein 2017). After the election, stories emerged about Trump's ties with Russian leader Putin and other Russian oligarchs. Trump and many of his supporters—both often consumers of FOX News—would claim "fake news!" whenever stories about such ties or other unflattering ones came out. Thus, "fake news" shifted from a label for actually made-up stories to a coverall for stories about inconvenient facts.

Platforms like Facebook often bring people together who share the same views. And similar people with similar views tend to share and spread similar news and ideas, whether scientific information or conspiracy theories. A study published by the *Proceedings of the National Academy of Sciences* (January 19, 2016), for example, found that networks of associations produced by sites like Facebook create a level of homogeneity of information and result in an echo chamber. Here, personal beliefs and news are spread and reinforced and contrary information is dismissed or does not even break through. So useful and effective is this tool that opposed sides of the political divide wield it against the other in spreading the desired information, whether factual or not (Del Vicario et al. 2016). Another study found that, although Facebook use itself was unrelated to political knowledge scores, the *more* people used it for news consumption and news sharing the *lower* they scored on measures of factual political knowledge (Cacciatore et al. 2017). Such conditions have driven commentators to claim that we now live in a "post-truth" world and not without reason.

But this is also not left to chance. On November 19, 2016, *The New York Times* published a story about Cambridge Analytica, a firm that uses Facebook quizzes and users' responses to news stories and other types of data to identify individuals—psychological profiling and "microtargeting" them—in order to manipulate their views and behaviors and to push a political agenda. Answers to quizzes provide demographic information and catalogs their knowledge of social issues and their political outlooks (Funk 2016; also see Cadwalladr 2018). Having already worked on the "Brexit" issue on the side of Britain leaving the European Union, the Trump campaign hired Cambridge Analytica (backed by billionaire Robert Mercer from the hedge fund industry) to round up voters via such online manipulation. One technique was a "dark post" only a receiver can see, i.e., it does not appear on the user's wall for others to view. Targeting users of specific demographic and political views, dark posts are meant to be shared with others with similar characteristics, to reinforce supporters' beliefs, or to be directed toward the opposition's base to spread disinformation there. An Ipsos survey of 3,015 US adults found that such techniques were successful, with 75% of Americans exposed to such fake news believing that the stories were accurate (Silverman and Singer Vine 2016). Though we might interpret such results with caution, little time and money would be spent on such efforts if they did not work to some degree. And, as such, reports in 2018 indicated that Trump campaign operatives were already working with ex-Cambridge employees on the 2020 presidential election cycle (Horwitz 2018).

In an inverted and mystified world, the powers-that-be and their sycophants can step into the gaps in our knowledge, sow dissension, misdirect us, or otherwise build upon the already mystified world we live in and experience. It takes careful observation and analysis to sort through the messages hitting us from all directions and the narrower and more uniform the sources of information available to us, the more controlled is our understanding of the world and the less likely it is that we act in a way contrary to what the powerful want. This is why twenty-first century politicians continue to find ways to control public discourse via shaping the rules of the media. In the United States (even before Donald Trump took office), politicians sponsored bills to repeal "net neutrality," which is the principle that internet service providers treat all data on the Internet equally. This effort at repeal was successful under the FCC leadership of Ajit Pai in 2018. Such changes in regulations allow internet service providers to charge greater fees for different websites, offer a slate of places one may visit online at different speeds for different costs, or even to refuse to allow linking to sites of the provider's choosing. Also, in 2018, the European Parliament's Committee on Legal Affairs passed Article 13, which could put an end to memes, remixes, other user-generated data, and require online platforms to pay publishers a fee to link to their news content. In short, efforts such as these can neutralize much of the democratic potential found in the way the Internet allows people to find and share information. Rather than have a state censor public information or restrict its flow, this task has been farmed out to the corporate community. It is not difficult to imagine what sort of information they have an interest in or what type of communication they will find contrary to those interests.[8]

---

8 An unattributed list posted to multiple webpages, blogs, boards, and so on, states the following: *What you should know about:* Why bats are dying by the millions; Why bees are dying by the billions; Why bird populations are plunging; Ocean acidification; Melting ice caps; Deforestation; Dangers of natural gas fracking; Tar sands pollution and its dangers; Mountain top removal; GMOs, Monsanto, and the problems caused by toxic farming practices; Potential food shortages due to drought, soil depletion, and a plunge in wildlife populations; Polluted and depleted aquifers; How to grow food; Hazards of industrial pollution; Government lies; Lies from the financial system; Lies about the tax system; How your rights are being violated; Aging nuclear power plants; The realities of war; Depleted uranium bomb residue from wars and how it is being spread by the weather; Growth of the prison industry; Lies about the War on Drugs; How to disconnect from fossil fuels; Permaculture and sustainable living; Importance of organic foods. *What the news media tells you about:* Who got murdered; Lindsay Lohan; Who said what that doesn't matter; Kanye West and Kim Kardashian; Car chases; Justin Bieber; Who is getting divorced; The First Lady's workout routine; Sex scandals; The stock report; Who is gay; How many cars are selling; Who got arrested; Drama in D.C.; The housing market; Sports drama; Misinformation about history; Who got an award; Courtroom scandals; Gas prices; "Reality" show drama; What's being built; Whatever subtly perpetuates fear; Travel and leisure stuff; Who bought something expensive; What haircut to get; A little about racism and sexism; Corporate products to buy; Who had a baby; Where to eat; What color to wear; Whatever will keep you tuned in. See (URL retrieved August 12, 2018): http://i.imgur.com/OLfcSaE.jpg.

CHAPTER 41

# Applying Chemistry to Industry and Agriculture

The application of scientific knowledge to production techniques—from mining to textiles to agriculture—was a key feature of the Industrial Revolution. This connection continues today, as we witness growing technological complexity from computers in factories to use of pesticides, fertilizers, hormones, and antibiotics in farming. The advantages of such things are widely known. The people of modernity have lifetime access to more commodities, medicines, and calories today than people at any other time in history, which, in part, is reflected in longer average lifespans. Modern society, just like any other, has little choice but to extract raw materials from nature to warm ourselves, to make our clothes, and to shelter and feed us (and so on), though *how* we accomplish that extraction and *why* are among its crucial distinguishing features. In modernity, the industrial apparatus churns out commodities not so much as a way to simply meet people's needs but rather as a consequence of the ever-increasing needs of capital accumulation. And, as a result, modern technology, our mode of production, patterns of energy, resource, and commodity consumption, and methods of disposing byproducts and other wastes have begun to threaten our collective well-being in multiple ways.

We extract coal, gas, and oil from the earth for our energy facilities, factories, planes, trains, cars, and homes. But such sources of energy are hardly clean and there is environmental fallout from their use. Perhaps the first and most obvious of these concerns is the quality of our air. Any mention of the words "industrial revolution," for instance, cannot help but conjure up images of billowing smoke stacks and factories choking the air of urban centers in nineteenth century Europe and North America. Such problems, however, were and are not time-locked.

In a famous case, between December 5–9, 1952, a heavy smog blanketed London, England, in possibly the worst instance over its long history with "pea soup" air. Several factors accounted for the event. First, an "anticyclone" (also known as a "thermal inversion") settled over a windless city, meaning cold air was trapped underneath a warmer layer that held it in place. Second, Londoners were experiencing a cold winter, leading many people to burn more coal (and that of a lower quality) than normal. Plus, many of the city's power stations, industrial facilities, and transportation systems relied on coal. As a result, the air was inundated with tons of smoke particles, hydrochloric acid, fluorine compounds, and sulphur dioxide. The number of deaths attributed

IMAGE 41.1  Black Country—Borinage (Belgium), by Constantin Meunier

IMAGE 41.2  Nant Y Glo, Monmouthshire, Wales—1830, by Henry G. Gastineau, 1791–1876—Samuel Lacey, fl. 1818–1857

to the Great Smog of 1952 is estimated between 4,000 and 12,000 people (with a greater number becoming sick from respiratory infections, hypoxia, and restricted airways) (Nielsen 2002; Stone 2002; Bell, Davis, and Fletcher 2004; Lean 2012; Met Office 2015; Onyanga-Omara 2016).

This was not a singular event. In 2014, scientists warned that China's air quality resembled that of a nuclear winter—e.g., the concentration of PM 2.5 particles (particulate matter that can penetrate the lungs and enter the bloodstream) was 505 micrograms per cubic meter, with the World Health Organization's (WHO) "safe level" being 25; this level could also slow photosynthesis in plants and threaten China's food supply (Kaiman 2014). Delhi, India, too, has experienced smog similar to that of China and of a type that also drew comparisons to London of 1952, some of it from cars and industry and other portions from burning excess left over from agricultural production (i.e., unsold crops, other wastes) (Kamal 2016). Researchers in England found particles from air pollution in the placentas of pregnant women (see Masters 2018 and reference therein). This issue of air quality is a global health problem. One study by the International Energy Agency estimated the global deaths per year from air pollution at 6.5 million (see Reed 2016 and references therein).

After more than 200 years of industrial development and with much of the easier-to-get-at sources of energy by now extracted or facing depletion—e.g., in the Arabian Peninsula and elsewhere (see Plumer 2011; Drum 2014; Miller and Sorrell 2014; *The Economist* 2016; Rowell 2017)—more draconian methods of coal and oil extraction have been developed. For instance, as deep well mining became less lucrative and accessible in Appalachia, coal industries began to remove mountain tops *en masse* to get at the remaining coal seams, which, in addition to traditional strip mining, resulted in destroying 1.5 million acres of trees between 1976 and 2015 (see Funes 2018 and references therein). In the mid-2010s, Canada and the United States experienced an oil and gas boom because of the use of hydraulic fracturing (or "fracking") and the extraction of oil from the Alberta Tar Sands—essentially scraping mass amounts of trees and land from the surface (Image 41.7). Both practices destroy ecosystems and put poisons into ground water—e.g., heavy metals such as antimony, beryllium,

IMAGE 41.3
Nelson's Column during the Great Smog of 1952, London, by N.T. Stobbs

IMAGE 41.4  Two Photos Taken in the Same Location in Beijing, August 2005, by Bobak. The photograph on the left was taken after it had rained for two days. The right photograph shows smog covering Beijing in what would otherwise be a sunny day.

IMAGE 41.5  Smog Near New Delhi, India, November, 2016, by Saurabh Kumar

IMAGE 41.6  New Delhi, India, November, 2017, by Sumitmpsd

cadmium, chlorine, chromium, cobalt, lead, manganese, nickel, selenium, arsenic and mercury from mountaintop removal and methanol and benzene from fracking. Outside of water, fracking is also connected to air pollution (see Smithies 2018 and references therein) and is a leading suspect in causing increased earthquake activity across areas where it is practiced (see Gilman 2016).[1]

---

1   Sometimes earthquakes from natural causes create avoidable environmental damage related to energy production. In April 2011, a massive earthquake hit Japan, severely damaging a nuclear power plant in Fukushima and causing several reactors to fail. Ocean water was poured into the reactors to prevent a meltdown and a potential nuclear reaction, with the resulting wastewater released into the ocean. Afterwards, ocean currents in the Pacific saw measurable increases in radiation associated with the accident. The overall danger is hard to

IMAGE 41.7  Alberta Tar Sands, 2008, by Howl Arts Collective

The carbon dioxide (CO2) and methane byproducts from burning fossil fuels that are pumped into the atmosphere have set us on a long-predicted and possibly irreversible global warming trend whose apex is yet to be determined but will likely be catastrophic within decades, not centuries, if unchecked (see Gills 2016). We cannot say we were not warned. In 1896, Swedish scientist, Svante Arrhenius, calculated that increasing CO2 output would cause Earth's temperature to rise 5°–6° C. Similar investigations continued over the next century. In 1972, John Sawyer published, *Man-made Carbon Dioxide and the 'Greenhouse' Effect*. In 1988, James Edward Hansen, a scientist specializing in radiative transfer, planetary atmospheres, and climate modeling, testified in front of the US Senate, stating that scientific research provided a "high degree

---

estimate, with no consistent scientific agreement on the extent of the problem, though by March 2016 reports of thyroid cancer in children living near Fukushima had spiked (Normile 2016). Still, even as the global public had been made little aware of the extent of the ongoing threat, Japan enacted laws to suppress reporting on the incident as state secrets (Hunziker 2016). As of 2018, radioactive water was still being released into the ocean from the site (*The Japan Times* 2018b).

of confidence" that greenhouse gasses cause global warming and that "It is already happening now" (see Shabecoff 1988).

Such warnings were little heeded and the problem has only grown. Data suggest we are adding $CO_2$ into the atmosphere 10x faster than during the hottest period of the last 66 million years (Lavell 2016). In February 2017, scientists warned that human activity was causing climate change 170x faster than natural forces (Davey 2017). In April-May of 2018, the Mauna Loa Observatory in Hawaii recorded all-time $CO_2$ highs (at least for the last 800,000 years they have records for from ice core samples), with trend data showing an ongoing increase.[2] Other climate scientists report that the amount of $CO_2$ put into the atmosphere is *exponentially* accelerating (see Hunziker 2018 and references therein).

Throughout the early-2000s, climate scientists, seemingly yearly, told us that we had just experienced the hottest recorded January or March ever and that 2015 and 2016 were the hottest known years since records have been kept (Tabary 2016). Even with that in the background, in late spring of 2018, "thousands" of temperature records were broken across the United States (see Jamail 2018 and references therein) and by that summer all-time records for high temperatures were set all over the world (see Harris 2018; Romm 2018; Samenow 2018b). Correspondingly, the amount of $CO_2$ and subsequent temperatures at the poles and other normally icy terrains also increased dramatically (Thomson 2016; Yulsman 2016).

Warm air melts ice sheets and glaciers, a reality already observed prior to the turn of the millennium and the subsequent ramping up of climate change concerns. In May of 2018, the temperature at the North Pole spiked to the melting point of 32° F (or 30°–35° F, 17°–19° C, above normal) and the region experienced the warmest temperature on record for that time of year (see Samenow 2018a and references therein). Worse yet, by July 2018, the temperature had reached over 86°–90° F inside the Arctic Circle, with wildfires contributing to additional heat as well as smoke in the region and exacerbating already thawing snow and ice cover (see Kahn 2018; Irfan 2018; Kaufman 2018, and references therein). At the polar opposite side of the planet, the loss of Antarctic ice sheets between 1992–2017 has been estimated at three-trillion tons (The IMBIE Team 2018). By 2018, loss of Antarctic ice was occurring faster than any

---

2  Data comes from the US National Oceanic and Atmospheric Administration's Earth System Research Laboratory, Global Monitoring System. Their publicly available website with this information can be found here (URL retrieved August 13, 2018): https://www.esrl.noaa.gov/gmd/ccgg/trends/index.html.

time in the previous 25 years and had tripled since 2012, while raising global sea levels .12 inches (3 millimeters) since that time (NASA 2018b).

As ice cover thaws, it releases additional methane—a more potent greenhouse gas than $CO_2$—into the atmosphere, a problem on top of industrial releases of methane that will only contribute more to global warming (see Berwyn 2017; Knoblauch et al. 2018). Not only does the Arctic have billions of cubic meters of methane in the ocean and trapped in once-frozen tundra, current measurements of methane gas releases have been on the conservative side, as a 2018 report found that methane releases in United States are 60% higher than previous Environmental Protection Agency estimates (*Science | Reports* 2018). There is now a fear of feedback loops and a runaway hothouse effect, where warming leads to melting which leads to additional $CO_2$ and methane releases. It should then be of no surprise that one study concluded that global warming might result in a temperature rise twice that of what conventional models have predicted (Fischer et al. 2018).

Increased levels of greenhouse gasses and rising temperatures, melting ice, and rising sea levels ripple throughout the ecosystem and have individual as well as collective impacts on human social, economic, and physical wellbeing. For instance, one study found that for every 1° C (1.8° F) temperature increase caused by $CO_2$, the associated air pollution would cause about 1000 additional deaths and more cases of respiratory illness and asthma in the United States (Jacobson 2008). Nearly 60,000 suicides of Indian farmers over three decades have been associated with increasing temperatures (Safi 2017). In 2018, the warmest May since 1900 cost Norway's citizens a $2.34 billion for additional power (Karagiannopoulos 2018). In the mid-summer of 2018, over 57,000 people in Japan were taken to the hospital in three months dealing with heat related issues (including new temperature highs), nearing a record set in 2013 that was expected to be broken (*The Japan Times* 2018a). At least 33 deaths in Montreal, Canada and an overall total of 54 in the Quebec Province were attributed to a heat wave there (Roy 2018). And by August of 2018, California experienced the largest wildfire in state history (Serna, Queally, and Tchekmedyian 2018), driven by heat and dry spells associated with climate change (see Alexander 2018).

Extreme weather events (e.g., heatwaves, floods, droughts) are a signature of global warming (e.g., because of its stalling effect on the jet stream) and these should persist or even increase in the future (see Carrington 2018c and references therein). The potential economic and human costs are difficult to estimate but several are sobering. A study in *Nature* concluded that methane output and Arctic melting could cost the world economy $60 trillion dollars or more (Whiteman, Hope, and Wadhams 2013). Another study concluded that

IMAGE 41.8 Methane Leaking Through the Cracks, 2009–2010, by NASA/JPL/Eric Kort, Alan Buis; NSF, NCAR, NOAA

by 2100, if greenhouse gas output continues at its current pace, three out of four people on Earth may experience the type of heat and humidity associated with deadly heat waves for at least 20 days per year (Mora et al. 2017). And so troublesome are the prospects, the US military—the world's largest polluter (see Webb 2017 and references therein) and not typically known as an environmental crusader—has diagnosed global warming as a national security threat (see Conca 2014).

There are other ripple effects from rising temperatures, melting ice, and rising sea levels. Increased ocean temperatures lead to increased surface evaporation, both of which add fuel to hurricane strength (Trenberth et al. 2018). One model predicts that coastal flooding associated with global warming will double in frequency by 2050 (Vitousek et al. 2017). Other damages from hurricanes are well-known: coastline erosion, crippled industries (such as oysters, fishing, tourism, oil refining), and destroyed cities. With the ocean's rise and coastlines encroached upon, freshwater plants living at this border unable to deal with the salinity begin to die off and turn into "ghost trees" (see Parry 2017), which can be an early sign of sea level rise. Also indicative of this is the fact that underground internet cables—once built 25 years ago parallel to highways and coastlines with no thought of how geography and climate would change in the future—are threatened with destruction by rising sea levels, sooner than specialists had originally thought (see Gabbatiss 2018b and reference therein).

More dramatically, several island nations are currently sinking below the ocean's currents (Guilford 2014) and evacuations of villages and even whole atolls have commenced, e.g., Kiribati and the Solomon Islands. In 2018, "unprecedented" flooding hit India, killing dozens and requiring 40,000 people to be evacuated (Pokharel and McKenzie 2018). Rising sea levels in South Florida have impinged on underground sources of freshwater there, a problem expected to get worse (*Miami Herald* Editorial Board 2018). Coastal communities in developed countries are making plans for current and future flooding of property related to the ocean's rise, e.g., instituting tax plans to build or buffer levees and/or even retreating from the coast altogether (see Brunhuber 2018; Schwartz 2018). One study found that flooding related to rising sea levels could, by 2100, cost the world economy $14–27 trillion if warming is not held to the 2° C limit agreed to during the Paris climate talks (2015)—and such costs will depend on how high the oceans actually rise and the amount, type, and level of success of adaptive measures taken (Jevrejeva et al. 2018).

Atmospheric $CO_2$ also ends up *in* the oceans, where it chemically reacts with seawater and increases its acidity, endangering phytoplankton (the world's largest source of oxygen) and the food chain (Brannen 2014). One study found that ocean acidification harms the smelling ability of fish, which can disrupt how they detect food or predators (Porteus et al. 2018; also see University of Exeter 2018). Researchers conclude that global warming could suppress marine biological productivity for a millennium (Moore et al. 2018). Toxins from manure and fertilizer make their way into waterways and facilitate larger and larger alga blooms, which deplete water of the oxygen aquatic animals need to live, i.e., eutrophication. As fish either die outright or move away from their more natural habitats to other waters with more oxygen, areas left become "dead zones" that have little, or are absent of, life (see Map 41.1.). Such changes can disrupt mating, the feeding habits of other animals that rely on them, and bring on local and international turf battles over fishing grounds (e.g., see Abel 2018). In 2017, the largest dead zone in the Gulf of Mexico (nearly 8,200 square miles) was recorded (Milman 2017). And in 2018, the largest dead zone yet, i.e., the size of Scotland, was discovered in the Gulf of Oman in the Arabian Sea and contained almost no oxygen (Embury-Dennis 2018a). That same year, a dead zone found in the Baltic Sea was also among the world's largest, with oxygen loss there described as "unprecedentedly severe" (see European Geosciences Union 2018 and reference therein). While such oceanic areas of low level oxygen have been expanding, researchers argue that current studies have underestimated the level of deoxygenation, which they conclude will

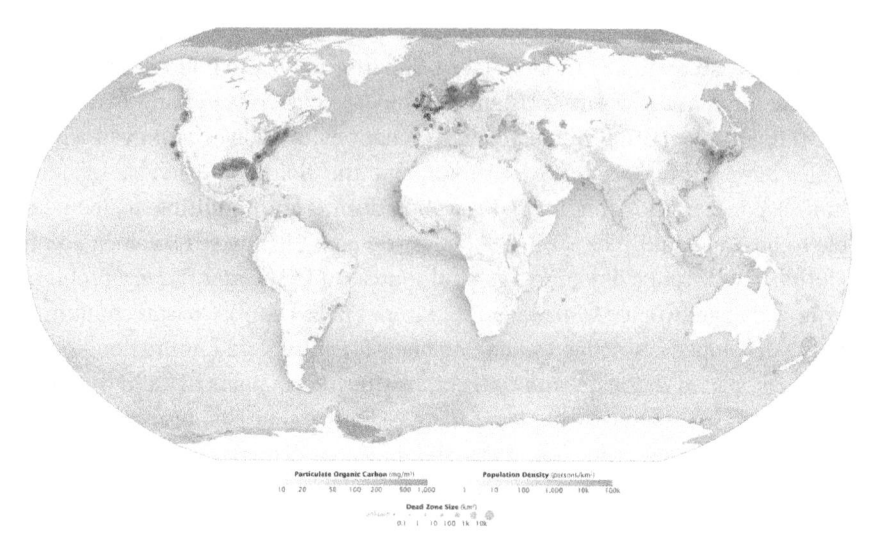

MAP 41.1    Aquatic Dead Zones, 2010, by Robert Simmon and Jesse Allen

continue and accelerate (Stramma et al. 2008; Helm, Bindoff, and Church 2011; Schmidtko, Stramma, and Visbeck 2017; Oschlies et al. 2018).

In the midst of such problems, governments struggle to do anything effective while carbon energy industries fund projects and propaganda meant to confuse and mislead the public about the threat (see Goldenberg and Bengtsson 2016). On top of these hurdles, scientists face the task of getting their findings taken seriously and altering hard-to-change lifestyle habits among the public (e.g., see Richardson 2015; Atkin 2017). For example, according to a report from the Food and Agriculture Organization of the United Nations, the livestock production chain associated with meat-based diets accounts for 14.5% of all human generated greenhouse gasses—distributed across feed and processing (45% of total), digestion (39%), manure decomposition (10%), and the rest from processing and transporting animal products (United Nations 2013). A shift from readymade fast food sandwiches to homemade ones would reduce the resulting carbon footprint by about half (Espinoza-Orias and Azapgic 2018). Each day in China alone, about 60 million takeaway food containers are thrown out, while Beijing itself produces about 25,000 tons of trash, most of it incinerated or going into landfills (Birtles 2018). In the UK, about 22 million tons of trash is thrown out each year, much of it shipped overseas with the goal of recycling it, though this is next to impossible for the government to monitor and it is feared a significant portion is dumped in landfills in places like Turkey and Malaysia (see Parveen 2018).

Much of this trash, including plastic, ends up in our waterways, streams, rivers, and oceans. Juxtaposed ocean currents that go in different directions across vast global regions produce a "gyre" (or a circulating pattern) that rounds up debris and concentrates it into more compact areas (Map 41.2). As a result of such currents, a huge garbage patch in the Pacific Ocean was discovered in 1997 and, despite being 16x larger than its original estimation, stands from somewhere between 3x the size of France to twice the size of the state of Texas (Schlanger 2018; Meredith 2018; Liu 2018). Other oceanic garbage patches have been found in the Indian Ocean between Africa and Australia (see L. Parker 2014) and in the South Pacific off the South American coast (see Pierre-Louis 2017). In 2018, the Dominican Republic made the news when a "wave" of plastic washed up on beaches after an offshore storm. Afterward, the activist group Parley picked up 30 tons of trash there in three days (see Yagoda 2018).

Plastics from such refuse break up into smaller and smaller parts, which birds and fish mistake for food, killing some and introducing these oil-based materials into our food chain inside sea-based animals that survive (Vaughn 2014; Plumer 2015; Forester 2016). Researchers have found microplastics in mussels (see Hoare 2018) and in seabirds to such an extent that the plastic leaves no room for food, leaving the birds to starve (see Gill 2018). We have

IMAGE 41.9
Image Microplastics, by NOAA Marine Debris Program

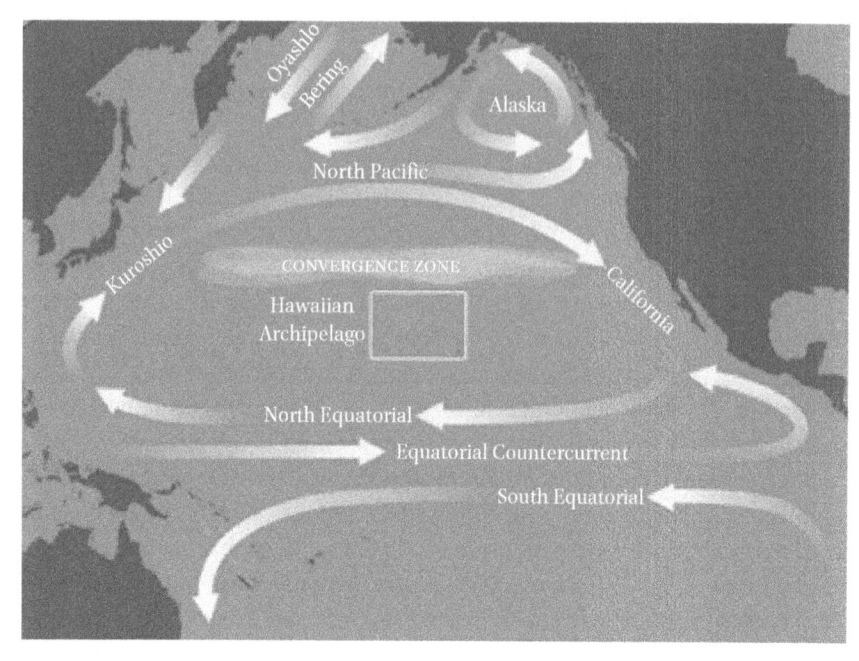

MAP 41.2    Map of the North Pacific Subtropical Convergence Zone (STCZ) within the North Pacific Gyre, by NOAA

IMAGE 41.10   The Great Pacific Garbage Patch, by Ray Boland

inundated the oceans with so much plastic that up to 26 microplastic particles per cubic meter were found in the waters at the most remote spot in the ocean—Point Nemo (over 1,000 miles in any direction from the nearest island) (*The Guardian* | Environment 2018).

That ecosystems need clean water (salt or fresh) and humans need drinkable water are both undeniable truths. But our methods of industrial production, commodity consumption, and waste elimination are threatening our ability to sustain these needs, such as in Europe in 2018, where only 40% of 130,000 waterways were found in a good ecological state, with agriculture, industry, and households the main culprits (see Nelson 2018 and references therein). And not only are pesticides and solid wastes ending up in our aquifers, watersheds, rivers, lakes, streams, and oceans, but we also are confronting issues we simply never imagined before:

- Medicines and birth control pills do not always get fully absorbed by the body and their leftovers get eliminated through waste products and make their way into waterways. These chemicals negatively affect fish and other natural aquatic wildlife, with some being born with multiple eyes or blind, hermaphroditic or neutered, and so on, e.g., male fish producing female eggs (see Konkel 2016; for review of literature, see Ebele, Abdallah, and Harrad 2017).
- Today, artificial plastic "microbeads" from makeup wash down the drain and into streams, tributaries, rivers, and oceans. One study (Rochman et al. 2015) estimated that 8 trillion microbeads (enough to cover 300 tennis courts) are introduced to US waters *per day*.
- The bleaching of and decline in coral of the Great Barrier Reef off the Australian coast has been described as "unprecedented," the result of poor turbidity (i.e., poor water quality due to particulate matter and sediment) and rising ocean temperatures (Smee 2018).
- The largest aquifer in America, the Ogallala, which cuts through several states (see Map 41.3) in the breadbasket of the Midwest and overlaps with fracking areas, is running dry from being used faster than it can refill itself (Jacobs et al. 2016). Scientists warn of impending water shortages in arid US states due to a 770% increase in water use and a 1440% growth of toxic waste water due to fracking between 2011–2016 (Gabbatiss 2018c).
- With 780 million people lacking access to safe drinking-water worldwide (United Nations) and with almost half the world predicted to live in high stress water areas by 2030, concerns about conflicts over grazing rights and water wars, present and future, do not seem unreasonable (see Arsenault 2012 and references therein; Ferguson 2015).
- Groundwater declines, soil collapses, and sinking urban areas have been observed in Beijing, Shanghai, and Mexico City, with growing problems

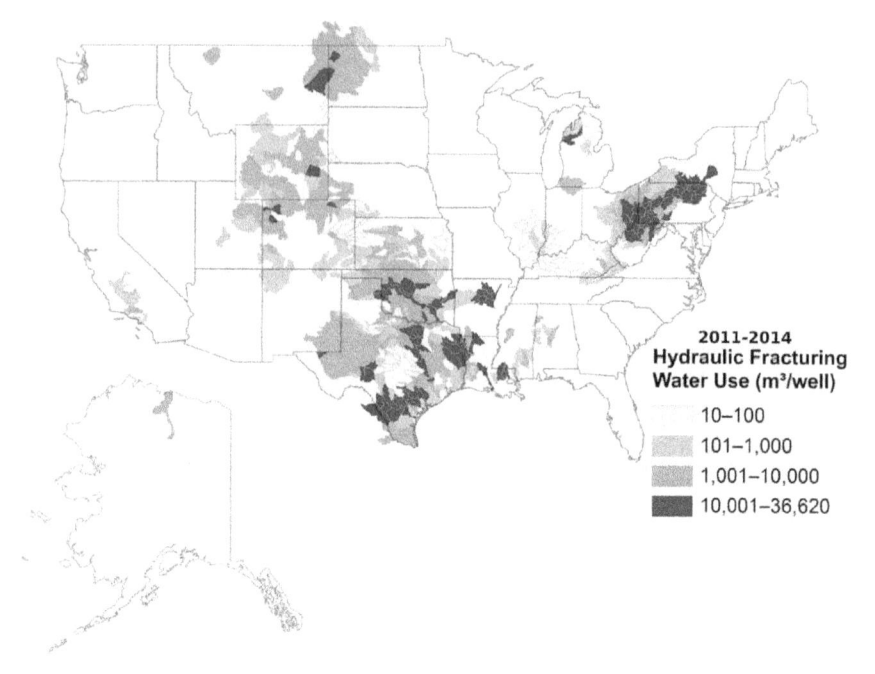

MAP 41.3   2011–2014 Hydraulic Fracturing Water Use (sq. meters/well), 2015, by US Geological Survey

predicted in over-stressed areas such as Saudi Arabia, Yemen, northwest India and Pakistan, and the Murzuk-Djado Basin in northern Africa (see L. Parker 2016).
- Bengaluru, Hyderabad, and New Delhi, India are among 21 cities predicted to run out of water by 2020 if current trends keep their pace, which would affect hundreds of millions of people (NITI Aayog 2018).
- In 2018, Cape Town, South Africa, was *within days* of becoming the first major city to run out of water.

Our treatment of land has not escaped the ravages we have visited upon the oceans. In cutting down deep-rooting forests and by replacing trees with weaker and shallower food crops, we court the loss of topsoil, floods, and new dust storms. According to a University of Maryland study, global loss of tree cover—from a combination of forest fires, agriculture, logging, and mining—in 2016 was estimated at 73.4 million acres, 51% higher than the previous year (see Weisse and Dow Goldman 2017 and references therein). In the United States, one study found that metropolitan areas were losing 36 million trees a year, or 175,000 acres in coverage (see Cassella 2018 and references therein). Another study examined both climate change and human land-use—individually and in tandem—and used models that incorporated an "optimistic" scenario of lower levels of warming (below 2° C), scenarios of a 2°–3° C and a 2.6°–3.7° C rise, and a "business-as-usual" scenario that predicts at 4°–6° C rise. Under the latter model, land-use practices are predicted to cause biodiversity losses of 2% and global warming to cause losses of 29%. Particularly susceptible are grasslands and savannas in southern Africa and southern America. Amphibians (which require both land and water) and reptiles (which use the external environment to regulate body temperature) are more threatened by global warming and land-use practices than mammals and birds (see Newbold 2018). Scientists similarly warn that hunting and loss of habitat, especially in Brazil, Indonesia, Madagascar, and the Democratic Republic of the Congo, are likely to push chimpanzees and orangutans (among other primates) to the brink of risk extinction by 2100 (Science Advances 2017; Johnston 2017; Gabbatiss 2018a).

In order to produce cars, plastics, clothes, refrigerators, food, and so on, we pump carcinogens and other chemicals into our land, air, water, and animals. In the 1980s, despite heated petroleum industry resistance, lead was banned from gasoline after scientists discovered its negative effects on human cognitive abilities.[3] Today, we are learning that air pollution can still result in a "huge" reduction in intelligence—equivalent to one year of education—especially for those over 64 years of age (see Carrington and Kuo 2018 and reference therein). And things like chlorine, lead, and PCBs inundate the environment to such an extent that they can be found in the food chain and our own bodies. Meat-based diets themselves require use of more water (2.9x), energy (2.5x), fertilizer (13x), and pesticides (1.4x) than vegetarian based diets (Marlow et al. 2009). Many of the fertilizers and pesticides we use for mass agriculture are known carcinogens rooted in petroleum-based technologies and we inject animals we eat with hormones and antibiotics, exposing ourselves to these chemicals at ever younger ages and tooling around with our bodies' chemistry.[4] Overuse of antibiotics (in both food and medicines) produces super-strains of bacteria we once could defeat, such as tuberculosis and gonorrhea, which are growing more and more immune to these weapons (see Centers for Disease Control n.d.a, n.d.b). In January 2017, a Reno, Nevada woman was reported to be the

---

3 Some have hypothesized this ban led to decreased crime rates decades later (see Casciani 2014).
4 It has been suggested that chemicals in the food supply account for early onset puberty in boys and girls in the Western world. As of yet, research is inconclusive. Similarly, sperm counts in America, Europe, Australia, and New Zealand have dropped more than 50% in just under the last 40 years, reasons for which are inconclusive but leading causal factors are suspected to be chemicals in the environment, obesity, smoking, and stress (see Kelland 2017).

first death from a bacterial infection that was resistant to all-known antibiotics (see Brink 2017). Today, experts warn that we are facing the "end of antibiotics" (see Begley 1994; Childress 2013) and an age looms when a simple cut and infection can again turn life-threatening.

In modern society's mass production, land, animals, and vegetation compete with human needs. Our favorite crops and gardening plants need protection against "weeds." Chemical companies produce herbicides—like Monsanto's Roundup, with the main ingredient glyphosate—to kill these weeds. In 2015, the World Health Organization decided that glyphosate was likely a carcinogen and, in 2018, a jury agreed, awarding a man with terminal cancer $289 million. Evidence at the trial convinced jurors that not only did Roundup contain carcinogenic chemicals but that Monsanto also knew this and failed to warn consumers (the number of additional plaintiffs and suits against the company number between 800 and 5,000) (see Bellon 2018; Corbett 2018c; Yan 2018). Insects such as bees pollinate flowering food-bearing plants—e.g., apples, almonds, grapefruit, pumpkins, peaches, pears, cherries, watermelons, and cucumbers, among others—and in the 2000s an epidemic of "colony collapse disorder" emerged, marked by millions of bee colonies suddenly dying and with pesticides such as neonicotinoids among the leading suspected culprits (Lu, Warchol, and Callahan 2014). One study found that glyphosate targets an enzyme in plants that is also contained in bees and this disrupts their gut biota and makes them susceptible to opportunistic pathogens they might otherwise have been able to fight off (Motta, Raymann, and Moran 2018). Further, there are multiple indications of declining insect populations as a whole, one of the cornerstones of the global ecosystem and without which there stands a significant threat of environmental collapse (see McKie 2018b and references therein).

The scientific community for years has warned the public and policymakers about these problems. There is, first off, the information and opinion found in the professional literature. For instance, in examining 11,944 abstracts of peer-reviewed scientific literature containing matching topics of "global climate change" or "global warming" published between 1991 and 2011, researchers found that 66.4% expressed no position on humans as a causal agent—i.e., anthropogenic global warming (AGW)—while 32.6% endorsed AGW, .7% rejected it, and .3% were uncertain. Among those expressing a position on AGW, 97.1% endorsed the "consensus" position that humans were the cause (Cook et al. 2013). Scientists also provide clear and easy to understand data lists of rising levels of $CO_2$ and the multiple ways we can document climate change, such as increasing temperatures, warming oceans, shrinking ice sheets, glacial retreat, decreased snow cover, declining Arctic sea ice, sea level rise, extreme events, and ocean acidification (see NASA 2018a). And groups like the Union of Concerned Scientists (2018) publish accessible while detailed explanations of how we know temperatures are rising, how human $CO_2$ output contributes to this, and how we can compare natural versus human drivers of climate change to sift out what is really behind it.

Our current situation is hardly sustainable in a world experiencing population growth (over 7.5 billion and growing by about 83 million people a year as of 2018). Biologists warn that our period marks the sixth "great extinction" event experienced on Earth and this time coming from human activity, with animal and plant species dying at a level (up to 50% of all individual animals lost in recent decades) and rate (up to 100x normal) unseen for millions of years prior (see Kolbert 2015; Carrington 2017, and references therein). And as more of the world adopts modern market practices, modern technology, and modern patterns of consumption and waste disposal, our predicaments will only expand, accelerate, and worsen. One study found that should the global population adopt USDA dietary guidelines, we would need additional land amounting to the size of Canada with current farming practices (Rizvi et al. 2018). By another estimate, we are already, per year, using the resources contained in approximately 1.7 Earths; that is, we are consuming nature's resources in a year—e.g., putting more carbon into the air than forests can sequester—faster than they can be replenished and are hitting this point earlier and earlier (in 2017, it was August 2, the earliest it had ever been).[5] And this means that even if we held our level of consumption at a steady state relative to today's conditions, we will still exhaust the natural resources upon which our society—as well as most of those in the global community—rests.

As such, politicians that play coy, unsure, or skeptical about ecological problems and climate change engage in bad faith at best, willful ignorance more charitably, and simple vain avariciousness more critically. And it would hardly be an exaggeration to describe the Trump administration as, at best, antagonistic stewards of environmental health. As President, Donald Trump doubled the record for the longest time to go without a science adviser (Folley 2018). In June 2017, Trump withdrew the United States from the Paris Climate Agreement and also slashed Obama-era rules that made it harder for companies to

---

[5] The same metric establishes the day on the calendar we globally "overshoot" this consumption and this has arrived earlier and earlier over the course of time this model has been used to collect data. See "Earth Overshoot Day" at this link (URL retrieved August 13, 2018): https://www.overshootday.org/.

emit greenhouse gasses (Meyer 2018b). He ended NASA's research into and monitoring of greenhouse gas cuts. A year later he repealed an Obama administration policy (put in after the British Petroleum Deepwater Horizon 87-day oil spill of 2010) to protect bordering oceans and the Great Lakes and adopted a policy that encourages more gas and oil drilling (Cama 2018). In July-August 2018, news came out that his administration wanted to revoke the state of California's authority to regulate greenhouse gas emission standards for automobiles and to extend the right to self-regulate pollution to several states, stoking fears of an additional 365 million tons of carbon being released into the atmosphere (Beene et al. 2018; Conley 2018b). His administration also ended efforts sponsored by the Obama administration to study the effect of pesticides on approximately 2,300 endangered species (Neilson 2018). And, in that same vein, he nominated Scott Hutchins, a former executive at Dow Chemical, to oversee science at the USDA (Philpott 2018) and named a climate change skeptic, William Happer, to his National Council as a senior director for emerging technologies (McLaughlin 2018).

Trump also placed Scott Pruitt at the head of the Environmental Protection Agency. A conservative and a member of the Southern Baptist Convention, Pruitt had previously stated that "There aren't sufficient scientific facts to establish the theory of evolution" and, on the Christian Broadcasting Network, argued in favor of a "biblical worldview" of the environment, where humans have a "responsibility to manage and cultivate, harvest the natural resources that we've been blessed with to truly bless our fellow mankind" (National Public Radio 2018). Reflecting such views, under Pruitt's leadership the EPA's Office of Science and Technology Policy deleted references to "science" and science-based standards from its mission statement. Pruitt also proposed, under the auspices of "transparency," that data available to EPA policy-makers only be from studies whose data was/is publicly available. Critics saw this as a way to eliminate scientific studies that had privacy restrictions on data as protections for respondents and subjects of research. Pruitt's proposal, in effect, would scuttle decades of public health studies done under traditional scientific protocols of respondent confidentiality and anonymity and open up the agency to greater possibilities of industrial deregulation (for discussion, see Rest and Benjamin 2018).

Under Pruitt, the EPA turned in such a pro-business direction and away from its mission to "protect human and environmental health" that analysts considered it a prelude to "regulatory capture" (Dillon et al. 2018), i.e., where the industry meant to be regulated by a government agency instead has one of its representatives placed at that agency's head. Pruitt refused to admit to any link between $CO_2$ and global warming, claiming the relationship between human input and climate is intricate and hard to measure (Chiacu and Volcovici 2018), while being provided briefings and documents that deny fossil fuel involvement in anthropogenic climate change by the Heritage Foundation, the Heartland Institute, the Manhattan Institute, and the CO2 Coalition, which are funded by the Mercer Family Foundation (of Cambridge Analytica fame) (Associated Press 2018a; S. Waldman 2018). In another example of environmental hostility, under his leadership, the EPA blocked CNN, E&E News, and Associated Press reporters from attending a May 2018 summit on water pollution (Corbett 2018b).

Pruitt was not the only senior Trump administration official and/or office undermining environmental stewardship. Here is a sampling:

- As a Senator, Trump's Attorney General, Jeff Sessions, helped block EPA action against a political donor requiring that he clean up pollution from a coal mining operation (Schwellenbach, Choma, and Zagorin 2018).
- In April 2018, the US Bureau of Land Management blocked at least 14 staff archaeologists and specialists from attending the gathering of the Society for American Archaeology, many of whom worked in Western states where the BLM manages millions of acres of land that are known to have artifacts on them. More than one observer viewed this an attempt by the administration to reduce the ability of such scientists to engage the public on matters of land development related to energy interests (Maffly 2018).
- At the G7 Summit in the summer of 2018, the United States (along with Japan) declined to sign an agreement to reduce plastic waste in the oceans (Zilio 2018).
- Also in June 2018, four Republican senators (Ted Cruz—Texas, Rand Paul—Kentucky, James Lankford—Oklahoma, and Jim Inhofe—Oklahoma) urged the National Science Foundation Inspector General (Allison Lerner) to scrutinize grants for its Climate Matters program, fearing it engaged in "propaganda" to "influence political and social debate" in its attempts to provide classes and webinars to television meteorologists (from where much of the public gets its weather and climate information).
- As another indicator of this anti-science approach, according to an analysis by Silencing Climate Science Tracker—a database run by Columbia University's Sabin Center law fellow Romany Webb—nearly 100 examples of global warming-related terms were scrubbed from government documents and policies, such as those found at the White House, NASA, the National Science Foundation, the EPA, the Federal Emergency Management Administration, and other agencies (see Waters 2018).

The health of the public and the natural world do not seem to be a variable in this administration's (and its associates in the Republican Party) policy calculations, which appear to be nothing other than an assault on environmental protection as an aid to the business class and its goal of capital accumulation.

As environmental problems are a product of class relations and class warfare, our analysis should not stop at political operatives. Business interests cloud public information on environmental issues in order to prolong the profitability of their investments, efforts at deception that appear to have worked (see P. Wright 2017). And not only is the public targeted for deception but they are also targeted for areas to either extract resources or to locate polluting industries. Below are just a few examples:

- Internal documents show that oil companies, such as Shell (see Gabbatiss 2018d), have known for decades that burning fossil fuels could cause climate change and sea level rise.
- Exxon understood the prospect of global warming and climate change at least as early as the early-1980s but nevertheless funded climate change deniers for decades (Goldenberg 2015).
- A company owned by Australia's wealthiest person, Gina Rinehart (estimated worth, $17.6 billion), donated $4.5 million to a climate change denying think tank (the Institute for Public Affairs) over a two-year period (Readfearn 2018).
- A 2018 analysis concluded that lobbying activities of 90% of the world's 200 largest firms and 75 trade groups directly or indirectly opposed policies geared to fight climate change (see Influence Map 2018). Measuring their sunken investments in oil extraction and refinement infrastructure, company executives weigh a cost-benefit analysis of when they should shift investments into activities less environmentally threatening (Warrick and Mufson 2014; Macalister 2015).
- Polluting industries have found that lower-income areas are more ideal places to locate their activities, given that such communities are less likely to garner the financial resources for successful lawsuits (Collins, Munoz, and Jaja 2016).
- Corporations like Nestlé use the law and lawyers to gain access to water from streams and aquifers—even at a time when it is widely known that same area is in drought conditions—arguing to state administrators that it has inherited rights to forest water dating back centuries (C. Weber 2018).

In short, the corporate energy community and their allies, in order to protect their investments and profits, distract and distort public knowledge of the reality of the situation while scientists predict and/or we witness changing weather patterns, increasing loss of ocean fronts, flooded coastal cities, submerged islands, contaminated water supplies, mass crop failure, loss of coral reefs, and increased drought and wildfire as well as more severe weather (Milman 2014, 2015; Morales 2014; Mooney 2015; Gertz 2016; Griffith 2016; Joyce 2016; Kratochwill 2016; Selzak 2016). And the costs of pollution—from clean-up of contaminated ecosystems to medical costs from illness and death related to pollution and other toxins—are "externalized" costs shunted off onto the public, either through governmental expenditure or through personal costs of health care and lost productivity, costs savings that add to the bottom line of the owning and investing classes. The situation does break out into public consciousness at times and neither fossil fuel nor chemical industries enjoy a good public image. In fact, in 2018, when Bayer acquired Monsanto via a merger, they made the decision to lose the "Monsanto" name, so poorly did the public view that company.

Our environmental problems are immense and so are the forces aligned against fixing them. They stem from a profit-making system that extracts resources, spurs consumption and population growth (which feed back on each other), both of which provide a motor to capital accumulation, the primary goal and task of the business class. Because they get rich in the process of feeding their business machine, there is every incentive—from both the professional side and the individual side—to not only produce more things and convince more people to consume more stuff, but also to eliminate ways that states might step in and regulate industry so that the water, air, and land that people and animals need are protected. If no organized force stops the business class from shaping state policy to its liking, there exists no counterweight to the forces of endless accumulation, while nature and human lives lay in the balance. Our environmental problems, then, are less a product of the individual person who might use too much water in a shower or buy a car with a bit less gas mileage than they could have, but rather they are a fundamental feature of the system from which these problems sprung. As such, it is very unlikely our environmental problems can be fixed from within that systemic context itself.

CHAPTER 42

# The Measure of Social Progress

Across history, humans have had to overcome limitations imposed on them by climate, weather, predators and disease, levels of technological development (or lack thereof), the struggles with and against their neighbors, and all manner of ignorance and other impositions determined by cultural norms, norms often shaped by the preceding list. The social position of women as compared to that of men has been one of these imposed limitations. For most of human history and for most cultures, men, more so than women, have sat atop of our social structures and institutions. This reality has not been a static one, though, as the variations have been many, with some cultures enforcing more draconian rules and circumscribed roles than others. Still, among those variations, there are patterns in this inequality we can discern. From where did it come and how has it developed over time?

First, it is important to recognize that inequality between men and women has not always been with us. In most, if not all, nomadic foraging societies, women and men were/are seen as relatively equal. *Almost* everywhere we find hunter-gatherers, we also find a division of labor where men do most of the hunting and women do most of the gathering (again, not without some variation). This allotment of tasks, however, did not usually translate into differential allotment of status, wealth, authority, and power in those societies. While men tend to have more muscle mass than women and can run, lift, and throw longer and farther than women (on average), superior strength is not the origin of hunter versus gatherer roles. Men's strength gives them little to no advantage hunting gazelle or wild boar. Men-as-hunters use weapons and do not simply arm-wrestle game or choke them out with their bare hands. And weapons are usually as such that either men or women could wield them.

The most relevant biological difference between men and women, for this issue, is the fact that women birth babies and men do not. And, though the mother of a child is always known, not all societies understood that there was a "father" much less who that person was (in some places, the woman's brother assumes the role of male caretaker and role-model). Also, women in such societies are often with child for a large portion of their adult lives and children have a long period of development during which they are dependent on adults for care. Though childcare duties could be shared among many *individuals* regardless of gender or familiar relation, when it comes to *social roles overall*, assigning hunting to women in general would make childcare more difficult or make it dangerous for children should they be brought along—e.g., problems with securing the feeding of infants, as some hunts last days or more as animals are chased. Further, given their role in reproduction, women are less disposable than men at the society-wide level. Men cannot give birth and, therefore, societies depend less on them than on women for sustaining their populations.[1]

These dynamics above explain the root of early differences in gender roles. But this is neither the whole story nor its end.

Eventually, as humans learned to grow food, they no longer had to travel very much (at least in comparison to nomadic societies). This meant building (relatively) permanent housing and the development of more sedentary living. Gathering could still be done close to home but also so could clearing fields, harvesting, cooking, and collecting water. Though many of these other duties could be allotted without regard to genitalia, gender assignment, or parenthood, it still made sense to keep hunting in men's hands for the same reasons it always had been. But once areas fit for growing food, hunting game, and collecting water are settled upon, there arises the increased probability of the need to defend resources and one's people from hostile outsiders. As a result, those already proficient in weaponry and those you can more afford to lose are assigned the primary defender and protector roles. And as an incentive to men for their potential sacrifice are titles, authority, resources (i.e., land, cattle, wives), and other honors. Thus, with the agrarian revolution, the social position of men—i.e., wealth, status and social power—was raised over women relative to the more egalitarian allotment found in hunter-gatherers and social inequality was born.

This sketch is not meant to describe each and every outcome for each and every hunter-gatherer system that transformed into a tribal / simple agricultural society, but as a form of social organization, institutional male dominance was selected for in many places at many times as different cultures adapted to its logic.

Social, economic, political, and cultural changes could mold this gender inequality in a variety of directions, some more extreme than others. Some

---

[1] For example, imagine two societies that suffer some devastating event that reduces its male-female ratio. Society A is left with 100 women and 1 man. Society B is left with 100 men and 1 woman. Which one is better positioned to repopulate itself the quickest and easiest? Clearly, it is society A. Thus, given women's crucial reproductive social roles, men are assigned the more dangerous tasks. Certainly equal allotment would make a little less sense in these societies, and doing the reverse—i.e., assigning the most dangerous tasks to women—would make the least sense of all.

places women were given general social protections and provisions so that their ability to raise the next generation was secured. Women could be viewed as liabilities in their families (e.g., an extra mouth to feed) until they started having children and their status would slowly rise with the number of children to which they gave birth (especially male heirs). Women—especially their sexuality—might be strictly and tightly controlled to maintain their marital worth (exchange-value) for her father and family line with things like prohibitions against premarital sex, child marriage, genital mutilation, and honor killing against transgressors. Further, the most powerful and high-status men often had their choice of women as sex partners, concubines, mates, and wives, sometimes creating harems or institutionalizing polygynous marriages. In such settings, a significant portion of men were excluded from sexual access and did not reproduce. For instance, a 2015 study in *Genome Research* found that after the advent of agriculture, for every 17 women that passed on their genes, only one male did (see Diep 2015 and reference therein). So male dominance rippled *across* relations between men and women, where it was not simply "men's" interests that were cultivated but those interests among men from more powerful and high-status groups.

Mass agriculture and city-states needed large numbers of men for labor (and women too, of course) while women enjoyed greater access than before to calories and other social provisions for childbearing. This might be considered when "civilization" was born—i.e., the first city-states (not the barbarism versus civilization of Chapter 27). Here, there needed to be incentives to get men to contribute labor (outside of slavery) and a lack of access to sexual mates would work against this. Thus, developed familial arrangements, where two sets of parents would agree to have their children married, often at very young ages. Such decisions may be based on social connections, future political alliances, access to shared resources (e.g., land, cattle), the size of a dowry, and whatnot. "Civilization" thus developed ways to pair men and women together so that most men and most women ended up in reproductive unions, i.e., the initial development of "marriage and the family." There was the sometimes explicit and sometimes implicit agreement that the male would provide for the woman (with his labor), protect the household (with his life, if necessary), and that their household wealth would pass down to their progeny. In turn, the woman would provide sexual access (with the expectation of fidelity), raise children resulting from the union (heirs), and keep a household viable for raising those children while preparing food and taking care of shelter for the husband. Though various feudal systems, such as those in Japan, China, and Europe, expanded on this model or amended it in various ways, the basis for these familial relations was based on sexual, reproductive, economic, and political considerations in ways that were geared toward creating a level of social stability and reproducing its populace.

This institutional arrangement has often been called "patriarchy" in that males were the dominant group politically and economically and women were often property of men (first their fathers and later their husbands), with less rights and privileges than their counterparts. The origin of patriarchy is a sociological event, though men never organized themselves and planned it out as a system of oppression per se. Rather, patriarchy resulted from a series of socio-historical-cultural responses to material conditions in which many different systems found themselves. And patriarchy was a relatively successful form of social organization—here "success" is used to only refer to the extent to which patriarchy provided higher odds of a *society* or *culture* perpetuating itself into the future, regardless of how it affected individual members—and this why it emerged in so many places that had little to no contact with one another. Even if many women and none-too-few men did not necessarily reap the benefits from the system, those at its apex did, and those societies that adopted such practices thrived more so than those that did not (matriarchal societies were/are fewer and tended to remain isolated and small, which, of course, has its own advantages). But patriarchy could have difficult outcomes for women, some incredibly negative. And thus, it should be no surprise that at some point this system was challenged and, in some places, changed significantly.

Patriarchy was compatible with and thus survived into and through Europe's feudal period. Modernity's socio-political-economic developments, however, would change relationships between men and women and the role each play in society. Early on, the modern factory system found that women and children made for easily exploitable laborers, pulling women out of their domestic role (at least temporarily at first) and putting them into the paid workforce. Though men initially were responsible for the actions of their wives just as they were for their children, over time women were seen as adults and legally responsible for their own actions. They could be charged with crimes and soon they could own property. In Europe and the United States, the oft standard bearers for modernity, women were crucial in early labor movements, reform of sanitariums and orphanages, and the abolition of slavery. Later, they fought for the right to vote, which they won. This was more than a victory for them. It continued and extended the idea that the franchise should not be limited by artificial impositions. Women were also involved in other changes in gender relations, such as responding when called upon to provide labor during wars and the implementation of laws against domestic violence.

The development of technology throughout this period also assisted the social position of women. In their domestic role, women benefitted from the invention of electrical wiring, can goods, gas and electric stoves, washing machines, and dish washers. All of these reduced the time for necessary household chores and freed up time for women to pursue other endeavors, none-too-few of them potentially outside the household. The advent of the birth control pill and its later public availability (1960 in the United States) shifted the balance of control of women's reproductive careers more into their own hands. It is probably not coincidental that in Europe and America the modern feminist movement gained members and momentum and achieved some modest success after these material changes. Soon, by the 1970s and 1980s, Western women were entering college and/or the workforce *en masse*. By the late 20th and early 21st centuries, the vast majority of modern women *expected* that an education and the possibility of a career were within reasonable reach, should they so choose such things.

What is "progress"? Progress is the overcoming of the conditioning a social structure places upon us in a way that increases the benefits that "society" can confer. More food, all things being equal, is progress. Less susceptibility to the weather and insulation from its threats is progress. Controlling and expanding access to clean water is progress. Increased freedom of choice for individuals to pursue their interests, goals, and talents and to not be shoe-horned into narrow and required social roles is progress. The average person in feudalism, regardless of sex, had few choices in his or her destiny in comparison to the average person in modernity. That is progress.

As civilization emerged, roles were placed upon both men and women for the good of collective survival. For most of social history, people did not really challenge their social roles, given the generalized sociological belief of "that's just the way the world works." If one is not exposed to alternatives, then those alternatives are not likely to enter the imagination. Or, further, if the alternatives are not even a practical possibility, they will not be imagined because they cannot be, as the foundation upon which imaginings are based does not yet exist.

This brings us to several interconnected questions. Once such a sexual division of labor allowed its society to flourish, what happens or happened next? When we could produce extensively more than we could eat, when we could create social roles not centered on production and reproduction but ideas and art and science, when society hit a level where participation in political decisions were not monopolized by kings or monarchs, what happened to other social relations? Modern societies have developed in ways that show all sorts of progress. And one of these is the extent to which women have been able to live lives less and less determined by patriarchal structures, structures that had previously served *societal survival* but not necessarily *women* as individuals or as a group. Certainly, being protected and provided for were benefits but that came with the cost of keeping women in a reproductive service capacity for society as a whole, sort of like a broodmare for their culture (and the patriarchal familial line). And women had little choice in the matter and were limited and more stifled than men in their life options. Social changes modernity makes possible and the social changes wrought upon it by its social movements have provided more and more women more equality in terms of their social standing and an element of choice in their lives, choices that were once made *for* them and not *by* them. That is social progress.

The social position of women plays a special role in *measuring* social progress. This is for several reasons. First, the inequality of women as compared to men is, perhaps, the oldest socially structured form of inequality (though it could be argued that parent-child is older, this is less the outcome of a social structure per se but rather the natural outcome of birth and aging). Second, this historical root of structured inequality means that it has had a long period of integration into multiple social institutions across multiple types of societies. Thus, third, the social position of women has changed with social structures but has also changed in ways where types of systems have shaped that inequality to their benefit. What this means is that it is a special form of social inequality that seems both compatible with and exploitable by a variety of other social structures. As such, it is an important observation worth tending to that inequality between men and women emerged in the first *class* systems and has continually morphed with them, suggesting a certain compatibility between these types of inequality, i.e., class and gender relations are intimately intertwined. Fourth, given the above, when we see the social position of women improve relative to its historical past, this gives us a measure of the progress attained and attainable within the structure in which this has occurred. Fifth, given the previous point, as a measure of social progress, the social position of women also reveals how much progress *has not been made* and how much more there is left to accomplish.

Some of the most severe forms of patriarchal control remain with us today, reflected in practices more akin to norms of pre-modern societies.

- The name of the Nigerian Islamic group, Boko Haram, loosely translated means, "non-Islamic education is a sin" (as in education imported from British colonialists). This group targets school children, often killing the boys and kidnapping the girls. In places like Afghanistan, South Sudan, and parts

of India, women's status is still similar to property and they are traded like cattle and/or sold as sex slaves (see Deutsche Welle 2013; Raza 2014; Bangura 2015; Dixon 2016; Jolley and Gooch 2016).
- Also in areas of rural India, women still experience child marriage, bride burning for insufficient dowries (Stone and James 1995), marital rape (Raj and McDougal 2014), gang rape, and general public marginalization.
- In places like Pakistan and Bangladesh (which has the world's highest amount), family disputes over land and property or refusal of sexual advances and/or marriage spur on acid attacks on women meant to disfigure their faces (often causing blindness) and publicly humiliate them (Haque and Ahsan 2014).
- While it appears to be on a decades-long decline (especially among younger women), female genital mutilation (FGM) still exists in several parts of the world, notably sub-Saharan Africa, and is even becoming more common in Burkina Faso, Chad, Guinea and Mali (Koski and Heymann 2017; Westcott 2017).
- In Indonesia in 2018, a 15-year-old girl was jailed for having an abortion when she became pregnant after her brother raped her (Agence France-Presse 2018a).
- In places like Venezuela, where abortion is illegal and contraceptive pills cost up to 10 months' salary at minimum wage, desperate women turn to government funded free sterilization programs, often while still in their teens and 20s (Marillier and Squires 2018).
- Not only are women still forced to wear the hijab in places like Iran and Saudi Arabia (places with very modernized economies), Turkish-backed militias have demanded that Kurdish women wear it as well (Cockburn 2018).

Patriarchy and its practices, such as those above, place women in a paradoxical position where they are property but also are depicted as a symbol of the worth and purity of their community and, thus, violence toward them can be a way to punish that community. By extension, in patriarchy, where men own their daughters and wives, to rape a woman is to commit a crime against her father (who can no longer find a husband for her), while a married woman who allows herself to be alone with another man dishonors her husband. A variety of crimes and punishments extend from such norms. Villages in India (and elsewhere) exist that sentence women to rape or even gang rape as a punishment for crimes committed by their brothers, husbands, or fathers (see Poon 2014). Seen as an insult to the family, especially the father, and as injecting impurity into a community, women who refuse arranged marriages, date outside their religion and/or culture, or have premarital or extra-marital sex can be punished with "honor" killings, which occur predominately in conservative Muslim countries, usually with some family participation (not seldom involving mothers and grandmothers) and sometimes involving torture (see Chesler 2010). Advocacy group, Honor Based Violence Awareness Network, estimates that about 5,000 such honor killings occur each a year.[2]

Saudi Arabia has a particularly noteworthy history of assaults on women's rights, autonomy, and well-being. In 2002, Saudi Arabia's religious police prevented young girls from exiting a burning building because they were not wearing the correct Islamic dress (BBC News 2012). In 2007, after she appealed her case in objection to lenient sentences given to the perpetrators, a judge increased a woman's sentence from 90 to 200 lashes and ordered her jailed for six months after being gang raped, her crime being a married woman who had allowed herself to be alone with a man who was not her relative (see Baker 2007). Saudi Arabian women were banned from driving until recently, while activists for lifting the ban remained in jail (Al Jazeera News 2018a). And still Saudi Arabian women must limit their public interaction with men unless a male relative is present, they are prohibited from making their own financial decisions, and cannot swim in public.

In those societies with modernity's mark stamped upon them to greater significance and effect, progress has been both mixed and incomplete. In Europe, Australia, and the United States, women are not owned as chattel by fathers or husbands and are *legally* equal citizens, taxpayers, and voters. Marital rape laws have been scrubbed from the books, but only in the last few decades. Though women still experience rape and sexual violence and a justice system that often treats them with suspicion, accused rapists are put on trial, those convicted are jailed, and their reputations pilloried in their communities.[3] The stigma against premarital sex has been declining for decades and the double-standard on sexual behavior has faded somewhat. Women have their

---

[2] You can find the Honor Based Violence Awareness Network website and research at (URL retrieved August 16, 2018): http://hbv-awareness.com/.

[3] Some additional detail may be relevant here. On one side, it would be inaccurate to leave the impression that only modernized parts of the world punish convicted rapists. In fact, convicted rapists are often jailed and sometimes very harshly punished in countries just discussed previously (e.g., India, Pakistan, Saudi Arabia, and so on). And these areas of the world share the difficulties in arresting and convicting accused rapists with the modern West, often because of culture and legal norms shaped by patriarchal institutions. On the other side, in the West the crime of rape is not a crime against the father, family, husband, or community but a crime against the woman. And once convicted, rapists in the modern Western prison system are among the lowest status prisoners, vilified, ostracized, and often placed just above child molesters in their loathsomeness to other inmates.

choice in marriage partners and are not legally barred from owning property or their own businesses. Women are not legally prohibited from holding office. More Western women today attend college than men. They are even increasingly expected to pursue work and careers and discriminating against them in such pursuits is now illegal.

This is in no way to say that gender equality has been achieved in modern societies; many new problems will develop due to past practices and other challenges still exist and are ahead. A few examples will provide a good indication of some of these issues. In 1980, China instituted a one-child policy for families. Like the vast majority of the world, Chinese culture was patriarchal in nature at the time and this resulted in families preferring boy children, which often encouraged things like sex-selective abortions and female infanticide. Over the decades a gender imbalance grew, with men outnumbering women, peaking around 1.22 to 1 in 2008 and with 30 million more marrying-age men than women expected by 2020. The US Department of State concluded that such imbalances played a significant role in the increase of the sex-trafficking of women into China from places like Myanmar (formerly Burma), Vietnam, Laos, Mongolia, and North Korea (see Fetterly 2014; Powell 2015, and references therein).[4] A 2018 UK government report concluded that sexual abuse of women and girls—including on the job sexual harassment, spreading of disease, unwanted pregnancies—at the hands of international aid workers was "endemic" and had persisted for years (see McKenzie 2018 and references therein). Also, in 2018, officials at Tokyo Medical University were alleged to have changed exam scores of female applicants to make sure no more than 30% of successful candidates were women (see Forrest 2018). This is just a sampling of the ways in which the patriarchal norms and imbalances of power, social status, and civil-rights-in-practice that modernity inherited have persisted despite increasing widespread recognition of how they violate women's rights, dignity, autonomy, and overall well-being.

Progress on the equality of women did not just happen, nor did the forces of modernity impose such changes as if some metaphysical force enacted them outside of human agency. First, there have been multiple women's movements that have both raised public awareness of the inequalities they face and put pressure on governments and other institutions to change their practices, norms, and beliefs. Some of these movements initially started with non-gendered goals in mind, such as working toward reforms of orphanages, child labor, and prisons; afterward, they turned their goals toward women's suffrage

---

[4] For the US Department of State's "Trafficking in Persons Report 2015," see (URL retrieved August 16, 2018): https://www.state.gov/j/tip/rls/tiprpt/2015/index.htm.

and then later focused on laws related to domestic violence, reproductive rights, and sexual harassment. Further, such movements are not confined to legislative actions but rather have influenced the broader culture, encouraging women to pursue education, develop marketable skills and establish careers, and change cultural sexual norms. Second, there have been individual women who have worked diligently for specific causes to improve women's lives and to change the societies in which they live. To name just one example, in 2018, Nice Nailantei Leng'ete was credited for saving as many at 15,000 African girls from the practice of genital mutilation and working to end child marriage there (see Bennett 2018).

Because progress is made does not mean a destination is reached. Rather, a "measure of social progress" tells us whether and/or how the present has progressed over the past. And the measure of the present is not the present but an imagined future, one where other forms of structured social inequality no longer impinge on the lives and destinies of individuals and freely chosen life-paths are available without external coercion. Modernity contains within it a set of possibilities and potentials that are progressive in nature. Examining the social position of women and comparing it to their pre-modern position is a testimony to the progress we can measure in modernity's arc. It is also how we can define what progress *has yet to occur* and what sort of changes are still required. This effort at redefining such social roles and learning how we can work toward those changes will determine how far we have come and how far there is yet to go.

CHAPTER 43

# Defiling Republics

Modernity is known for the levels of potential and actual wealth it produces. Part of this wealth production results from the way its production techniques can extract and refine raw materials and manufacture them into consumable goods. And human labor sets the extracting, refining, and manufacturing technology in motion. But this is not historically new, nor is exploitation of the human laboring capacity. The Roman and Greek empires, ancient societies in what we today call China and Indonesia, as well those in Central America and Africa all practiced slavery, with some of them highly dependent upon it. Modernity adopted this practice, too, and turned it toward new ends.

In modernity, slavery was and is a *profit-driven trade*. It was initially centered in the emerging nation-state system that included Portugal, Spain, Holland, France, Britain, and the United States (in the West) as well as central parts of the Arabic-Muslim world in North Africa and the Middle East. These slaving areas plundered the African continent, buying slaves from African tribes who had conquered, captured, and sold (in a sense) their neighbors. In the process, human beings became owned pieces of property, commodities to be bought, sold, used up, and discarded, just as you or I might own a plow, a power drill, or a hammer. As commodities and as pieces of property, slaves commanded different prices, were insured, exchanged as gifts, and passed down through inheritance. For some modern slavers—especially the traders and plantation owners—profits came from selling people and/or forcing them to plant, harvest, and transport cotton, corn, ores, sugarcane, tobacco, etc. For other modern slave owners, the economic end was household wealth, comfort, and status, using slaves to keep a home in order (thus preserving its value), to serve food, to make clothes, and to impress their peers. These were often upper-class individuals with a few house slaves and/or those with smaller farms and workforces, though there was clearly some overlap between this class of slave owners and the plantation-owning class. Grasping this history requires tracing of modern slavery from Africa to the European trade in the Caribbean and South America and the development of slavery in North America.[1]

---

1  Some of the following discussion borrows from Greg O'Malley (author of *Final Passages: The Intercolonial Slave Trade of British America*) and his online discussion (2015). See (URL retrieved August 17, 2018): https://www.reddit.com/r/AskHistorians/comments/3pcfaz/ama_the_atlantic_slave_trade_especially_human/.

IMAGE 43.1  Capture of Slaves in Africa by African Slavers

During the transatlantic slave trade, an estimated 12.5 million people were shipped from Africa, with about 10.5 million arriving in the "New World" and 2 million dying at sea. Initially, the people captured in the early slave period lived closer to the African coast. Over time, more and more people were taken from Africa's inland areas, with some even forced to travel a thousand or more miles before the Middle Passage across the Atlantic (see Map 43.1, Image 43.2). Within the continent itself, the power and culpability of African nations, though hard to firmly establish, was not inconsiderable. If African kingdoms worried about labor shortages and stopped selling slaves, early European traders could not force their hand. European traders also could not dictate the type of slave (man, woman, child) that was offered. As global demand for slaves increased, some African leaders started wars with neighbors for the purpose of taking slaves (the conquest of Africa in terms of European colonialism would come later, after steamships, better weapons, medicines to battle disease, etc. were available). The story of modern slavery begins here.

Modernity's mode of production turned people into tools to be worked, often to death in slavery's more abusive forms in the "New World." Portugal, Spain, England, Holland, and France competed for resources on many Caribbean islands and in South America. Slave owners running large sugar operations—the most profitable of the plantations—preferred male slaves and a lot of them, as they needed a constant replenishment of new slaves because death rates were highest on these plantations. Besides overwork and harsh living conditions, tropical regions also had dangerous disease environments, which made the enslaved vulnerable to yellow fever, malaria, and so on.

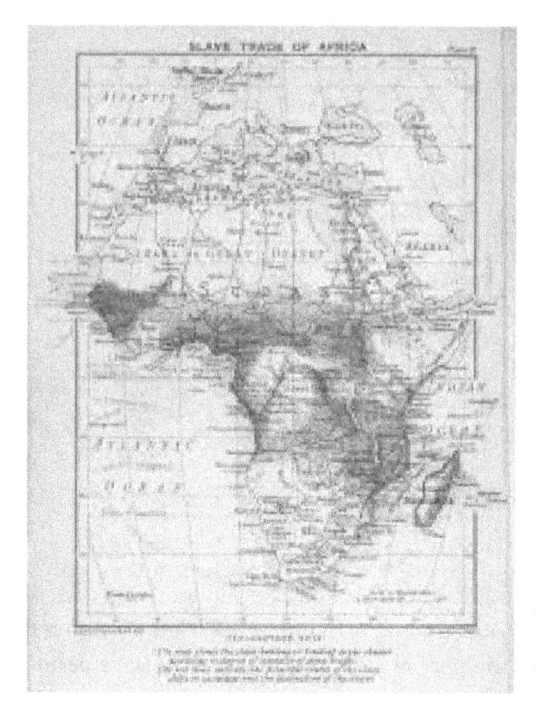

MAP 43.1
Slave Trade of Africa, 1899, Johnston, Harry Hamilton, Sir (1858–1927) (Author) Bartholomew, J.G. (John George) (1860–1920) (Cartographer)

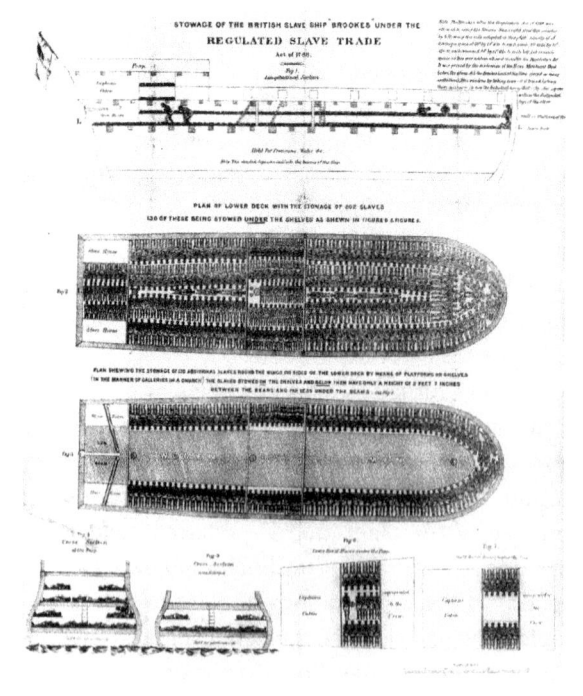

IMAGE 43.2
Slave Ship Poster, by Unknown Author

IMAGE 43.3
Sugarcane Cutters in Jamaica (after 1838 Abolition of Slavery), circa 1880, by Unknown Author

Further, Caribbean islands were more dependent on importing food, so they required a steady influx of trade-friendly ships. Combined, all of these factors augmented and enhanced the slave trade in the area.

The Spanish Empire did not trade much in Africa before the nineteenth century (due to the Treaty of Tordesillas) and often got slaves from the Portuguese, Dutch, French, and the British. With the Spanish controlling many Caribbean islands, they eventually granted monopoly trading rights (i.e., Asiento de Negros) to Britain to trade slaves there, who, in turn, created the South Sea Company to manage it. This trade allowed the British to use it as "cover" to smuggle other goods as well. The trade also extended between colonies. For instance, after being captured by fellow African tribes, sold to British slavers on the coast, the Middle Passage, and offloading in Barbados or Jamaica, slaves could be resold to other colonial holdings, to North America, Spanish America, or to the French Caribbean (e.g., Haiti, Martinique).

The British were the second leading slave trading nation behind Portugal, trading throughout the Caribbean, especially Jamaica and Barbados. By the 1780s, a movement sprang up in Britain to end slavery, including reform laws, abolition, banning trade with other countries (1806), and eliminating trade to British colonies (1808). Soon, fearing themselves at a competitive disadvantage, under pressure from Quakers and Methodists, and hoping to prevent the United States (just having won its Revolutionary War) from seizing the mantel of standing for "liberty" and "rights," Britain actively tried to thwart and diminish the international trade with warships patrolling the African coast and with diplomatic efforts.[2] As anti-slavery sentiment spread to the wider British

---

2 One interesting unintended consequence of the British patrolling for slave ships and trying to prevent the trade was increased mortality rates for those transported. The shipping routes got longer and longer to avoid the British navy and this allowed more time for diseases

IMAGE 43.4
Official Medallion of the British Anti-Slavery Society, 1795, by Josiah Wedgwood (1730–1795) and either William Hackwood or Henry Webber

IMAGE 43.5
Rescued Slaves Aboard the HMS Daphne, 1868, by The National Archives UK

to spread and also required more food and water (or increased the odds of running out of them). The British established Sierra Leone as an area to place those they had liberated and shipped others there from America who sought refuge with them during the Revolutionary War. None of this means slavery ended nicely for former slaves of the British Empire. For instance, in Britain, slave holders were compensated for their loss of property upon the emancipation of slaves but slaves themselves were released with only the clothes on their backs.

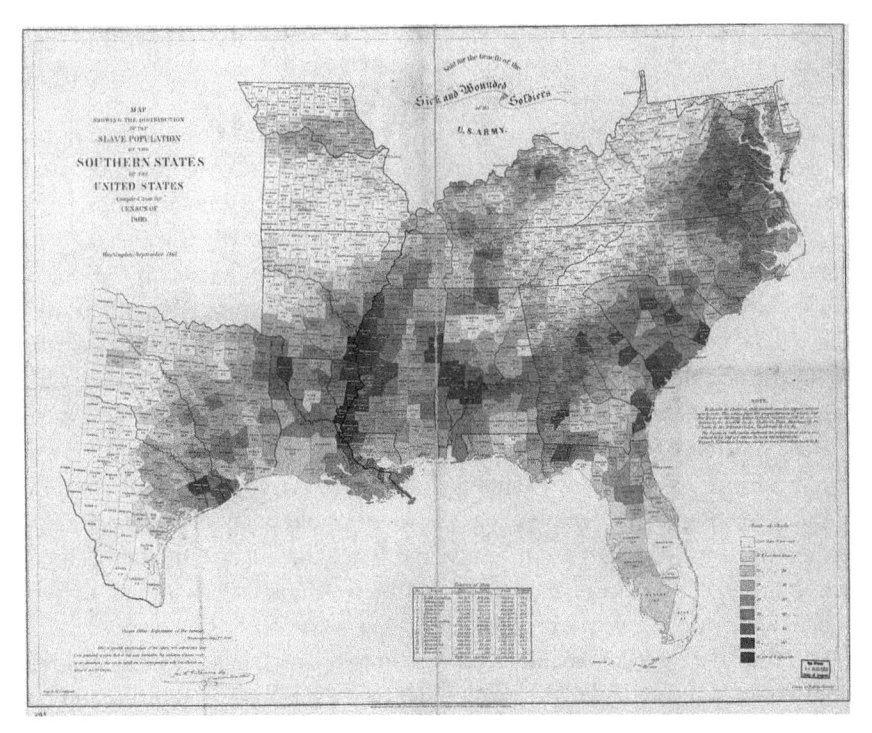

MAP 43.2   US Coast Guard Survey's Map of the Slaveholding States, by E. Hergesheimer (cartographer), Th. Leonhardt (engraver)

culture, social movements against it grew and, in one instance, textile workers in Manchester refused to touch cotton picked by US slaves, which helped enforce Lincoln's embargo on cotton exported from slave states to such an extent that he felt compelled to write them a letter of thanks (see Rodrigues 2013).

Some of the first slaves brought to North America (1619) came from pirates/privateers and the colonies would soon be significant participants in the institution, though not the major players in the trade. What would become the United States actually experienced a lower level of slave importation than much of the Caribbean and South America (the United States imported about 400,000 slaves in total of the 12.5 million transported from Africa). However, lacking a large importation of slaves, plantation owners had to ensure their own slave populations reproduced. Thus, US plantation owners imported more women and children than slavers in the Caribbean and had a more balanced gender ratio. As the United States outlawed importation of slaves in 1808 (but not slavery itself), they were in a position to "grow" their own slave population and by the eve of the Civil War, the United States was one of the largest slave-holding areas in the world (about 4 million, most native born) (see Map 43.2 for a look at the various densities of slaves versus free persons in US slaveholding states).

Though transporting slaves could be lucrative, the real money was in slave labor, especially on larger plantations. As both commodities and laborers, slaves were selected for certain traits. Western Africa was highly agricultural, so individuals from those regions that cultivated skills in growing crops, tending animals, carpentry, etc. were more valued in some US colonies (as well as in Brazil and Caribbean islands) than others. And, like in the Caribbean and South America, labor discipline was a regular concern. For instance, if a slave had been in a region for too long (often over six months) and were on the selling-block, they were likely to be seen as rebellious and troublesome. Many colonies placed burdensome duties on these "seasoned" slaves. In the United States, rebellious slaves could be threatened with being "sold down the river" from northern slave states (Kentucky, Virginia, Maryland) to southern ones (Alabama, Mississippi), where their treatment would putatively be worse. This threat to tear them from their friends and family had, it was thought, a great disciplining effect. Estimates are that between 1800 and 1860 about a million slaves were sold this way.

As the US republic expanded outwardly and developed inwardly, its pretense to democracy and liberty required that laws be made for and applied to slaves as a special class, e.g., they could not hold property, allowable separation of families, could not testify in court. Slowly, they were separated, differentiated, and institutionally unequal to other classes of exploited laborers, such as indentured servants. With the belief among some colonists that Christians were forbidden to enslave other Christians, some slaves tried conversion to Christianity as a path to liberation (with success for some). In response, colonial governments (e.g., Maryland) increasingly changed their laws so that "heathen ancestry" became the designation of servitude versus freedom. As it was previously divided between "Christians" and "Heathens" (or "Savages"), over time this change shifted the designation of who was potentially subject to a free versus unfree status to a white versus black distinction (see Fredrickson 1981). As such distinctions become common throughout the colonies, it drew a "color line"—dividing a working class into those with more social status and privileges (whites) than others (blacks)—something W.E.B. Du Bois (1903:19) claimed would be "the problem of the twentieth century" in the United States.

The people kidnapped, chained, transported, sold, and worked to exhaustion did not respond without resistance. Up against the law, armies, dogs, needing passes, being beaten, raped, and so on, slaves ran away, sabotaged tools, faked illnesses, killed overseers, and burned down masters' homes. Often led by religious leaders, an abolitionist movement arose across race and class lines and political conflict and divisions developed over the status (slave or free) of new states added to the Union. Slaving states in the South feared that, if a balance was not struck between when free versus slave states were added, then free states could outvote slave states at the federal level and outlaw the practice. But so lucrative was the institution that many US slaving states decided secession was preferable to losing a hostage workforce. It would take The Civil War and a later set of amendments to the US Constitution to finally eliminate legal slavery, at least to some extent.[3] After emancipation in the United States, many former slaves found themselves trapped by a corrupt legal system as well as by sharecropping and were sold to businesses and corporations as cheap labor (e.g., convict leasing), effectively keeping some form of legal labor exploitation in place. And lynching of freed slaves and their descendants was socially acceptable enough that crowds would participate and even pose with the victim's corpse. Pictures were sold on postcards up through the 1900s.[4]

After former slaves in the United States were freed, there were many attempts to put the genie back in the bottle, as it were. For instance, social segregation and lack of civil rights protections ruled for decades after The Civil War. The eugenics movement attempted to limit procreation between members of different supposed races (called "miscegenation") to "purify" races and improve society. The idea was that "mixing" of the races degraded the stronger

IMAGE 43.6  Convict Leasing, Children, 1903, by John L. Spivak

---

3   The 14th Amendment to the US Constitution made an exception for slavery as "punishment for a crime whereof the party shall have been duly convicted."
4   See the book and website, *Without Sanctuary*, and the link here (URL retrieved August 17, 2018): https://withoutsanctuary.org/.

308 CHAPTER 43

IMAGE 43.7 Sharecropper Sam Williams with Family Members and Laborers in Cotton Field, 1908, by Miscellaneous Items in High Demand, PPOC

IMAGE 43.8 Lynching and Burning of Will Brown, Nebraska, 1919, by Unknown Author

one, inevitably those sitting atop the political-economic pyramid.[5] Corporate interests such as the Carnegie Institution, the Rockefeller Foundation, the Harriman railroad fortune, and J.H. Kellogg (among others) funded the movement and supporters came from many quarters, some of which may surprise us (e.g., Margaret Sanger, W.E.B. Du Bois). Many US university classes included eugenics in their curricula and dozens of states enacted laws that restricted marriage partners, immigration by certain groups, and allowed (often forced) sterilization of the "unfit" (which fell disproportionately on non-white and working-class women). Voices from some quarters argued for euthanasia. "Scientific Baby Contests" were held by several organizations, even The National Association for the Advancement of Colored People (NAACP). Nazi Germany drew inspiration from the United States, went further, and executed many of the "unfit." Outside of eugenics, residential schools and forced assimilation were instituted as ways to forge people native to the land into a modern person, losing their cultural identity in the process.

For African-Americans today, a series of accumulated disadvantages associated with this history of slavery, racism, and discrimination produces social conditions that lower their average lifespans. Segregation and redlining, on top of wider racial and class inequalities, concentrate African-Americans at higher proportions in neighborhoods that cause multiple personal health problems: dilapidated housing infested with mice whose urine byproducts induce asthmatic reactions and with lead paint that causes neurological problems; stress from work or from needing to find it; poor quality food (food chains selling fresh produce invest less in such areas and fast food franchises invest more) and family stress that results in shortened telomeres and more rapid aging, less sleep and thus a greater risk of heart disease; and dangerous neighborhoods that spike adrenaline and cortisol, which can lead to heart problems and compromised immune systems (see Khazan 2018 and references therein). Blacks, especially those who are young and male, are approximately 3x more likely to be killed by police use of force than are whites (see Howard 2016 and references therein; Edwards, Esposito, and Lee 2018). The Drug War has resulted in arrest and incarceration levels of poor, urban, non-white men higher than their rate of drug use (see Ingraham 2014 and references therein).[6] Consequently, the number of black men in jail today rivals the number enslaved in the United States in 1850, conditions that have been called an era of "the new Jim Crow"

---

5  Eugenics laws were also passed restricting the liberties of people with birth defects, low IQ, and other "undesirable" traits.
6  Also see the ACLU's 2013 report, *The War on Marijuana in Black and White*, at (URL retrieved August 17, 2018): https://www.aclu.org/files/assets/aclu-thewaronmarijuana-rel2.pdf.

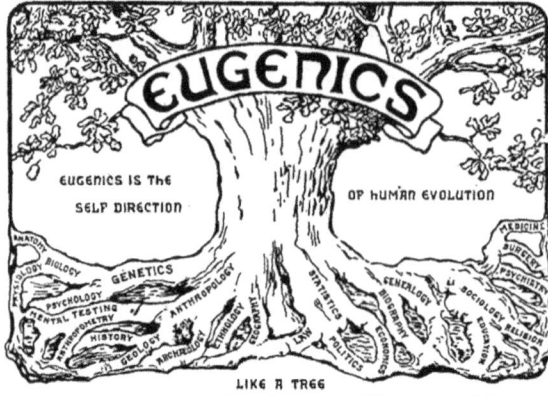

IMAGE 43.9
Logo from the Second International Congress on Eugenics, 1921

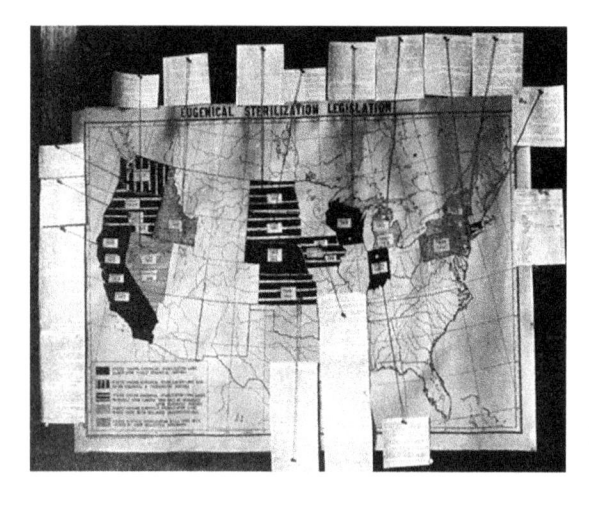

IMAGE 43.10
Map Indicating Sterilization Legislation in US States, 1921

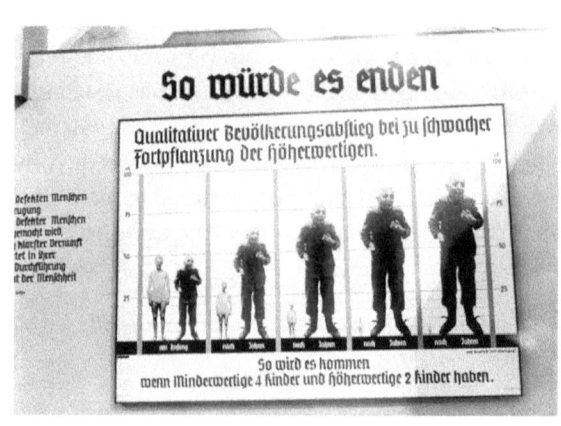

IMAGE 43.11
German Eugenics Propaganda, 1935

IMAGE 43.12  Tom Torlino, Native American Before and After Forced Assimilation, by John N. Choate (sometimes credited as J.N. Choate)

IMAGE 43.13  Rally at State Capitol, Protesting the Integration of Central High School, Little Rock, Arkansas, 1959. [This photograph is a work for hire created between 1952 and 1986 by one of the following staff photographers at *U.S. News & World Report*: Warren K. Leffler (WKL), Thomas J. O'Halloran (TOH), Marion S. Trikosko (MST), John Bledsoe (JTB), or Chick Harrity (CWH).]

IMAGE 43.14  US Marshals with Young Ruby Bridges on School Steps, William Frantz Elementary School, New Orleans, 1960, by Uncredited Department of Justice Photographer

(see Alexander 2010; Kilgore 2015).[7] Given levels of incarceration and single-motherhood, black neighborhoods are more likely to lack male role models, which negatively affects the mobility and incomes of young black men, even those born into households with average to above average wealth (see Badger et al. 2018 and references therein).

Racism, both individual and institutional, still grips much of the world. The modern ideas of separate, biologically-rooted racial categories and the assumption of their superiority / inferiority over others fit nicely within the xenophobic attitudes many cultures have historically had toward their neighbors and outsiders. In a recent poll (GlobalScan / BBC 2016) of 21 countries, when asked to choose between "national citizenship," "being a world citizen," "local community," "religious tradition," and "race or culture" as the "most important defining criteria of self-identity," while the global average for "race or culture" was 8%, the highest scores were South Korea (23%), China (15%), India (13%), Pakistan (11%), Indonesia (10%), and Germany (10%).[8] In the same poll, the highest five scores for "somewhat" to "strongly disapprove" of marriage between different races and ethnic groups were from India (34%), Pakistan (33%), South

---

7   Also see Michelle Alexander, *The New Jim Crow*, at (URL retrieved August 17, 2018): http://newjimcrow.com/.
8   The lowest were Australia (2%), France (3%), Canada (4%), The United States (4%), The United Kingdom (4%), Spain (5%), and Ghana (5%).

IMAGE 43.15 "Japanese Only" Sign at Yunohana Onsen, Otaru City, Hokkaido, Japan, 1999, by Olaf Karthaus and Dave Aldwinckle. [Rendered in Japanese, English and Russian, barring patrons not ethnically Japanese from using the bathing facilities.]

Korea and Russia (tied at 32%), Indonesia (27%), and China (22%). Beliefs in their own racial superiority toward each other are not uncommon among those in China, Japan, and South Korea, and people in all three will tend to place Indonesians, Laotians, Cambodians, and Vietnamese below themselves. The ideology of racial purity was the backdrop to ethnic cleansing (1990s) in Europe, where the bloodletting in Sarajevo harkened back to the brutal and racist practices of the past. This history of racism stands in contrast to modernity's ideal of equal treatment under the law and has worked its way into all manner of modern institutions.

Today, not only do modern nation-states still find that much of their social inequalities via social class weigh more heavily on the descendants of slaves, but the world continues to allow slavery to happen. In 2005, as part of a class action suit representing thousands of exploited individuals (and stemming from a 1997 UNICEF report's estimate of 200,000 children smuggled across borders in Benin, Burkina Faso, Mali, and Togo), three young men sued Archer Daniels Midland, Cargill, and Nestlé for their participation in the slave industry related to Ivory Coast's cocoa plantations (Chatterjee 2013). Nestlé later admitted to benefitting from forced labor in its supply chains in Thailand (Kelly 2016). Rather than isolated cases, according to the Walk Free Foundation (an Australian-based NGO), as of 2014, more than 35 million people worldwide were held in slavery, with five countries (14.29 million in India, 3.24 million in China, 2.06 million in Pakistan, 1.2 million in Uzbekistan, and 1.05 million in Russia) counting for 61% of the total (though all 167 countries studied had some form of slavery). Those with the highest proportion of their population enslaved were

Mauritania (4%), Uzbekistan (3.97%), Haiti (2.3%), Qatar (1.36%), and India (1.14%) (see Elliot 2014a).

Despite having twice elected Barack Hussein Obama as its President (the first non-white President in its history), the US electoral system then put Donald J. Trump in the seat. This was seen in some quarters as a racist backlash against Obama as a black man unworthy of the office. While measures of racial resentment in the United States have remained relatively steady since 1988 (when the following research began), what has increased since then are correlations between racial resentment and partisanship, ideological self-identification, voting Republican, attitudes about government spending, and private or public health insurance, which the authors believe is explained, in part, by politicians, party leaders, and mass media using "racial priming" or "subtle and not-so-subtle messages that encourage citizens to base their opinions at least in part on racial considerations" (see Enders and Scott 2018 and references therein). In another indicator of the pull of polarizing racial sentiments, research shows that climate change deniers are more likely to be older, white, and Republican (Benegal 2018) and that many American whites (predominately Republican) changed their opinions on national health care and on global warming / climate change once they learned that Barack Obama supported the former and wanted action on the latter (see H. Smith 2018 and references therein). It was this racialized atmosphere into which Trump tapped, as multiple studies showed that a potent mix of white evangelical conservatism (Pulliam Bailey 2016), fears of losing a preferred social status, and traditional racism played major roles in his election to office (see Lopez 2017; McElwee and McDaniel 2017; Jacobs 2018; Mutz 2018; Wadsworth 2018, and references therein).

Prior to his candidacy, Trump had a long-documented history of racially inflammatory statements and discriminatory behaviors, including avoiding renting apartments to African-Americans, claiming that "laziness is a trait in blacks," and once took out ads in the *New York Times* arguing for the death penalty against five black and Latino teenagers more than 10 years after DNA evidence had exonerated them of a rape. During his 2016 presidential campaign announcement, he called Mexican immigrants criminals and "rapists" (for a longer list of Trump's racist behavior, see Leonhardt and Philbrick 2018). Such rhetoric attracted enough voters, or at least did not repel enough of them, that he won the office.

Once in office, Trump's actions and words were hard to disconnect from racist overtones. Five instances are enough to demonstrate the point. First, when a "Take Back the Right" rally in Charlottesville, Virginia—majorly attended by white men and many carrying torches as well as Nazi and Confederate flags—resulted in a heavy police presence, public unrest, and the death of a counter protester at the hands of a rally participant, Trump, rather than condemning the event, publicly stated that there was "blame on both sides" and that each had "very fine people." Second, his response to hurricane relief efforts showed dramatic differences in Texas and Florida versus Puerto Rico, the latter which he repeatedly denigrated (see Merica 2017). Third, witnesses at a closed-door meeting reported that he had referred to Haiti and places in Africa as "shithole" countries and wondered why the United States could not have more immigrants from places like Norway. Fourth, in 2018, during a controversy over his separation and detention policies of (mostly Latino) refugee families coming to the United States at unapproved points of entry, Trump said such people "infest the country." Comparisons to Adolf Hitler's claim about "vermin" Jews were hard not to draw (e.g., see Sapolsky 2018). Fifth, in August 2018, after a former aide was fired and later wrote a book on her experiences in the administration, she claimed that she had secretly taped Trump at the White House and recorded him using racist epithets (i.e., the "n-word" in a less-explicit American vernacular). In a news conference, Sarah Huckabee Sanders, Trump's Press Secretary, admitted that she could not deny that such a tape could exist. In other words, Trump used racist language to such an extent that had someone recorded him in the White House it would be a fool's errand to claim that in no way would any such recording find him using racist language.

In modernity's promissory note, people would have the liberty of free movement, freedom of speech, religion, and conscience, and "the people" are the basis of governing, where open and fair elections stand for consent and thus governmental legitimacy. The presence of slavery, however, did more than make a mockery of such democratic pretensions. It defiled the aspirations of nations as putative free republics. So institutionally and culturally ingrained was modern slavery that the contemporary world has yet to recover from it, nor rid itself of it completely. But when profits come from labor exploitation, when organizations and individuals target the vulnerable for this labor exploitation, when governments reduce their oversight and regulation of commodity markets, and when the consuming public continues to make such goods profitable whether by ignorance or apathy, slavery springs back to life, suggesting it is not an exception to our modern political economy but one of its trade secrets. And the racism and racist institutional practices that sprang from slavery similarly defile putatively democratic republics, cultures that aspire to uphold values of social equality, and undermine the spirit of progress that the best of modernity promised as an inspiration to others. Moreover, so persistent have such things been that we must begin to ask if they are not, in fact, exceptions to modernity's promises but rather indicators of them, that rather than betraying modernity's principles perhaps they are a basis of them. Such questions are both difficult to ponder and portentous in their answers, and thus are seldom addressed at all for we often fear what that answer will be.

CHAPTER 44

# A Fetish Dark and Mysterious

To fetishize something is to attribute inherent characteristics to it that are in fact a product of human invention. Humans often produce social objects—idols, money, gods—and not only treat them as if they had natural powers but they also allow such things to control their actions, movements, and beliefs. But what if a fetish comes to us not connected to an object or an idea but to a relationship? We saw earlier how capital is the all-dominating force of modern society, one that has wide powers over us. But it is not a belief system like a religious dogma or a political ideology. Capital cannot be held in one's hand as might a candlestick or even a dollar bill. And though invisible, capital has real expressions we can see. A factory is capital put to use in production. Warehouses full of commodities that businesses can convert into sales and profits are also part of capital's reality. And so too are other assets a business legally owns, such as stocks, bonds, real estate, or cash. What is strange about all of this is that capital is real, but it is not a *thing* that can be seen or touched or smelled. It is a *relationship*, a *process*, and a *circuit* that has manifestations everywhere in modern society.

The traditional circuit of capital is where money is invested in the production process—i.e., buying of land, labor, raw materials, machinery, utilities, and some sort of physical plant. A factory is built, laborers are hired, raw materials are transformed into goods using labor and machinery, the products are sold on a free market, and the resulting profits are remitted back to the original owner of the money initially set out. One crucial feature of this system is that money cannot stagnate, it has to move and often in a direction whereby it retains or even increases its value. This pressure on money's growth differs whether a business is a small concern or of moderate or multinational size. All three are likely to experience price competition from other businesses while the latter two are more likely to have investors who want a return on their deposits. Set up as such, the capitalist has several options on what to do with their profits.

Profits can be pocketed as personal income for the capitalist. This is the case for all businesses, though the smaller the business the more likely this is the primary focus of profit-making.

After personal income is taken, profits that are left can be reinvested back into the original operation, which, because of market competition, often targets cheaper raw materials, labor-saving technology, research and development, and/or the search for new markets (i.e., advertising, new sales areas, etc.). This sort of reinvestment results in business growth and explains how some companies go from small and local to moderate and national to even very large and international.

The larger the business, the more likely it is that they have investors and, as such, a portion of profits have to be used as dividends promised to stockholders. Stockholders can move their money rather easily, so they invest where they hope for a certain rate of return and, should that not occur, they can move their money in search of returns more to their liking. This means that the need to satisfy investors often constrains businesses in what they do with their profits and other market strategies, lest their investors flee and find better profit-making opportunities elsewhere.

And business owners themselves can become stockholders in other companies just in the same way, using a portion of their profits to stake a claim on future gains made by another organization. Whether or not they decide to reinvest in their own companies for expanding production or into other investment vehicles depends on both the expected demand for their products as well as the comparative rate of return they can achieve there versus other investment opportunities, whether those be in other productive companies or in alternative investment ventures. That said, investing in stocks always carries a level of risk, so sometimes profits are reinvested in things that offer better odds of holding their value, such as government securities (which are guaranteed) or commercial real estate (which often, but not always, holds value better than stocks whose value ebb and flow with the market overall).

In any case, businesses are not limited to any single one of these options and often set out reinvestments in multiple directions. What is important for this discussion, however, is that normal market operations and investments in stocks have a dynamic that compels both buyers and sellers to act in certain ways. This dynamic is a combined product of (1) capitalism's necessity for profit-making in a competitive market, (2) the need to move money lest it stagnate and lose value, and, in light of the former two, (3) balancing the pressure to maximize returns (to make stockholders happy) versus assuming a certain level of risk (and thus loss of profits, investors, and capital). This dynamic, crucially, is not limited to market exchanges among owners and investors and sellers and buyers but rather extends into wider market and social relationships far and wide, as we shall see.

Investors move their money where they expect an acceptable rate of return, which may be determined by levels of risk versus chances of higher or lower returns in various markets. Investments in production and subsequent profits and reinvestments back into production are called "productive capital," while money invested into stocks, bonds, and other paper representatives of value-forms is "financial capital" or "interest-bearing capital." When the anticipated odds of a higher rate of return on investments in *financial capital* are better than those for investments in *productive capital*, many in the investing classes gravitate away from the latter and toward the former (all other things being equal). Phrased another way, if investors do not expect tangible things to be sold at a level high enough to produce acceptable profits (a function of the level of effective demand in the market, or overall consumer spending power), then they will often tend to reinvest in intangible things, i.e., less investment in production facilities and more in banks, stocks, and securities.

The growth in "value" that profits from financial capital are based on is, nevertheless, only on paper. What this means is that the value of an investment in financial capital is represented by abstract figures recorded in files and documents: I bought XYZ stock for $10 and sold it $20; I made $10 though I produced no actual tangible thing. As such, interest-bearing capital—as compared to productive capital—is *fictitious value*. Invisible as it is like any other capital—as only numbers expanding on a ledger sheet—financial capital is not connected directly to anything productively real. At the same time, it can be converted into money—i.e., withdrawn from circulation as cash profit—or used to buy/trade for other forms of value—i.e., stocks, bonds, securities, land, etc. If these descriptions make it sound more convoluted than the simple money-form this is because financial capital can, in fact, operate in mysterious ways, which we shall see.

In advanced capitalism, more and more firms and organizations become anchored, in whole or in part, in this interest-bearing capital. This is because of several interconnected reasons. First, there tends to be a polarization between the classes, where the wealth of society concentrates in its upper echelons. The result is lowered spending power and demand from consumer sectors as whole and lowered effective demand lowers expectations of profitability in the productive sector. And, second, if the financial sector promises a higher rate of return—at least temporarily—at such times, then more and more investors will tend to flock to it. As more and more economic actors orient their investments toward this financial capital, more and more do governments direct policies toward the interests of financial capital's holders. Society becomes more and more organized, ruled, and controlled less by visible money invested in producing tangible things but by invisible capital invested into fictitious things. This is why interest-bearing capital is a dark and mysterious fetish. As it produces wealth without real value, money, investors, and class/state dynamics spin around its gravity while publics caught within this vector have barely a chance to understand the forces to which they are subject, a subject to which we now turn.

In 2008, many experts were taken by surprise when the world's stock markets centered in New York, London, Frankfurt, and Tokyo tanked. These experts, after all, had been celebrating a long-term rise of stock values driven by an expanding US housing market (more below). The historical amnesia was astonishing. It was as if Chicago School and Ivy League economists had long forgotten what an overvalued market, or "bubble," looked like. When it burst, it took down many investors and institutions with it. The gist of it was something along the following...

After World War II, most of Europe and Japan were industrially incapacitated and the United States took the lead in rebuilding the world economy, with policies such as the Marshall Plan (rebuilding Europe) and the Bretton Woods Agreement (rebuilding the world financial system and providing loans to devastated economies). By the 1970s, Europe and Japan had been rebuilt and again competed with the United States and did so, in part, by using cheaper sources of labor. The United States responded by starting to offshore its production base in search of similar sources of cheap labor. This—plus more women, immigrants, and computers in the economy as well as declining unionization—initiated a process that drove down US wages while, at the same time, US productivity went up. As a result, corporate profits soared—e.g., extensive growth in CEO salaries—while by the mid-1970s and 1980s US standards of living began to stagnate. As a result of this increased class polarization, some workers started to borrow against their houses and increased their reliance on credit cards, both of which increased short-term profits for businesses. However, these practices also lowered long-term effective demand in the United States, leaving less money in circulation for purchases thus less profits available in the productive sector.[1]

In the 1980s and 1990s, with lots of cash in their coffers but expecting only modest demand, businesses set out on a process of "merger mania." But in this era mergers also led to cutting workforces, further exacerbating the problem of low effective demand, too—and *increasing* demand is necessary for an economy to rebound in times of stagnation. Trying to find other outlets for cash

---

[1] While it appears as if spending on credit creates demand, it only does so in the short-term and only if the creation of such debt is sustainable. In the long-term, repayment of credit card debt comes with interest and this interest is extracted from future earnings, earnings which would/could contribute to future demand but now cannot. And should previous debts continue to add up, then future spending and the demand it represents only becomes possible with an increase in future earnings, which is not guaranteed.

ready for (re)investment, more businesses began to put money into the growing tech-market. After an initial rush, the "dot-com bubble" eventually burst between 2000 and 2002.

In the late 1990s, American corporate practices shifted from production-oriented managers to earnings-oriented stockholders, where the trading price of corporate stock (i.e., speculating on its future value) as a criterion for where investors placed their money displaced the previous focus on hard assets and past dividend payouts (see Krier 2009). The political sphere responded in ways indicative of such a climate. The US Congress, under President Bill Clinton, repealed the Glass Steagall Act—a Depression era law that regulated financial and commercial banking functions—and passed the Gramm Leach Bliley Act (or the Financial Services Modernization Act). The FSM Act allowed for blurring the line between commercial and financial banking practices and reduced the amount of liquid assets (i.e., disposable cash) a company needed on hand in order to invest in stock. Prior to this repeal of Glass Steagall, a bank had to keep its commercial assets (i.e., what you or I would deposit as our savings) distinct from its financial assets (i.e., its riskier investments in stocks and securities) at some ratio determined by law. In a hypothetical example, say for every $100 in commercial assets, a bank could use only $10 of those for financial risks and thus the total risk the bank assumed would be low enough to not expose its depositors as a whole to such risk. The idea was to prevent a bank's potential failure in trading stocks from bleeding into its obligations to protect customer/consumer deposits (this is also why federal insurance, FDIC, was later created for commercial deposits). This was a problem leading up to the Depression and, in part, caused its implosion—e.g., panics, runs, and lines of depositors at banks, skyrocketing unemployment, soup kitchens, and so on—and was something Glass Steagall was later supposed to thwart in the future.

Adding fuel to the fire, during most of this time (1990s–2000s), the FIRE sector of the US economy (finance, insurance, real estate) made for an increasingly larger portion of national GDP, though profits made here are done so without producing tangible products or things. As the FIRE economy grew and became ever more profitable, the manufacturing sector—and thus productive capital—increasingly made up a smaller portion of the national economy and declined in its attractiveness to investors.

In response, some corporations moved into the lending business via offering mortgage backed securities to workers, e.g., GMAC from General Motors. As more and more companies got into the mortgage lending market, the ratcheted-up competition put a downward pressure on industry lending standards and, as a result, it became easier for more people across income brackets to get housing loans. As he wanted to direct investment away from the public sector (e.g., government), Chairman of the Federal Reserve, Alan Greenspan (1987–2006), lowered the US Treasury Bill rate to 1% in 2004, which encouraged more investors to place their money in the mortgage market. As money poured into housing, mortgage lenders increasingly gave out easy-to-get "subprime" loans, often requiring no down payment, collateral, or even proof of a job from borrowers. Borrowers who once could not afford a home, especially without a down payment, could now get a loan through an "Adjustable Rate Mortgage" (ARM).

An ARM allowed one to borrow the initial down payment on a house and roll it into the loan. At first, such a mortgage loan had a lower interest rate, but it would adjust upward after 3–5 years, which, in turn, raised the monthly mortgage repayment. Borrowers with sufficient income could meet such higher obligations, though borrowers were not always told of the risks, especially those in lower income brackets.[2] Other borrowers intended to resell their houses at a profit before the upward adjustment kicked in. More and more people participating in this practice produced an inflating bubble. By buying cheap and selling dear, housing prices rose, and this allowed lenders (and borrowers) to assume this risk. Though, on the surface, this seems like a reckless financial risk for all parties, "collateralized debt obligations"—a new financial tool—were created as a way to allow investors to profit from this debt by packaging it and selling it.

How did this work? In a nutshell, collateral debt obligations (CDOs) "bundled" hundreds, even thousands, of subprime loans into packages to sell to investors as one item, who could then resell them at higher price, i.e., I buy the debt of 100 people in a CDO and if enough of them payoff their mortgages, my CDO is now worth more money than I paid for it and I can make a profit from this by either selling it or using it as collateral for new investments (even rolling it over into additional CDO purchases). Some of these mortgage loans were safe and others were highly risky. However, it was difficult to decipher the safety to risk ratio in many of these CDOs. Still, they remained profitable for investors (e.g., investment banking firms) just as long as the market for housing kept expanding and people with risky loans sold (or resold) their houses at a profit—called "flipping"—and paid off their mortgages (that people with

---

[2] There were race and gender components to the crisis as well. In 2007, *The Futurist* reported that the Consumer Federation of America (CFA) found that women were 41% more likely than men to be given a subprime loan and the disparity between them rose with income; minority women were more likely to receive such loans regardless of income (Tucker 2007). And in 2017, JPMorgan Chase was hit with $53 million in fines for targeting African-American and Latino mortgage borrowers for disproportionately higher rates than those provided to whites (Mattera 2017b).

their income typically could not afford). And as long as home buyers with subprime loans could continue to find new buyers willing and able to purchase at a higher price, the values of CDOs would hold and even expand with market growth.

To help in the profit-making process, ratings agencies such as Standard & Poore rated these CDOs at a triple-A rating, their highest and safest evaluation. As many people bought houses and tried to turn them over (creating the bubble), this was profitable for investors and individuals if they got out of the market in time, otherwise they could lose big once the bubble burst (though many were taken in by the profit-euphoria and then seemed to forget about bubbles or denied one was in the making). In order to protect investors against this, "credit default swaps" were created. Basically, a "swap" insured that if you had invested in a certain stock and it lost price, you could redeem your swap for the original value of the stock you bought. As selling credit default swaps became a way to make money by insuring the investments of others, they became a market in their own right and contributed significantly to the storm clouds that were brewing (though unrecognized as such at the time).

In 2000, Senator Phil Gramm inserted a provision into the Commodity Futures Modernization Act that allowed credit default swaps to be exempt from regulatory provisions enforced by the Commodity Futures Trading Commission. Thus, all manner of creative and risky deals went unchecked. For instance, a swap could be bought on a swap or you could buy a swap on someone else's investment (sort of like buying insurance on someone else's house). Subsequent swap purchases expanded in all manner of directions. One estimate pegged swap market growth from $180 billion in 1998 to (based on Bank for International Settlements numbers) to $6 trillion in 2004, $57 trillion by June 2008, and $41 trillion by the end of 2008 (Stulz 2010). Another approximation suggested growth from $1 trillion in 2001 to $54.6 trillion in 2008 (Terzi and Uluçay 2011). This growth reflected, in part, an overvalued market. To wit: with a world 2008 GDP of around $60 trillion, and the value of US homes in 2007 at around $19.9 trillion, the housing market's CDOs were insured for over $60 trillion via the swap market by 2007 (Watkins n.d.).[3]

A powder keg was set, and the adjustable rate mortgage was the fuse. As ARMS adjusted upward, they ran into a limit set by effective real demand. First, with household wages remaining stagnant, the ability of homeowners to

---

[3] The $60 trillion figure is referenced regularly (e.g., Deutsche Bank Research 2009) and often attributed to a 2018 source from International Swaps and Derivatives Association (e.g., Terzi and Uluçay 2011; Watkins n.d.), though without specifying a title or link. Tracking down the specific source or study from ISDA proved unfruitful.

service their growing housing debt declined as their ARMs ticked upward. Second, the number of people entering the housing market was not potentially infinite and once there was a slowdown of new homebuyers, the ability of those intending to flip houses to do so also declined and with it so too declined the prices houses could fetch and thus with these the value of the housing market as a whole. Because of these factors, an inevitable crash loomed and once it hit in 2007–2008, CDOs lost value, swaps were cashed in, housing sales stagnated, and/or their prices declined, and the edifice propping up the paper value of multiple fictitious capitals came crashing down.

Because of the bleeding between the wall once separating financial and commercial banking practices and their over-investment in CDOs and swaps, several companies found themselves hemorrhaging cash to meet their obligations. The investing sectors—which had holdings in publicly relevant assets including university and corporate pensions and in productive businesses that had also invested the housing market—started sacrificing what they could, selling off assets when and where available. The disaster soon spread from the financial sector outward to the productive sector, e.g., General Motors and Chrysler of the US auto industry. Institutions such as Goldman Sachs and Lehman Brothers went under (with the former later enjoying a government bailout and the latter left to die) and soon commercial paper began to dry up. The whole financial system and the industrial system attached to it were on verge of collapse.[4]

A few days into the crisis, President Bush and Treasury Secretary Henry Paulson announced an emergency influx of over $700 billion of government money into the market to slow the hemorrhaging. Later, the Troubled Asset Relief Program (TARP) was enacted by the Bush administration and continued under President Obama. The goal was to plug the holes in investing markets by providing financial bailouts to corporations that were overextended in the CDO and swap markets. The public was told it would cost taxpayers about $800 billion, though independent investigator (and former Wall Street insider)

---

4   Commercial paper is a financial tool commonly used in day-in day-out business practice. The general idea is that large financial banks lend this paper in very short-term loans (overnight, a day or two, etc.) so that the borrower can meet payroll obligations, buy needed equipment and resources, and so on. Commercial paper undergirds national and international businesses and basically keeps the system afloat. If banks refuse to lend commercial paper it is usually because they do not have confidence that the borrower will be solvent enough to pay off the loan. Given that these loans are for a very short term and that the issuers of commercial paper started to refuse to lend tells us much about how dangerous, unstable, and risky they viewed the market crash and financial meltdown and its connections to the productive sector.

Nomi Prins ([2009] 2011) calculated the cost at about $14.4 trillion. The result was a transfer of public funds to the investing classes, a socialism for the rich that protected many of them from the vagaries of the market that the public at large must navigate without such government protection and subsidy.

The collapse of the mortgage market and the resulting financial crisis rippled across both the US and the world economy. In the United States, GDP declined, the stock market fell, unemployment shot up, government expenditures streamed toward bailouts and stimulus packages, national debt increased, median family income and net worth both dropped, home values fell off, foreclosures spiked, and the number of families falling under the poverty line rose steadily. A Brookings Institute analysis noted that the global financial crisis resulted in "the largest and sharpest drop in global economic activity of the modern era," with "devastating real effects" which still "reverberates around the world." Analysts McKibbin and Stoeckel (2009) noted the crisis's effects on global trade stemming from slowdowns in business and household demand, increased aversion to lending risks by banks (which hit smaller businesses harder than larger ones, which are considered less risky), and subsequent shrinking of capital flows and thus contracting surpluses.

Developed economies of the Eurozone went into recession, with bank failures, spiking unemployment, and growing government debt, which were often responded to with cutbacks and austerity measures—e.g., with Greece and Ireland hit hardest and Portugal, Italy, and Spain following behind. In an analysis focused on just China, Hong Kong, Singapore, and Taiwan for periods during and just after the crisis, in all four countries real GDP growth declined and consumer price inflation and unemployment went up (though the latter only marginally in China); increases in government debt also went up in all four countries (with less impacts on China and Hong Kong) (see Lin et al. 2013). In more concrete terms, across all countries touched by the crisis, state jobs and services were cut as tax bases from wages and salaries were squeezed, millions of people went bankrupt, lost their homes, and suffered other personal difficulties and traumas. Pensions disappeared, mortgages were foreclosed, people lost jobs, suicides increased, and so on.

Even with these widespread effects, the vast majority of people were anywhere from dimly to totally unaware of either the historical or the structural causes of the crisis in which they were ensnared. It was truly a dark and mysterious turn of events and what was left available as their explanation was to lay the blame at the feet of irresponsible buyers and lenders. Even Alan Greenspan, a disciple of free market ideology, was caught so off guard that he said, "Those of us who have looked to the self-interest of lending institutions to protect shareholders' equity (myself especially) are in a state of shocked disbelief." He explained to the House oversight committee: "I made a mistake in presuming that the self-interests of organizations, specifically banks and others, were such that they were best capable of protecting their own shareholders and their equity in the firms." It was as if the supporters of free market ideology and architects of deregulation approached their economic theories as a zealot would their religion, i.e., without question and with faith over logic and/or evidence. Spokespersons, economists, bankers, and free market defenders had convinced themselves that an unregulated market would be free from highly predictable and historically demonstrated market dynamics that had produced many bubbles already in the past.

In world run by capital, even solutions to economic problems end up serving capital and often exacerbate the very things that bring crises on in the first place. After the initial shock and Barack Obama's subsequent election, his administration continued to hire and rely on the same or similar policy-makers behind these problems, e.g., Timothy Geithner and Larry Summers. One of his administration's solutions was to continue President Bush's strategy of dumping billions of taxpayer dollars into capital markets, i.e., the Trouble Asset Relief Program. Obama's administration also failed to offer a clear, predictable, and forward-oriented tax policy, which the business class wants (in addition to expected demand) before they sink excess capital into future production projects (creating jobs in the process).[5] Further, the US Federal Reserve under Ben Bernanke's leadership undertook "quantitative easing," which provided debt relief and improved cash liquidity for banks and other financial institutions through injecting them with money based on the purchase of government securities, a socialism for banking institutions that relieves them of the fallout from the market they helped create and from which they benefitted.

In another example, according to co-founder of Washington-based financial services consulting firm Federal Financial Analytics Inc., Karen Petrou, bank regulations after the crisis increased social inequality—with the top 10% of the population gaining an additional 8.3% of the country's wealth and the other 90%'s share dropping 17%—because (1) with fewer middle class customers middle class banks become unprofitable and investments flow to more profitable banks and (2) in difficult financial times, small-business loans are riskier and more expensive for banks, who shift their priorities to wealth management services and cut back on both small-business loans and middle class

---

5 This sort of hesitancy and caution about major capital commitments is simply part of the contingencies of the market. For instance, German businesses such as BMW, Mercedes, ThyssenKrupp, and Lufthansa openly expressed reluctance about investing in Britain because of uncertainty of what would happen with the "Brexit" issue (see O'Carroll 2018).

mortgage lending (see Nocera 2018 and references therein).[6] More recently, US President Donald Trump rolled back banking regulations put in place after the 2007–2008 crisis. It is not unreasonable—as wealth continues to concentrate to unprecedented levels, as investors search for profitable outlets, and as governments deregulate safeguards between financial and commercial investment practices—to assume that such conditions could trigger another crisis.

Such behavior is not limited to policies made in reaction to such crises. For example, between 2008 and 2017, "cash-rich US companies" spent nearly $4 trillion on buying back their own stock (an illegal practice before the Reagan/Thatcher market deregulation of the 1980s) rather than in productive investment. Buybacks provide not only lucrative payments to executives and stockholders but also improve stock indices with an appearance of growth that artificially inflates national GDP through profitable transactions that produce no new tangible value or everyday jobs (see Byrne 2017). "In a three-year period ending in 2012," writes Byrne, "449 companies in the S&P 500 index deployed 54 percent of their earnings, or $2.4 trillion, buying back their own stock." During the middle of all this (2014), Paul Singer (head of Elliot Management Corp.), wrote that "Nobody can predict how long governments can get away with fake growth, fake money, fake jobs, fake financial stability, fake inflation numbers and fake income growth" (reported in Crudele 2014).

Singer's sentiments are as much on the mark as they are likely to be ignored. To wit: faced with the news of President Trump's 2018 plan to reduce the corporate tax rate from 35% to 21%, one CNBC survey of corporate executives found that they believed 36% of the windfall would go to stock buybacks and payments of dividends and only 12% would go to wages (Liesman 2018). According to CNN, as of February 2018, workers had received $6 billion of the tax cut, while shareholders received $171 billion, as buybacks soared to record highs and doubled their level from the same time as the year before (Egan 2018a). In June 2018, NBC News reported that S&P 500 companies had given their shareholders a record $1 trillion in dividends and buybacks during the previous year (Popken 2018). Reflecting this skewed set of financial priorities and capital's

---

6  Such factors as these create macro-economic dynamics that are hard to grasp for individuals caught in them but are nevertheless intimately felt. For example, during a crisis, employers might turn to machinery to lower labor costs and boost productivity and profitability. Further, with many people out of work, employers can raise their demands in hiring, from "some college" to "college graduate" or from "college graduate with three years of experience" to "five years of experience" or even find plenty of applicants with advanced degrees. This will often squeeze out middle-skilled and moderately educated workers, leaving them behind, often permanently as the economy restructures (for discussion, see Lowery 2017 and references therein).

dim view of expected future effective demand, the labor force participation rate at the same time hovered at 63%, or 27% of the workforce were out of work long-term and/or had quit looking for a job.[7] Thus, the uncertainty in the market remained and the financialization process of the national and global economy continued apace, as did their basis in fictitious capital.

In the era of neo-liberal globalization, the only imagined solution from policy-makers is to feed capital's insatiable appetite for money by throwing trillions of dollars at it, behavior not dissimilar from fetishistic idol worshippers (capitalists and politicians) continuing to fling virgins (money) into a volcano (fictitious capital) as the crops fail (the housing market and the productive sector). An alternative approach would have been filtering government funds in the direction paying off the mortgages of subprime borrowers, a more Keynesian method of dealing with economic crises. This would have had several similar as well as very different outcomes. First, it would have solved millions of personal bankruptcies at the bottom, while simultaneously plugging holes in CDOs at the top. Second, freeing homeowners from such debts and monthly mortgage payments would loosen consumer spending, which would stimulate sales, profits, and job growth. Third, instead of legislating tax cuts at the top (i.e., providing money for the 1% and the funding class), such a method would have contributed to political support across middle and working classes.

The middle and working classes, however, do not fund the political process and thus their interests were not catered too, while the solution that was provided—i.e., bailouts for banks, tax cuts, TARP, quantitative easing, and so on—only exacerbated inequalities in wealth between the classes. Corporations, investing classes, and elite households make a lot of their money off investments, especially in stocks. For middle and working classes, their largest investment is often their homes. When homeowners lost their homes, they were not able to share in the economic rebound observed in the decade after the crisis, which saw the DOW Jones hit all-time highs. Thus, the crisis and its aftermath made inequality in the United States even worse (see N. Smith 2018b and references therein).

But traditional Keynesian redistribution policies as a solution for inequality and eliminating a crisis are a limited option in the period of globalization and for reasons national capitals—as opposed to multinational capital—find troublesome. Keynesian stimulus is predicated on the principle that new spending

---

7  See: Statista, "Monthly Civilian Labor Force Participation Rate in the United States from May 2017 to May 2018 (Seasonally Adjusted)" at (URL retrieved August 17, 2018): https://www.statista.com/statistics/193961/seasonally-adjusted-monthly-civilian-labor-force-participation-rate-in-the-usa/.

based on redistribution will be focused on local, state, and/or national businesses, which is a model from a bygone era. In today's global market, should working and middle classes have extra cash to spend on consumer goods, much of that would likely flow toward the emerging industrial giants of China and India and elsewhere (for discussion, see Asimakopoulos 2009). And perhaps because of such dynamics of neo-liberalism and globalization, capital's political allies prefer to cut out the middleman of redistribution and simply hand over excess gains to the investing class directly without concern for the livelihoods of the population as a whole.

The events of the financial crisis of 2007–2008 and their aftermath are instructive. Their results were dark and mysterious to many—even policymakers—and they rippled across multiple societies. After the crisis burst into the open, transnational capital continued to offload the costs of their investment risks on citizens and conservative politicians kept pushing tax breaks with their additional cash flow for businesses and the wealthy. But this can never and has never solved wider market problems because no new demand has been stimulated, leaving the underlying malaise intact. And by late 2018, it appeared to more than one observer that economic storm clouds were again brewing. The Organization for Economic Cooperation and Development (OECD) warned that growth in the world economy had perhaps peaked, especially so given the ascending trade wars between major economies begun by the Trump administration (Elliot 2018a). There were fears of an impending new economic crisis, with leading potential sparks being some combination of high levels of student loan debt (as a drag on consumption and homeownership), growing corporate debt (which can lead to defaults), overinvestment in risky companies, over-indebtedness in emerging markets (made vulnerable should the US dollar grow stronger on international markets, which makes repayment more difficult), increased debt taken on by equity firms, hedge funds, and mortgage companies, and the prospect of cyberattacks by hackers (Phillips and Russell 2018). Outside this host of contributing factors, another analyst opined that continued interest rate increases from the Federal Reserve could lead to a bear market (Vlastelica 2018), and that such a development, according to a third, could be followed by flash crashes triggered by computerized trading, a crisis in liquidity (a measure of the ease and speed at which a financial instrument can be traded; cash is highly liquid), volatility (swings in the market), and even social unrest (see Kolanovic 2018).

Note that all of the above variables reduce to the fact that capital accumulation leads to concentrated wealth and overaccumulation, both of which lead to overinvestment in financial capital and a fundamental weakness in the productive sector. In such conditions, fictitious capital becomes destructive, as it scrambles to find a home with an acceptable rate of return and as such homes increasingly lose their profitability amid increased risk, the market returns to its dark, dangerous, and mysterious ways. For one analyst, this rise of modern finance represents the concentration of decision-making power running parallel to that of national sovereignty and bypassing democratic procedures, with citizens left behind and feeling it. Coming on top of the previous era of deindustrialization, financialization and globalization shape the fate of currencies, public infrastructure, and private savings and this creates a feeling of powerlessness among citizens and cultivates social conditions conducive for the rise of a strongman promising to fix things (Vogl 2017). Demagogues like Donald Trump (and Jean-Marie and Marine Le Pen in France, it should be said) step in and harness and redirect public anger toward immigrants and away from the financial sector and the climbing concentration of wealth among the top 1%, .05%, and .01% (see Foroohar 2016). After the WWII defeat of fascism in Italy and Nazi Germany, we hoped we had transcended such internal systemic threats. But the financial crisis of 2007–2008 and the response to it demonstrate modernity's continued bewitching by fictitious creations of its own making and with results similar to those prior to WWII again one of its possible futures.

CHAPTER 45

# The World Market

The term "globalization" was being used more and more in the 1990s and by the early 2000s it seemed like we had always used it. The term suggested that the world economy was developing in ways that signaled a new era, one in need of new thinking and approaches and eliciting excitement, even trepidation. Scholars debated whether this new reality was identified by the increasing speed and distance of information exchanges, growing cultural homogeneity, or more trade across more nations, or some combination of all of the above. None of these were recent developments, however, as they have always been features of the modern world. And neither is trade connecting far flung corners of the globe a particularly modern phenomenon. From approximately 120 BCE to 1460s CE, The Silk Road connected the Mediterranean with cultures to its east as far as Japan and Korea (and this was not the only long-distance trade route prior to modernity). But there is a key distinction between previous history and now. In prior eras, it was individuals, kingdoms, trading companies, privateers, and so on who took advantage of long-distance trade routes, while in modernity long-distance forms of production and exchange are *at the structural basis of its political-economic system.* And it has been this way since modernity's birth.

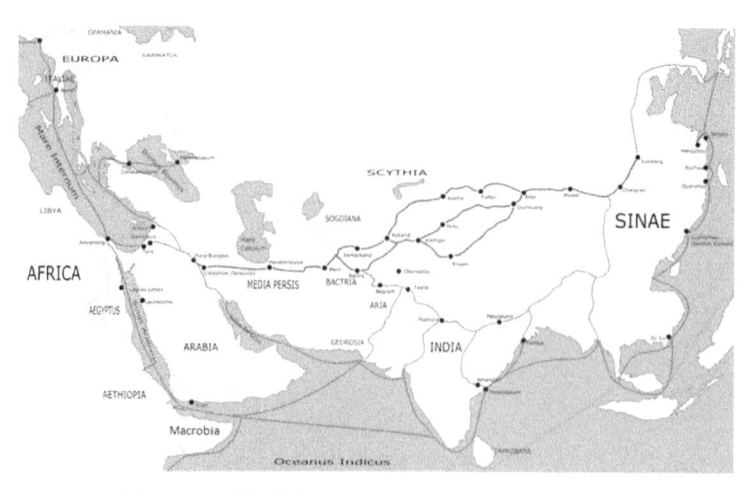

MAP 45.1    Transasian Silk Trading Routes, 500BC–500CE

The early colonial efforts of Portugal and Spain targeted the Caribbean and Central and South America. After them, the French, Dutch, and English embarked on global conquests, with the British Empire eventually coming out on top (at least for a while). And in the wake of global linkages that the British established did new nations rise—i.e., the United States, Canada, Australia, New Zealand, and Jamaica. European powers (including the British) also turned toward lands in South East Asia (India), the Middle East (Palestine), and the Far East (China), just to name a few. Competition among colonial powers over Africa later played a major role in the outbreak of World War I, a conflict that lasted until the end of World War II. The aftermath established the political-economic framework of the second half of the twentieth century, including the Cold War and what came after—the era "globalization." The world market was there throughout.

Much of the wealth and comfort of modern societies sitting atop the world market have been built on the backs of those at its bottom. In the colonial period, wood, rubber, gold, other metals and ores, and agricultural products (e.g., sugarcane) were the targets of production and extraction. Today, cars (as well as other transportation vehicles like trucks and planes), petroleum products, metals for transportation and computers (and their component parts), diamonds, and food and agricultural products like fish, soybeans, wheat, rice, and coffee are the most common globally traded products (see Desjardins 2018; Duddu 2014). Though some sources of these raw materials (and other components) are in more developed countries, such raw materials are also found in none-too-few moderately developed and poorer regions of the world:

- Oil—Russia (13%), Saudi Arabia (13%), USA (12%)
- Gas—USA (20%), Russia (16%), Iran (5%)
- Cement—China (51%), India (6%), USA (2%)
- Coal—China (47%), USA (13%), Indonesia (7%)
- Timber/lumber—USA (24%), Russia (9%), China (5%)
- Gold—China (14%), Australia (9%), Russia (8%)
- Iron—China (45%), Australia (22%), Brazil (10%)
- Sugar—China (29%), Brazil (24%), India (6%)
- Cotton—China (26%), India (20%), USA (14%)
- Rubber—Thailand (30%), Indonesia (12%), Malaysia (9%)
- Coffee beans—Brazil (33%), Vietnam (22%), Colombia (11%)
- Lead—China (52%), Australia (12%), USA (7%)
- Platinum—South Africa (71%), Russia (12%), Zimbabwe (7%) (see Desjardins 2016).

And it is similar with precious metals used in many modern technologies. For instance, according to data from the European Commission, the following countries enjoy the largest global production share of ...
- Cobalt (lithium batteries)—Canada (11%)
- Beryllium (computers and telecom products)—The United States (85%)
- Fluorspar (steel, paints, floor insulation, and high-performance optics)—Mexico (18%)
- Cobalt (computers)—Democratic Republic of Congo (41%)
- Niobium (structural steel, MRI scanners, pacemakers, other electronics)—Brazil (92%)
- Platinum (vehicles, electronics, and computer accessories)—Russia (11%)
- Magnesium (structural steel)—Turkey (12%)
- Indium (flat screen displays)—Japan (11%)
- Graphite (fuel cell technology)—India (13%)
- Platinum (catalytic converters, high-tech lab equipment)—South Africa (79%)

In addition, China has the world's majority reserves of rare earth minerals (97%) and the critical raw materials of antimony (91%), tungsten (78%), gallium (75%), germanium (72%), graphite (72%), fluorspar (59%), indium (58%), magnesium (56%), and beryllium (14%). And approximately $1 trillion worth of cobalt, niobium, rare earth minerals, copper, gold, and iron have been found in Afghanistan (see Rockwood 2010). As many of these resources are geographically locked, there is every reason to assume that such countries will continue to play a significant role in world affairs; and even if they are minor powers they will become a contested terrain for the major ones.

Interlocking global trade is not recent in modernity's history. Just as a man or a woman in Victorian England may have dressed in clothes made from cotton picked by slaves in the American South, heated their home with coal extracted by poorly paid workers in Wales, drank tea grown in and transported from India, and eased their pains with laudanum mixtures containing opium grown via an imperial conquest forced upon China, it is similar today. Today's conveniences such as cars, televisions, refrigerators, clothes, shoes, and cellphones often still find their points of origin—materially and/or through wage-labor—somewhere far afield from their point of sale. My coffee this morning was brewed from beans picked by poorly paid families and children grown a great distance from where I live in the United States, likely in Central or South America, or maybe Jamaica or Ethiopia. The clothes I dress myself with may come from textiles sewn together in sweatshops in Guatemala, Vietnam, or Indonesia. My car that takes me to work runs on gas that could have come from

MAP 45.2  The Modern World Market[1]

oil pumped in Saudi Arabia, Venezuela, Texas, Canada, or Iraq (among other places). For lunch I might eat prawns harvested from waters off of Thailand by workers whose labor conditions resemble that of slavery. After my dinner, my dessert could contain pistachios probably from Iran and chocolate from cocoa picked in the Ivory Coast by (often enslaved) children who likely have never tasted the finished product (see Anti-Slavery International 2004; Davis 2017; Rivero 2017; Food Empowerment Project 2018; Kelly 2018, and references therein).

But the world's poorer regions enrich its wealthier ones via more than simply the provisioning of goods through extraction of their raw materials and the use of labor in commodity production. Rich nations ship tons of solid wastes back to poor ones, especially an increasing amount of electronic waste associated with computer technology (see Breivik et al. 2014; Ellis-Petersen 2018), up to 90% of which is dumped or traded illegally (Nichols 2015). And developing

---

1  A note below the map in the original article states (p. 5): "Figure 2. Map of the land trading network. The color of the node shows to what extent a country is an importer (gray) or an exporter of land (red), and the size of the node represents the number of trading partners. The links represent the flow of land acquired by an importer from an exporter. Link colors are that of the importing node. Number of countries (nodes) = 126, while number of land trade relationships (links) = 471 (reflexive links shown, e.g., loop for China having a national partner involved in land trade along with international partners)."

countries are net-creditors to the developed world, providing tax havens and suffering balance of payment asymmetries that send wealth from poor nations to rich ones amounting to (if China is excluded) $11.7 trillion in net resource transfers since 1980 (Global Financial Integrity 2015). We cannot, then, understand the wealth and standard of living that modern societies enjoy outside of these broader linkages of the world market and the ways poor nations subsidize the rich.

The modern world market has always facilitated a movement of people across geographical space. Sometimes people migrate in search of economic opportunity, other times they flee political persecution or war in search of personal safety, and still other times they are caught up in the more nefarious trade of human trafficking. Though the United States was shaped significantly by European immigration, the Continent's expats also immigrated to places like Brazil and Argentina and in both places, slavery followed. As the colonial period drew down, Algerians came to France and Indians to England (their former colonizers, respectively). More recently, Poles have come to Britain, Germany has a large group of Turkish immigrants, and Canada, compared to all G8 countries, has the largest proportion of immigrants among its population. Outside the West, many Vietnamese people settle in China and South Koreans and Chinese in Japan. And Japanese, Koreans, Chinese, and Central Americans still set their sights on the United States. As a civil war devastated Syria in the 2010s, the reality was less "migration" than a mass exodus of refugees fleeing war, with so many people heading to Europe that it caused emergencies as well as social, political, and economic controversies.[2] And as a conduit of people and things, the modern world market continues to facilitate human trafficking of laborers, slaves, and the vulnerable forced into sexual exploitation, especially in those states either less concerned about today's international norms, outside the reach of global regulatory institutions, or just ignored by the powers that be that allow it to continue. Women (as well as children) from poverty-stricken countries may be raped by smugglers and/or coerced into prostitution in the service of sex tourism in brothels and hotels in major cities, even more

---

2   In places like Greece, camps were set up to handle the influx, where processing was often slow and conditions often deteriorated. The EU had no unified policy, with some countries resolutely strict on border controls (e.g., Poland, Austria), while others were actively more porous and open (e.g., Sweden, Germany). Still, even in places that could handle refugees better than others, their number and rate provoked an anti-immigrant backlash in multiple quarters. In the summer of 2018, as Italy balked over taking in additional refugees, the EU even proposed paying countries just over $7,000 for every person they took in (see Mohdin 2018).

modern ones (e.g., see Murray 2013; Pattisson 2014; Vick 2016; United Nations Office on Drugs and Crime 2018).[3]

The world market serves as the basis for economic crises in multiple ways. When the Great Depression struck in 1929, the crisis's repercussions were felt across the Atlantic and across the globe. As we saw in Chapter 44, it was similar with the 2007–2008 financial crisis. For 2018, which is considered the recovery's highpoint, the World Bank expected the world economy to grow at 3.1% and expressed concerns about sluggish global economic growth by the 2020s. A slowdown, in their view, could result from several growing risks: (1) financial markets (where price share valuations are comparable to the period before the dotcom bubble in 2000 and the Wall Street crash of 1929); (2) stock prices being higher relative to earnings (another sign of an overvalued market); (3) potential interest rate hikes to fight inflation that can burst a bubble and bring on recession; (4) an upsurge in protectionism; (5) geo-political tensions such as the Korean Peninsula, in the Middle East, or governance problems in the Eurozone; and (6) a slowdown in population growth (which has driven global GDP in prior decades) (see Wallace 2018 and references therein).[4] No modern nation is independent of what happens in others, as the world market is an interconnected web of political-economic activity.

---

3  For recent reports from the US Department of State's Office to Monitor and Combat Trafficking in Persons, see: Belarus (2017) (URL retrieved August 18, 2018): https://www.state.gov/j/tip/rls/tiprpt/countries/2017/271144.htm; Democratic People's Republic of Korea (2016) (URL retrieved August 18, 2018): https://www.state.gov/j/tip/rls/tiprpt/countries/2016/258797.htm; Libya (2017) (URL retrieved August 18, 2018): https://www.state.gov/j/tip/rls/tiprpt/countries/2017/271228.htm; Russia (2017) (URL retrieved August 18, 2018): https://www.state.gov/j/tip/rls/tiprpt/countries/2017/271269.htm; South Sudan (2017) (URL retrieved August 18, 2018): https://www.state.gov/j/tip/rls/tiprpt/countries/2017/271282.htm; Sudan (2017) (URL retrieved August 18, 2018): https://www.state.gov/j/tip/rls/tiprpt/countries/2017/271288.htm; Venezuela (2017) (URL retrieved August 18, 2018): https://www.state.gov/j/tip/rls/tiprpt/countries/2017/271312.htm; Yemen (2017) (URL retrieved August 18, 2018): https://www.state.gov/j/tip/rls/tiprpt/countries/2017/271314.htm.

4  Other problems facing the world economy include the way debt crises in moderately developed economies like Greece, Turkey, or Argentina can potentially spread to other developed economies as a whole. When such countries default on their debt, their central banking creditors either do not get paid and/or their debt is restructured under "austerity" plans which often weigh heavily on public funds, social conditions, and political stability. Should interest rates rise, countries like Italy would have loan payment problems that threaten the entire Eurozone. And should a new global recession hit (and they inevitably do), organizations like the International Monetary Fund warn that many countries will find themselves fiscally squeezed, especially if they have underfunded old-age pensions and health care programs. In addition, a slowdown in China could disrupt global markets, given the level of global investment there (for discussion of the above, see Rogoff 2018).

A core feature of the world market, then, is that what happens in markets in one part of the world can influence the fate of a country in another part of the world. And this is true for even secondary economies. For example, after the collapse of the Soviet Union in the early 1990s, Western financiers and states promised economic support that was contingent on the instituting of austerity measures, which caused a spike in Russian poverty and unemployment, as well as social unrest. A 1997 Asian financial crisis eventually reached Moscow by 1998 and, no longer able to keep the ruble propped up, Yeltsin's government eventually was forced to announce the ruble's devaluation (after which it lost two-thirds of its value), defaulted on domestic debts, and placed a moratorium on external debt payments. Inflation spiked, and unemployment and poverty rose even further. However, the devaluation of the ruble made imports more expensive and this helped domestic producers. A weak ruble was not good for banking and finance, but the rising global fossil fuel prices of the 2000s were a boon for Russia's oil, gas, and coal industries (GDP rose 7% annually). And this, as a consequence, was also a boon for the elites sitting atop these industries. Profits previously made by financial oligarchs were distributed more narrowly than the gains made by this new class of industrial wealth. And after a clique around Yeltsin orchestrated Putin's promotion to the head of the Russian state, this backdrop became a foundation for his subsequent popularity. After 2000, Putin worked to diminish the power of financial oligarchs while facilitating the wealth and power of oil and gas oligarchs. And though he initially reached out to establish good relations with the West (e.g., expressing interest in joining NATO, extending assistance to the United States after the September 11, 2001 terrorist attacks), such warming up of previously cold relations would not last (for discussion on the above, see Wood 2018).

The situation in Venezuela in the 2010s is another, and related, case in point. With the ascent of Hugo Chavez's government, Venezuela undertook a series of "socialist" policies that used the country's oil wealth to sell on the global market to finance its overall economy. Its state-owned oil company provided cheap gasoline to citizens and purchased commodities on the global market to fill its store shelves (here we will ignore previous efforts of successive US administrations to undermine its sovereignty and economy under Chavez from 1999–2013). On the other side of the world, Russian leader Vladimir Putin, trying to rebuild the nation's military might and wanting to project its sea power, needed warmer ports that could be open year-round and not easily constricted by foreign forces. He seized Crimea before Ukraine could join NATO; if he had tried afterward it would have been seen as an attack on all NATO members. Though Western powers felt fighting back militarily was impractical, the United States at roughly the same time set out on an oil production boom and its ally, Saudi Arabia, started to sell off reserves at prices less than the cost of pumping oil out of the ground, which combined sent the price of world oil downward (it is unclear if the latter events were spurred on by the former). As the Russian economy was not a diversified one, it a saw significant drop in its GDP (2013–2016). Though not a direct target, this also sent oil revenues in Venezuela on a downward spiral, which, when combined with the price controls that throttled its agriculture sector, put its economy on its heels.[5] Their struggles to recover appeared both desperate and likely to be ineffectual.[6]

One of the ways the likeness of capital is reflected in the realities of the world market is its constant flux and change, including of those who sit atop it. After Portugal and Spain had their period of market dominance, Holland replaced them, followed by England (though France contested this for over a century and Germany almost defeated the British as well), and then the United States. Each time, the world's leading political-economic nation found itself overextended militarily and heavily invested in economic resources the system was in the process of passing by for new frontiers. Spain focused much of its energy on extracting gold and transporting it back to the homeland, which became less of an economic advantage when they spent that wealth on cathedrals, palaces, and so on. Holland focused on timber and agriculture that

---

5  In another example of how the interconnections of separate parts of the world can cause ripple effects throughout, in August 2018, when Turkey experienced a currency crisis—plunging its lira to a record low—said to be due to President Erdogan's increasing control over the economy and Turkey's worsening relations with the United States (i.e., US President Trump had announced a doubling of tariffs on Turkish metals after Erdogan had asked citizens to convert their euros, dollars, and gold into lira), world equities markets also dropped—triggering fears of recession and a possible banking crisis—while German bonds and other more stable assets received a boost (see Imbert 2018c; Randall 2018).

6  In August of 2018, President Nicolás Maduro announced several measures to stabilize Venezuela's sagging economy: (1) to reduce reliance on trading in dollars, a single exchange rate was pegged to the country's petro cryptocurrency to which he would also peg salaries, pensions, and prices—even with a 96% devaluation; (2) boosting minimum wage over 3,000%; (3) increasing the corporate tax rate; and (4) increasing already highly subsidized gas prices. Given that additional printing of money is also expected, such moves sparked fears of hyperinflation. Further, in March of the same year, US President Trump signed an executive order barring US-based financial institutions from transactions involving Venezuela petro-rooted cryptocurrencies (CNBC 2018b). It is difficult to see a path forward given these policy choices and the limited options in front of them in the face of a hostile world power as well as a world market that can make or break a country's short-term future. By late August, Venezuelans were fleeing the country (2.3 million or 7% of the country since 2014) at a high enough level (thousands a day into Peru, Colombia, Ecuador, Brazil) that Brazil announced it was sending armed forces to keep order near the border area and Peru declared a public health emergency (see Chibber 2018; France 24 2018).

allowed them to build a massive fleet of trading ships that could dominate the world economy, albeit temporarily. While Holland was sinking its investments into the economy for its time, England took the lead in advancements in the use of coal and steam. Already an empire with oceanic reach, England came to dominate industrially, militarily, and politically up to and even somewhat after World War I. However, while England was deeply invested in coal, the United States pursued the new oil economy, shaping its industry and military to match. And it was this latter process—the rise of the oil economy—that thrust the Middle East to front and center in many of the twentieth and twenty-first centuries' geo-political conflicts.

We should expect this pattern—newcomers finding emerging arenas of investment while older powers have investments sunk in the prior economy—to continue, with China appearing best poised for future ascendance.[7] For instance, China has already far surpassed the United States in investment in, use of, and jobs involving solar and wind energy and is poised not only to survive the decline of fossil fuels but also to become the industrial center for producing renewable energy technology for the rest of the world.[8] Further, the next geo-political turn for global investment strategies in the world economy is likely toward Africa (as history repeats itself). By 2035, the number of working-age people there will exceed the rest of the world combined; by 2050, one in every four humans will be African and by century's end 40% of the world's population will reside there. Economically speaking, since 2000, at least one-half of countries that have had the highest annual growth rate have been African and, by 2030, 43% of its population is expected to move into the global middle and upper classes. And also, by 2030, household consumption is predicted to reach $2.5 trillion (over double from its 2015 figure of $1.1 trillion), while consumer and business spending combined are expected to reach $6.7 trillion. In the face of this potential future, China, the European Union, and others such as India,

---

[7] In 2018, the International Monetary Fund estimated India's GDP at $2.6 trillion, ranking it as the world's sixth largest economy, ahead of France and behind the United States, China, Japan, Germany, and the United Kingdom. However, it is unlikely that we will see India as a competitor for the next global leader, as extending its military geographically does not seem to be one of its core priorities.

[8] As of 2017, China had approximately 2.5 million people working in the solar power sector alone, compared to 260,000 in the United States. China is working on converting to renewables for internal energy sources, cutting about 1.3 million jobs from its coal industry. They are also directing resources—e.g., approximately $367 billion—toward renewable energy generation (solar, wind, hydro, and nuclear) by 2020. Externally, in just one example, between 2008 and 2013, world prices for solar panels crashed 80% due to a flood of Chinese products in the global market (see Pham and Rivers 2017 and references therein).

Brazil, Turkey, Japan, and the Gulf States have all initiated diplomatic, developmental, and economic initiatives in Africa.[9] The United States, on the other hand—from Bush to Obama to Trump—has increased its military presence there, signing 34 status of forces agreements with African countries, having military deployments in 50 out of its 54 countries, and with its military advisers outnumbering its diplomatic corps (Booker and Rickman 2018).

The world market has brought with it both great cataclysms and social changes, often hard to understand for those experiencing them, especially their after-the-fact ripple effects. Several rhetorical but nevertheless relevant questions and observations demonstrate the point:

- While many US citizens understood that the status of slavery in both the South and in new states brought into the Union was a catalyst that drove the nation to its Civil War, how many understood that little of this would have happened without the international demand for cheap US cotton?
- How many citizens during World War I understood that international instability in currency exchanges and the competition over colonizing African territory brought European powers to their continental war of mutual destruction?
- Before, during, and after these conflicts, the issues about which they were fought had a central role in how political powers drew and redrew state boundaries, particularly in the Middle East and Africa, events and dynamics which today are barely remembered (at least in the more developed parts of the world).
- Christians in the Western and Northern Hemispheres may embrace the resurgence of Christianity in Latin America but probably have little knowledge or memory of the terrorism sponsored there under the tutelage of the Reagan administration in the 1980s.
- And to what extent do publics at large understand how much of their job, pension, health, and educational insecurities in the 2000s are rooted in the deregulation policies rooted in that same Reagan administration, policies urged on in response to developments in the world economy going back at least to the post-World War II period, a period bookended on the other side

---

9 In April 2018, with a rising concern over growing US protectionism under US President Trump, Chinese foreign minister, Lu Kang, felt confident enough to identify India and China as the new vanguards of globalization (see Aneja 2018). Perhaps reflecting and/or buoying such confidence was the establishment of the Asian Infrastructure Investment Bank (AIIB), a Chinese effort—involving Kenya, Egypt, Ethiopia, and 86 other countries from six continents—to fund infrastructure projects and other initiatives in energy, transportation, agriculture, and telecommunications (among other things). This initiative is in addition to China's "One Belt, One Road" initiative, a project to spend around $3 trillion on roads, ports, and so on in 60 countries (Dahir 2018).

by how the world market ushered in conflicts between nation-states leading up to World War I?
- How many people today understand that their clothes and cellphones are manufactured in sweatshops by highly exploited laborers watched by an armed military working for dictators and paid for by taxes in wealthy democratic societies?

In addition to such macro-questions, other mystifications put in our way prevent us from understanding real life in the world market. Environmental activists tell us that it makes better ecological sense to "eat local" in order to reduce one's carbon footprint. While it is very hard to argue against that logic, in a global economy a tomato grown on a small farm 40 miles away might require more total energy to grow and get to the table than a mango grown halfway around the world brought to a Western market via a massive cargo container, i.e., the former might transport a few thousand units in a truck while the latter could involve hundreds of millions of them on a ship, an economy of scale that changes the equation.

Let us take a look at a couple of other examples of obstacles that confront a clearer understanding of the world market and claims made about it.

An analyst tells us that the "economy is humming" (citing low unemployment at 3.8%, predicted yearly wage-growth of 3%, and the second longest expansion in US history) and then explains why experts foresee a possible recession by 2020—e.g., higher energy, commodity, and asset prices, escalating trade conflicts, budget battles, and/or trouble overseas (see Davidson 2018). The problem here is *not* that such things would *not* trigger a market downturn, because they probably would. The problem is that the economy is *not* humming. Though the unemployment rate appears low, much of that is because the US workforce participation rate declined during and after the financial crisis and has never recovered—in 2018 down over 3% from 2008.[10] Though 3% does not sound like very much, for a country the size of the United States that comes to 5–10 million working-age people (depending on what variables are used to define that group). And the unemployment rate is not the only dodgy statistic that can mislead us about the state of economic conditions. The GDP is often included in measures of economic health and this, too, can be misleading. For example, stock buybacks (which were observed as a result of the Trump tax cut, discussed in Chapter 44) will contribute to GDP as they are measured as a form of profitable market exchanges. Similarly, intra-firm trade—e.g., if parts of a product are made by the same company in different factories across state

---

10   See US Bureau of Labor Statistics data here (URL retrieved August 21, 2018): https://data.bls.gov/timeseries/LNS11300000.

or international lines, then shipping those parts for assembly is accounted as part of trade and thus economic activity subsequently measures higher than if the whole product was made in only one country—will measure as a form of economic growth, even if it does not represent new jobs or additional wealth creation. In the era of neo-liberalism, the United States saw a growth in both of these practices and using such measures makes it appear as if there's more economic activity and growth than there really is. Again, these are not the only measures that do this.

Many economic observers had previously written off US job losses of the 2000s as primarily the result of mechanization and robotics while downplaying corporate offshoring of labor costs as being less a factor than was often claimed. However, the data on apparent US manufacturing output growth in the 2000s was distorted because it failed to include the massive gains in computer power. When economists look at long-term trends, they often statistically increase their valuation of sales or assets to take into account both price changes and improvements in quality from year-to-year. For example, if the quality of a car improves from year X to year Y, economists might add that into their calculation of efficiency and productivity via its price change and use that in their calculations of how much technology plays a role in output and thus the conditions of the job market. However, the quantitative-qualitative increases in computer efficiency and productivity have been accounted for by use of previous models, e.g., instead of hypothetically increasing measurements by a factor of 10 or 20 to account for computer and robotic acceleration of efficiency, economists' models use the same factor of 2 that they use for other industries. This makes it seem that US computer firms are producing and selling more than they actually are and when this industry is added into the overall economic numbers, it makes US manufacturing appear more productive than it really is. As a result, evidence suggests that the US manufacturing employment sector is 26% smaller than it was in 2000 and much of this is due to shipping jobs overseas to places like China, especially after its admittance into the World Trade Organization. In that period, the dollar strengthened while global investment gravitated toward lower-waged Chinese markets. The result of all of these trends was an overall overestimation of the health of the US manufacturing sector (see Guilford 2018 and references therein).

These realities above simply add to the complexity of the world market and what it takes to grasp it today. For instance, while it would seem logical that more developed economies could rebound more effectively from the 2007–2008 financial crisis than those less developed, indications suggest otherwise. One study for the period between 2006 and 2009 found measurable declines and rebounds in growth rates in all economies assessed, though the economic growth rate of "emerging economies" performed better than that of developed countries, likely because of more financialization of the economies in the latter and more investment in productive activity in the former (Long, Huiwen, and Cheng 2012).[11] In short, when a developed economy increasingly gravitates towards financial markets while offshoring much of its productive base, it will have a harder time recovering from financial shocks. Real production, no matter how lucrative short-term stock trades can be, will always be at the basis of the real economy.

Another reality of the world market is the inner-class dynamic between national capital versus international capital. The former is mostly composed of small to moderately sized firms that are often active in national politics and favor policies that prioritize their home markets and industries. The latter is represented most commonly by multinational corporations that are more interested in international trade, multilateral agreements and organizations, reducing obstacles represented by state borders and regulation, and so on. Individuals in this class of actors increasingly lack nationalist identities and loyalties and often find shared solidarity with other representatives of international capital. This, however, is not always so cut and dried. Some large businesses at the state level may support global free trade agreements in hope of taking advantage of them so that their own activities might enjoy an international reach. Conversely, sometimes members of the business community with international ties retain a strong nationalist streak. In any case, there is a push-pull dynamic extending from this national versus international capital relationship (for discussion, see Robinson 2012; Carroll 2012; Murray 2012).

For instance, as a businessman, Donald Trump had ventures in multiple countries, though as US President he set out on an "America First" initiative that appears not only counter to the global free trade project of neo-liberalism but also has taken aim at long-term US commitments and allies. During his campaign and after his election, he voiced opposition to the North American Free Trade Agreement (NAFTA) and threatened to pull the United States out of the World Trade Organization, two principle global relationships supported by his predecessors and wide sections of the business class. And Trump

---

11  The authors listed developed countries as (Major) United States, Japan, Germany, United Kingdom, France, Canada, Italy, (Other) Australia, Austria, Belgium, Denmark, Finland, The Netherlands, New Zealand, Norway, Sweden, Switzerland, Greece, Ireland, and Portugal. Emerging market countries included (Asian) India, Indonesia, South Korea, Malaysia, (European) Poland, Czech Republic, Hungary, Slovak Republic, Slovenia, Turkey, (Other) Mexico, Brazil, Chile, South Africa, and Russian Federation.

also initiated a trade war with crucial trading partners and historic friends (e.g., Canada and Mexico). In July 2018, likely observing such trends, Chinese officials described as him "opening fire" on the entire world. It was hard to disagree with that assessment. In early 2018, Trump had put $34 billion of tariffs on Chinese goods in protest of Beijing's policies toward foreign high-tech industries—there had been a concern that the Chinese government was pilfering technological secrets from foreign companies invested there. China responded with tariffs on the US agricultural sector—e.g., soy beans and pork—in an attempt to hurt Trump in US communities where he enjoyed political support. Trump then guaranteed those communities aid, though it was doubtful that the $12 billion promised to make up the shortfall—i.e., buying excess crops and subsidizing trade promotions to build new export markets—would cover US farmers' expenses for even one year, much less be a viable long-term solution. Not only did this portend immediate economic troubles, but, in a global market filled with agricultural producers, it will be incredibly difficult for American farmers to attract lost customers back—e.g., exporting to China (see Huifeng 2018)—after they have fled US tariffs.

Still, such trade wars indicated the direction of Trumpian economic policy, which historically has resulted in retaliation (and the need to spend government money on subsidizing industries hurt by such actions). In June of 2018, Canada reacted to Trump's tariffs on Canadian imports to the United States with $13 billion in retaliatory tariffs on US imports to Canada. Also, in June, India joined the European Union's $3 billion in tariffs by increasing their own tariffs to $241 million on more than two dozen US goods. In early August 2018, China put an additional 25% tariff on 333 US goods worth $16 billion, including large passenger cars, motorcycles, fuels, fiber optic cables, coal, asphalt, plastics, and recyclables, among other products, in what was widely seen as a "tit-for-tat" reaction to Trump's tariffs on Chinese imports (Imbert 2018b). By September 17, 2018, the US administration announced it would impose $200 billion in additional tariffs on Chinese goods, while the next day China responded with its own announcement of $60 billion in tariffs on US goods in response. Trump's larger threat amounted to around $500 billion in tariffs on China in total should it not agree to sweeping changes in the way it approached intellectual property, industrial subsidies, and its tariff structure.

The long-term outlook because of such moves is risky at best and a threat to the global economy at worst. In June 2018, global equity funds witnessed outflows of $12.4 billion, a level not seen since October 2008, i.e., during the financial crisis triggered by the collapse of the housing market. This movement was believed to result from concerns that the post-crisis expansion was slowing down, fears about the continued success of trade in emerging markets, and jitters about impending trade wars (see Cox 2018). Strategists at Morningstar Investment Management Europe said (on or about July 4/5 2018) that their "expectation at the moment is that you won't have any real return from US equities over the next 10 years" and that the US market "looks both extremely expensive and very unattractive relative to other markets" (see Reklaitis 2018). By August, however, reports claimed that US stocks were once again heading for new highs while world stock markets struggled, with analysts pointing to the culprits of an economic slowdown of the Chinese economy, the financial crisis in Turkey, and the high debts of emerging market countries, i.e., governments of emerging market economies often borrow in US dollars and, as it gets stronger against other currencies, this makes dollar-funded debt harder to repay (Franck 2018).

So even if financialization does not produce any *things*, it still can operate as the puller of strings on the global scene and influence those economies that are the bedrock of world production. In this day and age, as a result, we are increasingly dependent on what happens in corporate suites where money is moved, credit lines are established, and unknown policy-makers in powerful nation-states make the rules.

During the Great Depression, as Europe sank deeper into economic malaise, the German economy, still on its heels from the post-WWI settlement, was especially hit hard and its money was rendered almost worthless. This European malaise played a central role in the rise of fascism and Hitler's regime. When the housing market in the United States tanked and brought the financial system to its knees, the repercussions also were felt worldwide. Indeed, the global economy went into recession, but one made worse by the oil shocks of the same period, which are often overlooked (see Hamilton 2009 on the role of oil in that recessionary period). In the United States, both reactionary Tea Party conservatives and the leftist Occupy Wall Street movement were angered by the downward spiraling economy and the rule of the banking oligarchs. By 2016, the United States had "elected" Donald Trump, a political novice with a record of reactionary racial animosity, corruption, and apparent authoritarian aspirations.[12] And, in 2017, we witnessed an election in France that drifted in a similar direction, though the result did not. During his first years in office, Trump's tariffs on products from Mexico, Canada, Europe, and China, plans to

---

12  Quotation marks are used here to note that, because of the scheme that the US electoral system uses in presidential elections, a winning candidate can receive the majority of "electoral" votes (allotted via state winners) while losing the overall "popular" vote. In the case of Trump in 2016, he received approximately 2.9 million fewer votes than Hillary Clinton while winning the Electoral College vote by a margin of 304 to 227.

renegotiate the North American Free Trade Agreement (NAFTA) and perhaps withdraw from it, and suggestions he wanted to withdraw from the World Trade Organization provided no succor to global stock markets, investors, and central banks. And such moves could also very well bring on an already feared global recession. And the results of such a downturn, internally to the United States and externally for the world community, could be darkly portentous as they echo what we observed after WWI and the rise of the fascist belligerents behind WWII. If modernity is a society where capital creates a world in its likeness, then we must judge that likeness through what it presents to us. The gyrations and repetitions of history seen in the world market are one key locale to observe those features.

CHAPTER 46

# The Political Chessboard

The cause of World War I's outbreak is often traced to the assassination of Archduke Ferdinand of Austria. While this was certainly a major flashpoint for that war, European powers did not pick up arms only and/or simply in reaction to or in revenge of his killing. Prior to the assassination, many nations of Europe had been involved in "the scramble for Africa," a period of colonization that had a pronounced effect on which countries would be best situated for ascending to economic, and thus political, power. At the time, there existed multiple treaties and agreements between European nations and each was jockeying for positional advantage and protecting its flanks through alliances and self-militarization. Balances of power shifted unpredictably, as the Franco-Prussian War (1870–71) resulted in Germany's rise, tensions between Austria and Serbia ratcheted up, as did those between Russia and Austria (the Balkan Wars), the UK and Germany, and Italy and Austria. It was a complex and volatile situation. The Archduke's assassination set off this powder keg and the resulting war—with the German Empire, Austria-Hungary, Bulgaria, and the Ottoman Empire aligned in the Triple Alliance against the coalition of France, Russia, Britain, Canada, Italy, Belgium, and (eventually) the United States—really lasted until 1945.

After World War II, the United States and the Soviet Union emerged as the predominate world powers and engaged in a series of political, ideological, economic, and social struggles known as "The Cold War." As the most powerful of the war's victors, other countries had to contend with each and/or manage their relationships with them in some way for securing a more stable and lucrative future in the post-war period. The goal of each side was containing their opponent's reach and influence while maintaining loyalty and commitment from those on their own side.

After Germany's defeat, American (along with British and Canadian) and Soviet forces met each other somewhere near the middle of the Continent, i.e., especially Berlin and surrounding areas. They agreed at Potsdam (1945) on their respective spheres of influence, with Germany being split into East and West. But mutual cooperation would be short-lived. Though Berlin was well inside of Soviet-occupied Germany, the United States, France, and Britain controlled the western part of the city. In June 1948, the Soviets blockaded road, rail, and water access to areas controlled by the Allies, who in turn began dropping needed supplies to people trapped there in what became known as the "Berlin Airlift" (1948–49). Within about 12 years (August 13, 1961), Communist East Germany constructed a wall that divided the city and prevented unrestricted access between the city's halves. The Berlin Wall would stand for decades as both real and symbolic separation of their respective spheres of influence and control, with the United States (and the West) touting itself as the "Free World" and dominating the capitalist arena and the Soviet Bloc presenting itself as the promise of communism and as a check against "Western imperialism."

Throughout the Cold War, most countries of the world were compelled to pick a side and were provided inducements to do so. The United States wanted to keep Europe loyal and rebuild many of its countries while also trying to squelch any positive feelings there for Soviet-style development, e.g., some "Euro-communist" political parties received popular support and the United States worked to undermine them. In the process, the United States constructed a formidable military apparatus in Europe to dissuade the Soviets from considering invading Europe in a ground war. For their part, the Soviet Union worked to keep Eastern Europe in general lockdown, with limited to nonexistent civil liberties and closed borders to the West, while guaranteeing internal social provisions such as housing and employment. Demands from Eastern Bloc countries for the expansion of civil liberties and/or democratic reforms were often met with force, e.g., the 1968 Soviet crackdown on Czechoslovakia in the "Prague Spring." Both sides propagandized their own people and infiltrated the other with spy networks. The United States and its allies came to be known as "The First World," the Soviet and the Communist Bloc "The Second World," and all others "The Third World."

The Cold War shaped significant portions of the twentieth century in the Third World. Central Asia and Africa were targets for courting loyalties and extracting resources. None-too-few dictators and repressive regimes were either forced upon Africa or supported there and induced to align with the United States or the USSR and remain obedient, e.g., in Angola, Mozambique, and The Democratic Republic of Congo (see de Sousa 2016). A "Non-Aligned Movement" (1961) also emerged, which attempted to stay out of the fray, though many there were subverted and brought to heel (this movement is officially still in existence).

Asia, too, was caught between the contending sides. From 1950–1953, the United States fought a war in Korea, eventually drawing to a stalemate and with the country divided between the communist North and the capitalist South, a division that remains. After the French decided that holding on to its former colonial domain in Vietnam was not worth the trouble, the United States stepped in, first with military "advisers" and later escalating the conflict into a full-blown war. In the process, the United States spent a great deal of political capital worldwide, though they ultimately withdrew in ignominy. During the conflict, US President Nixon also ordered a secret bombing of neighboring Cambodia, a move that drove many people there to ally with the communist Khmer Rouge and Pol Pot's regime. The American people were told that communist expansion in these distant lands must be stopped using US soldiers and national treasure because, should the communists get a foothold in one country, they would march through one after the other and soon be on the border of Mexico and Texas (i.e., "the domino effect"). By the 2000s, Vietnam was entering the world market on the side of capitalist development, a long-term victory for the capitalist sphere pulled from the jaws of a seeming previous defeat.

Overlapping with the Vietnam conflict in this period was the overthrow of the Batista regime in Cuba in 1959 by Fidel Castro and his forces. Prior to the revolution, Cuba had been a center of multinational sugar production, had casinos owned by organized crime syndicates, and was a vacation hub for the jet-set, with many (but not all) of the main players originating from the United States. After the revolution, Castro initially appealed to the United States for development assistance but was rebuffed and this pushed him to more closely ally with the Soviets. Subsequent US administrations placed a trade embargo on Cuba, attempted to assassinate Castro multiple times, and generally worked to destabilize the island. This came to a head when US planes photographed the installation of Soviet nuclear missiles there, just 90 miles from the US coast. President John F. Kennedy responded by surrounding the island with US naval ships, both an escalation of tensions and a way to force Cuba and the Soviets to the bargaining table. Though the prospects for avoiding a military clash were tenuous and the tension ominous (many feared the outbreak of a US-Soviet nuclear exchange), cooler heads prevailed and the Soviets withdrew their warheads, though not their economic support.[1] Cuba remained an official enemy of the United States for decades afterward and relations only thawed after overtures from the Obama administration (2016).

---

1 During the crisis, a Soviet submarine (*B-59*) was in international waters near Cuba. The United States dropped depth-charges in order to try to force it to the surface. The Soviets then went into deep waters to avoid the charges but this left them unable to monitor radio traffic and commands from Moscow for several days and thus unable to determine if war had broken out. The captain of the submarine decided to order a nuclear missile launch on the United States. However, protocol required that the three senior commanders agreed on the action. Second in command, Vasili Arkhipov, cast the single vote against the launch, very likely preventing the outbreak of World War III or at least a significant nuclear exchange and untold numbers of deaths.

In 1980, Ronald Reagan was elected President of the United States. A staunch anti-communist, Reagan's budget reflected the belief that the United States needed to significantly increase its military spending as part of its Cold War strategy (which was also a gift to the military-industrial complex). The move was widely seen as provoking the Soviets into escalating its allocation of resources to its own military buildup. Because of the way it was politically and economically structured, the Soviet Union might not have been able to get enough bread and cheese to store shelves, but it could silo resources upward to its weapons manufacturing, drawing them away from the people's everyday needs. Because of such inefficiencies amid long-running promises from the political class that better standards of living would soon arrive (though they never did), the people of the Soviet Union (and Eastern Europe generally) grew increasingly impatient and restless. In 1989, a series of liberalization moves occurred in Eastern Bloc countries such as Poland, Austria, and Hungary that allowed freer movement of people between borders. This was the beginning of a tide that would spread to other countries in the region, including East Germany. Under Gorbachev, the Soviet Union had already embarked on policies of *Glasnost* (opening) and *Perestroika* (restructuring) to address perceived (and real) weaknesses in Soviet society (and thus, clearly, to stave off additional popular unrest). These developments would eventually lead to escalating the undoing of the Soviet Union and the Communist Bloc.[2]

By the late-1980s, the world was entering a period where the configuration of geo-political power of old would no longer be in place and a new one had yet to take shape.

Testing this "new world order," between December 1989 and January 1990, the United States invaded the Central American country of Panama. The public was told this was because its leader, General Manuel Noriega, had been involved in cocaine running and also was a violator of human rights (though he had once been a CIA asset). There had been prior negotiations under the Reagan administration to get Noriega to step down and they even pressured him

---

[2] And like the assassination of Archduke Ferdinand and World War I, a singular event had significant implications, though this one more curious. An East German official, Günter Schabowski, misspoke about when additional passages, now through the Berlin Wall, would be allowed. Reading a note that he was handed a few minutes earlier, though he was not involved in the initial planning, he made it sound like the Wall would immediately be opened up for free and easy passage. The public took this on face-value and soon crowds of people amassed on both sides, guards reading the situation as inevitable stepped aside, and soon the Wall was broken open and East Germany was again connected to West Germany. Moreover, this began a process whereby within the next year or so, the Soviet Union and the Eastern Bloc would crumble.

with drug charges in US courts. After a failed coup attempt, Noriega began to shift toward Cuba, Nicaragua, and Libya for military aid. Relations between the United States and Noriega continued to sour and the United States began plans for an invasion. Further, Noriega could no longer be relied on to secure the Panama Canal, a vital link for international commerce. The latter two issues (military aid and security of the Canal) were not criminal in nature, though the first two were and thus were used for the public explanation for US military action under the order of President George Bush (I).

In the early 1990s, Saddam Hussein of Iraq went to the United Nations and charged that Kuwait had been slant drilling underneath Iraqi territory and stealing its oil. Unable to find a satisfactory solution to his grievance, he began building up his military on their mutual border. US Ambassador, April Glaspie, informed Hussein that the United States had "no opinion on Arab-Arab conflicts, like your border dispute with Kuwait." This was widely interpreted as giving Hussein the greenlight to invade Kuwait. After Iraq invaded, President Bush (I) took to the airwaves, compared Hussein to Hitler, and claimed that, "this aggression will not stand." The United States went to war with Iraq and liberated Kuwait shortly thereafter.

After the fall of the Soviet Union (1991), the United States remained as the world's sole "superpower" in political, economic, and military spheres. Polish-born Zbigniew Brzezinski, counsellor to US President Lyndon Johnson and National Security Advisor to President Jimmy Carter, in considering this new geo-political landscape, took the opportunity to write, *The Grand Chessboard*. In it he argued that the fall of the Soviet Union created a sort of power-vacuum in some areas of the world, especially the resource rich Eurasia region (see Map 46.1) and, should no stabilizing force step in to create order, the world would see the area controlled by competing tribal factions of religious fanatics and radicals uninterested in the niceties of the world economy. Such a situation could allow such groups to hold the developed world hostage because of its need for natural gas, oil, and other resources. He argued that, as it now stood unmatched on the world stage as both an economic and a military power and with the former Soviet Union having its own internal problems with which to deal, the United States should use its military force to occupy the region—especially strategic areas surrounding the Caspian Sea—to ensure geo-political stability and the world's future access to needed energy sources. His prognostication would be shown to reflect similar thinking and action by a later US administration.

After the terrorist attacks in New York City and Washington, D.C., in 2001, the George W. Bush (II) administration sent military forces into Afghanistan to fight the Taliban under the presumption that they had provided safe haven to

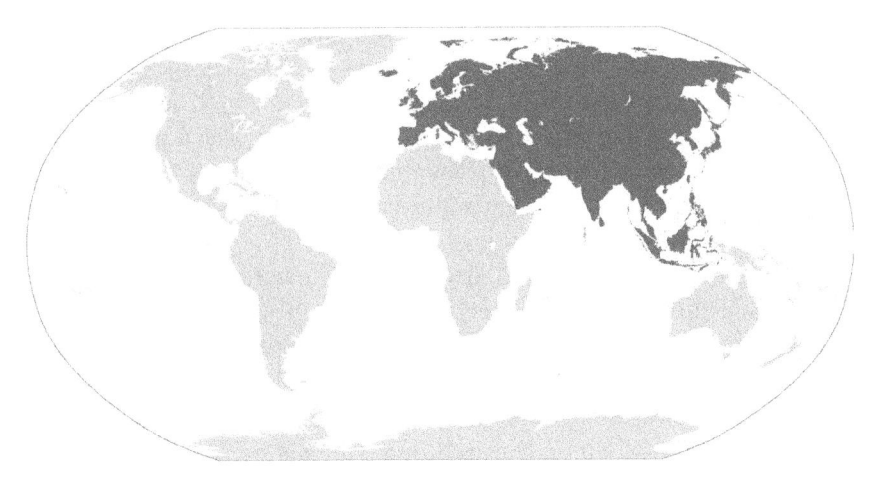

MAP 46.1   Eurasia

suspected mastermind, Osama bin Laden. But before that war was settled (and of this writing it still is not), Bush also ordered the US military into Iraq. Several justifications were floated—he was involved in the attacks on New York and Washington, D.C. and, later, that he still possessed weapons of mass destruction and could use them. After these two justifications proved unconvincing (the latter was rejected by the United Nations), the administration argued that the United States should intervene on the grounds that he was a human rights violator and that the United States would bring democracy to the country. Several aspects of this story were not told to the American public during the unveiling of these official justifications.

Prior to his taking office, several of George W. Bush's eventual cabinet members and advisors (Dick Cheney, Donald Rumsfeld, Paul Wolfowitz, and Richard Perle, among others) were members of the think tank/policy group, "Project for a New American Century." In 1998, they wrote an open letter to then-President Clinton urging him to invade Iraq and take out Saddam Hussein.[3] In 2000, the organization released a document entitled, *Rebuilding America's Defenses*, which argued that the United States should use its military force to secure its political and economic interests in the Balkans, the Persian Gulf,

---

[3] A copy of the Project's letter to President Clinton can be found at Information Clearing House, here (URL retrieved August 24, 2018): http://www.informationclearinghouse.info/article5527.htm.

Southwest Asia, and East Asia.[4] Hours after the September 11th attacks, US Defense Secretary, Donald Rumsfeld, argued for war with Iraq, even though no official culprit for the terrorist attacks had been identified yet. In the planning for the invasion of Iraq, Vice President Dick Cheney provided maps of Iraqi oilfields in making their strategic plans (Judicial Watch 2003). Little if any of this information made it into popularly consumed public discourse at the time (for discussion, see Paolucci 2009).

Observers have debated and tried to answer the question of why the United States invaded Iraq. While the official justifications made little sense, if the administration's plans were to simply "take" the oil, that does not explain why they opened up bidding on contracts to international energy companies. But if we think in terms of a geo-political chessboard, another answer emerges. The United States—for it to remain the international superpower that it was at the time and for its ruling class to remain strategically positioned as they were—had several tasks it needed to accomplish on the world stage. In the world market, one dominant country often assumes global leadership, even if temporarily—i.e., temporary because it is costly and as the leading power bears that cost, rising competitors often assume the mantel of dominance in new markets and resources (see Immanuel Wallerstein's models on the interstate system in the modern world economy). One task of global leadership is making sure international trading links and the flow of crucial commodities remain unencumbered. Further, global powers do not have the terms of trade dictated to them if they are to remain truly global powers. The United States could simply not leave to chance who would secure the oil fields and then just hope that whomever did would concede to keeping that oil flowing to world markets at a fair price. And even if another power did that, they could always either change the rate of oil output (which Saudi Arabia at times did), threaten to do so, or withdraw it altogether. In short, the United States could not risk having someone they could not control dictate to the world economy the terms of access to needed energy resources. Without a definitive account, such conclusions remain in the realm of speculation, though they do account for the known history better than the officially offered explanations.[5]

---

4   A copy of *Rebuilding America's Defenses* can be found at Information Clearing House, here (URL retrieved August 24, 2018): http://www.informationclearinghouse.info/pdf/Rebuilding AmericasDefenses.pdf.

5   One of the reasons Saddam Hussein was disliked by international power-brokers, such as the United States (among others), was that he often did not follow OPEC discipline. As the predominant OPEC country, Saudi Arabia would set quotas of production levels for member states. As an ally to the West, the United States could appeal to Saudi Arabia to raise or lower

The above is only a cursory overview of some of the historical elements of the global political chessboard, much of it from the view of the United States. But they are certainly not the only one playing the game. There have been regional rifts and rivalries, many not covered here. Still, moves on the chessboard that geo-political powers tend to make can be discerned. Prevent powers from rising when you can. Make advantageous political alliances and undermine those of your competitors. Transform economic power into political power. Economic coercion—e.g., manipulating currencies or using trade embargoes—may be necessary. Use your military strategically, countering other military forces as necessary but also locating your military to project your power forward, dominating regions that are economically vital, and using military spending as a way to force your enemy to expend theirs in ways they cannot afford. If possible, fund other nations to fight proxy wars for you. Deploy spies and propaganda abroad and, when necessary, at home. It's an unseemly game, one in which most people remain unaware of the moves, players, strategies, and outcomes until conflict presents itself at their doorstep.

In 2015, Jonathan Kirshner (author of, *American Power after the Financial Crisis*) wrote that the financial crisis of 2007–2008 would be a "watershed moment in world politics," where China experienced "buyer's remorse" for its "massive dollar holdings" and "the US is relatively less powerful and wields relatively less international political influence than it once did, trends that are likely to continue. But the roof is not falling in. Unless it does." He suggested three possible things could cause this falling roof: a new financial crisis, an implosion of the Euro system, and the stalling of Chinese growth (see Kirshner 2015). But these were/are all dangers to the world economy coming from *inside the economic system proper*, while triggering events could also come from the political arena first. And it is here we return to the 2016 election of Donald Trump as US President.

---

such quotas when strategically advantageous. However, if an actor like Hussein decided to raise (or lower) oil production, the economic interests and geo-political strategies of world powers could be undermined. As such, he remained an official enemy to the United States and other Western countries over the course of multiple administrations. That said, Saudi Arabia was not always on board with Western desires and could not necessarily be counted on to keep their oil production output at levels acceptable to other seats of economic power. They often grew resentful of Western demands to lower their production levels, especially when their capacity was much higher and therefore they had to concede to reduced cash flow at times. Because of such conditions, it was likely the prospect of having a friendly and compliant ally in Iraq encouraged US planners to implement their war plans.

Since the 2016 US Presidential election, the public learned several things that were not part of the typical news cycle during the campaign:
- The Kremlin preferred candidate Trump.
- Several Trump advisers had business dealings with the Russians prior to his run for office.
- Trump advisors had discussions with Russian intelligence agents prior to his selection as the Republican candidate for the presidency.
- After his election but prior to Trump taking office, National Security Adviser, Michael Flynn (and other members of the administration), contacted Russians about economic sanctions the Russians were facing because of their invasion of the Crimea in Ukraine (2014).

As this story began to unfold, other inconvenient facts about the political chessboard broke more and more into view. A dossier was reported to exist, worked on by British intelligence and elements of it endorsed by US intelligence agencies, that purportedly documented that Russia had tried to manipulate the election in favor of Trump. Other scuttlebutt included the claim that Trump was promised a lucrative share in the Russian oil company Rosneft if he could get sanctions against Russia lifted. Though reading intentions is murky business, it was believed that Putin wanted to secure Russia's domination of Arctic oil, keep the annexed Crimea (to secure sea access for Russia's Black Sea Fleet), and place friendly regimes into Eastern European governments as a buffer against Western Europe (which should be understood in the context of Ukraine's prior moves for closer ties to NATO and Western Europe). He thought an ally in the White House would help him in his goals.

Though attempts by Russians to influence US politics go back decades (and vice-versa), for insight to these events some observers pointed to *The Foundations of Geopolitics: The Foundations of Russia's Geopolitical Future* (1997) for insight. Perhaps Russia's corollary to Brzezinski's *The Grand Chessboard,* in this book Alexandr Dugin and Nikolai Klokotov (of Russia's General Staff Academy) argued that Russia must remain the center of the anti-bourgeois and anti-American revolution. Russia's overall goal should be to reject the influence of the Atlantic alliances, gain strategic control of the United States, and prevent liberal-democratic values from invading Russia. Use of subversion, destabilization, and disinformation tactics were to be preferred over military action and Russia's oil, gas, and other natural resources should be used against adversaries and other targets. Among several specific strategic tactics, the authors included the following:
- Push France and Germany into a tighter alliance.
- Isolate the UK from the rest of Europe.
- Absorb Finland into Russia.

- Grant special status to former Soviet countries to keep them more closely aligned to Moscow.
- Annex Ukraine.
- Ally with Middle Eastern and Islamic forces, which are already anti-Atlantic.
- Dismantle China to the extent possible.
- Provoke anti-Americanism in Japan and everywhere possible (i.e., make the United States a scapegoat).
- Encourage instability and separatism in the United States through...
  - Provoking "Afro-American racists."
  - Encouraging other racial and ethnic conflicts.
  - Supporting dissident movements.
  - Supporting sectarian groups.
  - Supporting isolationist tendencies in American politics.

Though how seriously this work should be taken as the actual playbook used by Putin is difficult to discern, much can be culled from using the outline above as a guide for reading Russia's moves during and after Trump's election.

During the 2016 US Presidential election, Russian President Putin had stated that he wanted Trump to win and his distaste for and hostility toward Hillary Clinton was no secret. Investigations after Trump's election revealed multiple moves by the Russians to help facilitate his installment into office:

- Establishing connections: There were contacts been Russians and the US religious right as early as 1995. There was a long-term effort costing millions of dollars to have Russian assets establish American identities and groups within US communities, using servers and VPNs based in the United States to hide their location. Foreign agents disguised as Americans were used to protest and/or to organize protests.
- Manipulating US social and news media: Pro-Trump messages by internet trolls were placed in social media—e.g., that Pope Francis endorsed Trump—and hackers planted false stories in the American news. There was a large-scale use of "Twitter bots" to generate dissention in internet discussions. Misleading ads and propaganda were posted on Facebook. Stories were created about (and/or paid agents engaged in) actions that emulated "radical" groups in order to associate them with the opposing side and harden public opinion of critics and stoke social divisions.
- Manipulating emails to create scandals: Leaked emails of top Democrats—e.g., some that showed how the Party's leadership favored Clinton over Bernie Sanders—infuriated some Sanders supporters and likely encouraged some to withhold their votes from Clinton once she secured the nomination. A WikiLeaks release of emails of Clinton campaign manager, John Podesta,

deflected attention away from a video released that showed Trump bragging about sexually assaulting women (the original hacks of Podesta's emails were traced back to Russian military intelligence). Constant media attention to emails forced the Clinton campaign off message, forcing them to react and make adjustments to the news cycle.

- Infiltrating US voting systems: The US Department of Homeland Security notified 50 state election organizations that Russia had targeted their election systems. Voting systems of at least seven states were broken into, including four of the five largest in terms of electoral votes—California (55), Texas (38), Florida (29), and Illinois (20); National Security Agency documents showed that people with connections to Putin breached voting machine manufacturers days prior to the 2016 election.[6]
- Manipulating voters: There were efforts to convince voters into non-participation, either through sowing internal dissention among Democrats (e.g., the emails related to Sanders) or by convincing others that their votes did not matter. Research showed that non-voters had as much to do with Trump winning as did actual voters. Non-voters in the 2016 presidential election tended to be young, less educated, less affluent, nonwhite; and Democratic non-voters composed about 55% of the total non-voting bloc, where an increase in those under-30 in key swing states could have swung the election to Clinton (on the above points, see Boot 2018; Harriot 2018; Hunt 2018; McKew 2018; Michel 2018; Shoot 2018, and references therein).

Using the outline from *The Foundations of Geopolitics* can also help us make sense of other goings-on during Trump's presidential campaign and afterward …

- Trump openly questioned the continued need for NATO, an organization created explicitly for the purpose of mutual self-defense between the United States and Europe against a Soviet threat and whose military mantra has always been, "An attack on one is an attack on all."
- He openly professed pro-Russian positions, including praising Putin's leadership and defending him against claims he had murdered political opponents.
- There were contacts between Trump's campaign staff and Russian operatives, including meetings in Trump Tower (attended by Donald Trump Jr., Trump son-in-law, Jared Kushner, and campaign chair, Paul Manafort) to

---

6  In Pennsylvania, their system that counts votes was discovered to contain remote access software that allows people who are not on the scene entry into the system and voters there complained that machines were changing their votes.

get dirt the Russians said they had on Democratic presidential candidate, Hillary Clinton.
- The Republican Party removed sanctions against Russia for its invasion of Ukraine from its platform at its National Convention.
- After his election, Trump broke with years of protocol and accepted a congratulatory call from the President of Taiwan just after his election (though he later claimed to support the "one China" policy).
- Soon after taking office, Trump moved to reduce or even eliminate US sanctions placed on Russia under Obama after the Russian invasion of Ukraine and their seizure of Crimea under Putin.
- Trump openly praised the British vote to leave the European Union—i.e., Brexit—and later made comments about an overvalued euro, which sent its value downward in international markets.

During his time in office, Trump and others in his administration made several geo-political moves that made little apparent sense if contextualized inside a traditional US-alliance model but did make sense when interpreted as if they were done to benefit Russia while undermining those same traditional alliances. A bill—ordered by Trump and drafted in May 2018—leaked that would announce the United States' withdrawal from World Trade Organization rules and would give Trump the ability to raise US tariffs on foreign imports at will (Swan 2018a). At the G7 Summit that June, he reportedly told the Group of Seven leaders that NATO was "as bad as NAFTA" and "much too costly for the US" (Swan 2018b). He left the summit and warned G7 members not to retaliate on tariffs he had imposed on them, threatened to cease doing business with US partners, and asked US representatives not to sign the joint communique put out by G7 leaders, while accusing the Canadian Prime Minister, Justin Trudeau, of making "false statements" to reporters. He then visited North Korea's Kim, leaving an impression that he preferred the company of authoritarian strongmen to traditional allies, according to a Brookings Institution observer (see Borger and Perkins 2018). At his meeting with Kim, Trump promised to end joint military exercises with South Korea, something wanted by North Korea, China, and Russia for decades. He got little if anything in return.

Ahead of a July 2018 NATO summit, the US Department of Defense was said to be investigating the possibility of removing US troops stationed in Germany—widely understood as a long-time deterrent to any Russian plans to invade Europe—after Trump had previously expressed support for such a move (Hudson et al. 2018). At the NATO summit, he accused Germany of being "totally controlled by Russia" because of their mutual energy supply agreements, while criticizing the Cold War ally for insufficiently funding NATO and instead relying on US contributions (Meredith and Turak 2018). Trump's demeanor toward the NATO alliance at the summit was frigid and skeptical—he again insulted Canada's Trudeau, calling him dishonest and weak.[7] After the summit, and in the wake of and in opposition to their own President's behavior, the US Senate voted 97–2 on a motion that affirmed US commitment to the organization (July 10, 2018).

Germany's defense minister, Ursula von der Leyen, complained that Trump had "no recognizable strategy" for dealing with President Putin of Russia and found especially troubling the fact that "nobody knows what was discussed or even agreed" to after Trump met privately with Putin in Helsinki (July 16, 2018) (Bowden 2018). But such concerns assumed that Trump was working on behalf of traditional Cold War geo-political alliances, one goal of which had been to contain Russian aspirations for a greater role in world affairs. However, though Trump's motives and goals were baffling inside this framework, such confusion is cleared away if he was working as a Russian asset. In fact, one former CIA Chief of Russian Operations called Trump Putin's "American oligarch," one similar to oligarchs in Russia "who do what [Putin] needs done and [after which he] then allows them to get really, really rich" (see Cizmar 2018).

And Trump was not the only apparent asset that Russia cultivated. In the face of the activities above—as well as observing (1) that conservatives continued to support Trump despite his visual subservience to Putin after the Helsinki meeting, (2) that his campaign was led by a political consultant (Paul Manafort, later convicted of felony bank and tax fraud) who had deep ties to Russian oligarchs and a Kremlin puppet in Ukraine and who was also responsible for softening the Republican platform on Russian sanctions, (3) that congressional leaders killed funds for states to bolster their election security, (4) that a Russian spy infiltrated the National Rifle Association (NRA), met with multiple conservative leaders, and wrote to her Russian handler that "I am ready for further orders" on the night of Trump's election, (5) that the NRA increased its donations from previous presidential campaigns to $30 million in order to elect Trump, (6) that the administration changed IRS rules so that groups like the NRA would no longer have to identify donors on tax forms and thus making them almost impossible to trace, (7) that multiple conservative congresspersons declared that Russian interference in the election either did not exist (despite widespread agreement among the intelligence community otherwise) or was so minor that investigations were unnecessary, (8) that FOX News consistently attacked the investigation into that interference and a majority of Republican voters polled said no such attacks actually occurred—one

---

7 Later that summer, when a dispute broke out between Saudi Arabia and Canada, the Trump administration refused to take Canada's side (see Chase 2018).

public commentator from the newspaper of record in the nation's capital concluded that "the entire Republican Party is becoming a Russian asset" (P. Waldman 2018).

While Putin's and Russia's chess moves seemed somewhat masterful (impressive at the least), perhaps the interest in closer ties was mutual? Though news broke throughout his first two years in office that Trump had ties to Russia going back longer than he had let on during the campaign, and though there were widespread suspicions and even reports that Putin had Trump "over a barrel" (see Tucker and Day 2018) and this forced him to do the Russian's bidding, he and his administration also received encouragement from one of America's longest and most influential global chess players—Henry Kissinger—to use better ties with Russia in order to counter the influence of a rising China (see Suebsaeng et al. 2018). It was not as if Kissinger was imagining things.

By 2016, and in comparison to other contenders, China was best positioned for a "post-American world order" (Gardels 2018) and appeared to have become so through multiple moves in prior years, which reflected overall goals that they continued to pursue thereafter. In 2015, China revealed its "Made in China 2025" program, which targeted ten tech-related areas for development, including advanced information technology, robotics and automated machine tools, pharmaceuticals/medical devices, aircraft, new energy vehicles, electrical generation, and advanced rail. Such a list would not surprise long-time observers of China's development. One widely believed strategy in its past (and likely future) plans was the acquisition of US and European companies in order to appropriate their technological innovations. After decades of specializing in low-end manufacturing of shoes and clothing, this program would continue recent wage increases in China (though it could also encourage firms that once found cost-effective labor in China to relocate elsewhere, something already seen with factory moves to Vietnam, Bangladesh, and India; for discussion, see The Editors of *The Epoch Times* 2018) and lead to its becoming an "innovation engine" that will likely compete with Silicon Valley (see Shmuel 2018)

In addition to China leading the world in developing renewable energy resources, its involvement with development projects in Africa, the Asian Infrastructure Investment Bank, and the Marshall Plan-like Belt and Road initiative—formerly, "One Belt, One Road," echoing The Silk Road of the past (see Chapter 45)—China is one of 16 Asian countries in negotiations to form the world's largest trading bloc (Pandey 2018). China also rallied the BRICS countries—Brazil, Russia, India, and South Africa (about 40% of the world population and a quarter of its output)—to fight protectionism together after a meeting at the G20 summit (Monteiro and Mbatha 2018). China made several moves reflecting this commitment to fight protectionism. With Trump's growing trade war, it made overtures to the European Union for a closer alliance, offering to open up more of the Chinese market to them in a goodwill gesture—though, it should be said, European representatives told them they would not side with Beijing against Washington (Emmott and Barkin 2018). During August of the 2018 trade war, the trading arm (Unipec) of the Chinese state oil company (Sinopec) and largest buyer of US oil suspended its imports of US crude, as other sources of affordable oil remained available from Europe and Africa (Paraskova 2018; Tan and Mason 2018). In their retaliatory tariffs, China targeted sectors of the US economy they believed would hurt Trump's political base and cause political divides (Thomsen 2018b). In another political-economic maneuver, in September of 2018, China and Russia announced that they would reduce their use of the US dollar in trade and instead use their own national currencies.

Reflecting changing geo-political power dynamics, the United States appeared to increasingly be ceding its forward projections of naval power to China in the South China Sea, with occasional territorial incursions in border regions and warnings sent between them but without an outbreak in violence (harkening back to the Cold War). Feeling emboldened in its changing global role, China increased its naval presence in the South China Sea, reportedly deploying anti-ship and surface-to-air missiles and electronic jammers, landing a nuclear-capable bomber at Woody Island, building operating bases on man-made islands, and consolidating its control over the strategic corridor between the Indian and Pacific Oceans, where about one-third of global trade ($5.3 trillion in 2017) passes through (Chellaney 2018). One US Admiral, surveying the situation, warned that only war would now prevent China's dominance over the region and the independent Taiwan, long wanted by China for reincorporating, stands as a significant potential flashpoint for such a scenario (Seidel 2018).

It is hard to see the developments above as anything but initial and perhaps significant fractures in the post-WWII Euro-America alliance as well as a shifting of the global power structure. Should the United States sever its post-war alliances with Europe, it basically cedes its geo-political standing as a sole and uncontested superpower. This is not the early twenty-first century's only potential fracturing point. The 2010s witnessed a groundswell of separatism in Europe, much of it in reaction to foreign immigration, though overall economic uncertainty and strain cannot be discounted as a contributor. This was the context of the 2016 "Brexit" vote as well, though growing evidence of Russian meddling must not be discounted, including promised lucrative financial deals with major British banks and investors (see Chait 2018; Gilbert 2018 and references therein).[8] As with Trump's fumbling and incoherent economic policy, a potential Brexit appeared unable to deliver the economic benefits its supporters expected, especially given its economy "slowed to a standstill" because of the initiative, with inflation surpassing wage gains, depressed GDP growth (.1% in first quarter of 2018), falling manufacturing output, and feared future austerity measures on the horizon (*The Economist* 2018b). In June 2018, reports also came from Sweden that nationalists there wanted to follow Britain's lead and leave the European Union, though their numbers were too politically impotent to push legislation while support for the EU had, in fact, grown after the results of the Brexit vote (*The Local* 2018). And all of this says nothing of the multiple—over a dozen—separatist movements active across the Continent in the early twenty-first century (see Henley et al. 2017).

Though the breakup of the post-World War II order and an emerging new one appeared to be a real potential in the late 2010s, modernity has historically undergone many prior shifts in economic, military, and political power. In the twenty-first century, however, this will likely be different than the Cold War, where two major superpowers positioned for advantage and rounded up and disciplined allies. The situation in the 2010s is more akin to Europe just before World War I, with global economic uncertainty and pockets of both malaise and growth, multiple power centers and contenders, shifting alliances, growing nationalist sentiment, and regional conflicts. For example, as the United States and Russia (among several others) play out a chess match in Syria, regional powers such as Israel, Turkey, Iran, and Iraq—as well as non-state entities represented by several rebel groups (the Free Syrian Army, ISIS/ISIL, Jabhat Fateh al-Sham, Hezbollah, and the Kurdish dominated Syrian Democratic Forces)—could play significant roles in how that conflict turns out.[9] Perhaps future historians of the twenty-first century will write about Syria in the same way they once did about Austria's role at the turn of the twentieth?

If not Syria, perhaps it will be Iran. Going back decades, the Americans, British, and the Soviets have all found reasons to meddle in Iranian society. In 1953, a combined effort of US and British intelligence overthrew Iran's democratically elected leader, Mohammad Mosaddegh, and installed the brutal regime of the Shah. In the 1970s, Iranian revolutionaries overthrew the Shah and

---

8 And with the help of Cambridge Analytica to rally a pro-Brexit vote, an organization discussed earlier in Chapter 40.
9 Accurately predicting endgames for such conflicts is always difficult, especially in the Syrian situation, which is incredibly complex even with a streamlined explainer helping one understand it (e.g., see Al Jazeera News 2018b).

seized the US embassy there, taking and holding hostages for 444 days. In the time since, tensions have waxed and waned and so have US-led international sanctions placed on Iran for its suspected support for terrorist organizations and, most recently, its nuclear program (which Iran claims is only for civilian energy purposes). Not only have successive US Presidents had aggressive postures toward Iran, but Iran is strategically placed to disrupt world energy markets. The Strait of Hormuz is between the Persian Gulf and the Gulf of Oman and is 21 miles across at its narrowest point (see Map 46.2). About one-fifth of the world's oil goes through the strait (which is about 35% of oil moved via the sea). Saudi Arabia, the United Arab Emirates, and Oman also have access to the Persian Gulf and the US Navy patrols it regularly. Should anyone attempt to disrupt oil trade through the area, or even should a minor military skirmish occur between contending navies on patrol, this potential flashpoint could transform into a wider military conflict, whether regional or even global.

There are portentous signs against future progress even if a global military conflagration is avoided. The American withdrawal from global leadership and the fracturing of former alliances provides greater latitude for countries like China and Russia to pursue illiberalism at home and abroad, e.g., Trump calls for Russia to be let into the G8 despite Russian election meddling and Putin's invasion of Georgia and Ukraine and his annexation of Crimea; China's Belt and Road Initiative promises billions of dollars in loans and developmental aid without required democratic assurances from recipient countries while Beijing promises non-interference in their domestic affairs (Amador 2018). With China's ascendance and with them (and the world economy) relying less on fossil fuels and shifting to more renewables, what sort of chess games we will see in the future appears to be a question with only speculative answers. It is

MAP 46.2
The Strait of Hormuz, by w:en:Kleptosquirrel (talk | contribs)

likely the United States will retain a certain position of advantage, power, and influence not only because of the size of its economy and its military might but also because of the fundamental role the dollar plays in the world economy, which it can use and has used as a weapon.[10] Perhaps formerly important chess pieces such as oil will lose their efficacy to move on the board, or perhaps countries such as the United States will make moves that retain the power of fossil fuel energy reserves in the global game, especially as their own growing extraction ability facilitates that potential.[11] No matter the case, games on the political chessboard we will no doubt continue to see. We can only hope the results in the early twenty-first century do not mirror those of the century prior.

---

10   The US dollar's role in currency exchange and trade—with more than half of global currency reserves and trade in US dollars and where the United States gets a cut for every dollar used—helps it finance trade and budget deficits, protects it against balance-of-payments crises, and allows it to weaponize payment flows via sanctions against persons (e.g., people doing business with official enemies, such as Iran, Cuba, and Sudan), entities, organizations (e.g., corporations, financial institutions), a regime, or even entire countries through its extraterritorial reach. The United States has used this weapon to fine several large corporations billions of dollars and suspended some from using the dollar. Such sanctions or even the threat of them can be used to depress stock and bond values of targeted organizations and to destabilize foreign currencies and entire economies. Should other countries become fed up with such pressures, they have few if any alternatives to which to turn. The euro lacks stability, the Japanese yen is backed by an economy stuck in two decades of stagnation, and both Chinese and Russian systems lack the transparency necessary for such an international currency (and the Chinse yuan is not fully convertible). Further, there is both an international financial infrastructure in place reliant on the dollar that would be hard to change and for any other country (e.g., Germany, Japan, China) to assume the US role would require running large trade deficits and fundamental changes in their mercantilist policies. The overall situation allows the United States to pursue its aims in trade, finance, and geo-politics outside the strictures of international law and institutions to which most other countries are subject (for this discussion, see Das 2018).

11   In June 2018, US oil production boomed to record levels (second highest in the world at 10.9 million barrels a day, behind Russia), as did its exports, which were higher than all OPEC countries except Saudi Arabia and Iraq (Domm 2018). By July of that year, Texas alone was set to surpass Iraq and Iran as the third largest oil producer in the world because of its Permian Basin oil field, which some believe rivals the Saudi Ghawar Field, the world's largest (Egan 2018b).

CHAPTER 47

# Throwing Dust in People's Eyes

In the history of international conflict, the use of misleading tactics to mobilize a nation's military and the lack of general public knowledge behind the thrust toward war are two common themes. In 1788, King Gustav III launched the 1788–1790 Russo-Swedish war—previously needing consent of the Swedish national assembly—using Swedish forces in fake Russian military uniforms to attack Puumala, their own outpost on the Russo-Swedish border. In 1931, Japanese officers blew up a section of railway in concocting a pretext to invade Manchuria and install a puppet government. During World War II, US citizens knew little of US corporate involvement in Hitler's rise to power nor about how the United States' blocking of needed supplies from reaching Japan was a backdrop to their attack on Pearl Harbor, which many Americans perceived as unilateral and unprovoked.

Not only are such deceits and information deficits not unique to our period, modern geo-politics also shares with the past the existence of leaders and their domains who need and desire land for natural resources, areas where their military power can oversee trade routes, and places they believe their forces will have strategic access for thwarting aspiring contenders. But modernity's tendency toward technological complexity is also directed toward producing ever more efficient forms of deadly force to secure the conditions of commodity production, world trade, and profit-making. Modern warfare, that is, is used less to convert the unbeliever or to takeover a rival kingdom's bounty but rather in pursuit of strategic geo-political position and to secure the conditions needed for capital accumulation, especially natural resources and trade routes. Political leaders, however, do not find these reasons helpful in mobilizing people in democratic societies to arms and thus they often find it necessary to appeal to tactics of deception.

Nazi war criminal, Hermann Göring, gave an interview to Gustave Gilbert in his jail cell while awaiting trial at Nuremberg. In that exchange, Göring stated:

> Of course the people don't want war. But after all, it's the leaders of the country who determine policy, and it's always a simple matter to drag the people along whether it's a democracy, a fascist dictatorship, or a parliament, or a communist dictatorship. Voice or no voice, the people can always be brought to the bidding of the leaders. That is easy. All you have

to do is tell them they are being attacked, and denounce the pacifists for lack of patriotism, and exposing the country to greater danger.

Göring here observes that human beings tend to rally around their leaders in reaction to an external threat, whether real or concocted. When a threat is real—when the Vandal hordes are sacking the city—a public will often readily mobilize for self-preservation. But the causes of modern war are often chosen rather than a reactionary self-defense and what has built up to it is often something out of most people's view. And once the violence has started, everyday people often have little ability, inclination, or appetite to discover the real causes behind it. Or, even if they do, the threat of personal destruction makes it difficult to discern truth from falsehood, where your side are "the good guys" by default. With its herd mentality and when its leadership embarks on military ambitions, the public gives leaders a pass and they can then proceed with little inspection as to their motives.

But this is not always true. With access to information and with oppositional political parties both increasingly the norm, government leaders are sometimes called to task and explanations are demanded. Such leaders cannot always rely solely on going to war to mobilize public opinion to support the cause, as Göring implied. For instance, above, Göring was possibly thinking of a staged attack on German assets made to appear as if carried out by Polish forces. In this "Gleiwitz Incident" (1939), Gestapo leadership had German soldiers dress in Polish uniforms and attack a German radio station. In doing so, they briefly broadcast anti-German propaganda, killed innocents, and used their corpses as proof of dead Polish combatants. Hitler pointed to the event as his justification for invading Poland, a major escalation leading up to World War II.

President Lyndon B. Johnson wished to escalate the United States' involvement in the Vietnam civil war. But the US population was weary. World War II was not too long behind it and it had recently fought to a stalemate in Korea, which ended with no official peace treaty. On August 2, 1964, North Vietnamese boats attacked the destroyer, the USS Maddox. Fire was exchanged on both sides. The National Security Agency claimed that two days later, on August 4, 1964, North Vietnam had again engaged US forces. President Johnson announced on television what had happened and that he would ask Congress for approval to use conventional forces in response (which would, in fact, mean war). Congress gave him their approval on August 7, 1964. But the second incident never happened and Johnson and his advisers knew it. This became known as the "Gulf of Tonkin Incident" and is now understood as a fabrication used for full-scale war in Vietnam. Millions of people subsequently died from the fighting, many civilians and draftees.

When President George Bush (I) planned to use US forces to invade Panama in 1989/1990—a country of no military threat to the United States—he provided the public a reason to justify the attack. In a televised address, Bush declared that Panamanian leader and strongman, General Manuel Noriega, was engaged in international cocaine running operations. In making his point, Bush presented a bag of cocaine said to have come from the easy access to drugs in the United States, which Noriega's dealings represented by implication. It later turned out that the cocaine was bought the day before from a young dealer in a park across the street from the White House.[1]

After Saddam Hussein's forces invaded Kuwait, President Bush (I) determined that the United States must lead an effort to turn back the Iraqi leader's aggression. In the process of gathering data on the Hussein regime, the Congressional Human Rights Caucus heard (October 10, 1990) from a 15-year-old girl only known by the name, "Nayirah." In her testimony, she claimed that Iraqi forces had pulled babies out of incubators, took the incubators, and left the babies to die. The imagery was both moving and horrific. And false. No evidence of her claims was corroborated (babies and patients did die but only because hospital staff had fled from the fighting). She was later revealed to be Nayirah al-Sabah, daughter of the Kuwaiti Ambassador to the United States. Her testimony was organized by Citizens for a Free Kuwait, a public relations campaign for the Kuwaiti government run by the American firm Hill & Knowlton (*New York Times* 1992).

The Project for a New American Century released its report, *Rebuilding America's Defenses*, in September, 2000, approximately a year before the terrorist attacks in New York City and Washington, D.C. In that report—which advocated for extending America's military forces into the Eurasian region— the authors argued that the public would have little stomach for US military adventurism without some sort of galvanizing event, like "a new Pearl Harbor."[2] While conspiracy theorists have used this as suggestive evidence that Bush's (II) administration was involved in those attacks, it is hard to argue against the idea that those attacks did provide them a usable excuse to further the agenda this earlier document had advocated. And though the US public

---

1  For insight on the US invasion of Panama, see Barbara Trent's 1992 documentary, *The Panama Deception*.
2  A copy of *Rebuilding America's Defenses* can be found at Information Clearing House, here (URL retrieved August 25, 2018): http://www.informationclearinghouse.info/pdf/Rebuilding AmericasDefenses.pdf.

probably needed little convincing for its military to go into Afghanistan, the administration had to deal with international resistance for its plans to attack Iraq. Though surveys (see Milbank and Deane 2003; Zeller 2003, and references therein) revealed that a significant portion of the US population believed Saddam Hussein was involved in 9/11 (despite the lack of any evidence), the international community, in this case the United Nations Security Council, was unconvinced Hussein had any culpability and that any danger he posed did not require US intervention. Bush administration Secretary of State, four-star General Colin Powell, presented evidence to the United Nations of Hussein's capabilities (February 5, 2003). Lawrence Wilkerson, retired Army Colonel and Chief of Staff to Powell, prepared the presentation for his boss. It turned out almost all of this evidence was either outdated, from suspect sources, false, or otherwise misleading. Wilkerson claimed that he was provided bogus information (which Powell was unaware of), that it was the "biggest mistake" of his life, and that he regretted not resigning over it. Even if we absolve Powell and Wilkerson of their misrepresentations, it is clear that the administration believed a case against Saddam was necessary for the public to accept aggression against a state that had not attacked it. And it was similar on the other side of the Atlantic. British Prime Minister, Tony Blair, told the public that Saddam Hussein had at least 20 missiles of chemical weapons that could reach British military assets in Cyprus, as well as Israel and NATO members Turkey and Greece within 45 minutes of the order. Evidence here, too, was lacking.

These are not the only examples where leaders threw dust in the eyes of their own people in the march to war. Unlike feudal lords who often did not need a publicly approved justification to send their soldiers off to fight, modern governments are presumed to be answerable to a voting citizenry. And in modern conditions, governments find statecraft and war useful and necessary tools in their competitive struggles with other nation-states in the world market. But very often the real reasons for wanting war are not usually a convincing, satisfying, or legitimate argument in the public's eyes, as they will be asked to provide the bulk of the money to pay for a war and the soldiers to fight it. And as long as the social realities behind modern war remain—i.e., the world market and its political chessboard along with governments expected to be answerable to publics—disguising the true motivations behind a march to war will likely be used again in the future. This too, it seems, is a built-in feature of the modern world.

CHAPTER 48

# Gravedigging Megalomaniacs

Those who stood atop the economic organizations pushing capitalist development forward were often pleased with their accomplishments and thus themselves in return. They built lavish mansions and funded public displays of grandiosity, such as statues and expositions. They financed dams that stopped rivers and destroyed communities, all in the name of progress. They transformed prairies into railroads, finishing off the remnants of indigenous societies in the process, who they accused of "not using the land." Ayn Rand called them "creators" and "makers" and those who needed the jobs they offered as the "takers." They believed that the masses required education in the splendor of their system and they assumed cultural leadership in building libraries and museums, establishing foundations, influencing the mass media, and shaping educational institutions. In doing so, they built a world in their own image. But in addition to these results they strove to see made manifest, the modern world is imbued with a host of unintended outcomes just as real as the former realities they forged.

An interesting sociological group dynamic is that an action beneficial for an individual can be detrimental for the group if done by all of its members. This is often called, "The Tragedy of the Commons" (stemming from an 1833 essay by the economist, William Forster Lloyd). It was once a British tradition to provide people access to "the commons" to graze their animals. It was in each individual's interest to make sure his or her animals ate enough so that they were well fed. However, should all those with access to the commons act similarly, the odds of over-grazing the fields increased, leaving them bare and fallow and thus risking the starvation of everyone's herds. It is a similar case with multiple facets of the modern economy. When only a few individuals with highly specialized skills migrate to a country where these skills are in high demand, they might find themselves handsomely rewarded for their talents and efforts. If more and more people with similar skills follow suit, then the pay that specialized labor fetches on the market will tend to decline. We can imagine the same dynamic for oceanic fishing stocks or choosing college majors.

Likewise, imagine business owners who have to hire laborers, buy raw materials, get the company moving forward in producing goods, and sell those goods for a profit. Their self-interest is growth in their money-investment for both their business concern and for their personal enrichment. But in the production process, all commodities are made to be sold and paying workers a wage that matches the value of commodities they produce will not produce the needed profits. So, we find two-edges to a singular sword: (1) by necessity, the total spending power possessed by workers-as-consumers is less than the total amount of money represented by the prices for all commodities available for sale added up and thus (2) a tendency toward "overproduction" of commodities in the market as a whole. When commodities cannot be sold, there is more supply than demand, which tends to put downward pressure on prices. And a downward trend in prices tends to produce a downward trend in profits, or at least profit rates. Decreased profits, or rates thereof, tend to result in pressure to lower the wage-bill, i.e., use labor-saving machinery, fire workers, and/or otherwise lower the cost of labor. Finally, this dynamic can spread across the entire economy, where the total wage-bill employers as a whole set out cannot purchase enough of the commodities produced and thus a spiral of depressed sales and profits commences that edges ever-closer to an economic crisis. And an economic crisis that is not reversed will threaten to spread and may even bring the whole system down, as its economic leaders continue to dig their own graves.

Unlike a small mom-and-pop business on Main Street, a large business might look to lands far beyond a nation's borders to sell their products. And the larger the business, the more likely it is they can and do sell in multiple countries. And further than selling, the larger the business, the easier it is for them to shift their production location and administrative staff from higher-wage geographical areas to lower-wage areas. Finally, higher-wage areas are often in countries with unions, pensions, health care mandates, more state regulations on product quality, worker safety, environmental protections, and so on. As a result, larger businesses—e.g., usually multinational corporations—often want the governments in countries in which they do business to enter into free trade agreements with each other. Free trade agreements often lower import tariffs, lower taxes on exports, allow for easier movement of investment capital across national borders and for the repatriation of profits, and tend to drive wages and regulations to their lowest common denominator across these international borders. The more equalized the terms of trade across nations, the more global areas that are opened up for production, distribution, and consumption, which thus means more profits for business enterprises as a whole. But such free trade agreements also mean instability in job markets for countries of origin, placing downward pressure on the wage-bill (thus reducing global effective demand), externalizing costs of environmental cleanup (including health costs) off onto states (creating expenditure of tax revenue problems), and rapid consumption of natural resources (e.g., trees, coal, oil). As a result, politicians that pass such free trade agreements at the behest of the corporate community for *short-term* gains do so to the *long-term* detriment of both their constituents and the corporate class.

If effective demand for a commodity is as such that investors expect that a company or an industry will experience growth (could be rapid, or slow but steady over the long-term), then that industry or company is likely to attract money from those investors. Or, when effective demand is at a level where the investing community collectively does not believe an increase in commodity purchasing is in the offing, they will tend to shift from investing in productive capital to investing in financial capital, as we have seen. When the value in a market for either productive or financial capital is relatively fresh and has not yet attracted many investors, it can experience a booming period where early entrants can see a significant rise in their stock values as new buying drives prices up. But these booms in both productive and financial stocks often overshoot the ratio of the level of real effective demand versus the amount of product that market can actualize. The result is the occasional blowing up of market bubbles, where the market is "overvalued" and then "resets" or "corrects" (in the economist's terms) or, worse, collapses. If an investor gets out in time—i.e., sells their stocks—they can make a handsome profit. However, if they fail to time it right, they can find themselves holding paper values that have significantly depreciated or are even worthless.

Today we are witnessing the new corporate strategy of stock buybacks (initially discussed in Chapter 44) to deal with money on hand when expected demand does not suggest investing in production will be profitable enough to satisfy investors. In order to grasp the systemic implication of this activity, we must first understand both the level of accumulation reached by the business class and changes in managerial culture that occurred during and after the 1980s.

The capitalist's aim is to make profits and then recycle a portion of those profits back into new investments, only to continue this recycling *ad infinitum*. Sometimes money can be reinvested directly into the original productive capital or into stocks of other productive businesses. Money also can be reinvested into financial instruments that promise an acceptable (or even higher) rate of return (but often at a higher risk). And still other times government bonds (relatively safe), currencies, or gold are a place to park investment capital. But what if all of these things are unlikely to provide a return high enough (compared to other options) or are just too risky? Risk might come from insufficient demand in the productive sector. Or it might come from overvalued bubble markets which threaten to burst. What is the business class to do with their money? Well, for one, they could hoard it. One report by Wealth-X and UBS, for instance, showed that in 2014, on average, $600 million (or 19%) of billionaires' assets were in the form of cash. By 2016, the Wealth-X Billionaire Census estimated that amount at $1.7 trillion (Egan 2014; Frank 2017). Such numbers suggest that neither expected effective demand for consumer goods nor stock market values provided enough risk-worthy opportunity to absorb this cash available for reinvestment.

Before 1982, US companies were not allowed to purchase their own shares. As part of the wider deregulation trend of the Reagan administration, the Securities and Exchange Commission eased these rules. This facilitated a shift in corporate governance of its bottom line from managerial control to the "cult of shareholder value," where investors' demands for maximizing returns increasingly held decision-making sway. One practice that emerged from this was corporations buying their own shares, thus pulling financial resources away from investments in production and research and development (and thus downsizing its labor force) and using this new liquidity to distribute to executives and shareholders. One investigation found that between 2010 and 2015, 60% of 3,297 publicly traded non-financial US companies bought back shares (buybacks which, in 2014, surpassed companies' combined net income for the first time other than in recessionary periods), and during a one-year period share purchases and dividends combined were $885 billion, more than their $847 billion in total net income. The result has been an increase in buybacks and dividends over investment in research and development, e.g., the proportion of net income spent on innovation shrank from over 60% in the 1990s to less than 50% in 2009 and then creeped up to 56% as net income fell. Executives making such decisions are not motivated simply by their own "greed" (though this element is not completely absent) but rather by activist investors who demand such returns or threaten to unseat executives who do not produce them. The managerial response with such buybacks, the study's authors suggest, are "signs that corporate America is undermining itself" (Brettell, Gaffen, and Rohde 2015).

Such practices double-back upon themselves and further reduce effective demand. But where are businesses supposed to reinvest profits if expected demand *is already insufficient* to justify plunging resources into new production and new jobs? They are left with mechanisms of "financialization," which often satisfy investors in the short-term but only make the problem worse in the long-term, especially as more and more corporations adopt similar practices. Research by the Organization for Economic Cooperation and Development (OECD) found that rising levels of inequality in the two decades after 1985 reduced economic growth in Mexico, New Zealand (by 10% each), the United Kingdom, Finland, Norway (by nearly 9% each), and the United States, Italy, and Sweden (between 6–7%) (Elliot 2014b). Another way to say this is: more concentration of wealth = less economic growth. And, indeed, just a few years later the OECD found that gains from a growing global economy went mainly to the top 1% while most of the global workforce experienced "unprecedented wage stagnation" (see Johnson 2018c and references therein).[1] And at some point, this concentration of wealth will undermine the very growth-dependent system that allows for accumulation of capital in the first place as the limits of that concentration are reached.

Should a corporation that makes goods go bankrupt, they often appeal to the government for a bailout, as Chrysler Motors did in 1979. Should a free trade treaty become a net negative for an industry, they often plead with the state for renegotiation. Should dozens of Wall Street banks fail because of their overinvestment in a bubble market, government stands behind them, e.g., as happened after the 2007–2008 crash when governmental regulators declared several banking institutions "too big to fail." It is in these times that the public can get a glimpse of which class the state actually works for. And most often it is not the public, which sees wages stagnate, prices rise, welfare provisions cut, schools underfunded, people losing their homes, water becoming undrinkable, and so on. In response, publics have often voted with their feet—e.g., Occupy Wall Street—though long hours at work, addiction to social media and entertainment, and constant bombardment of propaganda present compounding hurdles to sustained action.

At a macro-economic level, capitalism produces the greatest outpouring of goods and services history has ever seen. Because some of these goods are medicines, safer and more efficient forms of technology, and mass quantities of food, the capitalist system creates its own population dynamic. It is not by chance that a population explosion coincided with the Industrial Revolution (see Figure 48.1). Today, the world's population stands at over 7.5 billion people and grows by over 200,000 people every day. And with it grows the number of mouths to feed, bodies to clothe, families to house, and things to consume. And this in a world already teetering on an ecological precipice. Earth cannot indefinitely sustain this level of growth while having natural resources replenished sufficiently to continue this same way of life without end. Nor can our output of pollution remain at current levels without impinging on our ability to maintain modern production, consumption, and overall health. The system will have to draw back at some point, though it is not built in a way to do that

---

1  The "OED Employment Outlook, 2018" can be found here (URL retrieved August 25, 2018): https://read.oecd-ilibrary.org/employment/oecd-employment-outlook-2018_empl_outlook-2018-en#page7.

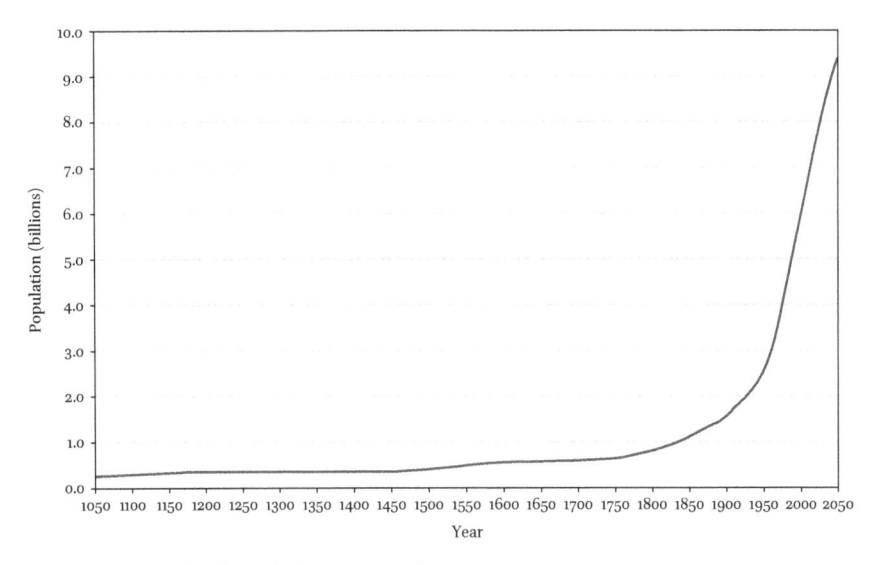

FIGURE 48.1  World population and growth rate curve

on its own. But if the system continues on its current path, it is digging our graves.

This intersection of megalomania and gravedigging broke open writ large with a new administration elected in the United States in 2016. Donald Trump made a handsome living in real estate and through other schemes—a university, steaks, vodka, casinos—many of which failed. But these failures did little if anything to shape his view of himself, a view with all the hallmarks of narcissism and visions of grandiosity. As a candidate, Trump harshly criticized free trade agreements such as The Trans-Pacific Partnership and NAFTA and promised to tear these up and, as President, he claimed they should be renegotiated. It was as if it was only the United States that could act with such economic authority and push around historically friendly countries. Trump promised to reinvigorate the coal industry at a time when the global trend is to turn away from environmentally dirty fuel sources and turn toward cleaner energy sources in solar and wind. This doubling down on the reliance on greenhouse gas producing fossil fuels comes at a time when scientists (and our own eyes) tell us that the Earth's climate is in a precarious balance and we will soon reach a point of no return, if we haven't already. Such policies not only court our own destruction but in fact threaten to hasten it. That might be as designed.

Several of Trump's closest administration members and/or appointees are "Dominionists" or have close associations with the movement. Dominionism is a radical Christian right theology/proto-organization. And similar to some radical Catholics in Trump's administration (e.g., campaign adviser, Steve Bannon), they do not believe in the separation of church and state and want Biblical law enforced in the United States. One of their spokespersons is worth quoting on these matters:

> World conquest. That's what Christ has commissioned us to accomplish. We must win the world with the power of the Gospel. And we must never settle for anything less. Thus, Christian politics has as its primary intent the conquest of the land—of men, families, institutions, bureaucracies, courts, and governments for the Kingdom of Christ. It is to reinstitute the authority of God's Word as supreme over all judgments, over all legislation, over all declarations, constitutions, and confederations.
>
> Christians have an obligation, a mandate, a commission, a holy responsibility to reclaim the land for Jesus Christ—to have dominion in the civil structures, just as in every other aspect of life and godliness. But it is dominion that we are after. Not just a voice. It is dominion we are after. Not just influence. It is dominion we are after. Not just equal time.
>
> *It is dominion we are after.*[2]

One could hardly imagine a sentiment so contrary to modern progress than this one, i.e., anti-democratic, theocratic, anti-intellectual, and authoritarian. This sentiment represents a turning back of the wheel to a time much prior to ours that only exists in the imagination. Worse yet, and like other Christian fundamentalists, Dominionists believe in a final global showdown between the Christian West and the Muslim world. They believe that a global conflagration—likely nuclear war—will bring Jesus back and initiate the Final Judgment of humanity on Earth. And they are convinced it is the job of believers like them to bring that about. With a more inflated sense of self-worth hardly imaginable, the idea of gravedigging megalomaniacs has shifted from a figurative turn of phrase to a literal reality.

There are other sectors of modern society that may not want such an outcome but believe that modernity is in the throes of collapse nonetheless. There are "doomsday preppers"—most commonly in America (but not solely) and made up of a mix of working class, middle class, and relatively affluent individuals and families—who buy rural land, stockpile arms, food, and other

---

2 George Grant. 1987. *Changing of the Guard.* Dominion Press. A PDF of Grant's book can be found online here: http://www.garynorth.com/freebooks/docs/pdf/the_changing_of_the_guard.pdf

items believed essential for surviving modern society's downfall, whether by war, economic chaos, and/or environmental collapse. One form of this sentiment can be seen in how some of the very rich, fearing an apocalypse, flocked to New Zealand to an extent that it drove up housing prices and created such a surge in homelessness that legislators initiated bans on foreign home ownership (see Dwyer 2018; Graham-McLay 2018). One cannot help but imagine the megalomania it takes to both flee from the world one helped create and demanded everyone else embrace while at the same time believing they would be safe from its repercussions by invading a distant island to which they were not invited. And should their worst fears come true once they set up homes there, they might find that their island safe haven has become a final home from which there is no escape, as either its habitants turn on them or they find themselves alone on estates surrounded by both wealth they cannot eat and other rich refugees they cannot trust. The irony would be amusing if the implications were not so grave.

CHAPTER 49

# The Sorcerer

The modern world is at once chaotic while operating with law-like processes that seem to unfold via their own internal logic. Think of the rhythms of the city, which wakes to joggers and delivery trucks that give way to rush hour and pedestrians that meld into a midday holding pattern of action and industry only to erupt into an end of the work-day rush hour that transforms into nightlife that eventually stalls out and the people of the street take over until dawn, only to start again. Among this flurry of activity, there is a rhythm and a cycle, and we can discern its patterns and its causes.

The modern world's marketplace is a product of multiple actors, actions, and sources. Producers make things to sell, these sales transform into profits, and profits saved, reinvested, and expanded transform into capital. Some of these businesses are small in nature, owned by an individual, maybe a family, and employ a handful of people. Other businesses are massive international concerns, employing thousands or even millions of people and selling goods on a global scale. And there are an untold number of middle-sized companies sitting in between. Workers at each location sell their labor for wages to pay rent, buy food and clothing, and, if they are lucky (and, increasingly, not many are), money is left over for entertainment, savings, long-term investments, or even retirement. The ratio of the total commodities produced, their prices, and the total wage-bill of the business class as a whole sets out determines the upper and lower limits of both supply and demand. And this dynamic shapes how and how many things businesses produce, the jobs they offer or cut, how much money workers can spend, and how capital is or is not accumulated. And these things all influence policies the contending classes try to push onto the state, how trade patterns develop, whether or not businesses that are large enough to move to lower-wage areas actually do so, and which areas of the world will be opened up for investment and resource extraction or will remain out of the sights of global investors and their state allies.

Economists are not the only ones to recognize cycles of boom-and-bust in capitalist economies. For most people, these are experienced as "good times" for employment alternating with "bad times" of job scarcity, both of which are temporally compact enough (several years each) to be perceived in daily life. But there are even larger 40–60 year "Kondratieff Cycles" of growth and contraction—e.g., a long period of expansion, a long period of decline, and long-term expansion returning and the wave beginning again. These waves

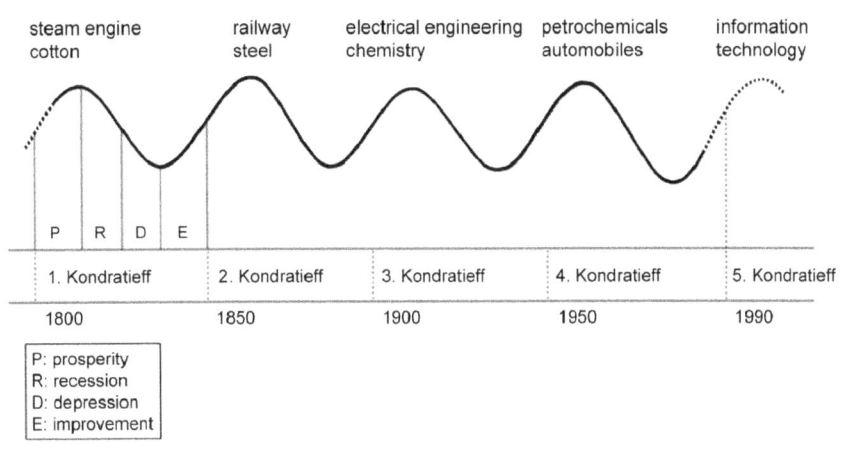

```
steam engine          railway      electrical engineering   petrochemicals   information
cotton                steel        chemistry                automobiles      technology
```

| P | R | D | E |
|---|---|---|---|

| 1. Kondratieff | 2. Kondratieff | 3. Kondratieff | 4. Kondratieff | 5. Kondratieff |
|---|---|---|---|---|
| 1800 | 1850 | 1900 | 1950 | 1990 |

P: prosperity
R: recession
D: depression
E: improvement

FIGURE 49.1   Kondratieff Wave

result from how economic organizations and states make short- to medium-run decisions (which is all they can really do) but, as these collectively add up over time, long-term trends and movements result (for discussion, see the work of Immanuel Wallerstein). These waves align with the introduction of new technologies and commodities to the world economy, such as cotton and steam engines used for mass production, railways and steel, petrochemicals and automobiles, and, more recently, information technology. Periods of decline are often followed by movements of states, businesses, and markets into new territories, ratcheted up competition over resources, and the non-rare regional war and sometimes world wars. And, as a consequence, these waves also witness the fall of once-great powers (i.e., Portugal and Spain) and the rise of new contenders to world authority (e.g., Britain, the United States, and today China and India).

As nations rise and fall and are thrown into competition with one another, they find old alliances stale and unproductive, make new ones, and even find themselves in conflict with still others. Suddenly, the money poured into technological development comes up with new devices, often dependent on materials from land once considered too arid or resource poor. The use of coal in manufacturing pushed Wales and Appalachia into the sights of developers and their thirst for resources. Oil crowned kings in the Arabian Peninsula where Bedouin tribes once ruled. Rare earth metals in Afghanistan and China promise to make these lands targets for extraction, as computers and cell phones are unlikely to go away anytime soon. Geo-politics has always followed behind these trajectories and has sometimes led them, only for nations to change places within the system once again.

Intellectual classes constantly reconfigure their theories and models in response to these dynamics of the world economy. At one moment, they effuse about the market's wonders as the apex of human development, a system that cannot be surpassed. The next moment, they scramble to theorize on how to fix what has failed. At a macro-economic level, laissez faire economic policy was supplanted by Keynesianism and now Keynesianism has been supplanted by neo-liberalism. At a meso-level, schools of thought differ on many things. Should monetarism be used and how? Are savings from workers a good or bad thing? Was going off the gold standard a good or bad thing? How do we stimulate investment in needed sectors? Should interest rates be higher, lower, about the same? Should we strive for full employment? Or is there a "natural rate"? And so on. Professional economists always seem a step behind, reacting to changes in the market and providing advice, new models, and suggestions on how to "tweak it" just right. For a system that is supposedly human nature made manifest, it has had an endless series of hiccups and spinouts and is in constant need for readjustments. They'll get it right one day, no doubt.

Except that they won't. The capitalist class is like the sorcerer who calls up forces from the underworld only to lose control of their spells, which

IMAGE 49.1 The Sorcerer Calls Up Spells He Cannot Fully Control - *The Witches of Warboyse*

sometimes come back to harm the master. The world market is not something that can be controlled, only tinkered with and responded to. It has its own momentum and movements and is in constant flux. As such, no person, organization, or country controls nor can control Kondratieff waves but can only become aware of and prepare for them (if they can) by adjusting their strategies accordingly. And this adjusting, very often, is in response to conditions as they unfold rather than precise plans for actions 40–60 years ahead of time. Whether during an upward or downward part of the wave-cycle, corporations and states try to position themselves best for either surviving the next round of gyrations or even taking advantage of the conditions that they can. With the multiple nation-states jockeying for positional advantage, with the thousands of multinational corporations doing the same, with hundreds of think tanks producing policy papers and statements, with dozens of international organizations writing regulations on trade and tariffs, the world market has become a thing with its own logic and momentum and cannot be reasoned with or even steered. The world market often seems in control of our destiny rather than the reverse, as we are carried along with it. It has a long-term direction that cannot be predicted with precision, especially the further into the future we try to aim our forecasts. It's an alchemy with only partially knowable formulae, one that produces elixirs that addict us and poisons whose antidotes elude us.

CHAPTER 50

# Prevailing Tendencies

Even if the world market is like a sorcerer who has lost control of his or her spells, we can discern certain of its patterns. Here we will focus on the implications of its system of economic value—that all products have prices, that a search for profits drives economic activity, and that the accumulation of capital is the name of the game. By reducing many economic activities down to such quantitative relationships, modernity's political economy has certain tendencies that tend to prevail.

But first it will be helpful to recount the elementary features of the system i.e., features that make it *a system as such*. First, there is the private ownership of the production process. Here, some individual or group (family, investors, etc.) legally owns the land, machinery, and raw materials (or their representations in "stock") that are used to produce commodities. This group is relatively small (historically, 1% or less of the population). Second, another group exists that does not own the production process and sells their labor-hours (and therefore a portion of their actual lives) to the first group for wages. Third, the production process produces commodities that business owners sell in a market where consumers and sellers meet. Fourth, this meeting of *many* different producers and sellers makes the market a competitive one in several ways—owners-as-producers compete for cheap labor, raw materials, and technological advantage and owners-as-sellers compete for buyers, market-share, and profits; workers as possessors of labor-power sell their labor to employers for the highest wages they can find for their skills and as consumers they are assumed to make decisions on the market-value of goods on which they spend their wages (though it is not always true that people spend their money rationally or with cost-benefit calculation). Fifth, commodities and profits are legally owned by the same individual/group who owns the business enterprise involved in the production and selling processes above. Sixth, profits in this system are used for (1) personal profit of the owners and investors and (2) for reinvestment back into production process in order to secure and/or improve market position relative to the fourth item above. Seventh, the logic of the system is set up as an infinite cycle of investment (raw material, land, labor, machinery) > production of commodities > sale > profits > accumulation of capital > reinvestment > production of commodities > and so on...*ad infinitum*.

There are several predictable outcomes built into a system such as this.[1]

*The business class is compelled to accumulate wealth (or capital).* Accumulating profits and/or capital is not really a choice or option for businesses in this system. If a company fails to accumulate profits and capital, they will quickly be disciplined by the market, whether this be through competition from others or from a loss of funds needed to run their business operation. What this means is that making profits and accumulating wealth in capitalism is less a product of individual "greed" than it is a systemic feature. The business class may experience greed within its ranks but the existence of that class and their never-ending search for profits and capital accumulation are not themselves the result of it. Should a producer not accumulate, they will be outpaced by other producers in the system and risk failure.

*Surplus-value extraction is a constant need for capitalists.* Because of competition in the market, because of the need for profits and capital accumulation, and because of the existence of wage-laborers, the business class must always be concerned with how much value they are getting out of their workers compared to the price it costs to employ them. First, they must always assure that their business enterprise is, on any typical day, getting more value out of their average worker than they are paying them in wages. Sometimes they get more or sometimes they break even and other times they may even take a loss but, overall, the extraction of value from labor over and above what laborers get paid must be there (note: there may be some job positions that are worth losing money on as long as this is made up for by other positions they extract enough wealth from to cover this cost).

Importantly, there is no real limit (beyond law and conscience) to the level of value-extraction business owners can enjoy for padding their profit margins. In a capitalist utopia, all other employers pay their workers well enough to purchase my products and I pay my workers as little as I can get away with. However, similar to the "Tragedy of the Commons" (discussed in Chapter 48), every other business owner has the same interest and if all of them could pay as little as possible or even nothing, there would in fact be no purchasers. Still, enjoying the least cost for labor (providing for the quality of that labor) while extracting maximum value is ideal for the capitalist. As a result, businesses in capitalist society search for all manner of ways to reduce labor costs, from keeping wages low, to speeding up machinery, to cutting labor hours, to requiring workers to do more than one job, or working overtime without pay, and so on. This also explains why employers oppose unions, resist paying for health

---

[1] For a summary of these prevailing tendencies, see Mandel (1990).

insurance and/or worker compensation and would rather eliminate pensions for retirees. And if such companies are large enough (i.e., possess enough capital assets) they can threaten to transfer jobs overseas to lower their own wage-bill (and increase their profits by actually doing so) as a way disciplining worker demands.

*There is a tendency toward technological advancements and complexity.* Because of competition between different producer-sellers (the same group at different periods of their activities), there will always be a need to become more "efficient" in either aspect—production or selling or both. As a result, capitalists have learned to calve off a portion of their profits to invest in new technology, often of the labor-saving type, which then reduces their costs of production as machines replace workers. Some companies work this into their cost of doing business in terms of creating "research and development" departments. Other times, businesses are happy to buy patents of inventors. And still other times someone invents a product and sets out on their own business venture. In all cases, we see in modernity a constant tendency toward new technological advances and increasingly complexity.

*Machinery tends to grow more complex and needs fewer and fewer laborers.* Above we noted the tendency for technological change, development, and complexity. We also noted the need for businesses to extract surplus-value from workers. Finally, we noted that businesses tend to be in competition with one another for purchasers and for market-share (of profits). Combined, what results is the tendency for businesses to invest money in more and more complex machinery that needs fewer and fewer workers over time. One result here is that such machinery can produce more goods and services more efficiently but at the cost of having less people overall working for wages doing the work the machines now do and/or staffing those machines.

Think of agriculture. Modern farmers no longer need draft animals to pull the plow, hands to plant seeds and pull weeds, nor similar hands to do the harvesting. Today, we have machines to till the soil and plant seed, automated watering mechanisms, extensive use of fertilizers and pesticides, and large machines for harvesting, to just name a few examples of the technological transformation of agriculture. This is the shift from human/animal power to mass production, a highly mechanized practice that needs vastly fewer workers. This reduction in paid workers creates the periodic problem of lowering effective consumer demand in the system, where there is a tendency for there to be not enough wages set out for workers to buy all the products made, products meant to be transformed into sales, profits and capital accumulation. As a result, …

*Profit rates will tend to periodically decline.* The dynamic above creates a particular problem for the system. If there is not enough money set out in wages as

IMAGE 50.1  Horse Drawn Plow, Ring of Kerry, 1963, by National Library of Ireland on The Commons

IMAGE 50.2  Wheat Harvest with a Claas Lexion before Sunset Near Branderslev, Lolland, Denmark, 2008, by Larsz/Lars Plougmann

a whole to buy up enough products, then supply outstrips demand. And, what every beginning economics student understands, when there is more supply than demand, prices tend to fall, sometimes to a point the rate of profit declines. And if a business owner holds commodity prices firm, they risk losing market-share to producers who do reduce prices. A decline in the rate of profit can occur for a single business, an industry, or even the business class as a whole. When it happens for any of these sectors, should it not be reversed, the outcome is often bankruptcy.

*Capital accumulation tends to concentrate and centralize.* Because of competition for profits and capital accumulation, the free market system systematically tends to concentrate capital in fewer and fewer hands (Figures 50.1 and 50.2). Those businesses that outcompete their competitors will tend to make more money, often to an extent that their rate of profit is higher. Over time, accumulation of capital feeds itself in two main ways. First, businesses can grow to the point where they reach "an economy of scale"—i.e., for larger businesses it is less costly to produce the same commodity per unit compared to smaller businesses, which allows them to out-compete rivals in price competition. If two businesses produce the exact same product but it costs one $1/10^{th}$ the amount of productive investment, then, assuming similar access to markets, they will vastly outstrip the other in profits and the smaller business will tend to be driven out of the market as the larger business enjoys the ability to offer lower sale-prices because of their lower investment costs and/or their more efficient methods of production and output.

Second, businesses with great stocks of wealth can buy up their competition. If you are a smaller business and a competitor offers to buy your company, and you are suffering from price-competition outlined above, you are more likely to accept that offer. In both cases, capital tends to concentrate in fewer hands over time and tend toward the formation of monopolies, a reality that undermines principles of the competitive market while being a product of those same principles, which is a contradiction at the heart of the system. As monopolies form and market principles become undermined, this makes it hard for wages to rise with productivity, creates commodity markets less and less responsive to the laws of supply and demand, and squeezes out room available for smaller businesses and thus limits the number of those who can enter the market, all of which double back and provide momentum to the force of continued monopolization.

What about centralization? Businesses will tend to flock to geographical areas attractive for their enterprises, areas often near each other. This may mean locating near financial centers (something more common in early capitalist development). Or this may mean going to where they can best access the natural resources they need, such as oil or diamonds or trees. Or this could mean shifting investments and/or production from higher-wage industrially developed countries to lower-wage emerging markets, e.g., moving from the United States to China to better access cheaper labor, a laxer regulatory climate, and areas with transportation to markets, including rail, rivers, and ports. Finally, businesses need to find consumers, which means locating their

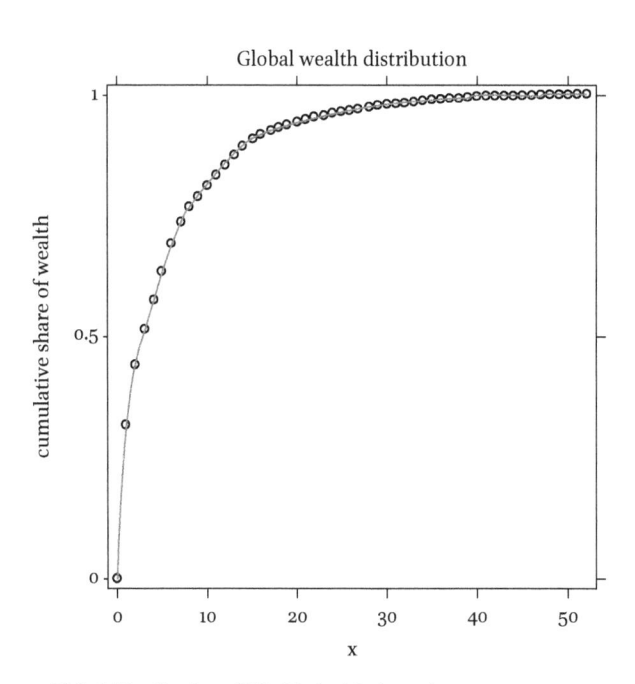

FIGURE 50.1   Global Distribution of Wealth, by Marius xplore

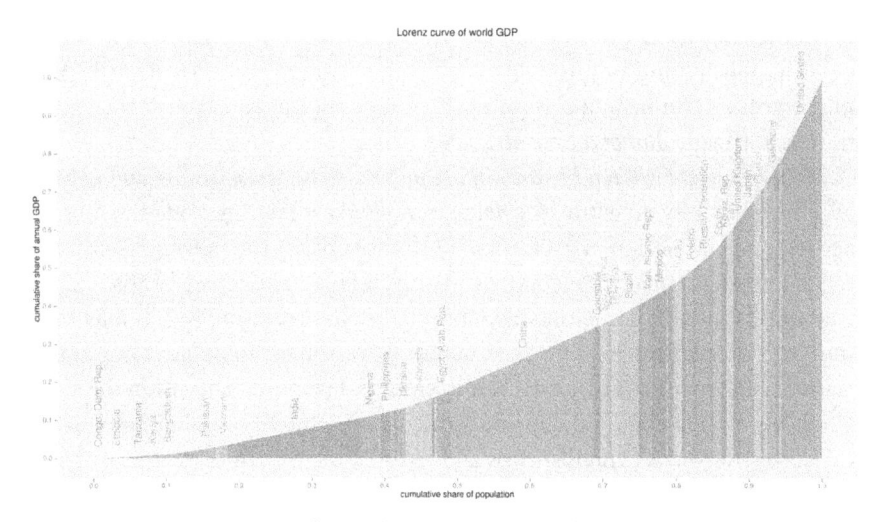

FIGURE 50.2   Lorenz Curve of Annual GDP Distribution in the World, 2013, by Tbap

products in more affluent areas. The result of all of these dynamics is that capital tends to become geographically concentrated, which generally produces urban centers teeming with great stocks of wealth amidst a mass of impoverished people (with some professionals sandwiched in between).

*Class struggle is inevitable.* The existence of classes is built into the structure of the capitalist system, as are their competing interests. Profits are built on the extraction of surplus-value from workers, who tend to receive less in wages than the value they produce for their employers. It would not be a leap to argue that workers would prefer (1) more job stability and economic security, (2) more wealth returned to them from their labor, and/or (3) the opportunity to own their own productive resources rather than working for those who do own them. Toward these ends, workers often organize themselves into unions and strike for a better wage-bill. Sometimes they even achieve control of the production process and work for themselves. Or, their political activity puts pressure on the state for favorable legislation. Occasionally, a working class engages in revolt or organizes itself into a political party and even takes the reins of power and steers the ship of state themselves.

Capitalists, however, are usually the main actors in the class struggle. They set the wage-bill as low as they can. They overcharge for products if they can. They collude on prices as long as regulators turn a blind eye. They hire managers to oversee the labor process on the shop floor. They resist the formation of unions. They threaten to ship jobs overseas if workers become pesky in their demands. They hire scabs and strike breakers. They buy off judges and diplomats. They fund the election campaigns of politicians to elicit friendly legislation. And they steer the ship of state in ways to benefit themselves in terms of trade policies and war. You might not know you are in a class struggle. You might not want to be in a class struggle. You might not consciously engage in the class struggle. *But in a class struggle you are.*

*Modern society will tend to grow more polarized.* Because profits and capital accumulation rely on extracting value from workers (setting aside the limited access to accumulation in the form of financial capital), the free market system tends to systematically concentrate wealth in fewer and fewer hands. This is true unless there is some outside, non-market intervention, which may take the form of changes in the tax structure, government mandated minimum wages, social security, socialized health care, and whatnot. Or, within the class struggle, workers can unionize and strike for a better wage-bill or, more radically, overthrow the capitalist class and redistribute wealth back to its original creators. In any case, the free market system left to its own accord—one without regulation or any form of redistribution such as welfare policies—will tend to see the rich get richer while the poor get poorer in a very real sense.

This polarization has an ideological component too, though this type of polarization does not always elegantly match up with class polarization. The business class has, at times, successfully gotten the working class to rally to its side, using a combination of media consolidation, propaganda, fear, appeals to religious and sexual prejudice, nationalism, and overall jingoism. Working class people vote for right-wing candidates that promise "jobs" by cutting taxes for the rich and to keep out unwanted "foreigners." Workers are told that government is the problem and a deregulated marketplace—e.g., reducing environmental laws, enacting free trade agreements and right to work legislation, keeping minimum wage increases suppressed, etc.—is the solution. On the other side, other factions in the middle classes have become more liberal, less and less religious, less xenophobic, more sexually liberated, and more environmentally conscious. This trend is not limited to workers or middle classes, as capitalists such as George Soros or Warren Buffet have voiced support for liberal causes such as environmental concerns, higher minimum wages, and higher taxes on corporate profits and executive salaries. Buffet has even been quoted as saying, "There's class warfare, all right, but it's my class, the rich class, that's making war, and we're winning" (see Stein 2006). And, increasingly, each side of the ideological divide views the other as succumbing to stupidity, ill-intent, and maliciousness. Not only is there a divide between contemporary ideological factions, but the gap between them is growing to the point where there is very little left in the center (see Pew Research Center 2014b; Bridges 2017; Foran 2017).

But this depiction of a polarized public entrenched between right-wing and left-wing positions can be misleading. What has happened is that the conservative, nationalist, free market extremes have continued to drift further to the right to the point of embracing fascism, while traditional liberalism has moved to the center, leaving less and less actual left political viewpoints, e.g., worker ownership of production facilities, socializing more productive and socially necessary activity, working class political parties, expanding access to higher public education, socialized health care, strong environmental protections, reducing the gap between the rich and the poor, strong social provisions for housing, and so on. The right flank has moved so far to the right and embraced reaction and fascism, while pulling liberals to the center. By the 2000s in the United States, however, the distance between the far right and centrist liberalism became greater than the distance between traditional conservatism and traditional liberalism. And US conservatism of the 2000s had moved so far in a right-wing direction that traditional liberalism appears to such conservatives as a far-left point of view, which liberalism hardly is.[2] This is how it looks from

---

2 One telling note of how extreme this has gotten is the fact that many conservative and far-right voters in the United States were convinced that Barack Obama was a "socialist," despite the corporatist make-up of his cabinet and the fact his administration proposed no recognizable socialist policies. For the right-wing of the twenty-first century, traditional liberal and

the United States, at least. Strong right-wing parties have also found electoral success in England, France, Italy, Hungary, and Turkey, while Russia and China make no pretense of their anti-democratic control of the levers of state, the occasional "election" notwithstanding.

*Economic crises are inevitable in capitalism.* Because of the transfer of value from the working class to the owning class, the imbalance of wealth distribution can reach a point where the market contracts instead of expands. Above we saw that there are periodic declines in profit rates and if these are not limited to a few businesses or industries but, in fact, spread system-wide, then the market goes into a recession. Severe and persistent recessions are "depressions" and, unless reversed, a depression can endanger the existence of the system, i.e., a "crisis" where capital is threatened with a permanent loss of its value across many sectors or even all markets as a whole. Basically, money loses value, credit dries up, businesses go under all around and soon this dynamic escalates and risks bringing down the entire market economy, with the 1929-1930s Great Depression and the 2007-2008 financial/housing crisis being the two most recent and memorable examples.

An economic crisis can lead to a political crisis. First, when people tend to get thrown out of work and suffer monetarily, they sometimes get harder to control, either from joining oppositional political parties to out-and-out rioting and revolt, e.g. 2011 riots in Greece over austerity measures. Second, if an economic crisis runs deep and long enough, the state will often respond in ways to alleviate the problem. How it does so is key. If the state responds by increasing its social welfare provisions, it stands a chance of increasing effective consumer demand in the system or at least appearing to try to do so. This will probably have somewhat of a palliative impact. However, states have often responded to crises by cutting interest rates on borrowing, encouraging free trade deals that assist in capital flight, providing tax breaks for the wealthy, and so on, while enforcing austerity measures and other forms of discipline on the working class, e.g., refusing to raise minimum wages, reducing social spending, raising taxes on wages, cutting government pensions, removal of price controls on inflation, devaluating currencies, and so on. Though the slate of measures above may help investors and the business class, it is a clear demonstration of who the state really works for. Thus, the people might turn their ire toward the

---

welfare-statist policies are now seen as "socialist" without a sense of history, irony, or shame, unquestionably an impressive victory for right-wing ideologists and propagandists. From an outsider's perspective, say coming from someone living in Europe, this depiction of Obama's centrist policies as "left" or "socialist" would appear patently absurd.

state for additional agitation, while, occasionally, they turn their ire toward the capitalists, e.g., the Occupy Wall Street movement of 2011-2012.

*The geographical boundaries of the system tend to expand.* Though we previously saw that capitalism has always had a world market, not all societies and regions have been "capitalist" per se. The stewards of the market system have learned that in order to turn back system-wide crises, finding cheaper sources of labor and raw materials is necessary. This has often meant expanding the boundaries of the system and taking over non-capitalist systems, i.e., colonialism and imperialism. The result has been an oscillating pattern of economic growth, a period of contraction, and later geographical expansion, often after some regional (and sometimes global) military conflagration. The system will often then experience a new period of profitability.[3]

*Increasing commodification of more and more of social life.* Another way to augment systemic profitability is to transform things not yet on the market for buying and selling into new commodities, into new markets for the investing classes in which to sink their money—whether start-up capital or prior profits. In early capitalism, the transformation of the commons in feudal Europe into privately owned property to be bought and sold was an early form of this. Other examples of commodification came in the form of transforming artists, teachers, and doctors (and others) into professions. More recently, we have seen the transformation of non-employed activities into non-paid activities employees used to do. Automatic Teller Machines (ATMs) and automatic checkout counters—just to name two examples—show how businesses have learned to "de-commodify" former labor done by workers and shift those duties to consumers, for no cost in wages.[4]

Another form of commodification is "privatizing" more and more services, organizations, and activities once outside of market forces. Prisons, once run by states, have been turned into profit-making businesses run by private companies. Profits here are boosted by having a steady flow of convicted criminals into prison, something that keeping drugs illegal does well. We have similarly seen a growth in charter and for-profit schools, the latter a case where young

---

[3] This section and the one that follows rely on insights from Immanuel Wallerstein's work on "world systems analysis," which also incorporates "Kondratieff waves" (as discussed in Chapter 49).

[4] This process of turning customers into unpaid workers has taken place in multiple sectors in the last several decades. In the early 1900s, grocery store employees both took items off of shelves that the customer wanted and rang up their bill. Up until the 1970s-1980s, gas was pumped by station employees who also would clean the windshield and check the engine's oil level. Many fast food franchises today hand cups to customers when they order their meal so that the buyer has to pour his or her own drink.

people are encouraged to take on significant debt burdens to gain devalued degrees at less-than-rigorous universities. And the cost of keeping traditional universities running is increasingly being shifted from state-supported funds to student tuition dollars, thus instituting a "student as consumer" model rather than a "public investment" model. Farmlands have been turned into commercial real estate and areas for advertising. Africa is currently undergoing a new land grab headed up by the Chinese looking for a place both for food security and in which to sink capital (Sy 2015).

And there are efforts to place things on the market that have never been before. As the human genome is increasingly mapped, there will likely be pressure for allowing it to be patented—though it cannot be in the United States as of 2018. The CEO of Nestlé argued that we should redefine water not as a human right but as a commodity for private owning and market selling (see McGraw 2013). With declining budgets, in 2018 NASA initiated a study on the viability of selling naming rights to spacecraft and rockets (K. Chang 2018). Commercials projected on the moon at some point are not an unreasonable expectation, as they have already been proposed in more than one quarter.

The prevailing tendencies described above result from the structure of the capitalist system and this system touches all areas of natural and social life. There are other tendencies we could also include here. The system's methods of resource extraction, energy use, commodity production and consumption, and waste disposal are directly related to environmental problems, which lurch from crisis to crisis, one building upon the last even as others get solved. A population administered by the capital-state nexus must be regularly counted, measured, and occasionally corralled and tamed, so methods of population control and monitoring grow increasingly sophisticated, moving from survey to census to education to psychological manipulation, behind which armed threat always stands.[5] The system lends itself to political crisis, corruption, and extremism, which bubble up regularly amidst periods of calm. The means of war grow increasingly sophisticated and lethal over time. The last world war

---

[5] Surveillance is an integral part of the process of capital accumulation. It happens in ways we either do not always recognize as surveillance per se or that have become so commonplace that they are the new normal. For instance, surveillance occurs in applying for jobs (which also allows for checks on credit history, debts, criminal background, social media history, and so on), at the workplace (at our work stations and through drug tests), over private property and places of production (video recording of land, buildings, and workers), over consumer behavior (purchases and credit card use), and between business competitors in the market (such as industrial spying) (for additional discussion, see Fuchs 2013).

ended with a glimpse of what the next one might look like and by today those lethal means are even more widespread.

We live in a system that is chaotic but knowable. It has laws and patterns. It has a trajectory that, while not always 100% predictable, is discernable. In order to know where we are going, we must know from where we have come and why. Grasping what modernity's prevailing tendencies are and why they exist are major steps in mapping out where we are and thus where we might go next and how we might get there.

CHAPTER 51

# Common Ruin

Prior to World War I, there was great enthusiasm for an international labor movement, where working people had no nation and whose common interests were opposed to those of capital. As the war broke out, however, national identity won out over class membership and workers picked up arms for their country and marched off to slaughter (though many of them were forced into such action through military impressment). It was a crushing blow for international labor solidarity, one from which it may have never recovered. It would not be the last time the forces of modernity threatened its contending classes with common ruin.

Though World War I was said to be "the war to end all wars," this was belied by World War II's outbreak, which some (such as French Marshall Ferdinand Foch) had predicted because of armistice measures forced upon Germany with the settlement of the first war. After Hitler's war of European conquest was halted in the East by the Soviets and in the West by combined American, British, Canadian, and French forces, Europe was left in shambles and it took decades for them to rebuild. In the Pacific theater, the Americans brought Japan to heel with atomic bombs in Hiroshima and Nagasaki (while the Soviets provided military pressure from the north). When tested prior to its use, some scientists believed the weapon might ignite the atmosphere; that it was considered worth the risk tells us much about the perceived gravity of the situation. In the Cuban missile crisis, a Soviet missile launch on the United States was narrowly averted because of the actions of one Russian officer (see Chapter 46, Note 1). Should that attack have taken place, the United States would have unleashed its nuclear force upon Russia to an extent that, it was hoped, the Soviet leadership would not or could not respond in kind. The world's population would have been trapped in a global nuclear exchange about which they had no say, nor from which could they escape. Ruination would have been common to all, except perhaps some of those living on isolated islands.

In his 1958 book, *The Causes of World War Three*, American sociologist C. Wright Mills argued that WWIII would be caused by the preparation for it. It would not be the last time such a conclusion would be offered. In January of 2017, Mikhail Gorbachev wrote in *Time* magazine that, "It all looks as if the world is preparing for war," observing that Russian and NATO forces faced each other at pointblank range rather than from a distance, that social spending was down while military spending was up, and that politicians world over sounded more and more belligerent. This was even before US President Donald Trump threatened a trade war by implementing tariffs against China, Europe, Canada, and Mexico. Further, Islamic and Christian radicals want a global faceoff between their factions, with each believing that Abrahamic prophesies foretell of destruction of those who do not believe exactly the way they do and that god's kingdom on Earth will be ushered in in the aftermath. And some of these believers have infiltrated state and military institutions in Pakistan, Saudi Arabia, Iran, and now the United States. Add in the weapons possessed by Britain, Israel, France, China, and India and you have a volatile and unpredictable mix. Moreover, in April of 2018, the United Nations warned that the world was facing an increased nuclear weapons threat, especially as the United States and North Korea escalated their belligerence toward one another. The idea that any one country or configuration of them could "win" such a war beggars belief. The world has inched toward common ruin before and in 2018 it appeared to be preparing to do so again.

In today's global and interconnected world, cultural exchange and sharing of information are sometimes thought to be bulwarks against the outbreak of conflicts like those we have seen in the past. But with social media being the current frontier of mass communication and a platform for mastering new techniques of public manipulation, it is perhaps reasonable to consider the opinion of a former executive from Facebook, Chamath Palihapitiya, on its social influence. Here is a quote from his talk at the Stanford Graduate School of Business (published on YouTube, November 13, 2017):

> I feel tremendous guilt. I think we all knew in the back of our minds—even though we feigned this whole line of, like, there probably aren't any really bad unintended consequences. I think in the back, deep, deep recesses of our minds, we kind of knew something bad could happen. ... We have created tools that are ripping apart the fabric of how society works. ... The short-term, dopamine-driven feedback loops we've created are destroying how society works. ... No civil discourse, no cooperation; misinformation, mistruth. And it's not an American problem—this is not about Russian ads. This is a global problem. ... It is eroding the core foundation of how people behave by and between each other. And I don't have a good solution. My solution is I just don't use these tools anymore. I haven't for years...[because I] innately didn't want to get programmed. ... Bad actors can now manipulate large swaths of people to do anything you want. It's a really, really bad state of affairs. And we compound the problem. We curate our lives around this perceived sense of perfection, because we get rewarded in these short-term signals: Hearts, likes, thumbs

up. And we conflate that with value and we conflate it with truth, and instead what it really is is fake, brittle popularity that's short-term and that leaves you even more, and admit it, vacant and empty before you did it. Because it forces you into this vicious cycle about what's the next thing I need to do, because I need it back. And think about that compounded by two billion people. ... You don't realize it but you are being programmed. It was unintentional, but now you've got to decide how much you want to give up.[1]

Palihapitiya's remarks bring to mind the analogy of the sorcerer we saw in Chapter 49, where a conjurer can no longer control the forces they have summoned up. Given the profit motive and capitalism's top-down control of such mass platforms, it is hard to imagine how everyday citizens can reverse such a trend outlined above, given the overall state of popular culture, our divisive politics, substandard education, an economy that rewards avarice and punishes altruism, and so on.

Speaking of everyday citizens, what of "the revolution"? Cannot workers of the world unite, seize the means of production and the state, dissolve the contending classes and usher in a new era, just as Karl Marx once so famously predicted? That *could* happen, in the sense that many things are possible. But today we see no international workers' movement or similar forms of solidarity, as working and middle classes remain in their nationalist camps and orbits. And the view from inside the United States looks similarly bleak; no real labor movement, party, or solidarity to speak of and its youth—that cohort known for creativity, rebellion, and a force for progressive social change—is similarly disaffected, fractured, and inert.[2] In an interview with Mark Karlin (2018), Henry Giroux had an analogous, if more dire, diagnosis:

> In an age when literacy and thinking become dangerous to the antidemocratic forces governing all the commanding economic and cultural institutions of the United States, truth is viewed as a liability, ignorance

---

1 A video of his comments can be found on YouTube at this link (URL retrieved June 16, 2018): https://www.youtube.com/watch?v=PMotykwoSIk&feature=youtu.be&t=21m21s.
2 One clinical psychologist diagnosed the lack of resistance from American youth of the 2000s as due to burdensome student loan debt, the medication of noncompliant behavior (the concocted "oppositional defiant disorder"), educational institutions training the young for obedience, the crushing of curiosity and creativity from standardized testing (No Child Left Behind policies from the Bush administration), the shaming of those who take education seriously, increased normalization of surveillance, television, religion, and consumerism (Levine 2011).

becomes a virtue, and informed judgments and critical thinking are demeaned and turned into rubble and ashes. Under the reign of this normalized architecture of alleged common sense, literacy is regarded with disdain, words are reduced to data and science is confused with pseudo-science. Traces of critical thought appear more and more at the margins of the culture as ignorance becomes the primary organizing principle of American society.

Under the 40-year reign of neoliberalism, civic culture has been commodified, shared citizenship eroded, self-interest and survival-of-the-fittest ethos elevated to a national ideal. In addition, language has been militarized, handed over to advertisers, and a politically and culturally embarrassing anti-intellectualism sanctioned by the White House. Couple this with a celebrity culture that produces an ecosystem of babble, shock and tawdry entertainment. Add on ... cruel and clownish anti-public intellectuals ... who defend inequality and infantile forms of masculinity, and define ignorance and a warrior mentality as part of the natural order, all the while dethroning any viable sense of agency and the political.

The culture of manufactured illiteracy is also reproduced through a media apparatus that trades in illusions and the spectacle of violence. Under these circumstances, illiteracy becomes the norm and education becomes central to a version of neoliberal zombie politics that functions largely to remove democratic values, social relations and compassion from the ideology, policies and commanding institutions that now control American society. In the age of manufactured illiteracy, there is more at work than simply an absence of learning, ideas or knowledge. Nor can the reign of manufactured illiteracy be solely attributed to the rise of the new social media, a culture of immediacy and a society that thrives on instant gratification. On the contrary, manufactured illiteracy is a political and educational project central to a right-wing corporatist ideology and set of policies that work aggressively to depoliticize people and make them complicitous with the neoliberal and racist political and economic forces that impose misery and suffering upon their lives. ... There is also the workings of a deeply malicious form of 21st century fascism and a culture of cruelty in which language is forced into the service of violence while waging a relentless attack on the ethical imagination and the notion of the common good. In the current historical moment, illiteracy and ignorance offer the pretense of a community in the form of right-wing populism, which provides a gift to the cloud of fascism that has descended upon the United States.

Giroux's pessimism does not seem unwarranted, especially when we consider the obstacles embedded in contemporary methods of communicating our shared dilemmas and what we can collectively do about them. Something must be done, no doubt, but our avenues of fruitful pursuit are neither clear, obvious, or unobstructed.

And should such trends be reversed, should there be active unrest and revolt, when have ruling classes not used the arms of state at their disposal for turning back challenges to their rule and authority? Ruling classes would fight their workers tooth-and-nail in order to not lose control of the system they sit atop. Police, national guard, the military, secret police, detention centers, martial law, new forms of crowd control, and so on await any new revolutionaries. Should either side succeed in such a conflict, what the aftermath they preside over may be something very different than what they originally fought for.

But what of a revolution that workers *actually win*? For starters, what likelihood is there that they will not follow a path of sectarian infighting, purges, and a drift toward authoritarianism? What is there to suggest such revolutionaries would avoid the problems that every political sect, just like religious ones, are subject to? History has already demonstrated how often this has happened in places like Russia and Cambodia. And though most are not cut from a Stalinist cloth, looking at the oppositional political landscape in the 2000s, one sees environmentalists, socialists, feminists, Marxists, anarchists, and other aspiring social progressives broken into dogmatic factions and camps—much like the People's Front of Judea versus The Judean People's Front.[3] The visions of the future they provide appear to outside observers as ranging from naïve utopianism to sectarian insularity. It only takes a cursory look at their views, actions, and factionalism to see that little exists there to inspire confidence that a peoples' revolution would result in progress instead of common ruin.

What happens if WWIII or a failed revolution do not take shape? What if the system continues on its current pattern and trajectory without war or rebellion? What happens if we keep raking Earth of its natural resources, mass producing commodities for mass consumption, and then discarding the wastes into the environment? Though we already have seen how grim the current situation is (see Chapter 41), it is set to get worse for the Earth's oceans, plants, air, and animals (including human beings) in our era of the neo-liberal global marketplace.[4]

---

3  A quick nod here to Monty Python's *The Life of Brian*.
4  In an era ruled by financial capital in a globalized neo-liberal market, one can think of it by way of an analogy to a swarm of locusts, scouring the environment for a place from which to extract needed resources. One example of this is with forests, where investment gravitates

Significant damage—loss of sea ice, dying coral reefs, growth of dead zones, increasing acidification, and crashing fish stocks from fishing fleets, global shipping, pollution, and agricultural run off—has reached almost all of our oceans, with only 13% left untouched by human activity (see Carrington 2018a and references therein).

Tropical forests in the Amazon—already ravaged by logging, burning, and agriculture (e.g., soy, beef, palm) and with about 16% deforested—have started to *release more carbon than they store*, which will reduce the amount of $CO_2$ that such forests can or will absorb and will be a problem for global carbon emissions controls as a whole (see Eaton 2018 and reference therein).

Studies have shown that the Earth has arguably entered its "sixth mass extinction" event, attributable to rapid loss of biodiversity over the last few centuries (Ceballos et al. 2015; Ceballos, Ehrlich, and Dirzo 2017). In a recent census of Earth's biomass, for instance, researchers concluded that the domestication of animals, the development of agriculture, and the later Industrial Revolution resulted in livestock and human biomass far surpassing that of wild mammals and outweighing all vertebrates combined (with the exception of fish)—wild land mammals have declined by a factor of seven, marine mammals by a factor of five, and a twofold decline in plant biomass, all from human activity (Bar-On, Phillips, and Milo 2018).

Our methods of growing, distributing, and consuming food are killing us collectively, from destroying land (e.g., rainforests), water (e.g., pesticide and fertilizer runoff producing dead zones), and air (e.g., releasing methane from meat production and carbon from transportation), with the wealthiest sectors of the world experiencing increased obesity, cancer, and heart disease while the poorest sectors go hungry and malnourished, one of cruelest contradictions of the modern world. Currently, more than 2 billion people lack safe drinking water (see Witze 2018 and references therein) and others must endure declines in the nutritional quality of fresh agricultural food products (see Conley 2018a and references therein) while mass farming techniques continue to use toxic pesticides and ship goods to world markets (Gross 2018).[5] A recent

---

toward resource sinks such as these driven by the rise of corporate management seeking to appease the demand for shareholder value, something happening both in the United States (Gunnoe and Gellert 2011) and especially in less developed countries that are more easily targeted for extraction and production in the context of their dependence on foreign investment (Jorgenson 2010).

5 Previously this book took note of how the way we service capital is comparable to the fabled "primitives" throwing virgins into a volcano to appease a god of their own making, believing this to be just the way things are. In another example of how this service to capital enwraps us like a religious devotion, in the face of climate disasters and crises at our poles, the melting

UN study found that, after three years of declines, the number of people globally undernourished rose to 821 million people (about 1 in 9) in 2017, with extreme climate events partly to blame (see Mundasad 2018 and reference therein). Another study found that for a planet of 7 billion people to achieve "high life satisfaction" based on our current environmental, technological, and economic relationships would require resource use 2-6x the sustainable level (O'Neill et al. 2018).

To study reporting on climate science is to encounter concepts such as "thresholds," "tipping-points," and "points of no return." Here are some sobering examples:

- With more of the world striving for modern forms of development, we have been reaching thresholds such as "Earth overshoot day" earlier every year (see Chapter 41).
- We are being warned that we are crossing other tipping-points, such as the loss of sea ice in the Barents Sea, which has historically been a barrier between the Arctic (colder) and the Atlantic (warmer) oceans but which now appears to be more an arm of the Atlantic. Such a change in oceanic circulation patterns will make it more difficult for Arctic sea ice to establish itself during the winter (see Timmer 2018 and reference therein).
- Rising temperatures in the Arctic also affect the circulation of the atmospheric jet stream, causing the stalling of summer weather patterns over Europe, North America, and parts of Asia, which can disrupt agricultural patterns and contribute to droughts and wildfires (Watts 2018b).
- As the planet warms and ice and tundra melt, additional methane is released and this can create a runaway feedback loop of additional gasses, more heat, more melting, and thus more gas releases. In 2018, for instance, NASA reported it had discovered lakes in Alaska and Siberia that were bubbling because of such methane releases (Osborne 2018).
- Related to the problem of carbon and methane releases acting as feedback loops on melting ice and permafrost and additional gas releases, another study concluded that we were on the brink of a "tipping point" especially considering that prior models used by governments in policy-making did not take into account how such loops accelerate climate change exponentially (they had used linear models, rendering such projections useless). Further, using these newer models suggested that we were much closer

---

of Arctic sea ice is being seen as a shipping opportunity, a new Northern Sea Route, to be used by and for commercial interests (see Booth and Ferris-Rotman 2018). The fact that the pole has melted enough to be used for new shipping lanes should be seen as a real-time disaster and a global wake-up call, not as an economic opportunity.

to exceeding the Paris Accord targets (i.e., limiting temperature increases to 1.5° C-2.0° C) than thought, ranging from having missed needed cuts in greenhouse gases 10 years ago (the worst case scenario) to having only about 20 years left to do so (see Batchelor 2018 and references therein).
- Another report explained that 125,000 years ago temperatures were not much different than they were in 2018 and in that prior period there was a major melting of the East Antarctic ice sheet and sea levels were 20 to 30 feet higher than the present time (see Mooney 2018 and references therein).

Unfortunately, data and prognostications such as these arrive to our consciousness as abstract things, every often, especially if one lives in the interior of a developed country. But people living on island nations have no such luxury, as they experience such developments in real time and in concrete ways as they evacuate their homes. Similarly, one photographer on assignment in the Arctic, Kalie Orlinsky, found conditions there so dire (as the ground did not freeze as it traditionally does over winter) that she "felt, in my bones, the weight of it all. I had never experienced a sense of real fear, for myself, for those I love most, and for all of humanity" (see Hughes 2018).

We are currently witnessing heat records set all over the planet, where the electrical grid becomes overloaded in places like France and California, the Arctic reached over 90° F in the summer of 2018, and additional heat waves and deaths associated with them are predicted to rise in the future. According to a 2018 University of Birmingham study, as the planet warms we will likely increasingly use air conditioning and other technology to cool ourselves, which, at current rates, will consume all of the renewable energy expected to exist by 2050 (see Hanley 2018 and reference therein).[6] And if that is the case, what energy sources outside fossil fuels will remain to power all of the other facets of our industrial architecture, homes, transportation, and whatnot? Still, time is running out and soon we will hit a "point of no return," if we have not passed it already—which depends on certain risk assumptions and trajectories of future output (see Aengenheyster et al. 2018). With all that said, should we not course correct immediately, nature will do that for us and this could very well mean the collapse of the ecosystem upon which all humans depend world over.

The era of fossil fuels served modern technological development well, but only temporarily. We have since learned of the environmental, political, and

---

6 See the University of Birmingham study, "A Cool World: Defining the Energy Conundrum of Cooling for All", here (URL retrieved August 26, 2018): https://www.birmingham.ac.uk/Documents/college-eps/energy/Publications/2018-clean-cold-report.pdf.

carcinogenic fallout from their use. Shifting modern manufacturing and other energy-dependent technologies from fossil fuels to cleaner sources such as solar, wind, hydraulic, and geothermal would be a significant environmental step forward, though for some scientists we are past the point of no return in respect to reversing the warming trend (Walker 2016). And we know that these climate conditions will get worse, as the warming associated with greenhouse gasses occurs about one decade after the initial emission (Ricke and Caldeira 2014). However, those with political and financial backing related to the fossil fuel industry have misrepresented claims of scientists, making their predictions, for example, from 30 years out appear off target when in fact their models were almost spot on (see Nuccitelli 2018). Such industry representatives appear content with passing down a bill for climate change to our children that stands at an estimated $8.8 trillion (see Chen 2016).

It is very possible that our past practices that came part and parcel with modernity and allowed it to thrive are practices that may make it so that modernity can no longer continue (see UN News 2016). In 1992, the Union of Concerned Scientists sent out a letter, "World Scientists' Warning to Humanity," that declared that the "environment is suffering critical stress" from a variety of pressures—e.g., air pollution and releases of carbon dioxide, ground water depletion, overfishing, erosion, forms of mass agriculture and animal husbandry, forest destruction, species loss, and the growing human population. And they warned that "No more than one or a few decades remain before the chance to avert the threats we now confront will be lost and the prospects for humanity immeasurably diminished."[7] They were not being hyperbolic. A study released in 2015 found that should nothing be done, if we continue on the current path and with current trends, we should expect catastrophic food shortages by 2040, possibly resulting in food riots and even societal collapse (see Doré 2015 and references therein). In 2017, "A Second Notice" was issued by the Union of Concerned Scientists. There they noted that, save stabilizing the ozone layer, the problems listed in their 1992 letter remain unaddressed and most have gotten worse.[8] Especially troubling, they said, was the trajectory of climate change due to fossil fuels, deforestation, and agricultural production (for meat in particular) and all of this on top of going through the sixth mass extinction event

---

7  A PDF copy of the Union's letter can be found here (URL retrieved August 25, 2018): https://www.ucsusa.org/sites/default/files/attach/2017/11/World%20Scientists%27%20Warning%20to%20Humanity%201992.pdf.

8  While often touted as a success, it must be noted that progress on things like ozone reduction can always be, and currently are being, undermined by industrial developments in countries disconnected from previous environmental initiatives (see Carrington 2018d; Montzka et al. 2018).

on Earth in 540 million years. It was signed by nearly 20,000 scientists (Griffin 2018).[9]

It might just be this environmental crisis that encourages modernity's ruling class to abandon the system rather than fight for it. Fearing unrest comparable to the Russian Revolution, bankers, investment fund managers, and other elites from places like New York and Silicon Valley are asking whether climate change or environmental collapse will impact Alaska or New Zealand the least, so that they can decide where to hedge their bets and buy property to escape to; they build bunkers, accumulate food, generators, ammunition, air infiltration systems, and gas masks; they fear civil war, resource depletion, nuclear explosions, or some other calamity; and they make plans for armed guards in their presumed safe havens but wonder how they will keep them loyal (see Osnos 2017; Rushkoff 2018). But those running away from civilizational collapse will not be able to run away from the current trajectory of a run-away "hothouse" Earth, while global warming and sea level rise will likely still continue even if we cut back on greenhouse gas emissions immediately (see Leahy 2018; Watts 2018a and references therein). These conditions do represent a real threat to life on the planet—human and non-human alike—and require *collective global* action, as evidence suggests that local actions—i.e., cities, states, and companies—will not be enough to offset the path set out for us by our current political-economic leadership (see Milman 2018 and references therein).

Of the multiple paths before us, several bring us to a similar destination. The world prepares for war. Political opposition has been rendered impotent and factionalized. The capitalist class hoards the world's wealth and dominates its governing structures. Our methods of production, consumption, and waste disposal fill up the natural world with pollutants, carcinogens, and carbon dioxide and methane, irrevocably changing the climate upon which we depend. These conditions are all predicted to get worse and spread to more people, as are the prospects of conflicts over resources and the potential for mass starvation. Our forms of communicating information about our problems and their possible solutions are intentionally filled with noise, distractions, disinformation, and ways to turn our ideas and personal information against us. If nothing is done, common ruin awaits all of the world's regions, nations, and classes. We are at a crossroads where the narrow paths modernity lays before us seem to lead to a land far away from the one of optimism and hope that it ushered in.

---

9 A PDF copy of the Union's "Second Notice" letter can be found here (URL retrieved August 25, 2018): http://scientists.forestry.oregonstate.edu/sites/sw/files/Warning_article_with_supp _11-13-17.pdf.

CHAPTER 52

# Chains, Riddles, Worlds

The modern world has always rested upon chains and remains dependent upon them. Perhaps the most readily grasped example comes from the history of slavery. As has been discussed, modernity did not invent slavery nor the idea of locking people up in order to control them. Still, a non-insignificant portion of modernity's wealth, infrastructure, law, and social relations were built upon chattel slavery. And this required capturing people in one part of the world and transporting them to another as cargo. The use of chains was ubiquitous throughout this process.

The world market connects one part of the world to another through "commodity chains," which are a central feature of modernity's system of production, distribution, and consumption (see Immanuel Wallerstein's work on the topic). The commodities in the wealthy "core" sectors of the world economy are often the end point of a process that began with corporations finding cheap labor and cheap raw materials in "peripheral" regions. Raw materials such as wood, fibers, ores, precious metals, fruits, vegetables, grains, diamonds, oil, and whatnot, are extracted from their natural environs, often by poorly paid laborers in more "traditional" societies with weak states. Such raw materials are then refined into cloth, boards, metals, food stuffs, etc. that can be sold to producers of clothes, furniture, and cars, or otherwise consumable goods.

IMAGE 52.1 Slavers Bringing Captives on Board a Slave Ship on Africa's West Coast, by Unspecified Author

CHAINS, RIDDLES, WORLDS 403

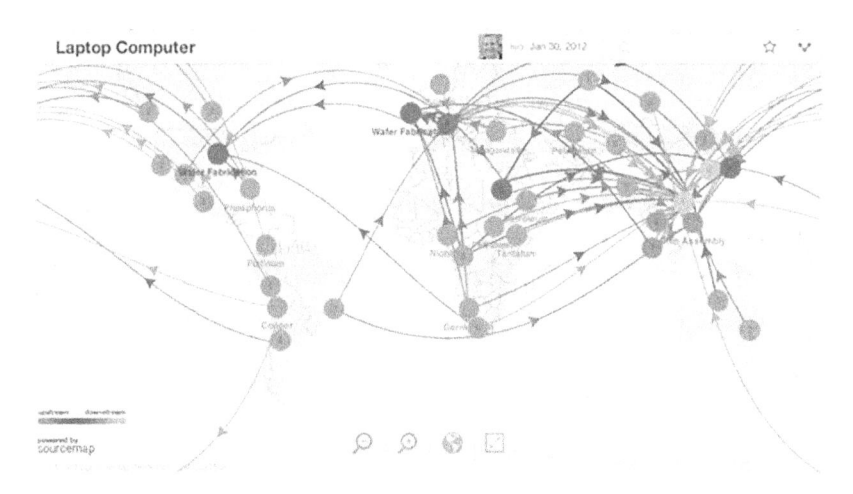

MAP 52.1   Supply Chain for a Laptop Computer, 2011, by leo

Each step "adds value" through this process from periphery to the core (where people enjoy higher standards of living). Like the relations of wealth appropriation and labor exploitation embedded between modern classes, the overall result here is a net transfer of wealth from poor areas of the world that are resource rich (periphery) to areas capital rich and materially complex (core).

In modernity, most of our wants and needs are taken of care for us. In our urban, suburban, and rural confines, the tools for survival—food production, warmth, shelter, water, and so on—are secured by external forces and, if they are not, we can visit the local gas station, discount store, fast food restaurant, and so on, to purchase prefabricated products that address our needs. And the modern world is increasingly coming to resemble these chains, especially as the techniques found in industries like fast food—efficiency, predictability, uniformity, and control—become adopted by other industries such as publishing, entertainment, housing, education, and so on (see Ritzer 2012). Modern society is inundated with these chain stores, and we grow dependent, corpulent, protected from insecurity, and, it seems, less and less challenged and more and more unhappy in our lives.

Freeing ourselves from humanly created mental shackles has been a time-honored goal and lament. In his *The Social Contract*, Rousseau wrote, "Man is born free and everywhere he is in chains." Voltaire warned us that "Those who can make you believe absurdities, can make you commit atrocities." As Noam Chomsky ([1998] 2002) has argued, "The smart way to keep people passive and obedient is to strictly limit the spectrum of acceptable opinion but allow very lively debate within that spectrum—even encourage the more critical and dissident views." That said, social and political discourse are always breaking free of the terms of debate set for them, as modernity provides us the first time in history where the question, "In what type of society do we wish to live?" is not something about which it is folly to ask. In prior periods, this question was sequestered to the halls of philosophical speculation, if asked at all. This is probably because the conditions of its possible resolution did not yet exist. Modernity makes this a real practical question, one in which it is not only reasonable to ask but possible to answer and, if we dare propose it, forge into reality.

What is it about modernity that makes this question not only more possible to ask but also *reasonable* to ask and even attempt to answer? Think of the pace of change in modern society. All that is solid melts into air, remember? We are always forging ahead with thoughts anew in modernity, whether we consciously realize it or not. To stand still is to be left behind. No other historical system outpaces its members this way. Thus, stability is not inherent to our modern consciousness and this means that we cannot have final faith in our system or even popular ideas. The system will never be stable and we must adapt with and to its flux.

This system creates new practical possibilities, both materially and mentally. A capitalist economy produces founts of wealth. It produces a constant stream of technological change, so much so that the average person literally has not the time to keep up with it all. And since our minds must adapt and update constantly, we can also see the cracks in the system, the alternatives it makes possible, and the ways it falls short better than people could in prior systems.

Think of democratic practice in modern society. On the one hand, capitalism swept away the feudal system, eroded social right by status, and created a civil society of freer movements as people pursue self-interest in the marketplace. Historically speaking, the societies that reached capitalist development earliest are those that pushed democratic reforms, some because their ruling class wanted such reforms and some because working classes forced democracy upon them. At the same time, ruling classes have wanted to limit democracy, as sharing state power with workers and the middle classes weakens their position in the class struggle. Modernity's ruling class just wanted power for themselves and to not have to share it with monarchs. And this has not changed all that much over time, which is why capitalists today fund politicians and work the levers of state—they want democracy but not too much of it and it should be run by them and/or their representatives. But the class of capital unleashed a political discourse and an economic system where the desire for a more equal and democratic world can find ever more fertile ground and today acceptance of these principles is commonplace and widespread. The ruling class cannot put this genie back in the bottle, no matter how hard they try.

Capitalism is a contradictory system. It creates massive stocks of wealth, technological innovation, and the possibility of democratic practice but it too creates a basis for new questions and their possible solutions. But capitalism undermines those very same solutions—it produces the most lopsided distribution of wealth the world has ever seen, uses technology to control labor, induces ecological crises, and has a ruling class that usurps incipient democracy when it can. What the system allows in a positive away, its internal operations and contradictions disallow to come to fruition. Even if this is the case, it does not negate the reality that people will still need and want solutions to their problems and such solutions cannot come from within the very system at the root of those problems.

Prior to capitalism, a social system by its very nature appeared normal and eternal. Capitalism, by its very nature *as a social system*, does this too but it also is the first and only system to date that also contains within it the vision and possibility of its transcendence and usurpation, even as its defenders try to deny that very possibility. A peasant of 1400 could not have imagined that the feudal system would give birth to a technologically complex, materially abundant society just 200–300 years down the line. But unlike feudalism, capitalist society internally develops its successor, and this provides us a vision of what a society after its dissolution might look like. This is truly historically unique. Apologists tell us there is no possible system after this one, a falsehood that, once grasped, makes the radical appear sane and makes the conservative modernity's Don Quixote.

Think about the broad sweep of human history. From our current historical vantage point, we can see transitory nature of class systems all too well. Each one—ancient societies like Egypt or Carthage, Asiatic and Europe feudalisms, slave systems world over, and so on—have all seen a period of ascension, geographical dominance, stagnation, and decline. All have been swept away. With its even more sharp contradictions and law-like patterns, there is every reason to assume capitalist society will follow this pattern. It is just another class system like the others, right? Well yes....and, more importantly, no.

Modernity sets the stage for human beings to reclaim their social relationships and to control their own destiny whereby those on the margins of and subject to power might escape domination and exploitation and freely exercise their creativity. Maybe this insight is what inspires its defenders? To the extent this is true, we should support that view. But modernity also creates the opposite conditions—increased domination, less freedom, and more physical and mental control. And this control of physical and mental conditioning is not an ideological divide. Remember what was said about religion, inverted worlds, mysticism, and ideology in prior chapters? These products of human alienation distort our thoughts on matters that require careful and rational deliberation. With capitalism's transcendence, the alienation that results from class exploitation should pass with the passing of its class relations, especially if we can build upon its benefits and create a new and improved world in which to live. Thus, modernity makes the goals for humans to structure their social lives to maximize their freedom to create in accordance with their needs and to guide this transformation toward collectively desired ends real practical possibilities. And it is from this vantage point that we can establish the basis for criticism of the conditions of our present. Are we moving toward or away from this freedom? Are we moving in ways that will facilitate it or undermine it?

Theologians and philosophers, armchair and professional, struggle with the question of the meaning of life. The way they approach such questions projects the range of possible answers as existing in the abstract realm of speculation. Pushed to its extreme, this speculative realm exists outside of us. Religion tells us that life's meaning comes from its gods, who can bring us utopia on Earth. Though philosophy approaches a similar question as answerable by reason, logic, and conjecture, this is still speculation. A materialist, on the other hand, is concerned not with dogma or speculation but with actual history and events and possibilities. Materialists are not here to guess at what an "ideal" society might look it. Utopian proposals have always been and will always be dangerous, naïve, and doomed to failure. What a realist-materialist proposes today is no more "utopian" than those in the past that demanded that slave masters be disenfranchised of their power and forced to step aside so that history may move on past them. From today's vantage point looking backward, this demand against slavery now seems so plainly obvious that most modern people would like to believe they would have been on the right side of history if given a chance to weigh in on the issue. A similar realist-materialist view would hold that capitalists now stand in the same place as slave owners once did—i.e., obsolete, socially parasitic, and in need of discarding. But this is a stance few people entertain today, with many seeing it as people *once* saw the demand to rid ourselves of slave masters—i.e., as naïve and extreme.

History has given us a riddle to solve. After we metaphorically crawled out of the mud and stood upright, we needed to cooperate for collective survival, learned to communicate in more complex ways, made up stories, and struggled for methods to sustain ourselves. Up until our current point in history, many of our solutions to our collective problems do not appear all that impressive, as they all seem to either cause suffering or have self-destruct mechanisms built into them. But history's riddle will not be solved by idols we invent nor is there a universal code to discover. We only have our planet and ourselves and, given our origins and evolutionary development, we must learn to create a world in which we can live, one which reduces want, fear, hunger, insecurity, violence, privation, and exploitation. This is and will remain a challenge, as people have yet to create a society that can sustain itself without conflict, superstition, and vulnerability. And if human beings are to move forward and advance a social system beyond capital, these are more than simply speculative or philosophical questions but real issues of practical resolve. In fact, a "society" is not something humans ever intentionally invented, though they will need to do so in a future after capitalism.

What is history's riddle? Simply put, can human beings create a world more than they are created by it? And can they create a world where most people, most of the time, are freed from toil, want, oppression, and the violence that comes with these things? Is it possible to construct a system of production, distribution, and consumption of goods and services where no cabal, group, or class monopolizes access to and control of the means and methods of that system? By extension, is it possible to organize a mass society, technologically complex, with an abundance of resources and services and with a democratic system of governance, without it becoming a system of control, oppression, and domination? Can human beings organize such a system where individual freedom and autonomy are not only respected but individual choice of freely chosen labor and creative activity is considered a paramount social desideratum? It is capitalism as a system that provides the preconditions and presuppositions that might allow us to forge answers to such questions into reality. To create a system that meets the above criteria, while moving beyond capitalism, is to answer history's riddle.

No system has lasted forever. That said, the modern mind is so shaped that imagining a life other than one in capitalist modernity, when prompted, is resisted by most. Within the confines of the acceptable is the idea that capitalism is simply the best we can do. It is not as if people believe and say, "Capitalism will last forever" but rather that they simply refuse to imagine that some other type of system after the current one is even thinkable. The irony, of course, is that capitalism is the only system that makes this question thinkable and, therefore, it takes money, education, and propaganda to prevent us from thinking it. But it was not always this way. There was once a lively labor movement in the modern world that clearly articulated the opposition of capital to labor, a point of view squelched in and exiled from popular modern discourse, a victory for modern elites by any measure. Such ideas today are mainly found in those domains (e.g., parts of Africa and South America) trying to extract themselves from the neo-colonial and neo-liberal order.

What sort of future worlds are being made possible by our present one? Just as our modern world incorporates elements of past systems into it, any new system will feature remnants of this one. This is especially true of material and technological things. Today, we see remnants of ancient pyramids used for tourism. We find housing made in agrarian and feudal systems still functioning today. We still use canals dug long ago. It would follow that the system that arises after ours will have railroads, highways, architecture, and so on, much in the same way.

The pursuit of the expansion of money invested allows for the conglomeration of accumulated wealth. Most people worldwide do not have enough money available to them in order to purchase productive assets, such as small businesses, stocks, etc. Most people have to rely on selling their mental and physical labor for salaries and wages. But a good number of businesses exist at local, regional, national, and international levels. We see these in buildings, office parks, hotels, shops, factories, malls, ports, banks, universities, etc. These conglomerations are increasingly in the same geographical areas where more and more people live (urbanization) and account for more and more of where social life happens. As the modern political-economic system orchestrates its own demise and births the possibilities of a new one, this infrastructure will likely remain, barring some catastrophic conflagration. Thus, those people who build the next system will not start from scratch, i.e., the business community is building it now. The question remains, once capitalism's demise is an inevitable practical reality, what system gets built next and who will build that system and how?

In one scenario, should the next system have no class that owns and monopolizes productive resources and thus does not operate on the basis of buying and selling people's labor, then what would this look like? Another way to say this would be, what sorts of things are the result of the class structure in our society and what would a world without it be like? While any definitive picture is impossible, one sketch of such a world must include a system where people are free to choose their labor, enjoy the fruits of that labor, and are actively and substantively involved in the major decisions that shape their lives. Such a system would not be one where a privileged few controls the lives of the many while benefitting off of that control. It should be materially abundant while containing mechanisms by which access to the means of life is not cutoff from people unless they labor in order to increase the riches of others. And it should be a world where humans approach nature via rational stewardship and conservation rather than treating it as a resource to be exploited.

In another scenario, those enjoying today's concentrations of wealth and power may refuse to give these up so that a new system can be born. Even if they do not organize the machinery of violence in an effort to save their class privileges, there remains the possibility that those with wealth, power, and knowledge today seize the reins of cultural, political, and economic leadership during the transition to a new system. After all, a portion of the old feudal ruling class saw the writing on the wall and positioned themselves as leaders of the new order. What is to stop today's ruling class from shaping things so that they also remain the next ruling class? As a result, the next system may not be capitalism as we know it, but it could be another class system, with all the trappings that implies—class inequality, exploitation, and control of the state.

Finally, another outcome on the slate of potential futures is that our global ecology collapses to the point where any semblance of a new complex society is unviable. Modernity could change the environment in ways that undermine building a new system before it can be conceived much less born. And, as we have seen, not only is this something that *could* happen in our lifetimes but in fact *is* a reality that *is* happening now. And this is something the rich seem to know while using their money to influence politicians and the babbling classes to convince us otherwise.

Some of these possible outcomes have their own problems and probabilities. The key variables will be the extent to which the various social classes understand the structural forces in which they find themselves and how these forces account for the decline of the system they are in, the extent to which they organize themselves as a class with particular interests different from and opposed to other classes, and their successes and/or failures in dismantling the current system and building a new one on its remnants. As capitalism and its social institutions slowly fail, fall, and morph, how the struggles between the contending classes turn out will determine who wins both the fight and the next world.

CHAPTER 53

# Socialist Sentimentalizing

Just as modernity was getting its sea legs under it, a variety of ideas for building new alternate social systems emerged, often in the form of utopian thinking. From Robert Owen to Charles Fourier to August Comte (who coined the term "sociology"), all manner of theorists formulated schemes on how to organize a non-class and/or non-capitalist society that would also be a world of peace and equality. Fourier's and Comte's plans stayed on the drawing board mostly, only manifesting themselves as writings in barely read books (though Fourier's plans did, it seems, find a few people interested in pursuing them). Only Owen made any headway in putting a plan into action and it still ultimately failed. And without a doubt, utopian schemes *are* doomed to failure. They imagine an idealized world of humanity living without struggle and instead only in harmony. This vision is simply not possible to make real for a variety of reasons.

Utopian schemes typically rely on a formal set of rules agreed upon prior to forging them into being and this means they must be built from the ground up. This requires that someone make the initial overture, organize confederates, and establish a way to make and enforce rules of order. Because of these factors, utopian schemes invite a dynamic where behavior is increasingly regulated and policed and where deviators are punished. In their search for peace and harmony, they become decidedly unfree and controlling, much in the same way religious cults do. As history has shown, all such attempts at utopias collapse, usually after turning inward on their members and/or because of the egomaniacal mendacity of a leadership that emerges and acts to enforce their preferred behavioral norms. But that is not how societies develop. A society is the product of a long evolution, where norms, values, and practices become institutionalized and internalized by individuals to such an extent that they feel like second nature. By creating a society from ground up you are asking for people to behave in a way that is not built into them in socio-evolutionary terms. You are also asking for a power struggle to develop over the building and the deciding, which lends itself to authoritarianism.

The impulse to create something out of modernity that is more equal in terms of class and status has not been relegated to history's dustbin, however. Another common entry in modernity's menu of progressive designs has been called "socialism," though socialist ideas, too, have often rested on high ideals of solidarity and equality and thus on a foundation not completely unlike utopian schemes. Such high ideals are not only notoriously hard to formulate and live up to in practice but they also invite a social dynamic where people must pass litmus tests of someone else's abstract formulation. It is not a far step from here to a committee on truth and/or evaluations of people's obedience to the cause, with criteria that tend to get narrower and narrower (see Chapter 38).

Morality and justice, too, are each forwarded as part of the edifice for socialist thinking. But whose morality are we to use? And what is "justice"? Why should the goal of a socialist society be "justice"? And while it is self-evident a society built on *injustice* sounds like an unpleasant contradiction, philosophers still debate what *justice* actually is and how to know it when you see it. This too seems like a gossamer-thin justification for socialism.

A realist view of socialism is not built on any of these things. As sentimentalizing about justice, equality, harmony, or peace directs us back to utopian thinking, a realist view understands that elements of socialism are already being constructed by capitalism. Capitalism has already built ports, roads, grade schools, sewage systems and canals, parks, and libraries, all through socializing the products of labor. If we expand our view, we find that health care and university education have been socialized in much of the modern Western world ("Western" here not limited specifically to geography). Capitalism has also produced housing, an electrical grid, satellites, and an untold number of factories. A realist and practical view of socialism asks the question: If history has shown we can live without feudal lords and slave masters who controlled the production system, can't we also live without the capitalist class? Are they needed to staff our social institutions, monitor and run the machines, till the fields, and bring goods to the market?

While a socialist system would be supportive of ridding ourselves of prejudice and discrimination based on race, gender, and sexuality, such status inequalities are not what socialism *is about*. Socialism is about dismantling the monopoly of class ownership of productive resources. To move past capitalism is to have those who do the labor be the ones who control the terms of that labor as well as owning the business enterprises in which they work. And those workers would necessarily be made from a cross-section of different genders, races, and sexualities. Socialism, simply put, is not about lofty ideals but rather about providing people control of their own productive activity and with it the future that this builds.

And, in this approach, individuality is not submerged into a nameless, faceless collective where people are numbers and a new state is a new ruling class that dominates and controls the productive forces of society. Rather, the people who do the labor are freely associated with each other and their work activity as both laborers and owners without an external, impersonal, and immovable force—the state—over them. Nor are they ruled by that invisible and abstract reality that rules everyone—classes and states—called "capital." In a realist-socialist understanding, people can gain control over the system they live in rather than the system controlling them. We take our current backward world and re-invert it ourselves.

A realist view does not assert life will be all harmony in socialism or that social problems would cease to exist. There will still be people whose ethics are suspect, who might turn violent or steal from their neighbors. There will still be roads that need to be paved and cleared of snow. There will be inequality, as people with specialized and scarce skills would be more rewarded for their efforts, given the time it takes to cultivate those skills and the limited time they would have to offer them. There will be people who put in more effort and energy into their productive and creative labor. Letting free riders exploit the work of others is to invite cynicism and withdrawal and thus more free riding. And there will be struggles over decision-making, not only because of disagreements but also because there will likely be people who try to use social institutions for their own personal benefit. There is no guarantee in a realist-socialist outlook that life in such a system will be without such obstacles and difficulties.

What a realist view of socialism *does* argue, however, is that a society that is no longer built upon class exploitation should significantly reduce the number of social problems related to class exploitation as such. There should be less poverty as the system is not built upon wealth appropriated from one class to another via forced labor—in capitalism, it is the threat of hunger and homelessness that forces people to sell their labor, not a sword in the back or the crack of a whip. Waste and pollution could be cut down in to a significant extent, as such a world would not be based on stimulating endless consumption nor would it have private interests blocking the path to cleaner methods of meeting societal needs. People will be less alienated from each other, as they are not competing for scarce jobs under threat of homelessness or starvation nor are they working so long that they have little time left for socializing or cultivating their interests and talents. The political system should become more representative, as without an elite class to buy the political process, more people can participate and, theoretically, *will* participate. Yes, there will be winners and losers, but the mass number of people will not be beholden to political elites that serve a dominant class.

A socialist outlook must be steely-eyed and not built on hopes for and dreams of an ideal utopia. A socialist is not out to exact revenge on individuals whose social status placed them as a member of some privileged status group in a prior system, as many of those individuals had no benefits conferred on them in the first place or, if they did, this was not something within their control. A socialist outlook does not demand ideological conformity to lofty ideals but simply demands that people are not controlled by systems that require they sell their labor so that others may build their wealth upon that labor. A socialist outlook rejects all forms of sentimentalizing and embraces the idea that people control their own economic destinies and reap the fruits of the work they do. If and when this outlook can be used to forge a new productive system in the wake of capitalism's waning years, we will have moved one step closer to solving *history's riddle*.

CHAPTER 54

# Whether We Want it or Not

The modern world is beset with pressing problems. We face a climate crisis that appears as unimaginable as it is unmanageable. We are rapidly consuming nature's bounty while our methods of production unleash pollution to such an extent that more and more ecological systems cannot recover. And we live in a political-economic system with exponential population growth that relies on *expanding* consumption while the way to deal with increasingly fouled air, water, and land requires both political will and a redirection of money for cleaner production methods and/or for cleaning up the mess already there. Addressing all of these problems means less money available for capital accumulation, which is directly against the objectives of the economic system and the business class that benefits from it and governs it. Thus, not only do we suffer from inertia in dealing with these social problems but we also confront an active and powerful faction opposed to doing anything about them that harms their interests.

Given the educational and ideological blinders with which we are fitted, when confronted with our political, economic, ecological, and geo-political problems, the average person is left with a host of unworkable and distracting hypotheses with which to work. If we are told that the solution lies only in changing consumptive activities like diet and trash disposal, then our strategies will simply target individuals for changing their personal behaviors—e.g., eat less meat and recycle our wastes. But this model for social change is unable to adequately address our environmental crises at the needed scale while it also ignores and arguably acquits the systemic sources of these same problems (for a discussion of how the era of neo-liberalism encouraged this approach, see Lukacs 2017). If one hones in on "greed" as the source of our problems, then this too is an individualistic approach that requires changing the behavior of enough people to fix those problems, which again obscures their systemic nature.[1]

---

[1] In 2018, premier billionaire investor, Warren Buffet, warned that another financial crisis was inevitable. For this "Oracle of Omaha," however, this inevitability did not stem from the systemic nature of crises but rather it was because people see "the guy next door, who they know is dumber than they are, getting rich and they aren't" and they feel pressure to "figure it out, too" and thus this behavior is "contagious" and "a permanent part of the system" (see Kim 2018). In this model, if we could just figure out a way to stop people from behaving on these irrational impulses, we could avoid bubbles and crises.

Accepting either or both of these approaches also means accepting a certain fatalism, as we must simply put up with a level of social dysfunction because we will always have trashy and/or greedy people. But behaviors such as diet, litter, and, especially, greed only exacerbate our modern social dilemmas; those dilemmas do not *originate* in these individualistic traits.[2] And if we hope for change, reform, and new progress via working through our established political parties, we rest our fate in the very same parties forged within the system, ruled by bureaucratic professionals and paid for by the business class and other elites.

With the above approaches being our dominant ones, it is no wonder that we are left with malaise, fatalism, and hopelessness as the system—whether in liberal or conservative policy guises—drives itself off a cliff and us with it. Such approaches deflect our inquiries from the most basic and obvious answer: our social problems come from the basic structure of our social system itself. From where else could they possibly come?

Are those who warn us of impending social problems tantamount to a contemporary Chicken Little, panicking themselves and the public over non-falling skies and pushing a not-so-hidden agenda? Though prophets of gloom and doom and predictions of society's crises have a long, mixed, and dicey record, there is no doubt about the following: that we are using up our oil and coal and the methods to extract what is left are increasingly draconian and ecologically disastrous; that the gasses we pump into the atmosphere because of our fossil fuel use raise global temperatures and this melts glaciers and ice packs and raises sea levels world over; that oceans rise as we watch the first island nations slip beneath the tides; that forests are being cut down for wood and grazing areas to service our meat-based diets (that require high levels of oil, water, land, and grain); that our population numbers continue to grow and we are likely to reach 10 billion at some point and if this were today we would have no way to feed everyone or provide them water; that should the rest of the world adopt levels of production and consumption found in the United States, Canada, Europe, Australia, and Japan, then the Earth's resources would be consumed in less than a year; that the capitalist class monopolizes the political institutions that could allow us to do something about these problems; that same class dominates the world economy, has mightily concentrated wealth in its hands, and only pursues the expansion of its capital without regard to

---

2   Similarly, if we account for our problems as a product of human sinfulness, then we are left with tools such as prayer, faithful supplication, and good works to remedy our society's ills. Again, the root of our problems is overlooked for surface treatments at best and ineffectual wishful thinking that prolongs or even exacerbates our difficulties at worst.

the common welfare of the population or the planet; and, finally, that none of these things can continue indefinitely without catastrophic results.

What is off the table in most discussions of modernity and its problems is the central organizing principle of the modern world, i.e., capital and its logic. The modern world is based on the production of goods, their sale/consumption, the rewarding of investors in terms of profit-taking, and the accumulation of profits as capital—only for the circuit to begin anew. To fail to see capital—with its multiple relationships and processes—as the key variable in modernity's problems requires the discipline comparable to a religious apologist. That is, the extent to which we are exposed to systemic criticism usually does not focus its attention on capital's internal logic but on its trappings, just as in commonplace religious criticism blind obedience is not the fault of religion in general or even a specific religion but rather specific priests abusing their authority. For *capital's* liberal and conservative apologists both, the system is fine but the people it produces have not yet mastered how to operate it.

When a discussion of the logic and implications of capital accumulation are off the table, its stewards are off the hook. Yes, sometimes greedy CEOs or the occasional Bernie Madoff is offered up for a ritual public sacrifice, but the logic of capital and its class of caretakers are mostly ignored and sometimes even celebrated. In their pursuit of profits and class power, the upper echelons of the business community drive the ecosystem into crisis and keep swaths of people impoverished, dependent, ignorant, and vulnerable. And this they know all too well, though to call them on it, ironically, is to risk being accused of fomenting class-hatred. They have orchestrated a very effective discourse to protect themselves, their class interests, and the system as a whole from inspection. And when critics question the system or even mention its fundamental problems, they are ignored or sidelined and when that fails they must be pilloried and have their sanity and integrity questioned.

In crisis periods, the public is presented with a variable set of "choices" about reform or non-reform. Regulate the free market or unleash it even further.[3] What cannot be discussed, and is not discussed, is the idea that the *normal* operation of the free market is the source of its crises. We live in a society where all the "good" that the system brings is willingly and intentionally and openly

---

3  There were some, amazingly, who claimed that the 2007–2008 financial crisis was the result of *government regulation* not the deregulation of markets (e.g., see Calabria 2009). This ideological belief is similar to the religious person who sees strife between factions of believers and concludes that *even more prayer* is just what is needed.

accredited to the system, while its problems, its faults, its disasters, its dangers, and the gun it points at our collective heads are explained by anything but the same. The fact that we have witnessed both crises and regulatory reforms, hundreds of economic theories, and multiple regional and world wars driven by capital's interests demonstrates the inherent chaos embedded in the system and that it needs constant taming.

To what extent are humans simply products of their social conditions and carried along with them versus to what extent are humans capable of imposing their creative will on the world and thus possess an element of free agency? Clearly, elements of both are in play and they will tend to oscillate from one to another given other variables. Some systems dominate their members more than others, while other systems provide for a greater potential for humans to act as free agents. And modernity possesses both traits but in a contradictory way. The institutional training and the relations of ruling in this society shapes individuals, as Michel Foucault (*Discipline and Punish*) noted, to be docile and useful. And capitalism shapes our consciousness to see the market as the outcome of the human animal being naturally acquisitive and competitive. As a system's contradictions develop and mature, they force things to the surface so that the surface appearance of things often gives way to their underlying causal essence. This can happen to the point where the causes of our problems become more and more available for our grasping, consciousness of our real social relations is acquired by ever more people, and, as a result, growing numbers come to understand and take action on our conditions.

Environmental activists often put their lives at risk for the common good and for the protection of the natural world—in the Philippines, 33 activists were killed in 2015, 28 in 2016, and 41 in 2017 (see Wei 2018 and references therein). Despite over 170 rangers losing their lives trying to protect them over the last 20 years and their numbers hitting a nadir of 242 in 1981, mountain gorillas in Africa are making a comeback due to conservation efforts—with an estimated population of more than 1,000 (see Bittel 2018 and references therein). These are the results of the activities of people who do not stand aside and let the external world pass them by. That is, these results are the outcome of human agency making a difference in response to a world in need of it.

Similarly, activists and governments are taking a variety of concrete steps to deal with air and solid waste pollution and climate change. Take the following sample:
– In August 2018, France became the first European country to ban all five pesticides suspected of a role in colony collapse disorder devastating bee populations (see Samuel 2018). Amsterdam—where they have constructed "insect

hotels" and banned the use of chemical pesticides on public lands—has seen a 45% increase in wild bee and honeybee species since 2000 (see Givetash 2018).
- Technological fixes for cleaning up the plastic in the ocean are in the works and ready to be tested (see Dalton 2018; Kart 2018). According to a UN environmental chief, the success of a ban on the manufacture, sale, transport, storage, and use of plastic in Mumbai, India has been "absolutely remarkable" (see Pinto 2018).
- Though the Great Barrier Reef off of Australia is in major crisis, in 2018 Belize received praise from UNESCO for its "visionary" plans (including a moratorium on oil exploration) to save its coral reef—the world's second largest—and it was taken off the endangered list.
- Because of both abandoned farms as well as government attempts to protect forests and their growth, the acreage of forests is increasing in parts of Europe over previous norms (e.g., in Spain, Greece, Italy, and Ireland), as well as observable growth occurring in Australia and America (see *The Economist* | J.B. 2017).
- In addition to the Paris Accords, 23 nations around the planet have agreed to accelerate their actions on climate change (Climate Action 2018a).
- Evidence suggests that China has been successful in reducing its sulfur emissions from power plants (Dizikes 2018).
- The UK is working on phasing out coal and even went past 1,000 hours without it and reduced its reliance on coal for generating electricity from two-fifths in 2012 to less than 6% in 2018 (Vaughn 2018a, 2018b); the City of London—the city within the city—was set to operate with 100% renewable energy in 2018 (Beach 2018).
- India has invested in a future that relies on more solar power (Climate Action 2018b).
- In 2015, Costa Rica generated 100% of its electricity needs on renewable energy for 299 days, for 271 days in 2017, and for 300 days in 2018, using a mixture of hydro, wind, geothermal, biomass, and solar. The government's plan is to be carbon neutral by 2021 (Chow 2018).
- The world's largest solar farm—the $2.8 billion Benban complex—is set to open in 2019 in the Egyptian desert, with the government's aim of getting 42% of the nation's electricity from there by 2025 (Scheier 2018).
- In August of 2018, Mexican President-elect, Andrés Manuel López Obrador, announced that he will ban fracking upon taking leadership.
- In parts of Europe (e.g., Germany, France, Belgium, Switzerland), wind and solar glut the energy network frequently enough (i.e., adding power to the grid) that energy from these renewable sources results in greater supply than demand—thus "power worth less than zero"—and this will

mean power reliant on fossil fuels increasingly needed less while operating at a loss and thus making a transition to renewables easier and more likely (Starn 2018a).
- Sweden's goal for renewal energy set for 2030 was already hit in 2018 (Starn 2018b).
- Spain generated 45% of all its electricity from renewable power in the first half of 2018 (Climate Action 2018c).
- Costs for solar electricity in Australia have "plunged" to "extraordinary" new lows (see Vorrath and Parkinson 2018 and references therein).
- In 2017, Germany broke a previous record when it obtained only 15% of its energy needs from coal and nuclear power (England 2017).
- Though it has lagged behind other countries, in 2018 the number of Americans who believe that current climate change is predominately human generated hit its highest level yet (Borick et al. 2018).
- The United States generated 10% of its power from wind and solar in the first four months of 2018 (Renewables Now 2018).
- As of the summer of 2018, California (with the fifth largest economy in the world, behind Germany and ahead of the UK) had a bill before its Assembly to reach 100% renewables and "zero-carbon" sources of electricity by 2045 (Roselund 2018) while its previous regulation of carbon industries and investment in solar and wind (2006) not only did not wreck its economy as some had predicted but rather the state experienced economic growth, cut emissions, and even generated energy surpluses (The Times Editorial Board 2018).
- Scientists at Stanford University have made advances on creating a rechargeable battery that can store power from solar and wind sources and provide energy to the grid quickly, efficiently, and at normal temperatures (Golden 2018).
- As of 2018, the state of Texas was on track for generating 86% of its power grid needs through solar or wind by 2020 (Weaver 2018).
- In 2017, Iowa, Oklahoma, Kansas, and South Dakota generated 30–37% of their electric through wind (Geuss 2018).
- Things like electric buses (and eventually automobiles) will increasingly reduce our reliance on oil (Hodges 2018).
- Given this direction, among other observations, the fossil fuel industry today is perhaps in a weaker position than it has ever been (see McKibben 2018).
- A recent paper on the threat of global warming and a "hothouse" future Earth was downloaded an "unprecedented" 270,000 times, numbers not seen since 2007, which was the year for both public warnings from Al Gore and the Intergovernmental Panel on Climate Change (see Watts 2018c).

And it appears as if the more people know, the more they aspire to act on that knowledge. Recent research has found that though political party affiliation and ideology correspond to concern about climate change predominately in the United States (as well as English-speaking democracies as a whole, though somewhat a lesser extent in western Europe), when measured at a global level both education and commitment to democratic values prove the variables most strongly correlated with climate concern (Lewis, Palm, and Feng 2018). It only follows that a more educated, more democratic world would be the path necessary to adequately deal with the environmental issues we face. This, however, would be only a first step, as it would not yet actually solve these problems.

Still, our environmental problems are not universally denied, even among the investing classes. Managers for investment firms can let their money talk and refuse to invest in companies resisting action on climate change, an action which one manager of a fund of over $1 trillion has already threatened (Selby-Green 2018). As head of a firm managing billions in assets, Jeremy Grantham, in a 2018 speech at a Morningstar Investment Conference in Chicago, said that, "Capitalism and mainstream economics simply cannot deal with these problems"—among which he mentioned deforestation, air and water pollution, and climate change—because "Anything that happens to a corporation over 25 years out doesn't exist for them, therefore, as I like to say, grandchildren have no value" to them. "A corporation's responsibility is to maximize profit, not to spend money and figure out how to save the planet. ... We are racing to protect much more than our portfolios. ... We are racing to protect our grandchildren and our species, so get to it" (see Imbert 2018a). While Grantham's call was for capitalism's reform, in 2018, scientists argued for a new Paris-style agreement for preservation of Earth's natural resources and habitats that would target both nations and the private sector, with one advocate presciently recognizing that, "We need to ... shift to an economic model that accounts for the fact that we operate within a close system—planet Earth—and that our economic growth is limited by the ecological limits of the planet" (see Hance 2018).

Socially and political speaking, people are growing impatient with old ways and embrace new possibilities. Despite racism in its past and the appearance of its racial climate under Trump, there is evidence that people in the United States are increasingly accepting of racial and ethnic diversity (Fingerhut 2018). And in a push back against its antagonism toward science on environmental matters, courts have ruled that Trump's EPA must provide evidence about its climate claims (Thomsen 2018a). A 2017 poll of Americans found that 4 out of 10 had favorable views of socialism, a view the poll's author found "alarming" and about which the *National Review* said, "threatens America's future" (see Nammo 2017 and references therein). Among the things to note here I would like to highlight two. First, the idea that the interests of the capitalist class are concomitant with the interests of the nation could hardly be stated more explicitly. Second, though perhaps sounding hyperbolic, the handwringing expressed by the *National Review* is not incorrect if what they meant by "America's future" is an unfettered capitalism existing in perpetuity.

Other survey results are troubling for class warriors such as these when examined through a generational lens. A poll of Australian millennials, from the Centre for Independent Studies (a right-wing think tank), found that 58% were favorable to socialism and 59% believed that capitalism had failed (see Boyle 2018 and reference therein). A 2018 Gallup poll of Americans found that 51% of younger Americans (18–29) viewed socialism favorably and only 45% had a favorable view of capitalism, a 12-point decline from the past two years and a decline from 68% in 2010 (see Elkins 2018 and references therein). In 2018, infamous libertarian capitalists, the Koch Brothers, commissioned a survey that, contrary to their presumable hopes, the following percentages of Americans viewed the below solutions to problems facing the country as "very" to "somewhat effective":

– Enforcing equal rights for all—84%
– Health care reform that puts doctors and patients in charge—83%
– Encouraging scientific and technological innovation—85%
– Ending the cronyism that leads to corporate welfare—74%
– Government paid college tuition—66%
– More regulation of Wall Street—69%
– Increased government assistance for childcare—69%
– A $15 minimum wage—65%

Other findings included 92% saying that growing health care costs were a problem and a combined 55% believing that a government-run health care system would be a very or somewhat effective policy solution (see Surgey and Jilani 2018 and reference therein).[4] True, these survey questions and answers from the Koch-sponsored survey mainly focused on liberal welfare-state approaches, so they should be interpreted within that context. And that said, by extension, the specific ideas of "socialism" respondents had in mind in the

---

4 A 2018 Reuters poll found that 70.1% of Americans support a Medicare-for-all single-payer health care plan—which broke down into 84.5% Democrat and 51.9% Republican support—and 60.1% support free college tuition paid for by taxing speculative trading—which broke down into 78.9% Democratic and 41.1% Republican support (see Stein, Cornwell, and Tanfani 2018).

preceding surveys are less important here than is the fact that such results reveal an understanding that capitalism is failing to meet the public's needs and new ways of approaching our socio-economic problems—including alternatives to traditional market-economy methods—are both needed and imaginable.

Opinions on the weaknesses and fundamental problems contained in set of social relations only are worthwhile if those social relations can be transformed through practice. If they cannot, then those opinions might as well be clouds we shout at. But if those social relations can in fact be changed and for the better, we do well to work toward those ends. However, we confront ideological hurdles all along the way meant to dissuade and confuse us and we must therefore remain vigilant. If social dysfunctions in modernity are the result of its specific social relations rather than human nature, inviolable laws of society, or god's law, then they can be changed and remedied. As such, scientific education and coordinated action will remain crucial for achieving additional progress on top of what modernity has already made possible. Researchers, for example, find that individuals with an expressed interest in science are more likely to overcome politically biased reasoning (Kahan et al. 2017), e.g., learning to trust climate scientists and their claims (Motta 2018). Those who are more comfortable with ambiguity and uncertainty are also more likely to develop prosocial behaviors that support and encourage others (Vives, Lluís, and Feldman Hall 2018). As more people challenge conventions and change their behavior, a tipping point (which varies based on the specific conditions in question) is reached where social conditions are as such that it becomes easier and more likely that others change their behavior as well (Centola et al. 2018). Given the dire conditions we find our planet in and the runaway force with which capitalism today seems to be working, we must become conscious of these conditions, their remedies, and the various options we have in front of us, whether we like it or not.

CHAPTER 55

# Afterword

A study of one's society requires consideration of its origins, history, structure, tendencies, and possible future(s). This book has strived to provide such an overview, though I cannot take credit for the origins of that view. The vast majority of this book's perspective I have adopted from elsewhere, though in the telling I saved referencing that inspiration until this second-to-last chapter. This was no oversight. I hoped the reader would consider this work's ideas on their own merits before passing judgment on their source. That is because this book's inspiration—in the person of Karl Marx—has been much misunderstood, vilified, and stereotyped and this still remains true today. Now that we are near our journey's send, it is time to make this issue clear, if was not already (though I suspect for many that it was).

Over the years I have studied and published several articles and books on the ideas and works of Marx. Most, if not all, of my writings, have been geared toward a professorial audience and, reflecting this, they are weighted down by abstract disciplinary language and this inherently limits their appeal typically to specialists. Consequently, more than once a colleague, friend, and/or family member has asked if I was ever going to write something for a more general audience. I thought it a good idea, should I afford myself the time. So, I did.

Why read Marx today? This question has been frequently asked and this book is but one of my answers to that question. There is no one thinker who grappled with the origins, logic, and destiny of modern society more than he. Further, he provides a point of view from which to grasp that modern society not only had origins but also has a trajectory, as well as a successor that remains to be seen. And Marx also helps us realize that we are involved in a political drama, whether or not we want to be and whether or not we like it. As such, we must understand our place in history, our place in the current social structure, and the options before us.

Marx provides an invaluable outlook for understanding the world in which we live. But we have to distill that value out of his works, which are not always easily understood. His record is too vast, complicated, and often filled with minutiae to interest much of a popular audience. As such, I hoped to have presented Marx's outlook on modernity from a perspective not often appreciated. Many treatments of Marx deal with his more commonly known terms and concepts, such as dialectics, the materialist conception of history, forces/relations/modes of production, the labor theory of value, the falling rate of profit, communism, etc. Though this book had no choice but to engage well-known concepts such as these, the method I used to prioritize my presentation focused on how he saw modernity as a whole and went about expressing that outlook.

Below, I take some time to reference and discuss from which of Marx's writings I took my chapter titles and themes, i.e., central texts and essays as well as footnotes, letters, or otherwise one-off comments. Some of these ideas have been extensively discussed in the scholarly canon, others are only somewhat known there and by laypersons, and still others are what I consider overlooked gems. For some chapter titles, I took authorial license and altered their wording to either shorten them, to reflect their core meaning, and/or just make the presentation of an idea pithy and/or reader-friendly. I will remain silent on my success, or lack thereof, on that score.

Before I introduce my sources, some words on what is here and what is not. Those with more experience with Marx likely recognized many of these ideas and sources as they read the book. After all, those familiar with his work could hardly fail to recognize "alienation," "class," "struggles," "opium," "the executive committee," "solids melting in air," "civilization versus barbarism," "rate of profit," "concentration of wealth," or "crisis theory." Other readers, however, may not be as schooled on Marx, but no matter. As you read through the sections below, you will find that the largest work represented is The Manifesto of the Communist Party. As this document contains numerous instances where Marx's phraseology captures a particular feature of modernity, it would be anywhere from difficult to impossible to write a book such as this without reliance on it. Perhaps my most uncommon and lesser read sources are Marx's private letters. In them you often find him expressing a view not written for a popular audience but nevertheless one full of insight on some feature of the modern world. Interestingly, as for *Capital*'s volumes, I referenced them in a few instances but did not rely heavily upon them.

In any case, here I must now give a nod to Marx and the sources from his work that animated the previous chapters.

*Chapter 1: No Rest Until Modernity Is Acquired.* The title of this chapter comes from an 1837 letter Marx wrote to his father during the early stages of his university education. It is a fascinating letter, as few of us today would write such prose and on such topics to a parent, especially as a college student. Not only do we not talk or write this way anymore, but the scope of his university inquiries is truly impressive; so is his self-awareness. In this letter, Marx outlines several topics he has studied, his false starts, his insights, his long-term goals, and so on. After this series of confessions, Marx (1975e, 19) declares, "I could not rest until I had acquired modernity and the outlook of contemporary science." This letter overall, and this passage in particular, inspires the rest of the book, as it expresses an interest he carried with him throughout his life.

*Chapter 2: Speculation Ends, Science Begins*. The inspiration for this chapter comes from a joint work of the young Karl Marx and Frederick Engels, *The German Ideology*. In outlining their materialist approach *contra* the idealists of their time, they declare that, "Where speculation ends, where real life starts, there consequently begins real, positive science" (Marx and Engels 1976: 37). The problem with speculative philosophy was its attempt to formulate "Truth" prior to empirical inquiry, a type of Truth similar to religious revelation that others simply have to accept.[1] Here we also see a young Marx's commitment to directing the scientific enterprise toward social questions and his willingness to critique established knowledge, a commitment he would never lose.

*Chapter 3: Divesting Philosophy's Ultimate Word*. Marx struggled with philosophy in several ways, eventually becoming generally dismissive of it, especially when and as it tended toward speculation. However, Georg Hegel's ideas he could not easily dimiss. There was a core insight there that could be used for empirical research and its presentation. To Ferdinand Lassalle, Marx (1983b: 316) noted, "I should, moreover, have liked to find in the text proper some *critical* indications as to your attitude to Hegelian dialectic. This dialectic is, to be sure, the ultimate word in philosophy and hence there is all the more need to divest it of the mystical aura given it by Hegel" (emphasis in the original). Marx became a dialectician through-and-through and deftly combined that outlook with that of positive science.

*Chapter 4: The Concept of Society.* Marx's revolutionary ideas about science and the study of society gained attention in certain circles. In his letters, you will find correspondence with kindred spirits or others curious about his ideas. Other times you can find Marx writing to authors he had read. To Ludwig Feuerbach (August 11, 1844), for instance, he writes to tell him that in Feuerbach's own work, the "concept of the human species [is] brought down from the heaven of abstraction to the real earth, what is this but the concept of *society!*" (Marx 1975g: 354). Here we find Marx endorsing the idea that to understand humans in a scientific way we must step back from speculative

---

[1] "On the other hand, it is precisely the advantage of the new trend that we do not dogmatically anticipate the world, but only want to find the new world through criticism of the old one. Hitherto philosophers have had the solution of all riddles lying in their writing-desks, and the stupid, exoteric world had only to open its mouth for the roast pigeons of absolute knowledge to fly into it" (Marx 1975f: 142).

philosophy and study our species in its social context if we are to produce any semblance of positive knowledge.

*Chapter 5: History and Human Development.* There are many places where Marx comments on history and human development. Perhaps the most well-known passage comes from his Preface to his *A Contribution to the Critique of Political Economy*.[2] Though that was not his first or only time to remark on such matters, it was perhaps his most systematic (and often misinterpreted).

---

2  "The general conclusion at which I arrived and which, once reached, continued to serve as the leading thread in my studies, may be briefly summed up as follows: In the social production which men carry on they enter into definite relations that are indispensable and independent of their will; these relations of production correspond to a definite stage of development of their material powers of production. The sum total of these relations of production constitutes the economic structure of society—the real foundation, on which rise legal and political superstructures and to which correspond definite forms of social consciousness. The mode of production in material life determines the general character of the social, political and spiritual processes of life. It is not the consciousness of men that determines their existence, but, on the contrary, their social existence determines their consciousness. At a certain stage of their development, the material forces of production in society come in conflict with the existing relations of production or—what is but a legal expression for the same thing—with the property relations within which they have been at work before. From forms of development of the forces of production these relations turn into their fetters. Then comes the period of social revolution. With the change in the economic foundation the entire immense superstructure is more or less rapidly transformed. In considering such transformations the distinction should always be made between the material transformation of the economic conditions of production which can be determined with the precision of natural science, and the legal, political, religious, aesthetic or philosophic—in short ideological forms in which men become conscious of this conflict and fight it out. Just as our opinion of an individual is not based on what he thinks of himself, so can we not judge of such a period of transformation by its own consciousness; on the contrary, this consciousness must rather be explained from the contradictions of material life, from the existing conflict between the social forces of production and the relations of production. No social order ever disappears before all the productive forces, for which there is room for it, have been developed; and new higher relations of production never appear before the material conditions for their existence have matured in the womb of the old society. Therefore, mankind always takes up only such tasks as it can solve; since, looking at the matter more closely, we will always find that the problem itself arises only when the material conditions necessary for its solution already exist or are at least in the process of formation. In broad outlines, we can designate the Asiatic, the ancient, the feudal and the modern bourgeois methods of production as so many epochs in the progress of the economic formation of society. The bourgeois relations of production are the last antagonistic form of the social process of production—antagonistic not in the sense of individual antagonism, but of one arising from conditions surrounding the life of individuals in society; at the same time the productive forces developing in the womb of bourgeois society create the material conditions for the solution of that antagonism. This social formation constitutes, therefore, the closing chapter of the prehistoric stage of human society" (Marx [1859] 1911: 11–13).

It is a view, nevertheless, that had been taking shape in his mind for years. For instance, in a series of notes and mini-essays later known as the *Economic and Philosophic Manuscripts of 1844*, he several times takes pause to consider human development from the point of view of human history. "Communism," Marx (1988a: 114) writes, "is the position as the negation of the negation, and is hence the *actual* phase necessary for the next stage of historical development in the process of human emancipation and recovery. *Communism* is the necessary pattern and the dynamic of the immediate future, but communism as such is not the goal of human development—the structure of human society" (emphases in the original). So, human development in its historical and social contexts are key questions for Marx. And this view would persist in his overall outlook.

*Chapter 6: A History of Struggles.* Marx and Engels were interested in how social class relations shape social systems and the history they foster. So central is the issue of classes and the struggle in which they are pitted that our writing duo placed a rather large claim at the beginning of their most publicly well-known work: "The history of all hitherto existing society is the history of class struggles" (Marx and Engels [1848] 1978d: 473). In later editions, having been exposed to emerging anthropological knowledge, Engels later felt the need to footnote this claim with the proviso that The Manifesto was referring to "written history," as knowledge of pre-historic peoples was hardly known when they initially wrote. For Marx, still, one can hardly make sense of written history without understanding the class structure upon which social systems rest.[3]

*Chapter 7: Mystical Consciousness.* Clear thinking is necessary for any and all scientific endeavors. Perhaps the greatest hurdle placed in front of the human sciences is the faulty forms of knowledge to which they and their subject matter are exposed. Rocks and fish do not have opinions, ideologies, or gods, after all. As such, in a letter in the *Deutsch-Franzosische Jahrbücher* which asserted that rational scientific knowledge should inform our political action, Marx (1975f: 144) argued for the "reform of consciousness not through dogmas, but by analyzing the mystical consciousness that is unintelligible to itself, whether it manifests itself in a religious or a political form." This comment is hardly alone in terms of his critical attitude toward mystical and mystifying knowledge, as "Nothing is easier than to invent mystical causes, i.e., phrases in which

---

3   It is important to note that Marx did not claim to be the first or only person to grasp the importance of studying classes: "Now as for myself, I do not claim to have discovered either the existence of classes in modern society or the class struggle between them. Long before me, bourgeois historians had described the historical development of this struggle between the classes, as had bourgeois economists their economic anatomy" (Marx 1983c: 62).

common sense is lacking" (Marx 1982: 96). In another instance, he criticizes Hegel's "pantheistic mysticism" as well as other forms of mysticism where "Reality is expressed not as itself but as another reality" (Marx 1975b: 7, 8).

*Chapter 8: Illusions to this Day.* Though people often interpret the typical behavior of their own time period as a product of human nature, this is an "illusion [that] has been common to each new epoch to this day" (Marx 1973b: 83). In modernity, it is the institutions "of bourgeois society, which economists try to pass off as natural and as such, eternal" (Marx [1847] n.d.: 121). This outlook stifles our ability to grasp modernity's origins, its historic uniqueness, and its contemporary limits and to think beyond them. Such mystifications are great aids to those who defend, benefit from, and/or rule such a system.

*Chapter 9: An Inverted World.* Not only do we suffer illusions common to this day but modernity presents us with forms of knowledge that are *backwards* in relation to their real causal relationships. In his Introduction to his *Contribution to the Critique of Hegel's Philosophy of Law*, Marx (1975c: 175) writes that "Man makes religion, religion does not make man. … This state, this society, produce religion, an inverted world-consciousness, because they are in an inverted world." And Marx and Engels (1976: 36) write in *The German Ideology*: "If in all ideology men and their relations appear upside-down as in a camera obscura, this phenomenon arises just as much from their historical life-process as the inversion of objects on the retina does from their physical life-process." In short, modern forms of knowledge not only can be illusory or mystifying but are in fact backward, particularly in terms of cause and effect. This theme of "inversion" takes a prominent place in Marx's outlook.[4]

---

4  For example: "The correct method is stood on its head. The simplest thing becomes the most complicated, and the most complicated the simplest. What ought to be the starting point becomes a mystical outcome, and what ought to be the rational outcome becomes the mystical starting point" (Marx 1975b: 40). One inversion that modernity tells itself, and thus us, is that it represents human beings overcoming their historical alienation from their true nature, which the market now reflects, when, in fact, we have actually reached a higher level of alienation than perhaps ever. Or, as Marx states, "Hence the greater and the more developed the social power appears to be within the private property relationship, the more egoistic, asocial, and estranged from his own nature does man become" (Marx 1975a: 220). Another form of this inversion is expressed in the belief that political power as found in the modern state is but a reflection of society in general's need for some sort of organized institution of authority and decision-making. The result here is the ideological belief that the modern state is but a representative of the necessity for any and all societies to have states. But, as Marx argues, "The abstraction of the *state as such* belongs only to modern times, because the abstraction of private life belongs only to modern times. The abstraction of the *political state* is a modern product" (Marx 1975b: 32).

*Chapter 10: Educating the Educator.* We often must take down our own idols once we realize an authority figure—father, mother, priest, teacher, governor—may not be any more knowledgeable than the jester, the fool, or the mad. As Marx (1978: 144), in his Theses on Feuerbach, wrote: "The materialist doctrine that men are products of circumstances and upbringing, and that, therefore, changed men are products of other circumstances and changed upbringing, forgets that it is men who change circumstances and that it is essential to educate the educator himself." Knowledge is rarely neutral and some supports the powers-that-be, whether that be a common illusion or an inverted belief. The educator, just as ourselves, must remain vigilant against knowledge that misleads.

*Chapter 11: Middle Class Snobbism.* Between the upper "bourgeois" class and a put-upon working "proletarian" class are the middle classes. Some of these are small business owners, others are educated professionals, and perhaps a few are well-paid laborers. In any case, the middle classes seem to identify more with their wealth accumulating superiors than their more closely connected working class compatriots. The middle classes in some ways even see themselves as superior to the upper classes, who they often view as decadent and vulgar. In any case, Marx (1985a: 377), despite growing up as one of them, sometimes found attitudes among the middle class as particularly irksome: "Moreover, although I had only read, or rather leafed through, very little of Schmidt's stuff, I have at heart always detested the chap as the quintessence of middle class snobbism, no less revolting in literature than elsewhere."

*Chapter 12: Windy Idealists and Frothy Youth.* Though it is not perfectly accurate to say that he saw this group as a "class," Marx (1989a: 85) nevertheless noted that "the windy idealists and frothy youths (the students at the Universities) of the middle class, bureaucracy and aristocracy" were a central part of the modern experience. And there can be no doubt that university students and their styles, tastes, artistic products, political behavior, and philosophies of life often leave a mark on other segments of society that ripple throughout generations after them, changing the world in innumerable ways.

*Chapter 13: Pauperism and the Artificially Impoverished.* We still treat poverty as if it is some mystery beyond our comprehension, even though it is produced by the very nature of modernity: "The modern laborer, on the contrary, instead of rising with the progress of industry, sinks deeper and deeper below the conditions of existence of his own class. He becomes a pauper, and pauperism develops more rapidly than population and wealth" (Marx and Engels [1848] 1978d: 483). While both then just as now we tend to blame and vilify the poor as authors of the conditions they suffer, for Marx, poverty follows the modern system wherever it establishes itself.[5] Poverty is both built into the system and can be inflated (or deflated) by acts of corporations or from state policies and, as such, some of those suffering poverty are "not the *naturally arising* poor but the *artificially impoverished*" (Marx 1975c: 186–187).

*Chapter 14: Social Scum.* Some people refuse to participate in the "normal" behavior associated with roles of their class station. Some people become involved in dealing drugs, graft, thievery, prostitution, and whatnot. In addition, this "'dangerous class,' the social scum, that passively rotting mass thrown off by the lowest layers of old society" can also become a "bribed tool of reactionary intrigue" (Marx and Engels [1848] 1978d: 482). The working class is not simply composed of noble toilers but, instead, such class conditions produce groups that prey upon the laboring people upon which everyone depends.

*Chapter 15: Of Souls, Sighs, and Opium.* If you were to ask the average person on the street to provide a quote from Marx, among the most common responses would be, "Religion is the opium of the people" (or some variation). Of course, Marx's stance toward religion was more nuanced and complex than that one quote allows but it does stand as a starting-point for grasping his critique of the institution. Here is his statement more fully: "*Religious* distress is at the same time the *expression* of real distress and also the *protest* against real distress. Religion is the sigh of the oppressed creature, the heart of a heartless world, just as it is the spirit of spiritless conditions. It is the *opium* of the people" (Marx 1975c: 175; emphases in the original). Marx sees religion as something shaped by material forces, in the present no less than in the past. And if those material forces celebrate the wealthy at the expense of the poor, then we should not be surprised at religion's adaptation to these structures of power and privilege.[6]

---

5   "At first, therefore, England tried to abolish pauperism by charity and administrative measures. Then it came to see in the progressive advance of pauperism not the inevitable consequence of modern industry but, on the contrary, the consequence of the English poor rate. It regarded the universal distress merely as a specific feature of English legislation. What was previously ascribed to a lack of charity now began to be attributed to an excess of charity. Finally, poverty came to be regarded as the fault of the poor themselves, and consequently they were punished for it" (Marx 1975d: 195).

6   For example: "The social principles of Christianity justified the slavery of antiquity, glorified serfdom of the Middle Ages and are capable, in case of need, of defending the oppression of the proletariat, even if with somewhat doleful grimaces.... The social principles of Christianity preach the necessity of a ruling and an oppressed class, and for the latter all they have to offer is the pious wish that the former may be charitable.... The social principles of Christianity declare all the vile acts of the oppressors against the oppressed to be either a just punishment for original sin and other sins, or trials which the Lord, in his infinite wisdom, ordains for the redeemed.... The social principles of Christianity preach cowardice, self-contempt, abasement, submissiveness and humbleness.... The social principles of Christianity are sneaking and hypocritical, and the proletariat is revolutionary" (Marx 1976a: 231).

*Chapter 16: The Cult of Nature.* Sometimes the prescience and range of material in Marx's writings are remarkable. For instance, both casual and even serious students might be surprised to see him (and Engels) commenting on the "cult of nature," filled with "mysterious hints and astonished philistine notions about Nostradamus' prophesies, second sight in Scotsmen and animal magnetism ... impotent expressions of fanatic malignity and a collection of Sancho Panza maxims and rules of wisdom ... such is the touching picture opened up to us by the religion of the new age" (Marx and Engels 1978c: 245–246). The spread mystical nonsense has been one of the hallmarks of modernity—no less evident in Marx's time than in ours—as human conditions of alienation persist and with religion both a consequence of this alienation and presenting itself as its solution.

*Chapter 17: World Literature.* By the turn of the millennium, we had heard the term "globalization" innumerable times. Different features have been identified as to what makes the world a "globalized" one. One regular claim concerns the increasing homogenization of the world's cultures. But this is nothing new: "And as in material, so also in intellectual production. The intellectual creations of individual nations become common property ... and from the numerous national and local literatures, there arises a world literature" (Marx and Engels [1848] 1978d: 476–477). Though this is not a recent development, today it has new leading progenitors e.g., Disney, Hollywood. In any case, the emergence of a world culture was something Marx clearly saw. And this process only accelerates with growth in the complexity and reach of modern technology—today's Internet is simply the most recent example.

*Chapter 18: Modern Society's All-Dominating Power.* The serious student of Marx knows that the topic he wrote most about was capitalism and its influence on modern society. It is a shame that many in the social sciences have reduced Marx's ideas down to "communism" and "Russia failed, and with it so did Marx," a sort of non-sequitur we would not tolerate in interpretations of any other scholar, classic or otherwise. In any case, Marx's *Grundrisse* is a massive set of notes he wrote between *A Contribution to the Critique of Political Economy* (1859) and *Capital* (1867). It is often read as a preparatory work for his latter magnum opus. And though such interpretations are not off the mark, the *Grundrisse* is its own piece, full of detailed exposition and insightful commentary. What perhaps unites all three works is the central role Marx sees capital playing in modern society and thus the central role its analysis must play in our own understanding of modernity: "Capital is the all-dominating economic power of bourgeois society. It must form the starting-point as well as the finishing point, and must be dealt with before landed property. After both have been examined in particular, their interrelation must be examined" (Marx 1973b:

107). Not to do so would be to misconceptualize a "theory of capital, that is the modern order of society" (Marx 1979b: 324). And, therefore, as capital and its market shape and dominate more and more social relations until they are *the* social relation, if you do not place capital at the center of your study, you are doing it wrong and you are likely to mistakenly find that problems of modernity are caused by some force outside the system. Thus, theorists in Marx's tradition should "detest the kind of explanation which solves a problem by consigning it to some other locality" (Marx 1991c: 78).

*Chapter 19: An Impulse Never Before Known.* As the modern market and its class of caretakers took shape in early capitalist development, they set in motion many things, and one of them was competition for labor and resources and they began to look outside of Europe for their endeavors. Their states took up this challenge with the establishment of colonies to enrich their ruling classes and the mother country, where "the increase in the means of exchange and in commodities generally, gave to commerce, to navigation, to industry, an impulse never before known, and thereby, to the revolutionary element in the tottering feudal society, a rapid development" (Marx and Engels [1848] 1978d: 474). Competition amongst the bourgeoisie and the states they created for colonial holdings set off a process where they could benefit themselves by subduing lands and people far and wide and put into motion both internal and external chain reactions that birthed the world market.

*Chapter 20: Head of the Movement.* When socio-structural-historical-institutional changes take place, where and when this happens and what the results will be are shaped by "the character of those who at first stand at the head of the movement" (Marx 1989d: 136–137). Capitalist development thus determined what sort of cultural norms would be adopted as the dominant ones. As a result, the European bourgeoisie brought with them their form of family, their forms of knowledge, language, religion, morality, technology, and so on everywhere they settled. But this process was and is uneven and thus the empirical conditions we examine today were and still are shaped by their timing and geography.

*Chapter 21: Absurd Epidemics.* Prior to modernity, an overproduction of goods was something to celebrate or take advantage of, a social boon even. In such an instance, a surplus might be distributed among people for consumption (for it may not last long), traded to gain other resources (as there are things we might need instead of extra wheat we cannot eat before it rots) or for political purposes (to build alliances), or even used for savings (for when harsh times return, as they always so). But in modernity, periodic crises of overproduction threaten "the existence of the entire bourgeois society," during which "a great part not only of the existing products, but also of the previously created productive forces, are periodically destroyed," emblematic of "an epidemic that, in all earlier epochs, would have seemed an absurdity—the epidemic of over-production ... there is too much civilization, too much means of subsistence, too much industry, too much commerce" (Marx and Engels [1848] 1978d: 478). And why? Too much stuff creates imbalances in the market, where supply outstrips demand, prices fall, profits collapse, and with them jobs and businesses—and when this demand continues to fall a crisis ensues. Such epidemics are another backward feature of our inverted modern world.

*Chapter 22: Swindling Joint-Stock Companies.* Today, we have what we call "blue-collar" crime and "white-collar" crime, the latter of which entails price fixing, collusion, bribery, fraud, graft, embezzlement, dumping dangerous products, among other things. Marx foresaw this pattern of "myriads of swindling joint stock companies ... springing up like mushrooms" (Marx 1985c: 551).[7] As a socially dominant class, the modern business class leads the way in committing criminal acts and getting away with them, as every criminologist knows.

*Chapter 23: Machines.* Sometimes sociologists, anthropologists, geographers, and/or historians categorize modern society not as a "capitalist" society but as an "industrial" or, commonly today, "post-industrial" society. What is important here is not so much the categorization (though that has its own problems, such as erasing "capital" from that categorization) but rather that machinery is at the center of what it means to be modern. For Marx ([1847] n.d.: 167–168), however, an analytical focus on machinery is diluted unless a class component accompanies it: "In England, strikes have regularly given rise to the invention and application of new machines. Machines were, it may be said, the weapon employed by the capitalists to quell the revolt of specialized labor." And this early observation about machines and class dynamics in capitalism is a topic he would return to in his mature work. Machines in a capitalist society are not neutral things but things capitalists use to control labor, to save money in

---

7 Also see: "The railways sprang up first as the *couronnement de l'oeuvre* in those countries where *modern industry was most developed,* England, United States, Belgium, France, etc. I call them the *'couronnement de l'oeuvre'* not only in the sense that they were at last (together with steamships for oceanic intercourse and the telegraphs) the *means of communication* adequate to the modern means of production, but also in so far as they were the basis of immense joint stock companies, forming at the same time a new starting point for all *other sorts* of joint stock companies, to commence by banking companies. They gave in one word, an impetus never before suspected to the *concentration of capital,* and also to the accelerated and immensely *enlarged cosmopolitan activity of loanable capital,* thus embracing the whole world in a network of financial swindling and mutual indebtedness, the capitalist form of 'international' brotherhood" (Marx 1991b: 356).

their expenditures on the production process, and, when they replace more and more workers, something that introduces a crisis of consumptive demand into the system. Machines and their use, then, express both the struggles and an internal contradiction within capitalist class relations.

*Chapter 24: Rule of the Towns.* Modernity has geographic relationships embedded in it. In modern society, "The bourgeoisie has subjected the country to the rule of the towns. It has created enormous cities, has greatly increased the urban population as compared with the rural, and has rescued a considerable part of the population from the idiocy of rural life" (Marx and Engels [1848] 1978d: 477). In short, urban life prevails and dominates over rural life. Farming is oriented toward feeding cities and their mineral resources are extracted for the industrial machine. Though we may debate whether it is accurate to describe "rural life" as a world of "idiocy" as Marx and Engels do here, it is true that the cosmopolitan character of city life is one of modernity's distinguishing features. There are more people, more cultures, languages, arts, ideas, beliefs, and styles of life in metropolitan centers than elsewhere. They are a central place where modernity is experienced.

*Chapter 25: Feverish Anxiety and Astonishment.* What is it like to experience modernity subjectively or psychologically? What sort of mental state do its material conditions elicit? Writing to his daughters, Marx (1989b: 154) described the reaction of several new arrivals to the city:

> Here in London life is just now dull enough. The cousins from the country are thronging its streets. You recognize them at once by their bewildered airs, their astonishment at everything they see and their feverish anxiety at the convolution of horses, cabs, omnibuses, people, babies, and dogs.

Here, prefacing Simmel's classic essay, "The Metropolis," Marx captures that moment of bewilderment that life in a city center can conjure. Upon first exposure, our sensory mechanisms are unprepared and have to catch up with urban conditions in their speed and the excitement and exhilaration that envelops us in return.

*Chapter 26: Solids Melting into Air.* The previous chapter considered what an individual's response to modernity might be in psychological or emotional terms. But if we imagine a sort of psychology for society at large, what might that experience be like? We find a possible answer in The Manifesto and it is worth quoting at length:

> The bourgeoisie cannot exist without constantly revolutionising the instruments of production, and thereby the relations of production, and

with them the whole relations of society. Conservation of the old modes of production in unaltered forms, was, on the contrary, the first condition of existence for all earlier industrial classes. Constant revolutionising of production, uninterrupted disturbance of all social conditions, everlasting uncertainty and agitation distinguish the bourgeois epoch from all earlier ones. All fixed, fast-frozen relations, with their train of ancient and venerable prejudices and opinions, are swept away, all new-formed ones become antiquated before they can ossify. All that is solid melts into air, all that is holy is profaned, and man is at last compelled to face with sober senses, his real conditions of life, and his relations with his kind.

MARX and ENGELS [1848] 1978d: 476

This evocative statement captures how modernity's living conditions produce a world without stability, in material and in mind. When people feel as if they never have sure footing in modernity, there is a real reason why.

*Chapter 27: Civilization and Barbarism.* Intentional and unintentional apologists for modernity have a habit of describing their world as civilization or "civilized." Or, at least that was the case early on (today, social scientists refer to Mesopotamia as the "cradle of civilization," generally meaning the first large-scale settlements). The nature of modernity "draws all, even the most barbarian, nations into civilization. The cheap prices of its commodities are the heavy artillery with which it batters down all Chinese walls, with which it forces the barbarians' intensely obstinate hatred of foreigners to capitulate. It compels all nations, on pain of extinction, to adopt the bourgeois mode of production; it compels them to introduce what it calls civilization into their midst, i.e., to become bourgeois themselves. In one word, it creates a world after its own image.... Just as it has made the country dependent on the towns, so it has made barbarian and semi-barbarian countries dependent on the civilized ones, nations of peasants on nations of bourgeois, the East on the West" (Marx and Engels [1848] 1978d: 477).[8] This juxtaposition of modern "civilized" peoples to non-modern "barbarian" societies was common in Marx's day. So-called barbarians sometimes did have practices we might find shocking today, including human sacrifice, child marriage, bride-stealing, and so on. However, it was and is easy to overstate such judgments, after all, many of those societies were able to keep their systems intact for an untold number of years. And yet

---

8   Also: "Rivers of Californian gold are pouring over America and the Asiatic coast of the Pacific Ocean, and dragging the most reluctant barbarian nations into world trade, into civilization" (Marx and Engels 1978b: 265).

one of "civilization's" highest values commonly prioritizes profits over people.[9] It is, it seems, easy to overstate how civilized "civilization" in fact is and understate what it shares with so-called "barbaric" practices we readily criticize.

*Chapter 28: Celebrating Orgies, Blood, and Fire.* This peculiar chapter title comes from two remarks Marx makes in *Capital*. The first is after he reviews how industry extended the working-day beyond 12 hours, introduced intensely violent machinery, exploited labor without regard to age, sex, day or night, and thus, "Capital celebrated its orgies" (Marx [1867] 1992: 264). Later, he highlights how the transformation of "slave, serf, and bondman" into a "free seller of labor-power" was a result of "their expropriation ... written in the annals of mankind in letters of blood and fire" (Marx [1867] 1992: 660). Like many of Marx's observations, these two are trenchant and pregnant with meaning, highlighting how the capitalist class goes about doing something that's incredibly destructive for one sector of society but very profitable for themselves. Given its history, the capitalist system appears reliant on this dynamic.

*Chapter 29: The Bureaucracy and the Bureaucrats.* Though many modern institutions rely on it, bureaucratic organization was, at one time, new enough that social thinkers remarked on and evaluated it. Sociology students learn that Max Weber first introduced the discussion of bureaucracy to the social sciences. But a short excerpt from Marx's work, *Contribution to the Critique of Hegel's Philosophy of Law*, dispels that notion, where he argues that, in the division of labor in the "business of government,"

> Individuals must prove their suitability for government service—i.e., pass examinations. The choice of specific individuals for public office is the prerogative of monarchial state authority.... The responsibility of office is the duty of civil servants and their life's vocation. They must therefore receive salaries from the state. The guarantee against the abuse of bureaucratic power is partly the hierarchical stature and accountability of the bureaucracy, and on the other hand the rights which communities and corporations possess. The humanity of the bureaucracy depends partly on the "direct moral and intellectual education," partly on the "size of the state." Officials form the "major part of the middle estate." Against their becoming an "aristocracy and arbitrary domination" protection is

---

9  For example: "Capital over here isn't as much subject to police supervision as on the Continent, and hence it's of no concern whatever to the railway directors how many people are killed during an excursion season, if only the balance looks to the comfortable side" (Marx 1985c: 551).

provided, partly by "the institutions of sovereignty working from above," and partly by "the corporate institutions' rights exercised from below." The "middle estate" is the estate of "education"....

The corporations are the materialism of the bureaucracy, and the bureaucracy is the spiritualism of the corporations. The corporation is the bureaucracy of civil society; the bureaucracy is the corporation of the state.... The same spirit which creates the corporation in society creates bureaucracy in the state. Hence, the attack on the spirit of the corporation is an attack on the spirit of the bureaucracy.

MARX 1975b: 44–45

As a form of organizing institutional authority and decision-making, bureaucracy is a "hierarchy of knowledge" and thus is highly involved in creating and perpetuating social inequality (Marx 1975b: 46, 60). Those with the knowledge to run the bureaucracy enjoy special status, authority, and influence. Finally, the last comment in the quote above tells us much about why some people react negatively toward criticism of the business class, as they and their companies are seen as embodiments of the nation, its identity, and thus to attack them is to attack the people.

*Chapter 30: The Economic Existence of the State.* Certainly no one likes paying taxes and everyone wishes they were less burdensome. However, taxes serve an important function in modern society: "Taxes are the existence of the state expressed in economic terms. Civil servants and priests, soldiers and ballet-dancers, schoolmasters and police constables, Greek museums and Gothic steeples, civil list and services list—the common seed within which all these fabulous beings slumber in embryo is *taxation*" (Marx 1976b: 328; emphasis in the original). And while "the state" often has connotations of the ruling class in Marx's writings, it is easy to forget that, once they are established, governments provide roads, ports, museums, libraries, public parks, grade schools, civil servants, and so on. Modern life would not be the one we know absent such things.

*Chapter 31: Democracy for their Truth.* The bourgeoisie has consistently flattered itself about its political system. But it is *their* system, not one of the people as a whole. As such, Marx (1975b: 31) tells us that, "Incidentally, it goes without saying that all forms of the state have democracy *for* their truth and that they are therefore untrue insofar as they are not democracy" (emphasis in the original). To the extent a state's own presentation to us—i.e., as a source of democracy and freedom—does not actually represent public participation and will is the extent to which political society is living a mystifying untruth.

*Chapter 32: Parliamentary Disease and the Holy Ghost*. It is commonly assumed that people in democratic societies get the governments they deserve. If the public voted them in, then the public gets the state representatives it wanted and the laws they enact reflect that public's will. As a result, us moderns seem to have "indeed been infected with the parliamentary disease, believing that, with the popular vote, the Holy Ghost is poured upon those elected, that meetings of the faction are transformed into infallible councils and factional resolutions into sacrosanct dogma" (Marx and Engels 1991: 400). If political parties serve a special interest that is not society as a whole, then who do they serve?[10] Formal voting is necessary but not sufficient for a society to be a democracy nor does it mean that its governing institutions represent the common interests, even though the existence of the franchise tends to make it look this way.

*Chapter 33: The Executive Committee*. The modern world is formally ruled by governments. But what sort of government and what is its main function?

> Each step in the development of the bourgeoisie was accompanied by a corresponding political advance of that class.... [T]he bourgeoisie has at last, since the establishment of Modern Industry and of the world market, conquered for itself, in the modern representative State, exclusive political sway. The executive of the modern State is but a committee for managing the common affairs of the whole bourgeoisie.
> MARX and ENGELS [1848] 1978d: 475

Modern society is managed by an organization of the business class and that organization—i.e., the state—is structured to serve the interests and needs of that same class, e.g., regulate labor, sign treaties, control a money supply, lend

---

10   "Far from desiring to transform the whole of society for the revolutionary proletarians, the democratic petty bourgeois strive for a change in social conditions by means of which the existing society will be made as tolerable and comfortable as possible for them. Hence they demand above all a diminution of state expenditure by curtailing the bureaucracy and shifting the bulk of the taxes on to the big landowners and bourgeois.... Even where there is no prospect whatever of their being elected, the workers must put up their own candidates in order to preserve their independence, to count their forces and to lay before the public their revolutionary attitude and party standpoint. In this connection they must now allow themselves to be bribed by such arguments of the democrats as, for example, that by so doing they are splitting the democratic party and giving the reactionaries the possibility of victory. The ultimate purpose of all such phrases is to dupe the proletariat. The advance which the proletarian party is bound to make by such independent action is infinitely more important than the disadvantage that might be incurred by the presence of a few reactionaries in the representative body" (Marx and Engels 1978a: 280, 284).

money and manage the national debt, and so on. To think the modern state is somehow something other than a "bourgeois" organization is to miss the truth of the matter.

*Chapter 34: Modern Mythology and its Goddesses.* Marx (1991a: 283) directed a broadside against classically liberal values, such as those held by a "whole gang of immature undergraduates and over-wise graduates who want to give socialism a 'higher, idealistic' orientation, i.e., substitute for the materialist basis (which calls for serious, objective study if one is to operate thereon) a modern mythology with its goddesses of Justice, Liberty, Equality and *Fraternité*" (emphasis in the original). Marx takes issue with justice, liberty, equality, and fraternity not so much as principles but instead shows little patience with "vulgar-democratic phraseology" (Marx 1987: 49) whereby "all classes melt away before the solemn concept of 'humanity'" (Marx 1976b: 330). Justice, liberty, equality, and fraternity are empty and hollow in a society where most people are free to work or starve, where capital's liberty takes away the liberty of others, and people's political representation is simply choosing from among bourgeois candidates to politically represent them under the banner of the nation and slogans of "All for one!"

*Chapter 35: Rolling Back the Wheel.* The middle and professional classes may at times "fight against the bourgeoisie, [but only] to save from extinction their existence as factions of the middle class." More importantly, in contrast with liberal philosophy, many in these classes tend "conservative. Nay more, they are reactionary, for they try to roll back the wheel of history" (Marx and Engels [1848] 1978d: 482). These groups believe that the highest value is self-interest and will sell out their working class compatriots if it means voting for a candidate who promises an additional .01% return on their bank notes or pensions or to lower their taxes; this, or inflicting religiously-endorsed restrictions of some group's civil liberties. And many conservatives are not simply fiscally so but are in fact politically "reactionary" in ways similar to defenders of monarchial power of old during revolutionary times.[11] They work to thwart forms of

---

11   "The violently reactionary role played by the rule of the princes only proves that in the pores of the old society a new society has taken shape, which furthermore cannot but feel the political shell—the natural covering of the old society—as an unnatural fetter and blow it sky-high. The more primitive these new elements of social decomposition, the more conservative will even the most vigorous reaction by the old political power appear. The more advanced these new elements of social decomposition, the more reactionary will even the most harmless attempt at conservation by the old political power appear. The reaction of the rule of the princes, instead of proving that it creates the old society, proves rather that its day is over as soon as the material conditions of the old society have become obsolete. Its reaction is at the same time the reaction of the old society which is

modern progress others desire, to turn back advances made, and/or to return to a mythic world that never existed in the first place.

*Chapter 36: The Goal of Popular Desire.* Why do we treat our national state executives as if they are kings, celebrities, and whatnot when they are, bureaucratically speaking, simply the highest ranked dog-catcher? Perhaps it is because we invest in the state and its head special qualities they do not inherently have: "Properly speaking *executive power*, e.g., rather than legislative power, the *metaphysical* state function, must be the goal of popular desire" (Marx 1975b: 119). We are still beholden to the aura of authority, something modernity has mystified with its cloak of popular participation. And the goal of that popular desire is for the top bureaucrat to not only be the repository of the people's hopes, dreams, and aspirations but also to personify their ideal image of their society reflected back at them, in some almost supernatural way.

*Chapter 37: National Egoism.* Pride in one's country is almost universally embraced in modernity. For some, it goes as far as patriotism and even nationalism: "In this article I also pilloried the French Republicans ... for saving, in their national egoism, all their colors for the Empire" (Marx 1989f: 475–476). Identifying oneself with a nationhood and its accomplishments, where our nation is part of our DNA, our personhood, or self-identity, is a modern phenomenon and another one of its mystifications, a sort of tribalism writ large.

*Chapter 38: Every Sect Is Religious.* There tends to be a narrow spectrum of acceptable opinion in politics, which means those parties which commit to serving the interests of the most powerful economic cohorts receive approval, funding, and access to the levers of state. But political views outside of this spectrum exist and tend to flourish, but with a certain sort of side-effect where "every sect is religious," especially those that make the "mistake of not seeking the real basis of ... agitation in the actual elements of the class movement, but of wishing, instead, to prescribe for that movement a course determined by a certain doctrinaire recipe" (Marx 1989c: 133). Political philosophies and organizations often become strict, controlling, and demanding of conformity and purity of thought. Even mainstream parties are susceptible, especially when ideologues work their way into positions of authority. Nevertheless, whether among extremist conservatives, libertarians, or dissident socialists, communists, and/or anarchists, one often finds hardline, rigid, and ideological factions immune to facts and resistant to questioning in ways comparable to religious

---

still the official society and therefore also still in *official possession* of power or in possession of *official power*" (Marx 1976b: 327–328).

sects. One thing you will see among them less often is a warning against the "superstitious belief in authority."[12]

*Chapter 39: Disgusting Despotism.* Some states make no such claims to democratic pretences. In fact, authoritarian and dictatorial states have been quite common. There are times and places where a powerful clique does not wish for any outside public participation:

> The mantle of liberalism has been discarded and the most disgusting despotism in all its nakedness is disclosed to the eyes of the whole world.... Despotism's sole idea is contempt for man, the dehumanized man, and this idea has the advantage over many others of being at the same time a fact. The despot always sees degraded people. They drown before his eyes and for his sake in the mire of ordinary life, from which, like toads, they constantly make their appearance anew.
> MARX 1975f: 133, 138

Modernity has birthed all manner of states and potentates that ruled with an iron fist that many a feudal lord would appreciate or even envy. But this dehumanizing of others is not exclusive to dictators and potentates; even democratically elected officials can succumb to it.

*Chapter 40: The Sycophantic Babblers.* Modernity's secular priesthood tries to convince us of untruths, fabrications, happy lies, convenient illusions, and so on. This priesthood is a professional class—educated, institutionalized—and is given a daily dais from which to make declarations about the necessity and perfection of the modern political-economic system and/or to prostrate themselves for a political leader. In expressing his disdain for this state of affairs, Marx (1988b: 69) wrote:

> Once interconnection has been revealed, all theoretical belief in the perpetual necessity of the existing conditions collapses, even before the collapse takes place in practice. Here, therefore, it is completely in the interests of the ruling classes to perpetuate the unthinking confusion. And for what other reason are the sycophantic babblers paid who have no other scientific trump to play except that, in political economy, one may not think at all!

---

[12] "When Engels and I first joined the secret communist society, we did so only on condition that anything conducive to a superstitious belief in authority be eliminated from the Rules. (Lassalle subsequently operated in the reverse direction)" (Marx 1991e: 288).

Back then, Marx could see capitalism's birth, maturation, and the structural forces that inevitably would lead to its decline. Very little has changed in the interim, except that the techniques of hoodwinking the public have only grown ever more sophisticated, professionally taught, and practiced, with technology always added to the effect.[13]

*Chapter 41: The Application of Chemistry to Industry and Agriculture.* The number of advances science has brought us is too long to count. But, like machines, Marx's outlook is sensitive to how the class dynamic of capitalism can take something supposedly neutral—such as scientific knowledge—and turn it towards its own ends: "Subjection of Nature's forces to man, machinery, application of chemistry to industry and agriculture, steam-navigation, railways, electric telegraphs, clearing of whole continents for cultivation, canalization of rivers, whole populations conjured out of the ground—what earlier century had even a presentiment that such productive forces slumbered in the lap of social labor?" (Marx and Engels [1848] 1978d: 477). This comment foreshadows what we would later come to know as our environmental crisis. It has been common to assume that Earth is just too large and humans too small for us to inflict any appreciable damaging influence on it. Of course, we now know this belief to be false. Today, capitalist forms of production, consumption, and waste are bringing us to ecological ruin.

*Chapter 42: The Measure of Social Progress.* It is often erroneously argued that Marx was only concerned with social class inequality and that he found questions of gender (and race) to be superfluous. As regards to gender, informed scholars understand very well that this issue was given over to Engels in their division of labor. Engels's *Origins of the Family, Private Property, and the State* is not only part of their overall outlook but is also a foundational text in gender studies. That said, one of Marx's (1979a: 259) comments on gender provides its own sociological insight: "Anybody who knows anything of history also knows that great social changes are impossible without the female ferment. Social progress can be measured exactly by the social status of the beautiful sex (the ugly ones included)." Gender relations have a central role in both evaluating the conditions of a society's progress as a whole and identifying the areas still requiring social change. Given where women's place historically has been, their place in modernity tells us much about the social progress contained in

---

13  "Up till now it has been thought that the emergence of the Christian myths during the Roman Empire was possible only because printing had not yet been invented. Precisely the contrary. The daily press and the telegraph, which in a moment spreads its inventions over the whole earth, fabricate more myths in one day (and the bourgeois cattle believe and propagate them still further), than could have previously been produced in a century" (Marx 1989e: 117).

the system, how much of this progress has come from their efforts, and how much modernity's potential progress remains unfulfilled.

*Chapter 43: Defiling Republics.* In representing the International Working Men's Association, Marx (2000) wrote a letter to US President Abraham Lincoln that contained the following passage:

> While the workingmen, the true political powers of the North, allowed slavery to defile their own republic, while before the Negro, mastered and sold without his concurrence, they boasted it the highest prerogative of the white-skinned laborer to sell himself and choose his own master, they were unable to attain the true freedom of labor, or to support their European brethren in their struggle for emancipation; but this barrier to progress has been swept off by the red sea of civil war.

The working class has its internal factions and some of these are nationally-centered and others are due to racial separation and ideology. Marx tells us that the existence of slavery, and racial slavery at that, defiles the republics in which it exists and their pretensions to freedom and democracy. Like gender, the extent to which a society has overcome such a racial past is a key to grasping its level of social progress. In his view, we should hold "That the emancipation of the producing class is that of all human beings without distinction of sex or race" (Marx 1989g: 340).

*Chapter 44: A Fetish Dark and Mysterious.* Some money invested in production becomes "capital" once its circuit is complete. But not all money invested goes into "productive capital." Some goes into "financial" capital or what Marx sometimes called "fictitious capital." This is today's financial sector, otherwise known as Wall Street, Frankfurt, Tokyo, and other trading centers. They trade in stocks and other bearers of interest. In *Theories of Surplus-Value*, Part III, we learn:

> [*I*]*nterest-bearing capital* is the perfect fetish. It is capital in its finished form—as such representing the unity of the production process and the circulation process—and therefore yields a definite profit in a definite period of time. In the form of interest-bearing capital only this function remains, without the mediation of either production process or circulation process. Memories of the past still remain in capital and profit, although because of the divergence of profit from surplus-value and the uniform profit yielded by all capitals—that is, the general rate of profit— capital becomes very much obscured, something dark and mysterious.
>
> MARX 1971: 454–455

The commodities traded on stock exchanges shape many things outside the trading room floor. Banks, corporations, pensions, neighborhoods, entire countries can be and are molded by what happens there. And the number of ways interest-bearing stocks and bonds can be packaged and sold can proliferate to the point where it becomes a strange and hardly knowable underworld that extends from those subterranean confines and touches lives far and wide. It is hard to develop and maintain a solid sense of our conditions of existence when the causal forces that shape our world are far outside our observational reach and day-to-day direct experience.

*Chapter 45: The World Market.* Readers of Marx and Engels ([1848] 1978d: 475–476) were told that we live in a globalized economy many years before modern theorists weighed in:

> Modern industry has established the world market, for which the discovery of America paved the way. This market has given an immense development to commerce, to navigation, to communication by land. This development has, in its turn, reacted on the extension of industry; and in proportion as industry, commerce, navigation, railways extended, in the same proportion the bourgeoisie developed, increased its capital, and pushed into the background every class handed down from the Middle Ages....
>
> The need of a constantly expanding market for its products chases the bourgeoisie over the whole surface of the globe. It must nestle everywhere, settle everywhere, establish connections everywhere.
>
> The bourgeoisie has through its exploitation of the world market given a cosmopolitan character to production and consumption in every country.

The world market, always part of the capitalist system, requires an analysis in its own right. "In place of the old local and national seclusion and self-sufficiency, we have intercourse in every direction, universal inter-dependence of nations" (Marx and Engels [1848] 1978d: 477). We see this concern follow Marx through to his mature works. In the *Grundrisse*'s Introduction, Marx (1973b: 108) discusses his overall project and says that the final investigative subject should be the "world market and crises." In *Capital,* Volume III, he writes:

> And when in the 16th, and partially still in the 17th, century the sudden expansion of commerce and emergence of a new world market overwhelmingly contributed to the fall of the old mode of production and

the rise of capitalist production, this was accomplished conversely on the basis of the already existing capitalist mode of production. The world market itself forms the basis for this mode of production. On the other hand, the immanent necessity of this mode of production to produce on an ever-enlarged scale tends to extend the world market continually, so that it is not commerce in this case which revolutionises industry, but industry which constantly revolutionises commerce. Commercial supremacy itself is now linked with the prevalence to a greater or lesser degree of conditions for a large industry.

MARX [1967] 1973a: 333

And, finally, in *Theories of Surplus-Value*, Part III, he argues that, "Capitalist production rests on the value or the transformation of the labor embodied in the product into social labor. But this is only [possible] on the basis of foreign trade and of the world market. This is at once the pre-condition and the result of capitalist production" (Marx 1971: 253). Clearly, the world market was a core feature of modernity's rise, structure, and development over time and grasping it was of the highest importance for Marx. And it still should be for us, too.

*Chapter 46: The Political Chessboard.* After the Peace of Westphalia (1648), the stage was set for the rise of nation-states as legal entities whose competitors mutually recognized each other's rights to territories, self-defense, and so on. Still, given their ruling class's interest in expansion for resources, labor, and profits, it would not take long for intrigue to set in. States have jostled with each other, made alliances, encroached on each other's territories, undermined their neighbors, stabbed each other in the back, waged war, etc. And they do so with strategy, cunning, boldness, and sometimes folly. "May God damn me if there be anything more stupid than this political chessboard!" (Marx 1985b: 513).

*Chapter 47: Throwing Dust in People's Eyes.* In modernity, it is usually nation-states that go to war and this is useful for the political class and who they represent. And because war is often unpopular, "There is no better way of throwing dust in people's eyes than to set armies marching, horses stamping, and cannon thundering" (Marx 1985b: 513). War makes people lose their sense of reason and adopt a callous view of potential casualties. And waging wars against a state's enemies becomes a political tactic used against one's own people to manipulate them for political ends. Sadly, it is easier to see how the powerful in other societies do this more than it is when our own leaders do it.

*Chapter 48: Gravedigging Megalomaniacs.* There is much we can learn about modernity if we watch what the ruling class does and what they think about themselves. As human personifications of capital occupying a structural location in the class system, business leaders are compelled to act in certain ways. As accumulators of wealth—wealth dependent on its appropriation from workers—capitalists rely on workers to spend their wages (that make-up an ever-declining share of the total cost of production) on goods. That dynamic cannot continue on indefinitely because of its own internal structural logic. But, because of the way the system operates through its own laws, it is not as if the business class has a choice. However, given repeated periods of overproduction, crises, and a return to calm, there also seems to be repeated amnesia and righteous "bourgeois megalomania" (Marx 1983a: 21) toward what brings crises into being in the first place. It is as if the bourgeoisie are compelled to repeat the same behaviors over and over all the while they "are digging their own graves!" (Marx 1991d: 299).[14]

*Chapter 49: The Sorcerer.* In folklore, a sorcerer calls up magical powers he has not yet mastered and loses control over them. Similarly, the bourgeoisie, with its market, its cultures, and its states, "has conjured up such gigantic means of production and of exchange, is like the sorcerer, who is no longer able to control the powers of the nether world whom he has called up by his spells" (Marx and Engels [1848] 1978d: 478). Not only does no one control the modern world market, there are no levers available that guarantee specific outcomes. Countries have their central banks, stock markets, interest rates, and so on, but these only manage things partially and temporarily. The ruling class can only do so much and sometimes the market eats members of that same class.

*Chapter 50: Prevailing Tendencies.* Scientists are interested in uncovering the law-like behaviors of their object of study. The same was true for Marx. In *Capital*, Volume III we find: "Under capitalist production, the general law acts as a prevailing tendency only in a very complicated and approximate manner, as a never ascertainable average of ceaseless fluctuations" and thus "There must be some counteracting influences at work, which cross and annul the effect of the general law, and which give it merely the characteristic of a tendency" (Marx [1967] 1973a: 161, 232).[15] Clearly, such law-like tendencies should be a core concern for any student who wants to make sense of what can seem capricious and chaotic in modern society. And this is true whether we are speaking about nameless bureaucrats working for world trade organizations

---

14  Also: "What the bourgeoisie, therefore, produces, above all, is its own grave-diggers" (Marx and Engels [1848] 1978d: 483).
15  Marx ([1867] 1992) also uses the term *laws of motion* to describe what he wants to uncover about capitalism as a system.

and on their associated treaties, policy-planners in nation-states, management of regional economic concerns, or the small business down on the street corner.

*Chapter 51: Common Ruin.* What happens if the working classes fail to unite and win the world? What if the ruling class, the middle class, and the working class all turn their aim on each other? History gives us its hints: "Freeman and slave, patrician and plebeian, lord and serf, guild-master and journeyman, in a word, oppressor and oppressed, stood in constant opposition to one another, carried on an uninterrupted, now hidden, now open fight, a fight that each time ended either in a revolutionary re-constitution of society at large, or in the common ruin of the contending classes" (Marx and Engels [1848] 1978d: 473–474). Today, "common ruin" could mean anything from a global conflagration that destroys civilization or the return of a more repressive fascist system. Or the classes could continue in their struggles while the environment collapses all around them. In any case, common ruin is one possible future that capitalism lays before us should we fail to navigate our way out of this system and into a more progressive successor.

*Chapter 52: Chains, Riddles, Worlds.* In the Manifesto, Marx and Engels ([1848] 1978d: 500) proclaim, "The proletarians have nothing to lose but their chains. They have a world to win." Not only would it be an oversight to omit this political call to action in any overview of Marx's outlook, some recognition of his approach to communism is also necessary in terms of how he sees it as answering history's "riddle."

> [C]ommunism already knows itself to be re-integration or return of man to himself ... the complete return of man to himself as a social (i.e., human) being ... [and a] resolution of the conflict between man and nature and between man and man—the true resolution of the strife between existence and essence, between objectification and self-confirmation, between freedom and necessity, between the individual and the species. Communism is the riddle of history solved, and it knows itself to be this solution.
> 
> MARX 1988a: 102–103

It was often Marx's habit to write in ways where many different meanings could be extracted from something he argued. Other times we are left a tantalizing comment but with little else to go on. This might be one of those times. I tried to give my view of what Marx was trying to get across in this chapter (the reader can decide on my success).

*Chapter 53: Socialist Sentimentalizing.* For Marx (1982: 104), the urge to push for socialism on moral grounds was not only a weak argument but counterproductive: "The *only point* upon which I am in complete agreement with Mr. Proudhon is the disgust he feels for socialist sentimentalizing" (Marx 1982: 104). One reason for this attitude is that "Whenever the class struggle is thrust aside as a distasteful, 'crude' manifestation, the only basis still left to socialism will be a 'true love of mankind' and empty phrases about 'justice'" (Marx and Engels 1991: 407). Marx (1976b: 322) believed that instead of "clichés about justice," socialism's potential reality rested on a practical grasp of capitalism's trajectory and unleashing the possibilities of and for socialism contained within it so that they could come into being. Appeals to peace, justice, or morality will not help this project.

*Chapter 54: Whether We Want It or Not.* The capitalist system—as a *system*—is going to do what it is going to do and it will carry the world with it. Being "in favor" or "against" capitalism sort of misses Marx's point. Capitalism's prevailing tendencies do not care and will develop and unfold regardless of our beliefs:

> In that case we do not confront the world in a doctrinaire way with a new principle: Here is the truth, kneel before it! We develop new principles for the world out of the world's own principles. We do not say to the world: Cease your struggles, they are foolish; we will give you the true slogan of struggle. We merely show the world what it is really fighting for, and consciousness is something that it *has to* acquire, even if it does not want to.
> MARX 1975f: 144; emphasis in the original

It also does not matter if one is in favor of "communism" as Marx understood it or as one of his followers understood/understands it. What *does* matter, though, is the extent to which one comes to understand (1) that the society he or she lives in will change invariably in a way where it becomes unsustainable in that same form, (2) that this eventuality is due to the inner-workings of that system and, as such, is inevitable, (3) that a new system will need to be built on the remnants of the old collapsing one, and (4) that new system can be as free or as repressive as people make it in their struggles to build anew. Marx's call is for us to not leave such outcomes to chance.

So, that's the recap of the book and the inspiration for its chapters. Professional Marxologists can decide whether it accurately reflects Marx's outlook on modernity. No doubt I omitted some elements that could have made the cut. But that said, I believe Marx's view provides us a good image of what modernity is, from where it came, and how it works and unfolds. I hope the reader agrees.

This book spent little space citing influences or in Marxian erudition in general (too much of the latter perhaps being a weakness of my previous writings on Marx). This was intentional as the goal of the book is to introduce new students and readers to modernity via Marx's overall outlook rather than to focus attention on Marx the person or Marx the scholar. But Marx is not the only thinker who has influenced my ideas and it therefore would be impossible not to have others' ideas seep into my own writing. It is perhaps appropriate to give them credit here. The works of Michel Foucault, Immanuel Wallerstein, and Bertell Ollman have each been influential on my grasp of modernity, Marx, and my writings on both. Foucault's *Madness and Civilization, Discipline and Punish, History of Sexuality*, and many of his published lectures have shaped my view of the modern world. Wallerstein's overall approach (world systems analysis) is also central to my understanding of it as well. And, my command of Marx—such as it is—would simply not be what it is without Ollman's *Alienation, Dialectical Investigations*, and *Dance of the Dialectic*, as well as several of his published articles. I am grateful for their work and owe them an unpayable debt for it.

Additionally, it would be remiss if I failed to mention Marshall Berman's, *All That's Solid Melts into Air: The Experience of Modernity*. While I did not consult that text directly in writing this book, after reading it during my first years in graduate school, his chapter on The Manifesto had an impact on my thinking about both modernity and Marx's thoughts on it. I do not remember much about that book other than how he portrayed Marx's words "all that is solid, melts into air" as a succinct encapsulation of the modern experience. That idea stuck with me ever since I read it. Not only was devoting a chapter to it no doubt a necessity, but it is perhaps *the* one past source that connected the idea of "modernity" in my mind with Marx's overall project.

This book is firmly rooted in the ideas of Marx, believes that his vision of the modern world was relatively accurate, and that that world is still with us. And when that modern world is obdurate and operates nakedly and openly in ways he described, on occasion mainstream media outlets take notice. For instance, in 2014, Sean McElwee published an article in *Rolling Stone* magazine (January 30), "Marx Was Right: Five Surprising Ways Karl Marx Predicted 2014." While no exegesis on the nature of modernity as a whole and Marx's take on it, *Rolling Stone* was not cowed by the boogieman Marx has always represented in modern America. In this piece, McElwee points out that Marx's models provide a grasp of the inherently chaotic nature of capitalism, especially as expressed in deepening inequality, the rise of fictitious capital, and the housing market crash of 2007–2009. He also recognizes how Marx understood capitalism's drive to unleash our imaginary appetites, this time for things like the newest iPhone (or other soon-to-be released gadgets). Finally, McElwee notes that Marx foresaw the globalization of capitalism (e.g., the International Monetary Fund), the trend toward predatory monopolies (e.g., Walmart), and the persistence of an industrial reserve army (e.g., low-wages and big profits). As seen in this article, it does not take a Ph.D. to understand that the modern world is still much like the one that Marx described. Marx's approach to sociological inquiry is a type of knowledge we must acquire if we are to demystify our own minds, embrace the fruits of the modern world, and build a bridge to a new one.

CHAPTER 56

# Postmodernism?

In the 1970s (though others date it earlier), the idea of "postmodernism" gained traction with intellectuals in the arts and sciences. For artists and architects, postmodernism referred to emergent styles coming after the period already designated as "modern." For social thinkers, the concept of postmodernism rested on the claim that "modernity" as a unique historical period had passed and that we subsequently needed new modes of thinking to capture the present moment (Lyotard [1979] 1984). To be taken seriously, such a claim must go beyond assertion; it must *demonstrate* that modernity is now behind us. But postmodern social theorists have never demonstrated any such thing, nor can they. Capital remains our social ordering principle. The development of the world market and of world culture continue apace. Cities rise out of the ground like they have in the past and they still house the rush of market society's pace and complexity. Nation-states wage war for reasons they always have. Capitalism's classes are still locked in the same struggle they have always been in. Despots still rise and later fall. None-too-few self-declared socialists still engage in sentimentalism and/or jingoism, as do the religious and the new agers and the system's liberal and conservative apologists.

Not only are postmodernist claims about modernity's passing flimsy at best, but the way postmodern thought has steered social inquiry is anti-Enlightenment, anti-science, and dangerous. If that claim sounds strong, consider the following interconnected ideas that postmodernists have pushed: anti-foundationalism, science as just one form of storytelling, and radical relativism. Below I address each of these issues in turn.

First, anti-foundationalism. In this claim, traditional social theory has tended to privilege some assumption about the nature of reality, often a "first assumption" as a sort of ontological foundation—e.g., What must we assume to be true before continuing with an investigation? What is at the basis of sociological realities in such a way that other things cannot really precede them? Marx, of course, thought that labor was at the foundation of society. Habermas (1981a, 1981b) accepted this premise and later added communicative action as a co-basis. So foundational assumptions starting here would be, "Without labor and communication there is simply no way humans could create a world in which to live." Postmodern theorists reject the consideration of such foundations. For them, our social relations are free-floating things without roots, beginnings, ends, and/or bases. But this argument is simply claims-making without either a demonstration of how previous positions were wrong or a justification of its own internal merits, which seem self-justifying and thus tautological.

Second, postmodern theory argues that all the methods that human beings have invented to get ideas across are simply and only forms of storytelling. And there are many ways to tell stories. Who gets to tell their stories has historically involved relations of power and privilege, with some people and groups getting silenced in the process. Who knows how many ways of viewing and understanding the world we will miss if we assume some forms of storytelling are better than others? Not only is that exclusionary but all stories are told from a point of view. And in the West, science emerged as the form of storytelling with the highest status. But science has been forged mainly by privileged (white, heterosexual, Western, colonialist) men in dominant institutions and this has excluded a wide variety of knowledge and experiences from the margins. And if science is just another form of storytelling and if all people have a right to speak, then there is no reason to privilege science over other forms of knowledge—or so goes the postmodernist's argument.

A common postmodern view, therefore, is the idea that science is simply a cultural prejudice and, specifically, a Western, male, heterosexual, colonial way of knowing. While it is true that science has been used and abused to service the interests and ends of dominant groups, to mistake these as *inherent* to the idea of science, rather than the biases of those practicing it, is a failure of imagination—and a failure to understand identity/difference—of the first order. Science requires logic, data, reason, debate, peer-review, values of objectivity, and so on. These were not plucked out of thin air and created because of a desire for repressing women or the people of the "New World." Rather, they were forged because Enlightenment scientists and philosophers began to understand how our senses fool us, how appeals to authority—e.g., The Church—make us believe falsehoods, and that our subjectivity, wishes, and dreams have from little to nothing to do with establishing how the world actually works. To say that science is simply a cultural prejudice leads us to overlook the ways it has helped us overcome superstition, ignorance, stupidity, vanity, lies, and so on. The idea that science is just another way to tell stories is a direct rejection of the progressive spirit embedded in these Enlightenment principles and the victories science long struggled to win against hostile authorities. Skepticism of science equates to skepticism of the scientific *method* and thus directly denies that there is a way we can produce higher order knowledge. And whether such skepticism comes from biblical literalists, flat-earthers, climate change deniers, or postmodern social theorists, these very different groups are in this apparently similar anti-intellectual boat.

Third, given the two points above, postmodern theorists tell us we must adopt a form of radical relativism. All things are relative. No one culture is inherently good or bad. No form of knowledge is better than another. In a world with as many points of view as people, we have no foundation on which to judge ideas and there is no way science can provide true objectivity. Perception is subjective, based on the experiences and viewpoints of the individual and, therefore, there is no way to ground knowledge with any level of certainty about which we might be confident. This sleight of hand—one that replaces *subjectivity* for the search for objectivity—is another abdication of Enlightenment values. One of the genuinely progressive ideas of Western society, one to cherish and fight for, not deride, is the idea that there can be a method of knowing that relies on evidence, testing, logic, reason, and hard, continual, rigorous investigation and does so in a way that minimizes, to the best extent that we can, our subjective biases. Postmodern theory casts this principle aside as somewhere between quaint, misguided, and/or a nuisance. But even if the idea that science cannot be 100% objective is an agreeable critique, it does not follow that we should no longer strive to consistently and progressively reduce biases as much as possible. The solution is not an embrace of subjectivity but a more rigorous objectivity, including reflexivity about cultural and institutional biases that can distort scientific knowledge.

This postmodern position, too, is internally contradictory. If knowledge is relative—which is an absolutist statement—on what basis is there to accept or believe that assertion in the first place? And if knowledge is reducible to storytelling, why should we entertain postmodernism's claims at all, as the very idea of positing an argument assumes that an element of internal validity exists. Postmodernism undermines itself because it cannot defend itself using its own principles.

A resulting implication from postmodern theory is that emotional appeal becomes part of a discourse's worthiness. If it feels true, it has truth-value. And who is to say this is a problem? Under postmodern assumptions, we cannot. It is the recipient of a truth-claim that determines its value. Thus, though postmodern theorists may not say so explicitly, for those swayed by its influence, feelings and political goals establish truth-value, and data, logic, or evidence of what is possible in the world are embraced only when they service these former ends, i.e., when convenient. Every person interested in manipulating groups *en masse*—whether public relations professional, preacher, cult leader, or despot—would agree.

When I first encountered postmodern social thought, I was a bit taken aback, then a bit intrigued, and then nonplussed when I saw how smitten so many in my discipline (and others associated with it) were with what I decided had become nonsense. My first exposure was through the writings of Jean Baudrillard, whom I first read sometime around 1990–1992. I was given an anthology of his writings (Baudrillard [1988] 1989) that began with his early Marxist work. As the book unfolded, I found him becoming more abstract, cantankerous, fed up, despairing, and speculative. I found it difficult to employ his concepts in my thinking with any clarity. As I learned more about postmodernism (and that his ideas were part of that movement), it seemed to me as if long-held and established norms of reason, science, and logic were being abandoned in favor of a "say whatever the hell you want" attitude.

I was later introduced to the work of Michel Foucault and learned that he too was considered, by some, as part of this intellectual fashion. Though I, like many, found him hard to understand at first, I found new and intriguing ideas in his works and still do (except for, perhaps, *The Order of Things*). I jumped head first into reading him and concluded that he did not easily fit into the mold of a "postmodernist." In fact, the more I studied him the more I found that he was clearly within the modernist tradition, a scholar who honored empirical information, the use of logical analyses, argumentation, and so on.

I found out later that I was correct by Foucault's own account. Before his death, Foucault aligned himself with traditions classically modern and questioned whether what the postmodernists were doing was in fact a worthwhile pursuit. I wrote an article demonstrating how he adopted many of Marx's methods and concepts though, as he admitted, he intentionally hid his usage of Marx (Paolucci 2003). He claimed many people, even Marxists, could not recognize Marx when they read him and that in order to be accepted in the "right" circles one had to cite the master's sacred texts. Foucault refused to play along, even claiming he deleted his prior citations of Marx in his manuscripts. As a result, many intellectuals assumed, incorrectly, that he was unfriendly to Marx. In any case, the postmodernists came to adopt Foucault as one of their own, an idea that could not be farther from the truth of his intents and goals, in my view.

Over time, I encountered other foundational thinkers for postmodern theory: Francois Lyotard, Jean Luc Lacan, Jacques Derrida, among others. Nonsense, the lot of it, I decided. I could not make heads or tails of what they were saying most of the time and, when I could, I found simply indemonstrable or unprovable assertions and jargon so obscure that only an intellectual could mistake it for substance. And in doing so, many intellectuals seemed to find postmodernism's sloppy reasoning acceptable if it appeared to conform with their own political biases and desires. It was only later that I learned of the

Sokal Affair, which was an incisive demonstration of the problem inherent in postmodern discourse.[1]

So, postmodernism presents us with a plethora of problems. First, the entire intellectual trend bases itself on a faulty premise: that that which makes "modernity" what it is has passed and a new era is upon us (a type of claim similar to those made by globalization theorists). The fact that the claim has been entertained at all demonstrates intellectuals' failure to grasp modern society adequately in the first place, i.e., they do not study and/or understand capital and why we must do both if we are to get a handle on comprehending the modern world. Second, the academy's gullibility on postmodernism has added to something on which it has, in part, always lived, i.e., the bandwagon of trendy ideas. High-minded thinkers are often easily seduced by impenetrable rhetoric. Postmodern theory contains plenty of that. And though its presence in mainstream academic circles is much less than it once was, with so many professionals and students having been caught under its sway, its influence has resulted in a great deal of time and energy lost in social thought. Third, the remnants of postmodernism's foundations are still with us academically and politically and some critics go so far to say it tends toward fascism, this time on the left, for reasons addressed below.

Today there are unaware students at expensive schools spouting anti-liberal values and anti-scientific rhetoric in the name of progress and equality. For instance, if we look at the 2010–2017 rise of the "new political correctness" on campus, we find that it merged postmodern ideas with identity politics. For postmodern theory, knowledge, in part, is inherently imbued with qualities of those who produce it. And while for too long Western institutions have marginalized the voices of the weak, the colonized, women, and so on, postmodernism brought its adherents to the conclusion that an idea or assertion can be

---

[1] In order to demonstrate that postmodernism not only did not make internal coherent sense but also that postmodernist scholars were likely to embrace work that simply appealed to their linguistic and political biases (i.e., what sounded good to their subjective proclivities rather than being based on sound science), in 1996 Alan Sokal submitted a fake paper to the journal, *Social Text*. He described the paper as filled with postmodern jargon and quasi-scientific terms and mathematical models that a first-year graduate student would find nonsensical on the surface. Providing it the equally jargon-filled but impressive title, "Transgressing the Boundaries: Toward a Transformative Hermeneutics of Quantum Gravity," his article argued that reality did not exist. It was published after peer-review. He immediately announced the hoax and the reasons behind it, subsequently receiving praise and criticism from multiple quarters. Sokal also proclaimed his goal was to take a jab at the direction taken by leftist ideas, as, being on the left himself, he found their trajectory problematic and antithetical to sound scientific thinking.

dismissed, or at least diminished, because of from where it comes, e.g., a "white cis-gendered heterosexual male." There are at least three interconnected logical failures here to note.

First, postmodern theory assumes that knowledge forms developed by any dominant group or its members are *prima facie* suspect and lacking because of that very structural position of privilege. For example, if it was men that once dominated science as a way of knowing, then traditional science's methods are "masculine" and, as such, biased. In short, if men predominated in developing something, it is "masculine" by definition and faulty by implication. Therefore, it follows, any problematic aspects of science are not because of its methods *per se* but because science is something *men developed* and this by default is biased against women at minimum and perhaps even harms them. This may not always be stated as explicitly as this (though sometimes it is) but multiple types of postmodern arguments put forth this line of reasoning.[2] And what we have in such cases is a sort of "ad hominem" logical fallacy writ large.

Second, even if the institutional structure has been one built on racial privilege, male dominance, and heteronormativity, what does that have to do with

---

2  Feminist scholar, Laura Parson (2016), made just this argument, one that received some perhaps unwanted attention, especially from conservative critics of feminist identity politics. In it, she argued that poststructuralism "rejects objectivity" (103) and "notions of absolute truth and a single reality, which is masculine" (105). In her analysis of syllabi from STEM classes, she argued that "language used in the syllabi reflects institutionalized STEM teaching practices and views about knowledge that are inherently discriminatory to women and minorities by promoting a view of knowledge as static and unchanging" (111). One thing she singles out for criticism is that "Syllabi promote the positivist view of knowledge by suggesting that there are correct conclusions that can be drawn with the right tools" (111). She describes as "a more feminist view of knowledge" the idea that "knowledge is constructed" and "subject to change" and depicts the "male-dominated view of knowledge as one that students acquire and use [to] make the correct decision" (111). The idea that scientists believe that scientific ideas are not subject to change is a failure of understanding the basics of science of the first order. At the very center of the scientific method is changing conclusions because new data is collected, debate amongst peers, constant testing of assumptions, and so on. Further, her argument also implies that the opposite of a masculinist "objectivity" is a preferable feminist "subjectivity," which has little to do with a firm foundation of knowledge. In this form of discourse, masculine is associated with "positivism" and both are rejected as neither sufficient nor necessary for the enterprise of knowing. This position contrasts with the idea that, even given all their faults, men and traditional science and its method provided society with *progress* in the ways of knowing that should be embraced, defended, and furthered. To attach fault to ideas *just because* men supposedly developed them is reactionary at base. A copy of Parson's discussion can be found here (URL retrieved August 27, 2018): https://nsuworks.nova.edu/cgi/viewcontent.cgi?referer=http://thefederalist.com/2016/09/29/feminist-phd-candidate-science-sexist-not-subjective/&httpsredir=1&article=2467&context=tqr.

any *specific* ideas or arguments? This is a classic ecological fallacy. Are violent crime rates highest in poor, non-white neighborhoods? If so, then should the next person you meet who is poor and non-white be considered a criminal? Certainly not. But identity politics, imbued with postmodern logic, does just this with Western, white, heterosexual, cis-gendered men and the institutions and practices in which they have historically been involved. In this logic, if the biases of Western, white, colonial, straight men can be found in some forms of scientific ideas, then *science itself* and all of its claims are similarly tainted. Not only is this a non-sequitur but it echoes prior claims made by racists and anti-Semites in more than one respect. Nazis claimed that some knowledge was to be rejected because it was "Jewish science." And both Nazis and US racists would condemn an individual if they had ancestry that included someone from a contaminated group. It is unlikely that those who embrace postmodern arguments realize the parallel (they likely have never thought of it) nor would they agree with such a critique, as it appears their liberal-left orientation self-shields them from entertaining that they might share forms of argumentation with groups they would find offensive and loathsome.

By extension, the third problem with the postmodern view of knowledge, and a mirror-image of the previous one, is that postmodern identity politics teaches us to not evaluate claims based on evidence and logic but on who is doing the speaking. Here, ideas and individuality become inseparably intertwined and, as a result, to disagree with someone because one of their claims lacks substance, requires more evidence, or fails a test of logic is to "silence" them. This is especially true if the claims-maker comes from a group identity politics prioritizes and the critic comes from some group deemed more privileged. Moreover, the fair and open debate demanded of science becomes one where critics—especially if they are white, male, cis, and straight—of an *idea* can be accused of racism or sexism or homophobia against *persons* and groups should they find a particular claim faulty. To the extent this depiction accurately reflects a form of postmodern discourse, it also reveals the extent to which that discourse relies on ad hominem arguments, hasty generalizations, and the use of non-sequiturs.

In all three instances above, the priorities and tactics of identity politics usurp a commitment to the scientific and progressive principles instilled in Enlightenment ideals, a dangerous game indeed. Though liberals traditionally see themselves as counterpoints to conservatives, they share with conservatives this reactionary tendency embedded in modern discourse.

The alliance of postmodern ideas and identity politics has produced a certain authoritarian streak in the latter's activists. Speech policing today is found the halls of the academy, beginning with a charge easy to get behind but leading to some unsettling prospects. It is a laudable idea that campuses should be safe, inviting, and inclusive. And certainly, there are rules against forms of hate speech meant to make sure historically oppressed populations feel welcomed. But the range of language that is allowable narrows more and more overtime, where previous well-thought out bans against ethnic slurs open the door for requirements to use a student's preferred (sometimes invented) pronouns, where everyone, presumably, is free to make up their own gender and demand the use of associated appellations. The issue here is not that challenges to the gender binary are illegitimate but rather that the list of possibilities is ambiguous, shifting, and perhaps endless while those who violate inchoate rules can be subject to opprobrium and even disciplinary action.[3] So finely-grained have the criteria available for interpersonal surveillance become that one can commit a "microaggression" of language use or physical comportment because of "unconscious bias." And when the aggrieved party gets to identify infractions defined as such, they can be almost anything and changed without regard to consistency (see Chapter 38, Note 2).

Many social activists appear to have become dogmatic in their thinking and in their demands on society and others. Given their embrace of the idea (not unfounded) that language shapes thoughts which shapes behavior, they remain on the lookout for the slightest perceived transgressions. But there is an emphasis here on policing and censoring ideas, words, and speech that has taken a peculiar turn. Where once there arose prohibitions against words meant to demean, belittle, and/or intimidate as insults and slurs, today there is a targeting of controversial and/or unpopular and/or unwanted opinions—which are entirely different—with a similar prohibition. The idea that you defeat ideas you disagree through additional ideas and speech is seemingly missed on postmodern identity politics. For example, campuses in the West are adopting speech codes, creating "safe spaces," establishing "bias teams" to censure

---

3   In the 2010s, Facebook changed and several times added to (and subtracted from) its list of gender identity options. Going well-beyond "male, female, non-binary, trans, and other," their list, depending on what date and source you use, ranged from 51 to 71 categories from which one could choose. Conservatives, of course, were outraged and mocked the company as well as the identity-based social trend associated with the proliferation of so many terms and categories. The point here, however, is simply to show that when personal subjectivity becomes the basis for knowledge, then havoc can result in the traditional function of language. If history is any measure, we are very likely going through a period of anomic change and uncertainty and in such times there is often an explosion of possibilities. In this particular case, what is also produced is conservative reactionary fear and liberal reactionary enforcement and censure of deviations. In time, it is very likely that such lists of multiple gender identities will be reduced via a combination of social debate and scientific endorsement to four or five or so and culture will adjust and such a list of categories will become the norm, one that will seem acceptable to future conservatives as it will be what they have always known.

those with the wrong (often admittedly offensive) ideas and no-platforming speakers with whom they disagree. However, the line that demarcates "offensive" constantly moves and is redefined, where even liberal and scientific allies are called to the carpet. Professors and some students on the left today openly ponder ways in which they want free speech stifled instead of protected, seemingly unaware of the contradiction they are constructing.[4] And they have targeted offenders and gone after peoples' jobs, families, and livelihoods when they are disagreed with. In true Machiavellian fashion, there is a sense among them that all of these methods are acceptable as long as their political goals are "equality," "inclusion," and "diversity," even if their approach to such things would fit nicely in with the political witch hunts of the McCarthy variety.

We are starting to see this sort of ill-liberal behavior on our campuses more and more. Harvard student, Sandra Y.L. Korn (2014), argued that we "should give up our obsessive reliance on the doctrine of academic freedom," which would help us "consider more thoughtfully what is just." To set aside the principle of academic freedom in favor of what is considered "just" (who gets to decide?) is tantamount to tossing a live grenade into the institutions of higher learning and hoping the results favors one's side. And that this idea would come from *inside* the halls of the ivory tower is a frightening testimony to the tendencies critics of identity politics have warned about. In fact, as if more evidence was needed, this new generation increasingly supports enforcement of what can or cannot be said in the name of social justice, which we will see below with a few examples.

At the University of California at Berkeley, in January 2015, students criticized the reliance on Plato, Aristotle, Hobbes, Locke, Hegel, Marx, Weber, and Foucault—because they were white, male, and economically privileged—and the omission of non-white, non-male, and other voices in class curricula. This argument has a surface logic to it that seems reasonable until one realizes that this was in a course on *classical* social theory. The argument seems to be that wealthy, educated men from elite positions historically have dominated social institutions and thus forms of education and learning and, therefore, teaching classical social theory today should require that students read people

---

4  For instance, opening the door to speech codes and limitations in principle would allow the same tactic to be used against one's interests should the fortunes of political-institutional power shift in another direction. The failure to see this in potential is a parallel to religious groups who want to dismantle the separation of church and state. In the latter case, having one's religious beliefs and practices shape state institutions is seen as a positive just so long as it is the religious beliefs and practices one favors. However, should such a political initiative be successful, once-dominant groups could find their institutions and beliefs repressed and/or usurped after another group achieves power and uses the precedent of religion in politics to their own favor.

who were not involved in that very form of learning itself. But the first point undermines the second. While it would not be unreasonable to inspect the Western, male, colonial biases of such authors (which these critics do argue), to suggest that a class on classical social theory is remiss to teach these authors to the exclusion of others seems curious. Outside of incorporating early feminist thought from writers such as Gilman or Wollstonecraft, what other authors from the "classical" period contributed to what social theory is today? That point notwithstanding, the editorial writers recommended that "instructors attend workshops on inclusivity in the classroom," that we "restructure the way social theory is taught," "dismantle the tyranny of the white male syllabus," and demanded "the inclusion of women, people of color and LGBTQ* authors on our curricula" (see Kazuo and Perret 2015). They made no suggestions for what authors to include on this latter issue.

In February 2015, Northwestern University Professor and self-described feminist who writes about gender, politics, and the psyche, Laura Kipnis (2015), published an article in *The Chronicle of Higher Education*. There she argued that sexual panic rules on campus, as exemplified by the quick use of Title IX inquiries. Students were outraged; their petition called her article "belittling" and "inflammatory" and demanded "swift, official condemnation of the sentiments expressed by Professor Kipnis [and...] that in the future, this sort of response comes automatically."[5] Kipnis was brought up on Title IX charges for her article. During the 72-day investigation, she was prohibited from confronting her accusers, could only have a "support person"—while the university had its own attorneys—and had a gag ordered enforced that prevented her from publicly speaking about the matter. These moves, ironically, seem to be the *opposite* of traditional norms of justice and appear more akin to a kangaroo court.

In 2015 (November 20), Pew Research published the findings of a survey that found that "40% of Millennials OK with limiting speech offensive to minorities," outpacing all other generations, and with Democrats scoring 17% higher (35%) than Republicans (18%) (Poushter 2015). But who decides what is offensive? Individuals, a committee, popular opinion? How often will that bar be moved? And not only have the roles reversed—with liberals answering more censoriously than conservatives—but past witch hunts come to mind as radical groups turn inward and eventually accuse their own of heresy. For instance, staunch feminist speakers such as Germaine Greer (no platformed at Cardiff University), Julie Bindel (no platformed by the National Union of Students), and a student reading group interested in Nietzsche (University College of

---

5  A copy of the students' petition can be found here (URL retrieved August 27, 2018): https://docs.google.com/forms/d/e/1FAIpQLScr34pXKmDVPSXbi4TQx2Ypo1Rar8HOImonxxAOUhUSp-6waw/viewform.

London) have been banned from campuses (for other examples, see O'Neill 2015). In 2015, a Yale professor—in response to the University's request for respectful costumes—argued in a campus-wide email that Halloween, universities, and the lives of youth were all places that allow for "maturation" through experimenting with the "obnoxious ... inappropriate or provocative or, yes, offensive ... [and should allow for a] regressive, or even transgressive experience" and that the University's costume recommendations represented an "institutional (which is to say: bureaucratic and administrative) exercise of implied control over college students" and expressed a worldview that turns colleges into "places of censure and prohibition." Student activists wanted none of this and called for her firing or resignation. When her colleague (and husband) defended her statement, they called for his firing too (Hudler 2015).

In their use of intimidation tactics to shut down campus and public speakers they do not like, such activists' strategy has not been to win the debate of ideas but to shout down opponents and directly or indirectly threaten them with violence.[6] In a 2016 incident at the University of Missouri, Assistant Professor Melissa Glick called for "muscle" to help her shoo away a reporter from a university paper covering on-campus protests. If conservatives were doing this to liberals on campus, the liberals would rightly decry this as the use of fascist tactics. It should not surprise us, then, when even neo-conservatives figure out that, "The Campus Left and the Alt-Right Are Natural Allies" (see Willick 2016). Liberal activists, however, usually imagine criticisms of them can only come from the right and not from a point of view further left than they are. Worse yet, there is a tendency to assume that criticism of their tactics means one supports sexism, racism, homophobia, and so on. One can certainly favor the political ends of equality such movements work toward while at the same time finding their tactics problematic.

And, disturbingly, the people doing the above come from some of the most privileged and well-off societies and groups in human history. Many of their problems have already been solved and they have no wars to fight, hunger to worry about, nor shelter to fear losing. In becoming reactionaries, they have adopted the *worst* of liberalism, rejected its strong points (e.g., open inquiry,

---

6 A telling, if melodramatic, instance of this was demonstrated at Portland State University (February 7, 2018) where students accused biologist—Heather Heying—a being a "piece of shit," "brainwashed," and spreading "fascism" which "should not be tolerated in civil society." This was because of her comments that men and women are biologically different and this shapes things like height, lactation, muscle mass, locations of fat deposits, and so on. They disrupted the panel, marched out of the hall, attempted to damage recording equipment in the process, called the panel Nazis, and shouted "power to the people" on their way out of the building. A video of the event can be found on YouTube here (URL retrieved September 15, 2018): https://www.youtube.com/watch?v=n5D_ltpw7CI.

debate, free speech), and have ignored useful ideas of radicalism—e.g., the harnessing of scientific principles in the critique of the existing order, faith in logic and reason, and so on. This at a time when the world is on the brink of ecological disaster and when the ruling class's grip on resources, production, and government is as strong as it has ever been and stands to grow ever stronger.

Postmodern theorists would likely vehemently deny the accusation of fascism, seeing themselves of the political left and radically opposed to right-wing ideology. But consider Kakutani's observations in a piece for *The Guardian*. Beginning with noting Hannah Arendt's claim in *The Origins of Totalitarianism* that "The ideal subject of totalitarian rule is not the convinced Nazi or the convinced communist, but people for whom the distinction between fact and fiction (i.e., the reality of experience) and the distinction between true and false (i.e., the standards of thought) no longer exist," Kakutani draws out several parallels between the postmodern-political-academic left and strategies of the Trump administration and its new right supporters (he also calls on Orwell's observations as well as tactics of Holocaust revisionists, creationists, and the tobacco industry that distort truth and manipulate the public). Below I recount several of his arguments.

Kakutani (2018) points out that we have long been suffering from "truth decay," where objectivity has increasingly fallen out of favor. The relativism embraced by the New Left of the 1960s was meant to expose the biases of Western, bourgeois, male-dominated ideas and postmodernism pushed this further in arguing there are no universal truths, only smaller personal ones and perceptions shaped by culture and society. Today, however, such a relativist notion of the true also has been embraced by the populist right. Both the reactionary right and the postmodern left are hostile toward established knowledge and believe that the wisdom of the crowd founds truth on egalitarian principles, where the disenfranchised are not only heard but are the litmus test for the validity of an idea or claim. Both the postmodern theorist and the anti-vaxxer no longer trust science or scientists. Climate change deniers and postmodern deconstructionists both use a discourse of "many sides," "different perspectives," "uncertainties," and "multiple ways of knowing," a strategy that could have been taken straight from the tobacco industry's playbook (which is true in the case of climate change denial industries). For both, broader truths are unfashionable and empirical evidence is regarded suspiciously and replaced with personal testimony and "positioning" as to the speaker's own race, religion, gender, and so on, that inform, skew, or ratify their ideas.

Here we return to Marx's warning about the mystifying influence of an inverted world and the need to recognize identity/difference in our analyses.

What both postmodernists and today's reactionary right share is the idea that you start with your political desires and conclusions, and then words, ideas, concepts, and so on are fitted to them. And if this means manipulating data, slandering and/or silencing critical views, using language as a weapon to do for you what you need and/or want it to do, shouting down opposing voices, and/or misrepresenting ideological rhetoric as actually being rooted in logic and reason, then so be it. Start at the end and make any pretense to science—to the extent it is honored at all—do the work you need it to do, instead of starting with scientific principles—e.g., ontological assumptions, epistemological procedures, developing of explanatory models, honest and open debate, etc.—and then coming to conclusions on how they might inform political action in the world. That is, both the postmodernist and the reactionary right approaches are *backward* and each court a fascist tendency, even if their political endpoints are different.

Postmodernism has set back social progress. It has infected the academic left and the intellectual class, even if we have passed its apex as a scholastic trend. Its remnants remain and they are imprinting their anti-Enlightenment and ill-liberal tendencies on a once-proud institution. And because their goals are now gender, sexual, and racial equality, standing up to their *political tactics* (as opposed to their goals) is to invite fear, censure, and opprobrium, as well as accusations of sexism, xenophobia, and racism. This form of politics, however, reduces itself to a Machiavellian set of techniques to establish equal opportunities for learning, employment, advancement, and social esteem but which ultimately mean providing equal opportunities to become middle and upper-class warriors, to join the ranks of the bourgeoisie and/or to serve them. This is liberalism's limit. Though eliminating status inequalities is agreeable, should it be accomplished sans a class-based tack and without a focus on the logic of capital, liberalism's overall approach is to make it so that women, non-whites, and the LGBTQ community all have equal opportunity to serve capital as its allies in the class struggle. And they have adopted the tactics of reaction in order to do so. This is a misleading type of progress, one whose categorical imperative masks its barren soul and vicious strategy.

Postmodernism should not be taken seriously, at least as a theoretical scientific model. And postmodernists should not be taken seriously either, at least as intellectuals. Touting such ideas is evidence of their lack of discernment and an inability to distinguish emotional appeal, jargon, and politics from real positive knowledge, which postmodern theory generally rejects. That said, *its trends and influence should be taken seriously*, as they are anti-science and set back the potential progress we find deep within the kernel of modernity. And not only that, postmodernism and identity politics, with their denial, rejection, or ignoring of a class-based model and outlook, promise no challenge to the ordering principle of modernity but actually facilitate its continued dominance. It would not be a stretch of meaning to see in postmodern thought and politics kindred spirits to the forces of reaction aspiring to conserve the modern order.

In 2017, a new "Sokal affair" was unveiled, one mainly academic in nature but, in an age of the Internet, one the public also had opportunity to witness. Professors Peter Boghossian (under the pseudonym, Peter Boyle) and James Lindsay (under the pseudonym, Jaimie Lindsay) submitted an article to the open access journal, *Cogent Social Sciences*, which editors published after peer-review (2017, Volume 3, Issue 1). Their article ("The Conceptual Penis as a Social Construct") claimed that "The penis *vis-à-vis* maleness is an incoherent construct. We argue that the *conceptual penis* is better understood not as an anatomical organ but as a gender-performative, highly fluid social construct." Like Sokal's 1996 paper that claimed reality did not exist, this paper seemed to take a postmodern/social justice activist position—i.e., that gender does not exist—to its logical conclusion: the penis does not exist (and that the conceptual penis was behind climate change). And similarly to Sokal's method, the authors used a pastiche of jargon and randomly chosen terminology to intentionally not make sense. Finally, also in Sokal's vein, the goal was to show that academic traditions like postmodernism and its allies are more interested in whether they agree with an author's political/social conclusions than they are about systematic method, empirical rigor, or sound theoretical reasoning. Praise and condemnation similar to what Sokal received were immediate and *Cogent Social Sciences* later retracted the article.[7]

---

7  See the *Cogent Social Sciences* website and its paper retraction here (URL retrieved August 3, 2017): http://www.tandfonline.com/doi/abs/10.1080/23311886.2017.1330439. For their comments and discussion of their hoax, see: Boghossian and Lindsay (2017).

# References

Abel, David. 2018. "Fish Wars Loom as Climate Change Pushes Lobster, Cod, and Other Species North." *Boston Globe*. June 21. Retrieved June 23, 2018 (https://www.bostonglobe.com/metro/2018/06/21/fish-wars-loom-climate-change-pushes-lobster-cod-and-other-species-north/4uCFNQKDz3dipGaZSD7WVP/story.html).

Aengenheyster, Matthias, Qing Yi Feng, Frederick van der Ploeg, and Henk A. Dijkstra. 2018. "The Point of No Return for Climate Action: Effects of Climate Uncertainty and Risk Tolerance." *Earth System Dynamics* (9): 1085–1095. doi.org/10.5194/esd-9-1085-2018.

Agence France-Presse. 2018a. "Indonesia Girl Jailed for Abortion After Being Raped by Brother." *The Guardian*. July 21. Retrieved August 15, 2018 (https://www.theguardian.com/world/2018/jul/21/indonesia-girl-jailed-for-abortion-after-being-raped-by-brother).

Agence France-Presse. 2018b. "Istanbul Gay Pride March Hit with Tear Gas as Turkish Police Try to Enforce Ban." *The Telegraph*. July 2. Retrieved August 8, 2018 (https://www.telegraph.co.uk/news/2018/07/02/istanbul-gay-pride-march-hit-tear-gas-turkish-police-try-enforce/).

Ahuja, Amit. 2016. "Why Caste Matters Less in Urban India." *The Hindu* | Business Line. July 19. Retrieved August 31, 2018 (https://www.thehindubusinessline.com/opinion/why-caste-matters-less-in-urban-india/article8871456.ece).

Albanese, Joe. 2017. "Is Big Ice Cream Trying to Hijack Our Democracy?" *The National Review*. September 12. Retrieved August 7, 2018 (https://www.nationalreview.com/2017/09/ben-cohen-ben-jerrys-magnate-mounts-dangerous-assault-constitutional-corporate-speech/).

Alexander, Kurtis. 2018. "Scientists See Fingerprints of Climate Change All over California's Wildfires." *San Francisco Chronicle*. August 3. Retrieved August 12, 2018 (https://www.sfchronicle.com/science/article/Scientists-see-fingerprints-of-climate-change-all-13128585.php).

Alexander, Michelle. 2010. *The New Jim Crow: Mass Incarceration in the Age of Colorblindness*. New York: The New Press.

Algar, Selim. 2014. "Major Banks Knowingly Funded Hezbollah Terror Operations: Suit." *New York Post*. November 10. Retrieved September 1, 2018 (https://nypost.com/2014/11/10/major-banks-knowingly-funded-hezbollah-terror-operations-uit/).

Al Jazeera News. 2018a. "Saudi Women Hit the Road as Driving Ban Lifted." Al Jazeera. June 24. Retrieved June 26, 2018 (https://www.aljazeera.com/news/2018/06/saudi-women-hit-road-driving-ban-lifted-180623215156740.html).

Al Jazeera News. 2018b. "Syria's Civil War Explained from the Beginning." Al Jazeera. April 14. Retrieved June 26, 2018 (https://www.aljazeera.com/news/2016/05/syria-civil-war-explained-160505084119966.html).

Allegretto, Sylvia, Anna Godoey, Carl Nadler, and Michael Reich. 2018. "The New Wave of Local Minimum Wage Policies: Evidence from Six Cities." Center on Wage and Employment Dynamics | Institute for Research and Labor and Employment. September 6. Retrieved September 22, 2018 (http://irle.berkeley.edu/files/2018/09/The-New-Wave-of-Local-Minimum-Wage-Policies.pdf).

Amador, Edward. 2018. "An American World Without American Hegemony." Arc Digital. June 13. Retrieved August 21, 2018 (https://arcdigital.media/an-american-world-without-american-hegemony-cb1316ed548d).

American Civil Liberties Union. 2014. "War Comes Home: The Excessive Militarization of American Policing." June. Retrieved August 7, 2018 (https://www.aclu.org/sites/default/files/assets/jus14-warcomeshome-report-web-rel1.pdf).

Amnesty International. 2018. "More than 7,000 Killed in the Philippines in Six Months, as President Encourages Murder." Amnesty International UK | Issues | Action for Individuals. January 12. Retrieved August 8, 2018 (https://www.amnesty.org.uk/philippines-president-duterte-war-on-drugs-thousands-killed).

Andone, Dakin, and Jessica Campisi. 2018. "There's Not a Single US State Where Minimum Wage Worker Can Afford a 2-Bedroom Rental, a Report Says." CNN. June 15. Retrieved July 24, 2018 (https://www.cnn.com/2018/06/14/us/minimum-wage-2-bedroom-trnd/index.html).

Aneja, Atul. 2018. "China, India Are New Vanguards of Globalization, Says Chinese Foreign Ministry." *The Hindu*. April 23. Retrieved June 29, 2018 (https://www.thehindu.com/news/international/china-india-are-new-vanguards-of-globalisation-says-chinese-foreign-ministry/article23648458.ece).

Anti-Slavery International. 2004. *The Cocoa Industry in West Africa: A History of Exploitation*. Retrieved August 20, 2018 (http://www.antislavery.org/wp-content/uploads/2017/01/1_cocoa_report_2004.pdf).

Appalachian Land Ownership Task Force. 1981. "Land Ownership Patterns and their Impacts on Appalachian Communities: A Survey of 80 Counties." Submitted to the Appalachian Regional Commission, February 1981. See: (http://files.eric.ed.gov/fulltext/ED325280.pdf).

Arendt, Hannah. [1963] 2006. *Eichmann in Jerusalem: A Report on the Banality of Evil.* New York: Penguin.

Arsenault, Chris. 2012. "Risk of Water Wars Rises with Scarcity." Al Jazeera. August 22. Retrieved June 25, 2018 (https://www.aljazeera.com/indepth/features/2011/06/2011622193147231653.html).

Ash, Lucy. 2015. "The Truth Behind the Rape of Berlin." *The Telegraph*. May 2. Retrieved September 5, 2018 (https://www.telegraph.co.uk/culture/tvandradio/11576601/The-truth-behind-The-Rape-of-Berlin.html).

Asimakopoulos, John. 2009. "Globally Segmented Labor Markets: The Coming of the Greatest Boom and Bust, Without the Boom." *Critical Sociology* 35 (2): 175–198.

REFERENCES

Associated Press. 2018a. "Senior EPA Officials Collaborated with Climate Change Denial Group, Emails Show." *The Guardian.* May 25. Retrieved June 20, 2018 (https://www.theguardian.com/environment/2018/may/26/senior-epa-officials-collaborated-with-climate-change-denial-group-emails-show).

Associated Press. 2018b. "UN Expert Calls US Income Inequality 'A Political Choice.'" AP News. June 4. Retrieved July 24, 2018 (https://apnews.com/amp/2f11091232a349f39cfe2e80e8c46545?__twitter_impression=true).

Atkin, Emily. 2017. "Guess Which World the EPA Just Deleted from Its Science Mission Statement." *Mother Jones.* March 7. Retrieved August 1, 2017 (http://www.motherjones.com/environment/2017/03/epa-science-technology-office-removed-science/).

Ayres, Sabra. 2018. "Russian Journalists Slain While Investigating Kremlin-Linked Company in Central African Republic." *Los Angeles Times.* August 1. Retrieved August 8, 2018 (http://www.latimes.com/world/la-fg-africa-russian-journalists-20180801-story.html).

Badger, Emily, Claire Cain Miller, Adam Pearce, and Kevin Quealy 2018. "Extensive Data Shows Punishing Reach of Racism for Black Boys." *New York Times.* March 19. Retrieved June 28, 2018 (https://www.nytimes.com/interactive/2018/03/19/upshot/race-class-white-and-black-men.html).

Bagdikian, Ben. [1983] 1997. *The Media Monopoly.* Boston: Beacon Press.

Baker, Vicky. 2007. "Rape Victim Sentenced to 200 Lashes and Six Months in Jail." *The Guardian.* November 17. Retrieved August 16, 2018 (https://www.theguardian.com/world/2007/nov/17/saudiarabia.international).

Baldwin, Clare. 2018. "Physicians Say Rohingya Scars 'High Consistent' with Myanmar Atrocity Reports." Reuters. July 5. Retrieved August 8, 2018 (https://www.reuters.com/article/us-myanmar-rohingya-phr/physicians-say-rohingya-scars-highly-consistent-with-myanmar-atrocity-reports-idUSKBN1JV1H3).

Bangura, Zainab Hawa. 2015. "We're Witnessing Revival of Slave Trade in the 21st Century." CNN. June 15. Retrieved August 15, 2018 (https://www.cnn.com/2015/06/11/opinions/bangura-isis-treatment-women/index.html).

Bar-On, Yinon M., Rob Phillips, and Ron Milo. 2018. "The Biomass Distribution on Earth." *Proceedings of the National Academy of Sciences* | Latest Articles. Retrieved June 20, 2018 (http://www.pnas.org/content/pnas/early/2018/05/15/1711842115.full.pdf).

Barker David, and Kathleen Knight. 2000. "Political Talk Radio and Public Opinion." *Public Opinion Quarterly* 64 (2): 149–170.

Batchelor, Tom. 2018. "Paris Global Warming Targets Could Be Exceeded Sooner than Expected Because of Melting Permafrost, Study Finds." *Independent.* September 18. Retrieved September 25, 2018 (https://www.independent.co.uk/environment/climate-change-paris-agreement-permafrost-melting-carbon-emissions-a8541686.html).

Bates, Clive, and Andy Rowell. 2004. Tobacco Explained...The Truth About the Tobacco Industry...In Its Own Words. *UCSF: Center for Tobacco Control Research and Education.* Retrieved July 29, 2018 (https://escholarship.org/uc/item/9fp6566b).

Baudrillard, Jean. [1988] 1989. *Jean Baudrillard: Selected Writings*, edited by Mark Poster. Cambridge: Polity Press.

BBC News. 2011. "Mau Mau Uprising: Bloody History of Kenya Conflict." April 7. Retrieved September 5, 2018 (https://www.bbc.com/news/uk-12997138).

BBC News. 2012. "Saudi Policy 'Stopped' Fire Rescue." March 15. Retrieved June 26, 2018 (http://news.bbc.co.uk/1/hi/world/middle_east/1874471.stm).

BBC News. 2018. "Peru Child Sacrifice Discovery May Be Largest in History." April 28. Retrieved July 23, 2018 (https://www.bbc.com/news/world-latin-america-43928277).

Beach, George. 2018. "The City of London Will Be Powered with 100% Renewable Energy by October 2018." Inhabitat. June 18. Retrieved July 5, 2018 (https://inhabitat.com/the-city-of-london-will-be-powered-with-100-renewable-energy-by-october-2018/).

Beene, Ryan, Jennifer A. Dlouhy, John Lippert, and Ari Natter. 2018. "Trump to Seek Repeal of California's Smog-Fighting Power." Bloomberg. July 23. Retrieved August 12, 2018 (https://www.bloomberg.com/news/articles/2018-07-23/trump-is-said-to-seek-repeal-of-california-s-smog-fighting-power).

Beevor, Antony. 2002. "They Raped Every German Female from Eight to 80." *The Guardian.* May 1. Retrieved September 5, 2018 (https://www.theguardian.com/books/2002/may/01/news.features11).

Begley, Sharon. 1994. "The End of Antibiotics." *Newsweek.* March 27, 1994. Retrieved June 18, 2018 (http://www.newsweek.com/end-antibiotics-185984).

Bell, David N.F., and David G. Blanchflower. 2018. "Underemployment in the US and Europe." NBER Working Paper No. 24927. National Bureau of Economic Research | International Finance and Macroeconomics, Labor Studies, Monetary Economics. DOI: 10.3386/w24927.

Bell, Michelle L., Devra L. Davis, and Tony Fletcher. 2004. "A Retrospective Assessment of Mortality from the London Smog Episode of 1952: The Role of Influenza and Pollution." *Environmental Health Perspectives* 112 (1): 6–8.

Bellon, Tina. 2018. "Monsanto Ordered to Pay $289 Million in World's First Roundup Cancer Trial." Reuters. August 10. Retrieved August 13, 2018 (https://www.reuters.com/article/us-monsanto-cancer-lawsuit/monsanto-ordered-to-pay-289-million-in-worlds-first-roundup-cancer-trial-idUSKBN1KV2HB).

Benedictus, Leo. 2014. "Sick Cities: Why Urban Living Can Be Bad for Your Mental Health." *The Guardian.* February 25. Retrieved July 30, 2018 (https://www.theguardian.com/cities/2014/feb/25/city-stress-mental-health-rural-kind).

Benegal, Salil D. 2018. "The Spillover of Race and Racial Attitudes into Public Opinion About Climate Change." *Environmental Politics* 27 (4): 733–756.

# REFERENCES

Bennett, Jessica. 2018. "Kenyan Woman Saves 15,000 Young Girls from Female Genital Mutilation." *Ebony.* July 26. Retrieved August 15, 2018 (https://www.ebony.com/news-views/kenyan-woman-saves-15000-young-girls-from-female-genital-mutilation).

Bernish, Claire. 2017. "Pablo Escobar's Son Reveals His Dad 'Worked for the CIA Selling Cocaine'—Media Silent." The Free Thought Project. February 17. Retrieved September 18, 2018 (https://thefreethoughtproject.com/escobar-son-cia-cocaine/).

Berwyn, Bob. 2017. "Methane Seeps Out as Arctic Permafrost Starts to Resemble Swiss Cheese." Inside Climate News. July 19. Retrieved August 13, 2018 (https://insideclimatenews.org/news/18072017/arctic-permafrost-melting-methane-emissions-geologic-sources-study).

Birtles, Bill. 2018. "Beijing Churns Out 25,000 Tonnes of Rubbish Every Day—Here's How It Deals with Its Waste Crisis." ABC News (Australia Broadcasting Corporation). August 5. Retrieved August 12, 2018 (http://www.abc.net.au/news/2018-08-07/how-beijing-deals-with-waste-crisis/10078026).

Bittel, Jason. 2018. "Against All Odds, Mountain Gorilla Numbers Are on the Rise." EcoWatch. June 30. Retrieved July 13, 2018 (https://www.ecowatch.com/mountain-gorilla-numbers-on-the-rise-2582376835.html).

Blendon, Robert J., and John M. Benson. 2001. "Americans' Views on Health Policy: A Fifty-Year Historical Perspective." *Health Affairs* 20 (2/March/April). doi.org/10.1377/hlthaff.20.2.33

Blitzer, Ronn. 2018. "President Trump Regrets Order Ending Family Separations, Report Says." Law and Crime. June 25. Retrieved August 8, 2018 (https://lawandcrime.com/immigration/president-trump-regrets-order-ending-family-separations-report-says/).

Bogdanich, Walt, and Eric Koli. 2003. "2 Paths of Bayer Drug in the 80s: Riskier One Steered Overseas." *New York Times.* May 22, 2003. Retrieved June 5, 2018 (https://www.nytimes.com/2003/05/22/business/2-paths-of-bayer-drug-in-80-s-riskier-one-steered-overseas.html).

Boghossian, Peter, and James Lindsay. 2017. "The Conceptual Penis as a Social Construct: A Sokal-Style Hoax on Gender Studies." *Skeptic.* Retrieved August 3, 2017 (http://www.skeptic.com/reading_room/conceptual-penis-social-contruct-sokal-style-hoax-on-gender-studies/).

Boissoneault, Lorraine. 2017. "There Never Was a Real Tulip Fever." Smithsonian.com. September 18. Retrieved June 5, 2018 (https://www.smithsonianmag.com/history/there-never-was-real-tulip-fever-180964915/).

Booker, Salih, and Ari Rickman. 2018. "The Future Is African—and the United States Is Not Prepared." *Washington Post.* June 6. Retrieved June 29, 2018 (https://www.washingtonpost.com/news/democracy-post/wp/2018/06/09/the-future-is

-african-and-the-united-states-is-not-prepared/?noredirect=on&utm_term=.742397b3a4bb).

Boot, Max. 2018. "Without the Russians, Trump Wouldn't Have Won." *Washington Post.* July 24. Retrieved August 21, 2018 (https://www.washingtonpost.com/opinions/without-the-russians-trump-wouldnt-have-won/2018/07/24/f4c87894-8f6b-11e8-bcd5-9d911c784c38_story.html?noredirect=on&utm_term=.233d2bdcd9eb).

Booth, William, and Amie Ferris-Rotman. 2018. "Russia's Suez Canal? Ships Start Plying a Less-Icy Arctic, Thanks to Climate Change." *Washington Post.* September 8. Retrieved September 20, 2018 (https://www.washingtonpost.com/world/europe/russias-suez-canal-ships-start-plying-an-ice-free-arctic-thanks-to-climate-change/2018/09/08/59d50986-ac5a-11e8-9a7d-cd30504ff902_story.html?noredirect=on&utm_term=.96ab4b982e11).

Borger, Julian, and Anne Perkins. 2018. "'My Touch, My Feel': Trump Shows His Contempt for G7 Allies." *The Guardian.* June 9. Retrieved July 1, 2018 (https://www.theguardian.com/us-news/2018/jun/09/trump-g7-allies-comments-russia-north-korea).

Borick, Christopher, Barry G. Rabe, Natalie B. Fitzpatrick, and Sarah B. Mills. 2018. "As Americans Experienced the Warmest May on Record Their Acceptance of Global Warming Reaches a New High." *Issues in Energy and Environmental Policy* 37 (July): 1–7.

Bouie, Jamelle. 2014. "Down and Out: The Single Fact that Powerfully Explains Why Black Americans Have Such a Hard Time Climbing the Economic Ladder." Slate. April 3. Retrieved August 4, 2017 (http://www.slate.com/articles/news_and_politics/politics/2014/04/desean_jackson_richard_sherman_and_black_american_economic_mobility_why.html).

Bowden, John. 2018. "German Defense Minister: Trump Has 'No Strategy' for Dealing with Putin." The Hill. July 28. Retrieved August 21, 2018 (http://thehill.com/policy/international/399361-german-defense-minister-trump-has-no-strategy-for-dealing-with-putin).

Boyle, Peter. 2018. "Poll Shows 58% of 'Millennials' in Australia Favourable to Socialism." Green Left Weekly. June 22. Retrieved July 13, 2018 (https://www.greenleft.org.au/content/poll-shows-58-%E2%80%98millennials%E2%80%99-australia-favourable-socialism).

Brailovskaia, Julia, and Jurgen Margraf. 2017. "Facebook Addiction Disorder (FAD) among German Students—A Longitudinal Approach." PL*oS One* 12 (12): e0189719. doi.org/10.1371/journal.pone.0189719.

Brandt, Allan M. 2012. "Inventing Conflicts of Interests: A History of Tobacco Industry Tactics." *American Journal of Public Health* 102 (1): 63–71.

Brannen, Peter. 2014. "Acid Trap: Earth's Oceans Are Beginning to Warm and Turn Acid, Endangering Plankton and the Entire Marine Food Chain." Aeon. February 18. Retrieved June 19, 2018 (https://aeon.co/essays/why-plankton-is-the-canary-in-the-coal-mine-of-our-oceans).

REFERENCES

Breaking News. 2018. "While World Watches Rohingya Crisis, Burma Christian Minority Faces 'Cleansing.'" April 25. Retrieved August 8, 2018 (https://www.breakingnews.ie/world/while-world-watches-rohingya-crisis-burma-christian-minority-faces-cleansing-839188.html).

Breivik, Knut, James M. Armitage, Frank Wania, and Kevin C. Jones. 2014. "Tracking the Global Generation and Exports of E-Waste. Do the Existing Estimates Add Up?" *Environmental Science &Technology* 48 (15): 8735–8743.

Brettell, Karen, David Gaffen, and David Rohde. 2015. "The Cannibalized Company: How the Cult of Shareholder Value Has Reshaped Corporate America." Reuters | Special Report. November 16. Retrieved July 2, 2018 (https://www.reuters.com/investigates/special-report/usa-buybacks-cannibalized/).

Bridges, Tristan. 2017. "This Is the Real Reason Why American Politics Is So Polarized, According to an Expert." Business Insider. March 14. Retrieved July 11, 2018 (http://www.businessinsider.com/sociology-explains-polarization-politics-2017-3).

Bridle, James. 2018. "Rise of the Machines: Has Technology Evolved Beyond Our Control?" *The Guardian*. June 15. Retrieved July 30, 2018 (https://www.theguardian.com/books/2018/jun/15/rise-of-the-machines-has-technology-evolved-beyond-our-control-).

Brink, Susan. 2017. "A Superbug that Resisted 26 Antibiotics." National Public Radio. January 17. Retrieved June 21, 2018 (https://www.npr.org/sections/goatsandsoda/2017/01/17/510227493/a-superbug-that-resisted-26-antibiotics).

Brown, Claire. 2018. "Amazon Gets Tax Breaks While Its Employees Rely on Food Stamps, New Data Shows." The Intercept. April 19. Retrieved July 23, 2018 (https://theintercept.com/2018/04/19/amazon-snap-subsidies-warehousing-wages/).

Brunhuber, Kim. 2018. "'Nobody Has that Much Money': One Sinking City's Fight Against Rising Sea Levels." CBC News. July 2. Retrieved August 12, 2018 (https://www.cbc.ca/news/world/rising-sea-levels-sfo-foster-city-1.4711621).

Buchheit, Paul. 2018. "What Just Happened? $30 Trillion to the Richest White Americans Since 2008." Common Dreams. September 3. Retrieved September 22, 2018 (https://www.commondreams.org/views/2018/09/03/what-just-happened-30-trillion-richest-white-americans-2008).

Bullard, Gabe. 2016. "World's Newest Major Religion: No Religion." *National Geographic*. April 22. Retrieved July 26, 2018 (https://news.nationalgeographic.com/2016/04/160422-atheism-agnostic-secular-nones-rising-religion/).

Bureau of Economic Analysis | Global Macro Monitor. 2011. "America's FIRE Economy." February 3. Retrieved August 7, 2017 (https://macromon.wordpress.com/2011/02/03/americas-fire-economy/).

Burke, Timothy. 2018. "How America's Largest Local TV Owner Turned Its News Anchors into Soldiers in Trump's War on the Media." Deadspin | The Concourse. March 31. Retrieved August 12, 2018 (https://theconcourse.deadspin.com/how-americas-largest-local-tv-owner-turned-its-news-anc-1824233490).

Burnett, Dean. 2018. "Delete Facebook? That's as Hard as Giving Up Sugar." *The Guardian*. March 23. Retrieved June 16, 2018 (https://www.theguardian.com/commentisfree/2018/mar/23/delete-facebook-giving-up-sugar-social-networks).

Burton, Tara Isabella. 2018. "Mike Pompeo, Trump's Pick for Secretary of State, Talks About Politics as a Battle of Good and Evil." Vox. March 15. Retrieved June 4, 2018 (https://www.vox.com/identities/2018/3/15/17117298/mike-pompeo-trump-secretary-of-state-politics-battle-evangelical-holy-war-christian).

Byrne, John Aidan. 2017. "US Companies Spent $4T Buying Back Their Own Stock." *New York Post*. August 19. Retrieved June 29, 2018 (https://nypost.com/2017/08/19/us-companies-spent-4t-buying-back-their-own-stock/).

Cacciatore, Michael A., Sara K. Yeo, Dietram A. Scheufele, Michael A. Xenos, Dominique Brossard, and Elizabeth A. Corley. 2017. "Is Facebook Making Us Dumber? Exploring Social Media Use as a Predictor of Political Knowledge." *Journalism & Mass Communication Quarterly* 95 (2): 404–424.

Cadwalladr, Carole. 2018. "'I Made Steve Bannon's Psychological Warfare Tool': Meet the Data War Whistleblower." *The Guardian*. March 18. Retrieved June 17, 2018 (https://www.theguardian.com/news/2018/mar/17/data-war-whistleblower-christopher-wylie-faceook-nix-bannon-trump).

Cain Miller, Claire. 2018. "Americans Are Having Fewer Babies. They Told Us Why." *New York Times*. July 5. Retrieved July 24, 2018 (https://www.nytimes.com/2018/07/05/upshot/americans-are-having-fewer-babies-they-told-us-why.html).

Calabria, Mark A. 2009. "Did Deregulation Cause the Financial Crisis?" The Cato Institute | Cato Policy Report. July / August. Retrieved July 13, 2018 (https://www.cato.org/policy-report/julyaugust-2009/did-deregulation-cause-financial-crisis).

Cama, Timothy. 2018. "Trump Rescinds Obama Policy Protecting Oceans." The Hill. June 20. Retrieved June 21, 2018 (http://thehill.com/policy/energy-environment/393213-trump-rescinds-obamas-policy-on-protecting-oceans).

Carlsen, Laura. 2013. "Under Nafta, Mexico Suffered, and the United States Felt Its Pain." *New York Times*. November 24. Retrieved September 6, 2018 (https://www.nytimes.com/roomfordebate/2013/11/24/what-weve-learned-from-nafta/under-nafta-mexico-suffered-and-the-united-states-felt-its-pain).

Carlson, Shawn. 1985. "A Double-Blind Test of Astrology." *Nature* 318 (6045): 419–435.

Carrington, Damian. 2017. "Earth's Sixth Mass Extinction Even Under Way, Scientists Warn." *The Guardian*. July 20. Retrieved August 14, 2018 (https://www.theguardian.com/environment/2017/jul/10/earths-sixth-mass-extinction-event-already-under-way-scientists-warn).

Carrington, Damian. 2018a. "Almost All of World's Oceans Damaged by Human Impact, Study Finds." *The Guardian*. July 26. Retrieved August 12, 2018 (https://www.theguardian.com/environment/2018/jul/26/just-13-of-global-oceans-undamaged-by-humanity-research-reveals).

Carrington, Damian. 2018b. "BBC Admits 'We Get Climate Change Coverage Wrong Too Often.'" *The Guardian*. September 7. Retrieved September 21, 2018 (https://www.theguardian.com/environment/2018/sep/07/bbc-we-get-climate-change-coverage-wrong-too-often).

Carrington, Damian. 2018c. "Extreme Global Weather Is 'the Face of Climate Change' Says Leading Scientist." *The Guardian*. July 27. Retrieved August 12, 2018 (https://www.theguardian.com/environment/2018/jul/27/extreme-global-weather-climate-change-michael-mann).

Carrington, Damian. 2018d. "Mysterious Source of Illegal Ozone-Killing Emissions Revealed, Say Investigators." *The Guardian*. July 8. Retrieved August 12, 2018 (https://www.theguardian.com/environment/2018/jul/09/mysterious-source-of-illegal-ozone-killing-emissions-revealed-say-investigators).

Carrington, Damian, and Lily Kuo. 2018. "Air Pollution Causes 'Huge' Reduction in Intelligence, Study Reveals." *The Guardian*. August 27. Retrieved September 12, 2018 (https://www.theguardian.com/environment/2018/aug/27/air-pollution-causes-huge-reduction-in-intelligence-study-reveals).

Carroll, William K. 2012. "Global, Transnational, Regional, National: The Need for Nuance in Theorizing Global Capitalism." *Critical Sociology* 38 (3): 365–371.

Cary, Peter. 2017. "The Public Favors Cutting Defense Spending, Not Adding Billions More, New Survey Finds." The Center for Public Integrity. March 23. Retrieved August 10, 2018 (https://www.publicintegrity.org/2017/03/23/20778/public-favors-cutting-defense-spending-not-adding-billions-more-new-survey-finds).

Casciani, Dominic. 2014. "Did Removing Lead from Petrol Spark a Decline in Crime?" BBC | Magazine. April 21. Retrieved August 2, 2017 (http://www.bbc.com/news/magazine-27067615).

Cassella, Carly. 2018. "A Mass Decimation of Forests Is Happening Across the US, and No One's Paying Attention." Science Alert. May 8. Retrieved June 20, 2018 (https://www.sciencealert.com/american-cities-losing-30-million-trees-every-single-year-in-stunning-decimation-tree-cover).

Ceballos, Gerardo, Paul Ehrlich, and Rodolfo Dirzo. 2017. "Biological Annihilation Via the Ongoing Sixth Mass Extinction Signaled by Vertebrate Population Losses and Declines." *Proceedings of the National Academy of Sciences* 114 (30): E6089–E6094. Retrieved August 2, 2017 (http://www.pnas.org/content/114/30/E6089.full.pdf).

Ceballos, Gerardo, Paul R. Ehrlich, Anthony D. Barnosky, Andrés Garcia, Robert M. Pringle, and Todd Palmer. 2015. "Accelerated Modern Human-Induced Species Losses: Entering the Sixth Mass Extinction." *Science Advances* 1 (5): 1–5. DOI: 10.1126/sciadv.1400253.

Centers for Disease Control. n.d.a. "Drug Resistant TB." Retrieved August 7, 2017 (https://www.cdc.gov/tb/topic/drtb/).

Centers for Disease Control. n.d.b. "Antibiotic-Resistant Gonorrhea." Retrieved August 7, 2017 (https://www.cdc.gov/std/gonorrhea/arg/default.htm).

Centers for Disease Control. 2018. "Suicide Rates Rising Across the US" June 7. Retrieved July 24, 2018 (https://www.cdc.gov/media/releases/2018/p0607-suicide-prevention.html).

Centola, Damon, Joshua Becker, Devon Brackbill, and Andrea Baronchelli. 2018. "Experimental Evidence for Tipping Points in Social Convention." *Science* 360 (June): 1116–1119.

Cha, Ariana Eunjung. 2016. "CDC Warns that Americans May Be Overmedicating Youngest Children with ADHD." *Washington Post.* May 3. Retrieved July 20, 2017 (https://www.washingtonpost.com/news/to-your-health/wp/2016/05/03/cdc-warns-that-americans-may-be-overmedicating-two-to-five-year-olds-with-adhd/?utm_term=.77c14177bdb).

Chait, Jonathan. 2018. "Britain Has a Russian Collusion Scandal Now. It Looks Exactly Like Trump's." *New York Magazine.* June 22. Retrieved July 1, 2018 (http://nymag.com/daily/intelligencer/2018/06/britains-russia-collusion-scandal-looks-just-like-trumps.html).

Chalmers, John 2018. "Special Report: How Myanmar Punished Two Reporters for Uncovering an Atrocity." Reuters. Sept 3. Retrieved September 22, 2018 (https://www.reuters.com/article/us-myanmar-journalists-trial-specialrepo/special-report-how-myanmar-punished-two-reporters-for-uncovering-an-atrocity-idUSKCN1LJ167).

Chamie. Joseph. 2018. "Premarital Sex: Increasing Worldwide." Inter Press Service. April 5. Retrieved September 3, 2018 (http://www.ipsnews.net/2018/04/premarital-sex-increasing-worldwide/).

Chan, Tara Francis. 2018. "Migrant Children Say They've Been Forcibly Drugged, Handcuffed, and Abused in US Government Detention." Business Insider. June 21. Retrieved August 8, 2018 (https://www.businessinsider.com/migrant-children-forcibly-drugged-abused-in-us-government-detention-2018-6).

Chang, Alvin. 2018. "Watch: Sinclair Forced Its TV Stations to Air Pro-Trump Propaganda on Family Separation." Vox. June 21. Retrieved August 11, 2018 (https://www.vox.com/2018/6/21/17488540/sinclair-tv-stations-family-separation-propaganda).

Chang, Kenneth. 2018. "Corporate Sponsors for NASA? Agency to Study Making Space for Brands." *New York Times.* September 11. Retrieved September 14, 2018 (https://www.nytimes.com/2018/09/11/science/nasa-corporate-sponsors.html).

Chase, Steven. 2018. "US Refuses to Back Canada in Saudi Arabia Dispute." *The Globe and Mail.* August 7. Retrieved August 21, 2018 (https://www.theglobeandmail.com/politics/article-us-sidesteps-getting-involved-in-escalating-saudi-canada-dispute/).

Chatterjee, Pratap. 2013. "Chocolate Slavery Case Against Nestlé Allowed to Proceed." CorpWatch Blog. December 24. Retrieved August 3, 2017 (http://www.corpwatch.org/article.php?id=15915).

Chellaney, Brahma. 2018. "Trump Is Losing the South China Sea." *The Japan Times*. June 19. Retrieved July 1, 2018 (https://www.japantimes.co.jp/opinion/2018/06/19/commentary/world-commentary/trump-losing-south-china-sea/#.WzjfINVKjIU).

Chen, Michelle. 2016. "Are You a Millennial? Congratulations! Climate Change Will Cost Your Generation $8.8 Trillion." *The Nation*. August 31. Retrieved August 1, 2017 (https://www.thenation.com/article/are-you-a-millennial-congratulations-climate-change-will-cost-your-generation-8-8-trillion/).

Chen, Tim. 2018. "Student Loans Have Become Our Modern-Day Debtors Prisons." *USA Today*. June 5. Retrieved July 24, 2018 (https://www.usatoday.com/story/opinion/2018/06/05/student-loans-crisis-allow-bankruptcy-investigate-abuses-column/640460002/).

Chesler, Phyllis. 2010. "Worldwide Trends in Honor Killings." Middle East Quarterly 17 (2): 3–11. Retrieved June 26, 2018 (https://www.meforum.org/articles/2010/worldwide-trends-in-honor-killings).

Chiacu, Doina, and Valerie Volcovici. 2018. "EPA Chief Pruitt Refuses to Link $CO_2$ and Global Warming." *The Atlantic*. (No Date). Retrieved August 12, 2018 (https://www.scientificamerican.com/article/epa-chief-pruitt-refuses-to-link-co2-and-global-warming/).

Chibber, Kabir. 2018. "Venezuela Has Lost 2.3 Million People—and It Could Get Even Worse." Quartz. August 28. Retrieved September 13, 2018 (https://qz.com/1371468/venezuela-has-lost-2-million-people-and-it-could-get-even-worse/).

Childress, Sarah. 2013. "Dr. Arjun Srinivasan: We've Reached 'The End of Antibiotics, Period.'" PBS | Frontline. October 22. Retrieved June 18, 2018 (https://www.pbs.org/wgbh/frontline/article/dr-arjun-srinivasan-weve-reached-the-end-of-antibiotics-period/).

Chomsky, Noam. [1998] 2002. *The Common Good*. Berkeley, California: Odonian Press.

Chomsky, Noam. 2015. *Year 501: The Conquest Continues*. Chicago: Haymarket.

Chomsky, Noam, and Edward Herman. [1988] 2002. *Manufacturing Consent: The Political Economy of the Mass Media*. New York: Pantheon Books.

Chow, Lorraine. 2018. "Costa Rica Runs Entirely on Renewable Energy for 300 Days." EcoWatch. November 21. Retrieved August 27, 2018 (https://www.ecowatch.com/costa-rica-renewables-2511342138.html).

Cizmar, Martin. 2018. "'Vladimir Putin Sees Trump as His American Oligarch': Former CIA Chief of Russia Operations Explains Relationship." Raw Story. July 14. Retrieved August 21, 2018 (https://www.rawstory.com/2018/07/vladimir-putin-sees-trump-american-oligarch-former-cia-chief-russia-operations-explains-relationship/).

Climate Action. 2018a. "23 Nations Sign Pledge to Step Up Action on Climate Change." June 22. Retrieved July 5, 2018 (http://www.climateactionprogramme.org/news/23-nations-sign-pledge-to-step-up-action-on-climate-change).

Climate Action. 2018b. "India to Bring Forward 100,000 Megawatts of New Solar Power." June 22. Retrieved July 5, 2018 (http://www.climateactionprogramme.org/news/india-to-bring-forward-100000-megawatts-of-new-solar-power).

Climate Action. 2018c. "Spain Hits 45% Renewable Power in First Half of 2018." July 13. Retrieved July 14, 2018 (http://www.climateactionprogramme.org/news/spain-hits-45-renewable-power-in-first-half-of-2018).

Clogston, Juanita "Frankie." 2016. "The Repeal of the Fairness Doctrine and the Irony of Talk Radio: A Story of Political Entrepreneurship, Risk, and Cover." *Journal of Policy History* 28 (2): 375–396. doi.org/10.1017/S0898030616000105.

CNBC. 2018b. "Maduro Orders 96 Percent Devaluation in Hyper-Inflation Stricken Venezuela." August 18. Retrieved August 18, 2018 (https://www.cnbc.com/2018/08/18/maduro-orders-96-percent-devaluation-in-venezuela.html).

Coca, Nithin. 2018. "Islamic Leaders Having Nothing to Say About China's Internment Camps for Muslims." *Foreign Policy*. July 24. Retrieved August 8, 2018 (https://foreignpolicy.com/2018/07/24/islamic-leaders-have-nothing-to-say-about-chinas-internment-camps-for-muslims/).

Cockburn, Alexander. 1998. *Whiteout: The CIA, Drugs, and the Press*. New York: Verso.

Cockburn, Patrick. 2018. "Kurdish Women Protest After Being Told by Turkish-Backed Militias to Wear the Hijab." *Independent*. June 14. Retrieved June 26, 2018 (https://www.independent.co.uk/news/world/middle-east/kurdish-woman-hijab-protest-turkey-militia-force-a8399206.html).

Cohn, Alain, Ernst Fair, and Michel André Maréchal. 2014. "Business Culture and Dishonesty in the Banking Industry." *Nature* 516 (December): 86–89. DOI:10.1038/nature13977.

Coleman, Murray. 2017. "Most-Read Client Retention Story: Wells Fargo Scandal Fallout Ripples Through Industry." Financial Advisor. December 26. Retrieved July 29, 2018 (https://financialadvisoriq.com/c/1824523/211663).

Collins, Chuck, and Josh Hoxie. 2015. *Billionaire Bonanza Report: The Forbes 400...and The Rest of Us*. Institute for Policy Studies. Washington, DC. See: (http://www.ips-dc.org/wp-content/uploads/2015/12/Billionaire-Bonanza-The-Forbes-400-and-the-Rest-of-Us-Dec1.pdf).

Collins, Mary B., Ian Munoz, and Joseph JaJa. 2016. "Linking 'Toxic Outliers' to Environmental Justice Communities." *Environmental Research Letters* 11 (1): 1–9. DOI: 10.1088.

Conca, James. 2014. "Does Our Military Know Something We Don't About Global Warming?" *Forbes*. November 14. Retrieved August 1, 2017 (https://www.forbes.com/sites/jamesconca/2014/11/14/does-our-military-know-something-we-dont-about-global-warming/#27fde0814567).

Conley, Julia. 2018a. "Climate Crisis to Cause Hundreds of Millions of Dangerous Nutrient Deficiencies—In Countries Least Responsible for Emissions." Common

Dreams. August 27. Retrieved September 15, 2018 (https://www.commondreams.org/news/2018/08/27/climate-crisis-cause-hundreds-millions-dangerous-nutrient-deficiencies-countries).

Conley, Julia. 2018b. "Trump's 'Immoral' Plan to Allow Coal States to Self-Regulate Could Send 365 Million Tons of Carbon into Atmosphere." Common Dreams. August 18. Retrieved September 12, 2018 (https://www.commondreams.org/news/2018/08/18/trumps-immoral-plan-allow-coal-states-self-regulate-could-send-365-million-tons).

Connor, John M., and C. Gustav Helmers. 2007. "Statistics on Modern Private International Cartels, 1990–2005." The American Antitrust Institute, AAI Working Paper No. 07-01. January 10. Retrieved July 15, 2018 (https://www.antitrustinstitute.org/content/aai-working-paper-no-07-01-statistics-modern-private-international-cartels-1990-2005).

Cook, John. 2011. "Roger Ailes' Secret Nixon-Era Blueprint for Fox News." Gawker. June 30. Retrieved September 11, 2018 (http://gawker.com/5814150/roger-ailes-secret-nixon-era-blueprint-for-fox-news).

Cook, John, Dana Nuccitelli, Sarah A. Green, Mark Richardson, Bärbel Winkler, Rob Painting, Robert Way, Peter Jacobs, and Andrew Skuce. 2013. "Quantifying the Consensus on Anthropogenic Global Warming in the Scientific Literature." *Environmental Research Letters* 8: 1–7. DOI: 10.1088/1748-9326/8/2/024024.

Cooley, Charles Horton. 1902. *Human Nature and the Social Order*. New York: Scribner's.

Cooper, Betsy, Daniel Cox, Rachel Lienesch, and Robert P. Jones. 2016. "Exodus: Why Americans Are Leaving Religion—and Why They're Unlikely to Come Back." PRRI. September 22. Retrieved July 26, 2018 (https://www.prri.org/research/prri-rns-poll-nones-atheist-leaving-religion/).

Copping, Jasper. 2012. "British Have Invaded Nine Out of Ten Countries—So Look Out Luxembourg." *The Telegraph*. November 4. Retrieved July 27, 2018 (https://www.telegraph.co.uk/history/9653497/British-have-invaded-nine-out-of-ten-countries-so-look-out-Luxembourg.html).

Corbett, Jessica. 2018a. "Sanders Slams US Inequality as Report Finds Nearly Half of Americans Can't Afford Basic Necessities." Common Dreams. May 18. Retrieved May 31, 2018 (https://www.commondreams.org/news/2018/05/18/sanders-slams-us-inequality-report-finds-nearly-half-americans-cant-afford-basic).

Corbett, Jessica. 2018b. "'This Is Not Ok': Guard Shoves Reporter as EPA Bars Multiple News Outlets from Water Pollution Event." Common Dreams. May 22. Retrieved June 20, 2018 (https://www.commondreams.org/news/2018/05/22/not-ok-guard-shoves-reporter-epa-bars-multiple-news-outlets-water-pollution-event).

Corbett, Jessica. 2018c. "With 'Mountainous' Evidence on Plaintiff's Side, Hundreds of Cancer Cases Against Monsanto Get Green Light." Common Dreams. July 20. Retrieved August 12, 2018 (https://www.commondreams.org/news/2018/07/10/

mountainous-evidence-plaintiffs-side-hundreds-cancer-cases-against-monsanto-get/).

Cox, Daniel. 2017. "Way More Americans May Be Atheists than We Thought." FiveThirtyEight. May 18. Retrieved July 26, 2018 (https://fivethirtyeight.com/features/way-more-americans-may-be-atheists-than-we-thought/).

Cox, Daniel, Rachel Lienesch, and Robert P. Jones. 2017. "Beyond Economics: Fears of Cultural Displacement Pushed the White Working Class to Trump." PRRI / *The Atlantic*. May 9. Retrieved June 12, 2018 (https://www.prri.org/research/white-working-class-attitudes-economy-trade-immigration-election-donald-trump/).

Cox, Jeff. 2018. "Investors Are Yanking Money Out of Global Stocks at Levels Not Seen Since the 2008 Financial Crisis." CNBC. June 28. Retrieved August 18, 2018 (https://www.cnbc.com/2018/06/28/global-stocks-see-biggest-loss-of-investor-cash-since-the-financial-cr.html).

Crandall, Christian S., Jason M. Miller, and Mark H. White. 2018. "Changing Norms Following the 2016 US Presidential Election." *Social Psychological and Personality Science* 9 (2): 186–192.

Croucher, Shane. 2017. "Western Banks, Terrorism and Isis: The Nihilism of Dark Finance Fuelling Global Insecurity." *International Business Times*. March 3. Retrieved September 1, 2018 (https://www.ibtimes.co.uk/western-banks-terrorism-isis-nihilism-dark-finance-fuelling-global-insecurity-1474508).

Crudele, John. 2014. "US Economic Growth Is All an Illusion." *New York Post*. November 6. Retrieved June 29, 2018 (https://nypost.com/2014/11/06/us-economic-growth-is-all-an-illusion/).

Cuthbertson, Anthony. 2017. "Rich Americans Live 15 Years Long than Poor Counterparts: Study." *Newsweek*. April 7. Retrieved July 24, 2018 (https://www.newsweek.com/rich-americans-live-15-years-longer-poor-study-580486/).

Dabla-Norris, Era, Kalpana Kochhar, Nujin Suphaphiphat, Frantisek Ricka, and Evridiki Tsounta. 2015 (June). "Causes and Consequences of Income Inequality: A Global Perspective." International Monetary Fund. Strategy, Policy, and Review Department. Retrieved July 15, 2018 (https://www.imf.org/external/pubs/ft/sdn/2015/sdn1513.pdf).

Dahir, Abdi Latif. 2018. "The Growing Membership of a China-Led Development Bank Challenges the IMF-World Bank Orthodoxy." Quartz | Africa. May 9. Retrieved June 29, 2018 (https://qz.com/1273424/kenya-joins-china-led-asian-infrastructure-investment-bank-aiib/).

Dale, Daniel. 2018. "Donald Trump Makes 100 False Claims for Second Consecutive Week." *The Star*. July 6. Retrieved August 8, 2018 (https://www.thestar.com/news/world/analysis/2018/07/06/donald-trump-makes-100-false-claims-for-second-consecutive-week.html).

Dalton, Jane. 2018. "World's First Ocean Plastic-Cleaning Machine Set to Tackle Great Pacific Garbage Patch." *Independent*. April 22. Retrieved July 5, 2018 (https://www.independent.co.uk/news/world/americas/ocean-plastic-cleanup-machine-great-pacific-garbage-patch-launch-boyan-slat-a8317226.html).

Darlington, Shasta, and Patrick Gillespie. 2017. "Mexican Farmer's Daughter: NAFTA Destroyed Us." CNN | Money. Retrieved September 6, 2018 (https://money.cnn.com/2017/02/09/news/economy/nafta-farming-mexico-us-corn-jobs/index.html).

Das, Satyajit. 2018. "How the US Has Weaponized the Dollar." Bloomberg. September 6. Retrieved September 23, 2018 (https://www.bloomberg.com/view/articles/2018-09-06/how-the-u-s-has-made-a-weapon-of-the-dollar).

Data for Progress. 2018. "Polling the Left Agenda." Retrieved August 10, 2018 (https://www.dataforprogress.org/polling-the-left-agenda/).

Davey, Melissa. 2017. "Humans Causing Climate to Change 170 Times Natural Forces." *The Guardian*. February 12. Retrieved August 7, 2017 (https://www.theguardian.com/environment/2017/feb/12/humans-causing-climate-to-change-170-times-faster-than-natural-forces).

Davidson, Paul. 2018. "The Economy Is Humming. So Why Do Experts Foresee a Recession in 2020?" *USA Today*. June 11. Retrieved August 20, 2018 (https://www.usatoday.com/story/money/2018/06/11/recession-2020-heres-why-economists-think-may-happen/686177002/).

Davies, Nicholas J.S. 2014. "35 Countries Where the US Has Supported Fascists, Drug Lords and Terrorists." AlterNet. March 4. Retrieved July 31, 2017 (http://www.alternet.org/world/35-countries-where-us-has-supported-fascists-druglords-and-terrorists).

Davis, Chelsea. 2017. "The Truth Behind the Chocolate Industry Will Leave a Bitter Taste in Your Mouth." Paste Magazine. February 15. Retrieved August 20, 2018 (https://www.pastemagazine.com/articles/2017/02/the-truth-behind-the-chocolate-industry-will-leave.html).

Dayen, David. 2018. "How America Broke its Economy." *New Republic*. May 8. Retrieved May 31, 2018 (https://newrepublic.com/article/148329/america-broke-economy).

Del Vicario, Michela, Alessandro Bessi, Fabiana Zollo, Fabio Petroni, Antonio Scala, Guido Caldarelli, H. Eugene Stanley, and Walter Quattrociocchi. 2016. "The Spreading of Misinformation Online." *Proceedings of the National Academy of Sciences* 113 (3): 554–559. doi.org/10.1073/pnas.1517441113.

DeParle, Jason. 2012. "Harder for Americans to Rise from Lower Rungs." *New York Times*. January 4. Retrieved August 4, 2017 (http://www.nytimes.com/2012/01/05/us/harder-for-americans-to-rise-from-lower-rungs.html?pagewanted=all).

Desai, Sonalde, and Amaresh Dubey. 2012. "Caste in 21st Century India: Competing Narratives." *Economic and Political Weekly* 46 (11): 40–49.

Desjardins, Jeff. 2016. "Where Do Raw Materials Come From?" The Visual Capitalist. November 16. Retrieved August 20, 2018 (http://www.visualcapitalist.com/where-do-raw-materials-come-from/).

Desjardins, Jeff. 2018. "These Are the World's Most Traded Goods." World Economic Forum. February 23. Retrieved August 20, 2018 (https://www.weforum.org/agenda/2018/02/the-top-importers-and-exporters-of-the-world-s-18-most-traded-goods).

de Sousa, Ana Naomi. 2016. "Between East and West: The Cold War's Legacy in Africa." Al Jazeera. February 22. Retrieved August 22, 2018 (https://www.aljazeera.com/indepth/features/2016/02/east-west-cold-war-legacy-africa-160214113015863.html).

Deutsche Bank Research. 2009. "Credit Default Swaps." December 21. Retrieved June 29, 2018 (http://citeseerx.ist.psu.edu/viewdoc/download?doi=10.1.1.353.2815&rep=rep1&type=pdf).

Deutsche Welle. 2013. "In Kabul, Trading Women Like Cattle." September 5. Retrieved August 15, 2018 (https://www.dw.com/en/in-kabul-trading-women-like-cattle/a-17059788).

Deutsche Welle. 2018. "Philippines: Rodrigo Duterte to Continue 'Relentless and Chilling' Drugs War." July 23. Retrieved August 8, 2018 (https://www.dw.com/en/philippines-rodrigo-duterte-to-continue-relentless-and-chilling-drugs-war/a-44798233).

Diep, Francie. 2015. "8,000 Years Ago 17 Women Reproduced for Everyone One Man." *Pacific Standard*. March 17. Retrieved August 6, 2017 (http://www.psmag.com/nature-and-technology/17-to-1-reproductive-success).

Dillon, Lindsey, Christopher Sellers, Vivian Underhill, Nicholas Shapiro, Jennifer Liss Ohayon, Marianne Sullivan, Phil Brown, Jill Harrison, Sara Wylie, and the "EPA Under Siege" Writing Group. 2018. "The Environmental Protection Agency in the Early Trump Administration: Prelude to Regulatory Capture." *American Journal of Public Health* 108 (S2): S89–S94. DOI: 10.2105/AJPH.2018.304360.

Dixon, Robyn. 2016. "Child Brides Sold for Cows: The Price of Being a Girl in South Sudan." *Los Angeles Times*. June 29. Retrieved August 15, 2018 (http://www.latimes.com/world/africa/la-fg-south-sudan-child-marriage-snap-story.html).

Dizikes, Peter. 2018. "Checking China's Pollution, by Satellite: Study Finds Reduction in Sulfur Emissions from Power Plants." MIT News. June 18. Retrieved July 5, 2018 (http://news.mit.edu/2018/checking-china-pollution-by-satellite-0618).

Domm, Patti. 2018. "US Oil Exports Boom to Record Level, Surpassing Most OPEC Nations." CNBC. June 27. Retrieved August 21, 2018 (https://www.cnbc.com/2018/06/27/us-oil-exports-boom-to-record-level-surpassing-most-opec-nations.html).

Doré, Louis. 2015. "Society Will Collapse by 2040 Due to Catastrophic Food Shortages, Says Study." *Independent*. June 22. Retrieved July 5, 2018 (https://www.independent.co.uk/environment/climate-change/society-will-collapse-by-2040-due-to-catastrophic-food-shortages-says-study-10336406.html).

Dowie, Mark. 1977. "Pinto Madness." *Mother Jones*. September/October. Retrieved June 5, 2018 (https://www.motherjones.com/politics/1977/09/pinto-madness/).

Doyle, Sady. 2015. "Season of the Witch: Why Young Women Are Flocking to the Ancient Craft." *The Guardian*. February 24. Retrieved June 3, 2018 (https://www.theguardian.com/world/2015/feb/24/witch-symbol-feminist-power-azealia-banks).

Drum, Kevin. 2014. "Chart of the Day: Oil Is Getting Harder and Harder to Find." *Mother Jones*. July 23. Retrieved August 13, 2018 (https://www.motherjones.com/kevin-drum/2014/07/chart-day-oil-getting-harder-and-harder-find/).

Du Bois, W.E.B. 1903. *The Souls of Black Folk*. New York: New American Library, Inc.

Duddu, Praveen. 2014. "The Ten Most Traded Food and Beverage Commodities." Food Processing Technology. February 20. Retrieved August 20, 2018 (https://www.foodprocessing-technology.com/features/featurethe-10-most-traded-food-and-beverage-commodities-4181217/).

Duncan, Greg J., and Richard J. Murnane, eds. 2011. *Whither Opportunity? Rising Inequality, Schools, and Children's Live Chances*. New York: Russell Sage Foundation and Chicago: Spencer Foundation.

Dwyer, Colin. 2018. "New Zealand Bans Home Sales to Most Foreigners: 'It's Not a Right, It's a Privilege.'" National Public Radio | World. August 15. Retrieved August 25, 2018 (https://www.npr.org/2018/08/15/638922391/new-zealand-bans-home-sales-to-most-foreigners-it-s-not-a-right-it-s-a-privilege).

Dynarski, Susan. 2018. "Fresh Proof that Strong Unions Help Reduce Income Inequality." *New York Times*. July 6. Retrieved July 24, 2018 (https://www.nytimes.com/2018/07/06/business/labor-unions-income-inequality.html).

Eaton, Sam. 2018. "Tropical Forests Are Flipping from Storing Carbon to Releasing It." *The Nation*. August 30. Retrieved September 20, 2018 (https://www.thenation.com/article/tropical-forests-are-flipping-from-storing-carbon-to-releasing-it/).

Ebele, Anekwe Jennifer, Mohamed Abou-Elwafa Abdallah, and Stuart Harrad. 2017. "Pharmaceuticals and Personal Care Products (PPCPs) in the Freshwater Aquatic Environment." *Emerging Contaminants* (3): 1–6. doi.org/10.1016/j.emcon.2016.12.004

Edwards, Frank, Michael H. Esposito, and Hedwig Lee. 2018. "Risk of Police-Involved Death by Race/Ethnicity and Place, United States, 2012–2018." *American Journal of Public Health* 108 (9): 1241–1248.

Egan, Matt. 2014. "Billionaires Are Hoarding More Cash." CNN | Money. September 23. Retrieved August 3, 2017 (http://money.cnn.com/2014/09/23/investing/billionaires-hoarding-cash-wealth-investing/index.html).

Egan, Matt. 2018a. "Tax Cut Scorecard: Workers $6 Billion; Shareholders $171 Billion." CNN | Your Money, Your America. February 16. Retrieved June 29, 2018 (http://money.cnn.com/2018/02/16/investing/stock-buybacks-tax-law-bonuses/index.html).

Egan, Matt. 2018b. "Texas to Pass Iraq and Iran as World's No. 3 Oil Producer." CNN. July 17. Retrieved August 21, 2018 (https://money.cnn.com/2018/07/17/investing/texas-oil-iran-iraq-permian-basin/index.html).

Ehrenreich, Barbara. 1989. *Fear of Falling: The Inner Life of the Middle Class.* New York: Pantheon Books.

Eilperin, Juliet, and Darla Cameron. [2017] 2018. "How Trump Is Rolling Back Obama's Legacy." *Washington Post.* March 24, 2017 (updated, January 20, 2018). Retrieved August 8, 2018 (https://www.washingtonpost.com/graphics/politics/trump-rolling-back-obama-rules/?noredirect=on&utm_term=.2656d9732934).

Elkins, Kathleen. 2018. "Most Young Americans Prefer Socialism to Capitalism, New Report Finds." CNBC. August 14. Retrieved August 27, 2018 (https://www.cnbc.com/2018/08/14/fewer-than-half-of-young-americans-are-positive-about-capitalism.html).

Elliot, Larry. 2014a. "Modern Slavery Affects More than 35 Million People, Report Finds." *The Guardian.* November 17. Retrieved August 3, 2017 (https://www.theguardian.com/world/2014/nov/17/modern-slavery-35-million-people-walk-free-foundation-report).

Elliot, Larry. 2014b. "Revealed: How the Wealth Gap Holds Back Economic Growth." *The Guardian.* December 8. Retrieved August 3, 2017 (https://www.theguardian.com/business/2014/dec/09/revealed-wealth-gap-oecd-report).

Elliot, Larry. 2018a. "Global Economic Growth Has Peaked, Warns OECD." *The Guardian.* September 20. Retrieved September 23, 2018 (https://www.theguardian.com/business/2018/sep/20/global-growth-has-peaked-warns-oecd-economic-outlook).

Elliot, Larry. 2018b. "World Bank Recommends Few Regulations Protecting Workers." *The Guardian.* April 20. Retrieved May 23, 2018 (https://www.theguardian.com/money/2018/apr/20/world-bank-fewer-regulations-protecting-workers).

Ellis, Blake. 2013. "Student Debt Delays Spending, Saving—and Marriage." CNN | Money. May 9. Retrieved August 31, 2018 (https://money.cnn.com/2013/05/09/pf/college/student-loan-debt/).

Ellis-Petersen, Hannah. 2018. "Deluge of Electronic Waste Turning Thailand into 'World's Rubbish Dump.'" *The Guardian.* June 28. Retrieved July 1, 2018 (https://www.theguardian.com/world/2018/jun/28/deluge-of-electronic-waste-turning-thailand-into-worlds-rubbish-dump).

Embury-Dennis, Tom. 2018a. "'Dead Zone' Larger than Scotland Found by Underwater Robots in Arabian Sea." *Independent.* April 27. Retrieved June 19, 2018 (https://www.independent.co.uk/environment/dead-zone-arabian-sea-gulf-oman-underwater-robots-ocean-pollution-discovery-a8325676.html).

Embury-Dennis, Tom. 2018b. "Donald Trump Threatens to 'Take Away Media's Credentials' over Negative News Stories About Him." *Independent.* May 9. Retrieved August 8, 2018 (https://www.independent.co.uk/news/world/americas/us-politics/donald-trump-media-credentials-twitter-threat-negative-news-stories-fake-network-a8342901.html).

REFERENCES

Emmott, Robin, and Noah Barkin. 2018. "Exclusive: China Presses Europe for Anti-US Alliance on Trade." Reuters. July 3. Retrieved August 21, 2018 (https://www.reuters.com/article/us-usa-trade-china-eu-exclusive/exclusive-china-presses-europe-for-anti-u-s-alliance-on-trade-idUSKBN1JT1KT).

Enders, Adam M., and Jamil S. Scott. 2018. "White Racial Resentment Has Been Gaining Political Power for Decades." *Washington Post*. January 15. Retrieved June 28, 2018 (https://www.washingtonpost.com/news/monkey-cage/wp/2018/01/15/white-racial-resentment-has-been-gaining-political-power-for-decades/?noredirect=on&utm_term=.4f3d71620b91).

Engels, Frederick. 1934. *The Dialectics of Nature*. Moscow, USSR: Progress Publishers.

England, Charlotte. 2017. "German Breaks Renewables Record with Coal and Nuclear Power Responsible for Only 15% of Country's Total Energy." *Independent*. May 5. Retrieved July 13, 2018 (https://www.independent.co.uk/news/world/europe/germany-renewable-energy-record-coal-nuclear-power-energiewende-low-carbon-goals-a7719006.html).

Erick V.S., Kasie Raymann, and Nancy A. Moran. 2018. "Glyphosate Perturbs the Gut Microbiota of Honey Bees." *Proceedings of the National Academy of Sciences*. Published ahead of print, September 24. doi.org/10.1073/pnas.1803880115.

Espinoza-Orias, Namy, and Adisa Azapagic. 2018. "Understanding the Impact on Climate change of Convenience Food: Carbon Footprint of Sandwiches." *Sustainable Production and Consumption* 15 (July): 1–15. doi.org/10.1016/j.spc.2017.12.002.

Essa, Azad, and Sarin Furcoi. 2017. "Malawi: People with Albinism 'Living in Fear.'" Al Jazeera. June 7. Retrieved July 23, 2018 (https://www.aljazeera.com/news/2017/04/malawi-people-albinism-living-fear-170419064018308.html).

European Geosciences Union. 2018. "New Study: Oxygen Loss in the Coastal Baltic Sea Is 'Unprecedentedly Severe.'" July 5. Retrieved August 12, 2018 (https://www.egu.eu/news/414/new-study-oxygen-loss-in-the-coastal-baltic-sea-is-unprecedentedly-severe/).

Eyre, Eric. 2016. "Drug Firms Poured 780M Painkillers into WV Amid Rise of Overdoses." *Charleston Gazette-Mail*. December 17. Retrieved June 1, 2018 (https://www.wvgazettemail.com/news/cops_and_courts/drug-firms-poured-m-painkillers-into-wv-amid-rise-of/article_99026dad-8ed5-5075-90fa-adb906a36214.html).

Fagen, Richard R. 1975. "The United States and Chile: Roots and Branches." *Foreign Affairs* (January). Retrieved July 31, 2018 (https://www.foreignaffairs.com/articles/chile/1975-01-01/united-states-and-chile-roots-and-branches).

Fahmy, Dalia. 2018. "Key Findings About American's Belief in God." Pew Research Center. April 25. Retrieved July 26, 2018 (http://www.pewresearch.org/fact-tank/2018/04/25/key-findings-about-americans-belief-in-god/).

Ferguson, James. 2015. "The World Will Soon Be at War over Water." *Newsweek*. April 24. Retrieved June 25, 2018 (http://www.newsweek.com/2015/05/01/world-will-soon-be-war-over-water-324328.html).

Ferguson, John Paul. 2017. "More Students, Young Americans Turn to Paganism." The College Fix. October 31. Retrieved June 3, 2018 (https://www.thecollegefix.com/post/38436/).

Fetterly, Madeline. 2014. "Sex Trafficking and China's One Child Policy." The Diplomat. November 6. Retrieved August 16, 2018 (https://thediplomat.com/2014/11/sex-trafficking-and-chinas-one-child-policy/).

Fine Maron, Dina. 2018. "A Conversation with the Only Scientist in Congress." *Scientific American*. July 31. Retrieved September 21, 2018 (https://www.scientificamerican.com/article/a-conversation-with-one-of-few-scientist-in-congress/).

Fingerhut, Hannah. 2018. "Most Americans Express Positive Views of Country's Growing Racial and Ethnic Diversity." Pew Research Center. June 14. Retrieved July 5, 2018 (http://www.pewresearch.org/fact-tank/2018/06/14/most-americans-express-positive-views-of-countrys-growing-racial-and-ethnic-diversity/).

Fischer, Hubertus et al. 2018. "Palaeoclimate Constraints on the Impact of 2°C Anthropogenic Warming and Beyond." *Nature Geoscience* 11: 474–485. DOI: 10.1038/s41561-018-0146-0.

Fitzgerald, Des, Nikolas Rose, and Ilina Singh. 2016. "Revitalizing Sociology: Urban Life and Mental Illness Between History and the Present." *British Journal of Sociology* 67 (1): 138–160.

Folley, Aris. 2018. "Trump Doubles Record for Longest Time Without Science Adviser." The Hill. July 27. Retrieved August 12, 2018 (http://thehill.com/blogs/blog-briefing-room/news/399230-trump-doubles-record-for-going-longest-time-without-science).

Food Empowerment Project. 2018. "Child Labor and Slavery in the Chocolate Industry." Retrieved August 20, 2018 (http://www.foodispower.org/slavery-chocolate/).

Foran, Clare. 2017. "America's Political Divide Intensified During Trump's First Year as President." *The Atlantic*. October 5. Retrieved July 11, 2018 (https://www.theatlantic.com/politics/archive/2017/10/trump-partisan-divide-republicans-democrats/541917/).

Forester, Katie. 2016. "Microplastics in the Sea a Growing Threat to Human Health, United Nations Warns." *Independent*. May 21. Retrieved August 1, 2017 (http://www.independent.co.uk/environment/microplastics-microbeads-ocean-sea-serious-health-risks-united-nations-warns-a7041036.html).

Foroohar, Rana. 2016. *Makers and Takers: The Rise of Finance and the Fall of American Business*. New York: Crown Business.

Forrest, Adam. 2018. "Tokyo Medical University 'Changed Women's Exam Results' to Limit the Number of Female Doctors." *Independent*. August 3. Retrieved August 15, 2018 (https://www.independent.co.uk/news/world/asia/tokyo-medical-exam-results-female-doctors-grades-changed-medicine-a8475966.html).

Fox, Maggie. 2018. "Suicide Rates Are Up 30 Percent Since 1999, CDC Says." NBC News. June 7. Retrieved July 24, 2018 (https://www.nbcnews.com/health/health-news/suicide-rates-are-30-percent-1999-cdc-says-n880926).

REFERENCES

France 24. 2018. "Brazil Deploys Army to Border as Venezuela Crisis Deepens." Reuters. August 29. Retrieved September 13, 2018 (https://www.france24.com/en/20180829-brazil-deploys-army-border-venezuela-crisis-deepens).

Franck, Thomas. 2018. "US Stocks Are Again Headed for New Highs While Rest of the World's Stock Market Struggles." CNBC. August 17. Retrieved August 21, 2018 (https://www.cnbc.com/2018/08/17/the-rest-of-the-world-is-feeling-pain-from-tariffs-and-a-strong-dollar.html).

Frank, Robert. 2017. "Billionaires Are Holding $1.7 Trillion in Cash." CNBC. August 10. Retrieved August 3, 2017 (https://www.cnbc.com/2016/08/10/billionaires-are-hoarding-cash.html).

Fredrickson, George M. 1981. *White Supremacy: A Comparative Study in American and South African History.* Oxford: Oxford University Press.

Fritze, John. 2018. "Novartis Says It Paid Trump Attorney Michael Cohen More than $1 Million for Nothing." *USA Today.* May 9. Retrieved July 29, 2018 (https://www.usatoday.com/story/news/politics/2018/05/09/novartis-questioned-mueller-ties-trump-attorney-michael-cohen/593732002/).

Frontline. 2002. "Bolivia—Leasing the Rain." Public Broadcasting System. June. Retrieved July 16, 2018 (http://www.pbs.org/frontlineworld/stories/bolivia/).

Fry, Richard. 2016. "For First Time in Modern Era, Living with Parents Edges Out Other Living Arrangements for 18- to 34-Year-Olds." Pew Research Center. May 24. Retrieved August 1, 2017 (http://www.pewsocialtrends.org/2016/05/24/for-first-time-in-modern-era-living-with-parents-edges-out-other-living-arrangements-for-18-to-34-year-olds/).

Fuchs, Christian. 2013. "Political Economy and Surveillance Theory." *Critical Sociology* 39 (5): 671–687.

Funes, Yessenia. 2018. "Coal Mining Has Destroyed 1.5 Million Acres of Appalachian Forest." Earther | Gizmodo. July 26. Retrieved August 12, 2018 (https://earther.gizmodo.com/coal-mining-has-destroyed-1-5-million-acres-of-appalach-1827892712).

Funk, McKenzie. 2016. "Cambridge Analytica and the Secret Agenda of a Facebook Quiz." *New York Times.* November 19. Retrieved June 17, 2018 (https://www.nytimes.com/2016/11/20/opinion/cambridge-analytica-facebook-quiz.html).

Gabbatiss, Josh. 2018a. "Chimps and Orangutans among Species in Danger of Being Wiped Out in Imminent Mass Extinction of Primates, Scientists Warn." *Independent.* June 15. Retrieved June 20, 2018 (https://www.independent.co.uk/environment/primates-mass-extinction-chimpanzees-gorillas-monkeys-scientist-warning-brazil-indonesia-a8400186.html).

Gabbatiss, Josh. 2018b. "Rising Sea Levels Will Soon Destroy Underground US Internet Cables, Scientists Warn." *Independent.* July 16. Retrieved August 12, 2018 (https://www.independent.co.uk/environment/sea-levels-rise-internet-cables-climate-change-underground-new-york-miami-a8449716.html).

Gabbatiss, Josh. 2018c. "Scientists Warn Fracking Could Cause Water Shortages after Usage Shoots Up by 800% in Parts of US." *Independent*. August 15. Retrieved September 12, 2018 (https://www.independent.co.uk/environment/fracking-water-shortage-drought-fossil-fuels-oil-gas-duke-university-a8493451.html).

Gabbatiss, Josh. 2018d. "Shell Predicted Dangers of Climate Change in 1980s and Knew Fossil Fuel Industry Was Responsible." *Independent*. April 8. Retrieved June 20, 2018 (https://www.independent.co.uk/news/business/news/shell-predicted-climate-change-fossil-fuel-industry-1980s-global-warming-oil-a8294636.html).

Gannon, Kathy. 2018. "Pashtuns Take to Streets to Accuse Pakistan Army of Abuses." The Quint. April 28. Retrieved August 8, 2018 (https://www.thequint.com/news/world/pashtun-rights-group-protest-against-atrocities-of-pakistani-army).

Gardels, Nathan. 2018. "China Is Laying the Groundwork for a Post-American World Order." *Washington Post*. July 27. Retrieved August 21, 2018 (https://www.washingtonpost.com/news/theworldpost/wp/2018/07/27/america-china/?noredirect=on&utm_term=.afb41aa1062a).

Germanos, Andrea. 2018. "99-Year-Old Nuremberg Prosecutor Calls Trump's Detention of Children a 'Crime Against Humanity.'" Common Dreams. August 8. Retrieved August 9, 2018 (https://www.commondreams.org/news/2018/08/08/99-year-old-nuremberg-prosecutor-calls-trumps-detention-children-crime-against).

Gerstein, Josh. 2017. "One Weird Court Case Linking Trump, Clinton, and a Billionaire Pedophile." Politico. May 4. Retrieved June 16, 2018 (https://www.politico.com/story/2017/05/04/jeffrey-epstein-trump-lawsuit-sex-trafficking-237983).

Gertz, Emily J. 2016. "750 Million People at Risk as Scientists Discover Contamination of One of the World's Biggest Freshwater Supplies." AlterNet. August 31. Retrieved August 1, 2017 (http://www.alternet.org/environment/contamination-threatens-one-worlds-biggest-freshwater-supplies).

Geuss, Megan. 2018. "In 2017, Four US States Generated More than 30% of Their Electricity from Wind." Ars Technica. August 27. Retrieved September 15, 2018 (https://arstechnica.com/information-technology/2018/08/in-2017-four-us-states-generated-more-than-30-of-their-electricity-from-wind/).

Ghilarducci, Teresa. 2018. "Why Wages Won't Rise When Unemployment Falls." *Forbes*. July 18. Retrieved August 31, 2018 (https://www.forbes.com/sites/teresaghilarducci/2018/07/18/why-wages-wont-rise-when-unemployment-falls/#dacoffb5d9df).

Gilbert, David. 2018. "Everything You Need to Know About the Bombshell Report Linking Russia to Brexit." Vice News. June 11. Retrieved July 1, 2018 (https://news.vice.com/en_us/article/zm8gz9/trump-russia-aaron-banks-brexit-farage).

Gilens, Martin, and Benjamin Page. 2014. "Testing Theories of American Politics: Elites, Interest Groups, and Average Citizens." *Perspectives on Politics* 12 (3/September): 564–581.

REFERENCES

Gill, Victoria. 2018. "Marine Plastic: Hundreds of Fragments in Dead Seabirds." BBC | Science and Environment. June 23. Retrieved June 25, 2018 (https://www.bbc.com/news/science-environment-44579422).

Gills, Justin. 2016. "Scientists Warn of Perilous Climate Shift Within Decades, Not Centuries." *New York Times*. March 22. Retrieved August 1, 2017 (https://www.nytimes.com/2016/03/23/science/global-warming-sea-level-carbon-dioxide-emissions.html).

Gilman, Sarah. 2016. "New Map Shows Increase in Human-Caused Earthquake Risk." *National Geographic*. March 28. Retrieved June 18, 2018 (http://news.nationalgeographic.com/2016/03/160328-earthquakes-map-risks-usgs-science/).

Gilson, David. 2010. "Capitol Hill's Top 75 Corporate Sponsors." *Mother Jones*. September / October. Retrieved August 7, 2018 (http://www.motherjones.com/politics/2010/09/capitol-hill-top-corporate-sponsors).

Givetash, Linda. 2018. "Bees Are Dying at an Alarming Rate. Amsterdam May Have the Answer." NBC News. September 7. Retrieve September 20, 2018 (https://www.nbcnews.com/news/world/bees-are-dying-alarming-rate-amsterdam-may-have-answer-n897856).

Global Financial Integrity. 2015. "Financial Flows and Tax Havens." Centre for Applied Research, Norwegian School of Economics, Global Financial Integrity, Jawaharlal Nehru University, Instituto de Estudos Socioeconômicos, and the Nigerian Institute of Social and Economic Research. December. Retrieved June 29, 2018 (http://www.gfintegrity.org/wp-content/uploads/2016/12/Financial_Flows-final.pdf).

GlobalScan / BBC. 2016. "Global Citizenship a Growing Sentiment among Citizens of Emerging Economies: Global Poll." BBC World Service Poll. Retrieved July 15, 2018 (https://globescan.com/wp-content/uploads/2016/04/BBC_GlobeScan_Identity_Season_Press_Release_April%2026.pdf).

Gold, Matea, and Anu Narayanswamy. 2016. "The New Gilded Age: Close to Half of All Super-Pac Money Comes from 50 Donors." *Washington Post*. April 15. Retrieved July 28, 2017 (https://www.washingtonpost.com/politics/the-new-gilded-age-close-to-half-of-all-super-pac-money-comes-from-50-donors/2016/04/15/63dc363c-01b4-11e6-9d36-33d198ea26c5_story.html?utm_term=.274de34828fc).

Golden, Mark. 2018. "Stanford Scientists Advance New Way to Store Wind and Solar Electricity on a Large Scale, Affordably and at Room Temperature." Stanford News Service. July 19. Retrieved August 27, 2018 (https://news.stanford.edu/press-releases/2018/07/19/liquid-metal-high-voltage-flow-battery/).

Goldenberg, Suzanne. 2003. "Bayer Division 'Knowingly Sold' HIV Infected Protein." *The Guardian*. May 23. Retrieved June 5, 2018 (https://www.theguardian.com/world/2003/may/23/aids.suzannegoldenberg).

Goldenberg, Suzanne. 2015. "Exxon Knew of Climate Change in 1981, Email Says—But It Funded Deniers for 27 More Years." *The Guardian*. July 8. Retrieved August 1, 2017 (https://www.theguardian.com/environment/2015/jul/08/exxon-climate-change-1981-climate-denier-funding).

Goldenberg, Suzanne, and Helena Bengtsson. 2016. "Biggest US Coal Company Funded Dozens of Groups Questioning Climate Change." *The Guardian.* June 13. Retrieved August 1, 2017 (https://www.theguardian.com/environment/2016/jun/13/peabody-energy-coal-mining-climate-change-denial-funding).

Goni, Uki. 2016. "Kissinger Hindered US Effort to End Mass Killings in Argentina, According to Files." *The Guardian.* August 9. Retrieved July 31, 2017 (https://www.theguardian.com/world/2016/aug/09/henry-kissinger-mass-killings-argentina-declassified-files).

Graham, Ruth. 2018. "Church of the Donald." Politico Magazine. May/June. Retrieved June 11, 2018 (https://www.politico.com/magazine/story/2018/04/22/trump-christian-evangelical-conservatives-television-tbn-cbn-218008).

Graham-McLay, Charlotte. 2018. "Foreigners Face Ban on Buying Homes in New Zealand After Apocalypse Bolthole Fad Hikes Prices." *The Telegraph.* August 10. Retrieved August 25, 2018 (https://www.telegraph.co.uk/news/2018/08/10/foreigners-face-ban-buying-homes-new-zealand-apocalypse-bolthole/).

Gramlich, John. 2017. "Few Americans Support Cuts to Most Government Programs, Including Medicaid." Pew Research Center. May 26. Retrieved August 10, 2018 (http://www.pewresearch.org/fact-tank/2017/05/26/few-americans-support-cuts-to-most-government-programs-including-medicaid/).

Grannum, Patricia. 2018. "One in Four Japanese Employees Admit to Wanting to Kill Their Boss, Survey Shows." Inquisitr. June 23. Retrieved July 24, 2018 (https://www.inquisitr.com/4955465/one-in-four-japanese-employees-admit-wanting-to-kill-their-boss-survey-shows/).

Griffin, Andrew. 2018. "20,000 Scientists Give Dire Warning About the Future in 'Letter to Humanity'—And the World Is Listening." *Independent.* March 7. Retrieved June 20, 2018 (https://www.independent.co.uk/environment/letter-to-humanity-scientists-warning-climate-change-global-warming-experts-a8243606.html).

Griffith, Hywel. 2016. "Great Barrier Reef Suffered Worst Bleaching on Record in 2016, Report Finds." BBC. November 28. Retrieved August 1, 2017 (http://www.bbc.com/news/world-australia-38127320).

Grit Post Editorial Board. 2018. "America Is on Fire, but Cable News Won't Mention Climate Change as the Culprit." Gritpost. July 31. 2018. Retrieved August 11, 2018 (https://gritpost.com/cable-news-climate-change/).

Gruebner, Oliver, Michael A. Rapp, Mazda Adli, Ulrike Kluge, Sandro Galea, and Andreas Heinz. 2017. "Cities and Mental Health." *Deutsches Ärzteblatt International* 114 (8): 121–127.

Guardian Staff and Agencies. 2018. "Four in 10 Americans Can't Cover a $400 Emergency Expense." *The Guardian.* May 22. Retrieved July 24, 2018 (https://www.theguardian

.com/business/2018/may/22/federal-reserve-emergency-expense-economic-survey).

Guilford, Gwynn. 2014. "An Entire Island Nation Is Preparing to Evacuate to Fiji before They Sink into the Pacific." Quartz. July 1. Retrieved August 2, 2017 (https://qz.com/228948/an-entire-island-nation-is-preparing-to-evacuate-to-fiji-before-they-sink-into-the-pacific/).

Guilford, Gwynn. 2018. "The Epic Mistake About Manufacturing That's Cost Americans Millions of Jobs." Quartz. May 3. Retrieved August 18, 2018 (https://qz.com/1269172/the-epic-mistake-about-manufacturing-thats-cost-americans-millions-of-jobs/).

Gunders, Dana. 2012. "Wasted: How America Is Losing Up to 40 Percent of Its Food from Farm to Fork to Landfill." National Resource Defense Council Issue Paper. August, IP: 12-06-B. Retrieved July 15, 2018 (https://assets.nrdc.org/sites/default/files/wasted-food-IP.pdf?_ga=2.215687700.2003740465.1531648473-1530218673.1531648473).

Gunnoe, Andrew, and Paul K. Gellert. 2011. "Financialization, Shareholder Value, and the Transformation of Timberland Ownership in the US." *Critical Sociology* 37 (3): 265–284.

Guterres, António. 2018. "The Rohingya Are Victims of Ethnic Cleansing. The World Has Failed Them." *Washington Post*. July 10. Retrieved August 8, 2018 (https://www.washingtonpost.com/opinions/the-rohingya-are-victims-of-ethnic-cleansing-the-world-has-failed-them/2018/07/10/08cab8a0-8447-11e8-9e80-403a221946a7_story.html?noredirect=on&utm_term=.65ba67f92e61).

Guttentag, Joseph, and Reuven S. Avi-Yonah. 2005. "Closing the International Tax Gap." Pp. 99–110 in *Bridging the Tax Gap: Addressing the Crisis in Federal Tax Administration*, edited by M.B. Sawicky. Washington, D.C.: Economic Policy Institute.

Habermas, Jürgen. 1981a. *Theory of Communicative Action, Volume One: Reason and the Rationalization of Society*. Boston: Beacon Press.

Habermas, Jürgen. 1981b. *Theory of Communicative Action, Volume Two: Lifeworld and System: A Critique of Functionalist Reason*. Boston: Beacon Press.

Hamilton, James D. 2009. "The Causes and Consequences of the Oil Shocks of 2007–2008." Brookings Papers on Economic Activity, Economic Studies Program, The Brookings Institute 40 (1/Spring): 215–283. DOI: 10.3386/w15002.

Hance, Jeremy. 2018. "Scientists Call for a Paris-Style Agreement to Save Life on Earth." *The Guardian*. June 28. Retrieved July 13, 2018 (https://www.theguardian.com/environment/radical-conservation/2018/jun/28/scientists-call-for-a-paris-style-agreement-to-save-life-on-earth).

Handwerk, Brian. 2016. "An Ancient, Brutal Massacre May Be the Earliest Evidence of War." Smithsonian.com. January 20. Retrieved July 23, 2018 (https://www.smithsonianmag.com/science-nature/ancient-brutal-massacre-may-be-earliest-evidence-war-180957884/).

Hanley, Steve. 2018. "Cooling People in a Hotter World Could Consume All of World's Renewable Energy by 2050." Clean Technica. July 13. Retrieved August 12, 2018 (https://cleantechnica.com/2018/07/13/cooling-people-in-a-hotter-world-could-consume-all-of-worlds-electricity-by-2050/).

Happiness Research Institute. 2015. "The Facebook Experiment: Does Social Media Affect the Quality of Our Lives?" Retrieved August 2, 2017 (https://docs.wixstatic.com/ugd/928487_680fc12644c8428eb728cde7d61b13e7.pdf).

Haque, Umair. 2018. "Why Didn't America Become Part of the Modern World?" Eudaimonia & Co. July 9. Retrieved August 27, 2018 (https://eand.co/why-didnt-america-become-part-of-the-modern-world-dac6d65e9015).

Haque, Sayed Emdadul, and Habibul Ahsan. 2014. "Human Rights Violations Against Women: Acid Violence in Bangladesh." *American Journal of Preventative Medicine* 46 (2): 216–217.

Harding, Luke. 2016. "What Are the Panama Papers? A Guide to History's Biggest Data Leak." *The Guardian*. April 5. Retrieved July 29, 2018 (https://www.theguardian.com/news/2016/apr/03/what-you-need-to-know-about-the-panama-papers).

Harriot, Michael. 2018. "Evidence Shows Hackers Changed Votes in the 2016 Election but No One Will Admit It." The Root. August 1. Retrieved August 21, 2018 (https://www.theroot.com/evidence-shows-hackers-changed-votes-in-the-2016-electi-1827871206).

Harris, Chris. 2018. "August in Europe 'Was the Warmest on Record.'" Euronews. September 5. Retrieved September 22, 2018 (https://www.euronews.com/2018/09/05/august-in-europe-was-the-warmest-on-record).

Harris, S.H. 2002. *Factories of Death. Japanese Biological Warfare, 1932—1945, and the American Cover-Up,* revised edition. New York: Routledge.

Hartmann, Margaret. 2018. "Trump Thought North Korea's State TV Was Even Better than Fox: Report." NYMag.com | Daily Intelligencer. June 15. Retrieved August 11, 2018 (http://nymag.com/daily/intelligencer/2018/06/trump-thought-north-korea-state-tv-was-even-better-than-fox.html).

Heath, Brad, Fredreka Schouten, Steve Reilly, Nick Penzenstadler, and Aamer Madhani. 2017. "Trump Gets Millions from Golf Members. CEOs and Lobbyists Get Access to President." *USA Today*. September 8. Retrieved July 29, 2018 (https://www.usatoday.com/story/news/2017/09/06/trump-gets-millions-golf-members-ceos-and-lobbyists-get-access-president/632505001/).

Hellman, Matilda. 2018. "Opioids, Opioids, Opioids: The Plague Among Middle-Aged White Americans.." *Nordic Studies on Alcohol and Drugs* 35 (5): 325–328.

Helm, Kieran P., Nathaniel L. Bindoff, and John A. Church. 2011. "Observed Decreases in Oxygen Content of the Global Ocean." *Geophysical Research Letters* 38: L23602. DOI: 10.1029/2011GL049513.

Helmore, Edward. 2017. "The American Dream? Top 20% Pulling Away from the Rest, Study Finds." *The Guardian*. June 4. Retrieved August 2, 2017 (https://www.theguardian.com/us-news/2017/jun/04/american-dream-economics-uppper-middle-class-study).

Henley, Jon, Finbarr Sheehy, Glenn Swann, and Chris Fenn. 2017. "Beyond Catalonia: Pro-Independence Movements in Europe." *The Guardian*. October 27. Retrieved September 24, 2018 (https://www.theguardian.com/world/ng-interactive/2017/oct/27/beyond-catalonia-pro-independence-movements-in-europe-map).

Hill, Lisa. 2001. "The Hidden Theology of Adam Smith." *European Journal of the History of Economic Thought* 8 (1): 1–29. doi.org/10.1080/713765225.

Hiltzik, Michael. 2018. "Employers Will Do Almost Anything to Find Workers to Fill Jobs—Except Pay Them More." *Los Angeles Times*. July 10. Retrieved July 24, 2018 (http://www.latimes.com/business/hiltzik/la-fi-hiltzik-employment-20180710-story.html).

Hincks, Joseph. 2018. "Duterte Is Assassinating Opponents Under the Cover of the Drug War, Philippine Rights Groups Say." *Time*. July 5. Retrieved August 8, 2018 (http://time.com/5330071/philippines-mayors-political-assassination-duterte/).

Hoare, Philip. 2018. "Microplastics in Our Mussels: The Sea Is Feeding Human Garbage Back to Us." *The Guardian*. June 8. Retrieved June 19, 2018 (https://www.theguardian.com/environment/shortcuts/2018/jun/08/microplastics-in-our-mussels-the-sea-is-feeding-human-garbage-back-to-us).

Hochschild, Adam. 1998. *King Leopold's Ghost*. New York: Mariner Books.

Hodges, Jeremy. 2018. "Electric Buses Are Hurting the Oil Industry." Bloomberg. April 23. Retrieved July 5, 2018 (https://www.bloomberg.com/news/articles/2018-04-23/electric-buses-are-hurting-the-oil-industry).

Holmes, Jacob. 2018. "To Supporters, Trump Isn't Just Right—He Controls the Truth." *Esquire*. July 31. Retrieved September 6, 2018 (https://www.esquire.com/news-politics/a22600827/donald-trump-supporters-believe-the-media/).

Horwitz, Jeff. 2018. "AP: Trump 2020 Working with ex-Cambridge Analytica Staffers." Associated Press News. June 15. Retrieved September 11, 2018 (https://apnews.com/96928216bdc341ada659447973a688e4).

Howard, Jacqueline. 2016. "Black Men Nearly 3 Times as Likely to Die from Police Use of Force, Study Says." CNN. December 20. Retrieved August 17, 2018 (https://www.cnn.com/2016/12/20/health/black-men-killed-by-police/index.html).

Hudler, Haley. 2015. "Yale Students Demand Resignations from Faculty Members over Halloween Email." The Fire: The Foundation for Individual Rights in Education. November 6. Retrieved August 3, 2017 (https://www.thefire.org/yale-students-demand-resignations-from-faculty-members-over-halloween-email/).

Hudson, John, Paul Sonne, Karen DeYoung, and Josh Dawsey. 2018. "US Assessing Cost of Keeping Troops in Germany as Trump Battles with Europe." *Washington Post*. June 29. Retrieved August 21, 2018 (https://www.washingtonpost.com/world/national-security/us-assessing-cost-of-keeping-troops-in-germany-as-trump-battles-with-europe/2018/06/29/94689094-ca9f-490c-b3be-b135970de3fc_story.html?noredirect=on&utm_term=.71392caaf3f4).

Hughes, Holly. 2018. "'A Sense of Real Fear': Climate Change Photog Katie Orlinsky on Documenting Arctic Melt." PND Pulse. August 30. Retrieved September 20, 2018 (https://pdnpulse.pdnonline.com/2018/08/a-sense-of-real-fear-climate-change-photog-katie-orlinsky-on-documenting-arctic-melt.html).

Huifeng, He. 2018. "China Says US Farmers May Never Regain Market Share Lost in Trade War." Politico. August 11. Retrieved August 18, 2018 (https://www.politico.com/story/2018/08/11/farmers-china-soy-bean-market-share-734773).

Hunt, Albert R. 2018. "Yes, Russian Election Sabotage Helped Trump Win." Bloomberg. July 24. Retrieved August 21, 2018 (https://www.bloomberg.com/view/articles/2018-07-24/russian-meddling-helped-trump-win-in-2016).

Hunziker, Robert. 2016. "Fukushima: Worse than a Disaster." *Counterpunch*. June 7. Retrieved August 1, 2017 (https://www.counterpunch.org/2016/06/07/fukushima-worse-than-a-disaster/).

Hunziker, Robert. 2018. "State of the Climate—It's Alarming!" *Counterpunch*. June 15. Retrieved June 19, 2018 (https://www.counterpunch.org/2018/06/15/state-of-the-climate-its-alarming/).

Hyun Choi, Jung, Jun Zhu, and Laurie Goodman. 2018. "The State of Millennial Homeownership." Urban Institute. July 11. Retrieved August 31, 2018 (https://www.urban.org/urban-wire/state-millennial-homeownership).

Imbert, Fred. 2018a. "Capitalism Is Killing the Planet and Needs to Change, Says Investor Jeremy Grantham." CNBC. June 13. Retrieved July 13, 2018 (https://www.cnbc.com/2018/06/13/gmos-grantham-capitalists-need-to-wake-up-to-climate-change-reality.html).

Imbert, Fred. 2018b. "China Slaps 25% Tariffs on $16 Billion Worth of US Goods." CNBC. August 8. Retrieved August 18, 2018 (https://www.cnbc.com/2018/08/08/china-announces-25percent-tariffs-on-16-billion-worth-of-us-goods-including.html).

Imbert, Fred. 2018c. "Turkish Lira Plunges 14% Versus Dollar After Trump Authorizes Doubling Metals Tariffs on Turkey." CNBC. August 10. Retrieved August 18, 2018 (https://www.cnbc.com/2018/08/10/turkish-lira-loss-deepens-as-pm-erdogan-calls-for-citizens-to-convert-.html).

Inagaki, Kazuyuki. 2010. "Income Inequality and the Suicide Rate in Japan: Evidence from Cointegration and LA-VAR." *Journal of Applied Economics* 13 (1): 113–133.

Influence Map. 2018. "Corporate Lobbying: How Companies Really Impact Progress on Climate." Retrieved September 22, 2018 (https://www.desmogblog.com/2018/09/12/report-90-percent-world-s-largest-200-industrial-companies-are-using-trade-associations-oppose-climate-policy).

Ingraham, Christopher. 2014. "White People Are More Likely to Deal Drugs, but Black People Are More Likely to Get Arrested for It." *Washington Post*. September 30. Retrieved August 3, 2017 (https://www.washingtonpost.com/news/wonk/wp/2014/09/30/white-people-are-more-likely-to-deal-drugs-but-black-people-are-more-likely-to-get-arrested-for-it/?utm_term=.961c72d72843).

Irfan, Umair. 2018. "Wildfires Have Ignited Inside the Arctic Circle." Vox. July 25. Retrieved August 12, 2018 (https://www.vox.com/2018/7/24/17607722/wildfires-greece-sweden-arctic-circle-heat-wave).

ITEP (Institute on Taxation and Economic Policy). 2017. "Fortune 500 Companies Hold a Record $2.6 Trillion Offshore." March 28. Retrieved September 25, 2018 (https://itep.org/fortune-500-companies-hold-a-record-26-trillion-offshore/).

Jacobs, Tom. 2018. "More Evidence that Racism and Sexism Were key to Trump's Victory." *Pacific Standard*. April 4. Retrieved September 12, 2018 (https://psmag.com/social-justice/more-evidence-that-racism-and-sexism-were-key-to-trump-victory).

Jacobs, Brian, Lauren E. James, Laura Parker, Kelsey Nowakowski, and Lawson Parker. 2016. "A Vanishing Aquifer: What Happens When the Water Runs Out?" *National Geographic*. August. Retrieved June 19, 2018 (https://www.nationalgeographic.com/magazine/2016/08/vanishing-aquifer-interactive-map/).

Jacobson, Mark Z. 2008. "The Causal Link Between Carbon Dioxide and Air Pollution Mortality." *Geophysical Research Letters* 35: L03808. DOI: 10.1029/2007GL031101.

Jamail, Dahr. 2018. "May 2018 Broke Thousands of Temperature Records Across the US." Truthout. June 18. Retrieved June 25, 2018 (https://truthout.org/articles/may-2018-broke-thousands-of-temperature-records-across-the-us/).

Jardine, Matthew. 1996. *East Timor: Genocide in Paradise*. Monroe, Maine: Odonian Press.

Jevrejeva, S., L.P. Jackson, A. Grinstead, D. Lincke, and B. Marzeion. 2018. "Flood Damage Costs Under the Sea Level Rise with Warming of 1.5° C and 2° C." *Environmental Research Letters* 13. doi.org/10.1088/1748-9326/aacc76.

Johnson, Jake. 2018a. "After Long Career Bailing Out Big Banks, Obama Treasury Secretary Tim Geithner Now Runs Predatory Firm That Exploits the Poor for Profit." Common Dreams. July 2. Retrieved August 31, 2018 (https://www.commondreams.org/news/2018/07/02/after-long-career-bailing-out-big-banks-obama-treasury-secretary-tim-geithner-now).

Johnson, Jake. 2018b. "As Bezos Becomes Richest Man in Modern History, Amazon Workers Mark #PrimeDay with Strikes against Low Pay and Brutal Conditions." Common Dreams. July 17. Retrieved August 31, 2018 (https://www.commondreams

.org/news/2018/07/17/bezos-becomes-richest-man-modern-history-amazon-workers-mark-primeday-strikes).

Johnson, Jake. 2018c. "As Global 1% Seize Economy's Gains, 'Unprecedented Wage Stagnation' for Everyone Else." Common Dreams. July 5. Retrieved July 11, 2018 (https://www.commondreams.org/news/2018/07/05/global-1-seize-economys-gains-unprecedented-wage-stagnation-everyone-else).

Johnston, Ian. 2017. "Gorillas, Monkeys and Other Primates Must Be Saved from 'Impending Extinction,' Urge 31 Scientists." *Independent.* January 18. Retrieved June 20, 2018 (https://www.independent.co.uk/environment/gorilla-monkeys-primates-save-from-impending-extinction-31-scientists-urge-a7533631.html).

Jolley, Mary Ann, and Liz Gooch. 2016. "'Sold Like Cows and Goats': India's Slave Brides." Al Jazeera. November 14. Retrieved August 15, 2018 (https://www.aljazeera.com/indepth/features/2016/11/cows-goats-india-slave-brides-161114084933017.html).

Jones, Jessica. 2015. "Lucía and Hugo Are Top Baby Names in Spain." *The Local.* May 21. Retrieved August 6, 2017 (https://www.thelocal.es/20150521/luca-and-hugo-top-baby-names-in-spain).

Jones, Sarah. 2016. "J.D. Vance, the False Prophet of Blue America." *New Republic.* November, 17. Retrieved July 16, 2018 (https://newrepublic.com/article/138717/jd-vance-false-prophet-blue-america).

Jorgenson, Andrew K. 2010. "World-Economic Integration, Supply Depots, and Environmental Degradation: A Study of Ecologically Unequal Exchange, Foreign Investment Dependence, and Deforestation in Less Developed Countries." *Critical Sociology* 36 (3): 453–477.

Joyce, Christopher. 2016. "Rising Seas Push Too Much Salt into the Florida Everglades." National Public Radio. May 25. Retrieved August 1, 2017 (http://www.npr.org/2016/05/25/477014085/rising-seas-push-too-much-salt-into-the-florida-everglades).

Judicial Watch. 2003. "Cheney Energy Task Force Documents Feature Map of Iraqi Oil Fields." July 17. Retrievred September 13, 2018 (https://www.judicialwatch.org/press-room/press-releases/cheney-energy-task-force-documents-feature-map-of-iraqi-oilfields/).

Just, Peter. 1980. "Time and Leisure in the Elaboration of Culture." *Journal of Anthropological Research* 36 (1): 105–115.

Kahan, Dan M., Asheley Landrum, Katie Carpenter, Laura Helft, and Kathleen Hall Jamieson. 2017. "Science Curiosity and Political Information Processing." *Advances in Political Psychology* 38 (S1): 179–199. doi.org/10.1111/pops/12396.

Kahn, Brian. 2018. "It's Ridiculously Hot and Smoky in Siberia Right Now." Earther | Gizmodo. July 5. Retrieved August 12, 2018 (https://earther.gizmodo.com/its-ridiculously-hot-and-smoky-in-siberia-right-now-1827364741).

Kaiman, Jonathan. 2014. "China's Toxic Air Pollution Resembles Nuclear Winter, Say Scientists." *The Guardian*. February 25. Retrieved August 1, 2017 (https://www.theguardian.com/world/2014/feb/25/china-toxic-air-pollution-nuclear-winter-scientists).

Kakutani, Michiko. 2018. "The Death of Truth: How We Gave Up on Facts and Ended Up with Trump." *The Guardian*. July 14. Retrieved August 27, 2018 (https://www.theguardian.com/books/2018/jul/14/the-death-of-truth-how-we-gave-up-on-facts-and-ended-up-with-trump).

Kamal, Hassan M. 2016. "Delhi Pollution: India Could Learn from London's Great Smog of 1952, Clean Air Act." *First Post*. November 9. Retrieved August 1, 2017 (http://www.firstpost.com/india/delhi-pollution-india-could-learn-from-londons-great-smog-of-1952-clean-air-act-3097430.html).

Kaplan, David. 2000. "The Darker Side of the 'Original Affluent Society.'" *Journal of Anthropological Research* 56 (3): 301–324.

Karagiannopoulos, Lefteris. 2018. "Warmest May Since 1900 to Cost Norwegians $2.34 Billion for More Power." Reuters. July 10. Retrieved August 12, 2018 (https://www.reuters.com/article/us-norway-power-prices/warmest-may-since-1900-to-cost-norwegians-2-34-billion-more-for-power-this-year-idUSKBN1K0257).

Karagueuzian, Hrayr S., Celia White, James Sayre, and Amos Normal. 2012. "Cigarette Smoke Radioactivity and Lung Cancer Risk." *Nicotine & Tobacco Research* 14 (1): 79–90.

Karlin, Mark. 2018. "Henry A. Giroux: The Nightmare of Neoliberal Fascism." Truthout. June 10. Retrieved July 5, 2018 (https://truthout.org/articles/henry-a-giroux-the-nightmare-of-neoliberal-fascism/).

Kart, Jeff. 2018. "The Ocean Cleanup Is Starting, Aims to Cut Garbage by 90% by 2040." Forbes. August 28. Retrieved September 15, 2018 (https://www.forbes.com/sites/jeffkart/2018/08/28/the-ocean-cleanup-is-starting-aims-to-cut-garbage-patch-by-90-by-2040/#71aa0cc9253e).

Katz, Josh. 2017. "Drug Deaths in America Are Rising Faster than Ever." *New York Times*. June 6. Retrieved August 2, 2017 (https://www.nytimes.com/interactive/2017/06/05/upshot/opioid-epidemic-drug-overdose-deaths-are-rising-faster-than-ever.html).

Kaufman, Mark. "It's 90 Degrees in the Arctic Circle this Week. Here's Why." 2018. Mashable. July 31. Retrieved August 13, 2018 (https://mashable.com/2018/07/31/arctic-heat-wave-climate-change/?utm_cid=hp-h-2#fVukBv.6taqX).

Kazuo, Rodrigo, and Meg Perret. 2015. "Occupy the Syllabus." *The Daily Californian | Opinion*. January 20. Retrieved July 13, 2018 (http://www.dailycal.org/2015/01/20/occupy-syllabus/).

Keiichi, Tsuneishi. 2005. "Unit 731 and the Japanese Imperial Army's Biological Warfare Program." *Asia-Pacific Journal* 3 (11/November), translated by John Junkerman. Retrieved September 5, 2018 (https://apjjf.org/-Tsuneishi-Keiichi/2194/article.html).

Kelland, Kate. 2017. "Sperm Count Dropping in Western World." *Scientific American | Reuters*. July 6. Retrieved September 12, 2018 (https://www.scientificamerican.com/article/sperm-count-dropping-in-western-world/).

Kelly, Annie. 2016. "Nestlé Admits Slavery in Thailand While Fighting Child Labour Lawsuit in Ivory Coast." *The Guardian*. February 1. Retrieved August 3, 2017 (https://www.theguardian.com/sustainable-business/2016/feb/01/nestle-slavery-thailand-fighting-child-labour-lawsuit-ivory-coast).

Kelly, Annie. 2018. "Thai Seafood: Are the Prawns on Your Plate Still Fished by Slaves?" *The Guardian*. January 23. Retrieved September 23, 2018 (https://www.theguardian.com/global-development/2018/jan/23/thai-seafood-industry-report-trafficking-rights-abuses).

Kennedy, John. 2016. "Barclays Says 2nd Circ. Terrorism Ruling Dooms Libor Suit." Law360. September 20. Retrieved September 1, 2018 (https://www.law360.com/articles/841934/barclays-says-2nd-circ-terrorism-ruling-dooms-libor-suit).

Khanna, Parag. 2016. "These 25 Companies Are More Powerful than Countries." *Foreign Policy*. Originally published the March/April 2016 issue. Retrieved July 24, 2017 (http://foreignpolicy.com/2016/03/15/these-25-companies-are-more-powerful-than-many-countries-multinational-corporate-wealth-power/).

Khazan, Olga. 2018. "Being Black in America Can Be Hazardous to Your Health." *The Atlantic*. July/August. Retrieved June 28, 2018 (https://www.theatlantic.com/magazine/archive/2018/07/being-black-in-america-can-be-hazardous-to-your-health/561740/).

Kilgore, James. 2015. "Mass Incarceration: Examining and Moving Beyond the New Jim Crow." *Critical Sociology* 41 (2): 283–295.

Kim, Tae. 2018. "Warren Buffet on Why Bubbles Happen: People See Neighbors 'Dumbing than They Are' Getting Rich." CNBC. September 12. Retrieved September 21, 2018 (https://www.cnbc.com/2018/09/12/warren-buffett-on-why-the-next-financial-crisis-is-unavoidable-greed.html).

Kipnis, Laura. 2015. "Sexual Paranoia Strikes Academe." *The Chronicle of Higher Education*. February 27. Retrieved July 13, 2018 (https://www.chronicle.com/article/Sexual-Paranoia-Strikes/190351).

Kirshner, Jonathan. 2015. "American Power and the Global Financial Crisis: How About Now?" Forbes. March 12. Retrieved August 21, 2018 (https://www.forbes.com/sites/jonathankirshner/2015/03/12/american-power-and-the-global-financial-crisis-how-about-now/#6b4452d47c54).

Knoblauch, Christian, Christian Beer, Susanne Liebner, Mikhail N. Grigoriev, and Eva-Maria Pfeiffer. 2018. "Methane Production as Key to the Greenhouse Gas Budget of Thawing Permafrost." *Nature Climate Change* 8 (April): 309–312.

Kodjak, Alison. 2017. "In Ads, Tobacco Companies Admit They Made Cigarettes More Addictive." National Public Radio | All Things Considered. November 27. Retrieved

July 29, 2018 (https://www.npr.org/sections/health-shots/2017/11/27/566014966/in-ads-tobacco-companies-admit-they-made-cigarettes-more-addictive).

Kolanovic, Marko. 2018. "JP Morgan's Top Quant Warns Next Crisis to Have Flash Crashes and Social Unrest Not Seen in 50 Years." CNBC | Finance. September 4. Retrieved September 23, 2018 (https://www.cnbc.com/2018/09/04/jpmorgan-says-next-crisis-will-feature-flash-crashes-and-social-unrest.html).

Kolbert, Elizabeth. 2015. "Will Humans Survive the Sixth Great Extinction?" *National Geographic*. June 23. Retrieved August 14, 2018 (https://news.nationalgeographic.com/2015/06/150623-sixth-extinction-kolbert-animals-conservation-science-world/).

Konkel, Lindsey. 2016. "Why Are These Male Fish Growing Eggs?" *National Geographic*. February 3. Retrieved June 22, 2018 (https://news.nationalgeographic.com/2016/02/160203-feminized-fish-endocrine-disruption-hormones-wildlife-refuges/).

Kopf, Dan. 2017. "American Poverty Is Moving to the Suburbs." Quartz. June 9. Retrieved August 2, 2017 (https://qz.com/1001261/american-poverty-is-moving-to-the-suburbs/).

Korn, Sandra Y.L. 2014. "The Doctrine of Academic Freedom: Let's Give Up on Academic Freedom in Favor of Justice." *The Harvard Crimson*. February 18. Retrieved July 13, 2018 (https://www.thecrimson.com/column/the-red-line/article/2014/2/18/academic-freedom-justice/).

Korte, Gregory. 2018. "In Hiring Michael Cohen, AT&T Betrays a Complicated Relationship with Trump." *USA Today*. May 9. Retrieved July 29, 2018 (https://www.usatoday.com/story/news/politics/2018/05/09/michael-cohen-payment-t-ceo-randall-stephensons-complicated-relationship-trump/594801002/).

Koski Alissa, and Jody Heymann. 2017. "Thirty-Year Trends in the Prevalence and Severity of Female Genital Mutilation: A Comparison of 22 Countries." *BMJ Global Health* 2 (4):e000467. doi.org/10.1136/bmjgh-2017-000467.

Kozik, Jessica. 2016. "Fracking Exec Reportedly Admits to Targeting the Poor, Because They Don't Have 'The Money to Fight.'" *In These Times*. April 19. Retrieved July 20, 2017 (http://inthesetimes.com/rural-america/entry/19069/exec-admits-fracking-targets-the-poor).

Kratochwill, Lindsey. 2016. "May Broke a New Record for Arctic Sea Ice Loss." *Popular Science*. June 10. Retrieved August 1, 2017 (http://www.popsci.com/may-breaks-new-record-for-arctic-sea-ice-loss).

Krier, Dan. 2009. "Speculative Profit Fetishism in the Age of Finance Capital." *Critical Sociology* 35 (5): 657–675.

Kristof, Nicholas D. 1995. "Unmasking Horror—A Special Report.; Japan Confronting Gruesome War Atrocity." *New York Times* | Archives. March 17. Retrieved September 5, 2018 (https://www.nytimes.com/1995/03/17/world/unmasking-horror

-a-special-report-japan-confronting-gruesome-war-atrocity.html?sec=health& pagewanted=print).

Krumei-Mancuso, Elizabeth J. 2018. "Intellectual Humility's Links to Religion and Spirituality and the Role of Authoritarianism." *Personality and Individual Differences* 130 (August): 65–75. doi.org/10.1016/j.paid.2018.03.037.

Kuek Ser, Kuang Keng. 2016. "Australia and the UK Have a Higher Proportion of Inmates in Private Prisons than the US." Public Radio International | The World. September 1. Retrieved September 6, 2018 (https://www.pri.org/stories/2016-09-01/australia-uk-have-higher-proportion-inmates-private-prisons-us).

Kwon, Diana. 2016. "Does City Life Pose a Risk to Mental Health?" *Scientific American.* May 20. Retrieved July 30, 2018 (https://www.scientificamerican.com/article/does-city-life-pose-a-risk-to-mental-health/).

Laporta, James, and Spencer Ackerman. 2018. "Detention Camps on Military Bases 'Smacks of Totalitarianism,' Troops Say." The Daily Beast. June 25. Retrieved August 8, 2018 (https://www.thedailybeast.com/detention-camps-on-military-bases-smacks-of-totalitarianism-troops-say).

Lartey, Jamiles. 2018. "Corporate Penalties Dropped as Much as 94% under Trump, Study Says." *The Guardian.* July 25. Retrieved September 2, 2018 (https://www.theguardian.com/us-news/2018/jul/25/trump-corporate-penalties-drop-public-citizen-study).

Lavell, Marianne. 2016. "Earth Hasn't Heated Up this Fast Since the Dinosaurs' End." *National Geographic.* March 21. Retrieved August 1, 2017 (http://news.nationalgeographic.com/2016/03/160321-climate-change-petm-global-warming-carbon-emission-rate/).

Lazarus, David. 2018. "The Economy May Be Booming, but Nearly Half of American's Can't Make Ends Meet." *Los Angeles Times.* August 31. Retrieved September 22, 2018 (http://www.latimes.com/business/lazarus/la-fi-lazarus-economy-stagnant-wages-20180831-story.html).

Leahy, Stephan. 2018. "Planet at Risk of Heading Towards Apocalyptic, Irreversible 'Hothouse Earth' State." Motherboard | Vice. August 6. Retrieved August 27, 2018 (https://motherboard.vice.com/en_us/article/8xbdnk/planet-at-risk-of-heading-towards-hothouse-earth).

Lean, Geoffrey. 2012. "The Great Smog of London: The Air was Thick with Apathy." *The Telegraph.* December 6. Retrieved June 23, 2018 (https://www.telegraph.co.uk/news/earth/countryside/9727128/The-Great-Smog-of-London-the-air-was-thick-with-apathy.html).

Lee, Sang-UK, In-Hwan Oh, Hong Jin Jeon, and Sungwon Roh. 2017. "Suicide Rates Across Income Levels: Retrospective Cohort Data on 1 Million Participants Collected Between 2003 and 2013 in South Korea." *Journal of Epidemiology* 6: 258–264. DOI: 10.1016/j.je.2016.06.008.

REFERENCES

Leonhardt, David, and Ian Prasad Philbrick. 2018. "Donald Trump's Racism: The Definitive List." *New York Times*. January 15. Retrieved June 28, 2018 (https://www.nytimes.com/interactive/2018/01/15/opinion/leonhardt-trump-racist.html).

Leslie, Ian 2016. "The Sugar Conspiracy." *The Guardian*. April 7. Retrieved September 1, 2018 (https://www.theguardian.com/society/2016/apr/07/the-sugar-conspiracy-robert-lustig-john-yudkin).

Levine, Bruce E. 2011. "8 Reasons Young Americans Don't Fight Back: How the US Crushed Youth Resistance." AlterNet. July 31. Retrieved July 5, 2018 (https://www.alternet.org/story/151850/8_reasons_young_americans_don%27t_fight_back%3A_how_the_us_crushed_youth_resistance).

Levine, David. 2017. "Are Cities Bad for Mental Health?" *US News & World Report*. July 4. Retrieved July 30, 2018 (https://health.usnews.com/health-care/patient-advice/articles/2017-07-04/are-cities-bad-for-mental-health).

Lewis, Gregory B., Risa Palm, and Bo Feng. 2018. "Cross-National Variation in Determinants of Climate Change Concern." *Environmental Politics*. doi.org/10.1080/09644016.2018.1512261.

Liesman, Steve. 2018. "Most of the Tax Cut Windfall Will Boost Buybacks and Dividends, Not Workers' Pockets, Survey Predicts." CNBC. January 30. Retrieved June 29, 2018 (https://www.cnbc.com/2018/01/30/cnbc-fed-survey-most-of-the-tax-cut-windfall-will-boost-buybacks-and-dividends.html).

Lin, Carol Yeh-Yun, Leif Edvinsson, Jeffery Chen, and Tord Beding. 2013. *National Intellectual Capital and the Financial Crisis in China, Hong Kong, Singapore, and Taiwan*. New York: Springer.

Liu, Marian. 2018. "Great Pacific Garbage Patch Now Three Times the Size of France." CNN. March 23. Retrieved June 18, 2018 (https://www.cnn.com/2018/03/23/world/plastic-great-pacific-garbage-patch-intl/index.html).

Lombroso, Daniel, and Yoni Appelbaum. 2016. "'Hail Trump!': White Nationalists Salute the President-Elect." *The Atlantic*. November 21. Retrieved August 20, 2018 (https://www.theatlantic.com/politics/archive/2016/11/richard-spencer-speech-npi/508379/).

Long, Heather. 2018. "Inflation Hits 6-Year High, Wiping Out Wage Gains for the Average American." *Washington Post*. July 13. Retrieved August 31, 2018 (https://www.washingtonpost.com/business/2018/07/12/inflation-hits-year-high-wiping-out-wage-gains-average-american/?noredirect=on&utm_term=.d6d4f778eb7a).

Long, Wen, Nan Li, Huiwen Wang, and Siwei Cheng. 2012. "Impact of US Financial Crisis on Different Countries: Based on the Method of Functional Analysis of Variance." *Procedia Computer Science* (9): 1292–1298. doi.org/10.1016/j.procs.2012.04.141.

Lopez, German. 2017. "The Past Year of Research Has Made It Very Clear: Trump Won Because of Racial Resentment." Vox. December 15. Retrieved September 12, 2018 (https://www.vox.com/identities/2017/12/15/16781222/trump-racism-economic-anxiety-study).

Lowery, Annie. 2017. "The Great Recession Is Still with Us." *The Atlantic.* December 1, 2107. Retrieved August 18, 2018 (https://www.theatlantic.com/business/archive/2017/12/great-recession-still-with-us/547268/).

Lu, Chensheng, Kenneth M. Warchol, and Richard A. Callahan. 2014. "Sub-Lethal Exposure to Neonicotinoids Impaired Honey Bees Winterization before Proceeding to Colony Collapse Disorder." *Bulletin of Insectology* 67 (1): 125–130.

Lukacs, Martin. 2017. "Neoliberalism Has Conned Us into Fighting Climate Change as Individuals." *The Guardian.* July 17. Retrieved September 21, 2018 (https://www.theguardian.com/environment/true-north/2017/jul/17/neoliberalism-has-conned-us-into-fighting-climate-change-as-individuals).

Lutz, Ashley. 2012. "These 6 Corporations Control 90% of the Media in America." *Business Insider.* July 14. Retrieved June 16, 2018 (http://www.businessinsider.com/these-6-corporations-control-90-of-the-media-in-america-2012-6?IR=T).

Lyotard, Jean-Francois. [1979] 1984. *The Postmodern Condition: A Report on Knowledge.* Minneapolis: University of Minnesota Press.

Macalister, Terry. 2015. "At Least One Major Oil Company Will Turn Its Back on Fossil Fuels, Says Scientist." *The Guardian.* January 11. Retrieved August 1, 2017 (https://www.theguardian.com/business/2015/jan/11/oil-company-fossil-fuels-jeremy-leggett-soaring-costs-risky-energy-projects).

Macdonald, Ted. 2018. "Major Broadcast TV Networks Mentioned Climate Change Just Once During Two Weeks of Heat-Wave Coverage." Media Matters for America. July 12. Retrieved July 24, 2018 (https://www.mediamatters.org/blog/2018/07/12/Major-broadcast-TV-networks-mentioned-climate-change-just-once-during-two-weeks-of-heat-wa/220651).

Mackintosh, Eliza. 2018. "Report Suggests Russia, Syria Deliberately Targeted Civilian Areas in Aleppo." CNN. February 13. Retrieved August 8, 2018 (https://www.cnn.com/2017/02/13/middleeast/syria-russia-aleppo-civilian-areas/index.html).

Maffly, Brian. 2018. "Feds Block Government Archaeologists from Speaking at a Major Science Conference." *The Salt Lake Tribune.* May 11. Retrieved June 20, 2018 (https://www.sltrib.com/news/environment/2018/05/11/feds-blocks-government-archaeologists-from-speaking-at-a-major-science-conference/).

Majumber, Maimuna. 2017. "Higher Rates of Hate Crimes Are Tied to Income Inequality." FiveThirtyEight. January 23. Retrieved August 2, 2017 (https://fivethirtyeight.com/features/higher-rates-of-hate-crimes-are-tied-to-income-inequality/).

Mandel, Ernest. 1990. "Karl Marx." Pp. 1–38 in *The New Palgrave Marxian Economics,* edited by John Eatwell, Murray Milgate, and Peter Newman. New York: W.W. Norton.

Marchin, Tim. 2018. "Nearly 60 Percent of Republicans Don't Want a Woman President in Their Lifetime, Poll Finds." *Newsweek.* April 26. Retrieved June 12, 2018 (http://www.newsweek.com/nearly-60-percent-republicans-dont-want-woman-president-lifetime-poll-902254).

Marillier, Lou, and Daisy Squires. 2018. "Lacking Birth Control Options, Desperate Venezuelan Women Turn to Sterilization and Illegal Abortion." The Intercept. June 10. Retrieved June 26, 2018 (https://theintercept.com/2018/06/10/venezuela-crisis-sterilization-women-abortion/).

Marlow, Harold J., William K. Hayes, Samuel Soret, Ronald L. Carter, Ernest R Schwab, and Joan Sabaté. 2009. "Diet and the Environment: Does What You Eat Matter?" *American Journal of Clinical Nutrition* 89 (5): 1699S–1703S. doi.org/10.3945/ajcn.2009.26736Z.

Marx, Karl. [1847] n.d. *The Poverty of Philosophy.* Moscow, USSR: Foreign Languages Publishing House.

Marx, Karl. [1859] 1911. Preface. *A Contribution to the Critique of Political Economy.* Chicago: Charles Kerr & Company.

Marx, Karl. 1971. *Theories of Surplus-Value,* Part III. Moscow: Progress Publishers.

Marx, Karl. [1967] 1973a. *Capital,* Vol. III. New York: International Publishers.

Marx, Karl. 1973b. *Grundrisse.* New York: Vintage.

Marx, Karl. 1975a. Comments on James Mill, *Élémens D Économie Politique.* Pp. 211–228 in *Karl Marx Frederick Engels: Collected Works,* Vol. 3. New York: Progress Publishers.

Marx, Karl. 1975b. *Contribution to the Critique of Hegel's Philosophy of Law.* Pp. 3–129 in Karl Marx Frederick Engels: Collected Works, Vol. 3. New York: Progress Publishers.

Marx, Karl. 1975c. *Contribution to the Critique of Hegel's Philosophy of Law:* "Introduction." Pp. 175–187 in *Karl Marx Frederick Engels: Collected Works,* Vol. 3. New York: Progress Publishers.

Marx, Karl. 1975d. "Critical Marginal Notes on the Article 'The King of Prussia and Social Reform. By a Prussian.'" Pp. 189–206 in *Karl Marx Frederick Engels: Collected Works,* Vol. 3. New York: International Publishers.

Marx, Karl. 1975e. Letter from Marx to His Father. November 10[-11], 1837. Pp. 10–21 in *Karl Marx Frederick Engels: Collected Works,* Vol. 1. New York: International Publishers.

Marx, Karl. 1975f. Letters from the *Deutsch-Französische Jahrbücher.* Pp. 133–145 in *Karl Marx Frederick Engels: Collected Works,* Vol. 3. New York: Progress Publishers.

Marx, Karl. 1975g. To Ludwig Feuerbach. August 11, 1844. Pp. 354–357 in *Karl Marx Frederick Engels: Collected Works,* Vol. 3. New York: Progress Publishers.

Marx, Karl. 1976a. "The Communism of the Rheinischer Beobachter." Pp. 220–234 in *Karl Marx Frederick Engels: Collected Works,* Vol. 6. New York: International Publishers.

Marx, Karl. 1976b. "Moralising Criticism and Critical Morality." Pp. 312–340 in *Karl Marx Frederick Engels: Collected Works*, Vol. 6. New York: Progress Publishers.

Marx, Karl. 1978. Theses on Feuerbach. Pp. 143–145 in *The Marx-Engels Reader*, edited by Robert C. Tucker. 2nd ed. New York: W.W. Norton.

Marx, Karl. 1979a. From Letter to Ludwig Kugelmann. December 12, 1868. P. 259 in *The Letters of Karl Marx*, edited by Saul Padover. Englewood Cliffs, New Jersey: Prentice-Hall.

Marx, Karl. 1979b. To Maxim Maximovich Kovalevsky. April 1879. Pp. 324–325 in *The Letters of Karl Marx*, edited by Saul Padover. Englewood Cliffs, New Jersey: Prentice-Hall.

Marx, Karl. 1982. Marx to Pavel Vasilyevich Annenkov. December 28, 1846. Pp. 95–106 in *Karl Marx Frederick Engels: Collected Works*, Vol. 38. New York: International Publishers.

Marx, Karl. 1983a. Marx to Engels. January 24, 1852. Pp. 20–21 in *Karl Marx Frederick Engels: Collected Works*, Vol. 39. New York: Progress Publishers.

Marx, Karl. 1983b. Marx to Ferdinand Lassalle. May 31, 1858. Pp. 315–316 in *Karl Marx Frederick Engels: Collected Works*, Vol. 40. New York: International Publishers.

Marx, Karl. 1983c. Marx to Joseph Weydemeyer. March 5, 1852. Pp. 60–66 in *Karl Marx Frederick Engels: Collected Works*, Vol. 39. New York: International Publishers.

Marx, Karl. 1985a. Marx to Ferdinand Lassalle. June 16, 1862. Pp. 376–379 in *Karl Marx Frederick Engels: Collected Works*, Vol. 41. New York: International Publishers.

Marx, Karl. 1985b. Marx to Lion Philips. April 14, 1864. Pp. 512–514 in *Karl Marx Frederick Engels: Collected Works*, Vol. 41. New York: International Publishers.

Marx, Karl. 1985c. Marx to Lion Philips. August 17, 1864. Pp. 550–551 in *Karl Marx Frederick Engels: Collected Works*, Vol. 41. New York: International Publishers.

Marx, Karl. 1987. Marx to Engels. December 2, 1864. Pp. 49–50 in *Karl Marx Frederick Engels: Collected Works*, Vol. 42. New York: International Publishers.

Marx, Karl. 1988a. *Economic and Philosophic Manuscripts of 1844*. New York: Prometheus Books.

Marx, Karl. 1988b. Marx to Ludwig Kugelmann. July 11, 1868. Pp. 67–70 in *Karl Marx Frederick Engels: Collected Works*, Vol. 43. New York: International Publishers.

Marx, Karl. 1989a. Marx to Edward Spencer Beesly. September 16, 1870. Pp. 84–85 in *Karl Marx Frederick Engels: Collected Works*, Vol. 44. New York: International Publishers.

Marx, Karl. 1989b. Marx to His Daughters Jenny, Laura and Eleanor. June 13, 1871. Pp. 153–155 in *Karl Marx Frederick Engels: Collected Works*, Vol. 44. New York: International Publishers.

Marx, Karl. 1989c. Marx to Johann Baptist von Schweitzer. October 13, 1868. Pp. 132–135 in *Karl Marx Frederick Engels: Collected Works*, Vol. 43. New York: International Publishers.

REFERENCES

Marx, Karl. 1989d. Marx to Ludwig Kugelmann. April 17, 1871. Pp. 136–137 in *Karl Marx Frederick Engels: Collected Works*, Vol. 44. New York: International Publishers.

Marx, Karl. 1989e. Marx to Ludwig Kugelmann. July 27, 1871. Pp. 176–177 in *Karl Marx Frederick Engels: Collected Works*, Vol. 44. New York: International Publishers.

Marx, Karl. 1989f. Marx to Sigfrid Meyer and August Vogt. April 9, 1870. Pp. 471–476 in *Karl Marx Frederick Engels: Collected Works*, Vol. 43. New York: International Publishers.

Marx, Karl. 1989g. Preamble to the Programme of the French Workers' Party. P. 340 in *Karl Marx Frederick Engels: Collected Works*, Vol. 24. New York: Progress Publishers.

Marx, Karl. 1991a. Marx to Friedrich Adolph Sorge. October 19, 1877. Pp. 282–284 in *Karl Marx Frederick Engels: Collected Works*, Vol. 45. New York: International Publishers.

Marx, Karl. 1991b. Marx to Nikolai Danielson. April 10, 1879. Pp. 353–358 in *Karl Marx Frederick Engels: Collected Works*, Vol. 45. New York: International Publishers.

Marx, Karl. 1991c. Marx to Pytor Lavrov. June 18, 1875. P. 78 in *Karl Marx Frederick Engels: Collected Works*, Vol. 45. New York: International Publishers.

Marx, Karl. 1991d. Marx to Thomas Allsop. February 4, 1878. Pp. 298–299 in *Karl Marx Frederick Engels: Collected Works*, Vol. 45. New York: International Publishers.

Marx, Karl. 1991e. Marx to Wilhelm Blos. November 10, 1877. P. 288 in *Karl Marx Frederick Engels: Collected Works*, Vol. 45. New York: International Publishers.

Marx, Karl. [1867] 1992. *Capital,* Vol. 1. New York: International Publishers.

Marx, Karl. 2000. Address of the International Working Men's Association to Abraham Lincoln, President of the United States of America. First published: The Bee-Hive Newspaper, No. 169, November 7, 1865. Marx & Engels Internet Archive. Retrieved December 28, 2015 (https://www.marxists.org/archive/marx/iwma/documents/1864/lincoln-letter.htm).

Marx, Karl, and Frederick Engels. 1976. *The German Ideology. Karl Marx Frederick Engels: Collected Works*, Vol. 5. Moscow/New York: International Publishers.

Marx, Karl, and Frederick Engels. 1978a. Address to the Central Authority to the League. March, 1850. Pp. 277–287 in *Karl Marx Frederick Engels: Collected Works*, Vol. 10. New York: Progress Publishers.

Marx, Karl, and Frederick Engels. 1978b. "Review." Pp. 257–270 in *Karl Marx Frederick Engels: Collected Works*, Vol. 10. New York: Progress Publishers.

Marx, Karl, and Frederick Engels. 1978c. Reviews from the Neue Rheinische Zeitung. Politisch-Ökonomische Revue No. 2. Pp. 241–246 in *Karl Marx Frederick Engels: Collected Works*, Vol. 10. New York: International Publishers.

Marx, Karl, and Frederick Engels. [1848] 1978d. The Manifesto of the Communist Party. Pp. 469–500 in *The Marx-Engels Reader*, edited by Robert C. Tucker. 2nd ed. New York: W.W. Norton & Company.

Marx, Karl, and Frederick Engels. 1991. Marx and Engels to August Bebel, Wilhelm Liebknecht, Wilhelm Bracke and Others. Mid-September, 1879. Pp. 394–408 in *Karl Marx Frederick Engels: Collected Works*, Vol. 45. New York: International Publishers.

Masters, James. 2018. "Air Pollution Particles Found in Mothers' Placentas, New Study Finds." CNN. September 17. Retrieved September 25, 2018 (https://www.cnn.com/2018/09/17/health/placenta-pollution-babies-intl/index.html).

Mattera, Philip. 2017a. "Citigroup." Corporate Research Project. June 1. Retrieved July 29, 2018 (https://www.corp-research.org/citigroup).

Mattera, Philip. 2017b. "JPMorgan Chase." Corporate Research Project. February 3. Retrieved June 29, 2018 (https://www.corp-research.org/jpmorganchase).

Matthews. Robert. 2003. "Astrologers Fail to Predict Proof They Are Wrong." *The Telegraph*. August 17, 2003. Retrieved June 3, 2018 (https://www.telegraph.co.uk/news/uknews/1439101/Astrologers-fail-to-predict-proof-they-are-wrong.html).

Maza, Cristina. 2018. "Donald Trump Lashed Out at Military for Not Making Money on Libya's Oil."*Newsweek*. September 6. Retrieved September 22, 2018 (https://www.newsweek.com/donald-trump-lashed-out-military-not-making-money-libyas-oil-1109684).

McCarthy, Niall. 2015. "Only 22 Countries Have Never Been Invaded by Britain." Statista: The Statistics Portal. April 29. Retrieved August 7, 2017 (https://www.statista.com/chart/3441/countries-never-invaded-by-britain/).

McCarthy, Niall. 2018. "Where Young Europeans Aren't Religious." Statista. March 26. Retrieved July 26, 2018 (https://www.statista.com/chart/13345/where-young-europeans-arent-religious/).

McCoy, Alfred. [1972] 2003. *The Politics of Heroin: CIA Complicity in the Global Drug Trade*. Chicago: Lawrence Hill Books.

McElwee Sean, and Jason McDaniel. 2017. "Economic Anxiety Didn't Make People Vote Trump, Racism Did." *The Nation*. May 8. Retrieved September 12, 2018 (https://www.thenation.com/article/economic-anxiety-didnt-make-people-vote-trump-racism-did/).

McGraw, George. 2013. "Nestlé Chairman Peter Brabeck Says We Don't Have a Right to Water, Believes We Do Have a Right to Water and Everyone's Confused." Huffington Post. April 25. Retrieved July 3, 2018 (http://www.huffingtonpost.com/george-mcgraw/nestle-chairman-peter-brabeck-water_b_3150150.html).

McGreal, Chris. 2016. "Financial Despair, Addiction and the Rise of Suicide in White America." *The Guardian*. February 7. Retrieved August 2, 2017 (https://www.theguardian.com/us-news/2016/feb/07/suicide-rates-rise-butte-montana-princeton-study).

McKenzie, Sheena. 2018. "Sexual Abuse 'Endemic' in International Aid Sector, Damning Report Finds." CNN. July 31. Retrieved August 16, 2018 (https://www.cnn.com/2018/07/30/uk/sexual-abuse-aid-sector-uk-report-intl/index.html).

McKew, Molly. 2018. "Did Russia Affect the 2016 Election? It's Now Undeniable." Wired. February 16. Retrieved August 23, 2018 (https://www.wired.com/story/did-russia-affect-the-2016-election-its-now-undeniable/).

McKibben, Bill. 2018. "Some Rare Good Climate News: The Fossil Fuel Industry Is Weaker than Ever." *The Guardian*. June 21. Retrieved July 5, 2018 (https://www.theguardian.com/commentisfree/2018/jun/21/climate-change-fossil-fuel-industry-never-been-weaker).

McKibben, Cameron. 2015. "NAFTA and Drug Trafficking: Perpetuating Violence and the Illicit Supply Chain." Council on Hemispheric Affairs. March 20. Retrieved September 6, 2018 (http://www.coha.org/nafta-and-drug-trafficking-perpetuating-violence-and-the-illicit-supply-chain/#_ednref).

McKibbin, Warwick J., and Andrew Stoeckel. 2009. "The Potential Impact of the Global Financial Crisis on World Trade." Brookings. August 31. Retrieved August 18, 2018 (https://www.brookings.edu/research/the-potential-impact-of-the-global-financial-crisis-on-world-trade/).

McKie, Robin. 2018a. "Climate Study 'Pulls Punches' to Keep Polluters on Board." *The Guardian*. September 23. Retrieved September 25, 2018 (https://www.theguardian.com/science/2018/sep/23/scientists-changing-global-warming-report-please-polluters).

McKie, Robin. 2018b. "Where Have All the Insects Gone?" *The Guardian*. June 17. Retrieved June 20, 2018 (https://www.theguardian.com/environment/2018/jun/17/where-have-insects-gone-climate-change-population-decline).

McLaughlin, Jenna. 2018. "Trump to Name Climate Change Skeptic as Adviser on Emerging Technologies." CNN. September 4. Retrieved September (https://www.cnn.com/2018/09/04/politics/happer-climate-denier-trump-adviser/index.html).

McLendon, Kim. 2016. "President Jimmy Carter Speaks Out: Calls the US an Oligarchy." Inquisitr. March 3. Retrieved July 28, 2017 (http://www.inquisitr.com/2850287/president-jimmy-carter-speaks-out-calls-the-u-s-an-oligarchy/).

Mead, George Herbert. 1934. *Mind, Self, and Society*. Chicago: University of Chicago Press.

Meixel, Brady, and Ross Eisenberry. 2014. "An Epidemic of Wage Theft Is Costing Workers Hundreds of Millions of Dollars a Year." Economic Policy Institute. September 11. Retrieved July 25 (http://www.epi.org/publication/epidemic-wage-theft-costing-workers-hundreds/).

Meredith, Sam. 2018. "'Great Pacific Garbage Patch' Has Grown to Twice the Size of Texas, Study Finds." CNBC. Retrieved June 18, 2018 (https://www.cnbc.com/2018/03/23/great-pacific-garbage-patch-has-grown-to-twice-the-size-of-texas-study-finds.html).

Meredith, Sam, and Natasha Turak. 2018. "Trump Slams Germany at NATO Summit: It's 'Totally Controlled by Russia.'" CNBC. July 11. Retrieved August 21, 2018 (https://www.cnbc.com/2018/07/11/trump-slams-germany-at-nato-summit-says-its-a-captive-of-russia.html).

Merica, Dan. 2017. "Trump Seems Ready to Pull Aid from Puerto Rico. He Took a Different Tone with Texas and Florida." CNN. October 12. Retrieved June 28, 2018 (https://www.cnn.com/2017/10/12/politics/trump-puerto-rico-texas-florida/index.html).

Merkelson, Suzanne. 2012. "INFOGRAPHIC: Million Dollar Gifts Accounted for Half of Super PAC's Money in 2011." Republic Report. April 5. Retrieved August 7, 2018 (https://www.republicreport.org/2012/infographic-million-dollar-gifts-accounted-for-half-of-super-pacs-money-in-2011/).

Merle, Ranae. 2016. "US Companies Are Saving $100 Billion a Year by Shifting Profits Overseas, Report Says." *Washington Post*. May 10. Retrieved September 25, 2018 (https://www.washingtonpost.com/news/business/wp/2016/05/10/u-s-companies-are-saving-100-billion-a-year-by-shifting-profits-overseas-report-says/?noredirect=on&utm_term=.574d44a5d617).

Met Office. 2015. "The Great Smog of 1952." April 20. Retrieved June 23, 2018 (https://www.metoffice.gov.uk/learning/learn-about-the-weather/weather-phenomena/case-studies/great-smog).

Meyer, Robinson. 2018a. "The Problem with *The New York Times*' Big Story on Climate Change." *The Atlantic*. August 1. Retrieved August 11, 2018 (https://www.theatlantic.com/science/archive/2018/08/nyt-mag-nathaniel-rich-climate-change/566525/).

Meyer, Robinson. 2018b. "Trump Has Done More than Pull Out of Paris." *The Atlantic*. July 2. Retrieved August 12, 2018 (https://www.theatlantic.com/science/archive/2018/07/trump-has-done-more-than-pull-out-of-paris/564212/).

*Miami Herald* Editorial Board. 2018. "Invading Sea Water Jeopardizes South Florida's Delicate Drinking Water Source, but We Can Lessen the Threat." *Miami Herald*. June 8. Retrieved June 19, 2018 (https://www.miamiherald.com/opinion/editorials/article212844644.html).

Michel, Casey. 2018. "Russians and the American Right Started Plotting in 1995. We Have the Notes from the First Meeting." ThinkProgress. June 19. Retrieved July 1, 2018 (https://thinkprogress.org/history-of-christian-fundamentalists-in-russia-and-the-us-a6bdd326841d/).

Milbank, Dana, and Claudia Deane. 2003. "Hussein Link to 9/11 Lingers in Many Minds." *Washington Post*. September 6, 2003. Retrieved July 11, 2018 (https://www.washingtonpost.com/archive/politics/2003/09/06/hussein-link-to-911-lingers-in-many-minds/7cd31079-21d1-42cf-8651-b67e93350fde/?utm_term=.2dede458030f).

Miles, Tom. 2018. "Mass Rape Cannibalism, Dismemberment: UN Team Finds Atrocities in Congo War,." Reuters. July 3. Retrieved July 31, 2018 (https://www.reuters

.com/article/us-congo-violence-un/mass-rape-cannibalism-dismemberment-u-n-team-finds-atrocities-in-congo-war-idUSKBN1JT2CF).

Miller, Richard G., and Steven R. Sorrell. 2014. "The Future of Oil Supply." *Philosophical Transactions of the Royal Society* 372: 1–27. doi.org/10.1098/rsta/2013.0179.

Milman, Oliver. 2014. "Sea Level Rise over Past Century Unmatched in 6,000 Years, Says Study." *The Guardian*. October 13. Retrieved August 1, 2017 (https://www.theguardian.com/environment/2014/oct/14/sea-level-rise-unmatched-6000-years-global-warming).

Milman, Oliver. 2015. "Earth Has Lost a Third of Arable Land in Past 40 Years, Scientists Say." *The Guardian*. December 2. Retrieved August 1, 2017 (https://www.theguardian.com/environment/2015/dec/02/arable-land-soil-food-security-shortage).

Milman, Oliver. 2017. "Meat Industry Blamed for Largest-Ever 'Dead Zone' in Gulf of Mexico." *The Guardian*. August 1. Retrieved August 2, 2017 (https://www.theguardian.com/environment/2017/aug/01/meat-industry-dead-zone-gulf-of-mexico-environment-pollution).

Milman, Oliver. 2018. "Climate Change: Local Efforts Won't Be Enough to Undo Trump's Inaction, Study Says." *The Guardian*. August 30. Retrieved September 20, 2018 (https://www.theguardian.com/environment/2018/aug/29/local-climate-efforts-wont-undo-trump-inaction).

Mindock, Clark. 2017. "Number of Hate Crimes Surges in Year of Trump's Election." *Independent*. November 14. Retrieved June 12, 2018 (https://www.independent.co.uk/news/world/americas/hate-crimes-us-trump-election-surge-rise-latest-figures-police-a8055026.html).

Mitchell, Amy, Jeffrey Gottfried, Jocelyn Kiley, and Katerina Eva Matsa. 2014. "Political Polarization & Media Habits." Pew Research Center. October 21. Retrieved September 21, 2018 (http://www.journalism.org/2014/10/21/political-polarization-media-habits/).

Mitchell, Amy, Jeffrey Gottfried, Michael Barthel, and Nami Sumida. 2018. "Distinguishing Between Factual and Opinion Statements in the News." Pew Research Center. June 18. Retrieved July 24, 2018 (http://www.journalism.org/2018/06/18/distinguishing-between-factual-and-opinion-statements-in-the-news/).

Mitchell, Josh. 2016. "More than 40% of Student Borrowers Aren't Making Payments." *Wall Street Journal*. April 7. Retrieved August 2, 2017 (https://www.wsj.com/articles/more-than-40-of-student-borrowers-arent-making-payments-1459971348).

Mitchell, Josh. 2018. "Rising US Consumer Prices Are Eroding Wage Gains." *Wall Street Journal*. August 10. Retrieved August 31, 2018 (https://www.wsj.com/articles/u-s-consumer-prices-rose-0-2-in-july-1533904402).

Mohdin, Aamna. 2018. "The EU Will Offer Member States €6,000 for Every Migrant They Take In." Quartz. July 24. Retrieved August 19, 2018 (https://qz.com/1335000/the-eu-will-offer-member-states-e6000-for-every-migrant-they-take-in/).

Monteiro, Ana, and Amogelang Mbatha. 2018. "China, BRICS Push to Shift World Order Amid Trade Threats." Bloomberg. July 27. Retrieved August 21, 2018 (https://www.bloomberg.com/news/articles/2018-07-27/china-brics-push-to-shift-world-order-amid-trump-trade-threats).

Montzka, Stephen A., Geoff S. Dutton, Pengfei Yu, Eric Ray, Robert W. Portmann, John S. Daniel, Lambert Kuijpers, Brad D. Hall, Debra Mondeel, Carolina Siso, J. David Nance, Matt Rigby, Alistair J. Manning, Lei Hu, Fred Moore, Ben R. Miller, and James W. Elkins. 2018. "An Unexpected and Persistent Increase in Global Emissions of Ozone-Depleting CFC-11." *Nature* 557: 413–417. doi.org/10.1038/s41586-018-0106-2.

Mooney, Chris. 2015. "The Melting of Antarctica Was Already Really Bad. It Just Got Worse." *Washington Post*. March 16. Retrieved August 1, 2017 (https://www.washingtonpost.com/news/energy-environment/wp/2015/03/16/the-melting-of-antarctica-was-already-really-bad-it-just-got-worse/?utm_term=.0bf783bc9c37).

Mooney, Chris. 2018. "At this Rate, Earth Risks Sea Level Rise of 20 to 30 Feet, Historical Analysis Shows." *Washington Post*. September 20. Retrieved September 25, 2018 (https://www.washingtonpost.com/energy-environment/2018/09/20/antarctica-warming-could-fuel-disastrous-sea-level-rise-study-finds/?noredirect=on&utm_term=.f336391ed906).

Moore, Keith J., Weiwei Fu, Francois Primeau, Gregory L. Britten, Keith Lindsay, Matthew Long, Scott C. Doney, Natalie Mahowald, Forrest Hoffman, and James T. Randerson. 2018. "Sustained Climate Warming Drives Declining Marine Biological Productivity." *Science* 359 (6380): 1139–1143. DOI: 10.1126/science.aao6379.

Mora, Camilo, Bénédicte Dousset, Iain R. Caldwell, Farrah E. Powell, Rollan C. Geronimo, Coral R. Bielecki, Chelsie W.W. Counsell, Bonnie S. Dietrich, Emily T. Johnston, Leo V. Louis, Matthew P. Lucas, Marie M. McKenzie, Alessandra G. Shea, Han Tseng, Thomas W. Giambelluca, Lisa R. Leon, Ed Hawkins, and Clay Trauernicht. 2017. "Global Risk of Deadly Heat." *Nature Climate Change* 7 (July): 501–507. DOI: 10.1038/NCLIMATE3322.

Morales, Alex. 2014. "Engulfed by Rising Seas, Islands Gain Moral Voice at UN." Bloomberg. December 10. Retrieved August 1, 2017 (https://www.bloomberg.com/news/articles/2014-12-10/engulfed-by-rising-seas-islands-gain-moral-voice-at-un).

Motta, Matthew. 2018. "The Enduring Effect of Scientific Interest on Trust in Climate Scientists in the United States." *Nature Climate Change* 8: 485–488. doi.org/10.1038/s41558-018-0126-9.

Mujezinovic, Damir. 2018. "Study: Right-Wing Authoritarianism Accounts for Correlation Between Religion and Lack of Intellectual Humility." Inquisitr. May 24. Retrieved June 12, 2018 (https://www.inquisitr.com/4912504/study-right-wing

-authoritarianism-accounts-for-correlation-between-religion-and-lack-of-intellectual-humility/).

Mummolo, Johnathan. 2018. "Militarization Fails to Enhance Police Safety or Reduce Crime but May Harm Police Reputation." *Proceedings of the National Academy of Sciences* (August). https://doi.org/10.1073/pnas.1805161115.

Mundasad, Smitha. 2018. "Global Hunger Increasing, UN Warns." BBC | News. September 11. Retrieved September 20, 2018 (https://www.bbc.com/news/health-45477930).

Murdock, Jason. 2018. "What Is Nametests? Facebook Quiz App 'Exposed Data of 120 Million Users'." *Newsweek*. June 28. Retrieved August 11, 2018 (https://www.newsweek.com/facebooks-new-leak-nametests-quiz-apps-120-million-users-exposed-user-data-999261).

Murray, Georgina. 2012. "The New Factionalism of the Ruling Class." *Critical Sociology* 38 (3): 381–387.

Murray, Rebecca. 2013. "Human Trafficking Networks Flourish in Yemen." Al Jazeera. January 10. Retrieved August 18, 2018 (https://www.aljazeera.com/indepth/features/2013/01/2013121476138266.html).

Mutz, Diana C. 2018. "Status Threat, Not Economic Hardship, Explains the 2016 Presidential Vote." *Proceedings of the National Academy of Sciences*. April 23. doi.org/10.1073/pnas.1718155115.

Nammo, Dave. 2017. "Socialism's Rising Popularity Threatens America's Future." *National Review*. March 18. Retrieved July 13, 2018 (https://www.nationalreview.com/2017/03/socialism-poll-american-culture-faith-institute-george-barna-tradition-liberty-capitalism/).

Nance-Nash, Sheryl. 2012. "Student Loan Debt: $1 Trillion and Counting." Forbes. March 22. Retrieved August 31, 2018 (https://www.forbes.com/sites/sherylnancenash/2012/03/22/student-loan-debt-1-trillion-and-counting/#69f9d3b77f18).

NASA. 2018a. "Climate Change: How Do We Know?" July 2. Retrieved August 12, 2018 (https://climate.nasa.gov/evidence/).

NASA. 2018b. "Ramp-Up in Antarctic Ice Loss Speeds Sea Level Rise." NASA | Jet Propulsion Laboratory, California Institute of Technology. June 13. Retrieved June 19, 2018 (https://www.nasa.gov/press-release/ramp-up-in-antarctic-ice-loss-speeds-sea-level-rise).

National Public Radio. 2018. "'On Fire for God's Work': How Scott Pruitt's Faith Drives His Politics." National Public Radio | Environment and Energy Collaborative. May 1. Retrieved June 20, 2018 (https://www.npr.org/2018/05/01/607181437/on-fire-for-gods-work-how-scott-pruitts-faith-drives-his-politics).

Neal, Jennifer Watling, C. Emily Durbin, Allison E. Gornik, and Sharon L. Lo. 2017. "Codevelopment of Preschoolers' Temperament Traits and Social Play Networks over an Entire School Year." *Journal of Personality and Social Psychology.* February. DOI: 10.1037/pspp0000135

Nebehay, Stephanie. 2018. "UN Says It Has Credible Reports that China Holds Million Uighurs in Secret Camps." Reuters. August 10. Retrieved September 7, 2018 (https://www.reuters.com/article/us-china-rights-un/u-n-says-it-has-credible-reports-that-china-holds-million-uighurs-in-secret-camps-idUSKBN1KV1SU).

Neilson, Susie. 2018. "The Pesticide Industry Has Wanted to Cut Endangered Species' Protections. Under Trump, It's Happening." *Mother Jones.* July 26. Retrieved August 12, 2018 (https://www.motherjones.com/environment/2018/07/thanks-to-trump-pesticide-companies-are-now-free-to-kill-all-the-endangered-species-they-want/).

Nelson, Arthur. 2018. "Most of Europe's Rivers and Lakes Fail Water Quality Tests—Report." *The Guardian.* July 3. Retrieved August 12, 2018 (https://www.theguardian.com/environment/2018/jul/03/most-of-europes-rivers-and-lakes-fail-water-quality-tests-report).

Newbold, Tim. 2018. "Future Effects of Climate and Land-Use Change on Terrestrial Vertebrate Community Diversity Under Different Scenarios." *Proceedings of the Royal Society B* 285 (20180792): 1–9. doi.org/10.1098/rspb.2018.0792.

*New York Times.* 1992. "Deception on Capitol Hill." *New York Times* Archives. January 15. Retrieved September 14, 2018 (https://www.nytimes.com/1992/01/15/opinion/deception-on-capitol-hill.html).

Nichols, Will. 2015. "Up to 90% of the World's Electronic Waste Illegally Dumped, Says UN." *The Guardian.* May 12. Retrieved July 1, 2018 (https://www.theguardian.com/environment/2015/may/12/up-to-90-of-worlds-electronic-waste-is-illegally-dumped-says-un).

Nielsen, John. 2002. "The Killer Fog of '52." National Public Radio | All Things Considered. December 11. Retrieved June 23, 2018 (https://www.npr.org/2002/12/11/873954/the-killer-fog-of-52).

Niewenhuis, Lucas. 2018. "China's Re-Education Camps for a Million Muslims: What Everyone Needs to Know." SupChina. August 22. Retrieved September 7, 2018 (https://supchina.com/2018/08/22/xinjiang-explainer-chinas-reeducation-camps-for-a-million-muslims/).

NITI Aayog. 2018. *Composite Water Management Index: A Tool for Water Management.* June 2018. Ministry of Water Resources, Ministry of Drinking Water & Sanitation, and Ministry of Rural Development, Government of India. Retrieved August 12, 2018 (http://www.niti.gov.in/writereaddata/files/document_publication/2018-05-18-Water-index-Report_vS6B.pdf).

Nitsche, Sara. 2012. "Bribing and Taking Bribes." CFO Insight. May 31. Retrieved August 6, 2017 (https://web.archive.org/web/20140409034706/http://www.cfo-insight.com/index.php?id=1083491).

Nocera, Joe. 2018. "We Wanted Safer Banks. We Got More Inequality." Bloomberg. August 6. Retrieved August 18, 2018 (https://www.bloomberg.com/view/articles/2018-08-06/inequality-why-bank-rules-and-fed-rates-hurt-middle-class).

Normile, Dennis. 2016. "Mystery Cancers Are Cropping Up in Children in Aftermath of Fukushima." *Science*. March 4. Retrieved June 18, 2018 (http://www.sciencemag.org/news/2016/03/mystery-cancers-are-cropping-children-aftermath-fukushima).

Norton, Ben. 2016. "'We Are the Death Merchant of the World': Ex-Bush Official Lawrence Wilkerson Condemns Military-Industrial Complex." Salon. March 29. Retrieved July 31, 2017 (http://www.salon.com/2016/03/29/we_are_the_death_merchant_of_the_world_ex_bush_official_lawrence_wilkerson_condemns_military_industrial_complex/).

Nuccitelli, Dana. 2018. "30 Years Later, Denier Are Still Lying About Hansen's Amazing Global Warming Prediction." *The Guardian*. June 25. Retrieved July 13, 2018 (https://www.theguardian.com/environment/climate-consensus-97-per-cent/2018/jun/25/30-years-later-deniers-are-still-lying-about-hansens-amazing-global-warming-prediction).

Nwanevu, Osita. 2018. "The Straightforwardly Popular Ideas of the Radical Left." Slate. August 7. Retrieved August 10, 2018 (https://slate.com/news-and-politics/2018/08/a-look-at-some-of-the-straightforwardly-popular-ideas-of-the-radical-left.html).

O'Brien, Matt. 2014. "Poor Kids Who Do Everything Right Don't Do Better than Rich Kids Who Do Everything Wrong." *Washington Post*. October 18. Retrieved August 4, 2017 (https://www.washingtonpost.com/news/wonk/wp/2014/10/18/poor-kids-who-do-everything-right-dont-do-better-than-rich-kids-who-do-everything-wrong/?utm_term=.f1fbdecf28f3).

O'Brien, Sarah. 2018. "Social Security Benefits Buy 34 Percent Less than in 2000, Study Shows." CNBC. June 21. Retrieved July 24, 2018 (https://www.cnbc.com/2018/06/21/social-security-benefits-buy-34-percent-less-than-in-2000-study-shows.html).

O'Carroll, Lisa. 2018. "German Businesses 'Reluctant' to Invest in UK over Brexit Uncertainty." *The Guardian*. July 5. Retrieved August 18, 2018 (https://www.theguardian.com/business/2018/jul/05/german-businesses-reluctant-to-invest-in-uk-over-brexit-uncertainty).

Omi, Michael, and Howard Winant. [1986] 2015. *Racial Formation in the United States*. New York: Routledge.

O'Neill, Brendan. 2015. "Trouble on Campus: The Rise of Ban-Happy Student Leaders." *The Telegraph*. October 31. Retrieved August 3, 2017 (http://www.telegraph.co.uk/education/universityeducation/11658770/Trouble-on-campus-the-rise-of-ban-happy-student-leaders.html).

O'Neill, Daniel W., Andrew L. Fanning, William F. Lamb, and Julia K. Steinberger. 2018. "A Good Life for all Within Planetary Boundaries." *Nature Sustainability* 1 (February): 88–95. doi.org/10.1038/s41893-018-0021-4.

Onyanga-Omara, Jane. 2016. "Mystery of London Fog that Killed 12,000 Finally Solved." *USA Today*. December 13. Retrieved June 23, 2018 (https://www.usatoday.com/story/news/world/2016/12/13/scientists-say-theyve-solved-mystery-1952-london-killer-fog/95375738/).

Osborne, Hannah. 2018. "NASA Has Discovered Arctic Lakes Bubbling with Methane—And That's Very Bad News." *Newsweek*. September 13. Retrieved September 20, 2018 (https://www.newsweek.com/arctic-permafrost-lakes-bubbling-methane-nasa-1119624).

Oschlies, Andreas, Peter Brandt, Lothar Stramma, and Sunke Schmidtko. 2018. "Drivers and Mechanisms of Ocean Deoxygenation." *Nature Geoscience* | Review Article. doi.org/10.1038/s41561-018-0152-2.

Osnos, Evan. 2017. "Doomsday Prep for the Super-Rich." *The New Yorker*. January 30. Retrieved August 27, 2018 (https://www.newyorker.com/magazine/2017/01/30/doomsday-prep-for-the-super-rich).

Oxfam International. 2016. "62 People Own the Same as Half the World, Reveals Oxfam Davos Report." January 18. Retrieved August 2, 2017 (https://www.oxfam.org/en/pressroom/pressreleases/2016-01-18/62-people-own-same-half-world-reveals-oxfam-davos-report).

Pandey, Erica. 2018. "16 Asian Countries Could Form the World's Largest Trading Bloc." Axios. July 1. Retrieved August 21, 2018 (https://www.axios.com/asian-trading-bloc-trump-trade-war-china-india-japan-000325a4-302f-46e3-931e-3072bcbbdd40.html).

Paolucci, Paul. 2003. "Foucault's Encounter with Marxism." *Current Perspectives in Social Theory* 22: 3–58.

Paolucci, Paul. 2009. "Public Discourse in an Age of Deception: Forging the Iraq War." *Critical Sociology* 35 (6): 863–886.

Paraskova, Tsvetana. 2018. "Chinese State Oil Major Suspends US Oil Imports Amid Trade War." Oilprice.com. August 3. Retrieved August 21, 2018 (https://oilprice.com/Latest-Energy-News/World-News/Chinese-State-Oil-Major-Suspends-US-Oil-Imports-Amid-Trade-War.html).

Parker, Clifton B. 2014. "Hallucinatory 'Voices' Shaped by Local Culture, Standord Anthropologist Says." Stanford | News. July 16. Retrieved, July 18, 2018 (https://news.stanford.edu/2014/07/16/voices-culture-luhrmann-071614/).

Parker, Laura. 2014. "Plane Search Shows World's Oceans Are Full of Trash." *National Geographic*. April 4. Retrieved June 25, 2018 (https://news.nationalgeographic.com/news/2014/04/140404-garbage-patch-indian-ocean-debris-malaysian-plane/).

Parker, Laura. 2016. "What You Need to Know About the World's Water Wars." *National Geographic*. July 14. Retrieved June 25, 2018 (https://news.nationalgeographic.com/2016/07/world-aquifers-water-wars/).

Parry, Wayne. 2017. "Climate Change before Your Eyes: Seas Rise and Trees Die." Associated Press | World. August 1. Retrieved August 2, 2017 https://apnews.com/7a8b498f 60034a8eb960900e08f7b4b8. Retrieved May 6, 2019.

Parson, Laura. 2016. "Are STEM Syllabi Gendered? A Feminist Critical Discourse Analysis." *The Qualitative Report* 21 (1): 102–116.

Parveen, Nazia. 2018. "UK's Plastic Waste May Be Dumped Overseas Instead of Recycled." *The Guardian*. July 22. Retrieved August 12, 2018 (https://www.theguardian.com/environment/2018/jul/23/uks-plastic-waste-may-be-dumped-overseas-instead-of-recycled).

Pashman, Manya Brachear, and Marwa Eltagouri. 2015. "Wheaton College Professor Says View of Islam, Not Hijab, Got Christian Teacher Suspended." *Chicago Tribune*. December 15. Retrieved August 6, 2017 (http://www.chicagotribune.com/news/local/breaking/ct-wheaton-college-professor-larycia-hawkins-20151216-story.html).

Pattisson, Pete. 2014. "North Koreans Working as 'State-Sponsored Slaves' in Qatar." *The Guardian*. November 7. Retrieved August 18, 2018 (https://www.theguardian.com/global-development/2014/nov/07/north-koreans-working-state-sponsored-slaves-qatar).

Pavid, Katie. 2018. "New Evidence of Ancient Child Sacrifice Found in Turkey." Natural History Museum. June 28. Retrieved July 23, 2018 (http://www.nhm.ac.uk/discover/news/2018/june/new-evidence-of-ancient-child-sacrifice-found-in-turkey.html).

Pengelly, Martin. 2017. "Donald Trump Repeats Respect for 'Killer' Putin in Fox Super Bowl Interview." *The Guardian*. February 6. Retrieved August 8, 2018 (https://www.theguardian.com/us-news/2017/feb/05/donald-trump-repeats-his-respect-for-killer-vladimir-putin).

Pennycook, Gordon, and David G. Rand. 2018. "Lazy, Not Biased: Susceptibility to Partisan Fake News Is Better Explained by Lack of Reasoning than by Motivated Reasoning." *Cognition*. doi.org/10.1016/j.cognition.2018.06.011.

Perlberg, Steven. 2018. "She Tried to Report on Climate Change, Sinclair Told Her to Be More 'Balanced.'" BuzzFeed News. April 22. Retrieved August 11, 2018 (https://www.buzzfeednews.com/article/stevenperlberg/sinclair-climate-change).

Petulla, Sam, Tammy Kupperman, and Jessica Schneider. 2017. "The Number of Hate Crimes Rose in 2016." CNN. November 13. Retrieved June 12, 2018 (https://www.cnn.com/2017/11/13/politics/hate-crimes-fbi-2016-rise/index.html).

Pew Research Center. 2014a. "Emerging and Developing Economies Much More Optimistic than Rich Countries About the Future." October 9. Retrieved August 4, 2017 (http://www.pewglobal.org/2014/10/09/emerging-and-developing-economies-much-more-optimistic-than-rich-countries-about-the-future/).

Pew Research Center. 2014b. "Political Polarization in the American Public." June 12. Retrieved July 11, 2018 (http://www.people-press.org/2014/06/12/political-polarization-in-the-american-public/).

Pew Research Center. 2016. "Low Approval of Trump's Transition but Outlook for His Presidency Improves." December 8. Retrieved August 10, 2018 (http://www.people-press.org/2016/12/08/3-political-values-government-regulation-environment-immigration-race-views-of-islam/).

Pew Research Center. 2017a. "More Americans Favor Raising than Lowering Tax Rates on Corporations, High Household Incomes." September 27. Retrieved August 10, 2018 (http://www.pewresearch.org/fact-tank/2017/09/27/more-americans-favor-raising-than-lowering-tax-rates-on-corporations-high-household-incomes/ft_17-0927_incometaxes_corporations_featured/).

Pew Research Center. 2017b. "Sharp Partisan Divisions in Views of National Institutions." July 10. Retrieved August 1, 2017 (http://www.people-press.org/2017/07/10/sharp-partisan-divisions-in-views-of-national-institutions/).

Pfeffer, Jeffrey. 2018. *Dying for a Paycheck*. New York: Harper-Collins.

Pham, Sherisse, and Matt Rivers. 2017. "China Is Crushing the US in Renewable Energy." CNN. July 18. Retrieved August 22, 2018 (https://money.cnn.com/2017/07/18/technology/china-us-clean-energy-solar-farm/index.html).

Phillips, Mark, and Karl Russell. 2018. "The Next Financial Calamity Is Coming. Here's What to Watch." *New York Times*. September 12. Retrieved September 23, 2018 (https://www.nytimes.com/interactive/2018/09/12/business/the-next-recession-financial-crisis.html).

Philpott, Tom. 2018. "Trump Just Nominated a Pesticide Exec to Oversee Science at the USDA." *Mother Jones*. July 18. Retrieved August 12, 2018 (https://www.motherjones.com/food/2018/07/trump-just-nominated-a-pesticide-exec-to-oversee-science-at-usda/).

Philstar.com. 2018. "US Working on Duterte-Trump Meeting in Washington." *Philippine Star*. July 4. Retrieved August 8, 2018 (https://www.philstar.com/headlines/2018/07/04/1830511/us-working-duterte-trump-meeting-washington).

Pickett, Kate, and Richard Wilkinson. 2017. "You're More Likely to Achieve the American Dream If You Live in Denmark." World Economic Forum | The Conversation. August 21. Retrieved May 31, 2018 (https://www.weforum.org/agenda/2017/08/youre-more-likely-to-achieve-the-american-dream-if-you-live-in-denmark).

Pierce, Charles P. 2016. "Drug Companies have been Pumping Opiates into West Virginia." *Esquire*. December 19. Retrieved, August 7, 2017 (http://www.esquire.com/news-politics/politics/news/a51673/drug-companies-opiates-west-virginia/).

Pierce, Charles P. 2018. "Oil Companies Want Taxpayer Dollars to Protect Their Facilities Against…Climate Change." *Esquire*. Retrieved September 6, 2018 (https://www.esquire.com/news-politics/politics/a22822288/texas-oil-refineries-climate-change-taxpayer-money/).

Pierre-Louis, Kendra. 2017. "Guess How Many Giant Patches of Garbage There Are in the Ocean Now?" *Popular Science*. July 21. Retrieved June 25, 2018 (https://www.popsci.com/south-pacific-garbage-patch).

REFERENCES

Pilkington, Ed. 2009. "Shell Pays Out $15.5m over Saro-Wiwa Killing." *The Guardian*. June 8. Retrieved July 31, 2018 (https://www.theguardian.com/world/2009/jun/08/nigeria-usa).

Pinto, Richa. 2018. "Mumbai Plastic Ban Working: UN Environment Chief." *The Times of India*. September 13. Retrieved September 20, 2018 (https://timesofindia.indiatimes.com/city/mumbai/mumbai-plastic-ban-working-un-environ-chief/articleshow/65788356.cms).

Plumer, Brad. 2011. "Oil's Getting Harder and Harder to Come By." *Washington Post*. December 13. Retrieved August 13, 2018 (https://www.washingtonpost.com/blogs/ezra-klein/post/most-of-the-worlds-oil-comes-from-aging-fields/2011/12/13/gIQAaM6CsO_blog.html?noredirect=on&utm_term=.ca1b9ed11a0d).

Plumer, Brad. 2015. "We Dump 8 Million Tons of Plastic into the Ocean Each Year. Where Does It All Go?" Vox. October 21. Retrieved August 1, 2017 (https://www.vox.com/2015/2/12/8028267/plastic-garbage-patch-oceans).

Pokharel, Sugam, and Sheena McKenzie. 2018. "'Unprecedented' Floods in Indian Tourist Hotspot Kill Dozens; 40,000 Evacuated." CNN. August 12. Retrieved September 12, 2018 (https://www.cnn.com/2018/08/12/asia/kerala-india-floods-intl/index.html).

Polimédio, Chayenne. 2018. "The Rise of the Brazilian Evangelicals." *The Atlantic*. January 24. Retrieved July 26, 2018 (https://www.theatlantic.com/international/archive/2018/01/the-evangelical-takeover-of-brazilian-politics/551423/).

Pomeroy, Ross. 2015. "Americans Greatly Overestimate Economic Mobility." Real Clear Science. November 13. Retrieved July 21, 2017 (http://www.realclearscience.com/journal_club/2015/11/13/americans_overestimate_social_class_mobility_and_the_effect_is_more_pronounced_among_conservatives_109450.html).

Poon, Linda. 2014. "Why a Village Leader Ordered the Rape of a 14-Year-Old in India." National Public Radio. July 15. Retrieved August 16, 2018 (https://www.npr.org/sections/goatsandsoda/2014/07/15/331347739/why-a-village-leader-ordered-the-rape-of-a-14-year-old-in-india).

Popken, Ben. 2018. "What Did Corporate America Do with that Tax Break? Buy Record Amounts of its Own Stock." NBC News. June 26. Retrieved August 18, 2018 (https://www.nbcnews.com/business/economy/what-did-corporate-america-do-tax-break-buy-record-amounts-n886621).

Porteus, Cosima S., Peter C. Hubbard, Tamsyn M. Uren Webster, Ronny van Aerle, Adelino V.M. Canário, Eduarda M. Santos, and Rod W. Wilson. 2018. "Near-Future CO2 Levels Impair the Olfactory System of Marine Fish." *Nature Climate Change* 8: 737–743. doi.org/10.1038/s41558-018-0224-8.

Poushter, Jacob. 2015. "40% of Millennials OK with Limiting Speech Offensive to Minorities." Pew Research Center. November 20. Retrieved July 6, 2018 (http://www.pewresearch.org/fact-tank/2015/11/20/40-of-millennials-ok-with-limiting-speech-offensive-to-minorities/).

Powell, Bill. 2015. "Gender Imbalance: How China's One-Child Law Backfired on Men." *Newsweek*. May 28. Retrieved August 16, 2018 (https://www.newsweek.com/2015/06/05/gender-imbalance-china-one-child-law-backfired-men-336435.html).

Price, Greg. 2018. "FOX News's Audience Almost Exclusively White as Network Faces Backlash Over Immigration Coverage." *Newsweek*. August 10. Retrieved September 21, 2018 (https://www.newsweek.com/fox-news-white-audience-immigration-1067807).

Prins, Nomi. [2009] 2011. *It Takes a Pillage: Behind the Bailouts, Bonuses, and Backroom Deal from Washington to Wall Street*. Hoboken, New Jersey: John Wiley & Sons, Inc.

Prins, Nomi. 2017. "The Next Financial Crisis Will Be Worse than the Last One." Truthdig. December 29. Retrieved July 29, 2018 (https://www.truthdig.com/articles/next-financial-crisis-will-worse-last-one/).

Project Censored. 2010. "The Media Can Legally Lie." April 29. Retrieved August 12, 2018 (https://projectcensored.org/11-the-media-can-legally-lie/).Pulliam Bailey, Sarah. 2016. "White Evangelicals Voted Overwhelmingly for Donald Trump, Exit Polls Show." *Washington Post*. November 9. Retrieved September 12, 2018 (https://www.washingtonpost.com/news/acts-of-faith/wp/2016/11/09/exit-polls-show-white-evangelicals-voted-overwhelmingly-for-donald-trump/?utm_term=.b74202c67d2b).

Raj, Anita, and Lotus McDougal. 2014. "Sexual Violence and Rape in India." *The Lancet* | Correspondence (383): 865. Retrieved June 26, 2018 (https://ac.els-cdn.com/S0140673614604359/1-s2.0-S0140673614604359-main.pdf?_tid=b22acbaa-fbfe-451e-a685-749e094e113a&acdnat=1530015151_6cdeccd860003512e533b9f86a9e9cd6).

Ramchandani, Ariel. 2018. "Forced Labor Is the Backbone of the World's Electronic Industry." *The Atlantic*. June 28. Retrieved August 31, 2018 (https://www.theatlantic.com/business/archive/2018/06/malaysia-forced-labor-electronics/563873/).

Randall, David. 2018. "World Equities Slip on Turkey Currency Woes." Reuters. August 12. Retrieved August 18, 2018 (https://www.reuters.com/article/us-global-markets/euro-on-defensive-as-turkish-crisis-sparks-rush-to-safety-idUSKBN1KX0SP?feedType=RSS&feedName=topNews&utm_source=reddit.com).

Rapley, John. 2017. "How Economics Became a Religion." *The Guardian*. July 11. Retrieved July 31, 2017 (https://www.theguardian.com/news/2017/jul/11/how-economics-became-a-religion).

Rauhala, Emily. 2018. "New Evidence Emerges of China Forcing Muslims into 'Reeducation Camps.'" *Washington Post*. August 10. Retrieved September 7, 2018 (https://www.washingtonpost.com/world/asia_pacific/new-evidence-emerges-that-china-is-forcing-muslims-into-reeducation-camps/2018/08/10/1d6d2f64-8dce-11e8-9b0d-749fb254bc3d_story.html?noredirect=on&utm_term=.aba7a227774a).

REFERENCES

Rawnsley, Andrew. 2018. "Madeleine Albright: 'The Things that Are Happening Are Genuinely, Seriously Bad.'" *The Guardian*. July 8. Retrieved August 8, 2018 (https://www.theguardian.com/books/2018/jul/08/madeleine-albright-fascism-is-not-an-ideology-its-a-method-interview-fascism-a-warning).

Raza, Danish. 2014. "When Women Come Cheaper than Cattle." *Hindustan Times*. March 23. Retrieved August 15, 2018 (https://www.hindustantimes.com/india/when-women-come-cheaper-than-cattle/story-EJD38cJ4kaTGVno3LJzUkJ.html).

Readfearn, Graham. 2018. "Gina Rinehart Company Revealed as $4.5m Donor to Climate Sceptic Thinkthank." *The Guardian*. July 20. Retrieved August 12, 2018 (https://www.theguardian.com/business/2018/jul/21/gina-rinehart-company-revealed-as-45m-donor-to-climate-sceptic-thinktank).

Reed, Brad. 2018. "Trump Tells Fox News He Wants Americans to Obey Him Like North Koreans Obey Kim Jong-un." Raw Story. June 15. Retrieved August 8, 2018 (https://www.rawstory.com/2018/06/trump-tells-fox-news-wants-americans-obey-like-north-koreans-obey-kim-jong-un/).

Reed, Stanley. 2016. "Study Links 6.5 Million Deaths Each Year to Air Pollution." *New York Times*. June 26. Retrieved August 1, 2017 (https://www.nytimes.com/2016/06/27/business/energy-environment/study-links-6-5-million-deaths-each-year-to-air-pollution.html).

Regencia, Ted. 2018. "Senator: Rodrigo Duterte's Drug War Has Killed 20,000." Al Jazeera. February 21. Retrieved August 8, 2018 (https://www.aljazeera.com/news/2018/02/senator-rodrigo-duterte-drug-war-killed-20000-180221134139202.html).

Reich, Robert. 2018. "Almost 80% of US Workers Live from Paycheck to Paycheck. Here's Why." *The Guardian*. July 29. Retrieved August 31, 2018 (https://www.theguardian.com/commentisfree/2018/jul/29/us-economy-workers-paycheck-robert-reich).

Reklaitis, Victor. 2018. "Brace for a Lost Decade for US Stocks, Warn Morningstar Strategists." MarketWatch. July 5. Retrieved August 18, 2018 (https://www.marketwatch.com/story/brace-for-a-lost-decade-for-us-stocks-warn-morningstar-strategists-2018-07-05).

Renewables Now. 2018. "Wind, Solar Farms Produce 10% of US Power in 4-Mo." June 27. Retrieved July 13, 2018 (https://renewablesnow.com/news/wind-solar-farms-produce-10-of-us-power-in-4-mo-617830/).

Rest, Kathleen, and Georges C. Benjamin. 2018. "Trump's EPA Puts Our Health at Risk." *Scientific American*. July 13. Retrieved August 12, 2018 (https://blogs.scientificamerican.com/observations/trumps-epa-puts-our-health-at-risk/).

Reynolds, Paul. 2018. "The Vetting Files: How the BBC Kept Out 'Subversives.'" BBC News. April 22. Retrieved June 16, 2018 (https://www.bbc.com/news/stories-43754737).

Richardson, John H. 2015. "When the End of Civilization Is Your Day Job." *Esquire*. July 7. Retrieved August 1, 2017 (http://www.esquire.com/news-politics/a36228/ballad-of-the-sad-climatologists-0815/).

Ricke, Katharine L., and Ken Caldeira. 2014. "Maximum Warming Occurs about One Decade after a Carbon Dioxide Emission." *Environmental Research Letters* 9 (12): 1–8. DOI: 10.1088/1748-9326/9/12/124002.

Ritzer, George. 2012. *The McDonaldization of Society*. Los Angeles: Sage.

Rivero, Anais. 2017. "Your Hershey's Chocolate Bar Was Made by Child Slaves." Affinity. August 4. Retrieved August 20, 2018 (http://affinitymagazine.us/2017/08/04/your-hersheys-chocolate-bar-was-made-by-child-slaves/).

Rizvi, Sarah, Chris Pagnutti, Evan Fraser, Chris T. Bauch, and Madhur Anand. 2018. "Global Land Use Implications of Dietary Trends." *PLoS One* 13(8): e0200781. doi.org/10.1371/journal.pone.0200781.

Robb, Alice. 2014. "Family Wealth Lasts for Ten to Fifteen Generations." *New Republic*. February 4. Retrieved August 2, 2017 (https://newrepublic.com/article/116462/family-wealth-lasts-ten-fifteen-generations).

Robinson, William I. 2012. "Global Capitalism Theory and the Emergence of Transnational Elites." *Critical Sociology* 38 (3): 349–363.

Rochman, Chelsea M., Sara M. Kross, Jonathan B. Armstrong, Michael T. Bogan, Emily S. Darling, Stephanie J. Green, Ashley R. Smyth, and Diogo Veríssimo. 2015. "Scientific Evidence Supports Ban on Microbeads." *Environmental Science & Technology* 49: 10759–10761. DOI: 10.1021/acs.est.5b03909.

Rockwood, Kate. 2010. "How a Handful of Countries Control the Earth's Most Precious Materials." Fast Company. November 1. Retrieved August 20, 2018 (https://www.fastcompany.com/1694164/how-handful-countries-control-earths-most-precious-materials).

Rodrigues, Jason. 2013. "Lincoln's Great Debt to Manchester." *The Guardian*. February 4. Retrieved June 27, 2018 (https://www.theguardian.com/theguardian/from-the-archive-blog/2013/feb/04/lincoln-oscars-manchester-cotton-abraham).

Rodriguez, Javier M. 2018. "Health Disparities, Politics, and the Maintenance of the Status Quo: A New Theory of Inequality." *Social Science & Medicine* 200 (March): 36–43.

Rogoff, Kenneth. 2018. "Are Debt Crises in Argentina and Turkey a Global Warning Sign?" *The Guardian*. June 11. Retrieved June 29, 2018 (https://www.theguardian.com/business/2018/jun/11/argentina-turkey-warning-advanced-economies).

Romm, Joe. 2018. "The US Just Suffered the Hottest May-June-July on Record." ThinkProgress. August 15. Retrieved September 12, 2018 (https://thinkprogress.org/hottest-may-june-july-in-us-history-ea200870459d/).

Rose Quandt, Katie. 2014. "College Has Gotten 12 Times More Expensive in One Generation." *Mother Jones*. September 3. Retrieved August 2, 2017 (http://www.motherjones.com/politics/2014/09/college-tuition-increased-1100-percent-since-1978/).

Roselund, Christian. 2018. "California 100% Renewable Energy Bill Heads to Assembly." PV Magazine. July 3. Retrieved July 13, 2018 (https://pv-magazine-usa.com/2018/07/03/california-100-renewable-energy-bill-heads-to-assembly/).

REFERENCES

Rowell, Andy. 2017. "As it Gets Harder to Find Oil, Norway Accelerates Arctic Drilling." Oil Change International. February 21. Retrieved August 13, 2018 (http://priceofoil.org/2017/02/21/as-it-gets-harder-to-find-oil-norway-accelerates-arctic-drilling/).

Roy, Gabriele. 2018. "Five More People Die of Heat in Montreal, Bringing city Total to 33." *The Globe and Mail*. July 7. Retrieved August 13, 2018 (https://www.theglobeandmail.com/canada/article-five-more-people-die-of-heat-in-montreal-bringing-city-total-to-33/).

Rugaber, Christopher S. 2017. "Pay Gap Between College Grads and Everyone Else at a Record." *USA Today*. January 12. Retrieved May 31, 2018 (https://www.usatoday.com/story/money/2017/01/12/pay-gap-between-college-grads-and-everyone-else-record/96493348/).

Rupar, Aaron. 2018. "Trump Administration's Efforts to Reject Comparisons with Nazis Are Not Going Well." ThinkProgress. June 19. Retrieved August 8, 2018 (https://thinkprogress.org/tom-homan-jeff-sessions-nazi-comparisons-nuremberg-defense-165249b9eb33-44e3856468c3-3b59877b1758/).

Rushkoff, Douglas. 2018. "Survival of the Richest." Medium. July 5. Retrieved August 27, 2018 (https://medium.com/s/futurehuman/survival-of-the-richest-9ef6cdddocc1).

Sadiq, Sheraz. n.d. "Timeline: Cochabamba Water Revolt." Frontline | World (PBS). Retrieved September 5, 2018 (http://www.pbs.org/frontlineworld/stories/bolivia/timeline.html).

Safi, Michael. 2017. "Suicides of Nearly 60,000 Indian Farmers Linked to Climate Change, Study Claims." *The Guardian*. July 31. Retrieved August 2, 2017 (https://www.theguardian.com/environment/2017/jul/31/suicides-of-nearly-60000-indian-farmers-linked-to-climate-change-study-claims).

Sahgal, Neha. 2018. "10 Key Findings About Religion in Western Europe." Pew Research Center. May 29. Retrieved July 26, 2018 (http://www.pewresearch.org/fact-tank/2018/05/29/10-key-findings-about-religion-in-western-europe/).

Samenow, Jason. 2018a. "Another Extreme Heat Wave Strikes the North Pole." *Washington Post*. May 7. Retrieved June 19, 2018 (https://www.washingtonpost.com/news/capital-weather-gang/wp/2018/05/07/another-extreme-heat-wave-strikes-the-north-pole/?noredirect=on&utm_term=.278a4a1b4f45).

Samenow, Jason. 2018b. "Red-Hot Planet: All-Time Heat Records Have Been Set All over the World During the Past Week." *Washington Post*. July 5. Retrieved August 12, 2018 (https://www.washingtonpost.com/news/capital-weather-gang/wp/2018/07/03/hot-planet-all-time-heat-records-have-been-set-all-over-the-world-in-last-week/?noredirect=on&utm_term=.c6c58c4513e9).

Samuel, Henry. 2018. "France Becomes First Country in Europe to Ban All Five Pesticides Killing Bees." *The Telegraph*. August 31. Retrieved September 20, 2018 (https://www.telegraph.co.uk/news/2018/08/31/france-first-ban-five-pesticides-killing-bees/).

Sapolsky, Robert M. 2018. "Be Alarmed When a Leader Tries to Make You Think of Humans as Vermin." CNN. July 9. Retrieved August 8, 2018 (https://www.cnn.com/2018/07/09/opinions/infest-insula-disgust-opinion-sapolsky/index.html).

Savage, Maddy. 2018. "Unlike Most Millennials, Norway's Are Rich." BBC | Capital. July 10. Retrieved July 24, 2018 (http://www.bbc.com/capital/story/20180709-unlike-most-millennials-norways-are-rich).

Scheier, Rachel. 2018. "The World's Largest Solar Farm Rises in the Remote Egyptian Desert." *Los Angeles Times*. July 30. Retrieved August 27, 2018 (http://www.latimes.com/world/middleeast/la-fg-egypt-green-power-20180730-story.html).

Schlanger, Zoë. 2018. "We Underestimated the Size of the Great Pacific Garbage Patch—By 16 Times." Quartz. March 22. Retrieved June 18, 2018 (https://qz.com/1234953/we-underestimated-the-size-of-the-great-pacific-garbage-patch-by-16-times/).

Schlesinger, Stephen C., and Stephen Kinzer. 2005. *Bitter Fruit: The Story of the American Coup in Guatemala*. Cambridge, Mass: Harvard University, David Rockefeller Center for Latin American Studies.

Schmidtko, Sunke, Lothar Stramma, and Martin Visbeck. 2017. "Decline in Global Oceanic Oxygen Content During the Past Five Decades." *Nature* 542: 335–339. DOI: 10.1038/nature21399.

Schor, Juliet. 1992. *The Overworked American: The Unexpected Decline of Leisure*. New York: Basic Books.

Schwartz, Jen. 2018. "Surrendering to Rising Seas." *Scientific American*. August 2018. Retrieved August 12, 2018 (https://www.scientificamerican.com/article/surrendering-to-rising-seas/).

Schwarz, Jon. 2015. "'Yes, We're Corrupt': A List of Politicians Admitting that Money Controls Politics." The Intercept. July 30. Retrieved August 7, 2018 (https://theintercept.com/2015/07/30/politicians-admitting-obvious-fact-money-affects-vote/).

Schwellenbach, Nick, Russ Choma, and Adam Zagorin 2018. "Bribery Trial Reveals Jeff Sessions' Role in Blocking EPA Action Targeting One of His Biggest Donors." *Mother Jones*. August 2. Retrieved August 12, 2018 (https://www.motherjones.com/politics/2018/08/bribery-trial-reveals-jeff-sessions-role-in-blocking-epa-action-targeting-one-of-his-biggest-donors/).

*Science Advances* (see author list therein). 2017. "Impending Extinction Crisis of the World's Primates: Why Primates Matter." *Science Advances* 3 (1): e1600946. DOI: 10.1126/sciadv.1600946.

*Science* | Reports. 2018. "Assessment of Methane Emissions from the US Oil and Gas Supply Chain." *Science* 361 (6398): 186–188. DOI: 10.1126/science/aar7204.

Scipioni, Jade. 2018. "Wells Fargo Hit with $2 Billion Fine over Faulty Mortgages." FOX Business. August 1. Retrieved September 1, 2018 (https://www.foxbusiness.com/features/wells-fargo-hit-with-2-billion-fine-over-faulty-mortgages).

REFERENCES

Scott-Clayton, Judith. 2018. "The Looming Student Loan Default Crisis Is Worse than We Thought." Brookings. January 11. Retrieved May 31, 2018 (https://www.brookings.edu/research/the-looming-student-loan-default-crisis-is-worse-than-we-thought/).

Seaquist, J.W., Emma Li Johansson, and Kimberly A. Nicholas. 2014. "Architecture of the Global Land Acquisition System: Applying the Tools of Network Science to Identify Key Vulnerabilities." *Environmental Research Letters* 9 (11): 1–13. DOI:10.1088/1748-9326/9/11/114006.

Seidel, Jamie. 2018. "US Admiral Warns: Only War Can Now Stop Beijing Controlling the South China Sea." News Corp Australia Network. April 22. Retrieved July 1, 2018 (https://www.news.com.au/world/us-admiral-warns-only-war-can-now-stop-beijing-controlling-the-south-china-sea/news-story/0f8f99c3fb44923 66cec09d234937ab2).

Selby-Green, Michael. 2018. "'Money Talks': A $1.2 Trillion Fund Manager Is About to Pull Investment from Companies that Won't Act on Climate Change." Business Insider. April 24. Retrieved July 5, 2018 (https://www.businessinsider.nl/legal-and-general-helena-morrisey-on-climate-change-2018-4/).

Selzak, Michael. 2016. "Coral Bleaching Even Now Biggest in History—And About to Get Worse." *The Guardian*. June 20. Retrieved August 1, 2017 (https://www.theguardian.com/environment/2016/jun/21/coral-bleaching-event-now-biggest-in-history-and-about-to-get-worse).

Serna, Joseph, James Queally, and Alene Tchekmedyian. 2018. "Mendocino Complex Fire Now Largest in California History, Capping Destructive Year." *Los Angeles Times*. August 6. Retrieved August 13, 2018 (http://www.latimes.com/local/lanow/la-me-ln-california-wildfires-danger-level-20180806-story.html).

Seymour, Richard. 2018. "The Apocalyptic Tone of Heatwave-Reporting Doesn't Go Far Enough—Not When the Issue Is Human Extinction." *Independent*. August 5. Retrieved August 11, 2018 (https://www.independent.co.uk/voices/heatwave-weather-report-human-extinction-issue-a8478271.html).

Shabecoff, Philip. 1988. "Global Warming Has Begun, Expert Tells US Senate." *New York Times*. June 24, 1988. Retrieved June 25, 2018 (https://www.nytimes.com/1988/06/24/us/global-warming-has-begun-expert-tells-senate.html).

Shaefer, H. Luke, and Kathryn Edin. 2012. "Extreme Poverty in the United States, 1996 to 2011." National Poverty Center | Policy Brief (#28, February). Gerald R. Ford School of Public Policy, University of Michigan. Retrieved August 4, 2017 (http://www.npc.umich.edu/publications/policy_briefs/brief28/policybrief28.pdf).

Shelbourne, Mallory. 2018. "Niki Haley: 'Ridiculous' for UN to Analyze Poverty in America." The Hill. June 22. Retrieved July 24, 2018 (http://thehill.com/policy/international/un-treaties/393659-nikki-haley-ridiculous-for-un-to-analyze-poverty-in-america).

Shen, Lucinda. 2016. "Goldman Sachs Finally Admits It Defrauded Investors During the Financial Crisis." *Fortune*. April 11. Retrieved July 25, 2017 (http://fortune.com/2016/04/11/goldman-sachs-doj-settlement/).

Shepherd, Christian. 2018. "In China, Universities Seek to Plant 'Xi Thought' in Minds of Students." Reuters. June 22. Retrieved August 11, 2018 (https://www.reuters.com/article/us-china-politics-education/in-china-universities-seek-to-plant-xi-thought-in-minds-of-students-idUSKBN1JI0I5).

Shermer, Michael. 2018. "The Number of Americans with No Religious Affiliation Is Rising." *Scientific American*. April 1. Retrieved July 26, 2018 (https://www.scientificamerican.com/article/the-number-of-americans-with-no-religious-affiliation-is-rising/).

Shmuel, John. 2018. "So Long, Silicon Valley, China Is the World's Innovation Engine." *Maclean's*. July 10. Retrieved August 21, 2018 (https://www.macleans.ca/news/world/so-long-silicon-valley-china-is-the-worlds-innovation-engine/).

Shoot, Brittany. 2018. "Who Helped Trump Most in the 2016 Presidential Election? Nonvoters, Pew Study Finds." Fortune. August 9. Retrieved August 23, 2018 (http://fortune.com/2018/08/09/nonvoters-trump-presidency-pew-study/).

Silverman, Craig, and Jeremy Singer Vine. 2016. "Most Americans Who See Fake News Believe It, New Survey Says." BuzzFeed News. December 6. Retrieved August 6, 2017 (https://www.buzzfeed.com/craigsilverman/fake-news-survey?utm_term=.hsZQ7LkMLg#.dezVyRW3RL).

Sinclair, Harriet. 2018. "Donald Trump Jr. Likes Tweet Suggesting Children Separated from Parents at Border Are Crisis Actors." *Newsweek*. June 18. Retrieved August 11, 2018 (https://www.newsweek.com/donald-trump-jr-likes-tweet-suggesting-children-separated-parents-border-are-981126).

Smee, Ben. 2018. "Coral Decline in Great Barrier Reef 'Unprecedented.'" *The Guardian*. June 5. Retrieved June 19, 2018 (https://www.theguardian.com/environment/2018/jun/05/coral-decline-in-great-barrier-reef-unprecedented).

Smith, David Norman, and Eric Hanley. 2018. "The Anger Games: Who Voted for Donald Trump in the 2016 Election, and Why?" *Critical Sociology* 44 (2): 195–212.

Smith, Heather. 2018. "Climate Deniers Are More Likely to Be Racist. Why?" *Sierra: The National Magazine of the Sierra Club*. June 18. Retrieved June 28, 2018 (https://www.sierraclub.org/sierra/climate-deniers-are-more-likely-be-racist-obama-trump-climate-change).

Smith, Noah. 2018a. "Everything Is Booming Except for Wages." Bloomberg. February 23. Retrieved August 31, 2018 (https://www.washingtonpost.com/business/on-small-business/everything-is-booming-except-for-americans-wages-noah-smith/2018/02/23/2f84964c-18b7-11e8-930c-45838ad0d77a_story.html?noredirect=on&utm_term=.a33c1b9a1288).

REFERENCES

Smith, Noah. 2018b. "Many Americans Still Feel the Sting of Lost Wealth." Bloomberg. August 8. Retrieved September 13, 2018 (https://www.bloomberg.com/view/articles/2018-08-08/many-americans-still-feel-the-sting-of-lost-wealth).

Smithies, John. 2018. "UK Government Report Shows Fracking Increases Air Pollution." *The Epoch Times*. August 5. Retrieved August 12, 2018 (https://www.theepochtimes.com/uk-government-report-shows-fracking-increases-air-pollution_2613949.html).

Southern Poverty Law Center | Hatewatch Staff. 2016. "Update: 1,094 Bias-Related Incidents in the Month Following the Election." Southern Poverty Law Center. December 16. Retrieved June 12, 2018 (https://www.splcenter.org/hatewatch/2016/12/16/update-1094-bias-related-incidents-month-following-election).

Squires, Nick. 2018. "Exorcisms Booming as Christian Faith Declines and Internet Offers Easy Access to Black Magic, Priests Told." *The Telegraph*. April 16. Retrieved July 26, 2018 (https://www.telegraph.co.uk/news/2018/04/16/casting-demons-catholic-priests-perform-exorcisms-phone-demand/).

Srivastava, Kalpana. 2009. "Urbanization and Mental Health." *Industrial Psychiatry Journal* 18 (2): 75–76. DOI: 10.4103/0972-6748.64028.

Starn, Jesper. 2018a. "Power Worth Less than Zero Spreads as Green Energy Floods the Grid." Bloomberg. August 6. Retrieved August 27, 2018 (https://www.bloomberg.com/news/articles/2018-08-06/negative-prices-in-power-market-as-wind-solar-cut-electricity).

Starn, Jesper. 2018b. "Sweden to Reach Its 2030 Renewable Energy Target this Year." BusinessDay. July 4. Retrieved July 6, 2018 (https://www.businesslive.co.za/bd/world/europe/2018-07-04-sweden-to-reach-its-2030-renewable-energy-target-this-year/).

Stech, Katy. 2017. "Judge Fines Bank of America $45 Million for 'Heartless' Treatment of Mortgage Borrowers." FOX Business. Retrieved July 29, 2018 (https://www.foxbusiness.com/features/judge-fines-bank-of-america-45-million-for-heartless-treatment-of-mortgage-borrowers).

Stein, Ben. 2006. "In Class Warfare, Guess Which Class Is Winning" *New York Times*. November 26. Retrieved August 25, 2018 (https://www.nytimes.com/2006/11/26/business/yourmoney/26every.html).

Stein, Jeff. 2018. "Across the Globe, Taxes on Corporations Plummet." *Washington Post*. July 24. Retrieved August 7, 2018 (https://www.washingtonpost.com/business/2018/07/24/across-globe-taxes-corporations-plummet/?noredirect=on&utm_term=.20fc65d0698c).

Stein, Letitia, Susan Cornwell, and Joseph Tanfani. 2018. "Inside the progressive movement roiling the Democratic Party." Reuters. August 23. Retrieved September 16, 2018 (https://www.reuters.com/investigates/special-report/usa-election-progressives/).

Stewart, Hadley. 2018. "'You Can't Be Out': Gay Egyptians Continue to Fear Persecution." NBC News. August 18. Retrieved September 7, 2018 (https://www.nbcnews.com/feature/nbc-out/hunt-has-never-stopped-gay-egyptians-continue-fear-persecution-n901886).

Stewart, Matthew. 2018. "The 9.9 Percent Is the New American Aristocracy." *The Atlantic*. June. Retrieved July 24, 2018 (https://www.theatlantic.com/magazine/archive/2018/06/the-birth-of-a-new-american-aristocracy/559130/).

Stone, Linda, and Caroline James. 1995. "Dowry, Bride-Burning, and Female Power in India." *Women's Studies International Forum* 18 (12): 125–134.

Stone, Richard. 2002. "Counting the Cost of London's Killer Smog." *Science* 298 (5601): 2106–2107. DOI: 10.1126/science.298.5601.2106b.

Stramma, Lothar, Gregory C. Johnson, Janet Sprintall, and Volker Morholz. 2008. "Expanding Oxygen-Minimum Zones in the Tropical Oceans." *Science* 320 (5876): 655–658, DOI: 10.1126/science.1153847.

Stulz, René M. 2010. "Credit Default Swaps and the Credit Crisis." *Journal of Economic Perspectives* 24 (1): 73–92.

Suebsaeng, Asawin, Andrew Desiderio, Sam Stein, and Bethan Allen-Ebrahimian. 2018. "Henry Kissinger Pushed Trump to Work with Russia to Box in China." The Daily Beast. July 25. Retrieved August 21, 2018 (https://www.thedailybeast.com/henry-kissinger-pushed-trump-to-work-with-russia-to-box-in-china).

Sura, Ajay. 2018. "Mass Castration: Dera Sacha Sauda Chief Gurmeet Ram Rahim Chargesheeted." *The Times of India*. February 2. Retrieved July 23, 2018 (https://timesofindia.indiatimes.com/india/mass-castration-dera-sacha-sauda-chief-gurmeet-ram-rahim-chargesheeted/articleshow/62748605.cms).

Surgey, Nick, and Zaid Jilani. 2018. "The Koch Brothers Commissioned a Survey of Americans and Found Most Like a $15 Minimum Wage, Free College, and Universal Health Care." The Intercept. August 9. Retrieved August 26, 2018 (https://theintercept.com/2018/08/09/koch-brothers-health-care-free-college/).

Swan, Jonathan. 2018a. "Exclusive: A Leaked Trump Bill to Blow Up the WTO." Axios. July 1. Retrieved August 21, 2018 (https://www.axios.com/trump-trade-war-leaked-bill-world-trade-organization-united-states-d51278d2-0516-4def-a4d3-ed676f4e0f83.html).

Swan, Jonathan. 2018b. "Scoop: Trump's Private NATO Trashing Rattles Allies." June 28. Axios. Retrieved July 1, 2018 (https://www.axios.com/donald-trump-foreign-policy-europe-nato-allies-worried-bd1e143a-e73a-415b-b688-d18ab2d902e7.html).

Sy, Amadou. 2015. "What Do We Know about the Chinese Land Grab in Africa?" Brookings. November 5. Retrieved July 3, 2018 (https://www.brookings.edu/blog/africa-in-focus/2015/11/05/what-do-we-know-about-the-chinese-land-grab-in-africa/).

REFERENCES

Tabary, Zoe. 2016. "Scientists Caught Off-Guard by Record Temperatures Linked to Climate Change." Reuters. July 26. Retrieved August 1, 2017 (http://www.reuters.com/article/us-weather-climatechange-science-idUSKCN1061RH).
Talking Points Memo. 2014. "GOP Rep. Acknowledges that Members Expect Donations for Votes." Talking Points Memo | Livewire. June 9. Retrieved July 28, 2017 (http://talkingpointsmemo.com/livewire/mcallister-contributions-votes).
Tan, Florence, and Josephine Mason. 2018. "China's Unipec Suspends US Oil Imports as Trade Spat Intensifies." Reuters. August 3. Retrieved August 21, 2018 (https://www.reuters.com/article/us-usa-trade-china-oil/chinas-unipec-suspends-us-oil-imports-as-trade-spat-intensifies-idUSKBN1KO0SB).
Tandoc, Edson C., Patrick Ferrucci, and Margaret Duffy. 2015. "Facebook, Envy, and Depression among College Students: Is Facebooking Depressing?" *Computers in Human Behavior* 43 (February): 139–146. doi.org/10.1016/j.chb.2014.10.053.
Temin, Peter. 2017. *The Vanishing Middle Class: Prejudice and Power in a Dual Economy*. Cambridge, Massachusetts: MIT Press.
Teo, Hsu-Ming. 1996. "The Continuum of Sexual Violence in Occupied Germany, 1945–49." *Women's History Review* 5 (2): 191–218. doi.org/10.1080/09612029600200111.
Terzi, Nuray, and Korkmaz Uluçay 2011. "The Role of Credit Default Swaps on Financial Market Stability." *Procedia Social and Behavioral Sciences* 24: 983–990. doi.org/10.1016/j.sbspro.2011.09.066.
Tett, Gillian. 2015. "Economists' Tribal Thinking." *The Atlantic*. September 1. Retrieved August 2, 2017 (https://www.theatlantic.com/business/archive/2015/09/economists-tribal-thinking/403075/).
*The Economist*. 2016. "The Future of Oil." November 26. Retrieved August 13, 2018 (https://www.economist.com/special-report/2016/11/26/the-future-of-oil).
*The Economist*. 2018a. "As Inequality Grows, So Does the Political Influence of the Rich." July 21. Retrieved August 7, 2018 (https://www.economist.com/finance-and-economics/2018/07/21/as-inequality-grows-so-does-the-political-influence-of-the-rich).
*The Economist*. 2018b. "Britain's Economy Has Slowed to a Standstill, Largely Because of Brexit." June 20. Retrieved July 1, 2018 (https://www.economist.com/britain/2018/06/21/the-economy-has-slowed-to-a-standstill-largely-because-of-brexit).
*The Economist*. 2018c. "Time Is Running Out for Nicaragua's President Daniel Ortega." June 9. Retrieved August 8, 2018 (https://www.economist.com/the-americas/2018/06/09/time-is-running-out-for-nicaraguas-president-daniel-ortega).
*The Economist* | J.B. 2017. "Why Forests Are Spreading in the Rich World." *The Economist*. December 12. Retrieved July 13, 2018 (https://www.economist.com/the-economist-explains/2017/12/12/why-forests-are-spreading-in-the-rich-world).

The Editors of *The Epoch Times*. 2018. "Why China Will Not Abandon Theft in Its Strategy to Surpass US Economy." *The Epoch Times*. April 29. Retrieved July 1, 2018 (https://www.theepochtimes.com/why-china-will-not-abandon-theft-in-its-strategy-to-surpass-us-economy_2502976.html).

*The Guardian* | Environment. 2018. "Point Nemo Is the Most Remote Oceanic Spot—Yet It Is Awash in Plastic." *The Guardian*. May 18. Retrieved June 22, 2018 (https://www.theguardian.com/environment/shortcuts/2018/may/18/point-nemo-is-the-most-remote-oceanic-spot-yet-its-still-awash-with-plastic).

The IMBIE Team. 2018. "Mass Balance of the Antarctic Ice Sheet from 1992 to 2017." *Nature* 558: 219–222. doi.org/10.1038/s41586-018-0179-y.

*The Japan Times*. 2018a. "Japan Nears Record Number of Hospitalizations for Heat-Related Issues." July 31. Retrieved August 12, 2018 (https://www.japantimes.co.jp/news/2018/07/31/national/japan-nears-record-number-hospitalizations-heat-related-issues/).

*The Japan Times*. 2018b. "Seven Years on, Radioactive Water at Fukushima Plant Still Flowing into Ocean, Study Finds." March 29. Retrieved August 12, 2018 (https://www.japantimes.co.jp/news/2018/03/29/national/seven-years-radioactive-water-fukushima-plant-still-flowing-ocean-study-finds/#.W3K4XM5KiUk).

*The Local*. 2018. "Sweden Democrats Call for Referendum on Swedish EU Membership after 2018 Election." June 18. Retrieved July 1, 2018 (https://www.thelocal.se/20180618/sweden-democrats-call-for-referendum-on-swedish-eu-membership-after-2018-election).

*The Times* Editorial Board. 2018. "Surprise! California Cracked Down on Carbon and Its Economy Is Still Booming." *Los Angeles Times*. June 13. Retrieved July 14, 2018 (http://www.latimes.com/opinion/editorials/la-ed-california-climate-change-20180713-story.html).

Thompson, Derek. 2014. "The Incredible Shrinking Incomes of Young Americans." *The Atlantic*. December 3. Retrieved August 1, 2017 (https://www.theatlantic.com/business/archive/2014/12/millennials-arent-saving-money-because-theyre-not-making-money/383338/).

Thomsen, Jacqueline. 2018a. "Judge Rules EPA Must Provide Evidence Used for Pruitt's Climate Change Claims." The Hill. June 7. Retrieved July 5, 2018 (http://thehill.com/policy/energy-environment/391130-judge-rules-pruitt-must-provide-evidence-used-for-climate-change).

Thomsen, Jacqueline. 2018b. "Leaked Documents Show China Using Tariffs to Target Trump's Base: Report." The Hill. July 3. Retrieved August 21, 2018 (http://thehill.com/policy/finance/international-taxes/395356-leaked-documents-show-china-using-tariffs-to-target-trumps).

Thomson, Jason. 2016. "Antarctic Carbon Dioxide Reaches Highest Levels in 4 Million Years." *The Christian Science Monitor*. June 18. Retrieved August 1, 2017

# REFERENCES

(https://www.csmonitor.com/Environment/2016/0618/Antarctic-carbon-dioxide-reaches-highest-levels-in-4-million-years).

Thum, Rian. 2018. "China's Mass Internment Camps Have No Clear End in Sight." *Foreign Policy*. August 22. Retrieved September 7, 2018 (https://foreignpolicy.com/2018/08/22/chinas-mass-internment-camps-have-no-clear-end-in-sight/).

Timmer, John. 2018. "Barents Sea Seems to Have Crossed a Climate Tipping Point." Ars Technica. June 26. Retrieved July 13, 2018 (https://arstechnica.com/science/2018/06/barents-sea-seems-to-have-crossed-a-climate-tipping-point/).

Toce, Sarah. 2018. "Republicans Vote to Make It Legal Nationwide to Ban Gays & Lesbians from Adopting." LGBTQ Nation. July 12. Retrieved August 8, 2018 (https://www.lgbtqnation.com/2018/07/rule-making-legal-ban-gays-lesbians-adopting-passes-house-committee/).

Tohti, Mehmet. 2018. "Uyghurs: Victims of 21st Century Concentration Camps." The Diplomat. May 18. Retrieved July 31, 2018 (https://thediplomat.com/2018/05/uyghurs-victims-of-21st-century-concentration-camps/).

Tracey, Emma. 2013. "Why Deaf People Sneeze Silently." BBC | Ouch. July 5. Retrieved May 25, 2018 (http://www.bbc.com/news/blogs-ouch-23162903).

Trenberth, Keven E., Lijing Cheng, Peter Jacobs, Yongxin Zhang, and John Fasullo. 2018. "Hurricane Harvey Links to Ocean Heat Content and Climate Change Adaptation." *Earth's Future* 6: 1–15. doi.org10.1029/.

Tromholt, Morten. 2016. "The Facebook Experiment: Quitting Facebook Leads to Higher Levels of Well-Being." *Cyberpsychology, Behavior and Social Networking* 19 (11): 661–666. doi.org/10.1089/cyber.2016.0259.

Tucker, Eric, and Chad Day. 2018. "AP Sources: Lawyer was Told Russia had 'Trump Over a Barrel.'" Associated Press News. Retrieved September 13, 2018 (https://www.apnews.com/4ac772445073491aa7d3ca9e558e0144).

Tucker, Patrick. 2007. "Subprime Lenders Target Women Unfairly." *The Futurist* (May/June): 7.

Union of Concerned Scientists. 2018. "How Do We Know that Humans Are the Major Cause of Global Warming?" July 6. Retrieved August 12, 2018 (https://www.ucsusa.org/global-warming/science-and-impacts/science/human-contribution-to-gw-faq.html).#.W3AmLs5KjIU).

United Nations. 2013. "Major Cuts of Greenhouse Gas Emissions from Livestock Within Reach." Food and Agriculture Organization of the United Nations. September 26. Retrieved June 22, 2018 (http://www.fao.org/news/story/en/item/197608/icode/).

United Nations. 2018. "Venezuela: Continued Impunity Amid Dismal Human Rights Situation-UN Report." United Nations Human Rights | Office of the High Commissioner. June 22. Retrieved July 31, 2018 (https://www.ohchr.org/EN/NewsEvents/Pages/DisplayNews.aspx?NewsID=23242&LangID=E).

United Nations Office on Drugs and Crime. 2018. "UNODC Report on Human Trafficking Exposes Modern Form of Slavery." Retrieved August 18, 2018 (http://www.unodc.org/unodc/en/frontpage/unodc-report-on-human-trafficking-exposes-modern-form-of-slavery-.html).

University of Exeter. 2018. "Acidic Oceans Cause Fish to Lose Their Sense of Smell." University of Exeter Research News. July 23. Retrieved August 12, 2018 (http://www.exeter.ac.uk/news/featurednews/title_672112_en.html).

UN News. 2016. "Earth's Health Declining 'Faster than Thought' but Actions by Governments Can Reverse Trend—UN." United Nations. May 19. Retrieved August 1, 2017 (http://www.un.org/apps/news/story.asp?NewsID=53981#.WYCCp4TyvIX).

Valenti, Denise. 2018. "Princeton Economists Find that Unions Had Historical Role in Helping Address Income Inequality." Office of Communications | Princeton University. June 21. Retrieved July 24, 2018 (https://www.princeton.edu/news/2018/06/21/princeton-economists-find-unions-had-historical-role-helping-address-income).

Vance, J.D. 2016. *Hillbilly Elegy*. New York: HarperCollins.

Vaughan, Liam. 2017. "How the Flash Crash Trader's $50 Million Fortune Vanished." Bloomberg. February 10. Retrieved August 18, 2018 (https://www.bloomberg.com/news/features/2017-02-10/how-the-flash-crash-trader-s-50-million-fortune-vanished).

Vaughn, Adam. 2014. "Microplastic Deposits Found Deep in World's Oceans and Seas." *The Guardian*. December 17. Retrieved August 1, 2017 (https://www.theguardian.com/environment/2014/dec/17/microplastic-deposits-found-deep-in-worlds-oceans-and-seas).

Vaughn, Adam. 2018a. "UK Passes 1,000 Hours Without Coal as Energy Shift Accelerates." *The Guardian*. July 13. Retrieved July 14, 2018 (https://www.theguardian.com/business/2018/jul/12/uk-to-pass-1000-hours-without-coal-as-energy-shift-accelerates).

Vaughn, Adam. 2018b. "UK Runs Without Coal Power for Three Days in a Row." *The Guardian*. April 24. Retrieved July 5, 2018 (https://www.theguardian.com/business/2018/apr/24/uk-power-generation-coal-free-gas-renewables-nuclear).

Vick, Karl. 2016. "Libya's Migrant Economy Is a Modern Day Slave Market." *Time*. October 21. Retrieved August 18, 2018 (http://time.com/4538445/libyas-migrant-economy-is-a-modern-day-slave-market/).

Victor, Jennifer. 2017. "Trump Uses Pay to Play. Here's Why and How to Fix It." Vox. September 6. Retrieved July 29, 2018 (https://www.vox.com/mischiefs-of-faction/2017/9/6/16262598/how-to-fix-pay-to-play).

Vidal, John. 2011. "Shell Oil Paid Nigerian Military to Put Down Protests, Court Documents Show." *The Guardian*. October 2. Retrieved July 31, 2018 (https://www.theguardian.com/world/2011/oct/03/shell-oil-paid-nigerian-military).

Vitousek, Sean, Patrick L. Barnard, Charles H. Fletcher, Neil Frazer, Li Erikson, and Curt D. Storlazzi. 2017. "Doubling of Coastal Flooding Frequency within Decades Due to Sea-Level Rise." *Scientific Reports* 7 (1399): 1–9. DOI: 10.1038/s41598-017-01362-7.

Vives, Marc Lluís, and Oriel Feldman Hall. 2018. "Tolerance to Ambiguous Uncertainty Predicts Prosocial Behavior." *Nature Communications* 9 (2156): 1–9. doi.org/10.1038/s41467-018-04631-9.

Vlastelica, Ryan. 2018. "Stocks Are in 'the Danger Zone,' and It Is 'Assured' that a Bear Market Will Occur in the Next Year, Analyst Warns." MarketWatch. September 10. Retrieved September 23, 2018 (https://www.marketwatch.com/story/stocks-are-in-the-danger-zone-and-it-is-assured-that-a-bear-market-will-occur-in-the-next-year-analyst-warns-2018-09-07).

Vogel, Pam. 2018. "Sinclair Stations Have Now Aired Six 'Must-Run' Segments Pushing for Brett Kavanaugh's Confirmation." Media Matters. July 30. Retrieved September 21, 2018 (https://www.mediamatters.org/blog/2018/07/30/sinclair-stations-have-now-aired-four-must-run-segments-pushing-brett-kavanaugh-s-confirmation/220837).

Vogl, Joseph. 2017. *The Ascendency of Finance*. Malden, Massachusetts: Polity Press.

Vorrath, Sophie, and Giles Parkinson. 2018. "Australia Solar Costs Hit 'Extraordinary' New Lows—$50s/MWh." RenewEconomy. June 27. Retrieved July 13, 2018 (https://reneweconomy.com.au/australia-solar-costs-hit-extraordinary-new-lows-50s-mwh-27007/).

Wadsworth, Nancy D. 2018. "The Racial Demons that Help Explain Evangelical Support for Trump." Vox. April 30. Retrieved September (https://www.vox.com/the-big-idea/2018/4/30/17301282/race-evangelicals-trump-support-gerson-atlantic-sexism-segregation-south).

Waldman, Paul. 2018. "The Entire Republican Party Is Becoming a Russian Asset." *Washington Post*. July 20. Retrieved August 21, 2018 (https://www.washingtonpost.com/blogs/plum-line/wp/2018/07/20/the-entire-republican-party-is-becoming-a-russian-asset/?noredirect=on&utm_term=.3794efcf1801).

Waldman, Scott. 2018. "Pruitt Got Climate Tips from Groups Backed by GOP Megadonors." E&E News | Politics. May 11. Retrieved June 20, 2018 (https://www.eenews.net/stories/1060081469).

Walker, Peter. 2016. "Climate Change Escalating So Fast It Is 'Beyond Point of No Return.'" *Independent*. December 1. Retrieved August 1, 2017 (http://www.independent.co.uk/news/science/donald-trump-climate-change-policy-global-warming-expert-thomas-crowther-a7450236.html).

Wallace, Tim. 2018. "Global Economy Set for Decade of Gloom as World Bank Predicts Recovery Will Fizzle Out." *The Telegraph*. January 9. Retrieved June 29, 2018 (https://www.telegraph.co.uk/business/2018/01/09/global-economy-set-decade-gloom-world-bank-predicts-recovery/).

Wallerstein, Immanuel. 1982. "Crisis as Transition." Pp. 11–54 in *Dynamics of Global Crisis*, edited by Samir Amin, Giovanni Arrighi, Andre Gunder Frank, and Immanuel Wallerstein. New York: Monthly Review Press.

Wallerstein, Immanuel. [1983] 1999. *Historical Capitalism*. New York: Verso.

Wallerstein, Immanuel. 2000. "The Construction of Peoplehood: Racism, Nationalism, Ethnicity." Pp. 293–309 in *The Essential Wallerstein*. New York: The New Press.

Warrick, Joby, and Steven Mufson. 2014. "Big Oil's Heirs Join Call for Action as Climate Summit Opens." *Washington Post*. September 21. Retrieved August 1, 2017 (https://www.washingtonpost.com/national/health-science/big-oils-heirs-join-call-for-action-as-climate-summit-opens/2014/09/21/ab27b1ce-40ea-11e4-b0ea-8141703bbf6f_story.html?utm_term=.fa5ca777fb70).

Waters, Hannah. 2018. "How the US Government Is Aggressively Censoring Climate Science." *Audubon*. Summer 2018. Retrieved August 12, 2018 (https://www.audubon.org/magazine/summer-2018/how-us-government-aggressively-censoring-climate).

Watkins, Thayer. n.d. "Credit Default Swaps and Their Role in the 2007–2008 Financial Crisis." San Jose State Department of Economics. Retrieved June 29, 2018 (http://www.sjsu.edu/faculty/watkins/CDS.htm).

Watts, Jonathan. 2018a. "Domino-Effect of Climate Events Could Move Earth into a 'Hothouse' State." *The Guardian*. August 7. Retrieved August 27, 2018 (https://www.theguardian.com/environment/2018/aug/06/domino-effect-of-climate-events-could-push-earth-into-a-hothouse-state).

Watts, Jonathan. 2018b. "Summer Weather Is Getting 'Stuck' Due to Arctic Warming." *The Guardian*. August 20. Retrieved September 15, 2018 (https://www.theguardian.com/environment/2018/aug/20/summer-weather-is-getting-stuck-due-to-arctic-warming).

Watts, Jonathan. 2018c. "World Is Finally Waking Up to Climate Change, Says 'Hothouse Earth' Author." *The Guardian*. August 19. Retrieved September 15, 2018 (https://www.theguardian.com/environment/2018/aug/17/world-waking-up-to-reality-climate-change-hothouse-earth-author).

Weale, Salley. 2014. "ADHD Drugs Increasingly Prescribed to Treat Hyperactivity in Pre-Schools." *The Guardian*. December 21. Retrieved July 20, 2017 (https://www.theguardian.com/society/2014/dec/21/adhd-medication-treat-hyperactivity-pre-school-children).

Weaver, John. 2018. "Texas Is Going Green: 86% of Future Capacity Solar or Wind, Zero Coal." PV Magazine. August 23. Retrieved September 15, 2018 (https://pv-magazine-usa.com/2018/08/23/texas-going-green-86-of-future-capacity-solar-or-wind-zero-coal/).

Webb, Gary. 1998. *Dark Alliance: The CIA, the Contras, and the Crack Cocaine Explosion*. New York: Seven Stories Press.

Webb, Whitney. 2017. "US Military World's Largest Polluter—Hundreds of Bases Gravely Contaminated." Mint Press News. May 15. Retrieved August 13, 2018 (https://www

.mintpressnews.com/u-s-military-is-worlds-largest-polluter-hundreds-of-bases-gravely-contaminated/227776/).

Weber, Christopher. 2018. "US Allows Nestle to Keep Taking Water from California Forest." AP News. June 28. Retrieved August 12, 2018 (https://apnews.com/67270f1105754f498bfab05e379bcee1).

Weber, Peter. 2018. "Watch Trump Shrug When Fox News Reminds Him Kim Jong Un 'Is a Killer' Who's 'Clearly Executing People.'" The Week. June 13. Retrieved August 8, 2018 (http://theweek.com/speedreads/778984/watch-trump-shrug-when-fox-news-reminds-kim-jong-un-killer-whos-clearly-executing-people).

Wei, Katherine. 2018. "What It's Like to Be an Environmental Defender in the Philippines." *Sierra: The National Magazine of the Sierra Club.* June 11. Retrieved June 21, 2018 (https://www.sierraclub.org/sierra/what-its-be-environmental-defender-philippines).

Weisbaum, Herb. 2016. "Putting Off Marriage, Not Buying a Home: How People Live with Student Debt." NBC News. July 9. Retrieved August 31, 2018 (https://www.nbcnews.com/feature/college-game-plan/putting-marriage-not-buying-home-how-people-live-student-debt-n612531).

Weisse, Mikaela, and Elizabeth Dow Goldman. 2017. "Global Tree Cover Loss Rose 51 Percent in 2016." World Resources Institute. October 23. Retrieved June 20, 2018 (http://www.wri.org/blog/2017/10/global-tree-cover-loss-rose-51-percent-2016).

Weissmann, Jordan. 2018. "Goldman Sachs Warns that Rising Wages Could Cut into Corporate Profits. *The Horror!*" Slate. July 9. Retrieved July 24, 2018 (https://slate.com/business/2018/07/goldman-sachs-warns-that-rising-wages-could-cut-into-corporate-profits-the-horror.html).

Wessel, David. 2015. "The Typical Male US Worker Earned Less in 2014 than in 1973." Brookings. September 18. Retrieved August 1, 2017 (https://www.brookings.edu/opinions/the-typical-male-u-s-worker-earned-less-in-2014-than-in-1973/).

Westcott, Lucy. 2017. "Female Genital Mutilation Declines Among Girls in Some Countries: Report." *Newsweek.* February 6. Retrieved September 12, 2018 (https://www.newsweek.com/fgm-female-gential-mutilation-decline-some-countries-553132).

White, Daniel. 2016. "Nearly 20% of Trump Fans Think Freeing the Slaves Was a Bad Idea." *Time.* February 24. Retrieved August 6, 2017 (http://time.com/4236640/donald-trump-racist-supporters/).

Whiteman, Gail, Chris Hope, and Peter Wadhams. 2013. "Climate Science: Vast Costs of Arctic Change." *Nature* 499 (July): 401–403. doi.org/10.1038/499401a.

Wierson, Arick, and Javier Arguello Lacayo. 2018. "Nicaragua Is on the Verge of Civil War. The Fallout Could Become the 'Biggest Wild Card' in the Midterm Elections." CNBC. August 10. Retrieved September 7, 2018 (https://www.cnbc.com/2018/08/10/midterm-elections-nicaragua-civil-war-crisis-wild-card.html).

Wigglesworth, Robin. 2018. "US Student Loan Debt Balloons Past $1.5tn." *Financial Times*. August 26. Retrieved August 31, 2018 (https://www.ft.com/content/18530da6-a637-11e8-926a-7342fe5e173f).

Willard, Jed. 2018. "What Europe Can Teach America About Russian Disinformation." *The Atlantic*. June 9. Retrieved July 24, 2018 (https://www.theatlantic.com/international/archive/2018/06/what-europe-can-teach-america-about-russian-disinformation/562121/).

Willick, Jason. 2016. "The Campus Left and the Alt-Right Are Natural Allies." *The American Interest*. September 1. Retrieved July 13, 2018 (https://www.the-american-interest.com/2016/09/01/the-campus-left-and-the-alt-right-are-natural-allies/).

Wines, Michael. 2018. "New Emails Show Michigan Republicans Plotting to Gerrymander Maps." *New York Times*. July 25. Retrieved August 7, 2018 (https://www.nytimes.com/2018/07/25/us/michigan-gerrymandering.html).

Wissman, Angela. 1998. "ADM Execs Nailed on Price-Fixing, May Do Time; Government Gets Watershed Convictions, But Company Still Dominates Lysine Market." *Illinois Legal Times*. October: 1.

Withnall, Adam. 2018. "Rohingya: UN Calls for Myanmar Generals to Be Prosecuted for Genocide, War Crimes and Crimes against Humanity." *Independent*. August 27. Retrieved September 7, 2018 (https://www.independent.co.uk/news/world/asia/un-investigators-myanmar-latest-news-prosecuted-genocide-investigated-a8509466.html).

Witze, Alexandra. 2018. "More than 2 Billion People Lack Safe Drinking Water. That Number Will Only Grow." Science News. August 16. Retrieved May 6, 2019 (https://www.sciencenews.org/article/future-will-people-have-enough-water-live).

Wojdyla, Ben. 2011. "The Top Automotive Engineering Failures: The Ford Pinto Fuel Tanks." *Popular Mechanics*. May 20. Retrieved June 5, 2018 (https://www.popularmechanics.com/cars/a6700/top-automotive-engineering-failures-ford-pinto-fuel-tanks/).

Wolff, Naomi. 2007. *The Shock Doctrine: The Rise of Disaster Capitalism*. New York: Picador.

Wood, Tony. 2018. "The Crisis that Created Putin." Jacobin Magazine. August 30. Retrieved September 23, 2018 (https://www.jacobinmag.com/2018/08/rouble-crash-yeltsin-putin-free-market).

Woolley, Suzanne. 2018. "Here's How Much Money You Need for Bankers to Think You're Rich." Bloomberg. May 23. Retrieved July 24, 2018 (https://www.bloomberg.com/news/articles/2018-05-23/bankers-don-t-think-you-re-rich-unless-you-have-25-million).

Wright, Jessica. 2017. "The Real Reasons Autism Rates Are Up in the US" *Scientific American*. March 3. Retrieved July 16, 2018 (https://www.scientificamerican.com/article/the-real-reasons-autism-rates-are-up-in-the-u-s/).

Wright, Pam. 2017. "87 Percent of Americans Unaware There's Scientific Consensus on Climate Change." The Weather Channel. July 11. Retrieved August 1, 2017 (https://

weather.com/science/environment/news/americans-climate-change-scientific-consensus).

Yagoda, Maya. 2018. "Wave of Plastic Pollution Off Coast of Dominican Republic Shows Extent of Global Damage." *Independent*. July 20. Retrieved August 13, 2018 (https://www.independent.co.uk/news/world/plastic-pollution-wave-video-dominican-republic-environment-parley-activist-santo-domingo-a8457251.html).

Yan, Holly. 2018. "Jurors Give $289 Million to a Man They Say Got Cancer from Monsanto's Roundup Weedkiller." CNN. August 11. Retrieved August 13, 2018 (https://www.cnn.com/2018/08/10/health/monsanto-johnson-trial-verdict/index.html).

Yates Sexton, Jared. 2017. "Hillbilly Sellout: The Politics of J.D. Vance's 'Hillbilly Elegy' Are Already Being Used to Gut the Working Poor." Salon. March 11. Retrieved July 16, 2018 (https://www.salon.com/2017/03/11/hillbilly-sellout-the-politics-of-j-d-vances-hillbilly-elegy-are-already-being-used-to-gut-the-working-poor/).

Yuhas, Alan. 2014. "One in 30 US Children Are Homeless as Rates Rise in 31 States, Report Finds." *The Guardian*. November 17. Retrieved August 2, 2017 (https://www.theguardian.com/us-news/2014/nov/17/report-one-in-30-us-children-homeless).

Yulsman, Tom. 2016. "Surface Melting of Snow and Ice in Greenland Explodes as Temperatures Soar to Record Levels." *Discover*. June 12. Retrieved August 1, 2017 (http://blogs.discovermagazine.com/imageo/2016/06/12/surface-melting-of-snow-and-ice-in-greenland-explodes/#.WYCBPoTyvIU).

Zeller, Tom. 2003. "The Nation; How Americans Link Iraq and Sept. 11." *New York Times*. March 2, 2003. Retrieved July 11, 2018 (https://www.nytimes.com/2003/03/02/weekinreview/the-nation-how-americans-link-iraq-and-sept-11.html).

Zilio, Michelle. 2018. "US, Japan Decline to Sign G7 Agreement to Reduce Plastic Waste in Oceans." *The Globe and Mail*. June 10. Retrieved June 19, 2018 (https://www.theglobeandmail.com/politics/article-us-japan-decline-to-sign-g7-agreement-to-reduce-plastic-waste-in/).

Zinn, Howard. 1980. *A People's History of the United States*. New York: HarperCollins.

Zoorob, Michael. 2018. "Does 'Right to Work' Imperil the Right to Health? The Effect of Labour Unions on Workplace Fatalities." *Occupational & Environmental Medicine* (June). DOI: 10.1136/oemed-2017-104747.

# Index

Accumulation (Accumulators)   25, 83, 123, 158, 370, 389, 446
   Of capital   120, 126, 134, 144, 159, 193, 196, 212, 212n, 217, 219, 221, 224, 227, 229, 269, 288, 289, 328, 364, 372, 376, 380, 381, 382, 384, 386, 390n, 414, 416, 429
   Of profit   125, 381, 416
   Of wealth   59, 76, 79–80, 125, 228, 342, 381, 408
   Overaccumulation of capital   140, 143, 328
   See also capital; capitalism; class; concentration (of capital, of wealth); crisis; inequality; labor; production (overproduction); profit
Afghanistan   63, 97, 141, 192, 230–231, 295, 323, 350, 367, 377
   Taliban   20, 63, 97, 192, 230, 350
   See also Bin Laden, Osama; drugs (opium); Eurasia; Soviet Union (invasion of Afghanistan); terrorism (September 11, 2001 attacks); war (Afghan War)
Africa   ix, 20, 36n, 41, 48n, 59, 112, 128, 130, 133, 187–188, 219, 237, 252, 282, 283, 296, 299, 300–303, 305, 306, 315, 331, 338–339, 346, 347, 359, 360, 390, 402, 407, 417
   North Africa   127, 230, 300
   See also colonialism; Congo; Egypt; Ivory Coast; Kenya; Libya; Nigeria; Sierra Leone; slavery; South Africa; South Sudan; Sudan; war (World War I—Scramble for Africa)
African-Americans   62, 152, 166n1, 182, 243n1, 309, 314, 321
   See also inequality; poverty; race and racism; slavery; violence (lynching)
Aggregate demand
   See economics (supply and demand)
Agricultural societies
   See societies (types of)
Ailes, Roger   259–260
   See also media (mass media—FOX News); Nixon, Richard; propaganda
Albright, Madeleine   183, 234
   See also Iraq
Alienation   60–61, 111, 406, 424, 428n, 431

   See also exploitation; labor; mystification; religion
Allende, Salvador   191, 248
   See also Chile; geo-politics; Kissinger, Henry; Pinochet, Augusto; socialism
Amazon (rainforest)
   See environmental crisis (forests)
America / American(s)   1n, 4, 5, 20, 29, 31, 49, 50n, 51, 58, 61, 62, 70, 78n, 79, 85, 86, 87, 91, 92, 93n, 95, 107, 109, 117, 128, 133, 135, 141, 151n5, 152, 166n1, 181, 182, 187, 189, 198, 211, 219, 225, 230, 232, 233, 235, 237, 243n2, 245–246, 253, 264n7, 266, 267, 281, 283, 283n4, 287, 294, 300, 303–304n, 309, 314, 315, 320, 321n, 332, 342, 343, 346, 348, 351, 352n4, 353, 355, 358, 359, 360, 361, 362, 364, 366, 366n2, 371, 374, 392, 393, 394n2, 395, 418, 419, 420–421, 421n4, 436n8, 444, 450
   American exceptionalism   68
   Colonial America   20, 189, 225
   See also Central America; Latin America; North America; South America; United States
Apollo missions   176–177
   See also technology (Moore's Law)
Appalachia   21n, 145, 189, 231, 271
   Appalachian Mountains   145, 189, 271
   Broad Form Deed   145
   See also coal; environmental crisis (and energy—mountain top removal); poverty
Appropriation of wealth   43–44, 388, 403, 412, 446
   See also accumulation; class; concentration (of capital, of wealth); exploitation; labor; pauperism; poverty; profit; value (surplus-value)
Arab Spring
   See social movement(s)
Arabia
   Arabian Peninsula   271, 377
   Arabian Sea / Gulf of Oman   277
   Arabic-Muslim world   300

INDEX 535

*See also* Kuwait; Qatar; Saudi Arabia; Yemen
Arctic
   *See* environmental crisis (global warming—melting ice sheets)
Argentina   128, 334, 335n4
   *See also* debt (debt crisis); South America
Arkhipov, Vasili   348n
   *See also* Cold War; Cuba (Cuban Missile Crisis)
Arrenhius, Svante   273
   *See also* environmental crisis (global warming)
Art (Artists)   98–99, 111, 241, 246, 294, 389, 429, 451
Asia (Asian / Asiatic)   60, 100, 128, 130, 142, 146, 179, 187, 259n2, 330, 336, 339n, 342, 347, 352, 359, 398, 405, 426n2, 436n8
   Central Asia   230, 347
   South East Asia   20, 331
   *See also* Bangladesh; Cambodia; China; colonialism; Hong Kong; India; Indonesia; Japan; Myanmar; North Korea; Pakistan; Philippines; Russia; South Korea; Taiwan; Vietnam
Assimilation   118, 309
   Forced assimilation and residential schools   309, 311
   *See also* barbarism; civilization
Asymptotic (Asymptotes)   165, 177, 194
   *See also* science; social change; social progress; technology (Moore's Law)
Atheism (Atheists)
   *See* religion
Austerity   222, 324, 335n4, 336, 361, 388
   *See also* debt crisis; development loans; international organizations (World Bank)
Australia   69n4, 107, 129, 181, 182, 223, 259, 279, 281, 283n4, 288, 297, 312n8, 313, 331, 342n11, 415, 418, 419, 421
   *See also* civilization; environmental crisis (oceans—Great Barrier Reef bleaching); Murdoch, Rupert
Austria   108, 235, 334n, 342n, 346, 349, 361
   Archduke Ferdinand of Austria   346, 349n

   *See also* Europe; war (World War I)
Authoritarianism   23, 72, 197, 198, 203, 251, 252, 253, 254, 254n4, 255, 257, 344, 396, 410, 441, 457
   *See also* despotism; fascism; governance

Bangladesh   128, 296, 359
   *See also* Asia
Banks (Bankers / Banking)   61, 76n, 77, 92, 95, 97n, 107, 121, 141, 150, 152, 159, 205, 219, 222, 318, 320, 321, 323, 323n, 324–327, 335n4, 336, 337n5, 344–345, 360, 372, 401, 408, 433–434n7, 444, 447
   Asian Infrastructure Investment Bank   339n9, 359
   Banking culture   150
   Bank of America   150, 152
   Bank of Credit and Commerce International   150
   Bank of New York Mellon   150
   Citigroup   150, 152
   Deutsche Bank   150, 322n
   Goldman Sachs   150, 209, 323
   HSBC   150
   J. P. Morgan Chase   150, 152, 321n
   Lehman Brothers   150, 323
   Morgan Stanley   150
   Wachovia   150
   Wells Fargo   150, 152
   *See also* capital (financial capital); capitalism; corporation(s); economics (interest); international organizations (Bank for International Settlements, World Bank); stocks; usury
Bannon, Steve   296, 374
   *See also* Trump, Donald (Trump administration)
Barbarism   179–185, 292
   Unit 731   67, 183
   *See also* civilization; colonialism; concentration camps; despotism; fascism; genocide; Nazism; poverty; race and racism; Sarajevo, Yugoslavia; Uyghur Muslims
Barter   3, 25, 28, 131, 192
Baudrillard, Jean   454
   *See also* postmodernism
Berman, Marshall   449

Bernays, Edward   264, 264n7
   *See also* media; propaganda; public
      relations
Bezos, Jeff   45, 61
   *See also* corporations(s) (Amazon)
Bible, The
   *See* religion
Bin Laden, Osama   192, 351
   *See also* Afghanistan (Taliban); terrorism
      (September 11, 2001 attacks); war
      (Afghan War)
Blair, Tony   367
   *See also* Britain; England; geo-politics;
      Hussein, Saddam; war (Iraq War)
Bolivia   63, 128, 191–192
   Aguas del Tunari   192
   Cochabamba   192
   *See also* debt (debt crisis); development
      loans; international organizations
      (World Bank); neo-liberalism; social
      movement(s); South America
Bolsonaro, Jair Messias   109
   *See also* Brazil; fascism; religion
      (fundamentalism)
Bosnia, Republic of
   *See* war (Bosnian War)
Bourgeois (Bourgeoisie)   241, 354, 426–
      427n2, 427n3, 429, 432, 433, 434, 435,
      436, 438, 438n, 439, 440, 442, 444, 445,
      446, 446n, 462, 463
   Bourgeois society   428, 432, 433
   *See also* accumulation; appropriation of
      wealth; capital; capitalism; capitalists;
      class; proletariat
Brazil   67, 109, 128, 187, 283, 306, 331, 332, 334,
      337n6, 339, 342n, 359
   *See also* Bolsonaro, Jair Messias;
      colonialism; South America
Bremmer, Paul   192
   Coalition Provisional Authority   192
   *See also* Bush (II), George W. (Bush (II)
      administration); terrorism (September
      11, 2001 attacks); war (Iraq War)
Bretton Woods Conference /
      Agreement   74–75, 319
   *See also* international organizations
      (International Monetary Fund, World
      Bank); war (World War II)
Brexit   267, 325n, 357, 360–361,
      361n8

   *See also* Britain; Cambridge Analytica;
      England; Mercer, Robert
Britain / British   20, 31, 67, 72, 86, 94, 112, 117,
      156, 189, 219, 223, 235, 237, 258, 267, 325,
      334, 337, 346, 354, 357, 360, 361, 367,
      368, 377, 392, 393
   British colonialism / empire   117, 129,
      129–130n, 134–135, 181, 182, 190, 225, 295,
      300, 300n, 303–304, 303–304n, 331
   *See also* Brexit; colonialism; England;
      Europe; feudalism; imperialism; India;
      Kenya; Scotland; United Kingdom;
      Wales; war (World War I, World War II)
Brzezinski, Zbigniew   350, 354
   *The Grand Chessboard*   354
   *See also* Afghanistan; Carter,
      Jimmy; Eurasia; geo-politics;
      Johnson, Lyndon
Buffet, Warren   387, 414n
Bureaucracy (Bureaucrats)   61, 75, 121, 126,
      136, 148, 160, 194–199, 203, 208, 215, 229,
      236, 248, 251, 263, 374, 415, 429, 437,
      438n, 440, 447, 461
   *See also* governance; nation-states; state;
      Weber, Max
Bush (I), George H.W.   235–236, 350, 366
   *See also* drugs (cocaine); Iraq; Kuwait;
      Panama; war (Gulf War)
Bush (II), George W.   206, 235, 323, 339,
      350–351, 366–367
   Bush (II) administration   192, 323,
      366–367, 394n2
   No Child Left Behind   394
   *See also* Afghanistan; crisis (financial
      crises—financial crisis of 2007–2008);
      Iraq; terrorism (September 11, 2001
      attacks), war (Iraq War)
Business class
   *See* class
Butler, Smedley   219, 219–220n
   *The Business Plot*   219
   *See also* imperialism; geo-politics; war

Cambodia   187, 241, 313, 348, 396
   *See also* Asia; genocide; Pol Pot; war
      (Vietnam War)
Cambridge Analytica   267, 287, 361n8
   *See also* Brexit; media (social media);
      Mercer, Robert; propaganda; Trump,
      Donald (Trump administration)

INDEX 537

Canada   107, 128, 129, 181, 182, 222, 258, 271, 275, 285, 321, 331, 332, 333, 334, 342n, 343, 344, 346, 357, 358n, 392, 393, 415
  *See also* environmental crisis (and energy—Alberta tar sands); Harper, Stephen; Trudeau, Justin
Candidate selection process   203–207
  Campaign financing / donations / funds   148, 149, 204–205n, 207, 217, 358
  *See also* Citizens United; class; policy (policy-makers and making); democracy; politics; voting
Capital   24, 90, 120, 123–125, 126, 134, 140, 142–144, 148, 153, 159, 182, 193, 196–197, 202, 205, 211, 212, 212n3, 215, 217, 218, 219, 219–220n, 221, 222, 224, 227, 269, 288, 289, 316, 317, 318, 320, 324, 325, 325n, 327–329, 337, 342, 345, 364, 368, 369, 370, 372, 376, 380, 381, 382–386, 388, 389, 390, 390n5, 392, 396n4, 397–398n5, 403, 404, 407, 412, 414, 415–416, 432, 433–434n, 434, 436, 436n9, 444, 446, 450, 451, 455, 463
  Basic structure of   120
  Capital flight   90, 388
  Centralization of   384–385
  Circuit of   120, 144, 316, 416, 444
  Financial capital   318, 328, 370, 386, 396–397n4, 444
    Fictitious capital   318, 328, 370, 386, 396–397n4, 444
    Financial deepening   80
    Financial globalization   80
    Financialization   327, 329, 342, 344, 372
    Interest-bearing capital   318, 444
  Investment capital   24, 90, 215, 369, 370
  National capital versus multinational / transnational capital   327–328, 342
  Productive capital   318, 320, 370, 444
  Social capital   125
  Start-up capital   153, 289
  *See also* accumulation (of capital, of profit, of wealth); class; crisis (financial crises); economics (interest); investment; labor; production (cycle of production and reinvestment); stocks

Capitalism   59, 124–125, 131, 135, 136, 137, 144, 185, 187, 202, 219, 242, 318, 372, 381, 388, 389, 404–407, 409, 411, 412, 417, 420, 421, 422, 432, 434, 442, 447n, 448
Capitalist development   134, 136, 137, 157, 171, 186, 348, 368, 384, 404, 432, 433
Capitalist society   122, 123, 124, 125, 136, 227, 228, 381, 405, 434
Fundamental contradictions of
  Competitive market leads to monopolies and concentrates wealth   384
  Encourages and undermines democracy   405
  Market society kills people through both obesity and starvation   397
  Massive production of wealth and poverty   405
  Tendency toward innovation and new machinery undermines demand   155–156
  Too much production creates economic crises   139–140
Prevailing tendencies
  Business is compelled to accumulate   381
  Capital tends to concentrate and centralize   384–385
  Class struggle   386
  Complex machinery needs fewer and fewer laborers   382
  Constant surplus-value extraction   381–382
  Economic crises   388–389
  Expansion of geographical boundaries   389
  Increasing commodification   389–390
  Periodic declines in profit rates   382–384
  Polarization of modern society   386–388
  Technological advancements   382
  *See also* accumulation; bourgeois; capital; class (class struggle); colonialism; commodities (commodification); concentration (of capital, of wealth); crisis; economics (bubbles); geography; investment; labor; profit (decline

Capitalism (cont.)
  in); technology (as method of lowering labor costs, development, growth, and level of complexity, innovation); value (surplus-value); world economy
Caribbean, The   IX, 128, 130, 187, 300, 301, 303, 305, 306, 331
  *See also* colonialism; Cuba; Haiti; Jamaica; slavery
Cartels
  *See* crime (drug cartels, corporate crime—corporate cartels)
Carter, Jimmy   22, 141, 210–211, 236, 350
  *See also* Brzezinski, Zbigniew
Caspian Sea   350
  *See also* Eurasia; geo-politics
Castro, Fidel   348
  *See also* Cuba
Catholic Church, The
  *See* religion
Central America   20, 63, 182, 189, 300, 334, 349
  *See also* Costa Rica; El Salvador; Guatemala; Honduras; Nicaragua; Panama
Chavez, Hugo   184, 336
  *See also* geo-politics; socialism; Venezuela
Cheney, Richard "Dick"   351–352
  *See also* Bush (II), George W. (Bush (II) administration); policy (foreign policy, policy-makers and making—think tanks and institutes—Project for a New American Century); war (Iraq War)
Chile   128, 191, 219, 248, 319
  *See also* Allende, Salvador; despotism; neo-liberalism; Pinochet, Augusto; South America
China   IX, 2, 4, 30, 44, 72, 94, 98, 128, 132–133, 136, 182, 183, 185, 219–220n, 241, 252, 271, 278, 292, 298, 300, 312, 313, 324, 328, 331, 332, 333n, 334, 335n4, 338n7, 338n8, 338–339, 339n, 341, 343–345, 353, 355, 357, 359–360, 362, 363n10, 377, 384, 388, 390, 393, 418
  Beijing   272, 278, 281, 343, 360, 362
  Belt and Road initiative   359, 362
  Chinese culture   298
  South China Sea   360
  Tiananmen Square   72–73, 182

  *See also* Asia; authoritarianism; concentration camps; despotism; geo-politics; globalization; neo-liberalism; slavery; Uyghur Muslims
Chomsky, Noam   36, 187n, 257
  *See also* human nature; language; media; propaganda
Christianity (Christians)
  *See* religion
Citizens United   204
  *See also* candidate selection process (campaign financing); democracy; freedom (free speech); politics; United States (US Government: branches and agencies—US Supreme Court)
City-states
  *See* societies (types of)
  *See also* nation-states
Civilization (Civilized society)   59n, 136, 179–183, 185, 424, 435–436
  *See also* barbarism; colonialism; genocide
Civil society   70, 119, 157, 212, 404, 437, 461n
Class (Classes)   2, 4, 25, 42–46, 71, 74–78, 79, 80, 82, 83, 84, 85, 86, 87, 91, 94, 95, 97, 134, 154–155, 156, 158, 184, 196, 197, 198, 201, 205, 212, 214, 215, 217, 218, 219, 220, 221, 222, 223, 224, 227, 228, 229, 258, 266, 288, 289, 295, 300, 306, 309, 313, 319, 325, 326, 327, 328, 336, 342, 352, 370, 372, 374, 377, 381, 383, 386, 387, 388, 392, 401, 404, 405, 407, 408, 409, 410, 411, 412, 413, 414, 415, 416, 421, 427, 429, 430, 431n, 432, 433, 434, 436, 438, 440, 441, 442, 443, 444, 446, 447, 448, 463
  Capitalist class and associated terms / categories
    Business class   88, 156, 158, 212n, 217, 218, 219, 220, 222, 228, 289, 325, 342, 370, 381, 383–384, 386, 414, 415, 433–434, 437, 446
    Capitalist class   125, 197, 198, 201, 205, 378, 386, 401, 415, 416, 421, 432, 436
    Corporate class   223, 370
    Investing class   328
    Owning class   217, 218, 229, 388
  Class-analytical concepts and terms
    Class consciousness   229
    Class dynamics   46, 125, 434, 441, 442
    Class interests   26, 228, 409, 416, 439

Class polarization 83–84, 319, 386
Class relations 227, 228, 229, 288, 406, 434
Class society 266
Class structure 42–43, 44–46, 74, 79, 80, 229, 408, 427
Class struggle 42–46, 91, 154–155, 215, 227, 427, 427n3, 434, 448, 463
Class struggle within the capitalist class 342
Class systems 42, 43, 44, 46, 295, 405, 409, 411, 446
Class consciousness 229
Class warfare 288, 387, 421
Middle class 21n, 25, 71, 74–78, 80, 82, 84–85, 86, 87, 196, 325–326, 374, 429–430, 440, 447
Non-class systems 45, 407–408, 410, 411
Poverty class / the poor 87, 91, 430
Ruling class 134, 184, 224, 228, 266, 352, 401, 404–405, 409, 411, 438, 446, 447
Underclass 82–83, 430
Upper-middle class 76, 76n
Upper class 358, 300
Working class 71, 76, 76n, 82, 85, 94, 95, 97, 212, 217, 221, 306, 327, 374, 386–388, 429, 440, 443, 447
*See also* accumulation; appropriation of wealth; bourgeois; capital; capitalism; concentration (of capital, of wealth); elites; inequality; labor; mobility; pauperism; poverty; proletariat
Climate change
*See* environmental crisis (climate change)
Clinton, Bill 235, 320, 351
Clinton administration 141, 183
Clinton, Hillary 244, 266, 344n, 355–356, 357
*See also* conspiracy theories (pizzagate), Trump, Donald
Coal
*See* fossil fuels
*See also* Appalachia; environment crisis (air pollution, and energy); Wales
Cocaine
*See* drugs
Cold War, The 46, 133, 171, 235, 257, 331, 346–347, 349, 357, 358, 360, 361
Domino effect 348

*See also* geo-politics; propaganda; Red Scare; Russia; Soviet Union; United States
College students
*See* education (college, students); social movement(s)
Colombia 63, 63n, 337n6
*See also* drugs (cocaine); Escobar, Pablo; South America
Colonialism IX, 20, 59, 112, 127–133, 134–137, 185, 189, 225, 247, 251, 295, 300n, 301, 303, 306, 331, 334, 347, 389, 432, 452, 457, 460
Decolonization 132, 135
*See also* barbarism; civilization; history and human development; imperialism; nation-states; slavery; war
Columbus, Christopher 187–188
*See also* genocide; New World
Commodities 24, 41, 119, 120, 121–124, 132, 138n, 139–144, 147, 149, 159–160, 162, 192, 220, 222, 228, 269, 281, 300, 315, 316, 333, 336, 340, 352, 364, 368–370, 376–377, 380, 384, 389–390, 396, 432, 444
Commodification 389
Commodity chains 402–403
Transformation of things and life into commodities 121–124
*See also* capitalism; consumption; free market; labor; neo-liberalism (privatization); production; profit; slavery
Communism 120, 171, 191, 241, 242, 248, 257, 347, 348, 349, 364, 397, 441, 462
Anti-communism (Reagan) 349
China 264
Euro-communism 397
Marx's communism 424, 427, 432, 441n, 447–448
*See also* Marx, Karl; North Korea; Pol Pot; socialism; Soviet Union
Competition 24, 25, 26, 45, 48, 56–57, 59, 88, 92, 120, 127, 132, 135, 138, 140, 147, 151, 154, 171, 204, 211, 217, 218, 219–220n, 221, 242, 257, 260, 303, 316, 317, 320, 331, 338n7, 339, 350, 352, 353, 367, 377, 380, 381, 382, 384, 386, 390n
*See also* capitalism; economics; free market; geo-politics; labor

Computers
See technology (computers and cybertechnology, Moore's Law)
See also internet
Comte, August 410
See also sociology
Concentration
  Of capital 211, 384–386, 433–434n
  Of wealth 79–80, 88, 242, 318, 326, 328, 329, 371–372, 415, 424
  See also accumulation (overaccumulation of capital); capital; capitalism; class; corporation(s); inequality; pauperism; poverty
Concentration camps 182, 185, 190, 248
  Internment of Japanese Americans 182
  Labor camps 248
  Soviet Siberian work camps 241
  See also despotism; genocide; Kenya (Mau Mau rebellion); Nazism; North Korea; Uyghur Muslims
Conditionality
  See development loans
  See also austerity; international organizations (International Monetary Fund, World Bank)
Congo 130, 184–185, 190
  Belgium Congo / Congo Free State 247
  Democratic Republic of Congo 247, 283, 332, 347
  See also Africa; barbarism; King Leopold of Belgium; violence
Congress (United States) 122n, 141, 191, 219, 232n, 242, 260, 320, 358, 365, 366
  See also United States (US Government: branches and agencies)
Conservatism (Conservatives) 59, 90, 109, 204–205n, 213, 222, 230, 232, 242, 244, 245, 257, 259, 259n2, 260, 275, 286, 297, 328, 344, 358, 387–388, 387–388n, 395, 405, 415, 416, 421, 440, 440n, 451, 456n, 458n, 460, 461, 462
  See also liberalism; Republicans
Conspiracy theories 119, 157, 267, 366
  Pizzagate 266
Consumption 21, 38, 63–64, 88, 123, 125, 145, 148, 150, 153, 155, 156, 212, 220, 222, 223, 228, 260, 266, 269, 281, 284, 285, 285n, 289, 300, 315, 318, 324, 327, 328, 338, 369, 371, 372, 380, 382, 384–385, 388, 389, 390, 390n, 394n2, 396, 397, 401, 402, 407, 412, 414, 415, 416, 433, 434, 443, 445
Conspicuous consumption 76
  See also commodities; economics (supply and demand); environmental crisis; production
Contras 63, 191
  See also drugs (cocaine), Nicaragua; Ortega, Daniel; Reagan, Ronald; Sandinistas
Corporate welfare
  See welfare
Corporation(s)
  Amazon 45, 118
  Archer Daniels Midland 147, 313
  Bayer 146, 289
  Bechtel 192
  British Petroleum 286
  Cargill 313
  Chrysler 323, 372
  Disney 117, 431
  Dow Chemical 286
  Dutch East India Company 187, 188
  Enron 149–150
  Exxon 288
  Ford (Ford Pinto) 146–150
  Fortune 500 151n5
  General Electric 151
  General Motors 320, 323
  Joint-stock companies 145, 433
  McDonald's 135
  Microsoft 153
  Monsanto 259n3, 268n, 284, 289
  Multinational corporations / capital 89, 148, 182, 187, 191, 222, 316, 327, 342, 348, 369, 379
  Nestlé 288, 313, 390
  Royal Dutch Shell 191
  United Fruit Company 189
  Walmart 45, 450
  See also accumulation; banks; capital; capitalism; capitalists; concentration (of capital, of wealth); economics; stocks; world economy
Costa Rica 128, 189, 418
  See also Central America
Crime 4, 55n3, 62, 109, 152, 162, 182, 191, 213, 224, 254, 296, 297, 297n3, 307n3, 348, 433, 457
  Arson 62

INDEX 541

Assault  62
Capital punishment  102, 232, 314
Corporate crime  152
   Bank fraud against homeowners  152
   Banks and laundering drug
      money  150
   Bid rigging  151
   Bribes and kickbacks  62, 148, 189,
      249, 433
   Conflicts of interest  150–151
   Corporate cartels  147n, 147–148
   Dangerous products  62, 146
      Ford Pinto  146–147
      HIV infected blood products  146
      Tobacco  146
   False advertising  145–146
   Insider trading  149, 150
   Manipulating the stock
      market  149–150
   Misrepresenting financial
      statements  149–150
   Pay to play  151
   Price fixing  62, 147
   Skimming  89, 148
   Tax evasion, tax havens and
      shelters  151
   Wage fraud  151–152
Crimes against humanity  251
Criminology  52
Drug cartels  63, 63n
Murder  20, 54, 62, 102, 183, 184, 190, 191,
   250, 251, 252, 253, 292, 295, 297
Rape and sexual assault  54, 55n3, 62, 102,
   183, 185, 187, 191, 245, 251, 356
Robbery and theft  62, 97, 182, 186, 191,
   248, 296–297, 297n3, 314
*See also* corporation(s); despotism;
   policing; stocks; violence
Crimea  336, 354, 357, 362
*See also* Eurasia; geo-politics; Putin,
   Vladimir; Russia; Ukraine
Crisis (Crises)  75, 141–142, 143, 144, 150, 158,
   222, 263, 520–529, 335, 337, 340, 341, 343,
   353, 369, 388, 390, 414n, 416, 424, 433, 434
   Economic crisis leads to political
      crisis  388–390
   Employer response to  326n
   Environmental crisis's relation to political-
      economic crisis  401
   Financial crises  353, 414n

   Asian financial crisis of 1997  336
   Financial crisis of 2007–2008  143,
      150, 222, 320–329, 335, 340–342, 343,
      353, 416n
      Adjustable Rate Mortgage
         (ARM)  321–322
      Collateralized Debt Obligations
         (CDOs)  320
      Commercial paper  323, 323n
      Financial Services Modernization
         Act (Gramm Leach Bliley
         Act)  320
      Gender and racial component to
         crisis  321n
      Housing market  143, 319, 322–323,
         327, 343, 344, 450
      International Swaps and
         Derivatives Association  322n
      Troubled Asset Relief Program
         (TARP)  323
   Turkey currency crisis  337n5, 344
   Venezuelan crisis  337n6
   Spiral and spread of a crisis  369, 414n, 433
   Relation of labor-saving machinery to
      a crisis  434
   *See also* accumulation (overaccumulation
      of capital); capital; debt (debt
      crisis); economics (bubbles); Great
      Depression; inequality; social
      movement(s) (Occupy
      Wall Street)
Cuba  120, 122n, 128, 187, 188, 348, 348n, 350,
   363n10
   Cuban Missile Crisis  348, 392
   *See also* Caribbean; Castro, Fidel; geo-
      politics North America; policy (foreign
      policy)
Cult of nature  112–116, 431
   *See also* religion (New Age movement)
Cult of personality  235, 245, 249
   *See also* despotism; Trump, Donald
Culture(s)  3, 5–7, 9, 21, 28–31, 36–37, 39, 45,
   47, 48, 50n2, 50n3, 51, 53, 55n4, 55–57,
   59n, 66–67, 76, 98–100, 102–104, 116, 131,
   160, 165–167, 237, 250, 256, 312, 330, 434
   American culture  135, 206, 235, 394–395
   Banking culture  150
   Chinese culture  298
   Cultural hegemony  135–136, 181–182, 309,
      368, 409, 433

Culture(s) (cont.)
  Cultural/social conditioning / learning   30–31, 35–37, 66, 110, 256, 294, 405
  Culture and patriarchy   290–299, 297n3
  Culture bound syndromes   36
  European culture   134–137
  Islamic culture   98
  Managerial culture   370
  Popular culture   136, 394
  Radical cultural relativism   453, 462
  Universal(s)   28, 36, 53, 55n4, 66, 98, 101, 111, 226, 406–407, 462
  Western culture   167, 452
  World / global culture   117–119, 330, 393, 431, 451
  See also colonialism; ethnocentrism; postmodernism; race and racism; socialization; societies (types of); xenophobia
Czech Republic   108, 342n
  Czechoslovakia and the Prague Spring   347
  See also Europe; Soviet Union (communist bloc)

Dead zones
  See environmental crisis (oceans)
Debt   83, 85, 87, 95, 143, 149, 150, 319n, 321, 323, 324, 325, 327, 328, 336, 390n, 434n, 439
  Debt crisis (also "debt trap")   89, 158, 192, 335n4, 344
    Greek debt crisis   158
  Student loans   75–76, 328, 390, 394n2
  See also austerity; class (middle class); crisis (financial crises—financial crisis of 2007–2008); development loans; international organizations (World Bank); pauperism; poverty
Democracy   23, 64–65n, 72, 119, 171, 190, 197, 198, 203–205, 208, 210–211, 213, 214–216, 219, 230, 246, 248, 251, 254, 256, 257, 264, 266, 268, 306, 315, 329, 340, 347, 351, 354, 361, 362, 364, 395, 404, 405, 407, 420, 438, 438n, 439, 441, 442, 443
  Anti-democratic   208, 374, 388
  See also authoritarianism; candidate selection process; freedom; liberalism (liberal democracy: theory and society); social movement(s); voting
Democrats (Democratic Party)   204–205n, 207, 244, 261, 355, 356, 357, 421n, 460
  See also conservatism; liberalism; Republicans
Denmark   86, 122, 130, 342n, 383
  See Europe; mobility
Deregulation
  See neo-liberalism
  See also banks; crisis (financial crises—financial crisis of 2007–2008); Great Depression; Reagan, Ronald; Thatcher, Margaret
Derrida, Jacques   454
  See also postmodernism
Despotism   106, 180, 230, 236, 247–255, 441, 451, 453
  Dictatorial power   20, 109, 150, 182, 189, 197, 198, 203, 245, 248, 254, 260, 340, 347, 364, 441, 442
  See also authoritarianism; barbarism; fascism; violence
Development loans   89, 148
  Conditionality   89
  See also colonialism; debt (debt crisis); history and human development; international organizations (International Monetary Fund, World Bank)
Dialectics   18–27, 22–23n, 27n, 423, 425
  Contradiction   25, 26, 50n3, 140, 155, 156, 384, 397, 405, 417, 426n, 434, 459
  Essence   22–24, 104, 417, 448
  Essentialism   23–24, 25, 43, 44, 46, 48
    Anti-essentialism   23–24
  Hegelian dialectic   18–19, 26, 425
  Negation   24–26, 182, 427
  Transformation   24–26, 28, 35, 38, 109, 121, 157, 171, 389, 406, 426n, 436, 445
    Quantitative to qualitative transformation   24–25, 99, 226, 341
  See also Hegel, Georg; Ollman, Bertell
Diversity   119, 124, 420, 459
  See also ethnicity; gender; postmodernism (identity politics); race and racism; sexuality; status hierarchies
Division of labor
  See labor

Drugs   21n, 62, 78, 94–95, 97, 107, 146, 148, 212, 366, 389, 340
　Cocaine   63, 63n, 94, 191, 349, 366
　　Crack cocaine   62
　Heroin   62–63, 94
　Hydrocodone and oxycodone   94
　Marijuana   65, 309n6
　Opium   63, 94, 107, 332, 424, 430–431
　　Opium Wars   94
　See also Bush (I), George H.W.; Contras; crime (drug cartels); Escobar, Pablo; Nicaragua; Noriega, Manuel; Panama; United States (US Government: branches and agencies—Central Intelligence Agency); war on drugs
Du Bois, W.E.B.   306, 309
　See also race and racism
Dutch, The
　See Holland; The Netherlands
Dutch East India Company
　See corporation(s)
Duterte, Rodrigo   252, 253
　See also authoritarianism; despotism; Philippines; war on drugs

East Timor
　See genocide
Ecology   2, 46, 79, 281, 285, 340, 372, 405, 409, 414, 415, 420, 442–443, 462
　See also environmental crisis
Economics (Economy)   3, 6, 7, 22, 25, 32, 51–52, 59, 60, 61, 62, 75, 80, 82, 83–93, 94, 96, 107, 109, 118, 120, 124, 125, 126–131, 134, 135, 136, 138n, 140, 141, 142, 143, 144, 145, 147, 148, 154–157, 159, 187, 192, 201, 208–212, 212n, 217, 219, 220–221, 221–222n, 222–224, 228, 230, 235–236, 238, 239, 242, 249, 259, 264, 275, 277, 291, 293, 300, 309, 315, 318–320, 324, 325–328, 330, 331, 334, 335, 335n4, 336–337, 337n5, 337n6, 338, 338n7, 339, 340–344, 346, 348, 349, 350, 351, 352, 353, 354, 360–363, 363n10, 368–369, 370, 371–372, 373, 375, 376–378, 380–389, 392, 394, 395, 398, 397–398n5, 401, 402, 404, 408, 409, 413, 414, 415, 417, 419, 420, 422, 426, 427n3, 430, 432, 438, 441, 442, 444, 447, 459

Advanced / developed economies   52n, 80–81, 108, 219, 296, 324, 328, 335n4, 337n7, 341, 342, 419
Bubbles   138, 143, 319, 320–322, 335, 370, 372, 414n
　The dot-com and/or the tech bubble   143, 320
　Tulip mania   138, 138n
Developing / emerging economies   80, 87, 167, 328, 333–334, 338, 342, 342n, 343–344
Economic conservatives   88, 90, 242, 259, 213, 222, 421
Economic crashes / crises   81, 91, 141, 143, 149, 150, 158, 323, 323n, 327–328, 335, 338n8, 369, 372, 388, 450
Economic power   25, 100, 145, 145n, 159, 187, 221, 346, 352–353n5, 353, 361, 432
Economic structure / system   59, 75, 92, 96, 124, 134, 136, 144, 331, 349, 353, 408, 414, 426n2
Economic theories as religion / market fundamentalism   242–243
Economist(s)   51, 84, 93n, 147, 220, 242, 319, 325, 341, 368, 370, 376, 378, 427n3, 428
Economy of scale   222, 340, 384
Expansion and contraction cycles / boom-and-bust   3, 74, 63, 124, 139–140, 143, 220–221, 222, 242, 319–320, 368–370, 376, 379, 388
　Kondratieff cycles / waves   376–377, 379, 389n
Export-based economy   89
FIRE economy (finance, insurance, real estate)   143, 358
Global economy   88, 141, 327, 340, 343, 344, 372, 444
Gross domestic product (GDP)   143, 320, 322, 326, 335, 336, 337, 338n7, 340, 361, 385
Inflation   79, 84, 88, 89, 90, 92, 141, 218, 221, 324, 326, 335, 336, 340, 361, 388
　Hyperinflation   184, 191, 337n6
Interest (interest rates)   92, 107, 141, 150, 217, 220–221, 319, 321, 328, 335, 335n4, 378, 388, 444, 447
Keynesian economics   220–222, 327–328
Laissez faire economics   59, 378
Macro-economic   75, 326n, 372, 378

Economics (Economy) (cont.)
  Market economy / system   25, 43, 59, 60,
    83, 88, 89, 107, 131, 139, 140, 143, 201, 220,
    224, 384, 386, 388, 389, 422
  Money economy   3, 107, 134, 143
  Rural economy   141, 159, 160–161, 222,
    235
  Supply and demand   5–6, 75, 96, 138–144,
    153–154, 155–156, 188, 220, 233, 247, 301,
    313, 317–320, 322, 324–325, 327, 328, 339,
    368, 369–371, 376–377, 382–384, 403,
    418, 433
    Aggregate demand   138
    Credit and demand   319n
    Effective demand   138, 139, 140, 144,
      156, 318–320, 327, 369–371, 382, 384
    Money supply   217–218, 221, 349
  See also accumulation (overaccumulation of capital); capital; capitalism; class; commodities; corporation(s); crisis (financial crises); exploitation; free market; history and human development; inflation; Keynes, John Maynard; labor; neo-liberalism; political economy; production (overproduction); profit; Smith, Adam; usury; wages; world economy
Ecuador   128, 189, 191, 337n6
  See also South America
Education   3, 7, 21n, 45, 57, 66–72, 74–75, 80,
    83, 84, 86, 87, 89, 97, 108, 110, 118, 122,
    124, 125, 134, 136, 153, 161, 171, 194, 197,
    205, 209, 211, 212, 227, 246, 283, 294, 295,
    299, 339, 368, 387, 390, 394, 394n2, 395,
    403, 407, 411, 420, 422, 424, 437, 459
  College   98, 108, 122, 167, 195, 227, 232,
    294, 298, 326n, 421, 421n
    Elite universities   125, 264
  Professor(s)   51, 53n, 147, 243, 243n2, 423,
    459, 460, 461, 464
  Students   23, 67–68, 71–73, 85, 230, 424,
    437, 455, 456n, 459, 460, 461, 461n
  The Educator   66–71, 429
  See also propaganda; social movement(s)
Effective demand
  See economics (supply and demand)
Egypt   ix, 46n, 60, 72, 98, 103, 252,
    339n, 405, 418
  See also Africa; Middle East; social
    movement(s) (Arab Spring)
Einstein, Albert   11, 14n
  On socialism   211
Eisenhower, Dwight D.   198, 198n
  See also military industrial complex
Elites (economic)   21, 89, 92, 151, 191, 205,
    207, 208, 209–210, 212–215, 227,
    235, 256, 327, 336, 401, 407, 412,
    415, 459
  Bilderberg meetings   219
  See also bourgeois; candidate selection
    process; class; democracy; policy
    (foreign policy, policy-makers and
    making—think tanks and institutes)
El Salvador   191
  See also Central America
Enclosure Laws   159
Engels, Frederick   425, 427, 428, 430, 431,
    434, 441n, 443, 444, 447
  See also Marx, Karl
England   ix, x, 108, 112, 115, 127, 128, 129, 131,
    134, 135, 160, 189, 190, 230, 252, 259, 269,
    301, 331–332, 334, 337–338, 388, 430n,
    433n, 434
  London   72, 159, 160, 189, 269–271, 418,
    435
    Piccadilly Circus   162
    Victorian England / London   94, 112,
      134, 332
  See also Brexit; Britain; colonialism;
    environmental crisis (air pollution—
    Great Smog of 1952); Europe; Scotland;
    Thatcher, Margaret; United Kingdom;
    Wales; war (World War I, World War II)
Enlightenment   10, 28, 452, 453, 457
  Anti-Enlightenment   451, 463
  See also science; philosophy;
    postmodernism
Environmental crisis
  Air pollution   269–271, 272, 275, 283,
    372, 400
    Beijing, China   272
    Great Smog of 1952 (London)   269–271
    Lead air pollution   283
    New Delhi   272
  And energy
    Alberta tar sands   268n, 271, 273

INDEX

Coal   269, 271, 287, 373, 415, 418, 419
   Mountain top removal   268n, 271
Fukushima nuclear
   accident   272–273n
Oil, modern industry, and the
   environment   89, 224n3, 269, 271,
   276, 286, 288, 369, 415, 418, 419
   Hydraulic fracturing
      (fracking)   268n, 271–272, 281,
      418
   Renewable energy   233, 338, 338n8,
      359, 362, 373, 399, 400, 418–419
Biodiversity   283, 397
   Decline in biomass   397
   Insects   284, 418
      Bees   268n, 284, 417–418
      Colony collapse disorder   284
   Species extinction   283
      Sixth great extinction   285, 297,
      400
Climate change   68, 68–69n3, 224n3, 257,
   257–258n, 258, 259, 274, 275, 282–283,
   284–287, 289, 314, 398–401, 417, 418, 419,
   420, 452, 464
   Climate change deniers   257–258n,
      259, 288, 314, 452
      Energy industry knowledge of and
         denial over   259, 278, 287–288,
         400
   Climate Matters program   287
   Intergovernmental Panel on Climate
      Change   419
   Paris climate accords   68–69n3, 277
   Scientific consensus on climate
      change   284–285
Diet and the environment   278, 283, 285,
   414–415
Environmental laws
   Attacks on   89, 215, 226, 387
   Public opinion about cost of   211
Exhaustion of resources   285
Freshwater   276–277
   Declining potable
      groundwater   281–282
   Groundwater contamination
      271–272
   Ogallala aquifer   281
   Saltwater contamination   276

Global warming   68n3, 69n4, 258,
   265, 273–277, 283, 284, 287, 288, 314,
   401, 419
   Extreme weather events   275
      Stronger hurricanes   276
   Greenhouse effect / gasses   68–69n3,
      274, 275, 276, 278, 286, 373, 399,
      400, 401
      Carbon dioxide   68–69n3,
         273–275, 277, 284–285, 287, 397,
         398, 400, 401, 418, 419
      Methane   273, 275, 276, 397,
         398, 401
      Arctic methane releases and
         runaway greenhouse effect   275
   Heat waves   275, 276, 399
   Arctic warming   274, 398–399
Land
   Deforestation   268n, 282–283, 397,
      400, 420
      Amazon rainforest   397
   Habitat loss and threat of
      extinction   283
   Pesticides and fertilizers   41, 141, 269,
      277, 281, 283, 284, 286, 382, 397,
      417–418
   Topsoil loss   282
Oceans
   Acidification   268n, 277–278, 285, 397
   British Petroleum Deepwater Horizon
      oil spill   286
   Dead zones   277–278, 397
   Great Barrier Reef bleaching   281, 418
   Oceanic garbage patches   279–280
   Plastic and Point Nemo   281
   Rising oceans, loss of ocean front,
      sinking island nations   276–277
   Warming and melting ice sheets / ice
      cover thaw
      Antarctica   274–275, 399
      Arctic   69n4, 274–275, 284–285,
         397–398n5, 398–399
Population growth   285, 289, 355,
   372–373, 414
Solid waste pollution   278–279
   Plastic   41, 279, 281, 283, 287, 343, 418
      Microbeads   281
      Microplastics   279

Environmental crisis (cont.)
    Trump administration anti-environmental policies   285–288
        Scott Pruitt at the EPA   286–287
        Union of Concerned Scientists   285, 400–401
        "World Scientists' Warning to Humanity" (1992)   400
        "A Second Notice" (2017)   400–401
    *See also* commodities; consumption; ecology; production
Epidemics
    *See* accumulation (overaccumulation of capital); crisis (financial crises); economics (bubbles); production (overproduction)
Equality
    *See* liberalism (liberal democracy: theory and society)
Erdogan, Recep Tayyip   253, 337n5
    *See also* authoritarianism; despotism; Turkey
Escobar, Pablo   63n
    *See also* drugs (cocaine); Colombia
Ethnicity (Ethnic)   2, 23, 56, 59, 132, 136–137, 183, 230, 237, 238, 243n2, 248, 312, 313, 355
    *See also* genocide; race and racism; status hierarchies
Ethnocentrism   56, 312
    *See also* race and racism; xenophobia
Eugenics
    *See* race and racism
Eurasia   350–351, 366
    *See also* Afghanistan; Brzezinski, Zbigniew; Caspian Sea; Crimea; geo-politics; Pakistan; policy (foreign policy); Turkey; Ukraine; Uzbekistan
Europe (European)   ix, 2, 4, 44, 45, 52n, 58, 59, 59n, 60, 70, 72, 75, 88, 91, 97, 98, 100, 107, 108, 112, 117, 122, 122n, 126, 127, 127n, 130–131, 132, 133, 134–137, 148, 159, 170, 171–175, 183, 187, 198, 213, 219n, 221, 242, 247, 259, 267, 268, 269, 281, 283n4, 292, 293, 294, 297, 300, 301, 313, 319, 331, 332, 334, 338, 339, 342n, 343, 344, 346, 347, 349, 354, 357, 359, 360, 361, 387–388n, 389, 392, 393, 398, 405, 415, 417, 418, 420, 432, 433, 443
Eastern Europe   242, 347, 349, 354
European Union   267, 338, 343, 357, 360, 361
Eurozone   324, 335, 335n4
Feudal / medieval Europe   1, 2, 3, 4, 6n, 43, 44, 60, 61, 74, 79, 92n, 98, 100, 112, 120, 126, 132, 134, 159, 171, 185, 223, 247, 292, 293, 294, 367, 389, 404, 405, 409, 411, 426n, 432, 441
Revolutions of 1848   72
    *See also* Austria; Britain; colonialism; culture (European culture); Czech Republic; Denmark; England; Finland; France; Germany; Greece; Holland; Hungary; imperialism; Ireland; Italy; Norway; Poland; Portugal; revolution(s); Scotland; Spain; Sweden; Switzerland; Turkey; Wales
Evolutionary theory   14–15, 30, 37, 110, 153, 178, 232, 286
Experimental model
    *See* science
Exploitation   61, 136, 189, 306, 307, 313, 340, 403, 406, 407, 409, 412, 436, 445
    Satanic Mills   189
    Sexual exploitation   334
    Sweatshops   155, 183, 192, 332, 340
    *See also* alienation; appropriation of wealth; barbarism; civilization; industry (industrial revolution); labor; profit; sexism and misogyny; slavery

Fascism   73, 230, 249, 254–255, 329, 344, 345, 364, 387, 395, 447, 455, 461, 461n, 462, 463
    *See also* authoritarianism; despotism; Nazism; race and racism; war (World War II)
Federal Reserve   87, 141, 156, 321, 325, 328
    *See also* crisis (financial crises—financial crisis of 2007–2008); Greenspan, Alan
Femininity
    *See* gender
Feminism
    *See* social movement(s)

INDEX

Feudalism
   See societies (types of)
   See also Europe (feudal / medieval Europe)
Financial crises
   See crisis
Finland   354, 371
   Helsinki   253, 358
   See also Europe; geo-politics; Putin, Vladimir; Trump, Donald
FIRE Economy
   See economics
First World   89, 347
   See also Cold War; Third World
Foch, Ferdinand   392
   See also Treaty of Versailles; war (World War I)
Foreign policy
   See policy
   See also geo-politics
Fossil fuels
   Coal   5, 82, 145, 155, 166, 189, 232, 233, 269, 271, 287, 331, 332, 336, 338, 338n8, 343, 369, 373, 377, 415, 418, 419
   Oil   89, 91, 166, 182–183, 190, 191, 192, 219, 244n3, 253, 259, 269, 271, 276, 279, 286–288, 331, 332–333, 336–338, 334, 344, 350, 352, 352–353n5, 354, 360, 362–363, 363n11, 369, 377, 384, 400, 402, 415, 418, 419
   See also corporation(s); environmental crisis (air pollution, and energy, climate change, global warming); industry; policy (foreign policy)
Foucault, Michel   417, 449, 454, 459
   See also postmodernism
Fourier, Charles   410
   See also utopianism
FOX News
   See media (mass media)
France   63, 72, 108, 127, 130, 131, 134, 181, 187, 190, 225, 230, 279, 300, 301, 303, 312n8, 329, 334, 337, 338n7, 331, 334, 342n, 346, 347, 354, 388, 392, 393, 399, 417, 418, 433n, 440
   Paris   68–69n3, 72, 160, 163, 285, 399, 418, 420
   See also colonialism; Europe; fascism; geo-politics; immigration; liberalism (liberal democracy: theory and society); revolution(s) (French Revolution)
France, Anatole   227
Fraternity
   See liberalism (liberal democracy: theory and society)
Free market (principles and systems)   21, 25, 59, 60, 61, 184, 205, 224, 316, 324, 325, 384, 386, 387, 416–417
   "the market"   26, 144, 158, 202, 220, 221, 224, 226, 227, 228, 317, 318, 321, 323, 323n, 324, 325, 325n, 327, 328, 329, 368, 369, 370, 378, 380, 381, 384, 388, 389, 390, 390n, 411, 417, 428–429n, 433, 447
   See also capitalism; commodities; competition; economics (laissez faire economics); free trade agreements; neo-liberalism; world economy
Free trade agreements   222–223, 342, 369–370, 373, 387
   North American Free Trade Agreement (NAFTA)   342, 345
   Trans-Pacific Partnership   222, 373
   See also free market; neo-liberalism
Freedom   4, 20–22, 64–65n, 72, 86, 124, 218, 225–229, 232, 241, 242, 245, 246, 248, 262, 294, 306, 405–407, 438, 443, 448
   Academic   459
   From external power   225
   Labor "freedom"   226–227, 228, 406
   Of assembly   227
   Of choice   294
   Of conscience   226, 227, 246, 315
   Of mind and body   227
   Of speech   55, 204, 226–227, 315, 459, 462
   Of the marketplace   226–227
   Of the press   254
   Of religion   226, 315
   See also democracy; liberalism (liberal democracy: theory and society); voting
French Revolution
   See France; liberalism–equality, fraternity, liberty); revolution(s)

Galilei, Galileo   11, 14n
   See also Enlightenment, science

Gender   2, 7, 23, 31, 56, 58, 97, 136, 137, 227, 229, 244, 290, 291, 293, 295, 298, 305, 411, 443, 456–458, 458n, 460, 462, 464
  Femininity   56, 167–168
  Cis-gender   456–457
  Gender equality / inequality   7, 291, 298, 299, 321n, 411, 443, 463
  Gender identity   458n
  Gender norms and roles   31, 56, 58, 97, 136, 137, 291
  Masculinity   56, 395, 456, 456n
  Non-binary   458n
  Transgender   230, 244n3
  See also patriarchy; sexism and misogyny; social movement(s) (feminist / women's movement)
Genocide   131, 181, 188, 198
  Armenian genocide   67
  East Timor   128, 190, 219–220n
    John Pilger's Death of a Nation   190
  Ethnic cleansing   183, 248, 313
  Holocaust, The   248, 462
  Hungarian Holodomor   248
  Native peoples of Australia, Canada, New Zealand, United States   181
  Rohingya Muslims   251
  See also barbarism; colonialism; Hitler, Adolf; Nazism; Rohingya; violence; war
Geography (Geographers)   4, 6, 31, 76, 78, 88, 119, 125, 126, 132, 208, 276–277, 332, 334, 338n7, 369, 384–385, 389, 405, 408, 411, 433, 434
  See also capital (centralization of); nation-states; world economy
Geo-politics   171, 208, 335–340, 342–344, 346–363
  See also Brzezinski, Zbigniew; colonialism; nation-states; policy (foreign policy); war; world economy
Germany   9, 9n, 91, 108, 117, 122, 127, 130, 131, 134, 190, 198, 221, 230, 248, 309, 312, 329, 334, 334n, 337, 338n7, 342, 346, 354, 357, 358, 363n10, 392, 418, 419
  Berlin   346
    Berlin Airlift   347
    Berlin Conference, 1884–1885   247
    Berlin Wall   347, 349n
  East Germany   347, 349, 349n
  Germanic tribes   112
  West Germany   349n
  See also Europe; fascism; Nazism; Hitler, Adolf; war (World War I, World War II)
Gerrymandering
  See voting
Giroux, Henry   394–396
  See also fascism; neo-liberalism
Glaspie, April   350
  See also Bush (I), George H.W.; Hussein, Saddam; war (Iraq War)
Global warming
  See environmental crisis
  See also Arrenhius, Svante; Hensen, James Edward
Globalization
  See economics (global economy); world economy
  See also neo-liberalism
Gorbachev, Mikhail   349, 392
  See also Russia; Soviet Union; war (World War III)
Göring, Hermann   364–365
  See also authoritarianism; fascism; Nazism; propaganda; war (World War II)
Governance (Government)   3, 4, 7, 20, 21, 22, 23, 35, 63, 67, 70, 75, 81, 83, 90, 91, 96, 110, 121, 122–123, 124, 129–130n, 134, 141, 142n, 143, 148, 151, 157, 167, 180, 182, 184–185, 189, 191, 197, 198, 200, 201, 203–204, 209–212, 214–219, 221–222n, 226–229, 234–236, 241, 242, 246, 249, 251, 252, 253, 258, 259n2, 260, 261–262, 266, 268n, 278, 285, 286, 287, 289, 296, 299, 306, 314, 315, 318, 323, 324, 325–327, 335, 336, 343, 344, 354, 365, 367, 369
  See also authoritarianism; democracy; despotism; freedom; liberalism (liberal democracy: theory and society); nation-states; policy; politics; state; United States (US Government: branches and agencies); voting
Gramm, Phil   149, 322
  See also corporation(s) (Enron); crisis (financial crises—financial crisis of 2007–2008—Financial Services

INDEX 549

Modernization Act); neo-liberalism (deregulation)
Great Barrier Reef
　See environmental crisis (oceans)
Great Depression　81–82, 141, 220, 221, 320, 335, 344, 388
　Glass Steagall Act　320
　US Agricultural Adjustment Act　141
　See also accumulation (overaccumulation of capital); crisis (financial crises); economics (economic crises); production (overproduction); welfare
Greece　100, 233, 234, 234n2, 335n4, 342, 367, 388, 418
　Ancient Greece / Greek empire　10, 40, 50, 300
　See also austerity; debt (debt crisis—Greek debt crisis); Europe; international organizations (International Monetary Fund, World Bank)
Greenhouse effect / gasses
　See environmental crisis (climate change, global warming)
Greenspan, Alan　321, 324
　See also crisis (financial crises—financial crisis of 2007–2008); Federal Reserve
Gross Domestic Product (GDP)
　See economics
Guatemala　128, 189, 191, 219, 332
　See also Central America; exploitation (sweatshops); geo-politics;
Gulf of Tonkin Incident　365–366
　See also geo-politics; Johnson, Lyndon; war (Vietnam War)

Habermas, Jürgen　451
　See also language
Haiti　128, 130, 187, 248, 303, 314
　See also Caribbean; colonialism; despotism; Duvalier, Francois ("Papa Doc"); North America
Haley, Niki　91
　See also Trump, Donald (Trump administration); United Nations
Hansen, James Edward　273–274
　See also environmental crisis (climate change, global warming)

Harper, Stephen　258
　See also Canada
Health and illness
　Cancer　6, 272–273n, 284, 397
　Diabetes　6
　Health care　45, 76, 84, 87, 122, 123, 125, 157, 194, 211, 223, 289, 369, 421
　Heart disease　6, 92, 397
　Obamacare　122n
　Obesity　5, 142n, 183, 283n4, 397
　Medicine　3, 9, 10, 16, 94, 182, 269, 281, 301, 372
　　Homeopathic medicine　6, 114
　　Overuse of antibiotics　283
　Mental illness　36, 164
　　Anxiety　75, 162, 164, 234, 435
　　Depression　8, 92, 118, 164
　　Schizophrenia　36, 36n
　National health care / socialized medicine　122, 212, 230, 314, 386, 387, 411, 421, 421n
　Stress　92, 283, 309
　Suicide　87, 92, 275, 324
　See also media (social media); poverty; socialism; urban
Hegel, Georg　18–19, 26, 28, 425, 428, 437, 459
　See also dialectics
Heroin
　See drugs
History and human development　7n, 16, 26, 27, 34, 35, 38–41, 60, 61, 71, 79, 98, 100–102, 106, 107, 111, 117, 134, 135–137, 153, 157, 159, 171, 290–294, 300, 330, 339, 348, 349, 359, 360, 368, 377, 384, 397, 399, 404, 407, 426n, 426–427, 427n3, 428, 431, 432, 433, 439, 444, 445
　See also capitalism (capitalist development); economics; revolution(s); social change; social movement(s); technology; war
Hitler, Adolf　73, 198, 235, 248, 254, 315, 344, 350, 364, 365, 392
　Beer Hall Putsch　235
　See also barbarism; concentration camps; despotism; fascism; genocide; Germany; Nazism; war (World War II)
Hobbes, Thomas　28, 74, 459

Holland   127, 128, 138, 138n, 300, 301, 337–338
  *See also* economics (bubbles—tulip mania); Europe; The Netherlands
Hollywood
  *See* media (mass media)
Honduras   189, 191
  *See also* Central America
Hong Kong   129, 324
  *See also* Asia; China; geo-politics
Houdini, Harry   112, 114
  *See also* religion (spiritualism)
Human nature   28, 32, 35–37, 57, 59–60, 131, 266, 378, 422, 428
  *See also* socialization
Human rights
  *See* rights
Human trafficking   96, 334–335
  *See also* exploitation; neo-liberalism; rights; slavery
Hungary   342n, 349, 388
  *See also* Europe; genocide (Hungarian Holodomor)
Hunger, undernourishment, malnourishment   89, 106, 144, 206, 220, 397, 398, 407, 412, 461
  Food storages   400
  *See also* commodities; poverty; world economy
Hunter-gatherers (Foragers)
  *See* societies (types of)
Hussein, Saddam   182, 350–351, 352–353, 352–353n5, 366–367
  *See also* despotism; geo-politics; Glaspie, April; Iraq; Kuwait; terrorism (September 11, 2001 attacks); war (Gulf War, Iraq War)

Idealism   18–19, 27, 425
  *See also* dialectics (Hegelian dialectic); Hegel, Georg; materialism; metaphysics; philosophy (speculative philosophy)
Identity politics
  *See* postmodernism
Ideology   21, 70, 124, 205n, 208, 214, 226, 237, 239, 242, 248, 263, 264, 313–314, 324, 325, 346, 395, 406, 413, 414, 416n, 420, 422, 426n, 427, 428, 428–429n, 441, 443, 462, 463

Capitalist market economies as "god's will"   59–60
In the university   256
"the economy" as ideological construct   51–52
  *See also* education; inversion; liberalism (liberal democracy: theory and society); meritocracy; mystification; national egoism; postmodernism (identity politics); race and racism
Immigration (Immigrants)   108, 119, 160, 167, 189, 213, 215, 232–233, 245, 253, 258, 309, 314, 315, 319, 329, 334, 334n2, 360
  *See also* migration; race and racism; Trump, Donald; xenophobia; world economy
Imperial Foods fire
  *See* violence
Imperialism   347, 389
  *See also* capitalism; colonialism; geo-politics; nation-state; policy (foreign policy); war
India   30, 36n, 48n, 51, 117, 128, 132, 187, 188, 275, 277, 282, 296, 297n3, 312, 313, 328, 331, 332, 334, 338, 338n7, 339n9, 342n11, 343, 359, 377, 393, 418
  Caste system   51
  New Delhi   371–272
  *See also* Asia; Britain; colonialism
Indians (American)
  *See* Native Americans
Individualistic reductionism
  *See* sociology
Indonesia   128, 182, 190, 283, 296, 300, 312, 313, 331, 332, 342n
  *See also* Asia; despotism; genocide (East Timor); Suharto
Industrial Revolution
  *See* industry
Industry   4, 35, 40, 41, 45, 71, 78, 80, 88, 96, 140, 142, 144, 146, 147–148n, 148, 154, 155–156, 158, 159, 180, 186, 188, 189, 193, 194, 198, 204–205n, 215, 218, 219, 220, 222, 224, 228, 248, 259, 268n, 269, 271, 273, 276, 278, 281, 283, 286, 288, 289, 313, 319, 323, 328, 336, 338, 338n8, 341, 342, 343, 370, 372, 373, 376, 383, 388, 390n, 399, 400, 400n8, 419, 430, 430n, 432, 433, 433–434n, 434, 435, 436, 439, 442, 444, 445, 450, 462
Deindustrialization   329

Industrial revolution 158, 188, 189, 194, 269, 372, 397
  New industrial revolution 156–157
  *See also* capital; capitalism; corporation(s); history and human development; military industrial complex; production (manufacture); societies (types of); technology
Inequality 44, 74, 79–81, 83, 87, 90, 93n, 213, 221, 223, 290, 291–292, 295, 299, 325, 327, 371, 395, 409, 412, 437, 443, 450
  Opportunity structure 74–75
  Privilege 59n, 70, 71, 78, 84, 125, 211, 214, 293, 306, 408–409, 412, 431, 451, 452, 456–457, 459, 461
  *See also* class; concentration (of wealth); mobility; patriarchy; pauperism; poverty; race and racism; sexism and misogyny; sexuality; status hierarchies
Inflation
  *See* economics
Innovation
  *See* technology (innovation)
  *See also* capitalism (prevailing tendencies); technology (Moore's Law)
Intelligent design 14–15
  *See also* evolutionary theory; science (falsification)
International law 131, 363n10
International Monetary Fund
  *See* international organizations
International organizations
  Bank for International Settlements 327
  G7 Summit 219, 287, 357
  International Criminal Court 251, 252
  International Energy Agency 271
  International Monetary Fund (IMF) 74, 80, 88, 335n4, 388n7
  Organization for Economic Cooperation and Development (OECD) 328, 371
  Oxfam International 79
  World Bank 74, 88, 148, 148n3, 192, 335
  World Economic Forum 156, 156n, 219
  World Health Organization (WHO) 271, 284
  World Trade Organization (WTO) 215, 341, 342, 345, 357
  *See also* free trade agreements; neo-liberalism; world economy

Interest (Interest rates)
  *See* economics
  *See also* capital (financial capital, interest-bearing capital); usury
Internet 5, 109, 118, 123, 142, 165, 170, 171n, 184, 212, 243, 252, 268, 276, 355, 432, 464
  Net neutrality 268
  *See also* media (social media); technology
Inversion 59–65, 428, 428–429n
  Backward ideas in our thinking 58, 428
    Advertising and consumption 63–64
    Appearance of modern world 228–339
    Capitalism, freedom, and labor alienation 60–61
    Capitalism, history, and human nature 59–60
    Crime 62
    Democracy, Kim Davis, and freedom of religion 64–65n
    Humans and society 58
    Love and marriage 61–62
    Origins of drugs and policy 62–63
    Postmodernism 463
    Poverty 92n, 92–93
    Racism and slavery 58–59
    Television and advertising 64
    Using concepts 101, 111
  Camera obscura 58, 428
  Inverted knowledge as general idea 62, 64, 70, 102, 267, 406, 428, 429, 462
  Reversing backward thought 412
  *See also* ideology; mystification
Investment (Investors) 20–21, 24, 44, 64, 80, 83, 88–90, 91, 96, 120, 121, 125, 135, 140, 143–145, 149, 150, 152, 153, 154, 159, 189, 190, 205, 215, 217, 219–220n, 221, 222, 223–224, 227, 228, 288, 289, 309, 316–328, 335n4, 337, 338, 339n, 341, 342, 343, 344, 345, 359, 360–361, 368, 369–372, 376, 378, 380, 382, 384, 388–389, 396–397n4, 401, 408, 414n, 416, 419, 420, 444
  *See also* capital; capitalism; production; profit; stocks
Iran ix, 157, 176, 182, 191, 230–231, 296, 331, 333, 361–362, 363n10, 363n11, 393
  Iranian Hostage Crisis 235
  Shah of Iran 230, 248, 361–362
  Strait of Hormuz 362

Iran (cont.)
    See also despotism; fossil fuels (oil); geo-politics; Middle East; Mossadegh, Mohammad; policy (foreign policy); revolution(s); sexism and misogyny; war (Iran-Iraq War)
Iraq   128, 182, 192, 219–220n, 235, 333, 350–352, 352–353n5, 361, 363n11, 366–367
    Invasion of Kuwait   350, 366
    See also geo-politics; Hussein, Saddam; Kuwait; Middle East; terrorism (September 11, 2001 attacks); war (Iran-Iraq War, Iraq War)
Ireland   59, 108, 128, 180, 324, 342n11, 383, 418
    Irish Potato Famine   160
    See also austerity; Europe
Israel   54n, 361, 367, 393
    Israeli-Palestinian conflict   265
    See also Middle East
Italy (Italian)   108, 127, 128, 130, 183, 324, 329, 334n, 335n4, 342, 346, 371, 388, 418
    Florence   159
    See also Europe; fascism; immigration; war (World War I, World War II)
Ivory Coast   130, 313, 333
    See also Africa; colonialism; slavery

Jamaica   128, 303, 331, 332
    See also Britain; colonialism; slavery
Japan   4, 6, 44, 67, 72, 75, 77n, 87, 88, 107, 128, 140, 147, 163, 183, 221, 259, 272–273n, 275, 287, 292, 313, 319, 330, 332, 334, 338n7, 339, 342n, 355, 363n10, 364, 392, 415
    Hiroshima and Nagasaki   392
Japan (Cont.)
    Tokyo   163, 319, 444
    See also Asia; environmental crisis (and energy); race and racism; urban; war (World War II)
Jinping, Xi   252, 264
    See also China
Johnson, Lyndon   350, 365
    See also geo-politics; Gulf of Tonkin Incident; war (Vietnam)
Joint-stock companies
    See corporations(s)
Jong-un, Kim
    See North Korea

Kant, Immanuel   11, 28
    See also Enlightenment
Kennedy, John F.   235, 348
    See also Cuba (Cuban Missile Crisis); cult of personality
Kenya   30, 128, 182, 190, 339n
    Mau Mau rebellion   190
    See also Africa; Britain
Keynes, John Maynard   138, 220, 222
    See also economics (Keynesian economics)
Khmer Rouge
    See Pol Pot
    See also Cambodia; genocide
King Leopold of Belgium   247
    See also barbarism; colonialism; Congo (Belgium Congo / Congo Free State); despotism; genocide; violence
Kissinger, Henry   191
    See also Cambodia; Chile; China; geo-politics; policy (foreign policy); Trump, Donald; war (Vietnam War)
Kondratieff cycles / waves
    See economics (expansion and contraction cycles / boom-and-bust)
Korean Peninsula
    See North Korea; South Korea; war (Korean War)
Ku Klux Klan
    See race and racism
Kuwait   128, 182, 350, 366
    See also Arabia; Bush (I), George H.W.; Glaspie, April; Hussein, Saddam; Middle East; war (Gulf War)

Labor   2, 24, 25–26, 31, 38–40, 43–45, 51, 52, 59, 60–61, 66, 70, 74, 77, 81, 83, 84, 85, 87, 89, 92, 94, 96, 97, 104, 121, 122–123, 124–125, 127, 132, 136, 140, 153, 154, 155, 156, 157, 158, 189, 190, 194, 201, 204–205n, 211, 218, 221, 223, 226, 227, 228, 247, 256, 290, 292, 293, 294, 299, 300, 301, 327n, 333, 340n, 341, 359, 368, 369, 371, 376, 380, 381, 382, 384, 386, 389, 392, 394, 402, 403, 405, 407, 408, 411, 412, 413, 424, 432, 434, 436, 437, 439, 442, 443, 445, 451
    As basis of society   38–40, 451
    Cheap labor   88, 127, 136, 190, 307, 319, 380, 384, 389, 402
    Child labor   44, 155, 189, 218, 299

INDEX    553

Division of labor   39, 66, 70, 74, 124, 153, 154, 211, 290, 294, 437, 443
Laborers   4, 25–26, 44, 215, 256, 293, 306, 308, 316, 334, 340, 368, 381, 402, 411, 429
Labor force   52, 89, 327, 371
   Labor force participation rate   52, 327, 327n
Labor market   51, 84, 85, 87, 89, 92, 125
Labor productivity   80, 83, 84–85, 89, 92, 157, 319, 326n, 341, 384
Labor theory of value / workers as producers of wealth   61, 424
Organized labor   81, 218
Pinkertons   189
Teleology of labor   104
Worker compensation   85, 155, 218, 382
*See also* accumulation; alienation; capital; class; commodities; exploitation; history and human development; pauperism; poverty; profit; proletariat; slavery; social movement(s); unions; wages
Lacan, Jean Luc   454
*See also* postmodernism
Language   6, 10, 18, 22, 24, 27, 29, 31, 35, 36–37, 48, 55, 58, 117, 131, 132, 134–135, 160, 171, 185, 190, 219, 232, 234, 237–238, 240, 243, 250, 253, 260–264, 315, 395, 423, 433, 434
   English-speaking world as remnant of colonial era   134–135
   Freedom of speech   55, 204, 213, 227, 315, 459, 462
   Gingrich Memo – Language: A Mechanism of Control   261–263
   Policing of language and ideas   240, 243–244, 243–244n2, 244n3, 457–459, 460, 463
   *See also* Chomsky, Noam; dialectics; Habermas, Jürgen; ideology; postmodernism (identity politics)
Latin America   142, 146, 339
   Latinas / Latinos / Hispanics   152, 232, 259n2, 314, 315, 321n
   *See also* Central America
Legitimacy   214, 215, 216, 224, 315
   *See also* ideology; liberalism (liberal democracy: theory and society); voting; Weber, Max
Leng'ete, Nice Nailantei

*See* sexism and misogyny (women's rights—female genital mutilation)
Lenin, Vladimir   241
   *See also* revolution(s) (October Revolution of 1917); Russia; Soviet Union
Liberalism (Liberal)   171, 203, 205, 213, 227, 229, 230, 235, 246, 254, 257, 264, 354, 362, 387, 387–388n, 416, 439, 440, 441, 451, 455, 458, 458n, 461, 463
   Equality   6, 7, 225, 227–229, 230, 243–244n2, 244, 295, 315, 410–411, 439, 455, 459, 461, 463
   Fraternity   225, 228–229, 230, 439
   Liberal democracy: theory and society   117, 203, 213, 246, 254, 257, 264, 354
   Liberty   225, 226, 227, 228, 229, 230, 242, 262, 303, 306, 315, 439
   *See also* conservativism; democracy; freedom; social progress
Liberty
   *See* liberalism
Libya   72, 130, 253, 335n3, 350
   *See also* social movement(s) (Arab Spring)
Lincoln, Abraham   305, 442
Literacy   170, 180, 394–395
   *See also* education; ideology; language; propaganda
Lyotard, Francois   451, 454
   *See also* postmodernism

Machines
   *See* technology (machines)
Maduro, Nicolas   337n6
   *See also* Venezuela
Malinowski, Bronislaw   179
   *See also* anthropology
Manafort, Paul   356, 358
   *See also* Trump, Donald (Trump administration)
Manufacture / manufacturing
   *See* production
Marcos, Ferdinand   248
   *See also* despotism; Philippines
Markets / market system
   *See* free market
Marriage and the family   61, 62, 101, 167, 246, 292, 298–299
   Arranged marriage   296

Marriage and the family (cont.)
   Nuclear family   134
   Same-sex marriage   64n, 108, 167
   See also inversion; sexism and misogyny (women's rights)
Marshall Plan, The   75, 319, 359
   See also Europe; GI Bill; war (World War II)
Marx, Karl   394, 423–450
   Marxian   428, 449
   Marxist(s)   396, 454
   Marxologists   449
   See also communism (Marx's communism); dialectics; Engels, Frederick; materialism; political economy; socialism
Masculinity
   See gender
McCarthy, Joseph
   See Red Scare
Marijuana
   See drugs
Materialism   17–19, 23–24, 26, 27n, 28, 31–33, 55n4, 99, 100–101, 109, 293, 294, 404, 406, 423–434, 425, 426–427, 429, 431, 435, 437, 439, 440n
   See also class; dialectics; economics; idealism; philosophy (speculative philosophy); technology
Mau Mau rebellion
   See Kenya
Media
   Mass media   21, 45, 62, 70, 118, 187, 190, 227, 246, 249, 252, 253, 256–260, 261, 265, 266, 268, 268n, 314, 355–356, 368, 386, 395, 450
   Bollywood   117
   Christian Broadcasting Network   244, 286
   Fairness Doctrine repeal and rise of conservative talk radio   257
   Fake news   70, 252, 266, 267
   FOX News   245, 259, 358
   Hollywood   117, 135, 242, 431
   Movies   118, 119, 123, 135, 265
   National Public Radio (NPR)   117
   Sinclair Broadcasting Group   257
   Telecommunications Act of 1996   257
   Telemundo   117
   Television   20, 41, 50–51, 64, 68, 117, 118, 119, 123, 135, 157, 183, 204, 245, 259, 260, 265, 287, 365, 394n2
   Social media   118, 335, 372, 390n, 393, 395
   Facebook   118, 257, 266, 267, 355, 393, 458n
   Reddit   118
   Twitter   119, 355
   State run media   248, 258
   See also internet; language; politics; propaganda; public relations
Mental illness
   See health and illness
Mercer, Robert   267
   Mercer Family Foundation   287
   See also Brexit; Cambridge Analytica; media; politics; propaganda; Trump, Donald (Trump administration)
Meritocracy   74, 205, 229, 266
   See also class; competition; education; elites; ideology; inequality; mobility; oligarchs
Mesoamerica   44
Mesopotamia   60, 98, 435
   See also societies (types of)
Metaphysics   26–27, 298, 440
   See also dialectics (Hegelian dialectic); Hegel, Georg; idealism; materialism; metaphysics; philosophy (speculative philosophy)
Mexico   72, 97, 128, 219n, 222, 232, 332, 342n, 343, 344, 348, 393
   Mexico City   281
   See also free trade agreements (North American Free Trade Agreement); North America
Middle class
   See class; education (college, students); inequality; meritocracy; mobility; poverty
Middle East   97, 118, 128, 130, 132, 182, 230, 300, 331, 335, 338, 355
   See also colonialism; Egypt; Iran; Iraq; Israel; Kuwait; Persian Gulf; policy (foreign policy); Qatar; Saudi Arabia; Syria; war (Gulf War, Iran-Iraq War, Iraq War, Syrian civil war); Yemen
Migration (Migrants)   2, 3, 7, 69n4, 78, 82, 118, 159, 160, 222

INDEX 555

See also immigration
Military industrial complex   198, 349
  See also Eisenhower, Dwight D.; policy
    (foreign policy); war
Mills, C. Wright   392
  See also sociology (sociological
    imagination)
Minimum wage
  See wages
Misogyny
  See sexism and misogyny
Mode of production
  See production; societies (types of)
Mobility   2, 74, 75, 78, 78n, 79–81, 84–87, 125,
    166, 256, 312
  Structural mobility   75
  See also class; competition; concentration
    (of wealth); education; inequality;
    labor; meritocracy
Modernity   ix, x, 1–7, 7n, 8, 27, 46, 51, 59, 59n,
    60, 61, 62, 65, 66, 71, 72, 74, 79, 82, 92,
    94, 97, 100–101, 107, 109, 111, 112, 114–116,
    117, 119, 120, 124, 125, 126, 130–133, 135,
    136, 159–161, 162, 164, 165, 166n2, 171,
    178, 179, 180, 181, 182, 185, 189, 194, 196,
    199, 211, 213, 214, 225, 227, 229, 230, 233,
    234, 236, 237–238, 247, 248, 251, 255,
    269, 293, 294–295, 297, 298–299, 300,
    301, 313, 315, 329, 330, 332, 345, 361, 364,
    374, 380, 382, 391, 392, 400, 401, 402,
    403, 404, 405–407, 409, 410, 416, 417,
    422, 423–425, 428, 428n, 430, 431, 432,
    433–435, 440, 441, 442, 443, 445, 446,
    449–450, 451, 455, 463
  Modern life   124, 157, 229, 438
  Modern society   4, 5, 6n, 8, 25, 30, 44, 46,
    48–49, 53, 63, 82, 108, 118, 120, 123, 125,
    136, 155, 160, 167, 196, 200, 201, 202, 203,
    212, 213, 217, 221, 224, 228, 229, 237, 239,
    265, 266, 269, 284, 294, 298, 316, 331,
    334, 374–375, 386, 403–404, 423, 427n3,
    432, 434, 439, 447, 455
  Modern world   1n, 2, 3, 5–8, 15–16, 24, 34,
    49, 97, 107, 114, 116, 119, 120, 125, 131, 140,
    158, 165, 183, 200, 223, 228–229, 247, 330,
    333, 334, 367, 368, 376, 397, 402, 403,
    407, 408, 414, 416, 424, 433, 439, 449,
    450, 455
    Modern world economy / market /
      system   44, 131, 156, 334, 352, 446

  See also capital; capitalism; civilization;
    colonialism; democracy; history
    and human development; world
    economy
Monopoly (Monopolization)   25, 88, 303,
    384, 407, 408, 411, 415, 450
  See also accumulation; competition;
    concentration (of capital, of wealth);
    corporation(s); economics
Moore's Law
  See technology
Morality   2, 36, 50, 50n3, 53–54, 54n, 55, 56,
    59, 59n, 76, 116, 178, 179, 206, 237–238,
    244, 253, 254, 262, 265, 411, 414, 433,
    437, 448
Mossadegh, Mohammad   151
  See also geo-politics; Iran; policy (foreign
    policy); United States (US Government:
    branches and agencies—Central
    Intelligence Agency)
Multinational corporations
  See corporation(s)
Murdoch, Rupert   259
  See also Ailes, Roger; media (mass
    media—FOX News)
Myanmar   128, 251, 298
  See also Asia; China; Rohingya
Mystification   10, 47–48, 51–52, 53, 55, 58, 61,
    67, 70, 101, 135, 226, 230, 243, 267–268,
    340, 427–428, 429, 438, 440–441
  Mystical / mystified consciousness
    47–52, 58, 216
  See also ideology; inversion

National Association for the Advancement of
  Colored People (NAACP)   309
National egoism   237, 238, 440
  Nationalism   108, 136, 228, 233, 237, 250,
    324, 361, 387, 394, 440
  Patriotism   234, 238, 250, 365, 440
  See also race and racism (white
    nationalism / supremacy)
Nationalism
  See national egoism
National Rifle Association (NRA)   358
Nation-states   3, 4, 96, 112, 126, 131–132, 160,
    236, 237, 313, 340, 344, 367, 379, 445,
    447, 451
  Modern nation-state system   300
  Peace of Westphalia   126, 445

Nation-states (cont.)
　See also capitalism; geo-politics; policy; politics; state; war; world economy
Native American(s)   59, 181, 189, 311
　Origin of "Indians"   187
NATO (North Atlantic Treaty Organization)   336, 354, 356, 357, 358, 367, 392
　See also geo-politics
Nature versus nurture
　See socialization
Nazism   117, 182, 198, 233, 248, 253, 309, 314, 329, 364–365, 457, 461n, 462
　Gleiwitz Incident   365
　Neo-nazis   97, 223, 314
　Nuremberg Trials   253–254, 364–365
　See also authoritarianism; concentration camps; despotism; fascism; genocide (Holocaust); Germany; Hitler, Adolf; race and racism; social movements(s) (Alt-Right); war (World War II)
Neo-liberalism   96, 221–222n, 221–224, 327–328, 341–342, 378, 396, 396n4, 407, 414
　Deregulation   286, 325, 326, 339, 371, 416n
　Free trade   21, 44, 96, 159, 180, 218, 222–223, 324, 342, 345, 369, 372, 373, 387, 388
　Privatization   89, 144, 192, 222–223, 389
　See also deregulation; free market; free trade agreements; Thatcher, Margaret; Reagan, Ronald; world economy (globalization)
Net Neutrality
　See internet
New Deal, The   81–82, 141–142, 219
　See also Great Depression; Roosevelt, Franklin D.; welfare
"New World"   104, 301, 452
New York City
　See United States
　See also urban
Nicaragua   63, 128, 191, 219–220n, 252, 350
　See also Central America; Contras; drugs (cocaine); Ortega, Daniel; policy (foreign policy); Reagan, Ronald; Sandinistas; terrorism
Nigeria   128, 130, 191, 295
　Boko Haram   295
　Ken Saro-Wiwa killing   191
　The Ogoni   191
　See also Africa; corporation(s) (Royal Dutch Shell)
Nixon, Richard   259, 348
　Watergate   235
　See also Ailes, Roger; Cambodia; conservativism; Kissinger, Henry; war (Vietnam War)
Nomadic societies
　See societies (types of)
Noriega, Manuel   349–350, 366
　See also Bush (I), George H.W.; drugs (cocaine); geo-politics; Panama; propaganda
North America   128, 130, 269, 300, 303, 305, 398
　See also Canada; Caribbean; Cuba; free trade agreements (North American Free Trade Agreement); Haiti; Jamaica; Mesoamerica; Mexico; slavery; United States
North American Free Trade Agreement (NAFTA)
　See free trade agreements
North Korea   120, 245, 248, 253, 260, 298, 357, 393
　Jong-un, Kim and the Kim family   245, 248, 253
　Korean Peninsula   248, 335
　See also Asia; authoritarianism; concentration camps; despotism; fascism; human trafficking; slavery; South Korea; Trump, Donald
Norway   91, 122, 130, 275, 315, 342, 371
　Nationalized oil policy   91
　See also Europe
Nouveau riche   76
　See also bourgeois; class; consumption (conspicuous consumption); elites

Obama, Barack   205–206, 232, 235, 245, 314, 323, 325, 339, 357, 387–388n
　Obama administration   92, 232, 286, 325, 348
　See also health and illness (health care—Obamacare)
October Revolution of 1917
　See revolution(s)
　See also Russia

Oil
  *See* fossil fuels; environmental crisis
Oligarchy (Oligarchs)   210–211, 252, 266, 336, 344, 358
  *See also* authoritarianism; democracy; despotism; elites; Putin, Vladimir; Russia; Trump, Donald
Ollman, Bertell   449
  *See also* dialectics
Opiates / Opioids / Opium
  *See* drugs (hydrocodone and oxycodone, opium)
Organization for Economic Cooperation and Development
  *See* international organizations
Ortega, Daniel   191, 252
  *See also* authoritarianism; Contras; Nicaragua; Reagan, Ronald; Sandinistas
Ottoman Empire   67, 127, 131, 346
  *See also* genocide (Armenian genocide); Turkey; war (World War I)
Overaccumulation of capital
  *See* accumulation
Overproduction
  *See* production
Owen, Robert   410
  *See also* socialism (realist-socialist); utopianism

Pakistan   132, 251, 282, 296, 297n3, 312, 313, 393
  *See also* Asia; authoritarianism; Eurasia; religion (Islam); sexism and misogyny (women's rights); slavery; social movement(s); violence
Panama   128, 151, 349, 366, 366n1
  Panama Canal   350
  *See also* Bush (I), George H.W.; Central America; drugs (cocaine); geo-politics; Noriega, Manuel; taxes (tax evasion, havens, and shelters)
Paris, France
  *See* France
  *See also* environmental crisis (climate change–Paris climate accords)
Pasteur, Louis   12
  *See also* science (experimental model)
Patriarchy   136–137, 292–293, 295–296
  Male dominance   291–292, 452, 456
  *See also* gender; sexism and misogyny

Patriotism
  *See* national egoism
Pauperism   93, 430, 430n
  Impoverishment   79, 81, 83, 88, 92, 95, 124, 131, 385, 416
  *See also* accumulation; class; concentration (of capital, of wealth); exploitation; inequality; labor; policy; poverty; profit
Persian Gulf   128, 182, 351, 362
  *See also* Arabia (Arabian Peninsula) fossil fuels (oil); Gulf of Oman; Iran; Middle East; policy (foreign policy); Saudi Arabia
Peru   30, 56, 128, 337n6
  *See also* South America
Philippines   30, 128, 253, 417
  *See also* Asia; Duterte, Rodrigo; Marcos, Ferdinand; war on drugs
Philosophy   17–19, 21, 26–27, 27n, 34, 40, 406, 425–426, 440
  Speculative philosophy   10–11, 17–18, 26–27, 27n, 28–29, 31, 32, 114, 404, 406, 407, 425, 426
  *See also* dialectics; idealism; materialism; politics (political ideals / philosophy / theory); science
Pinochet, Augusto   191, 248–249
  *See also* Allende, Salvador; Chile; despotism; fascism; Kissinger, Henry
Poland   108, 182, 198, 334, 342, 365
  *See also* Europe; Hitler, Adolf; Nazism (Gleiwitz Incident); war (World War II)
Polarization   83, 85, 125, 314, 318, 319, 386–387
  *See also* class; concentration (of capital, of wealth); ideology; politics
Policing (Police)   44, 62, 152, 200, 203, 218, 224, 251, 309, 314, 396
  Militarization of police   223–224
  Police state   223, 248, 410, 436n9, 438
  Religious police   248, 396
  Secret police   248, 396
  *See also* class (class struggle); crime
Policy   20, 21, 21n, 24, 26, 44, 59, 64, 75, 81, 83, 84n, 88, 90n2, 90n3, 91, 92, 96, 119, 122n, 122–123, 125, 141, 182, 194, 196, 197, 198, 201, 203, 204, 204n, 205, 207–216, 217, 219, 220–221, 221–222n, 222, 226, 232,

Policy (cont.)
    234–235, 238, 239, 242, 249, 253–254,
    258, 261, 265, 266, 284, 285, 286, 287, 288,
    298, 315, 318, 319, 325, 326, 327, 334, 336,
    337n6, 339, 342, 343, 344, 349, 351, 357,
    361, 353n10, 364–365, 373, 376, 379, 386,
    387–388n, 394n2, 395, 398, 415, 421, 430
  Foreign policy    198, 219, 258, 265
    Oil and foreign policy and
      relations    89, 182–183, 190, 191,
      192, 219, 253, 331, 332–333, 336–338,
      344, 350, 352, 352–353n5, 354, 360,
      362–363, 363n11, 369, 377, 384, 402
  Policy-makers and making    91, 92,
    204–205, 207–216, 219, 220–222, 226,
    253–254, 266, 284, 286, 288, 289, 318, 325,
    327, 328, 339, 342, 343, 344, 351, 364–365,
    376, 379, 386, 395, 398, 421, 430, 447
    Think tanks and institutes    21, 219,
      256, 264, 288, 379, 421
      Brookings Institute    219, 324, 357
      Centre for Independent
        Studies    421
      Heartland Institute    287
      Heritage Foundation    219, 287
      Institute for Public Affairs    288
      Manhattan Institute    287
      Project for a New American
        Century    351, 366
        *Rebuilding America's
          Defenses*    351–352, 352n4, 366,
          366n
      Rockefeller Foundation    308
      *See also* candidate selection
        process; elites; geo-politics;
        military industrial complex;
        nation-states; politics; state; war
Politics    2, 4, 11, 21, 27n, 31, 32, 33, 43, 45, 47,
  51, 61, 62, 68, 69, 70, 72, 90, 91, 92, 96,
  97, 100, 106, 109, 110, 120, 124, 125, 126,
  142n, 148, 151, 159, 178, 212, 212n, 213,
  214, 217, 218, 220, 221, 222, 225, 226, 227,
  228, 229, 230, 235, 236, 237, 238, 239,
  240, 241, 242, 243, 244, 243–244n2, 245,
  246, 248, 252, 254, 257, 258, 259, 259n2,
  259–260n3, 260, 261, 264, 267, 268, 285,
  287, 288, 291, 292, 293, 294, 307, 309,
  314, 316, 320, 327, 328, 334, 335n4, 338,
  339, 342, 343, 344, 346, 347, 349, 350,
  351, 353, 354, 355, 356, 358, 360, 361, 363,
  364, 365, 367, 369, 374, 386, 387, 388,
  390, 392, 394, 395, 396, 399–400, 401,
  404, 409, 412, 414, 415, 420, 423, 426n,
  427, 428, 429, 428–429n, 433, 438, 439,
  440, 440n, 441, 442, 443, 446, 447, 453,
  454, 455, 455n, 456n, 457–459, 460, 461,
  462, 463, 464
National politics    342
Political agenda    69, 72, 267
Political alliances / opponents    62, 109,
  130, 144, 228, 252, 253, 261, 292, 328, 346,
  353–354, 356, 357–358, 360–361, 362,
  377, 433, 446
Political aspirants / candidates    125, 204,
  204–205n, 205
Political authority / leaders / officials /
  representatives / rulers    2, 11, 43, 106,
  110, 148, 198, 208, 209, 248, 260, 314, 364,
  442
Political campaigns / candidates    125,
  148, 203–208, 214, 216–217, 228, 234–235,
  258, 261, 262, 327, 344, 387, 439
  Political action committees
    (PACs)    204, 204–205n, 206
    GOPAC    261
    Super PACs    204, 204–205n
  Political donations / donors /
    funds    148, 204–205n, 206, 207, 213,
    217, 287, 358, 386, 414
Political capital / influence    45, 126, 207,
  348, 353
Political class / elites    207, 235, 349, 412,
  446
Political corruption    148
Political crisis    388, 390
Political freedom    241
Political ideals / philosophy / theory    27,
  214, 225, 227, 230, 239, 243, 441
Political ideologies / orientation /
  views    70, 124, 203, 226, 237, 244, 264,
  267, 316, 428, 441
Political institutions / structure /
  system    31, 120, 210–211, 228, 236, 246,
  349, 412, 415, 426n, 438, 459n
Political knowledge / political
  discourse    207, 226, 267, 404
Political movements / participation    214,
  239

INDEX

Political operatives 288
Political party / parties 97, 203, 205, 206, 207, 208, 211, 214, 219, 239, 240–243, 244, 247, 252, 259, 261, 263, 264, 314, 347, 365, 386, 387, 388, 394, 415, 420, 438–439
Political power(s) 100, 213, 221, 242, 339, 346, 353, 360–361, 428–429n, 440n, 441, 443, 459n
Politicians 21, 45, 51, 92, 96, 97, 125, 148, 207, 207n, 260, 261, 264n6, 268, 285, 314, 327, 328, 369, 386, 392, 404, 409
Politics and media 257–259, 259n2, 259–260n3, 268n
*See also* candidate selection process; class; Democrats; elites; freedom; geopolitics; governance; liberalism (liberal democracy: theory and society); nation-states; policy; postmodernism (identity politics); Republicans; rights; social movement(s); state
Political economy (Political-economics) 100, 136, 212, 293, 309, 315, 330, 331, 335, 337, 360, 380, 401, 408, 414, 442
*See also* capital; capitalism; class; economics; policy; politics; profit
Pol Pot 241, 348
Khmer Rouge 348
*See also* Cambodia; despotism; war (Vietnam War)
Pompeo, Mike 110
*See also* religion (Christianity); Trump, Donald (Trump administration)
Popper, Karl 14
*See also* science (falsification)
Population growth
*See* environmental crisis
Portugal 127, 128, 181, 187, 190, 300, 301, 303, 324, 331, 337, 342n, 377
Lisbon 159
*See also* austerity; colonialism; Europe; slavery
Post-industrial society
*See* societies
Postmodernism 451–464
Alan Sokal Affair 455, 455n, 464
New Sokal affair 464
Anti-foundationalism 451
Anti-liberalism 455

Anti-science 451, 455, 463
Identity politics 455–459, 463
Identity politics and fascism 455, 461, 461n, 462–463
Germaine Greer, no platforming 460
Laci Green 243–244
Laura Kipnis, reaction to 460
Melissa Glick incident 461
New political correctness 455
Students call biologist Nazi, disrupt meeting 461n
Microaggressions 243, 243–244n2, 458
New political correctness 455
Social justice 243–244, 459, 464
Trans-exclusive radical feminists 243
Julie Bindel 460
*See also* class (class struggles); diversity; fascism; free speech; language; liberalism; social movement(s) (feminist / women's movement) status hierarchies
Poverty 4, 21n, 24, 69n4, 75–76, 76n, 78–83, 85–90, 90n3, 91–92, 92n, 94, 95, 110, 124, 131, 164, 183, 185, 227, 228, 229, 266, 324, 336, 385, 386, 397, 412, 430–431, 430n
*See also* accumulation; capitalism; class; concentration (of capital, of wealth); inequality; labor; meritocracy; pauperism; unemployment; wages
Powell, Colin 367
*See also* Bush (II), George W. (Bush (II) administration); terrorism (September 11, 2001 attacks); war (Iraq War); Wilkerson, Lawrence
Pre-modern peoples and societies 6, 6n, 57, 112, 179, 295, 299
Pre-modern people as "barbarian," "primitive," and/or "savage" 6, 59, 59n, 179–180, 183
*See also* societies (types of)
Prevailing tendencies (of capitalism)
*See* capitalism (prevailing tendencies)
Privatization
*See* neo-liberalism
Privilege
*See* inequality

Production   2, 3, 16, 26, 34, 44, 48, 58, 64, 81, 84, 85, 96, 120, 125, 135, 140, 141, 142, 143, 145, 154, 155, 156, 157, 159, 166n2, 211, 269, 271, 272n, 278, 281, 284, 294, 300, 301, 316, 317–318, 319, 325, 330, 331, 332, 333, 336, 342, 344, 348, 352–353n5, 363n11, 364, 368, 369, 370, 371, 372, 377, 380, 382, 384, 386, 387, 390, 390n, 396–397n, 397, 400, 401, 402, 403, 407, 411, 414, 415, 416, 424, 426n, 431, 435, 443, 444, 445, 446, 447, 462
   Cost of production   24, 120, 139, 148, 369, 381, 382, 389, 446
   Cycle of production and reinvestment   83, 120, 125, 135, 139–140, 143–144, 316–318, 370, 376, 380
   Manufacture (manufacturing)   85, 87, 138, 140, 142, 143, 148, 204–205n, 232, 300, 320, 340, 341, 359, 361, 377, 400
      As percent of GDP   143
      Downsizing   142, 371
      Just-in-time manufacture   140
      Lean manufacturing   142
      Sweatshops   155, 183, 192, 332, 340
      Weapons manufacturing   198, 349
   Mass production   16, 284, 377, 382
   Means of production   394, 433–434n, 446
   Mode of production   269, 301, 424, 426–427n, 436, 445
      Production system / forms of production   44, 58, 120, 157, 330, 402, 411, 441, 443
   Overproduction   63, 139–143, 369, 433, 446
   Production / assembly lines   140, 154
   Production methods / techniques   34, 48, 120, 140, 166n2, 269, 300, 401, 414, 426n
   Productive forces   424, 441, 426–427n, 433, 442
   Relations of production   426n, 435
   See also capital (circuit of, productive capital); capitalism; commodities; consumption; crisis; industry; labor; technology; world economy
Profit   25, 26, 44, 51–52, 63, 64, 83, 88, 89, 90, 91, 120, 122, 123, 124–125, 132, 135, 139–140, 143–144, 147, 147–148n2, 149, 150, 151, 151n5, 152, 154, 156, 159, 193, 201, 202, 212, 215, 217–218, 220, 221, 222–223, 226, 288, 289, 300, 301, 315, 316–318, 319, 320, 321, 322, 325–327, 329, 336, 340, 364, 368–369, 370–371, 376, 380, 381, 382–384, 386, 387, 388–389, 394, 416, 420, 433, 436, 444, 446, 450
   Decline in   143, 156, 382–384, 317, 319, 325, 326
      Potential downward cycle in profits leading to a crisis   369, 382–384, 388–389, 424, 433
   Labor exploitation as source of   124–125, 158, 201, 300, 315, 385
   Overproduction of   140
   Profitability (Profit rate)   63, 124, 139–140, 143–144, 152, 212, 217–218, 220, 221, 224, 288, 301, 317–318, 320, 322, 326, 326n6, 329, 369, 370, 384, 388–389, 420, 436, 444
   Reinvestment of   120, 125, 135, 140, 143, 144, 154, 316–318, 370, 371, 376, 380
   See also accumulation; capital; capital (circuit of); class; economics; exploitation; labor; value (surplus-value); production (overproduction); wages
Progress
   See social progress
Proletariat   429, 431n, 438–439n, 447
   See also bourgeois; class; class (class struggle); labor; revolution(s)
Propaganda   21, 70, 201, 204, 248, 257, 260, 264, 278, 310, 353, 355, 365, 372, 386, 407
   See also Bernays, Edward; geo-politics; language; media; public relations
Public relations   256, 264, 264n6, 366, 453
   Public consciousness   72, 119, 289
   See also Bernays, Edward; ideology; media; propaganda
Putin, Vladimir   252, 253, 266, 336–337, 354–356, 357, 358–359
   See also authoritarianism; Crimea; despotism; geo-politics; oligarchs; Russia; Trump, Donald; Ukraine

Qatar   128, 314
   See also Arabia; Middle East; slavery (contemporary slavery)

Race and racism   23, 56n, 58, 59, 85, 97, 132, 135, 136, 137, 183, 227, 229, 230, 232,

INDEX 561

234n2, 235, 306–307, 309, 312n, 312–315, 344, 355, 395, 411, 420, 443, 456, 462, 463
Anti-Semitism  457
Color line  59
Eugenics  182, 307, 309–310
Jim Crow laws  68, 309, 312, 312n
Ku Klux Klan  68
Lynching  182, 230, 307–308
Racial projects  136
Racial science  137
Segregation  68, 164, 230, 232, 307, 309
Sundown towns  166n1
White nationalism / supremacy  136, 233
See also Du Bois, W.E.B.; ethnicity; ethnocentrism; fascism; national egoism; Nazism; social movement(s) (Alt-Right); xenophobia
Reagan, Ronald  63, 113n, 222, 223, 232, 235, 326, 349
Reagan administration  90, 91, 191, 257, 339, 349–350, 371
See also conservatism; neo-liberalism; Republicans; Thatcher, Margaret
Redistribution  81, 219, 221, 222, 327–328, 386
See also appropriation of wealth; crisis; economics (Keynesian economics); welfare
Red Scare, The  242
McCarthy, Joseph  242
See also Cold War; Soviet Union; United States
Regulatory capture  286–287
See also neo-liberalism
Religion  4, 31, 34, 35, 42, 58, 100–111, 112, 124, 134, 185, 189, 237, 238, 242, 246, 296, 315, 325, 394n2, 406, 416, 428, 430–431, 459n, 462
Animism  34, 58, 100
Shaman  9, 14, 53, 100
Atheism / no religion  108–109
European Social Survey of religiosity  108
Buddhism (Buddhist)  12n4, 64–65n, 117, 251
Christianity (Christians)  29, 35, 53, 59, 64–65n, 101n, 102–103, 104, 105, 108–110
Assemblies of God  109
Bible, The  31, 54n, 104, 107, 108, 110

Biblical creationism  15, 462
Biblical worldview  286
The Ten Commandments  54n
Tree of Knowledge of Good and Evil  103
Catholicism  4, 12n4, 50n3, 76, 104, 171, 246, 248, 374
Church Militant  246
Second Vatican Council (Vatican II)  171
Vatican Conference (2018)  109
Christian Broadcasting Network  244, 286
Eastern Orthodox Church  104
Jesus  29, 104, 109, 110, 265, 374
Mormons  115
Prosperity Gospel  265
Protestantism (Protestants)  76
Dominionism  245–246, 374
Methodists  303
Quakers  303
Southern Baptist Convention  20, 104, 286
Fundamentalism  50n3, 104, 114, 231, 242, 374
Gods  28, 48, 49, 52, 53, 102, 111, 179, 237, 241, 256, 316, 406, 427
Abrahamic / Biblical god  53n, 108
Animist gods  2
Vedic gods  53
Hinduism (Hindus)  51, 53, 231
Islam (Muslims)  53n, 55, 60, 64–65n, 98, 102–103, 104, 105, 107, 108, 110, 117, 230, 231, 232, 233, 251, 252, 295, 297, 350, 355, 374, 393
Sharia law  97, 230
The Koran  104, 107
Judaism (Jews)  53, 104, 112, 182, 198, 231, 248, 253, 315, 457
Moses  54n, 112
The Torah  104, 107
Magic rites  100, 101
Monotheism  34, 102
New Age movement  114–115, 431, 451
Astrology  113, 113n, 114
Indigo children  114
Wicca / Witchcraft  114
Polytheism  34
Religious cults  115, 239, 245, 410, 453

Religion (cont.)
    Children of God   116
    Heaven's Gate   116
    People's Temple   115
    Raelians   116
    Scientology   115
    Religious hegemony   137
    Ritual   49–50, 50n2, 50n3, 55, 100, 105, 256
    Spiritualism   112–113
    Theocracy   4
    *See also* alienation; ideology; mystification; superstition
Republicans (Republican Party)   141, 198, 207, 209, 244, 245, 246, 257, 287, 288, 314, 345, 357, 358–359, 421n
    *See also* conservatism; Democrats
Revolution(s)
    Agricultural Revolution   104, 291, 408
    American Revolution   4, 303, 303–304n
    Anti-bourgeois revolution   354
    Cuban Revolution   348
    European revolutions of 1848   72
    French Revolution   4, 225, 228
    Iranian Revolution   230–231, 362
    Marx's theories of   426–427n, 432, 435, 439, 445, 447
    October Revolution of 1917 in Russia   241, 401
    Robotic revolution   140–141, 156–157
    Scientific revolution   3
    "The revolution", i.e., workers' revolution   394–396
    *See also* class (class struggle); history and human development; industry (industrial revolution); Marx, Karl; social change; social movement(s)
Rights   55, 61, 72, 91, 109, 130, 137, 184–85, 211, 214–215, 218, 227, 228, 230, 233, 251, 262, 263, 268n, 293, 297, 298, 299, 303, 307, 349, 351, 366, 421, 437, 445
    *See also* human trafficking; inequalities; politics; sexism and misogyny (women's rights); slavery (contemporary slavery); social movement(s)
Robotics
    *See* technology (robotics)
Rohingya   251
    *See also* China; genocide; Myanmar; violence

Rome (ancient)   2, 44, 46, 60, 96, 100, 110, 112, 179, 300, 442n
Roosevelt, Franklin D.   141–142
    *See also* Great Depression; New Deal
Rousseau, Jacques   403
    *See also* Enlightenment
Rumsfeld, Donald   351, 352
    *See also* Bush (II), George W.; war (Iraq War)
Rural   5, 74, 141, 159, 160–161, 162, 170, 200, 206, 222, 235, 296, 374, 403, 434
    *See also* urban
Russia   130, 142, 183, 245, 248, 252, 253, 266, 313, 331, 332, 335n3, 336, 337, 342, 346, 354–362n, 363n, 364, 388, 392–393, 396, 401, 432
    Moscow   336, 348n, 355
    *See also* Asia; Cold War; communism; geo-politics; Gorbachev, Mikhail; Lenin, Vladimir; oligarchs; Putin, Vladimir; revolution(s); Soviet Union; Stalin, Josef; Trump, Donald; Yeltsin, Boris

Sanders, Bernie   45, 91, 207, 335, 356
Sandinistas   191
    *See also* Contras; drugs (cocaine); Nicaragua; Ortega, Daniel; terrorism
Sarajevo, Yugoslavia   183–184, 313
    *See also* barbarism
Saudi Arabia   69n4, 109, 182, 192, 282, 296–297, 297n3, 331, 333, 337, 352, 352–353n5, 358n, 362, 363n11, 393
    Saudi Ghawar Field   363n11
    *See also* Arabia; despotism; Middle East; patriarchy; religion (atheism, Islam); sexism and misogyny
Science   3, 6, 9–12, 12n3, 12n4, 13–14, 14n, 15–16, 19, 23, 24, 27, 31, 32, 39, 40, 58, 66, 67, 68, 69, 69n4, 71, 82, 101, 102–104, 113, 120, 136, 137, 142n, 180, 226, 232, 242, 244n3, 257, 257–258n, 258, 259–260n3, 260, 264, 265, 267, 269, 271, 272–273n, 273–275, 277, 278, 281, 283, 284, 285, 286, 400, 401, 419, 420, 421, 422, 425, 426, 426n, 427, 431, 432, 435, 437, 442, 451, 452, 453, 454, 455, 455n, 456, 456n, 457, 458, 458n, 462, 463, 464
    Experiment   10, 11, 12, 13, 15
    Natural science   14, 32, 426n
    Philosophy of science   13

INDEX 563

Falsification 14, 16
Tautology 104, 452
Teleology 104, 105
Proto-science 40
Scientific revolution 3
Social science 13, 14, 23, 32, 67, 107, 264, 432, 437
*See also* dialectics; Enlightenment; sociology
Scotland 130, 223, 227
*See also* Britain; Europe; United Kingdom
Secularization 50n2, 100, 107–109, 110, 234, 246, 442
*See also* religion
Segregation (racial)
*See* race and racism
Semmelweiz, Ignaz 12
*See also* science
Sessions, Jeff 246, 287
*See also* Trump, Donald (Trump administration)
Sexism and misogyny 109, 136, 229, 232, 268n, 457, 461, 463
Women's rights 72, 297–298
Acid attacks 296
Bride burning 296
Child marriage 102, 292, 296, 299, 436
Domestic violence 293, 299
Dowry 62, 296
Female genital mutilation 292, 296, 299
Leng'ete, Nice Nailantei 299
Female infanticide 298
Honor killings 292, 296–297
Honor Based Violence Awareness Network 297, 297n2
Rape 54, 55n3, 62, 102, 183, 185, 187, 191, 248, 296, 297, 297n3
Reproductive rights 230
Abortion 108, 230, 233, 265, 296
Birth control 167, 230, 294
Roe v. Wade 233
Sex-selective abortion 298
Sex slaves / sex trafficking 296, 298
Sterilization (forced and otherwise) 181, 190, 296, 309, 310
Trading women 296
*See also* gender; inequality; patriarchy; sexuality

Sexuality 23, 72, 134, 137, 237, 227, 229, 292, 299, 441
Heterosexuality, heteronormativity / compulsory heterosexuality 134, 137, 452, 456, 457
Homosexuality / lgbtq community 52, 97, 182, 230, 232, 243n2, 248, 252, 265, 268n, 460, 463
Homophobia 109, 182, 229, 230, 232, 248, 265, 457, 461
*See also* gender; status hierarchies
Sierra Leone 303–304n4
*See also* Africa; slavery
Silicon Valley 359, 401
*See also* technology (computers and cyber-technology, innovation)
Simmel, Georg 435
*See also* urban (metropolitanism); sociology
Slavery 2, 20, 40, 43–44, 58–59, 60, 61, 96, 130, 181, 183, 187–188, 215, 224, 230, 238, 248, 292, 293, 296, 300–314, 315, 332, 333, 334, 339, 402, 405, 406, 411, 431n, 436, 443, 447
Asiento de Negros 303
Contemporary slavery 96, 248, 296, 313–314, 315, 333, 334
Pre-modern slavery 2, 40, 43–44, 60, 292, 300
Transatlantic slave trade 118, 301
*See also* colonialism; crime (crimes against humanity); exploitation; labor; race and racism; sexism and misogyny (women's rights—sex slaves / sex trafficking)
Smith, Adam 28, 59–61
*Wealth of Nations* 59
*See also* economics (laissez faire economics)
Social change 23, 27n, 42, 45–46, 72, 165, 229, 295, 339, 394, 443
*See also* asymptotic; class (class struggle); education (students); history and human development; revolution(s); social movement(s); social progress; societies (types of); technology (innovation)
Social movement(s) 44, 72, 167, 190, 192, 239, 240, 244, 246, 251, 293, 294, 295,

Social movement(s) (cont.)
　　298–299, 303, 305, 306, 307, 344, 347, 355, 361, 374, 392, 394
　　Abolition of slavery   293, 303, 306–307
　　Alt-Right   233, 461
　　　　Unite the Right Rally   233
　　Arab Spring   72, 73
　　Dominionism   246, 374
　　Eugenics movement   307–309
　　Feminist / women's movement   167, 243, 294, 298–299, 456n, 460
　　Islamic movements
　　　　Boko Haram   295
　　　　Islamic State   97, 192, 361
　　　　Mujahedeen   63
　　Labor movement   44, 293, 392, 394, 407
　　New Age movement   114
　　Non-Aligned Movement   347
　　Occupy Wall Street   344, 372, 389
　　Sectarian movements   239, 240, 241, 243–244n2, 355, 396
　　Separatists in Europe   361
　　Social justice   244, 459–463
　　*See also* education (students); Kenya (Mau Mau rebellion); revolution(s); social change
Social progress   6, 10, 37, 41, 46, 57, 69, 161, 229, 232, 233, 299, 315, 362, 368, 394, 396, 400n8, 410, 415, 422, 426n, 430, 440, 443, 447, 452, 453, 455, 456n, 457, 463
　　Social position of women as a measure of progress   290–299
　　*See also* democracy; freedom; gender; history and human development; societies (types of); technology (development, growth, and level of complexity); voting
Social Security   90n3, 122, 220, 221, 386
Socialism (Socialist)   184, 191, 220, 336, 387–388n, 396, 410, 411–412, 420, 421, 439, 441, 448, 451
　　Realist-socialist   411, 412
Socialism (Socialist) (Cont.)
　　Socialism for the rich   324, 325
　　Socialized / socialization of resources   122, 122n, 386, 387, 411
　　*See also* communism; Marx, Karl
Socialization   2, 36, 56n, 62, 101

Nature versus nurture   53, 58
Sense of self   8, 35
Societies (types of)
　　Agriculture (agrarian)   1, 23, 24, 39, 43, 44, 47, 66, 102, 106, 153, 291
　　City-states   2, 43, 66, 100, 292
　　Feudal   1, 2, 4, 6n, 43–44, 60, 61, 74, 79, 92n, 98, 100, 120, 132, 134, 159, 171, 185, 223, 247, 292, 293, 294
　　Horticulture   39, 43
　　Hunter-gatherer / foraging   1, 2, 6n, 23, 24, 34, 35, 39, 42, 43, 44, 46, 47, 57, 58, 66, 102, 120, 153, 179, 237, 290, 291, 298
　　Industrial   40, 66
　　Nomadic   33, 39, 42, 43, 102, 106, 165, 290, 291
　　Pastoralist   23, 39, 43, 58, 102
　　Post-industrial   434
　　Sedentary   39, 43, 291
　　Tribal   60, 112, 120, 179, 181, 291, 300, 303, 377
　　*See also* history and human development; revolution(s) (agricultural revolution)
Sociology   2, 6, 23, 33, 44, 48, 58, 88, 100, 101, 194, 392, 410, 434, 437
　　Individualistic reductionism   48, 414, 415
　　Sociological imagination   29
　　Sociological processes / variables   28–29, 35, 46, 55, 101, 102, 105, 138, 293, 294, 368, 443, 451
　　*See also* Comte, August; Marx, Karl; Mills, C. Wright; Simmel, Georg; Wallerstein, Immanuel; Weber, Max
Socrates   71
Sokal, Alan / Sokal Affair
　　*See* postmodernism
Soros, George   387
South Africa   128, 282, 331, 332, 342, 359
　　Cape Town   282
　　*See also* Africa; environmental crisis (freshwater)
South America   ix, 112, 128, 130, 219n, 279, 300, 301, 305, 306, 331, 332, 407
　　*See also* Argentina; Bolivia; Brazil; Chile; Colombia; colonialism; Ecuador; Peru; slavery; Venezuela
South Korea   118, 312–313, 357
　　Korean Peninsula   248, 335
　　*See also* Asia; North Korea; war (Korean War)

INDEX 565

South Sudan   295, 335n3
  *See also* Africa; sexism and misogyny
    (women's rights—sex slaves / sex
    trafficking)
Soviet Union   141, 171, 183, 235, 241, 242, 346,
    347, 348, 348n, 349, 349n, 356, 392
  Collapse of   336, 350
  Communist bloc   72, 171, 183, 347, 349,
    349n, 355
  Invasion and occupation of
    Afghanistan   63, 141, 230
  *See also* authoritarianism; Cold War; Cuba
    (Cuban Missile Crisis); Lenin, Vladimir;
    Russia; Stalin, Josef
Spain   60, 69, 117, 122, 128, 130, 134, 181, 187,
    230, 300, 301, 303, 312n8, 324, 331, 337,
    418, 419
  Madrid   159
  Spanish language   132
  *See also* colonialism; Europe; slavery
Speculation (financial)   143, 320, 421n
  *See also* capital (financial capital); crisis
    (financial crises); Great Depression;
    stocks
Speculation (philosophical)
  *See* philosophy (speculative philosophy)
Stalin, Josef   241, 248
  Stalinist   396
  *See also* authoritarianism; bureaucracy;
    Cold War; despotism; Lenin, Vladimir;
    North Korea; Soviet Union
State, The   4, 44, 48, 71, 82, 88, 95, 121, 187,
    196, 197, 198, 199, 201, 207, 208, 212, 213,
    214, 215, 217, 218, 222, 224, 226, 228, 237,
    248, 250, 255, 372, 376, 386, 388, 394,
    409, 412, 428–429n, 437, 438, 439, 440
  *See also* authoritarianism; bureaucracy;
    democracy; governance; nation-states;
    policy; politics; war
Status hierarchies   59, 59n, 75, 132, 194, 196,
    227, 229, 236, 290, 291, 292, 296, 298,
    300, 306, 307, 314, 404, 410, 411, 412, 437,
    443, 463
  *See also* gender; inequality; race and
    racism; sexuality
Stocks   145, 149–150, 158, 187, 217, 226, 268n,
    316–320, 322, 326–327, 335, 342, 344,
    363n, 368, 370, 380, 408, 444
  Bonds   316, 318, 337n5, 370, 444

Capital gains   222
Securities   149, 150, 317, 318, 320, 325
Shareholders   64, 90, 121, 145, 324, 325,
    326, 371, 396–397n4
  Cult of shareholder value   371,
    396–397n4
Stock buybacks   326–327, 340–341,
    370–371
Stock market / stock exchange   51, 81, 149,
    150, 158, 319, 324, 344–345, 371, 444, 447
  Wall Street   61, 158, 219, 244–245,
    323–324, 335, 372, 421, 444
Stock options   148
*See also* accumulation; banks; capital
    (financial capital—interest-bearing
    capital, productive capital); capitalism;
    class; corporations (joint-stock
    companies); crisis (financial crises);
    Great Depression; investment; social
    movement(s) (Occupy Wall Street);
    speculation (financial)
Students
  *See* education (college, students)
  *See also* class (middle class); debt (student
    loans); social movement(s)
Suburbs (Suburbanization)   87, 104,
    170, 403
  *See also* class (middle class); rural; urban
Sudan   128, 335n3, 363n10
  *See also* Africa; sexism and misogyny
    (women's rights—sex slaves / sex
    trafficking)
Suharto   190
  *See also* despotism; genocide (East Timor);
    Indonesia
Superstition   3, 38, 51, 60, 116, 180, 407, 452
  *See also* religion
Supply and demand
  *See* economics
Supreme Court, The
  *See* United States (US Government:
    branches and agencies)
Sweden   108, 122, 130, 334n, 342n, 361,
    371, 419
  *See also* Europe; war (Russo-Swedish War)
Switzerland   342n, 418
  *See also* Europe
Syria
  *See* Middle East; war (Syrian civil war)

Taiwan   128, 324, 357, 360
  *See also* Asia; China; geo-politics
Taliban, The
  *See* Afghanistan
Tautology
  *See* science
Taxes (Taxpayers)   57, 61, 67, 91, 95, 122, 148, 151, 151n5, 201, 206, 211–212, 215, 217, 221, 222–223, 224n, 263, 268n, 277, 297, 323, 324, 325, 337n6, 340, 358, 369, 386, 387, 388, 421n, 438, 438n, 440
  Tax evasion, havens, and shelters   151, 151n5, 158, 223, 334
    Mossack Fonseca   151
    Panama Papers   151
  *See also* welfare (corporate welfare: bailouts, subsidies, tax breaks and tax cuts)
Tech Bubble, The
  *See* economics (bubbles)
Technology   5, 6, 7n4, 10, 11, 24, 26, 34, 39, 40, 41, 42, 60, 67, 69, 79, 80, 83, 119, 132, 153, 155–158, 161, 165, 170, 177, 179, 180, 187, 189, 194, 211, 269, 283, 285, 286, 290, 294, 300, 317, 332, 333, 338, 341, 343, 359, 364, 372, 377, 380, 382, 389, 399, 400, 405, 407, 408, 418, 421, 432, 433, 442
  And health problems   155
  As environmental fix   400, 418
  As method of labor control   154–155, 405, 434, 436
  As method of lowering labor costs   155–157, 317, 326n6, 369, 381, 382, 434
  Biotechnology   157
  Computers and cyber-technology   5, 16, 35, 37–38, 40, 61, 85, 118, 142, 153–158, 165, 171, 176–177, 269, 319, 328, 331, 332, 333, 341, 377, 403
    Cyber-weapons   157, 328
  Deskilling   157
  Development, growth, and level of complexity   5, 6, 7n, 10, 34, 39, 40, 42, 60, 79, 80, 117, 119, 132, 140, 141, 144, 153, 155, 158, 161, 170, 179–180, 187, 194, 211, 269, 283, 285, 290, 294, 338, 364, 372, 377, 382, 398, 399, 400, 405, 407, 432, 442
  Domestic-labor saving machines   294
  Industrial technology   35, 40, 154–155, 189, 317, 332, 338, 359

  Information technology   117–119, 120, 142, 155, 184, 211, 287, 330, 359, 377, 390n, 393, 401
  Innovation   5, 359, 371, 405, 421
  Machines   34, 125, 140, 141, 144, 154, 153–158, 160, 176, 189, 194, 217, 226, 294, 316, 326, 359, 369, 380, 381, 382, 411, 434, 436, 442
    Moore's Law   171, 177
    Robotics   140–141, 154, 156–157, 341, 359
  *See also* asymptotic; history and human development; internet; materialism
Teleology
  *See* science
Terrorism   63, 68, 97n, 109, 182, 192, 336, 350, 352, 362, 366
  Islamic State / ISIS   97, 192
  September 11, 2001 attacks   63, 192, 336, 339, 350, 366
  *See also* Bin Laden, Osama; Bush (II), George W. (Bush (II) administration); fascism; geo-politics; policy (foreign policy); violence; war
Thatcher, Margaret   222, 223, 326
  *See also* Britain; conservativism; England; neo-liberalism; Reagan, Ronald
The Netherlands   108, 130, 187, 342n
  Amsterdam   159, 417
  *See also* economics (bubbles—tulip mania); Europe; Holland
Think tanks and institutes
  *See* policy (policy-makers and making)
Third World   88, 347
  *See also* First World
Tiananmen Square   72–73
  *See also* China; democracy; despotism; education (college, students); freedom; social movements(s)
Tragedy of the Commons   368, 381
  *See also* accumulation; capitalism (prevailing tendencies); commodities (commodification); production (overproduction)
Transcontinental Railroad   180–181
  *See also* barbarism
Trans-Pacific Partnership
  *See* free trade agreements
Treaty of Versailles   133

INDEX 567

See also Foch, Ferdinand; war
  (World War I, World War II)
Triangle Shirtwaist Factory fire
  See violence
Trudeau, Justin   357–358
  See also Canada
Trump, Donald   110, 119, 151n4, 207, 209,
  211, 232–233, 235, 244–245, 245n, 246,
  252–253, 253n, 254, 254n4, 257–258,
  260, 266–268, 286, 314–315, 326, 329,
  337n5, 339, 339n, 340, 342–344, 344n,
  353, 354–357, 358, 359–362, 373, 393, 420
  Trump administration   69, 119, 151n4,
    152, 253, 258, 285–287, 328, 357, 358n,
    374, 462
  See also authoritarianism; cult of
    personality; democracy; environmental
    crisis; fascism; Putin, Vladimir; Russia
Turkey   ix, 67, 252, 253, 278, 296, 332, 334,
  335n4, 337n5, 339, 342n, 344, 361, 367,
  388
  See also authoritarianism; debt (debt
    crisis); Erdogan, Recep Tayyip; Eurasia;
    Europe; financial crisis; genocide
    (Armenian genocide); geo-politics;
    Ottoman Empire
Twain, Mark   117, 238n, 247

Ukraine   336, 354, 355, 357, 358, 362
  See also Crimea; Eurasia; geo-politics;
    Putin, Vladimir; Trump, Donald
Unemployment   51–52, 52n, 81–87, 88,
  92, 109, 196, 218, 220–221, 320, 324,
  336, 340
  Underemployment   52, 52n
  See also class; crisis; economics (supply and
    demand); Great Depression; inequality;
    labor; pauperism; poverty; technology
    (as method of lowering labor costs)
Union of Concerned Scientists
  See environmental crisis
Unions (Unionization)   44, 45, 52, 81, 82,
  83, 86, 88, 91, 92, 155, 189, 191,
  204–205n, 205, 218, 224, 248, 263,
  319, 369, 381, 386
  Right to work laws   45, 92, 218, 387
  See also class (class struggle, working
    class); labor; proletariat; social
    movement(s)

United Kingdom (UK)   52n, 108, 278, 312n8,
  338n7, 342n, 346, 354, 418, 419
  See also Britain; England; Europe;
    Scotland; Wales
United Nations   91, 182, 183, 184–185, 278, 281,
  350, 351, 367, 393
  Food and Agriculture Organization of the
    United Nations   278
  UNICEF   313
  United Nations Security Council   367
  See also international organizations
United States   ix, x, 4, 14, 30, 36n, 45, 51, 52n,
  63, 63n, 68, 69n4, 72, 74, 75, 79, 81, 82,
  83, 84, 86–88, 90, 90n3, 91, 92, 97, 104,
  108, 112, 117, 122, 122n, 128n, 135, 140, 141,
  142, 143, 145, 147, 148, 149, 150, 151n5, 152,
  156–157, 158, 166n1, 166n2, 176, 180–182,
  183, 184, 189, 190, 191, 192, 197, 198, 204,
  205, 207n, 207–214, 219, 219–220n, 220,
  221, 222, 223, 224, 228, 230, 232, 233, 235,
  236, 242, 244, 245, 248, 252–253, 254,
  257, 259, 259n, 260–261, 266, 267, 268,
  271, 273–274, 275, 276, 281, 282, 285–287,
  293, 294, 297, 298, 300, 303, 305–307,
  307n3, 309, 310, 312, 312n8, 314, 315,
  319, 320–321, 322–326, 327, 327n, 328,
  331, 332, 334, 336–337, 337n5, 337n6,
  338, 338n7, 338n8, 339–341, 342, 342n,
  343–345, 346–348, 348n, 349–352, 352–
  353n5, 353–363, 363n, 364–366, 366n1,
  371–374, 377, 384, 387–388, 387–388n,
  390, 392–395, 396–397n4, 415, 419, 420,
  433–434n, 457
  Constitution of the United States   307,
    307n3
  New York City   63, 72, 94, 151, 160, 186, 192,
    264n7, 319, 350, 351, 366, 401
  Times Square   162–163
  US Government: branches and agencies
    Bureau of Land Management
      (BLM)   287
    Central Intelligence Agency
      (CIA)   63n, 190, 191, 219, 349, 358
    Commodity Futures Trading
      Commission   332
    Congressional Human Rights
      Caucus   366
    Consumer Financial Protection
      Bureau   152

United States (cont.)
  Environmental Protection Agency
    (EPA)   152n, 275, 286, 287, 420
  Federal Communications Commission
    (FCC)   152n, 257, 268
  National Aeronautics and Space
    Administration (NASA)   177n, 196,
    276, 287, 390, 398
  National Science Foundation
    (NSF)   287
  Office of Science and Technology
    Policy   286
  Securities and Exchange Commission
    (SEC)   152n, 371
  US Census Bureau   79, 84, 176
  US Department of State   298
  US House of Representatives   208,
    260, 325
  US Justice Department   147, 152n, 312
  US National Oceanic and Atmospheric
    Administration   274n
  US Senate   273, 358
  US Supreme Court   204, 209, 233, 258
  Washington, D.C.   63, 72, 73, 90, 191,
    192, 206, 253, 350, 351, 360, 366
  Urban (Urbanization)   5, 51, 87, 94, 95,
    143, 159, 160–161, 162–164, 170, 269, 281,
    309, 376, 385, 403, 408, 434–435
  Metropolitanism   5, 42, 90, 159, 162, 200,
    282, 434–435
  *See also* capital (centralization of);
    geography; rural; suburbs
Usury   107, 265
  *See also* economics (interest)
Utopianism   97, 239, 381, 396, 406, 410–411, 412
  *See also* Fourier, Charles; Owen, Robert;
    religion; socialism
Uyghur Muslims   185, 252
  *See also* China; concentration camps;
    despotism
Uzbekistan   313, 314
  *See also* Eurasia; slavery (contemporary
    slavery)

Value   24, 25, 61, 100, 149, 150, 292, 300, 316,
  317, 318, 320, 322, 323, 326, 369, 370, 371,
  380, 381–382, 386, 394, 397, 403, 420,
  444, 445

Surplus-value   381–382, 386, 388, 444
*See also* accumulation; appropriation
  of wealth; capital; capitalism;
  commodities; exploitation; labor;
  profit; wages
Venezuela   128, 184, 296, 333, 335n, 336–337,
  337n6
*See also* Maduro, Nicolas; South America
Vietnam   63, 72–73, 219–220n, 313, 332, 334,
  347–348, 359, 365–366
*See also* Asia; Gulf of Tonkin Incident;
  Johnson, Lyndon; Kissinger, Henry;
  Nixon, Richard; war (Vietnam War)
Violence   21, 47, 48, 87, 94, 96, 102, 106, 109,
  115, 130, 131, 132, 179–180, 183, 184, 185,
  186–187, 190, 192, 193, 203, 220, 224, 232,
  240, 247, 248, 252, 293, 296–297, 299,
  360, 365, 395, 407, 409, 412, 436, 440n,
  457, 461
  Imperial Foods fire   193
  Triangle Shirtwaist Factory fire   186, 193
  *See also* barbarism; capitalism (capitalist
    development); colonialism; crime;
    despotism; genocide; human nature;
    policing; race and racism (lynching);
    sexism and misogyny; social
    movement(s); terrorism; war
Voltaire   403
  *See also* Enlightenment
Voting   84, 137, 157, 203, 207, 213–216, 226,
  228, 234–235, 254, 260, 262, 293, 314, 344,
  348n, 356, 357, 360, 361, 387, 438, 440
  Franchise   180, 215, 293, 439
  Gerrymandering   208–209
  Voting Rights Act   230
  *See also* candidate selection process;
    democracy; liberalism (liberal
    democracy: theory and society)

Wages   20, 26, 44, 51–52, 52n, 60, 61, 63, 74,
  75, 80, 82–84, 84n, 85–86, 88, 89–90,
  90n2, 91, 91n, 92, 95, 96, 121, 122, 125, 143,
  151–152, 154, 155–156, 201, 212, 215, 218,
  220, 221, 222, 223, 226, 227, 296, 319, 322,
  324, 326, 332, 337n6, 340, 341, 359, 361,
  368–369, 372, 376, 380, 381, 382–383,
  384, 386, 388, 389, 408, 421, 446, 450
  Cost of living   90

INDEX

Minimum wage   44, 82, 84, 88, 90, 90n2, 91, 151, 218, 220, 226, 296, 337n6, 386, 387, 388, 421
   *See also* appropriation of wealth; class (working class); economics (inflation); inequality; labor; mobility; pauperism; poverty; proletariat
Wales   189, 223, 270, 332, 377
   *See also* Britain; England; Europe; fossil fuel (coal); Scotland; United Kingdom
Wall Street
   *See* stocks
Wallerstein, Immanuel   352, 377, 389n3, 402, 449
   *See also* sociology; world economy
War
   Afghan War   192, 350–351, 367
   Balkan Wars   346
   Bosnian War   183
   Gulf War   350, 366
   Iran-Iraq War   182
   Iraq War   192, 219–220n, 235, 351–352, 352–353n5, 367
   Korean War   248, 347, 365
   Russo-Swedish War   364
   Second Sino-Japanese War   183
   Syrian civil war   252, 334, 361n9
   US Civil War   305, 307, 339
   Vietnam War   63, 72–73, 219–220n, 347–348, 365–366
   World War I   132–133, 134, 219–220n, 231, 248, 331, 338, 339, 340, 346, 349, 361, 392
      Scramble for Africa   346
   World War II   46, 74, 88, 131, 133, 135, 141, 171, 183, 198, 219–220n, 231, 235, 253, 319, 331, 339, 346, 361, 364, 365, 390–391, 392
   World War III   348n, 392, 396
   *See also* geo-politics; nation-states; violence
War on drugs   253, 268n, 309, 309n
   *See also* crime; drugs; race and racism
Washington, D.C.
   *See* United States
   *See also* policy (foreign policy); United States

*Wealth of Nations*
   *See* Smith, Adam
Weber, Max   194, 203, 214, 246, 437, 439
   *See also* bureaucracy; legitimacy; sociology
Welfare (Welfare State)   61, 81, 82, 189, 220–222, 221–222n, 223, 263, 372, 386, 388, 421
   Corporate welfare: bailouts, subsidies, tax breaks and tax cuts   45, 89–90, 206, 218, 220, 222–223, 224n, 323–324, 326–328, 340, 343, 372, 387–388, 421
   Subsidies   141–142, 148, 218, 220, 222, 343
   *See also* economics (Keynesian economics)
White nationalism / supremacy
   *See* race and racism
   *See also* social movement(s) (Alt-Right)
Wilkerson, Lawrence   367
   *See also* Powell, Colin, war (Iraq War)
Women's rights
   *See* sexism and misogyny
Working class
   *See* class
World Bank, The
   *See* international organizations
World economy   3, 6, 88, 118, 131, 135, 135, 156, 219, 221, 275, 277, 319, 324, 328, 330, 335, 335n4, 338, 339, 350, 352, 353, 362, 363, 377, 378, 402, 415
   Global market and trade   3, 20, 21, 34, 88, 89, 96, 140, 141, 145, 147, 148, 150, 159, 192, 205, 215, 219, 219–220n, 222, 223, 233, 301, 324, 327, 328, 331, 332–336, 335n4, 338, 338n7, 338n8, 340–345, 352, 360, 361, 363, 363n10, 369, 372, 376, 385, 389, 396, 397, 444
   Globalization   80, 89, 327–329, 330, 331, 339n9, 393, 396n4, 431, 444, 450, 455
   World market   20, 81, 119, 218, 219–220n, 222, 330–345, 348, 352, 367, 379, 380, 389, 397, 402, 432, 444–445, 446, 451
   *See also* capitalism; colonialism; history and human development; neo-liberalism
World Health Organization
   *See* international organizations
World Trade Organization
   *See* international organizations

World War I
*See* war
World War II
*See* war

Xenophobia   59n, 118, 137, 237–238, 463
*See also* ethnocentrism; race and racism

Yeltsin, Boris   336
*See also* Putin, Vladimir; Russia; Soviet Union
Yemen   130, 282, 335n3
*See also* Arabia; human trafficking; Middle East

CPSIA information can be obtained
at www.ICGtesting.com
Printed in the USA
JSHW010604010720
6432JS00006B/10